357

2

HISTORY OF
MODERN COLLOQUIAL ENGLISH

A HISTORY OF MODERN COLLOQUIAL ENGLISH

By HENRY CECIL WYLD

AUTHOR OF 'THE HISTORICAL STUDY OF THE MOTHER TONGUE'
'A SHORT HISTORY OF ENGLISH'
'THE UNIVERSAL ENGLISH DICTIONARY,' ETC., ETC., ETC.

THIRD EDITION, WITH ADDITIONS

BASIL BLACKWELL
OXFORD
1956

First published . 1920
Second Edition . 1921
Third Impression 1925
Third Edition . 1936
Reprinted . . 1953
Reprinted . . 1956

PRINTED BY THE REPLIKA PROCESS
IN GREAT BRITAIN BY
LUND HUMPHRIES
LONDON · BRADFORD

PREFACE

THE collection of the material upon which this book is based, the arrangement of this, and the writing of the book itself have occupied about five years, during which I have also had many other distractions and occupations. Whatever may be the shortcomings and defects of the present treatment, it is vain to attempt to extenuate or excuse them in a short preface. On the other hand, such merits and new information as the book may possess may be left for the discriminating reader to discover for himself.

I offer no apology for having omitted any specific treatment of the history of the English Vocabulary, and of English Syntax, during the centuries between Chaucer's day and our own. Nor do I conceive that those who have a first-hand acquaintance with the subject will make it a ground of reproach to the author, that having, after all, done something, he has not attempted to do everything. It seems reasonable that a writer should select for himself the aspects of a subject with which he will deal. As I have myself not been altogether idle, during the last twenty years or so, in attempting to add to knowledge in various domains of the history of our language, I think I am entitled to invite others to give the world systematic treatises, even if these should be no more exhaustive than the treatment of other aspects in the present volume, upon historical English Syntax, and upon English Semantics. I have observed that these are branches of English studies which many people consider important for somebody else to tackle.

With regard to the present work, the facts here stated are with very few exceptions derived direct from the sources, that is from the documents themselves. The conclusions drawn from these, both the larger generalizations and the more minute points, are independently arrived at, and represent my own interpretation of the facts. I have not looked up specially everything that has previously been written upon the innumerable questions here discussed, but have preferred to make my own inferences from my own material. In all cases where I have taken facts or conclusions from others, I hope and believe that I have made full acknowledgement.

In the slight sketch of Middle English dialectal features given in

Chapter II, I have made use to some extent of the well-known mono-
graphs of Morsbach, Lekebusch, Dölle, and Frieshammer, but most of
the statements are based upon my own observations. As regards the
Modern Period, the credit due to a pioneer belongs to Dr. R. E.
Zachrisson, who in Chapter II of his important work on *The Pronunciation of English Vowels, from* 1400 *to* 1700, has emphasized the importance of what I have called *occasional spellings*, in the writings of the
fifteenth and sixteenth centuries. Dr. Zachrisson's collection of these
spellings, and his method of dealing with them, have resulted in the
need for a modification of the views previously held concerning the
chronology of sound changes characteristic of the Modern period. My
own treatment of the vowels in accented syllables is based primarily
upon the spellings of the kind referred to, and I am personally convinced that further investigations, over a wider period of time, will
vindicate more and more, in the main, the views first stated by
Dr. Zachrisson. I believe I differ from some of his conclusions—I have
not compared my results point by point with his—but it appears to me
incontestable that we must put the ' vowel shift ' much further back than
we were formerly accustomed to do. Future research into the history
of English pronunciation will, I think, concern itself rather with the
testimony of the unconsciously phonetic spellings in the documents of
the past, and with that of rhymes, than with the writings of the old
grammarians. It is often said that great caution is needed in using
rhymes to establish the existence of this or that pronunciation. This is
perfectly true, and the same might be said of every other source of
information concerning the speech of earlier generations. Great caution
is necessary in all research, and so are courage and imagination.

I have utilized the phonetic spellings of the earlier documents in an
attempt at the history of the pronunciation of vowels in unaccentuated
syllables, see Chapter VII, and in dealing with the changes undergone by consonantal sounds, see Chapter VIII.

It is satisfactory to find that many features of pronunciation hinted
at by the writers of the seventeenth and eighteenth centuries are often
expressed by the occasional spellings much earlier. The writers on
pronunciation not infrequently adopt, as a phonetic spelling to express
their meaning, forms practically identical with those occasional spellings,
into which writers of letters and other documents quoted below so often
slip unconsciously. Thus it is rather striking to find for instance
Porchmouth for ' Portsmouth ' mentioned by Elphinston as a vulgarism
in his day, to find the name spelt a hundred years earlier with -*ch*-, in
the Verney Memoirs, and again more than a hundred years earlier still
by Admiral Sir Thomas Howard (cf. p. 292, below). In the face of this

evidence, it is hardly possible to doubt that the pronunciation referred to
by Elphinston existed about two and a half centuries before his day.

The references to the old orthoepists and grammarians in this book
are taken either from my own notes, made some years ago from the copies
of these works in the Bodleian, from modern reprints, or, in a few cases,
from copies of the originals in my possession. The quotations from
Mulcaster's *Elementarie* are in all cases from a photographic reproduction of the Bodleian copy which my colleague Professor Campagnac
kindly lent me.

Books and collections of documents written in the fifteenth and
sixteenth centuries, from which forms are taken, are included in the
short Bibliography at the beginning of the book. I have not thought
it worth while to draw up a list of works belonging to the seventeenth
and eighteenth centuries, as it seemed most probable that all of these
would be known and accessible to readers of this book.

My gratitude is due to various friends who have helped me in
different ways. Dr. John Sampson read the first four chapters in manuscript and gave me the advantage of his advice on many important
points. His kindly interest in the work, continually displayed, and his
friendly encouragement, are not the least considerable benefits I have
received from him.

Professor Elton was so kind as to read the proofs of Chapters IV and
V, and to make many valuable criticisms and comments. I regret very
much that I was unable, owing to the stage which the work had reached,
to adopt many of his suggestions, or to develop further several interesting lines of investigation which he indicated. I can assure him that
I am none the less grateful to him, and that his informing remarks will
not be wasted.

To Professor R. H. Case I owe a peculiar debt. Not only have
I consulted him constantly on all kinds of minor points, chronological,
biographical, textual, and never in vain, but I have derived enduring
pleasure and inspiration, and much valuable information, from our frequent discussions concerning all manner of literary questions, both of
a general and special character. Mr. Case most generously placed not
only his stores of knowledge and the benefit of his highly cultivated taste,
but also his library at my disposal. To him I owe my acquaintance
with several important sixteenth- and seventeenth-century works, notably
Laneham's Letter, and the *Comparison of the Stages*; he also lent me
copies of these and several other rare books and tracts.

I offer my best thanks to Professor Campagnac for lending me his
photographs of Mulcaster, to Professor Foster Watson for bringing the
Correspondence of Dr. Basire to my knowledge, and for the loan of

the volume, and to Professor C. H. Firth for calling my attention to, and lending me, vol. 1 of the *Verney Papers*, and for pointing out the importance of the *State Papers* of Henry VIII. I tackled the latter too late in the day to do more than skim a few forms from the surface of a single volume. The references to the passages from *Boswell's Life of Johnson* on pp. 167 and 212 were most obligingly sent me by Mr. A. Okey Belfour of Belfast.

Miss Serjeantson of the University of Liverpool has helped me in many ways: in verifying and checking a large number of references, in copying out several rather long extracts from seventeenth- and eighteenth-century sources, and in some cases, by supplying me with actual forms—for instance a 3rd Pers. Sing. in -*s* in Bokenam which I had overlooked. For these not unimportant services, promptly and cheerfully rendered, my gratitude is now expressed.

In conclusion, I feel that if this book succeeds, on the one hand, in so interesting the general reader that he is impelled to study the subject for himself in the sources, and if, on the other, the special student of English should find in it such a collection of facts and inferences, and such a mapping-out of the ground as shall serve as the basis for further discussion and investigation, then the volume will have justified its existence.

HENRY CECIL WYLD.

THE UNIVERSITY OF LIVERPOOL.
December, 1919.

PREFATORY NOTE TO THE THIRD EDITION

THE new matter included in this Edition will be found chiefly in the appropriate places in the footnotes, though some have been incorporated in the text. When the additional material, and the discussion which this involves extend beyond the limits of a footnote, recourse is had to an Appendix. The new forms, and the topics dealt with for the first time in this book, are all indexed separately from the original Indices, which are left as they were.

The List of Sources, which in the earlier editions presented a somewhat confused appearance, has been recast, printed more clearly, and made to include later sources of the seventeenth and eighteenth centuries.

A brief list is added of some of the more important books which have appeared since this work was first published.

I am happy to think that the price of the present Edition may bring the book within the reach of many students of English who found the cost of the first two Editions prohibitive.

HENRY CECIL WYLD.

ALVESCOT.
March, 1936.

CONTENTS

ALPHABETICAL LIST OF SOURCES

FIFTEENTH TO EIGHTEENTH CENTURIES.

Alleyne, Edward, Memoirs of (1593-1626). Ed. Payne Collier, Shakespeare Society, 1843.
Alleyne Papers (1580-1661). Ed. Payne Collier, Shakespeare Society, 1843.
Aragon, see Catherine.
Ascham, Roger. Toxophilus, 1545 ; The Scholemaster, 1563.
Basire, Dr. and Mrs. Correspondence of (1634-75). Ed. Darnell, 1831.
Bath, Earl of. Letters, 1540, in Ellis' Orig. Letters, ser. 2, vol. ii, 157.
Beaufort, Margaret, 1443-1509. Ellis' Orig. Letters, 1. i. 46, &c.
Bekington, Bishop, see Margaret, Queen of Anjou.
Berners, Juliana. A Treatyse of Fysshynge, 1496. Wynkyn de Worde.
Berners, Lord. Translation of Froissart, 1520. Ed. W. P. Ker.
Bokenam, Osbern. Lives of Saints, 1443. Ed. Horstmann. Heilbronn, 1883.
Boleyn, Queen Anne. Letters, 1528, Ellis' Letters, i. 1 ; i. 2 ; ii. 2.
Booke of Quinte Essence, 1460-70. Ed. Furnivall, E.E.T.S., 1866.
Buckhurst, Thos. Sackville, Lord. Works. Ed. R. Sackville West. London, 1859.
Burghley, William Cecil, Lord. Letters in Ellis, cit. ser. vol. and p.
Burial of Edward IV, 1483. In Letters and Papers, vol. i.
Capgrave, John. Chronicle. Ed. Hingeston, Rolls Series, 1858.
Catherine of Aragon, Reception of, 1501. In Letters and Papers, vol. i, pp. 404, &c.
Cavendish. Life of Cardinal Wolsey, .1577. Kelmscott Press, 1893 (printed from Author's MS.).
Caxton, William. Life of Jason, 1477. Ed. Munro, E.E.T.S., 1913.
Celibacy, Vows of, 1459-1527. In Lincoln Diocesan Documents, q.v.
Cely Papers, 1473-88. Ed. Maldon, Camden Society, 1900.
Chetwynd Chartulary, 1490-4. Wm. Salt Archaeol. Society, vol. xii, 1891.
Constable of Dynevor Castle (temp. Hen. IV). Letter in Ellis, ii. 1.
Coventry Leet Book, from 1421. Ed. Reader Harris, E.E.T.S., 1901.
Cox, Captain, his Ballads and Books, see Laneham.
Cranmer, Archbishop. Letters, 1533-7, in Ellis, ser. 1, vol. ii, and ser. 3, vol. iii.
Creation of a Knight of the Bath, see York, Henry, Duke of.
Editha, Saint, Life of, 1420. Ed. Horstmann. Heilbronn, 1883.
Edward VI's First Prayer Book, 1549 ; Second Prayer Book, 1552.

Elizabeth, Queen. (1) Early Letters, in Ellis ; (2) Letters to James I, 1572–1602, Camden Society, 1849 ; (3) Letters in Bardon Papers, Camden Society, 1909 ; (4) Englishings (translations of Boethius, &c.), 1593. Ed. Pemberton, E.E.T.S., 1890.

Elyott, Sir Thomas. The Booke of the Gouernour, 1531. Ed. Croft, 2 vols., 1880.

Exeter Tailors' Gild, Ordinances of, 1466. Ed. Toulmin Smith, E.E.T.S., 1870.

Fisher, John, Bishop of Rochester (fl. 1459–1535). (1) English Works, ed. Mayor, E.E.T.S., 1876 ; (2) Letter in Ellis, iii. 2. 289.

Fortescue, Sir John. Governance of England, 1471–6. Ed. Plummer, Oxford, 1885.

Fox, Richard. Bishop of Durham and Winchester, Letters of, 1486–1527. Ed. P. S. and H. M. Allen, Oxford, 1929.

Gill, Alexander. Logonomia Anglica (2nd Ed.), 1627. Ed. Jiriczek, Q. and F. 90. Strassburg, 1903. (Important because Gill was Milton's headmaster at St. Paul's, and the poet adopted several of his spellings.)

Godstow, English Register of, 1450. Ed. A. Clark, E.E.T.S., 1905.

Googe, Barnabe. Eglogs, Epytaphes, and Sonnettes, 1563. Arber's Reprints.

Gosson, Stephen. The Schoole of Abuse, 1579. Arber's Reprints.

Gregory, William. Lord Mayor of London. Chronicle,in Historical Collections of a Citizen of London (before 1467). Ed. Gairdner, Camden Society, 1876.

Harley, Lady Brilliana. Letters, 1625–43. Camden Society, 1853.

Harvey, Gabriel. Letter Book of, 1573–80. Ed. C. J. L. Scott, Camden Society, 1884.

Henry VIII, King. Letters, 1515 and 1544, in Ellis' Orig. Letters, 1, vols. i and ii.

Howard, Lord Admiral Sir Edward. Letter to Henry VIII, 1513, in Ellis' Orig. Letters, ii. 1. 213.

Hungerford, Lady, Letters of, c. 1560–88, in Society in the Elizabethan Age. Hubert Hall, 1887.

Instructions to Lord Montjoie, 1483, in Letters and Papers, vol. i.

Ireland, English Conquest of, 1550. Ed. Furnival, E.E.T.S. 1896.

Ireland, State of, 1515, in State Papers of Henry VIII, Pt. III, 1834.

Irish Documents, 1489–93, in Letters and Papers, vol. i.

Knight, Bishop of Bath and Wells. Letters, 1515, in Ellis, ii. 1, and iii. 1.

Laneham, Robert, Letter from, 1575, in Captain Cox his Ballads and Books. Ed. Furnivall, Ballad Society, 1871.

Latimer, Bishop Hugh. (1) Seven Sermons ; (2) Sermon of the Plough, 1549. Arber's Reprints.

Layton, Richard, Dean of York. Letter to Lord Cromwell, 1535. Ellis, ii. 2, p. 60, &c.

Lever, Thomas. Sermons, 1550. Ed. Arber, 1895.

Lily, John. Euphues' Anatomy of Wit, 1579 ; Euphues and his England, 1580. Ed. Arber (in one vol.), 1895.

Lincoln Diocese Documents, 1451, &c. (Wills, Leases, Vows, &c.). Ed. A. Clark, E.E.T.S., 1914. Cit. L.D.D., Documents, date, and p.

Machyn, Henry. Diary, 1550-3. Ed. Nichols, Camden Society, 1848.

Margaret, Queen, of Anjou, and Bishop Bekinton. Letters, 1420-2. Camden Society.

Margaret, Queen of Scotland. Letters, 1503, Ellis, i. 1, p. 42.

Mary, Queen of Scots. Letters to Knollys, 1568, Ellis, i. 1. 253.

Mason, John. Letter, 1535, Ellis, ii. 2. 54, &c.

Milton (1) Autograph MS., 1637. Transcribed and printed with photographic facsimile, Cambridge Press, 1889. (2) Morgan MS. of Book I of Paradise Lost. Ed. with facsimile by Helen Darbishire. Contains elaborate Introduction and Notes. Clarendon Press, 1931.

Monk of Evesham, Revelation of, 1482. Arber's Reprints.

More, Sir Thomas. Letters, 1523-9, Ellis i. 1, and i. 2. Cit. p. See also Robynson, and Roper.

Mulcaster, Richard. Elementarie, 1582. Ed. Campagnac, Oxford, 1925. [Quoted from photographic copy of original in Bodleian.]

Oseney Abbey, Register of, 1460. Ed. A. Clark, E.E.T.S., 1907.

Palladius on Husbondry, 1421. Ed. Lodge, E.E.T.S., 1873. Cit. p. and line.

Paston, William (the Judge). Letters, 1425-30, P.L., vol. i.

Paston, Margaret. Letters in Paston Letters, 1440-70, in vols. i to iii. Ed. Gairdner.

Pecock, Bishop Reginald (of Chichester). The Repressor, 1425-30. Ed. Babington, Rolls Series, 2 vols., 1860.

Pery, Thomas. Letter to Mr. Ralph Vane, 1539, Ellis, ii. 2. 140, &c.

Puttenham, Richard (or George). The Arte of English Poesie, 1589. Arber's Reprints.

Raleigh, Sir Walter. Selections from his Historie of the World, his Letters, &c. Ed. G. E. Hadow, Oxford, 1917 ; also Works, 8 vols., Oxford, 1829.

Rawlyns, Richard, Warden of Merton. Letter of, 1515, in Letters of Bishop Fox, pp. 80-82.

Rede me and be not wroth, 1528. Arber's Reprints.

Rewle of Sustris Menouresses, c. 1450. Ed. Chambers, E.E.T.S., 1914.

Robynson, Raphe. English Translation of Sir Thomas More's Utopia, 1556. Ed. Lumby, Cambridge, 1891.

Rouen, Siege of, in Short English Chronicle, c. 1420.

Sackville, Thos., see Buckhurst.

Seymour, Sir Thomas. Letters, 1544, State Papers of Henry VIII, vol. 1.

Shillingford, John, Mayor of Exeter. Letters and Papers of, 1447-50. Ed. Moore, Camden Society, 1871.

Short English Chronicle, 1464. Ed. Gairdner, Camden Society, 1880.

Shrewsbury, Countess of. Letters, 1581-2, Ellis, ii. 2. 63, and ii. 3. 60, &c.

Sidney, Sir Philip. Miscellaneous Works. Ed. W. Gray, 1893 ; Complete Poems. Ed. Grosart. 2 vols., 1873.

Skelton, John. Magnyfycence, c. 1516. Ed. Ramsay, E.E.T.S., 1908.

Smith, Sir Thomas. (1) De Republica Anglorum (in English), 1565 ; (2) Letters, 1572-6, in Ellis, ii. 3 ; iii. 3.

Stonor Papers, 1290-1483 (2 vols). Ed. Kingsford, Camden Society, 1919.

Surrey, Thomas, Earl of. Letters to Wolsey, 1520, in State Papers of Henry VIII, Pt. III. **Surrey, Henry, Earl of.** Poems in Tottel's Miscellany. Arber's Reprints.

Suffolk Wills (Bury Wills and Inventories), 1463-1569. Ed. Tymms, Camden Society, 1850.

Udall, Nicholas. Roister Doister, 1553-6. Arber's Reprints.

Verney Family Letters. (1) Letters and Papers of, 15th century to 1639. Ed. Bruce, Camden Society, 1853 (Verney Papers). (2) Memoirs of the Verney Family, 1639-96. Ed. Lady Verney, 4 vols., 1894 (Verney Mems.). (3) Verney Letters of the Eighteenth Century, vol. i, 1696-1717 ; vol. ii, 1717-99 (Later Verney Letters. Ed. Lady Verney, 1930 (cit. name of writer, date, vol. and p.).

Wentworth Papers. Letters of Isabella, Lady Wentworth and her family, 1705-39. Ed. Cartwright, 1883.

Wilson, Thomas. The Arte of Rhetorique, 1585 (3rd Ed.). Ed. Mair, Oxford, 1909.

Wingfield, Sir Robert. Letter to Henry VIII, 1513, Ellis, ii. 1. 210.

Worcester, Ordinances of, 1467, in Toulmin Smith's English Gilds.

York, Henry, Duke of. Creation of a Knight of the Bath, 1494, in Letters and Papers, vol. 1, p. 388, &c.

RECENT WORKS ON THE ENGLISH OF FIFTEENTH AND LATER CENTURIES.

Darbishire, Helen. Introduction and Notes to Morgan MS. of Book I of Paradise Lost. See Milton (ii) in List of Sources. (Contains elaborate study of Milton's spelling.)

Davies, Constance. English Pronunciation from Fifteenth to Eighteenth Century. Dent, 1934.

Flasdieck, H. M. Forschungen z. Frühzeit der neu engl. Schriftspr. Halle, 1922.

Hitchcock, E. V. See Introductions to Bishop Pecok's Donet, E.E.T.S., 1921, and Folewer to the Donet, E.E.T.S., 1924.

Kilboom, Asta. Contributions to the Study of Fifteenth-century English Upsala, 1926.

Matthews, W. (1) Some Phonetic Spellings of the Eighteenth, Century, Rev. of Engl. Stud., Jan., 1936, pp. 42-60, and April, 1936, pp. 177-188. (2) William Tiffin. An Eighteenth Century Phonetician Engl. St. (Amsterdam) xviii, No. 3, June, 1936, pp. 97-114.

Wienke, H. Die Sprache Caxtons. (Kölner Anglist. Arbeiten ii Leipzig, 1930.

Wyld, H.C. (1) Studies in English Rhymes from Surrey to Pope, 1923. (2) A Short History of English (3rd Ed.), 1927. See especially Chapters vii. and viii.

Zachrisson, R. E.   The English Pronunciation at Shakespeare's Time, as taught by William Bullokar.   Upsala, 1927.

SOME RECENT WORKS ON M.E. DIALECTS.

Heuser, W.   Alt-London Dialek, &c.   Osnabrück, 1914.
Jordan, R.   Handbuch d. mittelengl. Grammatik, Pt. I.   Lautlehre. Heidelberg, 1925.
Mackenzie, B. A.   (1) Contributions to the History of the Early London Dialect.   Oxford, 1927.   (2) A Special Dialectal Development of O.E. *ea* in M.E., E. Studien, 61, 1927.
Reaney, P. H.   (1) On certain Phonological Features of the Dialect of London in the twelfth century.   (2) Dialect of London in thirteenth-century, E. Stud., 61, 9–23.   E. Studien, 59, pp. 321–45, 1925, 1926.
Serjeantson, M. S.   (1) Dialect of Earliest Complete Engl. Prose Ps. Engl. Studies (Amsterdam), vol. vi, pp. 177–99, Dec., 1924.   (2) The Dialect of the W. Midland in M.E.   Rev. Engl. Studies, vol. iii, Nos. 9, 10, 11, 1927.
Wild, F.   Sprache d. Wichtigeren Chaucer MS.   Wiener Beitr., 44. Leipzig, 1915.
Wright, J. and M. E.   An Elementary M.E. Gr. Oxford, 1925.
Wyld, H. C.   The Surrey Dialect of the thirteenth-century.   English Studies (Amsterdam), Apr., 1921.

REMARKS ON PHONETIC NOTATION

In a book like the present, which deals with a large number of questions connected with pronunciation and its changes, it is absolutely indispensable that we should be able to express rapidly, accurately, and unambiguously the precise sounds we are dealing with. This cannot be secured without the aid of Phonetic Notation.

The main essentials of a Phonetic Notation are : that there shall be a separate symbol for each separate sound ; that no symbol should be written if there is no sound to be expressed—e. g. no *r* is required in *part*, to express the pronunciation of most educated Englishmen at the present day ; we therefore write [pāt]; that the same symbol should always express one and the same sound—thus [s] is always the initial sound in *soap*, [z] always the final sound in *buzz*, &c.

When it is remembered, for instance, that the official spelling takes no cognizance of the many sound changes discussed in Chapters VI, VII, VIII, it is evident that '*spelling*' has nothing to do with the various problems involved, and that since we are dealing with *sounds*, we must have a simple and accurate means of expressing the phonetic facts we are considering. Thus the word *flood*, although often so spelt in the fifteenth and sixteenth centuries, may have, at a given time, three different pronunciations among different classes of speakers. In writing about these we can express the various sounds quite clearly by writing [ū, ŭ, a], but not by speaking about the '*oo*-sound'.

If the simple principles just enumerated be borne in mind, and if the reader does not associate the symbols in [ ] with the sounds which they express, often very inconsistently, in the traditional spelling, he will find very little difficulty in making out what sound is referred to. Even if he does experience some trouble at first in getting a clear idea of the sound intended, he may comfort himself by remembering, that if a phonetic notation were not used, he would be unable to gain any idea on the subject at all.

TABLE OF PHONETIC SYMBOLS USED IN THIS BOOK

Note that whenever phonetic symbols are used in the text they are enclosed in [ ].

VOWELS.

Symbol   *Sound expressed.*

[*i*] = English *i* as in *bit*.

[i] = English *ee* as in *see*; or French *i* in *si*. The vowel of the latter is short.)

[ɛ] = English *e* in *bet*; when long [ɛ̄] the French *è* before *r* as in *père*.

[e] = French *é* in *dé*; when long [ē] = German *e* in *lehnen*.

[æ] = English 'short *a*' as in *had*; [ǣ] = the same sound long.

[ū] = English *oo* as in *hoot*.

[u] = English *u* in *put*.

[ō] = German *o* as in *Bohne*.

[o] = French *o* in *fol*.

[ɔ] = English *aw* as in *Law*, or *a* in *hall*.

[ɔ] = English *o* in *not*.

[y] = French *u* in *bu*; when long [ȳ] = French *u* in *pure*.

[φ] = French *eu* as in *ceux*.

[œ] = French *eu* as before *r*—*peur*.

[a] = German short *a* in *hass*; when long, [ā] = English *a* in *hart* or in *father*.

[a] = English vowel in *cut*, &c.

[ə] = unstressed vowel in *water*, &c. This is one of the commonest vowel sounds in English; it occurs only in unaccented syllables.

[ʌ] = the vowel in the English words, *curd*, *term*, *heard*, *worm*, *bird*.

The diphthongs [ai, oi, ei, au, ou, ɛə, iə] are simply combinations of certain of the sounds mentioned in the table; they are heard in *bite*, *boy*, *cake*, *how*, *note*, *hare*, *here*, &c., respectively.

Definitions. The following technical terms for different kinds of sounds are often used :—*Back Vowel* = a vowel made with the back of tongue as [ā]; *Front Vowel*, one made in the front or middle of tongue as [ī]; *Rounded Vowel*, one in which the lips play a part, as [ū, ȳ], &c.; *Tense Vowel*, one made with the tongue, hard, braced, and muscularly tense [i]; *Slack Vowel*, one made with the tongue soft, and muscularly slack, as [ĭ]; *High, Mid, Low Vowels*: these terms refer to the different degrees of *height* of the tongue in articulation; [i, ɛ, æ] are respectively High, Mid, and Low, Front, Slack vowels. *Raising* refers to the movement of the tongue in passing, e. g. from [ē] to [ī].

CONSONANT SYMBOLS.

[χ] = sound of *ch* in Scotch *loch*.

[ʒ] = sound of *g* in German *sagen*.

[j] = sound of *y* in *yacht*, or *j* in German *jagen*, &c.

[j̇] = sound of *ch* in German -*ich*.

[w̥] = sound of *w* in English *wall*, &c.

[w̥] = sound of *wh* in Scotch or Irish *white*, &c.

[k] = sound of *k* as in *king*.

[g] = sound of *g* as in *good*.

[ŋ] = sound of *ng* as in *sing*.

B

[ʃ] = sound of *sh* as in *shoot*, &c.

[ž] = sound of *ge* in French *rouge*, or of *j* in *jamais*.

[t, d, b, p, n, m, l, r, f, v] express the same sounds as in ordinary spelling.

[þ] = sound of English *th* in *think*.

[ð] = sound of English *th* in *this*.

[s] = sound of *s* in *so*, or of *c* in *city*.

[z] = sound of *z* in *haze*, or of *s* in *is, was, easy*.

Definitions. A *Stop*, or *Stop Consonant*, is one in the pronunciation of which the air-passage is completely closed, or stopped, for a moment —p, t, k. These are sometimes called *explosives*. An *Open Consonant* is one in the articulation of which the air-passage is only *narrowed*, so as to allow a continual stream of air to pass—[f, s, þ, ʃ], &c. A *Voiced Consonant* is one during the articulation of which the vocal chords vibrate and produce a kind of 'buzz'—[z, v, ð, ž], &c., which may be contrasted with the *Voiceless*, or *Un-voiced*, corresponding sounds [s, f, þ, ʃ], &c.

[h], the aspirate, or ' rough breathing '—as in *hat*, &c.—is not included among the consonants because it is not consonantal in character.

CHAPTER I

INTRODUCTORY

WRITERS upon the history of language are very careful to insist that the process of development or evolution of speech takes place in the living, spoken language, and not in written documents. It is pointed out that language changes in the very act of speaking, that changes in pronunciation, accidence, and the rest come about gradually, and by imperceptible degrees, within the lifetime of a single generation, and in transmission from one generation to another. A history of a language is an account of these slight and gradual changes, the cumulative results of which, in the course of several generations, may be very remarkable. In a primitive age, the written form of a language is, in the main, a reproduction of the spoken form, and follows as nearly as may be, though often lagging somewhat behind, the changing fortunes of the latter. If a language ceases to be spoken as a normal, living means of intercourse between man and man, the written form can no longer change, but must remain fixed, since it must consist merely of a reproduction of ancient models; there is no longer a living, changing speech to mould its character and keep it up to date.

It is an unfortunate circumstance for students of the history of a language, but one from which there is no escape, that they are dependent upon written documents for a knowledge of all but the most recent developments, since, in the nature of things, they can gain no direct and personal access to the spoken language earlier than the speech of the oldest living person they may know. We are bound, therefore, to make the best use we can of the written records of the past, always bearing in mind that our question in respect to the writers of these documents is ever—How did they speak? What fact of pronunciation is revealed by, or concealed beneath, this or that spelling?

Our business in this book is mainly concerned with English as it has been spoken during the last four or five centuries; we are not attempting a history of literary form, and our interest in written documents, whether they rise to the dignity of works of literature, or be of a humbler character, is primarily in proportion to the light these compositions throw upon the spoken English of the period in which they were written. At the same time, in the course of our inquiry, we are bound to deal with the origin and character of the English of Literature and its historical relation to the spoken English of the various periods. If we turn for a moment to consider quite briefly the linguistic conditions in our own country at the present time, there are several outstanding facts which at once arrest attention. On the one hand, we have a written form of English which is common to all literary productions, and which is invariable as

regards spelling and grammar, both in books and private documents.
Written English is fixed and uniform. On the other hand, we find almost
endless variety in the spoken language. If we call up for a moment, in
no matter how hazy a manner, two or three different types of English
which we have heard spoken in as many widely separated areas in this
country, it is apparent at once that these types differ very much from each
other in almost every respect. Their sounds—that is, the ways in which
they are pronounced—are different; so, too, in many respects, are the
grammatical forms, and there are differences often in the names of quite
common objects. If we think of these different types of uttered speech
in relation to the written language we should perhaps find it difficult to
say which of them appeared to be least effectually expressed by our
present system of spelling. In any case it must be obvious to every one
that Literary English at the present time cannot be intended to represent equally the language as spoken locally, let us say in Devonshire,
Oxfordshire, or Yorkshire. Perhaps it was never intended to represent
any of these types, and, if not, it may well be asked, To what spoken type
does it correspond? Again, it is quite possible for an educated person
to speak with a very marked provincial accent, and yet to write perfectly
good English. In such a case the man may be said to speak one dialect
and to write another, and the character of his spoken dialect need not
influence his manner of writing to the smallest degree. Certainly no
indication of his peculiarities of pronunciation will be traceable in his
spelling. It is necessary to consider rather more closely the varieties
which exist in present-day Spoken English.

As a rule when we speak of the English Dialects we mean varieties or
English which are associated with particular geographical areas or counties.
Many of these types of English at the present time are distinguished,
according to the popular view, chiefly by possessing a more or less strange
pronunciation, and certain elements in their vocabulary which are not
current coin in every part of the country, and especially not among the
more educated portion of the community. Speech varieties of this kind,
confined to particular areas, it is proposed to call **Regional Dialects**.

By the side of these, there are numerous other types of English which
are not characteristic of any special geographical area, but rather of social
divisions or sections of the population. Of these the chief is the type
which most well-bred people think of when they speak of 'English'. At
the risk of offending certain susceptibilities this type of English must be
further described and particularized. As regards its name, it may be
called Good English, Well-bred English, Upper-class English, and it is
sometimes, too vaguely, referred to as Standard English. For reasons
which will soon appear, it is proposed here to call it **Received Standard
English**. This form of speech differs from the various Regional Dialects
in many ways, but most remarkably in this, that it is not confined to any
locality, nor associated in any one's mind with any special geographical
area; it is in origin, as we shall see, the product of social conditions, and is
essentially a **Class Dialect**. Received Standard is spoken, within certain
social boundaries, with an extraordinary degree of uniformity, all over the
country. It is not any more the English of London, as is sometimes
mistakenly maintained, than it is that of York, or Exeter, or Cirencester,

or Oxford, or Chester, or Leicester. In each and all of these places, and in many others throughout the length and breadth of England, Received Standard is spoken among the same kind of people, and it is spoken everywhere, allowing for individual idiosyncrasies, to all intents and purposes, in precisely the same way. It has been suggested that perhaps the main factor in this singular degree of uniformity is the custom of sending youths from certain social strata to the great public schools. If we were to say that Received English at the present day is **Public School English,** we should not be far wrong.

It has been said that Received Standard is one from among many forms of English which must be grouped under Class Dialects. By the side of this type there exist innumerable varieties, all more or less resembling Received Standard, but differing from it in all sorts of subtle ways, which the speaker of the latter might find it hard to analyse and specify, unless he happened to be a practised phonetician, but which he perceives easily enough. These varieties are certainly not Regional Dialects, and, just as certainly, they are not Received Standard. Until recently it has been usual to regard them as so far identical with this, that the differences might be ignored, and what we here call Received Standard, and a large part of these variants that we are now considering, were all grouped together under the general title of Standard English, or Educated English. This old classification of English Speech, as it now exists, into Provincial (Regional) Dialects, and Standard or Educated English, was very inadequate, since it ignored the existence of Class Dialects, or perhaps it would be more accurate to say that it ignored the existence of more than one Class Dialect, and included under a single title many varieties which differ as much from what we now call Received Standard as this does from the Regional Dialects. The fact is that these types of English, which are not Provincial or Regional Dialects, and which are also not Received Standard, are in reality offshoots or variants from the latter, which have sprung up through the factors of social isolation among classes of the community who formerly spoke, in most cases, some form of Regional Dialect. It is proposed to call these variants **Modified Standard,** in order to distinguish them from the genuine article. This additional term is a great gain to clear thinking, and it enables us to state briefly the fact that there are a large number of Social or Class Dialects, sprung from what is now Received Standard, and variously *modified* through the influence of Regional speech on the one hand, or, on the other, by tendencies which have arisen within certain social groups.

These forms of Modified Standard may, in some cases, differ but slightly from Received Standard, so that at the worst they are felt merely as eccentricities by speakers of the latter; in others they differ very considerably, and in several ways, from this type, and are regarded as vulgarisms. It is a grave error to assume that what are known as 'educated' people, meaning thereby highly trained, instructed, and learned persons, invariably speak Received Standard. Naturally, such speakers do not make 'mistakes' in grammar, they may have a high and keen perception of the right uses of words, but with all this they may, and often do, use a type of pronunciation which is quite alien to Received Standard, either in isolated words or in whole groups. These deviations from the habits of Received Standard may be shown just as readily in over-careful pronunciation, which aims at great 'correctness' or elegance —as when *t* is pronounced in *often*, or when initial *h* is scrupulously uttered (wherever written) before all personal pronouns, even when these are quite unemphasized in the sentence—as in a too careless and slipshod pronunciation—as when *buttered toast* is pronounced *butterd tose*, or *object* is called *objic*, and so on.

Again, the deviation from Received Standard may be in the direction neither of over-carefulness nor of over-slovenliness. There may be simply a difference of sound, as when *clerk* is made to rhyme with *shirk*, or *laugh* with *gaff*, or *valet* is pronounced without a -*t*, as if it were a French word. Or the difference may not have to do with pronunciation at all, but may consist in the inappropriate use of a word—say of *lady* or *gentleman*, or some other simple 'derangement of epitaphs'.

Different social grades have different standards of what is becoming in speech, as they have in dress and manners, or other questions of taste and fashion. Thus, for example, while some habitually use *'em*, *ain't*, *broke* (past participle), *shillin*, others would regard such usage with disapproval.

All these things and countless others of like nature are in no wise determined by 'education' in the sense of a knowledge of books, but by quite other factors. The manner of a man's speech from the point of view we are considering is not a matter of intellectual training, but of social opportunity and experience. It is of great importance for our purpose in this book that the distinction between Regional and Class Dialects should be clearly grasped, and also that the existence of Modified Standard, by the side of Received Standard, should be fully recognized. The very nature and origin of the English of Literature and of Received Standard Spoken English cannot be understood unless these facts be clearly before us. Both the latter and Literary English derive their origin from several Regional types, and have from time to time been influenced by others in minor respects. But, during the last two centuries at least, the modifications which have come about in the spoken language are the result of the influence not primarily of Regional but of Class Dialects.

Upon these influences, and their effects, it will be our business in this book to attempt to throw some light.

But the question will be asked, Where does Received Standard English come from? This question must be answered, at least in outline, at once.

It is evident that any form of language, whatever may be its subsequent history, must, in the beginning, have had a local habitation, an area over which it was habitually spoken, a community of actual speakers among whom it grew up and developed. In other words, if Received Standard is now a Class Dialect, and the starting-point of other Class Dialects, it must once have been a Regional Dialect.

If we examine the records of our language in the past, it appears that from the thirteenth century onwards a large number of writings exist which were produced in London, and apparently in the dialect of the capital. These documents are of various kinds, and include proclamations, charters, wills, parliamentary records, poems, and treatises. Among the latter we may reckon the works of Chaucer. The language of these

London writings agrees more closely with the form of English which was later recognized as the exclusive form for literary purposes than does the language of any other mediaeval English documents. So far, then, it appears that Chaucer used the dialect spoken in London for his prose and poetry ; this is proved by the agreement of his language with that of other documents of a literary or an official character, written in London before, during, and after his time. When, after the introduction of printing, a definite form of English becomes the only one used in literary composition, that form is on the whole, and in essential respects, the normal descendant of Chaucer's dialect, and of Caxton's. The latter writer specifically states that he uses the type of English *spoken* in London, and in the following century, Puttenham, to whom we shall again refer later, recommends, as the proper English for the writer, that which is *spoken* in London. London speech then, or one type of it, as it existed in the fourteenth century, is the ancestor of Literary English, and it is also the ancestor of our present-day Received Standard. Written Standard may be said to have existed from the end of the fourteenth century, although it was not used to the complete exclusion of other forms for another hundred years or so. It is more difficult to date the beginning of the existence of a spoken standard. It is certain that educated people continued to use local dialects long after they had given up attempting to put these local forms down on paper. This is true of the upper classes no less than of the humbler. As we shall see, there are plenty of proofs of this in literature. The question is, How soon did men begin to feel that such and such forms were 'right' in the spoken language, and that others should be avoided? for it is the existence of this feeling that constitutes the emergence of a favoured or standard dialect. The existence of such a standard of Spoken English is certainly established by remarks of grammarians and others in the sixteenth century, and it is highly probable that the first recognition of the superiority of one type over the others must be placed at least as early as the fifteenth century, and perhaps earlier still.

A further question, closely related to the above, but not quite identical with it, is, When did the ancestor of our present Received Standard become a Class Dialect? Another way of putting this question is to inquire how early do appreciable and recognized divergences appear between the speech of the upper and lower classes in London. There are general reasons for believing that social dialects would arise quite early in a large community; it may be possible, though not easy, to establish from documentary evidence a probability that they actually did exist in the fifteenth century ; it is quite certain that in the sixteenth century a difference was recognized between upper-class English and the language of the humbler order of the people, and we have the perfectly definite statement of Puttenham that this was the case.

A simpler problem, but one which must be touched upon here, is the diffusion of the common literary type of the written language on the one hand, and of the Spoken Standard English upon the other.

As we shall see, before the middle of the fifteenth century, long before printing was introduced, we find that the local dialects are less and less used in writing, whether in private more or less official documents, such as wills and letters, or in what we must regard as literary works in the special sense. This is due partly to the study of London official documents by scribes and lawyers and other officials, partly, in the case of literature proper, to the immense vogue of Chaucer.

With the advent of Caxton and his successors the spread of a know-ledge of the English in which he wrote became easy and natural.

The diffusion of the Spoken Standard was a much slower process. It is not complete at the present time, as we see from the fact that more or less pure Regional Dialects still linger on. The first classes, outside the metropolis, to acquire the Spoken Standard would be those representa-tives of the nobility and gentry who visited the Court for longer or shorter periods, and the higher officials: the great lawyers, statesmen, and ecclesiastics whose business brought them into contact with the King and his courtiers. Another influence was that of the Universities, who sent out the clergy into country parishes, and masters into the schools. The influ-ence of printed books was no doubt considerable, even in modifying actual speech, for although these could not affect pronunciation to any great extent, they made an ever-increasing public acquainted with the gram-matical forms and general structure of a dialect which had these features in common with what was becoming more and more the standard medium of intercourse in polite society.

Not less important than the above, in spreading the current coin of the form of English which has gradually taken the place of the old Regional Dialects nearly everywhere, are the activities of trade and commerce.

The necessity for intercourse between the great provincial centres of industry and the metropolis, and the extraordinary development of means of locomotion during the nineteenth century, which facilitated travel, have carried the speech of London into all parts of the country and made it the current form.

On the other hand, while the geographical diffusion of some form of Standard English has thus grown apace, its spread among all classes of the population has been secured by the breaking down of social boundaries and intermingling of classes, as well as by the development of education. In all the schools, in no matter what geographical area, or among what social grade, an attempt is made to eliminate the most marked pro-vincialisms and vulgarisms. Thus gradually the Regional Dialects are being extirpated, the coarser features of the vulgarer forms of Class Dialect are being softened, and the speech of the rising generation is being brought up to a certain pitch of refinement—or so it is believed. At any rate a process of modification is always going on.

Thus a form of speech which began as a Regional Dialect has become at once the sole recognized form used in writing, and has gradually extended its sway in colloquial use not merely all over the country, but among all classes.

But this latter process could not happen without a loss of uniformity, and thus a fresh differentiation has taken place, resulting in the large number of forms of Modified Standard which now exist.

Among the forms we may distinguish two main kinds—one kind which is definitely modified by some existing Regional Dialect, and another which seems to be more purely a Class Dialect with no characteristic

Regional influence that can be discovered. Of the former kind there are innumerable varieties, and they may be heard in the larger towns such as York, Manchester, Liverpool, and Birmingham, &c. The other kind of Modified Standard seems to exist chiefly among the more or less educated Middle Class of the South, especially within fifty miles or so of London, and, of course, in London itself. The distinctive character of the Modified Standard of the big towns remote from London consists chiefly in certain approximations in the pronunciation of vowel, and, to a lesser degree, of the consonantal sounds to those of the nearest Regional Dialect. This kind of English is often described as 'a provincial accent'. We ought probably to reckon the typical Cockney English of London, as spoken by educated Middle Class people, in the same class as the above, only here we should not speak of a 'provincial accent', but of a 'Cockney accent'. The peculiarities of this kind of London English, which distinguish it from Received Standard, are doubtless as much Regional in origin as are those of Liverpool or Manchester.

Much below these types in the social scale we have, both in London and in the big towns of the Midlands, other forms of Modified Standard, also influenced by the Regional Dialect, only more strongly so than the educated speech just referred to, various other Class Dialects which we should not hesitate to describe as vulgar. The London Cockney of the streets is an example of this genre.

The special type of Modified Standard spoken in such a centre as Liverpool or Manchester may become so well established that each of these and similar cities may form a starting-point whence linguistic influence spreads over an area coextensive with their social and economic influence.

Thus the process of differentiation is almost infinite, and the tendency of language is not, as it has sometimes been wrongly said, in the direction of uniformity, but of variety. The former view, which arose from a realization that the old Regional Dialects of England were disappearing, lost sight of the fact that their place was being taken by a totally different form of English, not developed normally from the several Regional Dialects, but one of different origin, acquired through external channels. The old dialects were not growing like each other, but were vanishing. In their places various forms of Modified Standard have arisen.

We may now briefly consider the dialectal character of the London English from the thirteenth and fourteenth centuries. Already in Henry III's Proclamation of 1258 we find that the dialect has both Southern and East Midland features, while Davie, about half a century later, and the fourteenth-century London Charters show the same mingling of type, and also have some specifically South-Eastern or Kentish forms. The East Midland characteristics become more marked, and the purely Southern less so. Chaucer's poetry shows a slight increase of the East Midland element, and a corresponding diminution of the Southern, and in his prose the Southern element is weaker still. Fifteenth-century official London documents and the language cf Caxton have very largely lost the purely Southern features, and henceforth the English of Literature and Standard Spoken English display less and less the characteristics of the old Southern Dialect, and an ever-growing proportion of typical East Midland peculiarities.. Thus London English has ever been a combination of elements characteristic of at least three Regional Dialect types, and while all three are still clearly traceable to-day, present-day English is very largely descended from the old East Midland type. Throughout the fifteenth and sixteenth centuries, however, purely Southern features, since discarded, crop up, here and there, in the published works and in the private correspondence of the best writers.

The history of London English since Davie, and later of Received Standard, has been a gradual shifting of the relative preponderance in the various Regional elements of which it is composed. The influence of· the Class Dialects probably began in the sixteenth century.

The mixed character of the dialect of London in the Middle Ages is not to be wondered at, having regard to the geographical position of the city. Further, the growing importance of London as a market brought traders into it from all parts of the country, and the strong East Midland influence probably came from the great business centre of Norwich.

A great deal has been said about different types of dialect, and it is well to be quite clear as to the nature of the distinctions which separate these. It will be convenient to deal with these under the three main heads of Pronunciation, Accidence, or Grammatical forms, and Vocabulary.

Perhaps the most important characteristic of dialect is its pronunciation. At the present time, it is certainly this feature which chiefly distinguishes Received Standard from the different kinds of Modified Standard, especially when the latter, as so often happens, is spoken by persons who are more or less highly educated. Such people will hardly differ in their grammar from Received Standard, and as regards Vocabulary, except in a limited number of familiar colloquialisms and slang which certainly do vary from class to class, it may be said that, on the whole, persons of the same kind or degree of instruction possess approximately the same range of words. This is largely determined by general culture and habits of reading. It is of course obvious that every occupation or profession has technical words of its own, which, while habitual to its members, are unfamiliar or perhaps unknown to those outside. These technical 'trade terms' are not under consideration for the moment.

To return to Pronunciation. In the older dialects, where conditions are less complex, the question resolves itself very largely into the special treatment, within a certain speech area, of an original sound. We must illustrate this point briefly. In Old English there was a diphthong (i.e. a combination of two vowel sounds) *eo* which, according to its origin, was long in some words and short in others. The dialects of the South-West, and West Midlands, by the middle of the thirteenth century at any rate, had altered this sound into one closely resembling the present French vowel in *du*. This vowel is written *u*, after the French method, in Middle English. On the other hand, the dialects of the East, especially the East Midlands (East Anglia), changed this old diphthong into a sound which was written *e*, which, when it represented the old long *eo*, was pronounced like Mod. French *é* in *dé*, and, when it corresponded to the old short *eo*, was pronounced like *è* as in *bête*.

Examples of these two types are :—O.E. *eorþe* (*þ* = '*th*'), M.E. on the

one hand *urþe*, and on the other *erþe* 'earth'; O.E. *ċeorl*, M.E. *churl(e)*
and *cherl(e)* 'churl'; O.E. *deorc* 'dark', M.E. *durk* and *derk*; O.E. *ċēōsan*
(inf.) 'choose', M.E. *chüsen* and *chēsen*; O.E. *lēod* 'people', M.E. *lüde*
and *lēde*. It is probable that the Mod. Eng. spelling *churl* and the now
obsolete spelling *chuse* are survivals of the old *ü*-type.

One other example of an old vowel, developed on different lines in
different dialects, is the O.E. sound *ā* (pronounced like the vowel in *hard*),
which in the M.E. dialects of the South and Midlands is written *o, oo, oa*,
representing no doubt some kind of long '*o*'-sound, but in the Northern
and Scotch M.E. dialects is still written *a* (or *ai*) and rhymes with an
'*ē*'-sound. We find these differences preserved to-day when we compare
stone, foe, hot, O.E. *stān, fā, hāt*, with the Scotch *stane, fae, het*. In the
latter word the vowel has been shortened, just as it has been in *hot*, earlier
written *hoate*, &c. These are examples of old differences which distinguish
different Regional Dialects.

Now in dealing with a mixed dialect like that of London in the
thirteenth century, the written and spoken forms of which later became
respectively the common literary language and Received Standard, the
problem arises of disentangling the various Regional types of which
these forms of English are composed. The variegated character of the
old London dialect is well exhibited in the developments therein found
of the Old English sound which was written *y*, but pronounced like
French *u* in *bu, lune*, &c. There are three possibilities.

In the larger part of the country, the South-West, the Central and
West Midlands as far north as Lancashire and Derbyshire, the old sound
remained apparently unaltered in the M.E. period, and was written with
the French symbol for this sound—*u*. In the South-East, Kent, Essex,
and a large part of East Anglia, the old sound appears in M.E. as *ě*,
indeed it had taken this form already in the ninth century in Kent;
but in the North, and in the East Midlands, including parts of Norfolk and Suffolk, O.E. *y* appears as *ĭ* in Middle English. Now the
London Dialect of the fourteenth century has all three developments of
this sound; indeed the same word may occur in more than one type,
showing that all three types were current in the London area. Examples
are:—O.E. *synne* 'sin', M.E. *sinne, sünne, senne*; O.E. *byrian* 'to bury',
M.E. *birie(n), bürie(n), berie(n)*; O.E. *bryċġ* 'bridge', M.E. *brigge, brügge,
bregge*; O.E. *cyssan* 'to kiss', M.E. *kisse(n), küsse(n), kesse(n)*.

In Present-day English we preserve all three types, although we do not
admit more than one form of any given word:—thus *kiss, sin, hill,
bridge, ridge, list* (vb.), &c., belong to the E. Midland type; *bundle, rush*
(the plant), *thrush, clutch, cudgel*, and some others, are derived from the
type having the French *u*-sound in Old and Middle English, though this
has changed since the latter period into quite a different sound; while *fledge,
knell, merry* represent the Kentish, South-Eastern, and East Anglian type.
It should be noted that our *bury* is spelt according to M.E. *ü*-type, and
pronounced according to the South-Eastern type, while *busy* is also spelt
according to the former type, but our pronunciation of it is derived from
the E. Midland *bisy*, very commonly found in M.E. and Early Modern.
All the above words have the vowel *y* in Old English.

It is quite possible, though at present difficult to establish, that the distribution of types in the above words depended originally upon Class Dialects. In any case the usage fluctuates, even in good writers, during the fifteenth and sixteenth centuries, and does not altogether agree with our present habits. One of the things which complicates our problems is that it is possible for a peculiarity which is Regional in origin to pass into London speech and Early Standard English through the channel of a particular class, so that so far as this particular form of English is concerned the feature begins as a characteristic of Class Dialect. From this starting-point it may gain wider and finally, perhaps, almost universal currency. An apparent example of this is the pronunciation of. *ĭ* as *ĕ*, e. g. *tell* for *till*, *sence* for *since*, *cetezen* for *citizen*, and so on. This peculiarity, to judge by the occasional spellings, gains ground gradually in London English from the late fifteenth century onwards. These *e*-spellings appear to be more numerous among the middle-class writers, in private letters, &c., than among the more distinguished members of society, though the latter are by no means free from them. In the eighteenth century *tell*, &c., is distinctly mentioned as a London vulgarism. So far as our evidence goes, these *e*-spellings, in words that originally had *i*, appear earliest, and are most frequent, in documents written in the extreme East—Essex, Suffolk, and Norfolk. If this is correct, then we have here a Regional character which was given currency through the lower and middle classes of the metropolis, and later, to judge from the spellings in the Verneys' and Lady Wentworth's Letters (cf. p. 229), must have been fairly widespread in the speech of the upper classes of that period. This peculiarity has apparently disappeared entirely from decent English, though a pronunciation something like *pen* for *pin*, &c., is common among vulgar speakers.

A rather more difficult problem is presented when in Received Standard two different types are found side by side, one of which is of comparatively late appearance, when this later type, being at one time exhibited by a large number of words, has at the present time become restricted to a much smaller group—when in fact the *distribution* of the types among words of one and the same original class has gradually been altered. A case in point is seen in the history of a large group of words which in Middle English contained the combination -*ĕr*-, the original pronunciation of which was approximately that of the Mod. German *er* 'he'. As regards the spelling of these words, present-day English writes sometimes -*er*-, as in *certain*, *servant*, &c., sometimes -*ear*-, as in *learn*, *heard*, &c., sometimes -*ar*-, as in *star*, *far*, *dark*, &c. We have two distinct vowel sounds in the above words, one that of the vowel in *bird*, the other that of the first vowel in *father*. All the words spelt -*ar*- are pronounced with this latter sound, and also some spelt -*er*-, as *clerk*, *Derby*, &c., and a certain number spelt -*ear*-, as *heart*, *hearth*. The rest, whether spelt -*ear*- or -*er*-, are pronounced with the sound heard in *bird*. Now all these words and many others were originally written with -*er*- in M.E. Why this diversity in pronunciation at the present time, a diversity which has actually to some extent been crystallized in the spelling? How has it come about that many of these words are now pronounced with the vowel as in *bird*, which in the sixteenth, seventeenth, and eighteenth centuries were pronounced, by good speakers, according to the '-*ar*-' type? That this was so is proved not only by the statements of writers on pronunciation, but by the spelling in private and published documents. Thus, to mention a few sixteenth-century instances, Bishop Latimer writes *swarving* 'swerving', *farventlye, clargie, hard* 'heard'; Ascham has *hard* 'heard'; Queen Elizabeth writes *harde* and *parson* 'person'; Thomas Wilson writes *darth* 'dearth'. (For a fuller treatment of this point, and evidence of -*ar*- pronunciations in the following centuries, see pp. 212–22, below.) At the present time the distribution of the -*er*- (vowel as in *bird*) and -*ar*- (vowel as in *father*) types is perfectly fixed in Received Standard, and none of the above pronunciations would be considered polite, though the list of -*ar*- pronunciations in the seventeenth and eighteenth centuries which differ from our own is even longer than that for the sixteenth (see pp. 165; 217–21). Between the last quarter of the eighteenth and the first quarter of the nineteenth century, it is evident that a very great shifting took place in Received Standard, in the distribution of the two types of pronunciation in words of this class. What is the reason for this? I think it is difficult, if not impossible, to suggest any other cause than the influence of Class dialect. The history of this question is very curious, and the details must be left for a later chapter, but it may be stated here in outline, and without proofs. The change of -*er*- to -*ar*- seems to have started in the dialects of the S. East (a few spellings occur in the thirteenth century), and to have spread to East Anglia; from 1460 onwards these forms are pretty numerous in the Regional dialect of Essex and Suffolk. The London Official dialect and the Literary dialect had but few -*ar*- forms before the fifteenth century, and they are rare before the end of this or the beginning of the following century. Their number increases with the advance of the century, and they are most numerous in the private documents of Middle Class writers down to the middle of the sixteenth century. The facts seem to point to the -*ar*- forms being importations from below into Upper Class English. They become increasingly fashionable until the last quarter of the eighteenth century, when they recede before the other type, leaving comparatively few survivors, and those chiefly, though not entirely, such words as *dark*, &c., where the -*ar*- spelling was by this time traditional and fixed. I believe that the explanation must be sought in the influence of cultivated Middle Class speakers, who were not content to abide by the now traditional pronunciation 'sarvice', 'vartue', 'sarmon', but preferred to adopt what they conceived to be the more 'correct' and 'refined' pronunciation suggested by the spelling, which by that time had long been fixed. If this view is the right one, and the facts seem to establish it, then we have here a linguistic feature which found its way from a Regional dialect into Middle Class London speech, passed thence into Received Standard, only to be ousted later by a fresh wave of Middle Class influence, this time in the direction of a deliberate attempt at elegance. In its inception, this innovation was probably considered as vulgar and finnicky, as we still consider 'fore-head' instead of 'forrid', or 'often' instead of 'offen', which last, by the way, Queen Elizabeth herself wrote, and doubtless pronounced.

While so many words formerly pronounced according to the -*ar*-type are now pronounced according to the -*er*- type, the former is still adhered to in *clerk*, *heart*, and in the proper names *Berkshire*, *Berkley*, *Bertie*, *Derby*, &c., and this in spite of the spelling. To pronounce these as with the vowel heard in *bird* is a vulgarism from the point of view of Received Standard, and in *heart* this pronunciation is probably never heard.

We may now pass to illustrate variations in Accidence associated with different dialect types. Good examples, of old standing, are the forms of the 3rd pers. Pres. Indic. sing., and the pl. of the same tense in verbs. In M.E. all the Southern and most of the Midland dialects used a 3rd pers. sing. in *-eth*, *cumeth*, &c., until we get pretty far north, to Lincolnshire, where forms in *-es*, *-is*, *cumes*, *cumis*, &c., were almost equally common. The Northern dialects always use *cumis*, *cums*, &c. At the present day the *-eth* forms are unknown in colloquial English anywhere, but are often used in poetry, chiefly because they provide an additional syllable for purposes of metre, and they are familiar to all through the Bible and the Prayer Book. These forms are, then, survivors of the old Southern and Midland usage. The *-s* forms, now universal, are originally Northern, but from the point of Modern English they may be regarded as Midland, since it is pretty clear that they have come into the language of everyday life from East Anglian sources. (On this point, however, see pp. 334–7, below.) Now these *-s* forms are practically unknown in London English, official, literary, and colloquial, during the whole of the fifteenth and the early part of the sixteenth century. In East Anglia, however, they appear, even in prose, during the latter part of the fifteenth century, and are found occasionally much earlier. They are very rare in Literary English prose or in private letters until quite late in the sixteenth century, though they are commoner in some writers, e. g. Latimer, Ascham, Wilson, than in others, and it may be noted that these three were all Cambridge men, and belonged respectively to Leicestershire, Yorkshire, and Lincolnshire. The *-s* forms are very common in Queen Elizabeth's letters written during the last twenty years of her life, but much rarer in the earlier ones, written when she was a girl. In poetry, in the first half of the sixteenth century, 3rd persons in *-s* are commoner than in the prose of the same period, showing that their use here at a time when they were not in common and familiar use is due to metrical reasons. It seems that by the beginning of the seventeenth century, however, these forms had become usual in familiar speech and private letters, though the *-eth* forms continued to be used not only in poetry, but in the more elevated prose style. This is well seen in the Authorized Version, and in such writers as Raleigh and Browne. The auxiliaries *hath* and *doth* continued in literary, and perhaps also in occasional colloquial, use throughout the eighteenth century.

The old M.E. Pres. Indic. plurals are as follows: in the South *-eth*, *we cumeþ*, or *cumeth*, &c.; in the Midlands *-en*, *we cumen*, &c.; in the North *-es*, or *-is*, *we cumis*, &c. The earliest London documents have the Southern forms exclusively, but as early as 1258 the Midland forms predominate (Hen. III's Proclamation), and Davie in 1327 has only one example of an *-eth* ending.

The later fourteenth-century documents, including the works of

Chaucer, have very many forms in *-en* or *-e*, and very few in *-eth*. Caxton's typical form is *-en*. Henceforth we may say that *-en* or the *-e* with the loss of *-n* is the characteristic form of Literary English, and this is the ancestor of our present form without ending. The *-n* is found only sporadically during the sixteenth century. By the side of these Midland forms, the Southern *-eth* occurs in private letters, and even in published literary works here and there throughout the sixteenth century, being found, for instance, occasionally in Euphues. (For details on the Pres. Indic. Sing. and Pl., see pp. 334–41, below.)

In the history of these verbal forms we see the gradual displacement and finally the complete elimination, in Literary and Standard Spoken English, of one dialectal type by another.

Turning now to Vocabulary as a feature of dialectal type, we find that in the older works on Modern Regional Dialect this is almost the only aspect dealt with; indeed most of these works are, in the main, mere glossaries of the various dialects. It is a fact that the present-day provincial dialects between them possess a very large number of words which either (*a*) are not used at all in Received Standard, or (*b*) which express different ideas in the dialects from those which they express in Received Standard. On the other hand, nearly all dialect glossaries contain numbers of words, assigned to the dialect, which are perfectly current in the best spoken and Literary English, and used everywhere in precisely the same sense. For an element of vocabulary to rank as a characteristic dialect feature, this element, or word, must be either unknown altogether in Literary and Received Standard English, or else must be used in different sense, with a different idiomatic value from those given to it in Spoken or Literary Standard. Such Scotch words as *neave* 'fist', *steek* 'to close', *ashet* 'dish', *jaw-box* 'sink', amongst thousands of others, fulfil the first of the above conditions—all of them would be entirely outlandish and incomprehensible to English people of the South—while Irish-English *after* in *he's after doing it* = 'he's just done it', Scotch and North of Ireland *to think long* meaning 'to feel lonely', Irish-English *to knock* in *the horse knocked him at the stone gap* = 'threw him at the stone wall', and *bold* in the sense of 'naughty', said of a child, fulfil the second condition.

As regards the earlier periods of English, a minute analysis of the characteristic regional distribution of vocabulary has yet to be made for Middle English. It is, however, a well-ascertained fact that in certain districts of the Midlands and North very large numbers of Scandinavian words were in use which were unknown in the South, and the occurrence of these in a text would be a safe test, apart from other considerations, by which to rule out a southern origin.

In Middle English it would seem that words often had a comparatively limited diffusion, if we may judge of this from the rarity of their occurrence. In such texts as the West Midland Alliterative Poems (Pearl, Patience, Cleanness, &c.) and Sir Gawayne and the Green Knight, there are dozens of words which seem to be peculiar to these texts, and to have died out of all dialects at the present time. The history of a very large part of the vocabulary of the present-day English dialects is still very obscure, and it is doubtful whether much of it is of any antiquity. So

far very little attempt has been made to sift the chaff from the grain in
that vast receptacle the English Dialect Dictionary, and to decide which
elements are really genuine 'corruptions' of words which the yokel has
heard from educated speakers, or read, misheard, or misread, and
ignorantly altered, and adopted, often with a slightly twisted significance.
Probably many hundreds of 'dialect' words are of this origin, and have
no historical value whatever, except inasmuch as they illustrate a general
principle in the modification of speech. Such words are not, as a rule,
characteristic of any Regional Dialect, although they may be ascribed
to one of these, simply because some collector of dialect forms has
happened to hear them in a particular area. They belong rather to
the category of 'mistakes' which any ignorant speaker may make,
and which such persons do make, again and again, in every part of
the country.

The question which chiefly concerns us here with regard to vocabulary
is how far Standard English, written and spoken, has been influenced by
provincial vocabulary during the last four or five hundred years. This
is a very difficult question to answer with any degree of certainty, but the
probability is that such influence has been very slight. After all, the
essentials of our vocabulary are pretty much the same as they are in
Chaucer or Caxton. Certain terms and idioms have become obsolete ;
certain affectations and preciosities which occur in Caxton have perished—
if indeed they ever lived in English, outside his works ; many new words
of learned origin, or learned concoctions, such as terms from Greek
elements to designate new scientific discoveries, many words from foreign
tongues, have become current in our speech since the beginning of the
fifteenth century ; but has there been any great influx of plain English
words from English provincial dialects ? Such words would necessarily
be terms connected with the simplest and most ordinary experiences of
everyday life, and life on rather a humble plane. But words of this kind
have not been renewed since the fifteenth century to any great extent,
and it is certain that it is not from the uncouth Regional dialects, already
falling into disrepute among both the learned and the polite, that the
rising Standard English would derive the means for a completer and subtler
expressiveness.

When at the present time we find that some word or expression,
claimed as a characteristic of some Regional dialect, is in ordinary use
either in good colloquial or Literary English, we shall probably do well
to believe, unless the contrary is proved, that the so-called 'dialectal'
term has been borrowed from one or other of the latter sources, rather
than that the reverse process has happened.

If we consider contemporary English, whether written or spoken, it
does not appear that the Regional dialects are exerting any appreciable
influence upon our vocabulary. It is certain that no one picks dialect
words and expressions out of a dictionary to introduce them into his
speech or his writings. There is the novel which contains large portions
of dialogue in dialect—sometimes genuine, perhaps oftener fictitious—
but the sporadic appearance of such works is not sufficient to give a wide
currency to new elements of vocabulary. It is doubtful whether even
Mr. Thomas Hardy, in spite of the considerable vogue of the Wessex

Novels, has imposed a new word from the West Country upon Literature, outside the circle of his imitators.   It may be that here and there a writer deliberately uses a dialect word which he has learnt either from Mr. Hardy or Louis Stevenson, for the sake of novelty or picturesqueness, but the occasional occurrence of such a word in a novel or a poem, a word which perhaps nine readers out of ten do not understand, is hardly sufficient to establish the claim—if indeed such a claim be made— that our present-day Literary English is being influenced as regards vocabulary by Regional dialect.

The great factor which nowadays destroys the value of Vocabulary as a specific characteristic of a given Regional dialect, is the migratory habits of the population.   Almost every village, even in districts remote from London or other great centres of population, contains several inhabitants who have come into it from some more or less distant county, either because they have married natives of the village, because they are in the service of local farmers or gentry, or the railway company, or because they were employed in the construction of the local railway line, and stayed on after this was completed.   These persons bring with them alien habits of speech, and their families form so many nuclei whence these spread to a wider circle.   This is certainly true of pronunciation and accidence, but probably to a lesser extent than of vocabulary, for this is far more readily acquired than new vowel sounds or a fresh grammatical system.

The influence of one Regional dialect upon another, brought about by the migration of individuals from one area to another, would be a curious chapter in the study of local dialect, which some day perhaps may be written.   So far nothing has been attempted upon this aspect of the subject, and it seems to be assumed, for the most part, that a Regional dialect is a pure dialect, except in so far as it is influenced by some form of Standard English.   The fact that this is far from being the case will become more and more apparent after the War.   When the soldiers return to their villages they will undoubtedly bring a greatly enlarged vocabulary, consisting partly of new technical terms, partly of the current slang of the Army, partly also of words picked up from their mates in the Regiment, who represent often a great variety of linguistic types. These returned heroes will naturally and properly enjoy a considerable prestige among their fellow villagers, and it would seem inevitable that much of their new jargon will become part and parcel of the speech of the rising generation.   It is thus not improbable that the War will have destroyed, in many areas, the last frail claims of Vocabulary to be considered a specific characteristic of the dialect.

But if the vocabulary of Regional dialects has not greatly influenced the English of Literature, neither has it *fait fortune* in Received Standard Spoken English.

Among speakers of this form of English, country dwellers alone have any direct contact with local dialect in the strict sense.   It is impossible to lead the life of the country, and to share its sports and interests, without coming into more or less close relations with persons whose normal speech is the Regional dialect of the place.   In this way, most speakers of Received Standard who live in the country gain, involuntarily, a very

c

fair knowledge of the local dialect in all its aspects. They can imitate the pronunciation, they know the characteristic grammatical 'mistakes', and they know a considerable number of the typical words and idioms. Yet, in the South and South Midlands at any rate, most persons whose natural speech is Received Standard would not dream of attempting to use the local dialect, pronunciation, and accidence in speaking with their humbler friends. If they did so it would be felt as an insult by the latter. The superior classes keep their excursions into dialect for occasions when they wish to reproduce an amusing thing that some villager has said, for the entertainment of their equals. On the other hand, while retaining his own mode of pronunciation and his own grammar, a speaker of Received Standard may employ, without offence, in his intercourse with all classes, a considerable number of words and expressions, relating to the everyday life of the country, drawn from the local dialect. Such words will for the most part be of a more or less technical character, and connected with agriculture, horses, cattle, and sport. But these terms will hardly be used apart from the scenes and occupations to which they naturally belong, and a man who might quite naturally speak in his own village of selling *tegs*, of finding a *yaffle's nest*, or, if he were an Irishman, of *lepping* a horse, would probably use the ordinary words *sheep, woodpecker, jump*, at a London dinner-table.

In such a case as this the knowledge and occasional use of dialect words could not be said to affect in any way the normal vocabulary of the speaker, any more than would the knowledge of the words of a foreign language, and the proper use of them when speaking that language. Of course if a speaker were unacquainted with the words current in Received Standard, and habitually made use of large numbers of dialect words, in all companies and places, it must be admitted that, even if he spoke ' good ' grammar and had the normal pronunciation, his speech had so far been modified by the Regional form. But, as a matter of fact, such a case is hardly conceivable. The exclusive use of a typical Regional dialect vocabulary, a use not confined to a few categories of words, but embracing expressions indispensable in every aspect of life, would not exist apart from the employment also of the typical pronunciation and grammatical forms of the dialect—in fact a speaker whose vocabulary is of this character will not be a speaker of Received Standard at all, but of Regional dialect pure and simple. To sum up, it is difficult to see how, in recent times, Regional dialect can exercise any considerable *direct* influence upon the vocabulary of Received Standard English. Such influence, in so far as it exists at all, must be *indirect*, and exerted through the medium of Class dialect—that is, through the various forms of Modified Standard. Just as we have seen that the other Class dialects have reacted and are continually reacting upon Received Standard, and thence upon the language of Literature, in respect of pronunciation and grammatical forms, so this is also true of Vocabulary. This brings us to a brief consideration of Vocabulary as a distinguishing and typical feature in Class Dialect.

We have already touched, in passing, upon this point (see p. 4, above). It is desirable to illustrate it rather more fully. It is a curious fact that the characteristic features of the colloquial vocabulary of Received

Standard at any given period consist rather in what is omitted than in what actually occurs. There exists a set of prohibitions and taboos which are quite rigidly, though unconsciously, observed by certain circles, just as in others they are quite as naturally and innocently ignored. We may begin from the point of view of Received Standard, and with this negative side of the case. It must be clearly borne in mind that, in the following and all remarks upon the subject of contemporary Received Standard, no attempt is made to dictate upon ' correctness' in speech, to set up canons of propriety, or to give instruction as to how people ' ought' to speak. We approach the subject merely as students and observers of linguistic facts, which happen to be closely related to social phenomena. We neither blame nor praise ; we are indifferent to what this or that authority may censure or approve. We are simply concerned with what exists among different sections of speakers, and our business is to record faithfully certain habits of speech, and not to exhibit our own preferences.

With these prefatory remarks we may begin our brief catalogue of curiosities, and we thus designate them not because of any inherent strangeness or eccentricity in the words themselves, but on account of the curious fact that what are normal and natural elements of speech in some circles, are regarded in others as ' vulgar' and laughable.

We may begin with what have been called ' shopwalker words', such as *vest* for *waistcoat*, *singlet* for *vest*, *neckwear* for *ties*, *footwear* for *boots and shoes*. It is possible that some regard all these terms as graceful and elegant modes of expression, far superior to the homelier words which they displace. On the other hand, there are many speakers who would as soon think of uttering horrible oaths before ladies, as of using such words seriously. Another word, less ' shoppy' and technical than the above, but used by some with a sense of refinement, is *serviette* instead of *napkin*, whereas others hardly know the word and would be slightly startled if one of their friends were to use it. A very curious usage belongs to that of the definite article before the names of complaints and maladies. The same speakers who might say ' the influenza', ' the measles ', ' the cholera', ' the stomach-ache', ' the scarlet fever ', would never dream of saying ' the bronchitis ', ' the headache ', ' the appendicitis ', ' the cough ', ' the cold ', ' the kidney disease ', while they might omit the article altogether before the entire list of aches and ills just enumerated. The use of the definite article before the names of diseases, &c., was formerly the fashion, and so great an authority on social propriety as Lord Chesterfield said ' the head-ach '. Again, other speakers would use the article before the name of every ill to which human flesh is heir. A word which many reprehended when the present writer was young is *gentlemanly*, *gentlemanlike* being considered the proper word. The latter is now apparently obsolescent in wide circles of speakers, and the former has nearly won the day. The censure formerly directed against *gentlemanly* arose solely from the feeling—right or wrong—that it belonged to the vocabulary of a lower social stratum and was therefore a vulgarism. An interesting reference occurs in a letter of Lord Macaulay of May 28, 1831, in which he records that Lady Holland objected to certain words, saying—' Then there is *talented, influential*, and *gentlemanly*. I never could break Sheridan of saying "*gentlemanly*" though he allowed it was wrong.' (See *Life and Letters of Macaulay*, Popular ed., pp. 150, 151.) Reference has already been made to the discrete and restricted use of the words *gentleman* and *lady* which many practise, preferring the terms *man* and *woman* in referring to the human male and female. On the other hand, many sections of the population now give to the former words an application so universal that more fastidious persons regard these as possessing distressing associations. Thus many would put quite differently the statement—'The party consisted only of my wife and one of her lady friends, myself and another gentleman.' A certain experience and dexterity, if instinct be lacking, are required in the use of the two words.

If it were necessary to attempt to formulate the general tendencies which have been discernible in Received Standard English during the last three centuries and a half, and which have been increasingly potent during the last hundred and fifty years, we should name two, which are to some extent opposed, but both of which are attributable to social causes. The first is the gradual decay of ceremoniousness and formality which has overtaken the speech and modes of address, no less than the manners, of good society. The second is the effort—sometimes conscious and deliberate, sometimes unconscious—after 'correctness' or correctitude, which, on the one hand, has almost eliminated the use of oaths and has softened away many coarsenesses and crudities of expression—as we should now feel them to be, however little squeamish we may be--while on the other it has, by a rigid appeal to the spelling—the very worst and most unreliable court for the purpose—definitely ruled out, as 'incorrect' or 'slipshod' or 'vulgar', many pronunciations and grammatical constructions which had arisen in the natural course of the development of English, and were formerly universal among the best speakers. Both of these tendencies are due primarily to the social, political, and economic events in our history which have resulted in bringing different classes of the population into positions of prominence and power in the State, and the consequent reduction in the influence of the older governing classes. Among these events, which we can only glance at here, are the break-up of the feudal system, which upset temporarily the old social conditions and relations; the extinction of most of the ancient baronial families in the Wars of the Roses; the disendowment of the monasteries, and the enriching of the king's tools and agents, which produced an entirely new class of territorial magnates in Henry VIII's time; the rise of the great merchants in the towns in the late Middle Ages, and the further growth of this class, which under Henry and Elizabeth produced men of the type of Gresham; the Parliamentary Wars and the social upheaval of the Protectorate; the enormous growth of commerce and industry, and the rise of banking during the eighteenth and early nineteenth centuries; and especially, perhaps, the development of steam in manufactures, and the building of railways. By these means many families, in the course of two generations, passed from the shop, the hand-loom, the plough-tail, or from trundling the wheelbarrow, into the great land-owning classes, and became endowed with political influence and even, occasionally, with political insight, one or both of which often rapidly led them to the peerage. In quite recent times the judicious exploitation of the gold and diamonds of South Africa has brought men from the meanest fortunes to great wealth, and therefore to positions of social prestige, within a few years.   Such are a few of the factors which have brought about a continual recruitment of the upper classes from below—often from the very depths.   We may add to these the growth of educational facilities—very much enhanced of late years—which increasingly throughout the last few centuries have enabled the young man of talent to carve for himself a way to fortune and importance, and to reach positions where he could be useful to the State or to the Church.   While the skeleton of the fabric of English society has remained the same since the break-up of the feudal system, the actual human elements in every section are being continually modified.   Applied to the time of Edward IV such phrases as 'baronial class', or Tenants in Chief, imply generally, the descendants of the companions of the Conqueror.   We still have a baronial class, but its members are not all the sons of these men. Every class is for ever being renewed from below, and though the old labels remain, they have largely lost their significance.

These social changes have inevitably brought with them corresponding changes in manners and in speech.   It may be said that the new arrivals within each social group would assimilate the speech and manners of those among whom they came, and this is no doubt largely true, but the speech and habits of a lifetime are not changed in a moment, as a vesture. Much of the old remains, and slowly and imperceptibly the new-comers react upon their environment, almost as much as they are influenced by it.   Thus, for instance, it is suggested that the Middle Class Puritan ideals have gradually brought about a greater reticence of expression and a more temperate use of expletives, and also a greater simplicity of manners, from which many of the airs and graces of the older order were eliminated. Again, a highly cultivated and intellectual section of the Middle Class have played a prominent part in Church and State since the time of Elizabeth.   We see, under that monarch, a generation of courtiers, statesmen, and prelates, who were also scholars, and even some who, like Sir Thomas Smith, were educational reformers and writers upon language, as well as statesmen.   The influence of these learned courtiers would be in the direction of correctness and elegance of utterance, in opposition to the more careless and unstudied speech of the mere man of fashion.   It is not forgotten that the English aristocracy of the older kind has always produced from time to time its Surreys, Sidneys, and Sackvilles.   There can be no better conditions for the formation of colloquial speech than a society in which the graces and lightness of the courtier are united to the good taste and sound knowledge of the scholar.   From such a circle we might expect a mode of speech as far removed from the mere frivolities of fashion, the careless and half-incoherent babble of the fop, as from the tedious preciousness of the pedant, or the lumbering and uncouth utterance of the boor.   Such a speech would be worthy to become the common standard of a great people, and the conditions under which it could arise existed, if anywhere, at the Court of Elizabeth.   Lord Chesterfield, with his usual sound sense, remarks in one of his letters: 'The common people of every country speak their own language very ill; the people of fashion (as they are called) speak it better, but not always correctly, because they are not always people of letters. Those who speak their own language the most accurately are those who have learning and are at the same time in the polite world; at least their language will be reckoned the standard of the language of that country' (Letter 103).

We have described one kind of result, of the mingling of classes, upon English manners and speech, but there is another which is less happy in its manifestations. It is one thing to bring naturalness to the manners of an age which has too many artificial airs and graces, by introducing an honest, independent simplicity of bearing; it is quite another thing to supplant a gay geniality, or a courtly and gracious ceremoniousness, by a loutish awkwardness which springs from an ignorance of how to behave, by a blatant and vulgar familiarity of address which knows no discrimination, or by a stiff-backed pomposity that ill conceals an uneasy self-conceit. These things neither attach nor charm.

Similarly, in the matter of speech, it is good to contribute a nice and accurate sense in the use of words, a clearness and precision of construction, a definite and unambiguous enunciation, when all these are combined with the ease, the lightness, the swiftness, and the complete absence of deliberately studied utterance which are the essentials of civilized colloquial speech.

It is quite another thing to be so haunted by the fear of not being 'correct' as to attempt an over-precise pronunciation—based for the most part upon the supposed force of the spelling—which departs so far from established usage as to suggest that the speaker is ignorant of this; to adopt words and locutions derived from books and in their place there, but unusual and misplaced in colloquial English; to aim at a sham refinement in pronunciation and vocabulary, to shun what is familiar through fear of being vulgar—in a word to be either artificial or pedantic.

Such are among the chief vices of Middle Class English at the present time, and such they have always been. These traits at first strike speakers who are unaccustomed to them as ridiculous and vulgar, but by force of habit, many of them gain, first tolerance, and then even acceptance, and the history of English, during the last couple of centuries at any rate, shows that many of these features have been imposed upon Received Standard and have taken the place of the old traditional forms, while others are in process of becoming accepted despite the contempt of the older generation. This is perhaps the natural result of the shifting standards of taste, manners, and speech which were inseparable from the social movements referred to. It is significant that while the Middle Classes used to insist upon being 'genteel', the very word has now fallen into disrepute, and is held to express a false ideal of breeding, a bogus refinement, far more vulgar than downright coarseness.

We may illustrate, in passing, the decay of ceremoniousness as exhibited in language, in the modes of address. It is certain that the plays, novels, as well as the private letters, diaries, and memoirs of the sixteenth, seventeenth, and eighteenth centuries reveal a state of manners and address among the superior classes far more stately and elaborate than anything that now obtains; even Miss Austen's novels occasionally exhibit a style of colloquial English which would now be felt as stilted and high-flown.

Taking the mode of addressing and referring to people, whether in conversation or in letters, we need only consider here the use of *Sir* and *Madam, My Lord, My Lady, Your Lordship,* and so on. How many sons and daughters would now use any of these forms to their parents? We may say that among persons who, without being intimate, meet or correspond on terms of anything like equality, and still more so among relations and intimate friends, all these modes of address are obsolete in private life, and survive only in formal letters to strangers, or, in uttered speech, only from the public platform, in courts of justice, and upon official ceremonial occasions.

How different was the custom in the eighteenth century may be gathered from one of Lord Chesterfield's letters, in which he says—'It is extremely rude to answer only Yes or No to anybody, without adding Sir, My Lord, Madam, according to the quality of the person you speak to.' Lady Mary Wortley Montagu, writing to her intimate friend Lady Bristol, makes constant use of polite formulas—'You'll wonder, Madam,' &c., 'I received your Ladyship's letter'; to Lady Rich she writes 'I have just received at Vienna your Ladyship's compliments'; again— 'you see, Madam,' and so on. Lady Lucy Wentworth, writing as a child, in 1739, to her 'Dear Papa', Lord Strafford, signs herself 'Your Lordship's most dutifull and most affectionet daughter', and adds a postscript, referring to her sister—'Lady Hariot beggs her duty to your Lordship.' Such graces of address have vanished from the friendly intercourse of intimates and relations, apparently with the triumph of 'the genteel thing', and it can hardly be temerarious to connect the modern off-hand style, and the decline in the external forms of politeness, which has been going on for a hundred years or more, with the rapid rise of a wealthy bourgeoisie and industrial class, who were perhaps inclined to attach too little value to externals. The social movements which have so profoundly affected Received Standard English, have changed it also in that aspect which is the outward expression of manners, and nowadays an off-hand informality and familiarity of address are considered a part of the natural and inevitable equipment of good breeding. No part of a language is perhaps more difficult for a stranger to acquire, and to apply with propriety, than the polite formulas which are current at a given moment in a particular society; nothing in speech is more intimately related than these to the social, moral, and cultural state of which language is the most vital expression.

With regard to the second tendency, that—at its best—towards greater decorum and less crudity in expression, or—in its less admirable light— towards 'gentility', sham refinement, and a mincing utterance, it has already been said that the Middle Class has so far won the day, for good or for ill, that that outspokenness which characterized the familiar speech of the seventeenth and eighteenth centuries has been considerably toned down. While among both the upper and the lower classes, as distinct from those which intervene, a freedom and frankness of thought and expression have always prevailed which differ widely from what the author of *The Decay in the Art of Lying* called 'the kind of conversation that goes on at a meat-tea in the house of a serious non-conformist family', it would be easy to cull from the plays and letters of the seventeenth and eighteenth centuries words and expressions placed in the mouths of well-bred ladies, or coming naturally from their pen in correspondence, which women of equal breeding nowadays would consider coarse and indelicate. Not many women at the present time would write—if they could—some of the poems of Lady Mary Montagu. We may take examples almost at random from the dramatists. 'I wonder, Sir Francis,' says Lady Heartfree in Vanbrugh's *Journey to London*—'I wonder you will allow the lad to swill his guts with such beastly lubberly liquour.' If the genuineness of this as a picture of the speech of a 'woman of quality' in the late seventeenth or early eighteenth century be doubted, we have ample confirmation in the Wentworth Papers of the first third of the latter century. 'My father is laid up with the gout;' writes young Lady Strafford, 'I believe I shall jumble my guts out between this and Russell Street, for since my father has been ill, I have gon every day.' Agàin, the same lady says, speaking of the abode of Prince Eugene in London—'I wonder Mons. Marshall can talk of his great liveing here, for they had a very indifferent lodging in St. James Street, and the house was keept the nastiest I ever see a house, and used to stink of your favorite dish onions, ready to kill me.' This is not elegant diction according to our present views, and few great ladies would now speak or write thus. (See further examples in Chap. X.)

Still more remote is all this from the speech of a bourgeoisie which, if it cannot aspire to the fine manners of its betters, dare not cultivate their freedom of expression, as it is not always sure of being able to distinguish true refinement from mere squeamishness. People who are anxious above all to be 'genteel' dare not run risks or play pranks in conversation. A very shrewd hit at the flimsy sham refinement, which was current already in the eighteenth century, is made by Goldsmith in the immortal dialogue of the alehouse revellers in *She Stoops to Conquer*, and the satire is all the more telling and laughable by reason of the incongruity of the fine sentiments expressed, and the vulgarity of the language in which they are couched.

Squire Lumpkin has just sung the stirring ballad of 'The Three Jolly Pigeons', which is greeted with great enthusiasm. When this has subsided the following comments are made by those present:

'I loves to hear him sink, bekeays he never gives us nothing that's low.—

'O damn anything that's low, I cannot bear it—

'The genteel thing is the genteel thing any time: if so be that a gentleman is in a concatenation accordingly.—

'I like the maxum of it master Muggins. What though I am obligated to dance a bear, a man may be a gentleman for all that. May this poison me if my bear ever dances but to the very genteelest tunes: "Water Parted", or "The minuet in Ariadne".'

'The genteel thing is the genteel thing'—'Damn anything that's low'—there is the whole gospel of a certain class of speakers. It may be put into any terms you please, but the sentiment is the same. The difficulty for them is just this, to be quite sure what is 'genteel' and what is 'low'. Shakespeare puts into the mouth of Hotspur, in *Henry IV*, a protest against a particular form of 'gentility' which has completely triumphed in our day, namely, the use of mild expressions of asseveration instead of

oaths of a more lurid character. While the following is directed specifically at the *bourgeois* habit of avoiding strong expressions of a particular
kind, its wider applicability to mincing and over-niceness in general can
hardly be doubted.
(The text and spelling are those of the First Folio.)

Hotspur. Come Ile haue your song too.
Lady. Not mine in good sooth.
Hotspur. Not yours in good sooth?
You sweare like a Comfit-makers Wife:
Not yours in good sooth; and, as true as I liue;
And, as God shall mend me; and, as sure as day:
And giuest such Sarcenet-suretie Oathes,
As if thou neuer walk'st further then Finsbury.
Sweare me, Kate, like a Lady as thou art,
A good mouth-filling Oath: and leaue in sooth,
And such protest of Pepper Ginger-bread,
To veluet-Guards, and Sunday-Citizens.
Act III, sc. i.

'Like a Comfit-maker's Wife'! 'Sunday-Citizens'; there is the whole
matter in a nutshell. 'Swear me like a Lady as thou art—a good mouth-
filling oath'—a very different school of manners this from that which
demands 'the genteel thing'. We shall return later to the subject of
fashionable oaths and expletives, the use and character of which varies
from age to age, and to some extent from individual to individual.

We may note here, by way of contrast with the above, that that very
great gentleman Lord Chesterfield, while admitting that 'you may sometimes hear some people, in good company, interlard their discourse with
oaths, by way of embellishment, as they think', adds—'but you must
observe, too, that those who do so are never those who contribute, in any
degree, to give that company the denomination of good company. They
are always subalterns, or people of low education; for that practice,
besides that it has no one temptation to plead, is as silly, and as illiberal,
as it is wicked' (Letter 166).

This pronouncement is at the other extreme from that of Hotspur.
It has a certain historical interest both on account of its author and of the
date at which it was written—1748. Even allowing for the century and
a quarter since Shakespeare, and the undoubted reaction in speech and
manners from the licence of the Restoration, there are reasons for thinking
that Lord Chesterfield, in this particular respect, was decidedly ahead of
the society—or, as he would have said, the 'company'—in which he lived.

One of the greatest charms of the historical study of a language lies
in the picture which it exhibits of the kaleidoscopic changes in the
standards of taste which prevail in civilized society from age to age.
Rightly interpreted, language is a mirror of the minds and manners of
those who speak it. It is at this point, perhaps, that the two studies of
'language', in the technical sense in which universities are apt to use
the term, and 'literature' seem most to meet and merge, so much so
that for a moment the interests appear one and the same. And yet, in
general, the aims, methods, and point of view of the pure philologist are
so different from those of the pure student of literature, that a foolish and

mischievous belief has arisen that these two great studies are in hostile opposition to each other. This view naturally finds most adherents among those who know least, or at any rate *understand* least, of either Literature or Philology. It is perfectly true that there is a conception of literature which seems remote from all human life and activity, and it is difficult to believe that such a conception, or the kind of study which is naturally based upon it, can appeal to, or interest any healthy and normal mind. It is unfortunately also true that there is an equally dismal and sinister hobgoblin which masquerades under the title of English Philology, and from this bogey, 'holy souls' at all times recoil with loathing and abhorrence. These two monsters, sham 'Literature' and dead 'Philology', may well be opposed to each other—very likely they are—but then they are equally unrelated to, and out of touch with, everything else in the world of realities, except the dreary minds which have conjured them up, and find therein a melancholy pleasure.

The invitation which a student of the history of a language utters to the companions of his voyage of discovery should be :

> 'Together let us beat this ample field,
> Try what the open, what the covert yield;
> The latent tracts, the giddy heights explore,
> Of all who blindly creep, or sightless soar;
> Eye nature's walks, shoot folly as it flies,
> And catch the manners living as they rise.'

This is a terribly high ideal to aim at, and one most difficult of attainment, but it is the true one. It means that the study of language is one line of approach to the knowledge of Man, and that fact is one we must never lose sight of.

It cannot be denied that, even in a more or less light-hearted study such as the present work, there is a certain amount of dry detail to be gone through, which many may find very dull. But let these believe that 'even the weariest river winds somewhere safe to sea', and that the 'horrible pit, the mire and clay', through which for a time they must pass, is only as a Wilderness in which they wander awhile—not for forty years but which leads to the promised land, 'a good land and a large, a land flowing with milk and honey'. This is the reward of a first-hand study of the subject itself. It is not always given to those who merely read books written about it.

To 'catch the manners living as they rise' is not easy when we attempt to do so through the language of generations which are dead and gone. Language as a whole, in all its aspects, its words and idioms, its coarseness and reticences, its pronunciation, and the very tones of voice, language in its completeness, is the most perfect mirror of the manners of the age. But how difficult to call up all this from the printed page, how more than difficult to convey to others some impression of those fragments which it may have been our good fortune to discover.

As we steep ourselves in the English of successive ages, we may gradually gain a sense of the spirit and genius of each, and feel the slow, almost imperceptible change which creeps on from age to age. Wherein precisely do the peculiar spirit and genius of each generation consist ? We may set forth the vocabulary, the turns of phrase, the clichés in vogue ; we may give an account of the inflexions, and describe the pronunciation of each period; but in none of these things severally or combined does the genius of the age completely reside.   Of course, it is too subtle for our analysis, and if we can dimly perceive it, we cannot, so to speak, decant it, and say 'here it is for all to taste'.   All we can do is to select some of the most obvious and least subtle aspects of language, the mere husks which contain part of the vital principle, and attempt to bring them before the reader.

CHAPTER II

DIALECT TYPES IN MIDDLE ENGLISH, AND THEIR SURVIVAL IN THE MODERN PERIOD

ALTHOUGH this book is concerned primarily with Modern English, and more particularly with the colloquial forms of speech, it is necessary to the intelligibility of the rather complex questions arising out of the composite character at once of Modern Literary English, and of Received Spoken English, to take a preliminary survey of the main types of English which were spoken and written prior to the establishment of one of these as the sole medium of literary expression, and the recognition of the same type as the Received Standard of the Spoken Language.

And first it is desirable to understand what we mean by the chronological labels which, for the sake of convenience, we attach to the language of different periods. When we speak of Old, Middle, and Modern periods, we must not be understood to imply that each of these has a perfectly clear-cut boundary which demarcates the English of each from that which goes before, and that which follows. Such sharp divisions do not occur in the history of a language.

Language is always changing, always in process of becoming different from what it was before. Just as the succeeding generations of mankind overlap, so that at any given moment there may exist, side by side, the old, the middle-aged, and the young, so do the characteristic features in the speech of each generation overlap and intermingle. Thus, at any given moment, we have the speech of the mature and effective generation, the central type which represents the average for the time being; but there is also heard the old generation which is passing away ; and, further, that of the rising youth who hold the promise of the future. There are no sudden breaks with the old tradition, but a gradual, continuous, and unperceived passage from what was to what is, and yet again foreshadowings of what is to be. We speak habitually of periods of Transition, as when the English of the twelfth century is called First Transition, that is from Old to Middle English, or when that of the fifteenth is thought of as the transition from Middle to Modern English. But in reality each period is one of transition, and if, in looking into the language of the past, we seem at times to get an impression of an abrupt and sudden change, it is because our record is imperfect, and our analysis not subtle enough, so that the sense of gradual development is lost.

As a matter of fact, the more minutely we study the documents from which our knowledge of the history of English is gained, the greater becomes our feeling of continuous development, and, consequently, the more reluctant are we to chop English up into periods, and affix labels to

each. It should be understood that whatever test we may take in deciding such a question as—when does the Modern period of English begin, and the Middle English period end ? and however we may answer the question, there is always this mental reserve, that, *so far as our available evidence goes*, this or that feature, which we choose to take as characteristic of Modern English, is not proved from the written documents to have existed before such and such a date. That it may have existed in actual speech much earlier, no sane person will deny; that it must have existed some time before it was sufficiently recognized to be recorded by the scribes, is certain.

Bearing these considerations in mind we shall realize that the chronological divisions which it is convenient, and indeed essential, to make are merely rough approximations to the actual fact. We may make such a rough-and-ready division as the following: **Old English,** from the earliest period down to about 1150; **Middle English,** which we may further subdivide into the Early, Central, and Late periods, from 1150 or so down to about 1400; **Modern English,** from the early fifteenth century to the present day. We should further distinguish **Early Modern,** from 1400 or so to the middle of the sixteenth century ; and after that it is often convenient to distinguish late sixteenth-century, seventeenth-century, eighteenth-century English, and in the same rough way we may consider Present-day English to begin towards the end of the eighteenth century.

It is proposed to give, as briefly as possible, an account of the main characteristics of those dialectal types which are represented in varying degrees in the London English of the fourteenth century, more especially the language of Chaucer. We shall then examine the leading features of fourteenth-century London English, emphasizing the different Regional constituents of this dialect.

The Middle English Dialects.

Considering the speech of England as a whole, from the twelfth to the fourteenth centuries inclusive, we are able to distinguish four main types, clearly separated from each other by different treatment of the older system of vowel sounds, and by different developments in the accidence, principally in connexion with the inflexion of verbs and pronouns.

The roughest and most general classification of the M.E. dialects is into Northern—including the speech of the Scottish Lowlands—Midland, South-Western, and South-Eastern, of which the Kentish dialect is the most marked and best represented in written documents. Midland may be further divided into East and West Midland, and each of these again varies in the northern and more southerly areas. The Southern group of dialects, while they all possess certain characteristics in common, are divided by definitely marked features according to their easterly or westerly situation, and we should further distinguish the central Southern dialects of Berkshire and Hampshire. The speech of the latter county, about which we know something in the M.E. period, shows on the whole the features of the west, but shares with the more easterly areas certain characteristics not possessed by the former. The dialects of Herefordshire, Worcestershire, Shropshire, and Oxfordshire seem to have been mainly Southern in character, but to have had also certain traits which we generally associate with Midland. This group is best regarded as South-West Midland.

The most important dialects for our present purpose—the making of Standard English—are those of the South (Central and Western), the South-Eastern (Kent and Essex), and the East Midland, especially the southern parts of this area—Suffolk and Norfolk. The Northern dialects have had very little direct influence upon Standard English, and those of the West Midlands still less.

(A list of some representative M.E. texts, arranged according to dialect, will be found in the *Bibliography*, p. 61.)

A few words are necessary concerning the pronunciation of M.E. It must ever be borne in mind that we are dealing primarily with *sounds* and not with *letters*. The Old English system of expressing vowel sounds was considerably modified by the Norman scribes. Sometimes sounds which had undergone little or no change since the O.E. period were expressed by a different spelling in M.E. Other sounds which had changed considerably were still written in the same way. Finally, some sounds which had come to be pronounced quite differently were gradually expressed by a new spelling, which shows that a change has taken place in the pronunciation.

M.E. spelling, though used according to method and custom, is not by any means perfectly consistent. It is to a certain extent phonetic, in that there is often a genuine attempt to express the sound as accurately as possible, but scribal custom soon hardens, and we must not expect to find minute shades of sound carefully distinguished. On the other hand, occasional lapses of the scribes from fixed habit may give us a valuable revelation of a change of sound. We may lay it down as a general principle that the alphabet as used by M.E. writers has what is called the 'continental values'—that is, the letter *a* (in the South and Midlands) represents roughly the same sound as in Italian or French, long or short as the case may be ; *e* represents either the sound of *e* in French *dé,* or that in *bête* ; *i* represents the vowel in French *vite;* *o* sometimes the vowel in French *beau,* sometimes approximately that in French *corps;* *u* never by any chance stands for the vowel in the Mod. Eng. *tune,* nor for that in English *but,* but either for the vowel in Mod. French *lune, but,* &c., or for the long vowel in Mod. Eng. *spoon.* This latter sound is more often written *ou* after the middle of the thirteenth century, according to the French habit. As a rule such combinations as *eu, ei, ai, au,* and sometimes *ou,* represent real diphthongs, that is *two distinct vowel sounds,* those which the letters of the combinations severally express.

Length of vowel is often expressed by doubling the symbol, as *goode, saaf,* and, by a few scribes, by marking the length above the letter. In this book long vowels in Old and Middle English words will always be marked in the usual way—*ā, ī,* &c.

As regards consonantal symbols, *ð* and *þ,* both inherited from O.E., represent indifferently the '*th*'-sound in *th*is or that in *th*ink ; *u* and *v* are used indifferently for the '*v*'-sound; *gh, h,* and sometimes *g,* represent either the sound of *ch* in German *ach,* or that in *ich* ; *ȝ,* a modification of an O.E.

letter, generally stands for the sound of *y* in *yacht*, but in many texts in the fourteenth century *y* is used for this sound; *r* is to be pronounced pretty much as in present-day Scotch wherever it is written; *wh* represents the sound of voiceless *w*, as in the Scotch pronunciation of *which, white*, &c.

We now proceed to indicate the chief characteristics of the various M.E. dialects both as regards sounds and accidence.

East Midland.

1. O.E. *ǣ* becomes *ă*, or when lengthened, *ā* :—O.E. *glæd*, M.E. *glăd*, O.E. *sæt*, M.E. *săt*, &c.; lengthened in :—O.E. *fǣder*, M.E. *fāder* 'father'.

2. O.E. *ǣ* becomes, according to its origin, either [ē] with sound of Mod. French *été*, or [ē] with sound of Mod. Fr. *bête*. The former occurs in M.E. *seed, sēde*; O.E. *sǣd* 'seed', the latter in M.E. *tēchen, teachen*, O.E. *tǣcan* 'teach'.

Note. The O.E. symbol *æ* represented the same vowel as the Mod. Eng. sound in *hat, mad*, &c. It occurred in O.E. both long and short.

The O.E. long *ǣ* had two distinct origins. (*a*) *ǣ* represents a Primitive O.E. vowel of very frequent occurrence. This vowel remained practically unchanged in the **West Saxon dialects** until the close of the O.E. period. In all the other dialects, North, Midland, and Kentish or S. Eastern, it became *ē* and is so written in the earliest records. We may refer to this sound as *ǣ*[1].

Examples of this are:—W. Saxon *sǣd* 'seed', non-W.S. *sēd*; W.S. Pret. Pl. *sǣton* 'they sat', *bǣron* 'they bore', *sprǣcon* 'they spoke', &c., non-W.S. *sēton, bēron, sprēcon*, &c. The existence of the latter type in words of this class in a M.E. text shows that it is not in an ideally pure W.S. dialect, though it does not fix it as definitely E. Midland, without other considerations. The proof of whether the Sthn. [ē] or the non-Sthn. [ē] exists in any given text cannot always be established with perfect certainty. The best proofs are (1) rhymes in which words which had this *ǣ* in O.E. rhyme with other words of a different class which are known to have either one or other of the two *ē*-sounds; or (2) the occurrence of the spelling *ea* which is never used for the tense [ē]. Thus if *rēde* 'council' should rhyme with *bēde*, 'prayer', it would establish the Southern type of pronunciation of *rēde*, O.E. *rǣd*, as *bēde*, O.E. (*ge*)*bedu*, had the long slack [ē] in all dialects. Again, such a spelling as *weaden* 'weeds, garments', O.E. *gewǣde*, which occurs in Ancren Riwle, also proves the Southern type of pronunciation. Such a rhyme as *dēde* with *ʒēde*, see extract B (*d*) below, shows Midland type, as *ʒēde*, O.E. *ʒe-eōde*, has always a tense *ē*.

(*b*) The other O.E. *ǣ* sound had a different origin, and a different fate. As regards its origin, it was developed in O.E. itself, before the historical period, from a long *ā* vowel, when this was followed by either -*i*-, or -*j*- in the next syllable. Thus O.E. *tǣcan* 'teach', fr. **tākjan*, cf. O.E. *tācn* 'sign'; O.E. *dǣlan* 'to divide', *dǣl* 'a part', fr. **dāljan, *dāli*, cf. the unaltered O.E. *dāl* 'a part' (our *dole*); O.E. *lǣdan* 'lead,' fr. **lādjan*, cf.

lād 'path', 'course'; *lǣran* 'to teach', fr. **lārjan*. cf. O.E. *lār* 'doctrine, lore', &c., &c. The *ǣ* of this origin we may refer to as *ǣ²*. This *ǣ* remains in every O.E. dialect except Kentish, where it is early, though subsequently to the change of the former *ǣ* just considered, changed to *ē*. In M.E. this characteristic difference between Kentish and the other dialects is preserved, and while the latter have the slack [ē] in words of this class, Kentish and South-Eastern have [ē]. This is well shown in the late fourteenth-century writings of Gower, a Kentishman. This writer, who, as we shall see, is on the whole remarkably free from provincialisms, habitually expresses the tense [*ē*], whatever its origin, by *ie*, and very conveniently for us, frequently writes *diel* 'part'; he also rhymes *tēchen* 'teach', with *sēchen* 'seek', where it is certain that tense *ē* is intended, as the latter word could have no other pronunciation. East Midland, then, agrees with all M.E. dialects except the Southern, Saxon dialects in having the tense sound for *ǣ¹*, and with all the dialects except Kentish in having the slack sound for *ǣ²*.

(3) O.E. *ȳ*, which had the sound of French *u* in *lune*, &c., becomes *ī* in East Midland as in the Northern dialects. Examples:—(short *ȳ*) O.E. *hyll*, M.E. *hill*, O.E. *bryċġ* 'bridge', M.E. *brigge*, O.E. *synn* 'sin', M.E. *sinne*, &c.; (long *ȳ*) O.E. *fȳr* 'five', M.E. *fīr*, O.E. *hȳdan* 'to hide', M.E. *hīden*, O.E. *(ge)mȳnd* 'mind, memory', M.E. *mīnd*. Note that the letter *y* is often used in M.E. for long or short *i*, and occurs often in the above words, but it never implies anything but the *i* sound. Note also that in some areas of the E. Midlands the old *ȳ* sound appears as *ē*. See further on this below, under Kentish and South-Eastern.

(4) O.E. *ĕo* becomes *ē*, always tense when it represents O.E. *ēo* in East Midland. Examples:—O.E. *eorþe* 'earth', M.E. *erþe*, O.E. *heorte* 'heart', M.E. *herte*; O.E. *ċēōsan* 'choose', M.E. *chēsen*, O.E. *hēōld* Pret. Sing. of *healdan* 'hold', M.E. *hēld*, O.E. *fēōll* Pret. Sing. of *feallan* 'fall', M.E. *fell*, &c., &c.

(5) O.E. *ea* before *r* and another cons. becomes *æ* in late O.E. and in M.E. appears in E. Midlands as *ar-*. Examples:—O.E. *earm* 'poor', later *ærm*, M.E. *arm*, O.E. *heard*, *hærd* 'hard, bold', M.E. *hard*, &c.; *ea* before *ll* becomes *all*, O.E. *eall* 'all', M.E. *all*. Bokenam, however, still has such belated forms as *sherp* 'sharp', *yerd* 'yard', perhaps through Essex influence.

(6) Southern O.E. *eald*, Late O.E. (Sthn.) *ǣld*, appears as *āld* in the Midland and Northern dialects already in O.E. This form becomes *ōld* in M.E. in the Midlands, through the change of *ā* to *ō*. Examples:— O.E. (Sthn.) *eald*, *ǣld*, Midland *āld* 'old', O.E. Southern *beald*, *bǣld* 'bold', Midland *bāld*, M.E. Midland *bōld*, O.E. Southern *ċeald*, *ċǣld* 'cold', Midland *cāld*, M.E. Midland *cōld*, &c. Norf. Guilds have the exceptional *hĕlden*, inf. and Bokenam *held* imperat. See the Southern and Kentish treatment of this sound below.

(7) O.E. *ĭe*. This diphthong, both long and short, is typical of the Southern, West Saxon dialects in O.E. In all the other dialects it appears as *ĕ* in the corresponding words already in the OE. period. From the point of view of the Midland and other non-Saxon dialects, therefore, including Kentish and South-Eastern, the starting-point is *ĕ*. This *ĕ* remains in Midland in M.E. See, however, under Southern below, the

fate of Old English (W. Saxon) *ĭe*. Examples of this in Midland M.E. are:—O.E. (non-Sax.) *ermþu*, West Saxon *iermþu* 'misery', M.E. Midland *ermþe*; O.E. (non-Sax.) *hēran* 'hear', West Saxon *hīeran*, M.E. Midland *hēren*, O.E. (non-Sax.) *lēsan* 'release, redeem', West Saxon *līesan*, M.E. Midland *lēsen*.

Points affecting the Accidence in East Midlands.

(8) Pres. Indic. 3rd Pers. Sing. ends in *-eþ*—*comeþ* 'comes', *tākeþ* 'takes', *þencheþ* 'thinks'. In the more northerly area (Lincolnshire, and even in Norfolk) the Northern ending *-es* often occurs, but, further south, this form gains ground slowly, and in the fifteenth century very few examples are found in Suffolk and Essex sources.

(9) Pres. Indic. Pl. ends in *-en*, or *-e*—*we hope*(*n*) 'hope', *we seye*(*n*) 'say', *we māke*(*n*) 'make'.

(10) Imperat. Pl. ends in *-eþ*—*comeþ* 'come', *lōkeþ* 'look', &c.

(11) Pres. Participle ends in *-end*(*e*)—*rennend*(*e*) 'running', *touchend*(*e*) 'touching'. In the northerly area of Lincolnshire, the typical Northern *-and* often occurs (Handlyng Synne). Even Norf. Guilds have *-and* at least once, by the side of the usual *-end*, and occasional *-yng*. The ending *-ing*, *-yng* is found occasionally quite early in the fourteenth century, and finally becomes the sole form.

(12) The Fem. Pers. Pron. *sche*, *she*, *scho*, &c., is found quite early—even Peterborough Chron. (*c.* 1154) has *scæ*. This form is Northern in origin, and usurps the place of the O.E. *heo*, M.E. *he*, *heo*, &c., &c.; cf. the Fem. Pron. in South-West and Kent below.

(13) The Pers. Pronouns in the Pl. are *hē*, and the Scandinavian *þei* 'they', and gradually, though later, *þeir*, &c., 'their', and *þeim* 'them', take the place of the O.E. *hie*, *heora*, *heom*, &c., M.E. *hī*, *hē*, *here*, *hem*. The Scandinavian forms apparently pass into Midland fr. the North, and the Nom. comes first. With the exception of Orm (1200), however, who has *þeȝȝ*, even this form is not much in use before 1300, after which date it apparently becomes almost, though not entirely, the only form in use. Norf. Guilds still have *he* by the side of the usual *þey*, &c. Orm has Dat. Pl. *þeȝȝm* by the side of the old *hemm*, and *hem* seems to be the typical form until the fifteenth century (Bokenam). The typical Possessive Pl. is *here*, only Orm having *þeȝȝre* (by the side of *heore*) before the fourteenth century. Early in this century Robt. of Brunne has occasional *þeyr*, by the side of the much more frequent *here*; Norfolk Guilds (1389) appear only to have *here*, but Bokenam in the next century has both the English and Scandinavian forms. Compare this with the state of things in South-West and South-East.

(14) Pres. Pl. *are*, *aren* of Verb 'to be'; also *bēn*.

(15) Loss of O.E. prefix *ge-*, M.E. *i-*, *y-*, in Past Participles, and retention of *-n* at the end of strong P. P.'s. This latter, however, is not universal:—*cumen*, *forbodyn* 'forbidden', *tolde* 'told'; cf. Southern *icume*, *itold*, &c.

The following short extracts from E. Midland texts give some idea of the dialect. The numbers attached to certain forms refer to the above

D

statements of the dialect features, and the words so numbered illustrate the feature described in the paragraph with the corresponding number.

It will be seen that in most cases there is a certain admixture of forms which do not belong strictly nor solely to E. Midland. This is rather disappointing and disconcerting to the student, who must remember that the speech of one area dovetails into that of another, as do the areas themselves.

Specimens of E. Midland.

A. FROM THE BESTIARY, CIRCA 1220.

(a) Wiles[1] þat weder is sō ille	at times the weather
þe[1] sipes[14] þat arn on[2.b.] sē fordriven[15]	ships that are driven about on the sea
lōð[13] hem is dēð[4], and lēf to liven	hateful to them is death, and dear to live
bilōken[9] hem[13], and sēn[9] ðis fis;	they look around
an ēilond hē[13] wēnen[9] it is	they think ('ween') it is an island
þerof[13] he aren[14] swið[1] fagen,	they are very glad thereof,
And mid here[13] migt þar[13] tō he dragen[9]	with their might towards it they draw
Sipes on festen	at anchor
And alle up gangen[9]	go
(b) Ðis devel is mikel wið wil and magt	
So wicches haven[9] in here[13] craft[1]	their
He doð[9] men hungren and haven ðrist[3]	he causes men to hunger and to have thirst
And mani ōðer[3] sinful list[3].	many other sinful desires

B. FROM ROBERT OF BRUNNE'S HANDLYNG SYNNE, C. 1303.

(a) Fro þat[1] tȳme þan wax Pers	
A man of sō feyre manérs	
Þat nō man myȝt yn hȳm fȳnde	
But to þe pōre bōþe mēke[4] & kȳnde[3];	
A mȳlder man ne myȝt nat bē	
Ne to þe pōre mōre of almes frē[4]	
And reuful of herte alsō he was,[1]	
Þat *mayst*[2.b.] þou hēre lēre yn þys pas.	learn
(b) Pērs stōde and dyd behōlde[6]	
How þe man þe kyrtyl sōlde[6]	
And[1] was þarwith[6] fērly wrōpe	wrapped up
Þat he sōlde sō sōne hys clōþe;	
He myȝt nō lenger for sorow stande,	
But ȝēde[4] hōme ful sōre grētand[11].	weeping

(c) Blessyd be alle pōre men
    For God almy3ty louep hem;
    And wēyl ys hem þat pōre are hēre   well
    Þey are with God bōþe lēʃe and dēre
    And ȳ shal fōnde, by ny3t and day   endeavour
    To bē pōre, 3yf þat ȳ may.

(d) Vnto a cherche bōþe þey 3ēde
    For to fulfylle hys wil yn dēde.

(e) Þe porter had hys spēche lōre   lost
    And hēryng alsō, syn hē was bōre.

Characteristics of Central Southern and South-Western Dialects in M.E.

(1) O.E. ǽ remains as a front vowel, written æ, ea, or e in the M.E. texts of the South, of the twelfth century and in those of the first half of the thirteenth, a being written only occasionally; from the beginning of the fourteenth century we find either a exclusively, or a-spellings with a certain sprinkling of e-spellings. This means that the original Southern type was gradually eliminated, even in the West, and its place taken by Midland forms. Thus Holy Rood Tree (c. 1170) generally has æ, occasionally e, once ea, and there is no doubt that all these spellings imply the same sound, probably something between [ɛ̆] and [ă]. This text only has a after w—in water. The Lambeth Homilies (c. 1190) has always e—efter, wes, feder, cweð, O.E. æfter, wæs, fæder, cwæð 'said'; Moral Poem (Egerton M.S.), c. 1200, has e; the Metrical Life of St. Juliana (Glos. 1300) has a few e-forms, spek 'spoke', O.E. spræc, 3ef 'gave', but mostly ă—wat 'what', O.E. hwæt, quað, 3af 'gave', O.E. g̈ef, was, glade, O.E. glæd 'glad', &c.; Robt. of Glos. (c. 1330) writes both a and e; Trevisa (1387) nearly always a, þat, blak 'black', O.E. blæc, schal 'shall', Late O.E. sc̈æl, &c., but creftes, O.E. cræftas. St. Editha (Wilts., c. 1420) has a alone.

This test is therefore only applicable to the early M.E. period, and then needs to be used with caution and combined with other tests. See the treatment of O.E. ǽ in Kentish below. We may note here, as we shall not devote a special section to the dialect, that the texts written in the Southern part of the W. Midland area—Oxfordshire, Worcestershire— St. Katherine, St. Juliana (prose), La3amon, Harleian Lyrics (Heref. 1300), and Piers Plowman, which all have many typical Southern traits, as well as other more typical Midland features, frequently have e as well as a. This may be owing to the Southerly situation of the counties whence these texts emanate, but it may also be an inheritance from O.E., since in a portion of the Mercian area ǽ had become ě already in that period.

(2) (a) O.E. ǣ¹, which normally remains in W. Saxon alone of all the

O.E. dialects, or in those areas over which this speech-influence extended, becomes [ē] when it survives into M.E., and is written either æ (in very early texts only), e or ea. The best proofs of the existence of this type in M.E. are the spelling ea, and rhymes of words of this class, with words whose vowel was of a different origin, but which are known to have had the [ē] sound.

It is pretty certain that the area over which the Southern type of this sound extended in Late O.E. and in M.E. was far wider than the original South-Western area of Wessex. On the other hand, the so-called ǣ- area seems later to have been restricted, and whereas, for instance, there are apparent traces of this sound in Southern West Midlands (St. Jul. Prose Life, Ancren Riwle, Harleian Lyrics, &c.), yet the evidence, even of the true Southern texts of the later period, shows that the other type with tense [ẹ̄] was also in use. Thus Metr. St. Jul. by the side of brẹþ rhyming with dẹþ, rēde with lēde 'lead' the metal, O.E. brǣþ, dēaþ, rǣd, lēad, also rhymes rēde, O.E. rǣd, with sēde 'said', and drede, O.E. drǣd, with neode where in each case the rhyming word must have had tense ẹ̄, and St. Editha rhymes þēre, O.E. þǣr 'there' with yfẹ̄re, Adv. 'together'. Cf. O.E. gefẹ̄ra; bēre 'bier', O.E. bǣr, with hēre 'here', O.E. hēr. On the other hand, Metr. St. Jul. rhymes breþ 'breath' with deþ 'death', O.E. brǣþ, dēaþ, rēde with lēde 'lead' vb., O.E. lǣdan, where the ǣ = ǣ² (see under E. Midlands above, 2 (b)).

(b) O.E. ǣ² remained as the slack long vowel [ē] throughout the Central Southern and South-Western areas. (See remarks under E. Midland 2 (b) above, and under Kentish, &c., 2 (b) below.)

(3) O.E. ȳ remains and is written u, or when long sometimes ui, or uy. In part of the Southern area O.E. ȳ becomes i already in the O.E. period before the 'front-consonants', O.E. čč, čğ, and perhaps sč, written ch, gge, sch in M.E. The present writer showed that this tendency was particularly strong in Devon, Dorset, Somerset, and Wilts., weaker in Hants, weaker still in Glos. See Short History of Eng., § 158 (f). There is also a strong probability that O.E. y was unrounded to i in part of Devon, independent of the influence of following consonants. The occurrence of i- forms in Southern texts, therefore, does not necessarily show impurity of dialect. The Southern area of the W. Midlands, whose dialect is represented in such texts as Laȝamon, Ancren Riwle ('Morton's text'), St. Jul. (Metr.), St. Katherine, Harl. Lyrics, and Piers Plowman, preserves the sound [y], both long and short, with great fidelity and consistency—huyden 'hide', fūr, fuyr 'fire', murhðe 'mirth', cunne 'kin', lüþer 'wicked', sunne 'sin', rug 'back, ridge', &c. &c.

(4) O.E. ēo seems to have become first of all [φ] as in German schön, and then [y] in a very large area of the South, South-West, and West Midlands. The sound, in texts from this wide area, is at first written eo, according to the O.E. scribal tradition, and then u, ue, or o. There are traces of this as far East as Surrey (Owl and Nightingale) and Hampshire, and Moral Ode (Egerton MS., Hants) writes duere 'dearly', suelfer 'silver'; Usages of Winchester (1389) still writes furþe, O.E. feorþa 'fourth'; fourteenth-century forms of Hants Place Names in Hundred Rlls. have Dūpe— 'deep', O.E. dēop, and Nuther—O.E. neoþer 'lower'. The u, o, or eo forms are further found in St. Jul. Metr. Life (only eo, generally ẹ̄, never u), Robt.

of Glos., Trevisa, St. Editha, and as late as 1447–50, in the letters of Shillingford, Mayor of Exeter. The texts from the South-West Midlands, Laȝamon, St. Jul. (Prose), Harl. Lyrics, &c., all have these forms in varying degrees of frequency. The development of O.E. *ēo* into *ē* on one hand, or into *ū* on the other, is one of the great dialectal tests between East and West (not between South and Midlands), and it would be rash to assign any text which has only *e* in words which had this diphthong in O.E., to an area farther west than the borders of Hampshire. Examples are *horte* ' heart '; *ilorned*, O.E. *geleorned* ' learnt '; *bōn* inf. ' be ', O.E. *bēōn*; *swore*, O.E. *sweor* ' neck ', &c., &c., Owl and Nightingale; *clupeþ* ' calls ', O.E. *cleopeþ*, *lume* ' limbs ', O.E. *leomu*, *brust* ' breast ', O.E. *brēōst*, in Robt. of Glos.; *suþþe* ' after ', O.E. *seoþþan*, *lūver*, O.E. *lēofor* ' dearer ', *luef* ' dear ', O.E. *lēof*, *pueves* ' thieves ', O.E. *þēofas*, &c., in Trevisa; *vrthe* = *urthe* ' earth ', O.E. *eorþe*, *dūre* ' dear ', O.E. *deor*, *būde* ' to offer ', O.E. *bēōdan*, in St. Editha. None of these texts is perfectly consistent, however, and *e*-spellings are fairly frequent in all, which perhaps shows that the easterly type was coming in, at any rate in the written language.

(5) O.E. *ea* followed by *r* + another consonant. The earliest South-Western texts, such as the Lambeth Homilies and others down to and into the thirteenth century, preserve the typical Southern *erm*, *herm*, O.E. *earm*, *æerm*, *hearm*, *hæerm*, but the Midland type *arm*, *harm*, &c., takes the place of these later. In this particular, as in so many others, the South-West Midland texts adhere to the Southern type. Similarly, before -*ll* we find *all* instead of Southern *æll* or *ell* very early. Thus, for instance, St. Jul. (Metr.) has *hard*, *harm*, *warm*, *ualleþ* ' falls ', *alle*. The South-Eastern translation of Palladius, however (Essex *c.* 1420), still preserves *e* in *hervest*, *herd* ' hard ', *yerdes*, &c.

(6) The O.E. combination *eald* in O.E. *eald* ' old ', *beald* ' bold ', *čeald* ' cold ', *wealdan* ' to rule, wield ', *healdan* ' hold ', appears in the early Southern texts in the typical forms -*eald*-, -*æld*-, -*eld*-, &c., which all = [ēld], but the Anglian type, O.E. *āld*, M.E. *ōld*, gets in very early, and as early as the twelfth century this substitution is beginning. In the thirteenth century and later there are only a few scattered survivals of the Southern type, such as *wælde* in Moral Ode, *wělde* in Prov. of Alfred, and so on. St. Jul. (Metr.) has only *ōld*, *hōlde*, &c. The South-Eastern dialects preserve the Southern form later, on which see below.

(7) O.E. *ǐe* in the Southern M.E. dialects. Already in O.E. we can distinguish, in the various Saxon texts, two dialectal types in the treatment of this old diphthong. In the later language some texts write *y* as *hyrde* ' shepherd ', earlier *hierde*, *sylf* ' self ', earlier *sielf*, *scyld* ' shield ', earlier *scield*, *hȳran* ' hear ', earlier *hīeran*, &c. Others write *i*: *hirde*, *silf*, *scild*, *hiran*. The former type appears as with *u* or *ui*, *uy* when long; in M.E. when retained the latter is written *i*. Thus M.E. *hurde* and *hirde*, *sulf* and *silf*, *schuld* and *schild*, *huyre(n)*, *huire(n)*, or *hūre(n)* by the side of *hire(n)*, are all typical Southern forms, as distinct from *hērde*, *schēld*, *hēren*, &c., which occur in all the dialects other than the South-Western.

The Southern conditions are more faithfully preserved in the treatment of the original short diphthong than in that of the long, and many texts, which in other respects are quite South-Western in type, have only traces of *ut* in the verb 'to hear', and many more examples of *ĕ*. St. Jul. (Metr.), Robt. of Glos., and Trevisa adhere most faithfully to the Saxon types both in long and short, though all have some *e-* forms. St. Editha has only *e*, though otherwise very Southern in character. St. Jul. (Metr.) has *hurde* (Pret.), but *bileue* from O.E. *līefan*; *bizite* 'obtaine', but *ʒĕlde* 'pay' Inf., W. Saxon *gieldan*.

The South-West Midland texts of the thirteenth century have certain traces of the *u-* forms.

Points connected with the Inflexions.

(8) The 3rd Pers. Sing. of the Pres. Indic. of verbs is universally *-eþ*, *-iþ*, or *-þ*, and we do not find the *-es*, *-s* endings as we do in E. Midland texts. A very curious exception, *louys* 'loves', occurs in St. Editha (2228), and there are a few other *-s* forms in this text.

(9) The Pres. Pl. Indic. normally ends in *-eþ* or *-iþ*.

This Southern peculiarity is shared by the dialect of the Prose St. Jul., and also by the Herefordshire (Harleian) Lyrics, though the latter has some examples of the Midland *-en*.

(10) The Imperat. Pl. ends in *-eþ* and *-iþ*, as in E. Midland.

(11) The Pres. Participle ends in *-ind(e)*. The later *-ing* participles develop rather later than in E. Midland. The South-West Midland texts, while exhibiting examples of the Southern *-inde*, have also the Midland *-ende*.

(12) The Fem. Pers. Pron. Nom. is always, in the South, some form derived from O.E. *hēo*.

The E. Midland and Northern *she, sche* forms are unknown, except for the quite exceptional *sse* in Robt. of Glos., and a few examples in Trevisa, who generally uses the typical *heo, hue*. Robt. of Glos. has *ʒo* frequently, also *heo*, and St. Jul. (Metr.) has *he, heo*. Other forms of these in Southern texts are the unstressed *ha*, while *he, hee, hoe* appear in St. Editha.

(13) The Pers. Pronouns of the Pl. are Nom. *hi, heo*, the unstressed *ha* and *a* (Lamb. Homs., Moral Ode, Saules Warde, Owl and Nightingale, Robt. of Glos.), and the weak *a* in Trevisa. St. Editha seems to have only the Scandinavian forms, *þey, þai, þay*, and this is the first appearance of these forms in the South. The Possessives are *hor(e)* (Gōd Ureisun, St. Jul. (Metr.), and Robt. of Glos.), *heore* (Lamb. Homs., Moral Ode), the weak *eore* (O. and N.), *here* (Robt. of Glos., Trevisa, and St. Editha), *her, hure, hurre* (St. Editha). Acc. and Dative *heom* (Lamb. Homs., Moral Ode, O. and N.); *hem* (St. Jul. (Metr.), Robt. of Glos., St. Editha); *hom* (Robt. of Glos., St. Editha); *ham* (Lamb. Homs., Gōd Ur., and Trevisa).

(14) The Pres. Pl. of Verb 'to be' is normally *bēoþ, bēþ, buþ*. Usages of Winchester has the two last, Robt. of Glos. has *bēþ*, Trevisa the last. St. Editha has the Midland *bēn* and *arne*. The South-West Midland Harleian Lyrics has both Southern *buþ*, and Midland *aren*.

(15) In O.E. the particle *ge-* is prefixed commonly to the P. P. of verbs, both strong and weak, when uncompounded. The P. P. of Strong Verbs ends in *-n*. In M.E. in the South and South-West Midlands the prefix is generally retained, being written *i-* or *y-*. All Southern texts

from the earliest M.E. to St. Editha write *ychōse, yslawe* 'slain', *yfounde,* &c., &c., with loss of final *-n.* Ancren Riwle, St. Jul. (Prose), St. Katherine, and Harl. Lyrics generally retain the prefix *y-*, but adhere to the Midland type in conserving also the *-n* in strong P. P.'s, e. g. *ikumen,* &c. The prefix is often used in the Pret. in O.E. and in Southern M.E., and indeed may be used before any part of a verb, often with no particular force, though it also has the function of making intransitive verbs transitive.

(16) Infinitives end in *-an* and *-ian* in O.E. In M.E. these become *-en*, or *-e*, and *-ien, ie* respectively. The latter type is often written merely *-y*, or *-i*. It is typical of the South, both East and West, but disappears before the encroachments of the *-an* type in E. Midlands. Examples: O.E. *lōkian* 'look', M.E. *lōkie, lōki, lōky*; *to susteni,* and *somony* 'to summon' both occur in Robt. of Glos. This suffix is also used with Vbs. of French origin. The loss of the final *-n* in the Inf. is a typical Southern feature.

Extracts illustrative of Southern Dialect.

* Note that in the South and South-Western area, initial *f-* is often, though not with complete consistency, written *v* or *u*, implying a voiced pronunciation.

(a) *From Moral Ode (Egerton MS.)* (Hants, *circa* 1200).

Muchele luwe he us cudde, wolde we it understonde

Þat vre eldrene misduden we habbet vuele on honde

Dieð cōm in þis middenerd þurh þe calde deofles onde
And synne and sorȝe and ȝeswinch a watere and ēc a londe

Vres formes faderes gult we abigget alle

Al his ofsprung after him in herme is bifalle.

Þurst and hunger, chule and hete, eche and al unelþe
Þurh dieð cōm in þis middenerd and oþer vnisalþe.

Notes. vuele = uvele, 'evil', O.E. *yfel. middenerd =* O.E. (W. Sax.) *middangeard* 'earth' (late O.E. *-ġerd).* The ending *-eþ* is written *-et* in this text in *habbet, abigget* 'purchase'. *chule =* W. Sax. *ċiele* 'cold' (late O.E. *ċyle,* whence *chule).* *Dieð,* instead of *dēþ,* as the other MSS. have, may be the result of Kentish influence in the scribe. *v* and *u* are interchangeable, hence *vre = ūre* 'our'; *vres = ūres,* gen. Line 5. 'the guilt *of our* first father'. Note the loss of *h* in *unelþe,* lit. 'unhealth', 'sickness'.

(b) *From Proverbs of Alfred* (1200).

Þus queþ Alured:

Wis child is fader blisse.

If hit so bitȳdeþ

Þat þu bern ibidest

Þe hwile hit is lȳtel

lēr him mon-þēwes

Þanne hit is wexynde

hit schal wende þar o.

Þe betere hit schal iwurþe

ēuer buuen eorþe.

Notes. Line 1. *u* written for *v* in Alured, O.E. *Ælfred.*
4. *bern* = O.E. *bearn* 'child'; *ibīdest* 'await, expect'.
7. = O.E. *weaxan* 'grow' (Late W. Sax. *wexan*).
8. = 'it shall turn then to'.
N.B. In late W. Sax. *weorþan* often becomes *wurþan*, but this could not rhyme with *eorþe. iwurþe* is from O.E. *ʒeweorþan*, and the spelling shows the M.E. change of *eo* to [yʲ]. This rhymes with *eorþe*, which shows that this word, too, had undergone the change in spite of the old spelling.

(c) *From Robert of Gloucester* (*c.* 1298).

(1) Þo þis chīld was an vrþe ibōre, his freond nome þerto hēde,

Hi lēte hit dō to Glastnebury to norichi and to fēde
To tēche him ēke his bilēue, pater-noster and crēde.

Þe child wax and wel iþeʒ, for hit mōste nēde.

Lūte ʒēme he nōm to þe wordle, to alle godnisse he drouʒ.

(2) In chirche he was devout inow vor him ne ssolde no day abide

Þat he ne hurde masse and matines and ēuesong and ech tide.

(3) And þe Normans ne couþe spēke þō bote hor ōwe spēche

And spēke French as hii dude atóm and hor children dude also tēche
So þat hēiemen of þis lond þat of hor blōd cōme

Hōldeþ alle þulke speche þa hii of hom nome

Vor bote a man conne Frenss me telþ of him lūte

Ac lōwe men holdeþ to Engliss and to hor ōwe spēche ʒute.

(4) . . . . . . þe gode quene Mold

Þat quene was of Engelond as me aþ er ytōld

Þa gōderhēle al Engelond was heo euere ybōre

Notes. (1) l. 2. *hi* = 'they'.   l. 4. *iþeʒ*, fr. O.E. *ʒeþeah, ʒeþah.*   l. 5. *wordle* = 'world' shows metathesis of *ld.*
(2) l. 1. *vor* = 'for'.
(3) ll. 1–2. Note rhyme.   l. 2. *atóm* = 'at home', still so pronounced by many good speakers.   l. 5. *me*, indef. Pron. = 'one'.
(4) l. 2. = 'as one has told before'.   l. 3. *gōderhēle*, adv. = 'fortunately for'.   *heo* = 'she'.

(d) *From the Metrical Life of St. Juliana*
(Gloucestershire *c.* 1300).

(1) Swīþe sōri was þis lūþer man þat he ne miʒte hire þoʒt wende

To habbe conseil of hire fāder after him he let sende.

And fōndede hire clēne þoʒt to chaunge þoru vair biheste.

Þō hī spēke uairest wiþ hire, þis maide hem ȝaf answere:—
Icholle hōlde þa ichabbe itake; ȝē ne dōþ me þērof nō dēre;
At ō word ȝē ne turneþ mē noȝt, þēr aboute ȝē spilleþ brēþ;
Dōþ me wat pȳne ȝe wolleþ, uor I ne drēde noȝt þen dēþ.
Þe hī sēie þat þis maide hire þoȝt chaungī nōlde,
Hire fāder bitōk hire þe justīce to dō wiþ hire wat he wōlde.

(2) We ne scholle þis foule wiche ouercome wiþ no dēde
ȝif no fūr ne mai hire brenne, in lēde we scholle hire brēde
A chetel hē sette ouer þe fūr and fulde it uol of lēde
Þis maide isei þis lēd boili, heo nas nōþing in drēde.
Anon so hēo was þerinne idō, þat fūr bigan to sprēde.
Fram þe chetel it hupte aboute, in lengþe and in brēde.
Sixti men and seuentēne it barnde in þe plāce
Of lūþer men þat stōde þer bī: þer was godes grāce.
Amydde þe chetel þis maide stōde, al hōl wiþþoute harm ;
Þat lēd þat bolynde was, ᴠnnēþe it þoȝte hire warm.

(3) Ne spāreþ noȝt he sēde, ac heieþ uaste þat heo of dāwe be.
Nabbeþ of hire namōre reuþe þen heo hadde of me.
Nōlde heo nōþing spāre me of al þat ich hire bʌd,
Vnnēþe ich dar on hire lōke, so sōre icham adrad.
Þo þis maide hūrde þis, hire ēien up heo caste,
A, out! out! þe deuel sēde hōldeþ hire nou uaste.

(e) *From Trevisa's translation of Higden's Polychronicon* (1387).

(1) Þar ẏs grēt plente of smal fysch and of eeles, so þat cherles in som
place feedeþ sowes wiþ fysch. Þar buþ ofte ȳtāke delphyns and
sē-calues and balenes (grēt fysch as it wēre of whāāles kūnde) and
dyuers maner schȳl-fysch among þe whoche schȳl-fysch buþ
moskles þat habbeþ wiþ-ynne ham margery perles of a
manere colour of hūȝ.

(2) Lond, hony, mylk, chȳse
þis īlond schal bēre þe prise

(3) Harold cōme vram werre of Noreganes and hūrde
tȳþȳnges hereof, and hyede wel vast and hadde
bote veāw knyȝtes aboute hym; vor he
hadde ȳlost meny stalword me in þe rāþer
batayl and he had noȝt ysent vor mōre help; and þeyȝ

a hadde, men were wrōþe and wolde hāue wyþdrawe,[15]
ham, vor hy moste hāue nō part of the prayes atte
batayl of Noreganes. Bote Harold sent vorþ spies vor
to aweyte and sē þe number and þe stringþe of hys enymyes. Duc
William touk þues[4] spyes and ladde ham aboute hys tentes
and hys pauylons, and vedde ham ryȝt realyche, and sent ham
to Harold aȝé.

Notes. (1) l. 4. *schyl,* fr. O.E. (W. Sax.) *sciell* 'shell'; this is the Southern *i*-type.
(2) l. 1. *chyse,* fr. O.E. (W. Sax.) *cūse,* later *cīsé* 'cheese'; the other dialects had
cēse in O.E., *chēse* in M.E.
(3) l. 1. *vram = fram* 'from'.   l. 3. *veaw* = O.E. *feawe* 'few'.   l. 6.
a = he, weak form. *þeyȝ* = O.E. *þeāh* 'though'. *atte* = 'at the'   l. 10. *þues,*
O.E. *þeōs* 'these'.   *vedde = fedde* 'fed'.

(f) From St. Editha (Wilts. c. 1420).

Bot hē[12] hurre-selff dwelte at Wylton stylle
Wit hurre mōder as y sayde ȝōwe ēre;
For hurre mōder to serue was hōlyche hurre wylle
Wel lēuer[4] þen ony ōther grēt stāte to bēre;
And also for hē was norysshut vp in þat plāce
And furste[3] y-ōrdryd[15] he was þēre þertō,
And many miracles þorow goddus grāce
For hurre wērone dōne þēre alsō.

. . . .

When he hadde regnyd here syxtene ȝēre
Fullyche complete wit somewhat mōre
And syxtene ȝēre hōlde and somewhat mōre y trōwe he wēre
When he was kyng furst[3] y-kōre[15]
Bote of his deth and also his burynge[3]
Ychāue[15] y-writon ȝōwe herebyfōre
And somewhat of his gōde gouernynge;
And þat is cause þat y wrȳte hēre nomōre.

Note. l. 1. *hē* = 'she'. l. 11. *hōlde* = 'old'.

Dialect Features of Kentish and South-Eastern.

(1) O.E. *ǽ* is retained as a fronted [ɛ] sound longer and more consistently
in Kentish than in the more Westerly Southern dialects. But even here, and
that as early as 1150 (Vespas. Homilies), the Anglian *a* appears. Vesp.
Homs. has *cwed̄,* O.E. *cwæþ; fedme* 'bosom', O.E. *fed̄m; weter* 'water',
but also *was, fader.* Laud Sermons (*c.* 1250) has *efter,* O.E. *æfter; þet,*
O.E. *þæt,* but *spac,* O.E. *spræc* 'spoke'; *hedde* 'had', O.E. *hæfde,* but
habbeþ, haþ, O.E. *hæþþ; wat,* O.E. *hwæt* 'what'; *water,* O.E. *wæter,*
and so on. Will. of Shoreham (1320) has a good number of *e* spellings:
wet, O.E. *hwæt; þet, schal* 'shall', *creft,* O.E. *cræft, heþ* 'hath', *wetere,*
&c.; on the other hand *wat, schal, water, glas,* &c. The total number of

a spellings is greater than those with *e*. Ayenbite (1340), the latest and on the whole the most typical example of Kentish, has *eppel*, O.E. *æppel* 'apple', *huet* 'what', *gled* 'glad', *gles* 'glass', &c., but also occasionally *a* as in *uader*.

(2) O.E. *æ*[1] and *æ*[2] have both the same (tense) *ē*-sound in Kentish. See remarks on this sound under the E. Midland characteristics above. The spellings with *ie* seem to prove tenseness in both original sounds: Will. of Shoreham has *ʒier* 'year', Prim. O.E. *gēr*, O. Kentish *gēr*, and Ayenbite has *cliene* 'clean' which has O.E. *æ*[2] (see E. Midlands 2).

(3) O.E. *ȳ*, as has already been mentioned (pp. 9, 30, 34, above), appears *ē* in Kentish and South-Eastern. There is further reason to believe that this peculiarity occurred also in a large area of the E. Midlands. It is found in Suffolk Charters in the late tenth century, cf. also p. 78, below. Examples from Kentish texts: *senne* 'sin', *felþe* or *velþe* 'filth', O.E. (Sax. and Angl.) *fȳlþe*; *keþþe* 'family', &c., O.E. *cȳþþe*, *werchen* 'work', O.E. *wyrċan*, *merie* 'merry', O.E. *myrig*, &c., &c.

(4) O.E. *ēo* never appears in Kentish as a rounded vowel (*u*, *oe*, &c.), as in the West and South-West, but, especially the long *ēo*, is either written *ie*, *ye*, *io*, *yo*, or *e*. It is rather doubtful whether the *ie*, *ye* spellings imply a diphthongal sound or whether they merely represent a tense *ē*. The Vesp. Homs. writes *bien*, O. W. Sax. *bēon* 'be'; *chiesen* inf. 'choose', O.E. *ċēosan*, *dier*-, O.E. *dēor* 'animal', *diofles*, O.E. *dēoflas* 'devils'. Laud Homilies has *bieþ* 'are', *bien* (inf.), but *sterre* 'star', O.E. *steorra*; *herte*, O.E. *heorte* 'heart'. Will. of Shoreham nearly always writes *ee* or *e* for *ēo* : *dēpe*, *crēpe*, *feende* 'enemy', but has also *soeþ*, O.E. *seoþ* 'see' (Western influence?), *bȳ* = *bēon* (inf.). Ayenbite writes *herte*, *erþe*, also *yerthe*, *yerne* 'run', O.E. *eornan*. For the long, *dyeule*, O.E. *dēofle*, *uryend*, *uriend* 'friend', O.E. *frēond*, *uyend*, O.E. *fēond* 'enemy'; *diere*, *dyere* 'dear', O.E. *dēora*, &c. By the side of these usual spellings, *e* and *ee* are also written occasionally. In view of the fact that most of the Kentish texts write *ie* for tense *ē*, as in *hier*, O.E. *hēr* 'here', and *hieren* 'to hear', Old Kentish *hēren*, and also that they all often write *ee* for O.E. *ēo*, it seems not improbable that the spelling means no more than tense [ē]. In the writings of Gower *ie* is a recognized symbol for [ē]. See remarks on p. 57.

(5) O.E. *-eall-*, *-earm-*, *-eard-* are written with *ea*, *æ*, or *e*, longer than in the South-Western. Vesp. Homs. has *ælra*, *ælmihti*; Will. of Shoreham *earmes* 'arms', *þou ert* 'art', *hermy* inf. 'to harm', but also *scharpe*, *harde*; Ayenbite seems to have the Anglian *-arm-*, *-ard-*.

(6) O.E. *-eald-* retains the front vowel of the old Southern type in Kentish, as against the Anglian *-ōld-* type, still more thoroughly than the combinations *-earm-*, *-eall-*, &c. Vesp. Homs. has *sælde* 'gave', 'sold', O.E. *sealde* ; *healde*, inf. 'hold', O.E. *healdan*; Will. of Shoreham has *chēld* 'cold', O.E. *ċeald*, *ċæld* ; *tealde* Pret., and *y-teld*, p.p. 'told', Late O.E. *iælde*, &c. ; *to hēlde* 'to hold', *ēlde* 'old', Late O.E. *æld*, &c., &c. ; Ayenbite has *ealde* and *yealde* 'old', *chealde* 'cold', *tealde* 'told', *healde* 'hold'. The typical Anglian forms with *-old-* do not seem to occur in the last text, nor are they at all frequent in any Kentish text.

(7) O.E. *ēa in Kentish*. The late treatment, at least in spelling, of this long diphthong deserves a few words, as it is typical. In most dialects O.E. *ēa* became *æ* in the Late O.E. period, and this *ē* [ē] in M.E., when

it is often written *ea—deaþ* = [*dēþ*], &c.   In Ayenbite, however, we get *dyaf* 'deaf', O.E. *deāf*; *dyaþ* and *dyeaþ* 'death', *dyed* 'dead'; *lyaf* 'leaf', O.E. *lēāf*; *lyas* pret. 'lost', O.E. *-lēās*, &c.   Will. of Shoreham has traces of these spellings in *lias* pret. 'lost', *senne-lyas* · sinless ', O.E. *lēās*, but otherwise writes *ea—deaþes, reaue*, &c.   The Laud Homs. has *diadlich* 'deadly', *diaþ* 'death', *be-liaue* 'faith', O.E. *ġe-leāfa*, all of which occur frequently, by the side of occasional *be-leaue*, &c.   Vesp. Homs. has *dēādlic, eadinesse*, O.E. *ēādiġ-*, *æac*, O.E. *ēāc* 'also', but also *ġeċas* 'chose', O.E. *ċēās*; *brad* 'bread', O.E. *brēad*; *admodi-*, O.E. *ēādmōdiġ* 'humble', &c.   Whether *ea, ia, ya* all represent some sound like [ǣ] or [ē̆], or whether they really represent a combination such as [ja], it seems impossible to say.   *a* in *brad* can hardly represent anything but [ǣ] or [ē̆], and this may well have been the sound in all these words.   If this were so, Kentish would only differ from the other dialects in employing a special graphic device.

(8) Initial *s-* and *f* often appear voiced in Kentish. This is particularly systematic in Ayenbite, where *u* (for *v*) is regularly written at the beginning of English words *uolc* 'people', *uor* 'for', *uoul* 'foul', &c., &c., also before cons. *uram, uryend*, &c., &c.   In French words *f-* is written: *fauour* 'figure', *flour* 'flower', *frut* 'fruit', &c., &c.   Note *uals* 'false', &c., however.   Initial *s-* is written *z* in English words, only before vowels, except in the old combination *sw-*, which is written *zu- —zuyn*, O.E. *swīn* 'swine', *zuēte* 'sweet', O.E. *swēte*, &c., also *zēche*, O.E. *sēċan* 'seek', *zenne* 'sin', &c., &c.   Before consonants *s* is written in English words : *strēme* 'stream', *strengþi* 'strengthen', and in French words *s* is written everywhere.   All the earlier Kentish texts write *s-* ; as regards O.E. initial *f-*, Vesp. Homs. seems always to write *f-*, Laud Homs. has occasional *v—vaire* 'fair', O.E. *fæġer* ; *uuluelden* lit. 'fulfilled, filled full', but more often *f-*, while Will. of Shoreham generally writes *f-*, but has also *uader* 'father', *vedeþ* 'feeds', *velþ* 'filth', &c.   Thus Kentish, apart from Ayenbite, does not use the voiced sound for initial *f-* nearly so commonly as South-Western, while the latter is far behind Ayenbite in the use of the voiced sound for *s-*.

Points connected with the Inflexions in Kentish.

(9) The 3rd Pers. Sing. Pres. Indic. ends in *-eþ, -þ* as in the rest of the Southern area. An exceptional *-s* form, *letes*, occurs in Vespas. Homs. however.

(10) The Pl. Pres. Indic. ends in *-eþ* as in Southern generally.

(11) The Imperat. Pl. ends in *-eþ, -þ* as in Southern generally, and E. Midlands.

(12) The Pres. Part. ends in *-inde* (with occasional *-ende*) as in South-Western.

(13) The Fem. Pron. Nom. is usually *hi*, never *sche*, &c.

(14) Pl. of 3rd Pers. Pronoun. Kentish agrees with the rest of the Southern in having no *þ-* or *th-* forms. A characteristic Kentish or South-Eastern form *his* is in the Acc. Pl. (= 'them') in Vesp. Homs., Shoreham, and Ayenbite. This is also found in some of the earlier E. Midland texts, e.g. Genesis and Exodus.

(15) The characteristic *bieþ*, Pl. Pres. Indic. of *bien* ' to be ', is found in Ayenbite.

(16) The statements concerning the prefix *i-* in verbs, especially the P. P., and the termination *-e*, without *-n*, which are made above with regard to South-Western, apply on the whole to Kentish.

(17) The *-ie*, *-y* endings in Inf. of Vbs. are very frequent in Kentish as in South-Western.

Illustrative Extracts from M.E. Kentish Texts.

(a) *From the* (*Vespasian A.* 22) *Kentish Sermons* (*c.* 1150).

(1) An þesser beoð[3] bedeles and laðieres to berie[3] archebiscopes and biscopes, prēstes and hare[14] ȝegeng. Ac þah we fif næmmie alle[6] hit on godes wille, and elc of ham[14] ȝestrēnð[3] and fulfeleþ[3][9] oðre. Of þesses fif ceþen[10] and of hare[14] bedeles we habbeþ[3] ȝeu[1][10] ȝesēd.[16] Of þe folce we siggeþ[10] þat[1] hit cumþ fastlice,[1] fram midden-ardes anginn alse fele alse deāde[7] beoð[15] alse fele beoð[15] to berie[3] icome,[16] wat frēnd,[1] wat fā,[1] and ēlce deȝie þicce þringeð.[1]

(2) Þan seied ham[14] god þe gelty[3] mannen ȝē[3] seneȝden an ȝeur ēcenesse, and ȝe scule birne an mire ecenisse. Ȝe seneȝden[3] alse lange alse ȝe lefede and ȝe scule birne alse longe as ic lefie. Witeð[11] into ēce fēr,[3] þe is ȝæarcod mine fō, and his ȝegeng. Sōn hi wrðeð abrōden of his ȝesecþe.

(b) *From the Laud Homilies* (*c.* 1250).

(1) Nu lordinges þis[1] is þe[1] miracle þet þet godspel of te dai us telþ.[9] ac great is þe tokeningge. Se leprus signifieþ[9] þo senuulle me;[3][8] ȝi lepre þo[3] sennen. Þet scab bitokneþ[9] þo litle sennen,[9] si lepre bitokneþ þo grete[7] sennen þet[1] biedh[4][15] diadliche.[7] . . . Nu ye habbeð[10][16] iherd þe[1] miracle and wet hit bitokned.[9] No lōke we yef we bīeþ[4][-15] clēne[2][[2]] of þise lepre, þat is to siggen[7] of diadliche[3] senne.

(2) And bi þet[1] hi[14] offrede gold þet[1] is cuuenable yeftte to kinge, scawede[1] þet he was sothfast Kink. And bi þet[1] hi[14] offrede Stor[14] þet me offrede wylem be þo[6] ialde laghe to here[14] godes sacrefise,[1] seawede þet he was verray prest. And be þet[1] hi[14] offrede Mirre þet[1] is biter þing,[9] signifieth[1][14] þet[1] hi[7] hedde beliaue þet[1] he was diadlich[7] þet[17] diath solde suffri[17] for man-ken.[1]

(c) *From William of Shoreham* (1310–20).

(1) Onneþe creft eny þat stāt
Ac some crefteþ þat halue
And for siknesse lēche creft
And for þe goute sealue
Me mākeþ.

For wanne man drāwiþ into ōldeward
Wel oft his bōnes ākeþ.
And bē a man nēuer so sprind
ʒef he schel libbe to ēlde
Be him wel siker þerto he schal
And his dēþes dette ʒēlde
To gile.
ʒet meni ʒong man wēneþ longe liue
And lēueþ wel litle wȳle.

(2) Lēue dāme, say me now
Wy heþ god forbōde hyt ʒow
Þet ʒē ne mōte
Ēten of al þat frūt þat hys
Hēre grōwynde in paradȳs
To ʒoure bōte?

We ēteþ y-nou quaþ ēue, ywis
Of alle þe trōwes of paradȳs
And bēþ wel gled;
Bote þys trōw mōte we nauʒt tāke,
For bōþe mē and mȳnne māke
God hyt forbede.

(d) *From the Ayénbite* (1340).

Ayē þe uondingges of þe dyēule: zay þis þet uolʒeþ: Zuēte
iesu þīn hōly blōd/þet þou sseddest ane þe rōd/uor mē
and uor mankēnde: Ich bidde þe hit bȳ my ssēld/auoreye
þe wycked uēnd: al to mi lyues ēnde. zuō bȳ hit.

þis bōc is dan Michelis of Nothgate, y-write an englis
of his ōʒene hand; þet hatte Ayenbyte of Inwyt. And is of
þe bōchouse of saynt Austines of Canterberie.

Hōly archangle Mīchael
Saynt gābriel and Rāphael
Ye brenge me to þō castel
Þer alle zaulen vāreþ wel.

Lhord ihesu almiȝti Kyng, þet mādest and lōkest alle þyng,
Me þet am þī makyng to þīne blisse me þou bryng. Amen.

Blīnd and dȳaf and alsuo domb, of zeuenty yēr al uol rond.
Ne ssolle by drāȝe tō þe grōnd, uor peny, uor mark ne uor pōnd.

We have now concluded our brief survey of the principal distinguishing features which characterize the Regional types that go to the composition of the dialect of London during the M.E. period, that is to say, the South-Eastern (especially Kent and Essex), the Central and more Westerly Southern, and the East Midland. The illustrative extracts from texts written in the various dialects furnish examples, in the actual living sentence, of most of our points, though possibly not of all. Outside the distinguishing marks of dialect, which are here selected as most typical, it will be observed that there is much that is common to all, and which belongs to the whole of English south of the Thames, and north, at least as far as Lincolnshire, in the East. We have omitted from our survey the Northern English, and Scotch dialects, and that large area, to the West, rather vaguely known as ' West Midland ' among students of Middle English. It is obvious that the dialects of these regions can have had no direct influence upon the speech of London, and as a matter of fact there are no typically Northern or West Midland elements in Literary or Standard Spoken English at the present day, nor were there any in the M.E. dialect from which these have sprung. It is hardly necessary to say that there are many features of grammar, sounds, and vocabulary which belong to English as a whole, which therefore occur in North, South, South-Eastern, East, and West Midland alike. There are also certain features, such as -s in the 3rd Pers. Sing. Present of verbs, which were originally Northern, but which subsequently passed into the North Midland English as a whole, in the first place, and later, from East Midland, probably through Essex, into London English. But, so far as the latter is concerned, these features are to be regarded as East Midland. See, however, pp. 334–7. below.

There are many other points of considerable importance, besides those above discussed under the various dialect headings, which arise in the detailed and minute study of the texts from which our illustrative extracts are drawn, but are passed over in silence here, because they would take us further into the minutiae of Old and Middle English grammar than it would be permissible to go in a book of this kind. It is believed, however, that this omission will not impair the general argument of the book, and the omission is deliberate.

The Dialect of London down to the Death of Chaucer.

We now pass to consider the dialect of London itself, down to the close of the fourteenth century and the beginning of the fifteenth.

It must be assumed that the reader has grasped the foregoing statement and enumeration of the various dialectal features of the different regions dealt with ; at any rate, the tables and examples can easily be referred to, and the references given to the various points dealt with will reduce the reader's labour to a minimum. The abbreviations E. Midl., Sthn., Kt., refer to the dialect areas as treated above, pp. 29–43, &c., and the numbers to the particular points. Thus E. Midl. 6 refers to the paragraph above under the heading E. Midl. in which the O.E. Midland combination -āld-, which in the Southern O.E. dialects is represented by -eald-, later -æld-, is dealt with.

We may first give some examples of documents written in London, from the time of the Conqueror down to Chaucer.

Illustrative Specimens of the Dialect of London from the Conquest to Chaucer.

(a) *William the Conqueror's Charter* (1066). From Liebermann's Gesetze d. Angelsachsen, vol. i, p. 486.

Willelm Kyng grēt Willelm bisceop and Gosfregð portirefan and ealle þa burhwaru binnan Londone Frencisce and Englisce freondlice. And ic kyðe eow þæt ic wylle þæt ģet beon eallra þæra laga weorðe þe gȳt wæran on Eadwerdes dæge Kynges. And ic wylle þæt ælc ċyld beo his fæder yrfnume æfter his fæder dæge and ic nelle geþolian þæt ænig man ēow ænig þrang bēode. God eow ġehealde.

(b) *Proclamation of Henry III* (1258). From Patent Rolls. Printed Ellis, Early English Pronunciation, Pt. II, pp. 501, &c., and Emerson's *M.E. Reader*.

Henri þur3 godes fultume King on Engleneloand, Lhoauerd on Yrloand, Dūk on Norm' on Aquitain' and eorl on Aniow Send igrētinge to alle hise hōlde, ilǣrde and ileawede on Huntendonschir' þæt witen 3ē wel alle þæt we willen and unnen þæt, þæt v̄re rǣdesmen alle oþer þe moare dæl of heom þæt beōþ ichōsen þur3 us and þur3 þæt loandes folk on vre Kuneriche habbeþ idon and schullen don in þe worþnesse of gode and on vre treowþe, for þe freme of þe loande, þur3 þe besi3te of þan toforen iseide rēdesmen. beō stedefæst and ilestinde in alle þinge abuten ænde. And we hoaten alle vre treowe in þe trēowþe þæt heo vs ōgen þæt heo stedefæstliche hēalden and swerien to hēalden and to werien þō isetnesses þæt beōn imakede and beōn to makien þur3 þan to foreniseide rǣdesmen ōþer þur3 þe mōare dæl of heom alswō alse hit is biforen iseid. And þæt æhc ōþer helpe þæt for to dōne bi þan ilche ōþe a3ēnes alle men. Ri3t for to done and to fōangen. And nōan ne nime of lōande ne of e3te wherþur3 þis besi3te mu3e beon ilet ōþer iwersed on ōnie wīse. And 3if ōni, ōþer ōnie cumen her on3ēnes, we willen and hoaten þæt alle v̄re treowe heom healden deadliche ifōan. And for þaet we willen þæt þisbeo stedefæst and lestinde, we senden 3ew þis writ open iseined wiþ v̄re seel, to hālden amanges 3ew ine hord. Witnesse v̄s seluen æt Lunden' þane E3tetenþe day on þe mōnþe of Octobr'. In þe two and fowerti3þe 3eare of vre crūninge. And in þis wes idōn ætforen vre isworene rēdesmen. And al on þō ilche worden is isend into ævriche ōþre schīre ōver al þære kuneriche on Engleneloande, and ēk intel Irelonde.
(N.B. Pl. Name, Hurtford (Earl of) among signatories.)

(c) *Adam Davy* (c. 1307-27).

(1) His name is ihōte Sir Edward þe Kyng
Prince of Wales, Engelonde þe faire þing.[1]
Me mette [2] þat he was armed wēl
Bōþe wiþ ȳrne and wiþ stēl,
And on his helme þat was of stēl
A coroune of gōld bicom hym wēl.
Bifōre þe shryne of Seint Edward he stood
Myd glad chēre and mylde of mood,
Mid twō Kniȝttes armed on eiþer sīde
Þat he ne miȝt þennes goo ne rīde
Hetilich hii leiden hym upon [3]
Als hii miȝtten myd swerde dōn.

(2) Þe Þursday nēxt þe beryng of our Lefdy
Me þouȝht an aungel cōm Sir Edward bȳ ;
Þe aungel bitook Sir Edward on hōnde
Al blēdyng þe foure forþer clawes sō wēre of þe Lōmbe.
At Caunterbiry, bifōre þe heiȝe autere, þe Kyng stood,
Yclōþed al in rēde murre ; he was of þat blee rēd as blood.
God, þat was on gōde Frīday dōn on þe rōde
So turne my swevene night and day to mychel gōde.
Tweye poynts þere bēn þat bēn unschēwed
For me ne worþe to clerk ne lēwed ;
Bot to Sir Edward oure Kyng
Hym wil iche shewe þilk mētyng.

[1] *þing* = 'creature'.   [2] Me mette = 'I dreamt'.
[3] This phrase is very like ou: 'laid into him'.

(d) Extract from 'A petition from the folk of Mercerye' (1386).

Rolls of Parliament, vol. iii, p. 225, &c. ; Morsbach, Engl. Schriftspr., p. 171.

And yif in general his falsenesse were ayeinsaide as of v̄s togydre of the
Mercerye or othere craftes or ony conseille wolde hāue tāken to ayeinstande
it, or as tyme out of mynde hath be vsed, wē wōlden companye togydre how
lawful so it wēre for owre nēde or profite were anon apēched for arrysers
ayeins the pees, and falsly many of vs that yet stonden endited and we bēn
ōpenlich disclaundred, hōlden vntrewe and traitours to owre Kyng.   for the
same Nichol said bifor Mair Aldermen and owre craft bifor hem gadred in
place of recorde that xx or xxx of vs wēre worthy to be drawen and hanged,
the which thyng lȳke to yowre worthy lordship bȳ and ēuen Juge to be
prōued or disprōued the whether that trowthe may shēwe for trowthe
amonges vs of fewe or elles no man many day dorst be shēwed. And nought
oonlich vnshēwed or hidde it hath be by no man now, but also of bifōre tȳme,
the moost profitable poyntes of trewe gouernaunce of the citee compīled to-
gidre bi longe labour of discrēte and wȳse men wythout conseille of trewe
men : for thei sholde nought be knōwen ne contynued in the tyme of Nichol
Exton outerliche wēre brent.

(e) *From Chaucer's Pardoner's Tale.*

'Ye, goddes armes,' quod this ryotour,
'Is it swich peril with him for to mēte ?
I shal him sēke by wey and eek by strēte,
I make avow to goddes digne bōnes !
Herkneth, felawes, we three been al ōnes ;

E

Lat ēch of us hōlde up his hōnd til ōther,
And ēch of us bicomen ōtheres brōther,
And we wol sleen this false traytour Deeth;
He shal be slayn, which that so many sleeth,
By goddes dignitee, ēr it be night.'
Togidres han thise three her trouthes plight,
To live and dȳen ēch of hem for ōther,
As though hē wēre his ōwene ybōren brōther.
And up they sterte al dronken, in this rage,
And forth they goon towardes that villáge,
Of which the taverner had spōke biforn,
And many a grisly ooth than han they sworn,
And Crīstes blessed body they to-rente—
' Deeth shal be deed, if that they may him hente.'
Whan they han goon nat fully half a mȳle
Right as they wolde han troden over a stȳle,
An ōld man and a pōvre with hem mette.
This ōlde man ful mēkely hem grette,
And seyde thus, ' now, lordes, god yow see!'
The proudest of thise ryotoures three
Answerde agayn, ' what? carl, with sory grāce,
Why artow al forwrapped sāve thy fāce?
Why livestow so lōnge in sō greet āge?'
This ōlde man gan lōke in his visāge,
And seyde thus, ' for I ne can nat fīnde
A man, though that I walked into Inde
Neither in citee nor in nō villāge,
That wōlde chaunge his youthe for myn āge;
And therfore moot I han myn āge stille,
As lōnge time as it is goddes wille.
Ne deeth, allas! ne wol nat han my lyf;
Thus walke I, lyk a restelees caitýf,
And on the ground, which is my mōdres gāte,
I knokke with my staf, bothe erly and lāte,
And seye, "leve mōder, leet me in!
Lo how I vanish, flesh, and blood, and skin!
Allas whan shul my bones been at reste?
Mōder with yow wolde I chaunge my cheste,
That in my chāmbre lōnge tȳme hath bē,
Ye! for an heyre clout to wrappe mē!"
But yet to me she wol nat do that grāce,
For which ful pāle and welked is my fāce.
But, sirs, to yow it is nō curteisye
To spēken to an ōld man vileinye,
But he trespasse in worde, or elles in dēde.
In hōly writ ye may your-self wel rēde,
"Agayns an ōld man, hoor upon his heed,
Ye shōlde arȳse;" wherfor I yeve yow reed,
Ne dooth unto an ōld man noon harm now,
Namōre than yē wōlde men dide to yow
In āge, if that yē sō lōng abyde;
And god be with yow, wher yē gō or rȳde.
I moot go thider as I hāve to gō.'

(f) *From Chaucer's Persones Tale.*

Wherfore as seith Seint Anselm: ' ful gret angwissh shul the sinful folk
have at that tyme; ther shal the sterne and wrothe juge sitte above, and

under him the horrible put of helle open to destroyen him that moot biknowen hise sinnes, which sinnes openly been shewed biforn god and biforn every creature. And on the left syde mo develes than herte may bithinke, for to harie and drawe the sinful soules to the pyne of helle. And with-inne the hertes of folk shal be the bytinge conscience and withouteforth shal be the world al brenninge.

Whider shal thanne the wrecched sinful man flee to hyden him? Certes, he may nat hyden him; he moste come forth and shewen him. . . . Now sothly, who-so wel remembreth him of thise thinges, I gesse that his sinne shal nat turne him into delyt, but to greet sorwe, for drede of the peyne of helle. And therfore seith Iob to god: 'suffre, lord, that I may a whyle biwaille and wepe, er I go with-oute returning to the derke lond, covered with the derknesse of deeth; to the lond of misese and of derknesse, where-as is the shadwe of deeth; where-as ther is noon ordre or ordinance, but grisly drede that evere shal laste.' . . .

. . . And therfore seith Seint Iohn the Evangelist: 'they shullen folwe deeth, and they shul nat finde him, and they shul desyren to dye, and deeth shal fle fro hem.' . . . For as seith seint Basilie: 'the brenninge of the fyr of this world shal god yeven in helle to hem that been dampned; but the light and the cleernesse shal be yeven in hevene to hise children; right as the gode man yeveth flesh to hise children, and bones to his houndes.'

The first document is given here chiefly on account of its intrinsic historical interest. It does not prove very much from a linguistic point of view. The form is to all intents and purposes Old English, and, like most other documents written in the eleventh century, is no doubt very archaic from the point of view of the English then spoken. It is the conventional Late Old English of the scribes, showing, it is true, some signs of departure from that of the classical period, but still giving no true picture of the changes which time must already have wrought in uttered speech. As regards dialect, the charter is certainly Southern English, and such forms as *yrf-*(nume) and *wǣran* (Sthn. 2 a) are characteristic of what we are accustomed to call West Saxon. We have, unfortunately, no reliable knowledge of the differences and points of agreement between the English of Wessex and that of Middlesex. Probably there were more of the former than of the latter. The forms *ealle, eallre*, and *gehealde* could not occur in a Northern or Midland dialect, though they might just as well be Kentish as 'Saxon' (Sthn. 6, Kt. 6). The fact is that all O.E. documents of the later period, with very few exceptions, are written in a common form which in all essential features is W. Saxon—though this particular charter has only two absolutely test forms—*yrf-, wǣran*—so much so that it is now commonly assumed that after Ælfred's time the prestige of Wessex in Government, Arms, and Letters, was such that the dialect of that area became a literary κοινή in universal use in written documents. That this was true of official London documents this charter, so far as it goes, is a proof. The fact that æ is retained in *fæder, þæt, dæge*, &c., tends to show a W. Saxon character, since *e* was typical in these words in Kent (Kt. 1) and in part of the Mercian area. On the other hand, Late Kentish scribes often write the letter æ for the *e*-sound. But the form *kȳðe* is certainly not Kentish, for this dialect would have *kēþe* (Kt. 3).

The written dialect of London, then, in the eleventh century was definitely Southern in character, and South-Western, rather than South-

Eastern. It may be asked whether the actual speech of the metropolis at this period is represented by this charter. It is largely a question of probabilities, but it is highly probable, if not absolutely certain, that this document—apart from chronological inconsistencies with the spoken language, to which allusion has already been made—does represent the type of dialect which was actually spoken in London when it was written. If that be so, the speech of London in the eleventh century was Southern in character, and, more exactly, approximated to South-Western, having as yet, so far. as our evidence goes, no purely South-Eastern features.

Passing now to extract (b), the **Proclamation of Henry III,** which is nearly two hundred years later than the above charter, we notice a considerable difference in its dialect constituents, as compared with the latter. We now observe the characteristic blending of Midland elements with those which are typically Southern, and in some cases the Southern and Midland forms of the same word or grammatical ending both occur.

Among the characteristically Southern forms are the following:—O.E. *ǣ* preserved as *e* or *æ* in *æt, þæt, wes* (Sthn. 1); O.E. *ǣ*[1] written *æ* in *rǣdesmen* 'councillors' (Sthn. 2 a); O.E. *y* preserved in sound, and written *u* in *Kuneriche* 'kingdom' (Sthn. 3); O.E. *-eald-* written *-eald-* as distinct from Midland *-ōld-* in to *healden* = [hēlden]. This belongs to the South-East and Kent as well (see Sthn. 6 and Kt. 6). Its survival here may be due to Kentish influence. The frequent *ēo* as in *hēo, bēoþ, trēowe,* &c., may be more than a traditional spelling, which, indeed, is unlikely so long after the Conquest, and may represent the Western rounded vowel often written *u* (Sthn. 4). It is possible that this sound never reached, in London, the stage represented by South-Western *u,* but was simply unrounded to *ē* previously.

The spelling *Hurtford* 'Hertford', O.E. *Heor*(*o*)*t*-, occurs among the signatures to the document, which is clearly a South-West or South-West Midland form, but this proves nothing concerning London speech.

Other Southern features are the common use of the prefix *i-* in *imakede* 'made' (Pret.), *-iseid*(*e*) 'said' P.P., *ilet* 'hindered' P.P., *iseened* 'signed' P.P., *igretinge* 'greeting', *idōn* 'done', *ichosen* 'chosen', *ilestinde* 'lasting', &c. (Sthn. 15); the Pres. Indic. Pl. in *-þ* as in *bēoþ, habbeþ* (Sthn. 9 and 14); the Pres. Part. in *-inde, ilestinde* (Sthn. 11); the Inf. in *-ien, to mākien* (Sthn. 16). This last may also be Kentish (Kt. 17). The Southern Pl. Pronouns *heo, heom,* are not decisive as to dialect at this period, since even in E. Midland texts the *th*-forms are not found so early as this. (See E. Midl. 13.)

The Midland forms in the Proclamation are *alle, halden* (we should expect *hōlden,* see E. Midl. 5); the Pres. Indic. Pl. in *-en, beon, cumen, willen, halden, hoaten* 'command', *unnen* 'grant', *senden* (E. Midl. 9); the P.P. of the Strong Vbs. *chēsen* 'chose', *swēren* 'swear', and of the anomalous *dōn* 'do'—*ichōsen, isworene, idōn*—retain the final *-n* (E. Midl. 15), though all these forms also agree with the Southern type in preserving the prefix *i-.* The spelling *wherþurȝ,* where Southern texts very frequently write *wer-* (*w-* for O.E. *hw*) and Midland texts more often *wh-,* seems characteristic of London documents, both official and literary, during the whole M.E. period, though, as we shall see, the spelling *w-* is fairly common later on.

The only Kentish or South-Eastern elements in this text appear to be *iwersed* 'worsened', O.E. *gewyrsed*, where *y* is best explained as the original O.E. sound from earliest **wursi-*, and *ænd* 'end', where *æ* is a curious scribal survival of a Kentish spelling not infrequent in some O.E. texts which show Kentish influence in other respects also. Other O.E. dialects usually write *ende*.

There seems no reason to doubt that this interesting document represents pretty fairly the London dialect of the period, allowing for the scribal•archaisms of spelling.

We now come to a specimen of London English written during the first quarter of the fourteenth century, taken from the so-called *Five Dreams* of the monk **Adam Davie**. From a literary point of view these 'poems' are of small interest, and they show no poetical talent of any kind. For the purposes of the student of the history of our language, however, they are of the greatest value, far more so indeed than many of the M.E. 'Set Books' often prescribed for young persons at our universities, and certainly the literary interest is hardly less.

The Southern element is still considerable, but the Midland element is larger than in either of the texts hitherto examined by us here.

It was impossible to choose short extracts which should show all the dialectal features contained in the poems, and we shall therefore base our statement upon an examination of the work as a whole and not confine ourselves to the forms in the extracts given above. The most typical Southern phonological feature is perhaps the retention of the long 'slack' [ē] for O.E. *ǣ*[1], which is proved by the rhymes *wēren* (O.E. *wǣron*) with *ēren* 'ears', O.E. *ēaran*, and of *drēde*, O.E. *drǣd*, 'doubt, fear' with *rēde* 'red', O.E. *rēad*. On the other hand the spelling *Stretford*, where the first element can only represent a non-W. Saxon or non-Central Southern *strēt* 'street' (W. Saxon *strǣt*), and the rhyme *drēde* with *mēde* 'meed, reward', which points to the E. Midland or South-Eastern [*drēd*]. This shows, as we have seen before, that the same word was current in both types. Another very typical South-Westernism is the *i* in the verb *shilde* (Sthn. 7) 'to shield', instead of the Midland or S.E. *shēlde*, and this type is represented more frequently than the former, as in *stēl* 'steel', *hēren* 'hear', *ȝēlde* vb. 'yield', W.S. *gieldan*. O.E. *y* in Davie shows apparently only the E. Midland type: *synne* ' sin ', Caunter*biry* (O.E. *byriȝ*), *yuel* 'evil', O.E. *yfel* (E. Midl. 3). O.E. *ēo* is always written *e*, except the S.E. form *to bīen* (Kt. 4). Otherwise *leue* 'dear', O.E. *lēofa*, *dērworþ* 'precious', O.E. *dēor*.

The Pres. Pl. has the Southern *-eþ* in *willeþ* (Sthn. 9), but the verb 'to be' has *bēn* (E. Midl. 9).

The Pers. Pron. Pl. *hij*, *hii* is the only form of the Nom., and this is about the last time we meet it in London documents. (See the forms of Pers. Pron. Pl. in E. Midland and Southern.) The form *ich* instead of E. Midland *ic* or *i* 'I' is typical of the Southern dialect at this period. The characteristic Southern p.p. with *i-*, or *y-*, occurs—*yknowe*, *ihote*, *ychosen*, *ywonden* 'wound', and the first two of these are specially Southern in the omission of final *-n*. This feature is also found in *bore*, *write* 'written', where, however, the prefix is lost, and in *awreke* 'avenged'.

We see, then, that in Davie's time the Midland elements were gaining ground, though many purely Southern features still lingered which, as we shall see, disappear later on, or are reduced to a minimum.

The next specimen, which was written in Chaucer's lifetime, shows a form of English practically identical with that of the poet. The general appearance of the document (**Petition from the folk of Mercerye**) is very much more modern and familiar to the average reader of the present day than anything we have so far discussed. The reason is that London English had by this time practically settled down into a definite blending of the various dialectal elements, and these (that is, the *Regional* elements) have not altered much since in their distribution.

Compared with Davie, the most striking points are perhaps the use of *thei* instead of *hij*, the consistent Pers. Pl. in -*en* (no forms in -*th*), the loss of *i-* in the P.P.; the usual retention of final -*n* in this part of the verb— *bēn, stonden,* &c., though *be* is used instead of *bēn*. Compared with the English of to-day, putting aside differences due to normal sound changes, there is very little difference to indicate—we have here, to all intents and purposes, the exact ancestor of Modern Standard English. The form *shēwe* is a different type from that which has produced Mod. *show,* but this is probably not a regional feature, and the same is true of *togydre* compared with *together,* and *ayein* compared with *again.* Incidentally, we may note how near the spelling is to that of the present day, but we must not be deceived into supposing that it represented the same pronunciation as our own. The similarity merely shows that it was really the M.E. official scribes who fixed the chief features of English spelling which have lasted down to our own day. It cannot be too often insisted that the English fourteenth-century spelling of the official documents, and of the Chaucer MSS., which was virtually continued into the next century, and taken over with no vital changes by Caxton, and so handed on to us, was already unphonetic, and no longer represented adequately the facts of pronunciation in Chaucer's day.

We now pass to the language of **Chaucer** himself, and this, from the importance of the subject, will demand a rather special treatment, though we shall endeavour to make our remarks as brief as possible.

We may say generally that the dialectal type found in Chaucer's writings, especially in his prose works, agrees very closely with that of the official London documents of his day.

The dialect of the poetry contains more purely Southern and South-Eastern elements than that of the prose works. The language of the latter, therefore, presents a greater contrast to that of the earlier London documents than does the language of the poetry, and, consequently, Chaucer's prose is nearer in actual dialect to Caxton, and to the English of a still later date, than his poetry.

It need not surprise us that there should be this difference between the prose and poetry of the same writer at this period. In the first place, the language of English poetry is always slightly archaic—at any rate it has always been so until quite recently. Now, to be archaic in speech in Chaucer's day meant that the writer or speaker made use of more Southern elements than was the actual contemporary usage in either spelling or writing business documents. We must take it that many Southern forms still lingered on in the speech of the older generation, and though obsolescent, they were perfectly familiar to every one. A freedom in the use of dialectal variants was obviously a great convenience to a poet, since it increased the number of his rhymes, and sometimes made his versification more supple and varied. It is also probable that the actual Court speech of Chaucer's time was rather more Southern in type than that of the people, or than that of the official scribes. It is certain that various Southernisms crop up from time to time in private letters, and even in literature, during the fifteenth and sixteenth centuries, which shows that this element lingered on in the usage of many who spoke and wrote Standard English.

Another point is that Chaucer's poetry shows a far larger number of Kenticisms—especially in the use of *e* instead of E. Midland *i* for O.E. *y*, in such words as *kesse* 'kiss', *fest* 'fist', *berie* 'bury' (verb), *fulfelle* 'fulfil', *fēry* 'fiery', &c.—than is found either in the London documents of all kinds before his day, or in the official documents written during his life-time. This may be explained to some extent by the fact that Chaucer lived for several years at Greenwich, but also perhaps from these Kenticisms being in vogue in Court English. At any rate the use of *e*-forms by the side of *i*-forms in the above and many other words was tolerated in the best English throughout the fifteenth and sixteenth centuries. Many of these forms are fixed in our language to-day, but many others, now no longer used, are continually cropping up, as occasional variants, in writings for nearly two centuries after Chaucer's death. This feature need not therefore be considered a personal peculiarity of the poet. When it is remembered that the *e*-forms obtained not only in Kent, but also in part of Essex, and Suffolk, and, to judge by the Norfolk Guild Records of 1387, also to some extent in Norfolk, it is not surprising that they should gain ground at a time when the Regional influence upon Standard English was predominatingly Eastern. It is curious that in the word *bury* we write the Southern but pronounce the S.E. type, and this latter form seems to preponderate greatly even in official documents.

In Chaucer's poetry a considerable number of words of this class occur at least once in the *e*-form, some with *e* and *i*, some with *e*, *i*, and *u*. The *i*-forms taken all round are the most frequent, the *u*-forms the least; indeed there are fewer of these than in the official documents.

Among the *e*-forms, now lost, which occur in Chaucer's poetry are—*besie* 'busy' (we still write the Southern type and pronounce the E. Midland), also *bisie*; *shette* 'shut', also an *i*-form; *thenne* 'thin', also *thinne*; *dreye* 'dry', and *drye*; *kesse* 'to kiss', and *kisse*; *lest* 'list', vb. (over thirty times), and *list* 'desire', vb. (over fifty times); *meri, myrie,* and *murie*; *melle* 'mill', and *mille*; *knette* and *knitte*; *fulfelle* and *fulfille*; *fēr, fēry* 'fire, fiery'; *fest* 'fist', and *fist*. Among the *u*-forms which are now lost are—*burth* 'birth', and *birth*; *bulde*, and *bilde* 'build'; *murthe* 'mirth', also *mirthe*; *put* 'pit', and *pit* (three times each); *furst* and *first*. *Evel*, O.E. *yfel*, 'evil' ('Kentish'), the prevailing form in Chaucer, is not necessarily lost, see p. 207. This list is given with some fullness because we shall find nearly all these forms occurring much later.

Besides the Southern features already alluded to, we must note the extremely frequent retention of the prefix *y-* in Past Participles.

We pass now to the E. Midland features of Chaucer's dialect.

(1) The O.E. combination -*eald*- always appears as -*old*-, except in three cases—*hĕlde* inf., *hĕlde* Pres. Ind. Pl., and *behelde* inf. We should probably put these very exceptional forms down to Kentish influence, as it seems very doubtful from the evidence of the purely Southern texts whether they would survive anywhere but in Kent at this period.

(2) O.E. (Sax.) *ie*, non-Sax. *ĕ* (see above, Sthn. 7), is often *e* by the side of *i*, so that we get *shĕld* (n.) and *shĕlde* (vb.) 'shield', and *shilde*, *hĕren* 'hear' (always), *herde* 'shepherd' (always), *yĕlden* 'yield, pay', and *yilden*, *yĕve* 'give', and *yive*; *yf* and *yif* 'if', *yit* 'yet', appear still only with the Southern forms. *Yelpe* 'boast', W. Sax. *ġielpan*, appears only in the non-Southern form.

(3) O.E. (Sthn.) *ēā* + *g* or *h* becomes *ē* in Anglian in O.E., and this is later raised to *i* before *g* (later *y*) and *h*. In Chaucer we get *eyen* 'eyes', O.E. *ēāgan*, *ĕgan*, as the usual written form, but occasionally *yën*, and the rhymes show that the latter was the form intended; similarly, in spite of the spelling *heighe*, O.E. *hēāh*, 'high', *heye*, &c., we also find *hȳe*, and the rhymes generally point to this as the pronunciation; O.E. *nēāh* 'near' is written *neye*, *neyh*, and *ny(e)*, but the word does not occur in rhyme. Our present forms are derived from M.E. *ȳe*, *hȳe*, *nȳe*, and these can only be Midland forms.

(4) O.E. *ǣ*[1] is shown by the rhymes to have had both the Southern pronunciation [ē] and the Midland and Kentish [ĕ]. Chaucer, therefore, used both types, and, as it happens, the Southern type predominates in rhyme. This does not necessarily prove that Chaucer heard or used this type in ordinary speech more than the non-Southern type. The frequency of its occurrence may be due to the exigencies of rhyme, or at least to convenience.

(5) Another test of the original type in use is found in the spelling of the shortened form of this vowel. The shortening of Southern *ǣ* produced *ǣ*, which, together with all *ǣ*-sounds, later took the Midland form *ǎ* and was so spelt, whereas the Old non-Southern *ĕ*-type when shortened underwent no essential change in spelling. The word *drādde*, p.p., &c., is frequent in rhymes by the side of *dredde*, the former being more frequent. Therefore Chaucer used both forms, and, while still retaining the original Southern, occasionally at least employed the non-Southern form.

The following are chief words with the unshortened vowel : (*a*) those which rhyme both with [ē] and [ē]—*dede* 'deed', *drēde*, &c., vb. and n., 'doubt', &c., *euen* 'evening', *rēde* vb. 'counsel'; (*b*) those which rhyme always with [ē]—*beheestes*, *seed*, *threed* 'thread', *weete* 'wet', *where*.

(6) O.E. *ĕŏ* always appears as *ĕ*. There is no trace of a rounded vowel.

(7) The Pers. Pronoun Pl. *thei* is the only form of the Nom. The old Southern *hij*, &c., has disappeared.

(8) The Fem. Pronoun *she* is the only form used.

(9) The Pres. Indic. Pl. usually ends in -*e* or -*en*, very rarely in the Southern -*eth*.

(10) The P.P. of Strong Vbs. usually retains the -*n* of the ending. -*e* is rarer.

(11) The Pl. Pres. Indic. of Vb. 'to be' is usually *been*, more rarely *bĕ*, occasionally *arn*. The Southern *bĕth* also occurs occasionally.

A word or two upon Chaucer's position in regard to Literary English may not be out of place. This is frequently misconceived, though less so now, even among those who are not professional students of English, than formerly. To put it briefly and bluntly, Chaucer did not create the English of Literature, he found it ready to his hand and used it. He used it far better than any English poet before him had ever done, and than any who came after him before Sackville and Spenser, for the simple reason that he was the first English poet of real genius who ever wrote. In saying this we are considering only poets since the Conquest, and will not discuss the intrinsic value, as literature, of Old English poetry. Chaucer was hailed with one voice by his contemporaries, as the supreme singer of all who had yet appeared in English; and by his immediate followers he was worshipped 'on this side of idolatry'. Except for a period during part of the seventeenth and eighteenth centuries, when men were so rash as to attempt to patronize him, all true lovers of poetry have turned to Chaucer again and again, with a delight which is ever renewed, for they find in him a gaiety, a tenderness, and a humanity which have never been surpassed, the fragrance of the woodland in spring, and a magic which resides only in the music of the greatest poets. In this sense Chaucer was, as the discerning, if disreputable, Hoccleve said, ' the firste finder of oure faire langage '— not that he invented or created it, but that he did with it what no one had ever done before. There is no mystery in the instrument which Chaucer uses—that had been gradually becoming what it was in his day, during the centuries of law-giving, and preaching, and chaffering, and gossiping, in court, church, and palace, in market and tavern, which had passed in London since the Conquest. The only mystery is that which surrounds every great poet. Who shall say why this particular kind of genius should arise just when and where it does? No amount of grammatical investigation will explain Chaucer, any more than it will explain Spenser, or Milton, or Keats, or Swinburne. Neither literary historians, nor grammarians, have yet explained why such a poet is just what he is, nor, probably, will the students of the japes and pranks which heredity plays upon mankind be able to do so. But if Chaucer neither created the English of Literature by vamping diverse dialectal elements together, as some have thought, to make himself more widely intelligible, nor yet perverted it, as others have maintained, by introducing new and foreign elements into its vocabulary, it may be asserted that, without any question, he certainly did give to that mixed dialect in which he wrote a prestige, a glory, a vogue, as a literary medium, which neither the most industrious of versifiers devoid of genius, nor the most punctiliously exact scribe in a Government office, could ever have given it. The dialect of London would, in any case, have become, nay, it was already becoming, the chief form of English used in writings of every kind, and that from the pressure of political, economic, and social factors; but there can be no doubt that the process was greatly hastened, so far as pure literature is concerned, by the popularity of Chaucer—as shown by the number of MSS. of his writings in existence, and, afterwards, by the number of printed editions, as well as by the frequent expressions of reverence for him scattered through literature, and by the irresistible impulse among poets to imitate his style, his turns of phrase, and his actual grammatical forms.

But we must return from this digression to the immediate and more prosaic business before us, and sum up briefly the main purport of our narrative in this chapter. We have attempted to set forth first some of the main distinguishing features of the chief dialectal types of Middle English which are found blended in the dialect of London during the same period. We have illustrated each type by short extracts from representative works covering between three and four hundred years. We then approached the language of London itself, through the rather scrappy remains of the earliest period after the Conquest, and examined the dialectal features of a few documents written in London from the time of the Conqueror down to Chaucer. We found that London English was, in its earlier phases, of a definitely Southern type, and more particularly of a Central, rather than an East Southern type. We witnessed the gradual appearance of more and more East Midland elements, and of some South Eastern, or Kentish, peculiarities. The E. Midland elements gain ground more and more, sometimes being used alongside of the corresponding Southern elements, sometimes exclusively, instead of the latter. By the end of the fourteenth century we found that London speech had become predominantly E. Midland in character, and that the purely Central Southern elements were very greatly reduced, though still in excess of what they are in Standard or Written English at the present time. We noticed further that certain Kentish features had become more frequent than in the earlier documents, and that in some cases Chaucer makes greater use of these than we do at the present time. There we leave London English then, at the end of the fourteenth century, rapidly approaching to our own speech so far as the general character of the dialectal elements is concerned, which make it up. But it still differs from our own usage, not only in the relative proportion of the different elements, but also as to the specific distribution of the types among particular words.

We cannot close this brief survey of the English dialects of the South and of the E. Midlands down to the close of the fourteenth century without glancing at the language of the three best-known writers among Chaucer's contemporaries—Gower, Wyclif, and the author of Piers Plowman. Each of these men has strong claims upon our interest. Each wrote voluminously and each exhibits in his writings different phases of the social or religious life of his age. They come from three widely separated areas of England, and their training and experience of life was different. Gower was a native of Kent, Wyclif of Yorkshire, William Langland of Shropshire. It is natural to inquire how far the language of these writers shows signs of conforming to a common literary type, or how far each preserves a strictly Regional dialect. The position of Gower in this respect is particularly interesting. If the reader compares the language of Gower's Confessio Amantis with that of the Ayenbite, written in Kent about fifty or sixty years earlier, he will at once note the absence from the former of most of the typical Kenticisms. Gower, born c. 1325, died 1408, was a Kentish country gentleman, a member of a Kentish territorial family, but the dialect of his gigantic English poem, with a few notable exceptions which we shall note directly, is practically that of Chaucer, that is to say, the London dialect   One feature, the ending *-ende*, which is his chief form of the Pres. Participle, is distinctly E. Midland, the Kentish form and Southern form generally being *-inde*, which was also the London form before Chaucer. (Cf. remarks on Davy above.) Chaucer, however, has given up this in favour of the new forms in *-ing*. Gower is in this respect archaic. The forms of the Pers. Pronouns are not those of Ayenbite (see p. 44, *ante*), but *sche* (occasionally *scheo*) for the Fem., and *þei* in the Nom. Pl., while the typical Kent *hise*, Acc. Pl. 'them', is not found, *hem* being used as by Chaucer. The Pres. Pl. Indic. of verbs ends in *-en* as in London, instead of the Kent and Southern *-eþ*. Gower has no trace of the Kent spelling *dyaþ*, &c., with *ya* for O.E. *ēa* (see above, Kt. 7). For old *ēo* he often writes *ie*; which, however, is not altogether on a footing with earlier Kent *ie*, *ye* (see Kt. 4), but quite clearly implies simply a long tense [ē] sound. This spelling, therefore, though hitherto chiefly found in Kentish, as a representative of old *ēo*, is in Gower merely a convenient graphic device, which in words like *briest*, O.E. *brēost*, 'breast', *behield* 'behold', O.E. *behǣld*, represents a typical E. Midland type, possibly by this time current also in Kent, but quite in accordance with the London type. Short *eŏ* as in O.E. *heorte*, &c., is always written *e*, *herte*, &c., as in E. Midland and in the London dialect. The spelling *dradde* 'feared' instead of Kent or E. Midland *dredde* is Southern and has the retention of the shortened form of W. Saxon *ǣ*[1] rather than of the Anglian *ē*; and the rhyme *brēþ*, O.E. *brǣþ* 'breath' with *dēþ* proves quite clearly that the former word retained the Southern type of the long vowel, and *ladde* 'led', by the side of the Kent *ledde*, Late Saxon *lǣdde*, shows the non-Kentish *ă* for earlier *ǣ*. This Midland *ă* is the regular form in Gower, in all words which formerly had *ǣ*. All these are non-Kentish features, whether they be Saxon or E. Midland, and they are shared by Chaucer and the London documents. Gower has no trace of the typical initial *z-* and *v-*, for *s-*, *f-*, which are so characteristic of Ayenbite. Now for the other side of the picture, the purely Kentish features of Gower's dialect. We must not attach too much weight to the fact that the poet has many examples of *e* for O.E. *y*, since, as we have seen above, these are very common in Chaucer's verse, and fairly frequent in other London documents. Besides, Gower has both *i* and *u* forms as well—as *fȳr* 'fire', *pitt, gilt* 'guilt', *hide* 'hide' vb., O.E. *hȳdan, sinne* 'sin'. *fille* 'fill', *þinne* 'thin', *first*; also *gulte, gulteless, hull* 'hill', O.E. *hyll, þurst* 'thirst', O.E. *þyrst*. The *e*-forms, however, appear to predominate in words having the short vowel—*besie, bregge* 'bridge', *hell* 'hill', *kertell*, O.E. *cyrtel*, 'kirtle', *keste* 'kissed', *merie* 'merry', *pet* 'pit', O.E. *pytt, senne* 'sin', *first*. Most of these forms occur, however, in Chaucer, several are found, much later, in the writings of persons who apparently spoke the Standard English of their day, and some survive at the present time. Much more important than these forms is the undoubted use by Gower of the specifically Kentish tense [ē] in words containing O.E. *ǣ*[2] (see above, Kt. 2). This is proved both by rhymes and by the spelling of these words with *ie*—e.g. *tēche* from O.E. *tǣċan* 'teach' from *tākjan*, rhyming with *besēche*, and *diel* 'part', O.E. *dǣl*, from *dāli*. Thus those essentially typical Kenticisms in Gower, which are not found also, to some extent at least, in London speech of the fourteenth century, are reducible to this simple peculiarity.

The results of this brief examination are remarkable, since they prove that in the fourteenth century already, a Kentishman did not necessarily write in his native dialect, but adopted the London form of English. This fact is capable of two interpretations. One is that people of a certain social standing in the shires in the neighbourhood of London already *spoke*, with certain provincial modifications, the Court dialect, and there-fore used it in their writings. The other is that the literary use of the London written form was already becoming established among the better educated, although they still retained their provincial forms in actual speech.

Possibly the truth, in the case of Gower, lies between these two suggestions.

Concerning the author of the remarkable work known as the *Vision of Piers Plowman* much has been conjectured, where nothing is known with certainty. Such details of his life as are asserted by recent writers, even his name—**William Langland**—are based upon statements which occur scattered through the poem itself, and are believed to be of an autobiographical character. How far they are really intended to refer to the author, and, if they do, how far they are reliable, is a pure matter of conjecture, like much else in the so-called literary history of the early period. That the poet lived in the South-West Midlands seems certain— apart from other arguments—from the dialect of his work ; that he had been bred up as an ecclesiastic, and knew the ins and outs of the lives of the monks and clerics of his day, seems equally certain from the character of the poem itself. Who his father was, whether he was married, whether he was a priest or only in minor orders, or not in orders at all, and other details regarding which many cobwebs have been spun, are speculations which have engaged many earnest minds, but they seem to have no bearing upon the literary merit of his work, and they certainly have still less from our present point of view. That he spent some part of his life in London, if we could be sure of it, would be of importance for us, and still more so to know in what world he lived. When we turn to the poem itself, which exists in three versions and innumerable manuscripts, we find small traces of any London influence upon the language. The dialect is rustic and archaic, and the metre is alliterative, and unrhymed. The main dialectal features—allowing for differences between the versions and manuscripts—are distinctly Western, and are coloured with that suggestion of Southernism which we are accustomed to find in texts written in Shropshire or Worcestershire. O.E. *ȳ* very commonly appears as *u* or *ui*—*buggen* 'buy', *huiden* 'hide'. O.E. *ēo* is still so written—as in *eorþe* by the side of *erthe*, *beoth* by the side of *bēth*. The old Fem. Pronoun *hē* 'she' is still used by the side of *shē*, and the Pl. Pronoun *heo* 'they' occurs as well as *they* and *þey*. In the Possess. and Dat. only *here* and *hem* are found. In verbs the prefix *i-* is often retained in P.P.'s ; the Pres. Indic. Pl., while generally ending in *-en*, often has the Southern *-eth*. The Pres. Part. is always in *-yng*. The Pl. Pres. of 'to be' is *bēn*, *bēth*, *bēoth*, and *aren*. The old combination *-an-* usually appears as *-on-* after the Western manner. The blend of Southern elements with those of Midland character is typical of the dialect of the area from which the poem emanates, and there appears to be no reason for supposing that this apparent mixture does not represent a genuine spoken dialect.

A thorough investigation of all the manuscripts of the three versions of Piers Plowman would be a long and tedious task, but it is one which ought to be undertaken. It is probable that from such an examination a pretty clear view of the precise dialect of the original would emerge, and further that this dialect would be found to show the characteristic blending of Southern with W. Midland features which is sometimes mistakenly supposed to be due to the influence of various scribes, but which is none the less a genuine dialectal type, just as much as in the mixed dialect of London itself. Probably, if Worcester or Shrewsbury or Oxford had been the capital of England, Piers Plowman would play the same important part in the history of English that the works of Chaucer actually do : it would represent what would in this case be the ancestral dialect of Standard Spoken and Literary English. As it is, however, the language of Langland has no historical relation with these types, is quite unaffected by the London English of his day, and agrees with this only in such features as have a wide Regional distribution.

Wyclif, who was born *circa* 1320, died in 1385. He was, therefore, a contemporary of Chaucer, though rather older than the poet. A North-countryman by birth, Wyclif lived many years in Oxford, where he was Fellow of Balliol in *c.* 1345, and Master of Balliol 1361. From 1374 to 1384 he was Rector of Lutterworth in Leicestershire.

His writings, apart from the translation of the Bible which bears his name, are very voluminous. A large collection of sermons and contro-versial treatises is edited by Thomas Arnold, Oxford, 1871, under the title *Select English Works of John Wyclif* (3 vols.). A very brief account of the language of this remarkable man must suffice here. The following remarks are based upon an examination of Vol. III of the *Select Works*. The first thing to say is that on the whole the language is very Midland in character, and has hardly any purely Southern, and apparently no Kentish features. The reader should compare the language of these tracts with that of Chaucer's prose. Although the treatises in Arnold's edition are taken from various manuscripts, written no doubt at different periods and in different places, and possibly in no case giving Wyclif's own dialect with perfect fidelity, the various treatises seem all to agree to a remarkable extent in the main characteristics. Perhaps the first thing that strikes the student is the extreme frequency of *i* in suffixes, *-is, -iþ, -id,* and occasionally *-in,* where Chaucer usually has *-es, -eþ,* &c. With the exception of *-in,* these forms of the suffixes enormously predominate over any others, though *-es,* &c., and more rarely *-us* do occur. So far as our evidence goes, therefore, we are apparently justified in assuming that Wyclif said *byndiþ,* &c. The vowel system on the whole agrees with that of Chaucer, except that whereas the latter has all three forms *u, i, e,* representing O.E. *y,* Wyclif, in the volume under consideration, seems to have *i,* and this East Midland or Northern form only—*synne, birien* 'bury', *bisi, gilti, fulfilliþ, siche* 'such', and so on. The only exception appears to be *werse,* but this may be otherwise explained than as corre-sponding to W. Saxon *wyrse* 'worse'. O.E. *ĕŏ* is always *ĕ,* and there seems to be no example of *hurte* 'heart', or *hŭld* 'held', O.E. *hĕŏld.*

These two points alone seem to rule out much South-West Midland influence, such as we might expect to find from a residence in Oxford. On the other hand the Southern *i* for O.E. *ie* occurs in *ʒitte*, O.E. *ʒiĕt*, þei *sillen* 'sell', O.E. *siellan, sillan, silf*, O.E. *sielf, silf* 'self'. The Inf. of the verb 'to give' is *ʒĕve*, which is Midland or S. Eastern or Northern, in place of the Southern *ʒive*; in 3rd Sing. both *ʒiuiþ* and *ʒĕueþ* occur. *Mon* 'man' and *con* 'can' are rather Western than Eastern. Turning to the accidence, we find *þei* always for the 3rd Pers. Pl. Nom.; in the Possess. *here, hore, hor*, which are the usual forms, but occasionally *þer*; in the Dat. Acc. *hem* and *hom*. Thus Wyclif agrees with Chaucer in having *þei*, but differs from him in having *ber*. This must be put down either to E. Midland or Northern influence. The Fem. Sing. is always *schĕ*, and incidentally we may note the interesting Possess. *hern* 'hers', used absolutely—'*þe child was hern þat wolde have it on lyve, and not hern þat wolde have it deed*', p. 310. The verbal endings are :— 3rd Pers. Sing. Pres. Indic. in some of the pieces *-iþ, -eþ*, in others *-is, -s*, &c.; for instance Fifty Heresies, Twenty-five Articles, and Seven Deadly Sins all have the latter type, while the Church and her Members, and Wedded Men have the former. The *-s* forms point to the North or North-East Midland; the Pl. Pres. ends in *-en* with extraordinary regularity, the *-n* being very rarely omitted. A few examples of *-eþ* occur in Tract XXI—'*þay loveþ Goddis care*', &c., p. 247. The P.P. of Strong Verbs is generally *-n* after the Midland fashion. The prefix *y-* does not occur. The Pl. Pres. of 'to be' is almost invariably *bĕn* or *been, bĕþ* being very rare (see p. 247, Tract XXI). The Pres. Part. of verbs ends in *-ynge*.

There are certain indications of Northern influence. A rather striking one is the writing of *u* and *oi* for O.E. *ō*, both common Northern spellings indicating a quite different development from that which this sound had in the South and Midlands, namely, towards a sound closely resembling, if not identical with, French *ü*—the sound in fact which in the South is generally expressed by *u* or *ui*. The examples I have noted in Wyclif are *mut*, O.E. *mōt*, 'must', pp. 342, 343; *sunner* 'sooner', p. 344; and *soiþ* 'true', O.E. *sōþ*, pp. 343 and 345.

The Pres. Pl. *schewis* 'shows'—*her werkes shewis þis wel*, p. 175, and doubtless there are other examples—is a striking Northern feature, especially as it is surrounded on the same page by Midland Pls. in *-en*. The Scand. *ʒōuen* P. P. of *ʒiuen* occurs, rather pointing to Northern or E. Midland, though the form occurs in Gower. To sum up this very brief sketch of Wyclif's literary dialect: he adopted, no doubt, the form of English current in the University of Oxford in his day, a form which differed from the surrounding Regional dialect to some extent, in that the most typical provincialisms were eliminated in favour of a more Easterly type approximating more to that of London. At the same time certain Northern peculiarities certainly clung to his speech, as they do to that of certain members of Oxford University in our own day, and some of these occasionally slip out in his writings. In point of prose style we must count Wyclif among the great masters—perhaps the greatest of his day and before it. There is nothing stilted or creaking in his sentences, which are those of a skilful and competent writer, with an instrument that he thoroughly understands, adequate for all his wants. He reminds one of Latimer by the nature and force of his prejudices, but he is a more polished writer, without that excellent bishop's violence, and occasional vulgarity of thought and expression.

> Crīstes lōre and his apostles twelve
> He taughte, and first he folwed it himselve.

Thus the fourteenth century closes without anything like a general acceptance of a uniform type of English among writers whose native dialect was not that of the metropolis or of the surrounding shires. It appears, however, from the works of Wyclif, that the type of speech, uttered and written, in vogue in the University of Oxford was definitely influenced by a more Easterly dialect, and we must suppose that this influence was exerted through the medium of London.

SHORT LIST OF MIDDLE ENGLISH TEXTS IN VARIOUS DIALECTS.

East Midland.

Peterborough Chronicle (Laud MS.), 1121–54.   Ed. Plummer.
Ormulum, c. 1200.   Ed. Holt, 1878.
Bestiary, c. 1250.   See O.E. Miscellany, Ed. Morris, E.E.T.S., 1872.
Genesis and Exodus, c. 1250.   Morris. E.E.T.S., 1873.
Robt. of Brunne's Handlyng Synne, c. 1300.   Furnivall, Pt. I, 1901 ; Pt. II, 1902.
Norfolk Gilds, 1389.   L. Toulmin Smith, E.E.T.S., 1870 (in *English Gilds*).
(*Bokenam's Lives of Saints*, c. 1430, is chiefly dealt with as Early Modern English in this book.   It was edited by Horstmann, Heilbronn, 1883.)

Southern.

Lambeth Homilies, before 1200.   Morris, in O.E. Homilies, E.E.F.S., 1868, Pt. I.
Moral Ode, Trinity MS. before 1200 ; Jesus MS. 1250 (both in O.E. Misc.) ; Egerton MS. 1200, in Morris's O.E. Homs., I.
Wooing of Our Lord, c. 1200 ; also *God Ureisun* and *Sawles Ward* of same date, all in O.E. Homs., I.
Owl and Nightingale, 1246–50.   Ed. Wells.
Proverbs of Alfred, 1250.   O.E. Misc.
Robt. of Gloucester, 1298.   Wright, Rolls Series, 2 vols., 1887.
St. Juliana (Metrical Life of), 1300.   Cockayne, E.E.T.S., 1872.
Trevisa (Translation of Higden's Polychronicon), 1387.   Vols. I and II, Babington ; III and IV, Lumley, 1865–86.   Rolls Series.   Extracts are given in Morris and Skeat's *Specimens*, II.
Usages of Winchester, 1389.   In Toulmin Smith's *English Gilds*.
(*The Life of St. Editha*, c. 1420, is regarded in this book as Early Modern English.   It was edited by Horstmann, in 1883.)

Kentish.

Vespasian Homilies, c. 1150.   Morris, O.E. Homs., I.
Kentish Sermons (MS. Laud), before 1250.   Morris, O.E. Miscellany.
William of Shoreham's Poems, 1307.   Conrath, E.E.T.S., 1902.
Ayenbite of Inwyt ('Remorse of Conscience'), 1340.   Morris, E.E.T.S., 1866.

Some of the chief texts in the London Dialect before Chaucer are illustrated above, pp. 46–9, with references for each extract.

CHAPTER III

THE ENGLISH OF THE FIFTEENTH CENTURY

THE student of English literature, and the student of the history of our language, will naturally take very different views of the fifteenth century. For the former, at least as regards poetry, this age will appear one of the dreariest in our annals—'The builders were with want of genius cursed'—and from the conventional dullness of Hoccleve and Lydgate he turns to Scotland, and finds something to cherish in the very genuine poetic gift of the versatile and humorous, if rather sumptuous, Dunbar. In prose there are competent and solid, if hardly entertaining, writers, such as Bishop Pecok, Sir John Fortescue, and Capgrave, and there is Sir Thomas Malory, the glowing pages of whose *Morte d'Arthur* redeem the century from the chill dullness which generally surrounds its literature. This noble work, which breathes the spirit and fragrance of Romance, makes alive the Knights and Ladies of the age of Chivalry which had already faded, and by the side of this world of heroes and champions, the figures of the earlier romances seem mere puppets and shadows. Caxton, the first English printer, occupies of right a place apart in the literary history of his day. His fame rests upon his activities as a printer, and the sound sense which he showed in the selection of books to print, rather than upon his productions as a writer and translator, though these are by no means contemptible. Much nonsense has been written about Caxton's creation of a dialect, and still more about his creation of a prose style. After what has been said in the former chapter it is unnecessary to explain here that Caxton did not concoct an artificial medley of dialects in which to clothe his translations. Language does not grow up in that way. As to the other claim, it could hardly be made by those who were acquainted with Caxton's writings, and with those of some of his predecessors and contemporaries. In point of beauty and dignity of style, Malory is incomparably Caxton's superior, while in ease and raciness the latter is at least equalled by some of the anonymous writers of what are practically official documents, such as the directions for the funeral of an English king, of which we give a specimen below (p. 89), and the account of the creation of the Duke of York (afterwards Henry VIII) a Knight of the Bath. Both of these entertaining, and often picturesque, pieces of English prose are contained in Vol. I of *Letters and Papers*, &c., edited by Gairdner.

We shall have more to say later on concerning Caxton, from the point of view which more immediately concerns us here.

For the student of the development of the English language, apart from its use as a means of literary expression, the fifteenth century is one of extraordinary interest.

The reasons for this are chiefly the following :—

(1) There is a large increase in the number of persons who can write, and therefore in the number of purely private documents which have come down to us. As a result of writing being more widespread, and consequently, freed from the shackles of the professional scribe, we seem during this century, almost for the first time, to overhear, as it were, real people actually speaking. That is to say, we find a great variety of spelling, and, what is more, new varieties of this, which often show such divergence from the convention of the scribes that it becomes plain that what we are accustomed to regard as the Middle English system of pronunciation has undergone, or is undergoing, very remarkable changes.

(2) On account of the sound changes whose existence is indicated by these occasional departures from the old spelling, on account of the modification in the inflexional system which the written documents show, and by reason of the whole complexion of the sentence, we are constantly forced to admit, in reading fifteenth-century documents, that Modern English has begun.

(3) During this century the use of Regional dialect in writing, both in private and public documents—official and purely literary—gradually dies out, and that variety of English whose rise we discussed in the last chapter, comes slowly but surely into practically universal currency. This is traceable before the introduction of printing.

(4) Lastly, printing is introduced, and a new era opens, bringing conditions hitherto unknown, and providing facilities for the spread of London English, whose predominance, if it were not so already, is henceforth absolutely assured.

These are important points, and must be dealt with successively in some detail. They may serve us as headings for our present treatment of the subject of this chapter. We must first, however, say something concerning the general character of the various classes of documents upon which our knowledge of fifteenth-century English is based. We may distinguish (1) official documents; (2) works which have some pretensions to be literature ; and (3) private letters. The first may again be divided into **Public** documents—Records, Instructions to Ministers. &c., Descriptions of Historical Events, like those just alluded to in Gairdner's *Letters and Papers*, &c. ; and **Private** documents such as Wills, and Inventories of Property. English Rules for Monastic Orders and Monastic Chartularies should, perhaps, be ranked as Private Official Documents.

In works of literature proper, we naturally distinguish between composition in Prose and Verse. Passing to the Private Letters, which in many respects are the most valuable of all for our purpose, we may distinguish between the more conventionally written missives of highly educated persons, such as Bishop Bekinton, Judge Paston, and John Shillingford, and those of comparatively uneducated people such as the Cely family (*Cely Papers*), Edmond de la Pole, Earl of Suffolk (in Ellis's *Letters Illustrative of Eng. Hist.*, Ser. III, Vol. I), and Margaret Paston, the judge's daughter-in-law.

It is rather difficult to classify Gregory's Chronicle (late fifteenth century), which is hardly a work of literature, and not quite a private diary.

F

A further division is necessary according to dialect. From this point of view we may distinguish: documents written in the London or Literary dialect; those, at the other extreme, written in a more or less pure form of Regional dialect; and those which are, in the main, in the London dialect, but which show some provincial influence.

A classification of this kind cuts right across the other, based upon the nature of the documents. It would be easy to select writings of each genre in all of the three dialectal categories just given.

The poems of Hoccleve and the prose of Caxton represent the London dialect among works of literature proper; so do not only, as we might expect, the official documents written in London, but also many from widely separated parts of the country—e.g. the English Registers 'of the Abbeys of Godstow (1450) and Oseney (1460), both near Oxford; the English Wills and Charters in the Chetwynd Chartulary (Staffs. *c.* 1440–90); the Coventry Leet Book (from 1420); the Ordinances of Worcester (1467); Ordinances of the Gild of Tailors of Exeter (1466); various documents of an official nature, written in Ireland by Irish Lords to Henry VII (1484–93). All these appear to be written in a form of English hardly distinguishable, on the whole, from that in use in London at this period. Among private letters written in this common form, may be mentioned those of Bishop Bekinton (1442), of Sir William Paston the judge (1425–30), and many others from Kings, Queens, Princes, and Ministers of State, printed by Ellis. Coming to writings in various more or less pure Regional dialects, we may mention here the Life of St. Editha (Wilts. *c.* 1420, in verse), the English version of Palladius on Husbandry (Essex *c.* 1420), the poems of Bokenam (Suffolk *c.* 1443), Awdeley's Poems (Shropshire *c.* 1420). In prose, literary writings in pure dialect are rare in this century, but in the private letters of the Cely family (1475–88), a wealthy middle-class family, we apparently have a pretty pure example of the Essex dialect; and the fifteenth-century Bury Wills are in many cases fairly close to the language of Bokenam. The Letters of Margaret Paston (1440–70), which I have examined in detail, are also, on the whole, in the dialect of Suffolk.

Finally, we come to the large class of writings, very fully represented in fifteenth-century English, which are, to all intents and purposes, in Common English, as we may perhaps now call it, but which, nevertheless, show certain deviations from it, due to the influence of Regional dialect. This influence varies very much in extent, and some of the works mentioned in the preceding group might perhaps be included here, such as the Letters of Margaret Paston and some of the Bury Wills.

Among poets Lydgate, 'the Monk of Bury', though undoubtedly a highly cultivated person, shows distinct E. Midland, we might say East Coast, influence. This Eastern influence—from Norfolk and Suffolk—is traceable in a certain number of prose writers of this period who belong by birth to these counties. Thus it occurs in the language of Capgrave (died 1464), who lived most of his life at Lynn, and in Thomas Gregory's Chronicle, the author of which was Lord Mayor of London in 1451-2, and died in r467. He was a native of Mildenhall in Suffolk, and of an armigerous family. In the language of Sir John Fortescue (supposed to have died 1476) we may perhaps note slight traces of South-Western influence. Sir John was the son of a gentleman of Devonshire, and was at one time Lord Chief Justice of England. The Regional influence in his *Governaunce of England* is so slight, however, that he would perhaps be more suitably included among the writers of Common Literary English. Rather more definite in his divergence from the London type is Bishop Pecok, whose *Repressor* (1449) is sometimes said to represent the 'Oxford type' of English. Reginald Pecok was a Welshman by birth, was a Fellow of Oriel in 1417, Bishop of St. Asaph in 1444, and of Chichester in 1450.

Passing to private letters, the most remarkable are perhaps those of John Shillingford, Mayor of Exeter in 1447–50. He fought the Bishop and Chapter of Exeter in the interests of his city, and his letters are written to his friends at home, describing his fortunes on a visit which he paid to London, to urge his case with the Chancellor in person. He was of gentle birth, had evidently received an excellent education, and was a man of self-possession and breeding. He was able to crack jokes and cap Latin quotations with the Chancellor, and he writes a style at once shrewd and humorous. His letters are remarkable as showing the spread of the Literary Standard in his day among persons of education and standing, for they approach very closely to that Standard, and exhibit but few provincialisms. A number of Lincolnshire Wills of this period show strong Regional influence in vocabulary, verbal forms, and occasionally also in the sounds, so far as these can be inferred from the spelling.

Such are a few of the sources of our knowledge of the various forms of English current in the fifteenth century.

We now pass to consider in order, and in more detail, those general characteristics indicated above, of the language of the period, and also the documents from which our knowledge of it is based.

(1) Deviations in Spelling from the Scribal Tradition which throw light upon Pronunciation.

The comparative frequency with which these occasional spellings occur in the fifteenth century is, no doubt, primarily due, as has been pointed out, to the spread of the art of writing beyond the circle of the professional scribe, and the increasing habit of using the art in familiar private correspondence. On the other hand, while these 'lapses' in spelling are commoner in documents of this latter class, where the writers are more off their guard than they would be in inditing works of more formal and permanent character, these occasional 'phonetic' spellings are by no means confined to private letters, but occur to a greater or less degree in writings of all kinds—official records, wills, and even in literary compositions in both prose and verse.

Even in the printed books of Caxton, usually so conservative and conventional, certain peculiarities creep in, here and there, which are certainly unconscious adaptations of spelling to suit the sound.

The question arises how far these indications of pronunciation imply that this, which, to judge from the ordinary scribal spelling, has shown but little sign of change for several centuries, has just begun now to move in the direction of Modern English. How far are we entitled to regard the fifteenth century as a great landmark in our linguistic history, a period of transition and change?

This question needs great caution in answering. A very large number of the spellings which appear to herald a new speech-era can, as a matter of fact, be shown to occur, here and there, several centuries earlier, in the full M.E. period, though they are far rarer and much harder to find. In such cases, the new pronunciation can hardly be claimed to have only just begun at the moment when we first find frequent instances of its expression, in the spelling, in the fifteenth century.

It is probable that a more thorough and minute examination of the varieties in M.E. spelling would reveal stronger proof than we have at present, of the existence in this period, of the development of certain sound changes which we have up to now assumed to be much later.

It is wiser, therefore, in those cases where we are not sure, to leave the question of the period at which the change began open, and content ourselves with the knowledge that it is *at least as early* as the date at which the spelling gives sure and frequent indication that such and such a new sound is intended.

It may, of course, be argued quite reasonably, that if a spelling occurs only once or twice in M.E. records, whereas it is comparatively common in the fifteenth century, this shows that in the latter period the sound change had been completed, and a definite new development reached, while in the former period the change was only beginning, and the uneasiness shown by the varieties of spelling merely indicates that the old sound had begun to be modified in the new direction, so that the scribe felt that the old spelling was no longer adequate.

It is true that the M.E. scribal vagaries suggest rather a more or less deliberate and tentative groping after a phonetic rendering, than the unconscious and spontaneous rendering of a specific sound in a more or less natural way, which is the impression very often made by the fifteenth-century departures from tradition.

On the whole, therefore, it is probable that the appearance of so many graphic expressions of a new form of pronunciation in the fifteenth century is misleading in so far as it suggests a sudden development. The fifteenth century is probably no more an age of transition than every age is such. Many sound changes had already come about, or at least had begun long before. By the fifteenth century the new sounds were definitely established, their incompatibility with the old spelling was obvious, and the fact that a larger number of writers were endeavouring to put down their thoughts upon paper or parchment, writers unshackled by tradition, leads to the new pronunciation being more often expressed in the spelling than heretofore.

To come now to closer quarters with the facts, we may say generally, that light is thrown by the occasional spellings of the fifteenth century, and, as we shall see later, also by those of the sixteenth century, upon the following points of pronunciation :—(A) (1) the quality, and (2) quantity, of vowel sounds in stressed (' accented ') syllables ; (B) upon the treatment of old vowels and diphthongs in unstressed syllables ; (C) upon the loss of consonants when final, or before other consonants, in cases where several consonants occur in a group ; (D) upon the development

of so-called parasitic consonants, after others, chiefly at the end of words;
(*E*) upon many other consonant pronunciations.

We shall briefly illustrate each of these points here; the fuller treatment and illustrations will come in their proper place in the chapter which deals with Changes in Pronunciation.

A (1) Indications as to the Quality of Vowels.

(*a*) M.E. tense *ē* is often written with *i* or *y*, which had the sound [ī] of Mod. Eng. '*ee*' in *meet*:—Shillingford: *myte* 'meet', *dyme* 'deem', &c.; Margaret Paston: *agryed* 'agreed', *symed* 'seemed', *wypyng* 'weeping', &c., &c.; Gregory's Chron.: *slyves* 'sleeves', *stypylle* 'steeple', &c. These spellings show that the Mod. sound had already developed out of the old *ē*, which had the sound of French *é* in *été*.

(*b*) O.E. tense *ō* is occasionally written *u* or *ou*, implying the sound [ū] as in Mod. *boot*:—Palladius: *must*, M.E. *mōste*; Margaret Paston: *must, Munday*; Pecok: *muste*; Bokenam: *suthly* 'truly', *forsuk, stude* 'stood', &c.; Cely Papers: *mwste, tuk* 'took'. These spellings show that [ū], or this sound shortened, was already pronounced.

A (2) Indications of Quantity.

Short vowels are often indicated by doubling the following consonant symbol:—Bokenam: *clennere* 'cleaner' compar.; St. Editha: *gretter* 'greater'; *flodde* 'flood', *delle* 'part'; Palladius: *woddes* 'woods', *watter* 'to water', *sonner* 'sooner'; Cely Papers: *breckefaste*.

B. The Treatment of Vowels and Diphthongs in Unstressed Syllables.

This is a rather intricate subject and will demand later a chapter to itself. The habit of pronouncing vowels differently, and more shortly, where they occur in unaccented syllables than when in fully stressed syllables is firmly engrained in English, though at the present time many people are in favour of pronouncing 'full' vowels in unaccented syllables. That this is against the genius of English is shown by ordinary, natural speech; that the habit is an old one the following examples will show. To pronounce the second syllable of *Oxford* like the word *ford*, and the second syllable of *porpoise* like the word *poise*, may be agreeable or the reverse, but it is certainly an eccentric novelty. Already in very Early Middle English we find that O.E. *a, u, o, e* were all pronounced alike when not accented, and are written *e*. O.E. long vowels were shortened in M.E. when unstressed, and short or shortened vowels often disappeared from pronunciation altogether. Thus, for instance, as early as St. Juliana (Prose, thirteenth century), we find O.E. **þær æfter* 'thereafter' written *brefter*, when the old *æ* has first been shortened and then eliminated. This process of 'reduction' of the vowels in unstressed syllables continued during the whole M.E. period, and in the fifteenth century we find numerous spellings which suggest a pronunciation not very unlike that of the present day. Indeed, in some cases a form, apparently from an unreduced type, is now pronounced habitually, through the influence of the desire to speak ' correctly' and ' according to the spelling' so common since the early nineteenth century. The M.E. process of 'reduction' whose results are reflected in the fifteenth-century spellings included the unstressed vowels in Scandinavian and Norman-French words, and affected every vowel and diphthong in this position. The following are a few examples which illustrate (*a*) mere uncertainty how to write the vowel of the unstressed syllable, (*b*) more or less definite methods of recording a specific sound.

(*a*) The following examples of indecision in writing the vowel in an unstressed syllable are all taken from the Cely Papers, but the same thing is found more or less in all the fifteenth-century texts.

Middle English -*en* :—(1) Written -*en* :—*taken, wretten* P. P.; (2)· Written -*yn* :—*wryttyn, lynyn* ' linen', *gevyn* P. P., *hosyn,* &c.; (3) Written -*on* :—*happon, hofton* ' often'.

Middle English -*el* :—(1) Written -*el* :—*fardel, stapel*; (2) Written -*yl* :—*myddyl, saddyl, cradyll, stapyl*; Written (3) -*al* :—*stapal*; (4) Written -*ul* :—*stapul.*

Middle English -*er* :—(1) Written -*er* :—*better, fader* ' father', *mother,* &c.; (2) Written -*yr* :—*bettyr, nwmbyr, ovyr, dowtyr,* &c., &c.; (3) Written -*or* :—*mannor* ' manner', *sumor, octobor,* &c.; (4) Written -*ar* :— *dynar* ' dinner', *manar* ' manner', *finar* ' finer'; (5) Written -*ur* :—*brocur* ' broker'.

This variety and hesitation point to an 'indeterminate' vowel, as it is often falsely called; that is, the sound [ə], which we now have in the second syllable of *father,* and in many thousands of unstressed syllables, whatever is written.

(*b*) As illustrations of the treatment of unstressed vowels which appears to be quite clearly and definitely expressed by occasional spellings from several sources, we take two points.

(1) *Rounded Vowels are unrounded.* French *u* [y] as in Mod. French *lune* is written *i, y,* or *e,* implying probably a sound closely resembling our vowel in the second syllable of *pity.* Examples :—Palladius : *moister* ' moisture'; Shillingford : *commyne* ' common', fr. *commune*; M. Paston : *repelacion* ' reputation'; Cely Papers : *aventer* ' adventure', the *venter* ' venture', *condyte* ' conduit', *byskitt* ' biscuit'; Gregory : *condytte, comyners, comeners*; Letters and Papers (1501) : *mynite* 'minute' in sense of a ' note'. The above spellings represent a pronunciation pretty much the same as our own in the words *conduit, biscuit, minute.*

M.E. *o* and *u* unstressed written *a* :—Cely Papers : *abedyensses* ' obedience', *sapose* ' suppose', *apon, appon* ' upon'; Shillingford : *apon* (also Letters and Papers, Gregory, Fortescue, &c.).

(2) *Diphthongs are simplified. oi* and *ei* often written *e, y* : *porpys* ' porpoise', Gregory; *toorkes* ' turquoise', Bury Wills (1501); *Synt Stevyn, Sent Paull, curtessy, certyn,* Shillingford; M.E. *seint, curteisie, certein*; *Syn Lenarde, Syn John,* men*tayne,* M.E. *meynteyne,* &c.; *Sent* Stephin, Rewle of Sustris Menouresses.

The examples are enough to establish the reality of the sound changes suggested by the spellings, and in the following century indications pointing in the same direction become still commoner in unstudied writing. Present-day pronunciation confirms the indications of these early spellings as regards *ei*, though *oi* is sometimes restored in unstressed syllables through the influence of the conventional spelling which later became fixed.

C. Occasional Spellings which reveal Losses of Consonants.

(1) *Loss of final consonant.*   M. Paston:—*nex* 'next', *husbon* 'husband', *hunder* 'hundred'; Cely Papers :—*My Lor*; Gregory :—*Braban*; Official account of entry of Catherine of Aragon (1503):—*uprigh.*

(2) *Loss of consonants in groups, before one or more consonants.*   Archbp. Chichele (1418):—*Lamhyth* 'Lambeth'; St. Editha:—*twolthe* 'twelfth', *twolmonth* 'twelvemonth', *bleynasse* 'blindness', *whyssonweke*; Shillingford :—*myssomer* 'midsummer', *Crichurch* 'Christchurch'; M. Paston:—*Wensday, morgage, Quessontyde* 'Whitsuntide'; Gregory :—*Wanysday* 'Wednesday', *halpeny, sepukyr* 'sepulchre'.

(3) *Loss of consonants between vowels.*   St. Editha :—*senty* 'seventy', *swene* 'dream', earlier *sweven, pament* 'pavement'; Caxton :—*pament.*

D. Addition of Consonants.

(1) *Finally, generally after* l, r, n; also after *s.*
Palladius :—*Spaniald* 'Spaniard', cf. Fr. *Espagnol*; St. Editha:—*jaylardes* 'jailors'; Margaret Paston:—*wyld* 'will'; Short Eng. Chron. (1464):—*Lymoste* 'Lymehouse'; Gregory :—*loste* 'loss'; Capgrave :—*ylde* 'isle', *lynand* 'linen'.

(2) *Development of parasitic consonant between other consonants.*   St. Editha:—*sump tyme* for *sum tyme* 'some time'; Cely Papers :—*Mongwmbre* for *Mongumry* 'Montgomery', *rembnant* 'remnant'.

Some of the tendencies expressed in these examples have left survivals at the present day : e. g. the loss of final -*d* in *lawn*, earlier *laund*; accretion of final -*t* after -*n, margent*, a poetical variant of *margin*.   Both loss and addition are very common in Vulgar Speech (Modified Standard). We shall see most of these forms in the sixteenth and seventeenth centuries, in use in the English of the politest persons.

The loss of consonants in groups still belongs to the best speech ; thus [wenzdɪ, weskət] are more common among good speakers than the rococco [weɪstkout, wednzdɪ].   We shall find many examples of such losses or assimilations of consonants in groups in the sixteenth, seventeenth, and eighteenth centuries.

E. Various Consonant Pronunciations.

(1) *The combination written* -si-, -sci-, *or* -ti- *pronounced '* -sh-' [ʃ] *as at present.*
Margaret Paston :—*sesschons* 'sessions', *conschens* 'conscience; Cely Papers :—*prosesschon* 'procession', *fessychens* 'physicians', *restytuschon* 'restitution', &c., &c.; Letters and Papers (1501):—*huisshers*, French *huissiers* 'ushers'.   In the last instance we actually retain a phonetic spelling of the word.

(2) *Final* -ing *pronounced* -in, *as with many speakers at present.*
Margaret Paston :—*wrytyn* (Noun), *kepyn* (N.), *gidyn* 'guiding' (N.),

hangyn (Pres. Part.) ; Gregory :—*blasyn* 'blazing' (Pres. Part.), *hayryn* 'herring'.

(3) *Miscellaneous.* -*b*- for -*p*- between vowels :—*Jubiter*, Bk. of Quinte Essence (1460–70) ; *jeberdy* 'jeopardy', Cely Papers ; *juberle*, Cr. of Knt. of Bth.

-*l*- lost before -*f*- :—*behaf* 'behalf', Bp. Bekynton (1442) ; before -*k*- :— *fawkyner* 'falconer', Cely Papers ; *Fauconbryge*, Gregory.

-*r*- lost in combination -*rs*- :—*wosted qwischons* 'worsted cushions', Will of Joan Buckland (Lincs. 1440) ; *passell*, Cely Papers.

-*gh*- not pronounced in middle of word before -*t*- or finally ; this is shown in Margaret Paston's omission of any symbol for the original sound in *myt* 'might', *kawt* 'caught', and also by such spellings as *howghe* 'how', *wright* 'write', *ought* 'out', &c., &c., when she would not have written the letters -*gh*- if they had represented any sound. Further, *smyht* 'smite', Rle. of Sustris Menouresses.

h- initially where it does not historically belong :—*herand* 'errand', *hought* 'ought', *hese* 'ease', Margaret Paston ; *hasche* 'ash tree', Gregory. (On all these points see Ch. VIII below.)

We have now illustrated some of the principal spellings found in fifteenth-century, or very early sixteenth-century documents, which are new departures, and suggest a different pronunciation from that usually held to be normal in M.E. These spellings are scattered through dozens of letters and other documents, and some of them might pass for slips of the pen, were they isolated. Many of them occur, however, in several documents of this period, and all of them are found with much greater frequency in writings of the sixteenth century, and are further confirmed much later, either by writers on pronunciation, by later (seventeenth and eighteenth century) spellings, or by survivals in our own day. When a writer departs from the traditional spelling in the manner shown by the above examples, we can hardly doubt that this eccentricity records some fact of pronunciation ; when we get confirmation of the kind just stated, we do not doubt at all.

Many of the pronunciations thus expressed are now obsolete, old-fashioned, or vulgar. The influence of the archaic system of spelling, insisted upon by the early printers and by their successors, has been too strong. We shall have occasion to see later how comparatively recent many of our present-day 'restored' pronunciations are. Other pronunciations again, such as the loss of -*l*- before certain consonants, as in *half, walk*, &c., are accepted facts, and at present no one has ventured upon a restoration ; perhaps the lettered democracy of the future, seeking 'the genteel thing', will introduce this, among other novelties, into our speech.

(2) Modern English begins at least as early as the second half of the fifteenth century.

Nothing is more difficult, as has already been urged repeatedly, than to fix upon a date for the beginning of a new era in speech ; indeed this can only be done approximately. All we shall endeavour to show here is that although some of the points of development adduced in support of the view may be considerably older, the net result of an examination of English speech as a whole during the fifteenth century leads us to the conclusion that before the close of that century, not to attempt more particular definition, the Modern Period of our language had begun. One of the surprises of a close study of the history of a language is the early date at which certain features occur in the texts—often far earlier than we should expect. Another surprise is the lateness of the occurrence of certain other features, which survive, here and there, much longer than we perhaps thought possible. In order to enjoy both kinds of astonishment it is clearly necessary to make not only a fairly minute study—since what is new in speech and just coming in is but infrequently, and only by scattered examples, discoverable in the written records, while the obsolescent is often equally hard to come by—but we must also take a rather wide survey in point of time, and roam over the written records of several centuries. The rewards of such a labour are the pleasant surprises just referred to, and a gradual gain of a sense of the continuity between the earlier and later periods. For the purpose which we have in view—to establish the modernity of fifteenth-century English—it is useful to take present-day English as a point of comparison, ai d to inquire how far some of the most characteristic features of our actual language are found already in the century we are now considering. It is also useful to indicate the points in which present-day English differs from that of the fifteenth century, since it is by no means suggested that the two forms are identical in all respects. In our brief analysis of Early Modern English, we confine ourselves primarily to London writings, and to those works produced either in the East Midlands or the South of England.

Our examination will deal chiefly with the Pronunciation ; the Accidence during the greater part of the century is still rather M.E. in character, and only a few points are here dealt with.

English Pronunciation in the Fifteenth Century.

The following are some of the chief differences between the pronunciation of vowels in the M.E. period and that of the present day :—

(1) M.E. *ā*, in *bāke(n)* 'to bake', *fāme* 'fame', &c., &c., has become [e*i*].

(2) M.E. *ă* which had the sound of French *a* in *patte*, &c., has become [æ] as in M.E. *băk*, present-day *back*, *fat*, adj., &c. &c.

(3) M.E. *ē*¹ = [ē] tense has become [ī] as in M.E. *fēlen—feel*, *seed*, *sede—seed*, &c., &c.

(4) M.E. *ē*² = [ɛ̄] has also become [ī], M.E. *hēte—heat*, *mēte—meat*, &c., &c.

(5) M.E. *ī* has been diphthongized to [a*i*], M.E. *wīf—wife*, *blīnd—blind*, &c., &c.

(6) M.E. *ū* has been diphthongized to [au], M.E. *hous* = [hūs]—*house*, M.E. *foule—foul*, &c., &c.

(7) M.E. *ŭ* has been unrounded to [a] as in M.E. *dust* = [dŭst], present-day *dust* = [dast], &c., &c.

(8) M.E. *ō* tense has become [ū] as in M.E. *mōne—moon* = [mūn], M.E. *fōde—food* = [fūd], &c.

(9) M.E. *au*, which was a genuine diphthong [*au*], has been monophthongized to [ō] written *au* or *aw*, as in *cause, hawk,* &c., &c.

(10) M.E. *ai, ei*, both pronounced [*ai*] in the later period, have become first [ǣ], then [ē̆], then [ē], and finally, in Standard English [e*i*] *rain, day, vein,* &c., &c.

(11) M.E. [ȳ] written *u* or *ui* has become [*i*ū, jū], e.g. *tune, fume, suit*; after *l, r*, the older [jū] has generally become [ū], e.g. *lute* (also [ljūt]), *fruit, rude,* &c., &c.

(12) M.E. [y̆] has been retracted to [ŭ] and then unrounded like other short *ŭ*-sounds to [a], e.g. *judge, bundle, rush* (the plant), *cudgel,* &c., &c.

(13) M.E. *-er* has become [ā̆(r)], M.E. *herte*—*heart*, M.E. *fer*—*far*, &c., &c.

(14) M.E. *wa-* has become [wɔ-] in *was, swan, swallow,* &c., &c.

The above list of changes is formidable enough, but it makes no pretence at completeness. It will, however, serve our turn for the moment.

Of the above changes, Nos. 3, 8, and 13 were shown, p. 67, above, to be expressed in fifteenth-century spellings. In 3 and 8 it seems certain that the full present-day stage had already been reached. As regards 14, *wosse* = ' was ' in Cely Papers leaves small room for doubt. It is extremely probable that the same may be said of Nos. 1, 2— such spellings as *begen* for *began*, and *fend* ' found ', M.E. *fand* (Paston Letters), point to a fronting in the former case, while *credyl* ' cradle ' in Bokenam, *teke* = *take*, *fēder* M.E. *fāder* ' father' in Paston Letters, and *ceme* ' came ' in Cely Papers seem to indicate the same process for the long vowel.

The first process involving M.E. *ē*² (No. 4) the change [ē̄<ē], began very shortly after the shifting of the vowel in No. 3. Cf. p. 209, below.

The spelling *gannes* ' guns ' in Paston Letters seems to show that short *ŭ*, No. 7, had at least started upon the path which was to lead to the present sound, if it had not fully attained it; the spelling *sadanly* ' suddenly' in Fortescue points in the same direction. If this be so, then No. 7 must have taken place still earlier. No. 5, the diphthonging of long *i* is more than hinted at by the spellings *bleynd* ' blind ', *myeld* ' mild ', in St. Editha, though it is improbable that the present sound had been reached.

The diphthonging of *ū*, No. 6, is suggested by the spelling *sauthe* ' south', Reg. of Godstow, Zachrisson, E. St. 52. 309. The spelling *awffer* ' offer' in Cely Papers is sometimes regarded as an inverted spelling showing that *aw* no longer necessarily indicated a diphthong, which would be impossible in this word. The only sound apparently which it could represent here is [ō]. If this is so then No. 9 also is a process already complete among some speakers in the fifteenth century. The monophthonging of *ai* (No. 10) is suggested in an undated letter of Marg. Beaufort (1443–1509), who writes *sa* for *say*. This lady was the mother of Henry VII. Apart from spellings in regard to Nos. 5 and 6, it must further be pointed out that if we once admit that old [ē] had become [ī], and that [ō] had become [ū], we must perforce assume that some change had affected the old [ī] and [ū], since if these had remained unaltered down to the period by which the new [ī, ū] developed, the latter would have been identical with them, and the subsequent history of both would have been the same. This, however, has not happened. Hence we must suppose that the change of [i and ū] was actually earlier than the change of [fēd] to [fīd] and of [mōne] to [mūn(e)]. But while this is certain, we have no definite evidence as to how far the diphthonging had gone, nor what was its precise character in the fifteenth century. The certainty is merely that these sounds had changed from their original form and started upon their new career.

Thus of the fourteen typical vowel changes which distinguish present-day English from that of the M.E. period, all but one are shown, by the direct evidence of occasional spellings, by inference drawn from other facts, or from both sources, either to have been completed, or at least to have begun, before the close of the fifteenth century.

The change in No. 11, so far as our evidence goes at present, cannot be proved to have started. On this point see p. 244, below.

It must be insisted upon that it is by no means proved, because a pronunciation is shown with considerable probability, or in some cases with certainty, to have existed at a given period among certain groups of speakers, that this pronunciation was universal. On the contrary, a change generally starts in one area, or among a class of speakers, and spreads to other areas and classes. Many of the above changes had probably not yet spread, in the fifteenth century, to the Court dialect, that is, to the ancestor of present-day Received Standard; others certainly had not. In most cases the novelties of pronunciation are made probable by forms taken from the Paston Letters, or the Cely Papers, and though this may be a coincidence due to our possessing in these documents a considerable body of more or less phonetically-written English, which it is difficult to match in documents known to have been written in London, the fact remains that our earliest evidence for many of the modern sound changes, or their inception, comes from the East Midlands or South-East. We shall see, however, that London English and Standard English show increasingly this Eastern influence, and we are entitled to say that in the popular speech of the South-East and South-East Midlands we find in the fifteenth century the germ of those changes which we regard as characteristic of Modern English, although, in some respects, the best London English was rather more archaic, so far as our evidence goes. This may, however, be illusory, and the more faithful adherents of scribal tradition who are the writers of the official and literary documents in London English, being more lettered persons than the Celys, and even than most of the Pastons, may conceal beneath their conventional spelling with its infrequent lapses into phonetic rendering, changes as remarkable as those made manifest by the less careful writers of Essex and Suffolk, and as remarkable as some of those which they themselves do reveal to us in their weaker moments.

It is significant that, in discussing the above changes, we are forced in each case to use a phonetic notation in order to make the sound change clear. In all the cases under review there has been practically no change in the received spelling since the M.E. period—none at any rate which records the very considerable changes in pronunciation that have occurred. The only exceptions to this are a few words like *far* where the -*ar*- spelling has been fixed in place of M.E. *fer*. But even this class of words is not consistent, and we write *Derby, hearth,* &c. When we find the constant individual departures from the convention, in favour of a more phonetic rendering, during the fifteenth and sixteenth centuries, it is clear that the English persistence in clinging to an outworn system of spelling, one which private writers were constantly infringing, must be put to the credit, or the reverse, of the printers. For about 450 years these worthies have dictated to us how we are to spell, in the same way that fashionable ladies are said to have their fashions prescribed for them by their dressmakers, who allow their customers small voice in the matter. Some may think that it is a good thing to have a thoroughly unphonetic spelling such as ours, and consider that any attempt to alter it would be a mistake. Others have an uneasy feeling that our system is inconsistent and misleading, and they therefore found societies for amending it—according to principles which it is often difficult to understand. It is impossible to say at present whether any of the numerous groups of reformers will win, or whether we shall insist on sticking to our old and familiar muddle. No spelling reformers have hitherto succeeded in this country. Those of us, however, who prefer our present system, bad as it is, because we know it, rather than a new system which is only very faintly phonetic in character, would do well to remember that our bad old spelling is chiefly defensible on the ground of custom, and not for any pretended historical merit. We should remember that it is the printers who have imposed it upon us. Had Caxton and his followers been more enterprising, it is highly probable that our spelling would have been less widely divorced from the facts of pronunciation than is actually the case.

The Vowels in Unstressed Syllables.

We have already indicated (p. 67, &c.) some of the more remarkable facts under this head which are observable in the fifteenth century, and the whole subject will receive a fuller treatment later on (Chap. VII). Enough has perhaps been said, and sufficient examples have already been adduced, to show that by the fifteenth century at any rate, not only was the habit of reducing vowels in unstressed syllables fully developed, but in many cases it seems certain that the results were already practically identical with the state of things with which we are familiar at the present time.

Changes in Consonant Sounds, Isolative, and in Combinations.

The changes indicated on p. 69, &c., above, are sufficiently striking, and it is unnecessary here to enter more fully into this matter, as the Consonants will be discussed in detail in their proper place (Chap. VIII below). It is enough to point out that such usages as the ' dropping ' of initial aspirates, the addition of these where they do not belong, the interchange of initial *w* and *v*, the loss of *l* before -*k*, &c., the pronunciation of '*sh*' in such words as *procession,* the loss of *d* in *Wednesday,* the addition of a final consonant in such forms as *ylde* for *isle,* and a dozen other practices which are proved by abundant evidence to have existed in the fifteenth century, are all very modern in character. Some of these are now vulgarisms, but none the less real for that; others have been lost, even among vulgar speakers, through the influence of 'education'; others may now be regarded as slipshod, though not vulgar, by the precise; many are part and parcel of the natural speech of the most meticulous.

Points in English Accidence of the Fifteenth Century.

(1) **Nouns.** The most modern feature in the inflexion of Nouns in this period is the use of such a construction as—*þe erle of Wyltones wyf*, which is found already in St. Editha, instead of the old form *þe erles wyf of Wylton*, which survives now in the well-known song *The Bailiff's daughter of Islington.* The 'group inflexion', as it is called, is by no means common in the writings of the fifteenth century, but that it occurs at all proves that it was in use, though probably it was still felt as collo-quial, and it is usually avoided, often by omitting the possessive inflexion altogether, as in *without my brother Roaf assent* (Ld. Hastings in Paston Letters, iii, p. 108, *c.* 1470). Even in the middle of the next century many writers dodge the 'group possessive' in one way or another (see p. 318). There is a very modern-sounding construction in the Creation of Duke of York Knight of the Bath (1494)—*sett in like maner as therle of Suffokis*, and in the account of the Reception of Catharine of Aragon (1501) we find *the Archebishoppe of Cauntreburys barge.* Other par-ticulars of the Inflexion of Nouns in fifteenth-century English will be recorded in due course (pp. 314–24). They are rather of the nature of survivals than of modernisms, such as the old uninflected Feminine Possessive Singulars—*ure ladye belle*, &c. (Shillingford), the innumerable Pls. in *-en* (or *-yn*, &c.), and such a mutated Pl. as *geet* 'goats'.

(2) **Personal Pronouns.** Whereas Chaucer and those of his con-temporaries who write London English still adhere to the old, English *her, hem,* as the exclusive forms of the Possessive and Dative Pl., the fifteenth-century literary and official writings in this dialect show an increasing use of *their, ther* in the Possessive and *theim, them* in the Dative. The former *her* is practically extinct in literary, and presumably in colloquial, use by the end of the century, though isolated instances occur as late as the middle of the next century. *Hem,* and the unstressed *em,* are far commoner, and indeed the latter under the disguise of *'em* is very common indeed, even in the lofty style, far into the eighteenth century, and is in frequent colloquial use at the present day. The form *hem* is very rarely found with the initial aspirate after the end of the fifteenth century, except in the form *'hem,* and it is pretty clear, as the subsequent writing with the apostrophe shows, that speakers and writers using *em* thought it was a reduced form of *them.*

Another modernism in the forms of Pronouns, though it occurs much earlier here and there, is the loss of the initial lip-consonant in *who,* which is found written *ho* and *hoo* in Siege of Rouen, Letters of Mary Paston, Gregory, Creation of Duke of York, &c.

A very common survival from M.E. usage in the fifteenth century is *tho, thoo,* the old Pl. Nom. of the Def. Art. used in the purely demon-strative sense 'those'.

See, on all these and other points, the treatment of the Pronouns in Chap. IX.

(3) Verbal Endings. In London documents of all kinds the 3rd Pers. S. Pres. Indic. ends in *-eth*, or *-ith*, almost without exception. The Pl. usually has the typical Midland *-en* or *-in*, *-yn*, but towards the end of the century the final *-n* becomes more and more rare, so that we get our present flexionless form. The Southern Pl. in *-eth*, *-ith* crops up with fair frequency apart from purely official documents, and indeed continues to be used occasionally far into the following century. The Pres. Part. is always either *-ing*, *-yng*, or occasionally *-eng*.

The Southern prefix *y-* or *i-* falls into desuetude in the Past Part., and the Southern endings without, and the Midland ending with, the final *-n* both occur in Strong Vbs. as at present, though the distribution of these forms is not fixed.

The distinction between Sing. and Pl. Pret. of Strong Vbs. of certain classes is lost towards the end of the century, and whereas Chaucer has *fond* 'I found', &c., and *funden* 'we found', Caxton uses the Sing. type *fond* for both numbers.

(3) The Passing of Regional Dialect in Written English.

We have seen that it is still possible during the fifteenth century to find, both in works of literature proper, in private letters, wills, &c., and even in official documents, the influence of Regional dialect.

As has been said, there are still a certain number of writings of this period which represent a more or less pure form of Regional dialect, and there are others which show traces of the author's native dialect while being, in the main, according to the London type of English.

We must be careful not to over-estimate the rapidity of the spread of a common form of Literary English. Many dialect features may still be traced in works written in nearly pure London English, such as Shillingford's letters. Writers on Modern English dialects, therefore, will do well in future to search diligently in the documents of the fifteenth century, and even later, and not to give up all hope of finding, after the fourteenth century, ancestral forms of the dialect which they are describing. This habit, which is far too common, has the unfortunate result of leaving a gap in the history of the dialect of some five hundred years! It is true that by the fifteenth century, in the huge area covered by the Midlands as a whole, there was spoken, or at least written, a type of English which, apart from certain rather minute points, often rather scattered, and hard to discover without a painful examination of the documents, was fairly uniform. This Midland type, in its broad outlines, agreed pretty much with London English, and when we consider more particularly the very large body of documents of all kinds written in the East Midlands, the differences between the written speech of this area and that of London appear at first sight so trifling, that some recent writers have been, rather too hastily perhaps, led to believe and to teach that dialectal differences had disappeared from written English, at least by the middle of the fifteenth century. A more careful examination of the sources, however, shows that this is far from being the case, even in the East, and although it appears that the language of most of the documents which we possess from this period has been, to some degree at least,

influenced by London English, a considerable amount of dialectal divergence exists in points of detail.

In the following brief survey of the question, we shall attempt to
show both the survivals of Regional dialect and the influence exerted by
the London dialect.

In considering London English at this period, it must be borne
in mind that the distribution of the competing dialectal elements was
not yet finally fixed. It is evident that many Southern features now
lost co-existed in the speech of the metropolis with those of E. Midland
and South-Eastern type. The appearance of such features in a document therefore does not necessarily show direct regional influence. The
precise blend of the various dialect elements varies within certain limits
from writer to writer, and each of these blends represents an existing
mode of speech.

Again, in examining E. Midland, or South-Eastern texts, we come
across features which we are justified in considering as characteristic of
these areas, although many or all of them may be found also in
London English of the period. The differences between E. Midland
and London English in the fifteenth century are comparatively slight,
since the latter was becoming more and more E. Midland in character,
and at this time was distinguished from pure E. Midland chiefly by the
survival of certain purely Southern features which did not normally
occur in the speech of Norfolk or Suffolk. We may put it in this
way :—there were few typically E. Midland features which did not occur
in London speech, but this contained also many others (Sthn.) which
were unknown to the E. Midlands.

We begin with two texts in which the Regional dialect is pretty
strongly marked, Bokenam's Lives of Saints (*c.* 1443), which the author
definitely tells us is written in the speech of Suffolk, and the Life of
St. Editha, written in the monastery of Wilton in Wiltshire about 1420.

Bokenam's is naturally a typical E. Midland text, and, as in other
texts from this area, we find several features which, absent from earlier
London documents, gain more and more ground during the century in
the speech of the capital.

The combination -*er*- is generally so written, but a certain number of
-*ar*- spellings are found, more than occur in the London documents of this
period so early in the century: *marcyfully, warkys, garlondys.* O.E.
slack æ̃ sometimes rhymes with tense *ē* :—*tēche* with *sēche, clēne* with *sene*
'seen', and *wene.* This treatment of æ̃² is regarded as typically Kentish
or South-Eastern in O. and M.E. It is interesting to note its spread to
Suffolk. There are indications, however, already in M.E. that this feature
was shared by E. Midland. It is apparently still alien to London speech.

Bokenam, like other E. Midland writers, often has *e* for old *i.* We
must distinguish two classes of words: words of two or more syllables,
where the sound occurs in ' open syllables ', that is at the end of a syllable,
when a single consonant intervenes between the following syllable. In
this class it is possible that lengthening has taken place, and that we
should regard the vowel as *ē*, e. g. *pete* ' pity ', *wretyn* ' written', *queknyn,*
inf. The other case is where *e* for *i* occurs in ' close syllables ', that is
before double consonants, or combinations of consonants, or in words of

one syllable ending in a consonant, e. g. *menstralsy, smet*, &c.   The first class offers some difficulties in interpretation, and views differ as to the origin of the change.   (See discussion, p. 226, &c., below.)   On the whole, it seems at present more likely that both classes can be brought under one heading—the lowering of *ĭ* to *ĕ*.   If this view be accepted, we may add *flekerynge* (where *e* should be short in any case), and *merour* 'mirror', a common form in Early Mod. Eng.   Both types of words occur with *e* frequently in E. Midlands in M.E., and become increasingly common in London English in the fifteenth and following centuries.   Those words where the vowel was certainly short have now been eliminated from Standard English.   Bokenam shares with other writers from Suffolk, Essex, and to some extent from Norfolk, the characteristic use of *e* for O.E. *ȳ*, generally considered South-Eastern, to which frequent reference has been made (see pp. 9, 41 (3), &c.).   Examples of the long vowel are *mende* 'mind', &c., *feer* 'fire'; and of the short, *berth*, 'birth', *kechyn* 'kitchen', *werst* 'worst'.   It may be noted that the spelling *fyre* also occurs, but the word rhymes with *chĕre*, thus showing the pronunciation.   The long *ē*-forms are not common in London English, though as we have seen the *ĕ*-forms are very frequent.   By the side of these, other spellings with *i*, *y* occur in Bokenam.

The Pronouns do not differ from the usage of London English.   The P. P.'s of Strong Verbs generally end in *-yn* (with *-n* according to Midland usage).

Turning to **St. Editha**, we find, as might be expected, far more differences from London English.   The very characteristic Western *u* for old *ēo* is frequent—*vrthe* 'earth', *hulte* 'held', O.E. *hēold*, *dūre* 'dear', O.E. *dēor*.   A couple of examples occur of the typical South-Western unrounding of *ŏ* to *ă*—*starm* for 'storm', and *crasse* for 'cross'.   This South-Western feature penetrated into Received Standard English in the sixteenth century, and became for a time a fashionable habit in the seventeenth (see p. 240); it has left a few survivals in Mod. Eng., e. g. *strap* by the side of *strop*, &c.   We find non-South-Western *hēre* 'hear' instead of *huire* as we might expect, but this need not be attributed to the indirect influence of London English, as the form seems to have been characteristic of the South-West Midland speech of Oxfordshire, Worcestershire, Herefordshire, &c.   The old Southern [*ē*] for *ǣ²* has disappeared, as is shown by the rhymes *pēre—yfēre, bēre* 'bier'—*hēre*, &c.   Short *ĕ* (or *ē̆*?) for older *i-* in open syllables is fairly common—*leuynge, pety, cete* 'city', *weke* 'week', *thēke* 'thick', &c.   It is doubtful how these forms should be explained (see p. 207, &c.).   Western *on, om* for *an, am* occur in *nomlyche* 'namely', *mon* 'man', *bonk* 'bank', *thonk* 'thank'.   Past Participles very commonly have the Southern ending without *-n*, *ybrōke*, *ychōse, ycōre*, &c., and, as we see from these examples, the Southern prefix *y-* was frequently preserved.   The Southern inf. ending in *-y* is found in *to correcty*.   The Pers. Pronouns preserve the old Southern form *yche* 'I', and the archaic Southern forms of the Fem. *he, hee* for 'she'.   The Midland Nom. Pl. *þey*, &c. seems the only form, and this may possibly be attributable to the influence of the predominating type, but in the other cases of the 3rd Pers. Pl. the *th-* or *þ-*forms are unknown in this text.   The unstressed suffix *-es*, &c., often appears as *-us*, after the manner of South-West Midland, by the side of *-ys* and *-es*.   In the Pres. Pl. of Vbs. *-yth* occurs by the side of the Midland *-e*.

St. Editha still retains the original distinction between Sing. and Pl. in those classes of Strong Vbs. where this existed: *drēf—drevyn* (earlier *drivon*) 'drove', *satte—sēton* 'sat', *borst—burst, brāke—brĕkon*, &c., &c.

These two texts illustrate respectively the Eastern and the Western types of English.

There is a considerable group of Eastern documents belonging to the fifteenth century, of which some account may be given.

The doggerel translation of **Palladius on Husbandry** possesses the characteristics of the Essex dialect. It resembles Kentish on the one hand, and E. Midland on the other. As regards the treatment of O.E. *ў*, this dialect normally has both *u* and *e* forms. Thus, in Palladius we find *curnels* 'kernels', *brustels* 'bristles', *busely*, &c., also *brēsid* 'bruised', *wermes* 'worms', *bey* 'buy'. By the side of these this text has many, perhaps a predominating number, of the *i*-forms, after the manner of the London dialect. Here, as in the Suffolk documents, *e* for *i* is frequent. Typically South-Eastern is the preservation of *e* (O.E. *ǣ*) in *bledders* 'bladders', *eddres* 'adders', *wex* 'wax', *sedness, yerd*. The Pres. Pl. generally has the Southern suffix *-eth*, and the prefix *y-* occurs generally in Past Part. The **Cely Papers**, from which various examples have been taken to illustrate fifteenth-century pronunciation, are also written by Essex people, but about fifty years later than Palladius. They are chiefly remarkable for the admirable freedom of the writers from scribal tradition, and give, on the whole, the impression of being the work of very uncultivated persons, and they perhaps illustrate Class, rather than a Regional dialect. They have several features which become increasingly common in the London dialect as the fifteenth century advances, and in the following century. Among these features, in addition to the numerous *e* for *i* spellings— *contenew, sweffte* 'swift', *wettnes, medyll*, &c.—we find a large number of *-ar-* for *-er-*forms—*starlyng* 'sterling', *sarten* 'certain', *desarve* 'deserve', *hard* 'heard', &c.; *wo-* for *wa-*, as in *wos* 'was', &c.; loss of *r-* before consonants, *passel* for 'parcel' (see also p. 70, above); misplacing of initial *h-*, *howllde* 'old', *hayssched* 'asked', &c.

For the rest, the final *-n* of Strong P. P.'s is often omitted—*wrete, spoke, undoe*, &c.; and the prefix *y-* is common—*y-wreten, y-yeuen*, &c. The younger Celys constantly use *-s* in the 3rd Singular Present, but the father and uncle have *-yth*, &c., far more commonly. The *-s* suffix is coming in, presumably from the Midlands, in the more northerly areas of which it had long been in use.

A typical letter from one of the Cely family will illustrate the general character of this collection of papers.

From a letter of Richard Cely the younger (1481). Cely Papers, pp. 58, &c.

Riught uterly whelbelovyd brother, I recomend me hartely onto you thankyng you of aull good brotherhod that ȝe have scheuyd to me at all tymms. . . . I met Roger Wyxton athysayd Northehamton and he desyryd me to do so myche as drynke wᵗ hys whyfe at Laysetter and after that I met wᵗ Wylliam Dalton and he gave me a tokyn to hys mother, and at Laysetter I met wᵗ Rafe Daulton and he brahut me to hys mother and ther I delyvyrd

G

my tokyn and sche prayd me to come to brekefast on the morow and so
I ded, and Plomton both; and ther whe had a gret whelfar, and ther whos
feyr oste and I pray yow thanke them for me Syr and ʒe be remembyrd whe
thaulkyd togydyr in hour bed of Dawltonys syster, and ʒe ferryd the con-
dyscyons of father and brethyrn, byt ʒe neyd not.   I saw hyr, and sche
whos at brekefaste wᵗ hyr mother and ws sche ys as goodly a ʒeung
whomane as fayr as whelbodyd and as sad as I se hany thys vij ʒeyr, and
a good haythe.   And I pray God that hyt may be impryntyd in yur
mynd to sette yowr harte ther Syr.   Hour father and I comende togydyr
in new orchard on Fryday laste and a askyd me many qwestyonys of
gyu, and I towlde hym aull as hyt whos . . . and of the good whyll that
the Whegyston- and Dawltons hows (= ' use '?) to yow and how I lykyd
the ʒeunge gentyllwhoman and he comaunded me to whryte to yow, and
he whowlde gladly that hyt whor brohut abohut and that ʒe laborde hyt
betymys. . . . No mor to yow at thys tyme.   Jhesu kepe you.
   Wrytyn at London the iiijᵗʰᵉ day of Juyn.   per yur brother.

                                                    Rychard Cely.

¹ **Margaret Paston,** whose letters cover the period from 1440 to 1470,
thus ending about the time the Cely Papers begin, is a Norfolk lady, socially
far above the Celys, but very much their equal in education; she writes a
slip-shod style, and evidently sets down as far as possible the forms of her
ordinary speech.   Her language has a curious resemblance to that of the
Celys.   One feature distinguishes her dialect both from theirs and from
that of London, namely, that except in the word *such*, she seems to use
no *u*-spellings for old *y*, writing either *i*, *y*—*lȳtil, hyrdyllys, gyrdill*; or
e—*beryid, bey, mēnd* ' mind '.   A very large number of cases of *e* for old
i are found in this lady's letters—*wete* ' know ', *wretyn* P. P., *Trenyte*,
chene ' chin ', *Beshopys, Welyam* ' William ', *preson* ' prison ', &c., &c.   The
spelling *-ar-* for old *-er-*, as has been already noted, becomes more frequent after the year 1461.   These spellings are less frequent on the whole
in the letters of Mistress Paston than in those of the Cely family.   Margaret
Paston uses *-yn, -e* (Midl.), and occasionally the Southern *-yth* in the
Pres. Pl.
   The language of the **Suffolk Wills** (Bury Wills and Inventories) of the
last quarter of the fifteenth century calls for little remark from the point
of view of Regional dialect.   These documents present the typical
E. Midland English of the foregoing, and it is hard to say that any
features here observable are alien to London.
   The interesting collection of fifteenth-century Lincolnshire Wills and
Vows of Celibacy (**Linc. Dioc. Documents**) deserves to be mentioned,
and demands a far closer study than is practicable here.   The influence of
Official London English is seen in the frequent use of *-yth* in the 3rd
Sing. Present, by the side of the local *-ys* or *-es*, which occurs in *ligges*
(Will of Richard Welby, 1465). ' The form *furst* with *u* ' first ' must also
be due to this influence (W. of Sir T. Comberworth, 1451).   North
Midland features are seen in *āwes* ' owes ', *sāwle* ' soul ', the use of *giff*
' give ' instead of *gēve* or *yēve*, the spelling *qwhite* ' white ' and such elements of vocabulary as *at* ' that ', *to gar pray for, kirk* ' church ', *quye*
' cow ', all from Comberworth's Will.   The Agreement between Barlings
Abbey, Lincs., and the Vicar of Reepham (1509) contains the Scandinavian words *laithe* ' barn ', *thack* and *thackyng* ' thatch ', &c.   It seems that

---

¹ Miss Kilboom, *Contributions*, p. xiii, having inspected the MS., states that
this lady nearly always employed a secretary, and that only very few of her
letters are in her own hand.

the remoter a district from the metropolis, the weaker the influence of London English in written documents, even when these are based upon official models. The Lincs. Wills really belong to that large class of documents surviving from this period, in which the intention is clearly to write the official dialect of London, but in which the lapses into the Regional dialect of the writer, in isolated forms, are fairly frequent.

We may now leave the consideration of writings which possess a considerable provincial flavour, and pass to those where this occurs only here and there, in isolated words and forms.

In the **Ordinances of Worcester** (1467) the lapses are very rare, and on that account we placed them in our general enumeration above (p. 64) among the documents in pure London Official English, but such forms as *fuyre* 'fire', *putts* 'pits', *brugge* 'bridge', *huydes* 'hides, skins'—all containing original O.E. $\bar{y}$—call for mention here, and we may perhaps regard *hur* 'their', O.E. *heora*, as an example of a typical Western *u* for O.E. *eo*.

Most remarkable, perhaps, of all the private letters of this period, in the fidelity with which they adhere to the London type, are those of **John Shillingford** (1447–50). Here, if anywhere, we might expect to find an almost pure Regional dialect. Shillingford had apparently lived in his native Devon continuously; most of his letters were not official reports, but private missives written to his friends at home, and yet, on the whole, he consisten ly avoids the forms of his local dialect and writes Standard English. His vowel spellings, his verbal forms, and his Pers. Pronouns are generally those of London English. Fortunately, however, for our knowledge of his native speech, that is the Devonshire dialect, he lifts the veil occasionally and drops into provincialisms. The following are the chief: The retention of the old South-Western type in *hurde* 'heard', *u* for O.E. *eo* in *durer* 'dearer', the shortened form of West Saxon $\bar{æ}^1$ in *radde* 'read' 'advised', unrounding of δ in *aftetymes* 'oft-times' (see remarks on p. 78 in connexion with St. Editha), and the very frequent retention of the prefix *y-* in P. P.'s, which, though common in Chaucer (see p. 53), was by this time dying out in London. The points noted concerning the vowels (except *radde*) are certainly pretty broad provincialisms, judged by the London Standard, and they, no doubt, indicate Shillingford's natural pronunciation, not only in the words quoted but in the whole of the classes to which they severally belong. We have, naturally, no means of knowing how far the excellent Mayor, having mastered another manner of writing, was able to adhere, in speaking, to the type which he records, on the whole so faithfully, on paper. We may, perhaps, conclude from the above forms that he spoke with a pretty strong Devonshire accent.

Less provincial still, as we might expect, is the language of **Bishop Pecok's** *Repressor for over much blaming for the Clergy* (*c.* 1449), which, written with the best intentions, led, together with other works from his pen, to its author being very much blamed *by* the clergy, and ultimately to his being tried and condemned for heresy. Pecok's style in the above book is clear and sound, although the philosophical argument which pervades it makes it rather tough reading. The dialect may be generally described as more or less colourless, and contains few deviations from the

current London written English beyond the absence of the more character-
istic Easternisms.   For instance, Pecok has practically no *ĕ*-forms (for
O E. *y̆*)—I have only noted *ungerd* ' ungirt ' in Vol. I—he uses a preponderance of *i*-forms in this class of words—*wirche* ' to work ', *girdele*
' girdle ', *birthe, biried, kind,* and a few *u*-forms such as *buried, duller.*
The Verbal forms are the normal Midland type: he uses *fill* (as in
Chaucer) for the Pret. of *fall*; he still distinguishes between the Sing. and
Pl. in Str. Vbs.—*brake—breken,* &c.; he has no *y-* prefix in Past Participles; and these in Str. Vbs. sometimes end in *-en,* or occasionally *-un—
sungun, foundun, writun,* &c., though more commonly in *-e.*   The
Pronoun of the 3rd Person in the Pl. is *thei, her, hem.*   He differs from
London English in having no *their, them,* &c.   Among provincialisms we
should probably reckon diphthonging before *-sch—waische* ' wash ', *aischis,*
fleisch ' flesh ',—and the interesting form *swope* ' soap ', O.E. *sāpe—waish-
ing with oyle and swope.*   The form *swope* will occupy our attention
again later on (p. 307).

As last examples of the class of writers we are at present considering,
that is those who use what is practically London official or literary English
with a certain provincial flavouring, we will take the Monk of Bury (*circa*
1370–1451) and a letter of Edmond de la Pole.   The language of
Lydgate is indeed hardly distinguishable from his contemporary Hoccleve,
or from the official London Eng. of the period, except for the occurrence
of rather more *ĕ*-forms for O.E. *y̆*.   Thus Lydgate, by the side of *fȳres,*
mirth, mynde, kynde, bysynesse, and *fuyre* ' fire ', writes also *vnkende*
' unkind ', *felthe* ' filth ', *sterid* ' stirred ', *besynesse.*   He also has a certain
number of *ĕ* for *ĭ* spellings, which, as we have seen (pp. 77–78), are common
in the Suffolk dialect of Bokenam, and in Essex—*velenye, merour, glemeryng, wedow.*   Like Chaucer, he uses both the Southern and E. Midland
forms of O.E. *ǣ*[1] in his rhymes—*breth—deth,* but also *drēde—spēde* (Vb.).
Seeing the unsettled state of London English at this time, in the first and
last of these particulars, it is rather doubtful whether they ought to be
ascribed in Lydgate to special E. Midland influence, as both are found in
Chaucer and other London writers—though it should be noted that the
Southern *brēth,* &c., with [ē] predominates in Chaucer's rhymes, whereas
it is rarer in Lydgate—and they were clearly current in London speech.
The *e* for *i* forms are more doubtful so early in the century, and they
seem to be absent from Chaucer's English.   It may, perhaps, be said that
Lydgate shows Eastern influence more by the absence of purely Southern
forms which at this period still abounded in London English, than by
the use of any typically E. Midland forms which are not found in the
latter.

Edmond de la Pole, Earl of Suffolk, was born about 1473, and exe-
cuted for high treason in 1513.   This ill-starred and illiterate nobleman
had the misfortune to spring from the ' sceptred race ' of York, his mother
being the sister of King Edward IV.

The following letter, written from the Continent to an unknown correspondent, in or before 1505, is a fitting close to our short survey of
writers who depart from London English undefiled.   Such definite
dialectal peculiarities as it possesses are clearly E. Midland, but its chief
interest lies in its illustration of how a man of the writer's quality might

write his mother tongue at the beginning of the sixteenth century. If the Earl spoke at all as he wrote, his must have been a queer lingo, due, no doubt, partly to a residence of some years abroad, away from English speakers.

'Cosen I deser yov to chohove (show) to my lord my cosen that yt vold ples hem to remember I kame to hem for the lovef and strouste (trust) I had to hem a bovef (above) ale hedder (all other) prenses, ver for I povt (put) my boddy yn ys hand, ver apone he gavef me ys chavfcondet to com ynto ys land, as vane I spake with heme he promes me as he vas a nobovle mane ys land chovld be free fore me, and noe (now) I have bein here one yeer and a haalvf and hame as ner nove (now) of my departeng hennes as I vas the frerst dae. And also yov came to me and desored me to povt my matter yn my lord my cosen hand, and he vold point me a dae ef he . . . a nend be teven (between) K. H. and me, vel ef nat my lord my Cosen promissed me be ys letters be sent John dae last passed he vold geevf me lessens (license) to de parte ys land ver yt plessed me; and thest have yov promes me for my lord my cosen wches (wishes) I have foufeled at the deser of my lord my cosen. Nove my day ys passed and a cordeng to my lord my cosen I deser of yov yovr lesens as yov be come of nobovele boveld (noble blood) and as yov be a trove jengtleman I deser yov to ch . . . yovr s . . . fochet to let me depart ascordeng to my lord my Coson letters and to yovr promes that yov have mad me. I strest (trust) my lord my Coson vele (will) nat beevef my her yn thest danger ef ys Heines come heyder; wches I thoke vele ef I vare yn ther handes I vare bovt as a mane hone done (undone). As ale (all) for be kaves (because) of my lord my Coson yn to hem for schol . . . (shelter?) ys . . . And also has done at my cosen deser that I vold nat do at ther der I strest my lord my cosen vele remember my goot hart that I have had and vele have to heme as nat to leev me her as a man leftf. Also ef yt ples hem to set me a dae of to ore iij monthes so I be yn some severte (surety) ver yt ples heme. I hame conten or and ef yt ples my lord my Coson that I mae be with hem and be at my lebertte I vel be glad to bed hes pleser. And to bed ys plas a yer or to thake chevf fortovn as ples God to send to heme, my parte I hame vele content to thake for Affter thest manner as I ame a cerstene man I vele nott bed to dee for yt, ver for Cossen as yov be a trove Jengtilmane do fore me as I hau geve yov kawes and thet I be not lost thovrt (through) the promes and chavef condded (safeconduct) of my lord my Coson and your proier for my good vell.' (Ellis's Letters, Ser. III, Vol. i, pp. 127, &c.)

It cannot be denied that the Earl must have been a very tedious correspondent, that he lacked charm, and that he was not very successful in expressing his ideas on paper with complete clearness. The style and diction of the above is typical of the rest of his correspondence collected by Ellis. We notice *e* for O.E. *y*, *e* for *i*, initial *v* for *w*, and initial *h*- inserted where it has no business, features which are fairly common in the other E. Midland writers we have considered.

All these things are common in London English before the end of the century, and increasingly so in the next century. They are found among writers of all classes, but some, especially the misplacement of *h*-, and *v* for *w*, appear to be more frequent among the less cultivated and less highly placed.

It must be admitted with regard to several of the sources considered above, as representing what we may call Modified London English, that not a little doubt arises as to whether we should not be better advised to regard them as representing a definite type of London speech. The difficulty appears mainly in respect of those texts and documents which have a distinct E. Midland or South-Eastern tinge. We have more than once emphasized the fact that these elements occur in undoubted London English, and it is largely the degree to which they are present which inclines us to classify a document as pure London, or as Modified London. It seems likely that there were at least two types of English actually spoken in London, one strongly tinged with E. Midland and South-Eastern characteristics, the other possessing less of the former, at any rate, and more of purely Southern features.

If this view were accepted we could regard all but the above documents, apart from the Western traits which some possess, and the North-East Midland of others, as representing actual types of Spoken London English, and group them as under the Eastern type of this dialect. The English of the official documents, and on the whole of Caxton, would occupy a central position between these two types, possessing several of the features of both, but in different relative proportion.

I am inclined to hazard the hypothesis that the spoken language of the Court and upper classes belonged rather to the Southern type of London English, that of the lower, and to a slightly less extent perhaps, that of the middle classes, to the Eastern type.

We turn now to consider some of the poetry, official records, and private documents actually written by Londoners in London during the fifteenth century, among which we include the writings of the Kentish Caxton who definitely adopted London speech as his basis. We begin with **Hoccleve** or Occleve, supposed to have been born about 1370 and to have died about 1450. Hoccleve was a merry companion, given, according to his own account, to haunting ale-houses and frequenting more or less disreputable company. He was a clerk in the office of the Privy Seal '*for his sustinaunce*', and the money so earned he dispensed, like Villon, ' tout aux tavernes et aux filles '. As a poet he lacks inspiration, but is not without a versifying skill of an imitative kind, and here and there a robust animal vigour of character. He gives, besides, a valuable picture of certain phases of London life. But his best claim to be remembered is his piety for Chaucer's memory, and the fact that one of the MSS. of his works (Harleian 4866) contains what is considered the best portrait—a kind of miniature—of his great predecessor. The passages referring to Chaucer which are quoted below are not without a certain dignity, and a pathos which is not all convention.

The spelling of the Hoccleve MSS. is very conventional, and there are but few spellings which indicate a change from the M.E. vowel system, though we may mention the form *musten*, which points to the important change of O.E. *ō* to *ū*. The language agrees in the main with that London type seen in Chaucer's writings, though there appear to be far fewer *e*-forms for O.E. *ў*. This class of words generally has the *i*-type— *bisynesse, knytte* (Vb.), *filthe, pittes, schitte* ' shut ', *fist*; *mankȳnde, fȳre, mȳnde, drȳe* (Vb. Inf.), *kȳþe* (Inf.), *bilde*, &c. By the side of these we have *unschete* (Inf.) ' to open ', *velthy* ' filthy ', *mery, beried, thēmel* ' thimble ' O.E. *þȳmel*, and further *suche, burdon cusse* (N.) on analogy of Vb. *cusse*, and *thursteth*. O.E. *ǣ*[1], to judge from the rhymes, occurs both in the Saxon and non-Saxon types:—*dēde* ' deed ' and *rēde* ' counsel ' both rhyming with *heed* ' head ', *rēde* (Vb.) with *lēde* (Vb.); on the other hand, *street* and *weet* ' wet ' rhyme with *feet*, and *dēde* and *rēde* with *forbēde* (O.E. *forbēodan*). The rhyme *spēeche* and *teeche* is ambiguous, since *ǣ*[2] in *brēde* ' breadth ' also rhymes with *spēde* ' speed ', the vowel of which was certainly tense. This looks as if Hoccleve may have used the Kentish-South-Eastern tense pronunciation of *ǣ*[2] (see p. 41, No. 2). The E. Midland *merour* and *wretyn*, *lenage* ' lineage ' occur. M.E.-*ĕr*- rarely occurs with the spelling -*ar*-. Note, however, *astarte* rhyming with *herte*, *merte*. The Pers. Pronouns in the Pl. are *þey*, *thei*, *here*, *hir*, &c., and *hem* usually, though I have noted *themselfe*. The Pres. Indic. Pl. ends in *n* (never -*th*); the P.P.'s of Strong Vbs. have both -*e* and -*en*—*knowe*, and with the prefix *y*-, *i*-, *itake*, *ifalle*; but *standen*, *waxen*, &c. The prefix *i*- is used also in Wk. Vbs.—*iþynchid*, *yput*. In unstressed syllables -*i*- (-*y*-) is very frequent before consonants—*puttith*, *tokyn*, *synkyn* (Inf.), *werkys* ' works ' which rhymes with *derk is*, *fēlist*, &c., &c. These -*i*- spellings become more and more common as the century advances.

The following brief specimens, taken from the *Regement of Princes*, illustrate Hoccleve's language sufficiently, and contain the well-known references to Chaucer, so often quoted scrappily at second-hand.

lines 1958–81.

> But weylaway! so is myn herte wo
> That þe honour of englyssh tonge is deed
> Of which I wont was hav consail and reed.
> O maister deere and fader reuerent!
> Mi maister Chaucer, flour of eloquence
> Mirour of fructuous entendement,
> O vniuersel fadir in science!
> Allas! þat þou thyn excellent prudence
> In þi bed mortal myhtist naght by-quethe;
> What eyled deth? allas! whi wolde he sle the?

> O deth! þou didest naght harme singuleer,
> In slaghtere of him; but al þis land it smertith;
> But nathelees, yit has þou no power
> His name sle; his hy vertu astertith
> Vnslayn fro þe, which ay vs lyfly hertyth
> With bookes of his ornat endytyng,
> That is to al þis land enlumynyng.

> Hast þou nat eeke my maister Gower slayn,
> Whos vertu I am insufficient
> ffor to descryue? I wote wel in certayn,
> ffor to sleen all þis world þou haust yment;
> But syn our lorde Crist was obedient
> To þe, in feith I can no ferther seye;
> His creatures mosten þe obeye.

4978   The firste fyndere of our faire langage

4982   Alasse my fadir fro þe world is goo

On Chaucer's portrait.   (Harl. MS. 4866 has the
best portrait according to Furnival.)

Al-þogh his lyfe be queynt,[1] þe resemblaunce
Of him haþ in me so fressh lyflynesse,
Þat to put othir men in remembraunce
Of his persone, I haue heere his lyknesse
Do[2] make, to þis ende in soth fastnesse
Þat þei þat haue of him lest þought and mynde,
By þis peynture may ageyn him fynde.

4992–8.

The language of **Sir John Fortescue** would appear to be a model of
propriety, and to be quite free from those occasional provincialisms which
we observed in his fellow Devonian, Shillingford.   His vowels are of
the normal London type, and call for very little remark.   O.E. *y* is represented by both *i* and *u*, but *e*-forms are very scarce, *meryer* being the
only one there noted.   On the other hand, he has a few examples of *e*
for *i*—*wech* 'which', *lemited*, *openion*, *contenually*, &c.   He usually retains
the old spelling *-er-*, but has *hartes*, *warre*.   He occasionally uses the old
forms of the Pers. Pron. *her*, *hem*, but more commonly *thair*, *thaim*, and,
of course, *they* always.   In the Pres. Pl. Indic. of Vbs. he has never *-th*,
but always the Midland *-en*, *-yn*, or *-e*.   In the P. P. of Strong Vbs. *-en*,
&c., is more frequent than *-e*, and no Vbs. of this class have the prefix *i-*
or *y-*, though I have noted *iblissed*.   It would almost seem as if Fortescue
had deliberately avoided even those Southernisms which were still in use
in London, such as Pres. Pls. in *-th*, and affected rather the Eastern type
of London English.

A more Southern type is found in the **Rewle of Sustris Menouresses**
(*circa* 1450).   Here we find, alongside of pretty frequent *-yn*, &c., also
very commonly *-yth*, &c., in the Pres. Pl., and the prefix *i-* fairly often
retained, though not generally in Str. Vbs.   The Pl. of the Pers. Pronouns is *þei* in the Nom., but knows only *her(e)* and *hem* in the Possess.
and Dat.

We pass now to **Caxton.**   The language of London was not wholly
natural to Caxton, who was a Kentishman.   Nor was he of the knightly
class to which, in the previous century, the Kentish Gower had belonged,
to whom the speech of the Court and its denizens was familiar.   This is
why, perhaps, we feel in reading Caxton a certain constraint and lack of
ease.   The style of the Prefaces is less high-flown than that of the translations themselves, but it is wanting in fluency and elegance, while that of
the latter is too often pompous when it is meant to be courtly, and merely
stodgy where it should be magnificent.   Caxton was not an innovator.
He followed entirely the scribal tradition in spelling, so that a novice
reading him and comparing his writings with the English of, say, Margaret
Paston or Gregory, might gain the impression that the language had
jumped back into Middle English again as regards pronunciation.   Yet,
as we have seen, in these writers and many others, earlier and contempo-
raneous, the development of several new features since the M.E. period,
in fact, the beginning of the Modern system of vowel pronunciation,

---

[1] quenched.   [2] *Do* is P. P. = 'caused'.

can be clearly traced. Of this Caxton lets us see next to nothing. His spelling, therefore, gives a very imperfect guide to the realities of English speech in his day, and conveys the impression that English was still much nearer to the M.E. stage than was actually the case. Even in the spelling of unstressed syllables, when the private documents of Shillingford—a quarter of a century earlier—and still more those of the Pastons and Celys, prove clearly by their spellings, that reduction of full vowels—shortening of long vowels, unrounding of rounded sounds, simplification of diphthongs—had already taken place, Caxton tells us practically nothing which we do not learn already from M.E. scribes, and though his varying spelling suggests, it is true, a hesitation how to express the reduced unaccented vowel, it would be difficult, if not impossible, to formulate any definite laws for the treatment of unstressed syllables from his writings. The frequent spellings *-id*, *-is*, &c., in flexional syllables may be noted.

In regard to inflexional endings Caxton appears to be very much at the stage of Chaucer. Like Chaucer and other M.E. writers he has the Inf. in *-en*, though he omits the ending more often than is common in the full M.E. period; he has the Midland *-en* Pl. in Pres. Indic. of Verbs; he has some very archaic forms of the Strong Verbs: e. g. *bote*, Pret. of *to bite*, and the P. P. *seten* of *to sit*; he retains the old Pret. of *find, fond* (as in Chaucer), though he does not appear to distinguish any longer between the Sing. and Pl. of the Pret. in Strong Verbs of this and other classes; he uses, as does Chaucer, the archaic *faught* as the Pret. of *fight*, which represents O.E. *fæht*, Early M.E. *faht*, as distinct from the P. P. *foughten* from earlier *fohten*; he uses, with remarkable consistency, the suffix *-en* in P. P.'s of Strong Verbs, and the prefix *y-* hardly occurs. By the side of *gave* he uses also the older *gaf*, and he agrees with Chaucer in using the difficult *fill* as the Pret. of *fall*. By the side of *their* and *them* Caxton has, though less frequently than these, *her* and *hem* for the Possess. and Dat. Pl. of the Pers. Pronoun.

Coming to the dialectal characteristics of vowels in Caxton's English, it is perhaps surprising that well-marked Kenticisms are not more frequent. The most characteristic feature of Kentish and the South-Eastern dialects is the appearance of *ĕ* for O.E. *ў̆*. Of these forms Caxton has not more than are commonly found in London speech, and those which he does use can all be found in other writers of Literary or Court English of this period. From our present point of view, among the most interesting are *seche* 'such', *knette* 'knit', and *shette* 'shut'.

Like Chaucer, Caxton, and many writers at a later date, use the South-Western *-on-* instead of the Eastern *-an-* in *lond, understond*, &c. Among other specifically South-Western forms, which earlier were more common in the London dialect, and many of which survived for a century after Caxton, we may note *silfe* 'self', and perhaps under this head would come the vowel in Inf. *gyue*, and P. P. *gyuen*, where Chaucer more commonly has the non-W. Saxon *yeue, yeuen*. There was a long hesitation regarding the forms of this word, the *e*-forms being perhaps the most usual during the fifteenth and sixteenth centuries, and lasting even into the early eighteenth among good speakers. The E. Midland *ĕ* for *i* occurs in *Phelip, wreton* (P. P.), *to wete* 'to know', *euyll*, &c. M.E. *-er-* is generally so written, but we find *warres, smarting, parill* 'peril'. This feature, as has been said (p. 11), is probably S.E. or E. Midland in or gin, and probably got into London at this period, with increasing frequency, from the latter area. On the whole Caxton's English is distinctly more Midland in character than Chaucer's. We have unfortunately no means of testing whether O.E. $\tilde{æ}^1$ had the Southern or Midland sound. His type of London English is distinctly of the Eastern brand, and nearer to that of Norfolk than of Kent or Essex, and still farther from the pure Southern of Surrey.

With regard to Caxton's use of the London dialect, there are two interesting points to be noted. One is that he tells us in one of his Prefaces (to his translation of the *Aeneid*, 1482) that he hesitates, he 'stands abasshed' what form to use, which implies two things, first that Caxton did not naturally write without taking thought, as Fortescue or Shillingford did, in London English, and secondly. (and this follows from the first) that he did not habitually use the type of English in ordinary speech. The other point is that in the Preface to the *Histories of Troy*, he tells us that when he had finished this translation, he showed it to 'my most redoubted Lady My Lady Margaret' Duchess of Bur-gundy, 'sister unto the King of England and of France, my sovereign lord' (Edward IV). 'Her good grace' having seen the work '*anon she found a default in my English which she commanded me to amend*'. It would be interesting to know on what ground this 'right high excellent and right virtuous princess' found fault. Was it that she objected to the style? (as well she might if she wanted an easy and flowing narrative). Or did she disapprove of Caxton's dialect? If the latter, it might mean either that he at first wrote in his native dialect, or that, having attempted the Court form of English, there were still too many broad provincialisms for a 'woman of her fashion'. This may well have been so, for in the same Preface Caxton says that he was born and learnt his English in Kent, in the Weald, 'where I doubt not is spoken as broad and rude English as in any place of England'. Another statement of Caxton's (Preface to Transl. of *Aeneid*) is worth recording. It is to the effect that the English used—he does not say where—when he wrote, was very different from that in use when he was born. Does this mean that English as a whole underwent a somewhat rapid change between 1422 or so and 1475 or so? Or does it refer only to the London dialect, and mean that the dialectal elements had come to be differently distributed, and in different relative proportion, during that period? We have no proof of the former ; in fact, there is every reason to think that English was developing then, as always, gradually and normally. As for the latter possibility, we do know that the E. Midland elements were gaining ground to the suppression of the Southern elements.

The following dialogue from Jason is typical of the kind of talk which fills the volume. It is 'genteel' to a fault, and so frigid and remote from reality, that it is quite unconvincing as a specimen of real colloquial English. It is certain that people did not speak to each other in this strain, even in the fifteenth century. Compare it with much of the dialogue in the *Canterbury Tales*, and the artificiality is felt to be not of an age only, but of all time. Caxton's style, when he tries the grand manner, is as bad as *Euphues* at its worst, except that Lyly sometimes drops his mannerisms, and makes his characters talk like human beings, which Caxton never does. Poor illiterate, stammering Edmond de la Pole, with his ' I strest my lord my cosen vele remember my goot hart that I have had—as not to leev me her as a man leftf', touches us far more than the icy and mincing heroics of Caxton.

From Caxton's History of Jason, from the French of Raoul Le Fevre, p. 82 (Furnival's Ed.), line 24, &c.

Whan thenne she apperceyuyd that Jason retorned vn to his logyyng at this time she wente agaynst him and toke him by the hand and lad him into one of her chambres. where she shewd to him grete partie of her richesses and tresours. And after she saide to him in this manere Right noble and valiant knight all thise richesses ben alle onely at your commandement and also my body wyth all. wherof I make now to you the ghifte and present Ander furthermore I haue nothing of valeur but that ye shal haue at your abandon and will to thende that I may deserue honourably your grace. Thenne when the preu Iason had vnderstande this that sayd is. he ansuerde to the lady sayng My dere lady I thanke you right humbly of your curtoysye And I declare vnto you that in no facion I haue deseruyd the hye honour that ye presente to me. Ha a gentill knight saide thenne the lady. hit is well in your power for to deserue all if it be your plaisir. In goode trouble madame ansuerde thenne Iason if ther be ony seruice or plaisire that I may do vnto you I commande ye it and I shal accomplisshe hit frely and with goode herte. ' How fair sire' sayd she thenne. ' wil ye accomplisshe my commandement.' ' Certes madame' sayd he ' I shal not faile in no point if hit be to me possible. And ther fore declare ye to me your good playsyr and desire. And after that ye shall parceyue howe I shall employe my self therto.

But enough of this.

The next document of which we give a specimen is an account of the way to carry an English king to his tomb. Its meaning is clear and unambiguous, and its style perfectly business-like. It is an admirable example of an official document of the period and of the type of London English in which these were written. The phonology and accidence are curiously like our own, and almost the only form which calls for remark is *shilde* ' shield ', which represents a Southern type as distinct from the Midland M.E. *sheelde*, from which our present form is derived. It will be noted that the -*n* of the Pres. Pl. and of the Inf. of Verbs is entirely absent.

Funeral of Edward the Fourth (1483).

Here foloith the Ordenances which shalbe done in the observaunce at the deth and buryall of a annoynted king.

When that a king annoynted ys deceassed, after his body spurged, it most be washed and clensed by a bishop for his holy annoyntment. Then the body must be bamed if it may be goton, and wrapped in lawne or raynes, then hosen, shertes, and a pair of shone of redde lether, and do over hym his surcote of clothe, his cap of estate over his hede, and then laie hym on a faire burde covered with clothe of gold, his one hand upon his bely, and a septur in the other hand, and on his face a kerchief and so shewid to his nobles by the space of ij dayes and more if the weder will it suffre. And when he may not goodly lenger endure, take hym away, and bowell hym and then eftsones bame hym, wrappe hym in raynes well trameled in cordis of silke, then in tartryne trameled, and then in velvet, and then in clothe of gold well trameled; and then lede hym[1] and coffre hym, and in his lede with hym a plait of his still, name and date of our, &c. And if ye care[2] hym, make a ymage like hym, clothed in a surcote with mantil of estat, the laices goodly lyeng on his bely, his septur in his hand and his crown on his hede, and so carry him in a chair opon, with lightes and baners, accompanyed with lordys and estates as the counsaill can best devyse, havyng the horse of that chair traped with dyvers trapers, or els with blacke trapers with scochons richely beten and his officers of armes abowt hym in his cottes of armes.

And then a lord or a knyght with a courser traped of his armes upon hym, his salet or basnet on his hede crowned, a shilde, and a spere, tyll he come to his place of his entring.[3] And at masse the same to be offered by noble princes.

[The rest of this very interesting document consists of an account of the rites observed at the funeral of King Edward IV.]

Naturally, so brief an extract does not give quite a complete picture of the language of the period, and we will therefore conclude our examination of official London English with some particulars of two documents already mentioned—(1) the **Creation of Henry Duke of York a Knight of the Bath** (1494), and (2) the **Reception of Catherine of Aragon** (1501). In the following account notice is chiefly taken of points in which the above documents differ from present-day usage, or of those in which, while agreement exists with our present speech, it is interesting to find so early. As regards vowel sounds, M.E. -er- generally survives as such, even in cases where we now have the -ar- or some other type; thus No. 1 has *sergent, swerde, kerved, kerver* 'carved', &c., *werke*, but No. 2 has, on the other hand, *Barmondsey, warning*. O.E. $\bar{y}$ is represented on the whole as at the present time, except *furst* 'first' (1), *bruge* 'bridge' (2), and *lift* 'left' (hand) (1). *e* for *i* is found in *shreven* P. P. (1). The early fronting of M.E. *a* to [æ] is perhaps indicated by the spellings[4]*weshed* 'washed' (1), and *es for* 'as for' (2). The rounding of *ă* after *w-* is shown in the spelling *wos* 'was' (1). Initial M.E. $\bar{e}$ [ē] appears as *ye-* in *yēst* 'east' (1). The name of our country was pronounced as at the present time, as is seen by the spelling *Ingland* (2), where *e* becomes *i* before -*ng*. M.E. tense $\bar{e}$ was probably already pronounced as at present, as is shown by the spellings *sien* 'seen', *indied* 'indeed', both in (1).

In the combination -*ns*- *n* is dropped as in *Westmester* (1); -*d* is added finally after -*l*-, *felde* 'fell' (1). Initial *wh*- was pronounced as at present all over the South of England—*wiche* 'which', *weroff* 'whereof', *wen* 'when' (1). The Pron. *who* was pronounced without *w*-, as at present, and is written *hoo* (1). One example of Group Possessives has already been quoted (p. 75), and another, *the abbot of Westminsters barge*, occurs in 2. The Possessive is found used absolutely—*sett in like maner as therle of Suffolkis* (1). The Pl. forms of the Pers. Pronouns are *thei, thaire, thaim*. Pres. Pls. in -*th, geuythe, hathe*, are found. The P. P.'s of Strong Verbs usually end in -*n*, and the prefix *i-, y-* is not used. The P.P. of 'be' is *been*, and *be*, and the same forms also occur in the Pres.

---

[1] i.e. put him in a casket of lead.   [2] carry.   [3] interment.

[4] *e* in *weshed* is from a M.E. type ; *es* is more probably a form with reduced vowel in an unstressed position.

Pl. Inflexional syllables very constantly have *i* or *y*—*kyngis* (Possess.), *actis* (Pl.), *purposithe*, *fairyst* (Superl.), *brokyn* (P. P.). The consonant *r* was probably still strongly trilled in the middle of words before consonants, to judge by the spelling *therell* = 'the earl', which suggests a pronunciation like that heard from Scotchmen at the present day.

Such are the main points which call for remark in these typical documents, and we see that the distribution of dialect elements is approaching that of our own day.

A few words should perhaps be said upon the language of literature proper at the close of the century, and we may take **John Skelton's** *Magnyfycence* as typical. Although Skelton lived until 1529, he must be regarded as a fifteenth-century poet. Few people read Skelton nowadays except Professors of Literature, not even those who attend their lectures, nor perhaps ever will again. 'Beastly Skelton Heads of Houses quote', said Pope, and this line—probably untrue in Pope's day, and an absurdity in our own—has possibly helped to preserve the poet's very name from decent oblivion, though the curious may have noted, tucked away in histories of English poetry, the couplet

> For though the dayes be nevir so long
> At last the belles ringeth to evensong,[1]

which is worth remembering as expressing a thought that has been expressed a hundred times in as many different ways, and also because it contains a Pres. Pl. in -*th*. Skelton's English as represented by *Magnyfycence*, written about 1516, is by no means uninteresting from our present point of view. It is of the Southern type of London English of the period, and exhibits that individuality in the use of dialectal elements which characterized the speech of cultivated persons, who were yet not provincials, at the end of the fifteenth century and much later. While in the main the language conforms pretty closely to the official London dialect, we find occasional divergencies from this. Thus *praty* 'pretty' preserves the Southern form of O.E. *æ*[1], shortened to *ĕ*, and then becoming *ă*, instead of the Midland of South-East *e*, the Southern *wokys* 'weeks' (W. Sax. *wucu*, fr. *weocu*), the Southern *herdely* 'hardly' with *e*, fr. O.E. *heard*, *hærd*, which in Midland became *hard* (cf. p. 33, No. 1); the archaic Southern *iche* for 'I' Pers. Pron.; the Southern prefix *y-* in the P. P. *ywet*, *storm ybeten*, and the Pres. Pl. in -*th*—*your clokes smellyth musty*. On the other hand, the typical present-day distribution of *i* and *e* in *mery*, *mirth*, *bysy* (also *besy*), and *i* also in *lyther* O.E. *lȳþer* 'bad'; the Eastern *e* for *i* in *glettering*, and the occasional use of E. Midland -*ys* in the 3rd Sing. Pres.—*lokys* 'looks', *reckys* 'recks', by the side of the usual -*yth*, &c. These -*s* forms, which were all but unknown among the best London writers—and speakers—for nearly another hundred years, except when used in mid-sixteenth century and after, to save a syllable in verse, may have got into the poet's language at Cambridge. Skelton has, for the time, a fair number of -*ar*- spellings for M.E. -*er*-, and rhymes which indicate that he pronounced -*ar*- sometimes when he does not write it—*harde* 'heard' P. P., *harte*, *swarue* 'swerve', *clark*, *barke* Vb., but also *herde*, *ferther*, *herke* 'hark'; further *enferre* 'infer' rhyming with

[1] This couplet, which is by Stephen Hawes, is wrongly attributed to Skelton here.

debarre, and *herk* rhyming with *clarke*. This peculiarity, already frequently
alluded to as occurring in other writers, becomes more and more common
in London English from the beginning of the second half of the century,
and probably started in Kent and Essex. An interesting example of it in
Magnyfycence occurs in the phrase—*All is out of harre*, where the last word
is from O.E. *heorra* ' hinge ', M.E. *herre*. The phrase means ' the times
are out of joint ', and the idiom is exactly equivalent to the French *hors
des gonds*. In inflexional syllables Skelton makes frequent use of *-ys*,
-yth, *-yd*, which, as we have seen, were before this time becoming
characteristic of London English, as they have remained so of the
Received Standard type of pronunciation to the present time.

We shall conclude this survey of fifteenth-century English with an
account of the language of **Gregory's Chronicle**. Some few particulars
have already been given of William Gregory (p. 64). As to the work
itself, it may have been completed somewhere about 1470, since it was
continued after Gregory's death in 1467. The MS., according to
Mr. Gairdner, is all in one hand, and that certainly of the fifteenth
century. In some ways this work is the most interesting for our purpose
of all those referred to in this chapter. It has an air of unstudied naturalness about its forms and style, and we may take it to represent pretty
faithfully the ordinary everyday speech of the better Middle Classes of
London, comparable to that of Machyn about a hundred years later, but
representing probably the English of a social *couche* superior to his, if
distinctly below the standard of the Court. It is the most considerable
document of its kind belonging to this age, and gives an extensive picture
of colloquial speech in the Metropolis.

The vowel system agrees on the whole with that of other London
documents of the period, but certain features are more strongly marked
than in other London documents. While from Gregory's origin we might
expect the E. Midland elements to be very strongly represented, to the
exclusion of most of the typically Southern, as a matter of fact, although
the former element is quite definitely present, some very interesting
Southern features also occur. This rather leads one to the opinion that
the presence of the Eastern characteristics is not primarily due to
Gregory's Suffolk birth, but to the fact that they were in use in the
Middle Class London speech of the time, rather more frequently than in
that of the superior ranks. In other words, Gregory wrote the genuine
London English of the class among whom he lived, and not a form
modified by Suffolk dialect. Had he done the latter, he would hardly
have made use of Southernisms which he could not have known from his
native dialect, but which were in use in London.

To begin with O.E. *ў*, Gregory has comparatively few *e*-forms, and
these are all known to have been in use in genuine London English—
berriyd, *steryd* 'stirred', *besely*, and *evylle*, which, however, may be
differently explained (p. 207). The *i*-forms greatly predominate—
first, *bylde*, *lyfte* ' left ' (hand), *byryd*, *syche* ' such ', *schytte* (Pret.) ' shut ',
lytylle. There are but few *u*-forms—*buryd*, *suche*, *muche*, *brūsyd* ' bruised '.
The M.E. combination *-er-* is written *-ar-* more frequently than in any
other London text of this time, that I have examined—*warre* ' war ',
Barkeley, *starre*, *sargent*, *clargy*, *marcy*, *sartayne* ' certain ', *sarmon*,

sarvyce; but, on the other hand, *-er-* is also well represented—*werre* 'war', *ferme* 'farm', *sterre, erthe, derke, herte, Clerkynwelle, ferther, kervyr* 'carver', *Colde Herborowe, person* = 'parson'. We know that the *-ar-* forms were coming into official London English about the middle of the fifteenth century, and that nearly all writers have some, but even at the end of the century they are not so frequent in any other document, official or literary, as here, and the Suffolk Wills of the third quarter of the century have but few, which is evidently due to the influence of official London English. We find more in the Paston Letters and the Cely Papers, and we are justified, I think, in regarding *sarmon,* &c., as having started in the South-East and E. Midlands, and having passed into London through Lower and Middle Class English, of which they became a characteristic feature. Another feature found in nearly all London documents to some extent, but peculiarly typical of the East (see Bokenam, Marg. Paston, Cely Papers, &c.), is *e* for *i,* but probably no other London document has so many of these spellings as Gregory. Of those which may be long we have—*preson, levyd* 'lived', *wete* 'know', *lemytyd, levyn* (Inf.) 'live', *letany, leverays* 'liveries', *wedowe, petefullyste, rever* 'river'; almost certainly short are *schelyngys* 'shillings', *pejon* 'pigeon', *pelory, denyr. Chekyns* may come under this group, but may also be differently explained. The following interesting Southern forms occur:—*dradde* (P. P.), *radde* (Pret.), which are both found in Chaucer, *praty* 'pretty', where *a* is a shortened O.E. *ǣ*[1] (cf. p. 29 (1); 33 (2)). Further :—*schylde* 'shield', *yldyste* 'eldest', *sylle* 'to sell', where we have the representations of Southern *scield, ieldest, siellan* (cf. p. 35 (7)). Before *-ng* and *-nch e* becomes *i*:—*Inglond, Kyngs Bynche,* both of which words, however, also occur written with the traditional *e.* A curious Westernism occurs in [1]*schute* 'shoot' O.E. *sceōtan,* which is found at least twice (cf. p. 34 (4)). The typical Eastern form is found in *Schēter Hylle* 'Shooter's Hill'. The combination *-an-* is often written *-on-,* not only before *nd, mb, ng,* which lengthenedt he vowel—*lond, stonde, lombe* 'lamb', *stronge, hongyd, longage* 'language', but also in *thonke* 'thanks', *thonkyd* 'thanked'. The *-an-* spellings are also found—*hanggyd, lambe,* and *land.* The new pronunciation of M.E. *ē* is expressed by *i* and *y*:—*hire* 'hear', *hirde* 'heard', *dyre* 'dear', *stypylle* 'steeple' (which may possibly be a Southernism for O.E. *y (īe)*), *slyvys* 'sleeves'. It is possible that the spellings *becheler* 'bachelor', *iesper* 'jasper', *fethem* 'fathom', indicate that M.E. *ă* had already undergone the modern shifting.

Passing to consonants, we find loss of consonants in *Braban* for 'Brabant', *Edwar the iiij* for 'Edward', *Wanysday* 'Wednesday', *halpeny, sowdyer* 'soldier', *Raffe* 'Ralph', *Fauconbrygge, sepukyr* 'sepulchre', and *Westmyster,* a very common form here, and in other documents. A final consonant is added in *patent* 'paten', *losste* 'loss'; *n* is intercalated in *massynger,* earlier *messager,* where we have kept the *n.* Old *-ht-* has become *-ft-* in *unsoffethe* 'unsought'. Initial *wh* is written *w-* in *werefore, wete* 'wheat', *wile* 'while'. Final *-th* is once written *f* in *Lambeffe* 'Lambeth'. The sound *r* was evidently lost before *-s-,* as is shown by the spellings *mosselle* 'morsel', *Ferys of Groby* = 'Ferrers'. Final *-ng* appears as *-n* in *blasyn sterre* 'comet', *hayryn* 'herring'. Interchange of *v* and *w* occurs in *wery* 'very', and *Prynce*

---

[1] The *u* in lines 27-8, *schute* is more probably from an O.E. type *sceōtan,* M.E. *schōten,* Early Mod. [shute], than a Western type with [y] for O.E. *eo.*

of Valys = 'Wales'. The Southern initial *v-* for *f-* occurs in *a valle* 'a fall'.

-t- between vowels is sometimes written *-d-*:—*radyfyde, depudyd, dalmadyke.* This records a genuine pronunciation which we later find described by writers on pronunciation, and regarded as a Cockney vulgarism. Other instances of the same process—voicing between vowels—are given (pp. 312–13). Rounding of *ă* after *v* occurs in *Syn Volantynys.*

In unstressed syllables Gregory shows the same tendency to put *i* or *y* in flexional syllables which we have noted in all the London writings of this period, and in many others as well. He also reduces vowels and diphthongs generally in this position. Thus, for M.E. *ei* in *seint* he writes *Syn* before a personal name—*Syn Lenarde, Syn John,* where the stress falls on the name. He writes *e* in the second syllable of M.E. *felow* 'fellow' in *felechype.* Unstressed syllables are sometimes lost altogether—*cytsyns* 'citizens', *unt hym* 'unto him'. French *u* or *ui* [*ȳ*] is unrounded when unstressed:—*comeners, comyners, condytte* 'conduit', *contymacy* 'contumacy'.

Turning to the Accidence, Strong Nouns either take the Pl. suffix *-ys*—*namys, howsys, eggys, treys,* &c., or merely *-s*—*strangers;* the only Wk. Pls. I have noted are *oxyn* and *schone* 'shoes'. Irregulars are *kyne* 'cows', *wemmen, bretheryn;* mutated forms—*fete, tethe.* Nouns expressing measure in time and space are frequently unaltered in the Pl.—*viij yere, iij fote, iiij fethem;* also some old Neuters—*hors, swyne, alle thynge, schippe, sheppe* 'sheep'. The Possessive Sing. of Nouns is commonly formed with the suffix *-ys*—*kyngys,* &c., or with *-s* alone—*waterberers;* another very common form in the fifteenth and sixteenth centuries, very frequent in Gregory, is the addition of the separate particle *ys* after the Noun—*Syn Edmonde ys Bury,* &c. This was doubtless the ordinary Possessive suffix in origin, but was frequently (or always) identified with the weak (unstressed) form of the Possessive Pronoun, and indeed is often written *hys, his* just as we still have it in our Prayer Book—*for Jesus Christ his sake,* &c. That this is a new formation, based upon the absolute identity in sound of the unstressed Possessive of the Pres. Pronoun (*h*)*ys,* and the Possessive suffix, is shown by such phrases—very common in all colloquial writings—as the *queene ys moder,* side by side with *the Queenys party.* In group constructions this detached *ys* is often used in the fifteenth century, and Gregory has *my lorde of Warwycke ys brother.* Note the phrase *no schoo apon no man ys fote.* When we should now inflect the group by adding the Possessive *'s* to the last word, e. g. *the Duke of Norfolk's daughter,* Gregory uses such constructions as *the dukys doughter of Northefolke,* or *the lordys wyffe Nevyle* 'Lord Nevil's wife'. The Possessive in *-ys* can be used absolutely—*a cepture in hys hond of the quenys.*

Finally, we may mention the uninflected Possessives—on which see at length pp. 316–18—which may be old Feminines such as *Mary Mavdelyn Evyn,* or old weak Pls. in *-n* as in *Alle Halowe day.* A frequent construction at this period is the expression of quantity without either inflexion or preposition between the two nouns, as *every sacke wolle,* which is like the German *ein sack wolle, ein glas wasser,* &c.

The following forms of the Pers. Pronouns may be mentioned. The Possess. Sing. of the 3rd Pers. Sing. Masc. is very commonly written *ys*

when unstressed—*the Prynce was jugge* (judge) *ys owne sylfe*, which
is the natural pronunciation to-day, and is found recorded as early as the
thirteenth century at least. The Neut. Sing. is generally *hit*. The 3rd
Pl. is Nom. *þey, they*, and the unstressed form *the*; Possess. *hir, hyr,
here*, and (rarely) *there*; the Dat. and Acc. is generally -*hem*, with the
weak form *em—ax of em that felde* (felt) *the strokys*, and, rarely, *them*.
In the Pl. of the 2nd Pers. *ye* and *you* are kept distinct, the former being
kept for the Nom., the latter for the oblique cases. The Relative Pronoun
'who' is occasionally written *hoo*, and the Dat. and Acc. *home*, showing
that *w* was not pronounced; the Gen., however, is written *whos* according
to the traditional spelling. There is in Gregory, as in several other fifteenth-
century texts, a Dat. *wham* which must be an unstressed form with early
shortening of the vowel in O.E. *hwām*. The now extinct Pl. Demonstr.
thoo 'those', fr. O.E. *þā* the Pl. of Def. Art., is frequent, also *thosse*.
The Indef. Art. is *a*, which is often used in this century and later before
words beginning with vowels—*a Englyssche squyer*. The emphatic *oon*,
and, before cons., *oo* 'a single, one', are used as in M.E. The M.E.
form *everychone* 'every one' occurs, divided *every chone*. The now
obsolete or vulgar *who som evyr* still survives.

The Pres. Sing. of Vbs. ends in -*yth*; the Pl. has commonly -*yn*,
belevyn, deputyn, folowyn, &c., occasionally -*e* as *behote* 'they promise',
and at least once -*yth(e), longythe*. The Inf. very commonly retains the
ending -*en*, or more usually -*yn—procedyn, ben, beryn, setten, settynne*, &c.,
sometimes loses the -*n* as in *to saye, to speke*, &c. The forms *answery,
ymageny* look rather like survivals of the old Southern Inf. (see p. 37 (16)).
The prefix *i*- is occasionally used both in Weak and Strong P. P.'s—
i-callyd, i-halowyde, igeve 'given', *i-knowe* 'known', &c. The ending
of the P. P. in Strong Vbs. has both -*yn* and -*e*, the latter being perhaps
more frequent—*drawe* and *drawyn, geve* and *gevyn, smete* and *smetyn,
founde* and *foundyn*, &c., &c. At least one use of the prefix *i*- occurs
in the Pret. *isong* 'sang'. The old distinction between Pret. Sing. and
Pl. seems to have vanished with the exception of *fauht* (Sing.) 'fought',
Pl. *fought*. So far as I can see, the type of the Pret. used in both Sing.
and Pl. is that of the Singular, even more generally than at the present
day, and not that of the P. P., so that Gregory and his contemporaries
use *bare, brake, bote* 'bit', and not *bore, broke, bit*, on the model of the
P. P. As regards Auxiliary and Irregular Vbs., *drust* (with metathesis)
is the Pret. of *dare*, 'shall' has *schalle* in Sing., and both *shulle* and
shalle in the Pl.; *ar* is used as well as *ben(e)* in the Pl. Pres. of 'to be';
may retains the old Pl. *mowen* as in Chaucer; the Pret. of *can* is still
couthe, the *l* not yet occurring in the spelling. The Pret. of 'to go' is
the archaic *yēde* and *yōde* (O.E. *ge-ēōde*).

A few phrases and constructions may be noted. 'On the morning of
Candlemas day' is rendered *on Candylmasday in the mornynge*, which
to us is strongly reminiscent of the Christmas carol 'There were three
ships came sailing by'.

The old habit of putting one adjective before a noun and the other
after, where used predicatively, which with us survives only in a few
fossilized phrases—'a good man and true'—is seen in *a pesabylle yere and
a plentefulle*.

H

I have gone thus into detail concerning the language of Gregory, because his Chronicle appears to be a very genuine record of how people actually spoke in the middle of the fifteenth century, more so than any other London document we possess. The picture gives rise in our minds to both kinds of surprise referred to on p. 71. We are alternately astonished at finding certain pronunciations and forms so early in use, and amazed at the survival of so many archaisms. Gregory may well be said to stand at the parting of the ways between the new and the old. In some ways he is more archaic than the classical language of Literature or of official writings, and in others he appears more modern. It is probable that the latter impression is largely due to the fact that his unstudied spelling and style reveal more of the truth regarding contemporary speech. On the other hand, it must be remembered that he represents a social class different from any we have hitherto examined except the Celys, who are definitely provincials. It is often urged as a merit of popular and dialect speech at the present day by its votaries, that it is more conservative of ancient forms than Received Standard English, but this is a one-sided view. Vulgar, popular, and Regional speech may each and all preserve certain ancient features which Good English has lost, but that is not the whole truth. They have also lost other features which the latter has preserved. The fact is that innovations are found in all forms of English, but they are not the same innovations; all forms of English likewise preserve certain old features, but they have not all preserved the same features. Gregory's value for us is none the less that he is the chief example, in the fifteenth century, of the Middle Class English of the capital. Doubtless the 'redoubted princess' who found fault with Caxton's parts of speech would have been equally down on Gregory; but whereas Caxton 'amended' his English, Gregory did not, for which we may be duly thankful. Caxton's English is a less true picture of the speech of his time than Gregory's because he slavishly copied the scribes, and apparently the scribes of an earlier day than his own. The result is that Caxton is in many important respects farther from the Spoken English of to-day than Gregory. Many of the latter's vulgarisms have become current even in the politest form of English, while much of Caxton's 'correctness' was obsolete in his own day in any form of English whatsoever.

We have now surveyed Literary English and London English from Chaucer to Skelton, and have glanced at some of the provincial forms during the same period.

We may draw this long chapter to a close with an attempt to summarize the main general results which emerge from our examination.

Already fairly early in the century, it is evident from the occasional spellings of the less conventional writers that the Middle English accented vowels have started upon that series of changes which has led to our present-day pronunciation. The vowels of unstressed syllables have been still further 'reduced' since the weakenings which took place in Late O.E. and Early Middle English. We notice, on the one hand, a variety of tentative methods of expressing these vowels, which points at least to an obscuration of the earlier sound, and on the other a certain consistency, which points to 'reduction' in a definite direction.

Certain typical Modern alterations in the pronunciation of consonants
are observable.   Turning to the question of Regional dialect and the
Standard Language, it is clear from many indications that Regional
dialect was still spoken, more or less by all classes.   In the written
language, we find an extended use of the London dialect in both private
and official documents ; but during the first three quarters of the century
at least, the local and natural dialect of the writer breaks out here and
there, in documents which conform on the whole to the London type.

On the other hand, there is room for surprise that a quarter of a century
before the introduction of printing, the Devonian Shillingford should
allow his native speech to show itself so little in his letters, while the
other and more important Devonian Sir John Fortescue has broken
away completely from Regional dialect.   In the early part of the
century several works of Literature proper, both in prose and verse,
preserve with very fair consistency the Regional dialect of the writers.

As regards the character of the London dialect, fast becoming the
recognized vehicle for all English which was written down, the South-
Eastern, and especially the E. Midland, elements gain an increasing
ascendancy, though many typically Southern features, or scattered forms
derived from the purely Southern type of English, still linger.   It seems
that we can distinguish among the documents written in London at
least two types of dialect—an Easterly and a more Southerly type.   It
is evident that both types were accepted and recognized in the speech of
London itself, and poets (e. g. Skelton) found it convenient to avail themselves of a latitude in the distribution of forms from both of these types,
fully as great as that enjoyed by Chaucer.   This latitude makes it
difficult to assert that a given form which is clearly E. Midland in origin
was not current in some type of London speech, and it is probable that
few of the typical Easternisms which we find in Lydgate would strike
a Londoner of the period as strange.

Thus the precise Regional dialect constituents of London English were
not finally fixed in their present proportion and distribution during the
fifteenth century, nor indeed for some time after the beginning of the
following century.

As regards social dialect, while it is pretty certain that an upper and
a lower class type of English were recognized, it is very difficult to be
sure exactly where to draw the line.   Some of the peculiarities of Gregory's
English are undoubtedly described as London vulgarisms at a later date,
but we cannot be quite sure that they were so felt at the time in which
he wrote, since most, if not all of them, can be paralleled from the
writings of persons far more highly placed than he.   It may be said,
however, that in Gregory we have a combination of peculiarities, which
probably do not occur in the same mass, and with the same frequency,
in writers of higher social status.   The letters of Edmond de la Pole
are not a fair sample of the speech of the higher English Nobility of his
age, since they produce the impression of being written not only by a
very ignorant man, but by one who has largely forgotten his native
tongue, at any rate any decent method of putting it down on paper.

Finally, we recognize the unsettled state of Literary and Standard
Spoken English in the curious individualism which makes it necessary

to describe the peculiarities of so many separate writers.   It is this, more than anything else, which makes us hesitate to claim for this century the existence of a definite Standard of Speech, or to say definitely where it is to be found.   It would be interesting to know whether the conception of vulgarism in speech already existed, and if so, what particular vagaries were brought under this head, and by whom.   No doubt there was a certain standard of 'correctness', but this is quite different from the existence of an upper class dialect as distinct from a lower.   We have quoted the rather vague statement of Caxton concerning the opinion which the Duchess of Burgundy took of his English, and have indicated that we may here have a hint of a social differentiation of speech, but this is quite uncertain.   We have to wait till the following century for more definite evidence.   After all, Gregory is our best hope if we ever expect to establish the existence of Class dialect at this period, meaning by the term a variety of London English, which may indeed have been partly Regional in origin, but which had come to be felt as an inferior variant of the language in vogue at the Court.

CHAPTER IV

THE ENGLISH LANGUAGE FROM HENRY VIII
TO JAMES I

THE sixteenth century is memorable for the student of the history of the language, not least, among many other reasons, because he now finds for the first time undoubted evidence, in specific statement, of the existence of a standard of speech. The dialect of the Court is definitely stated to be the 'best' form of English, the one to be acquired, and as far as possible to be used in the writing of poetry, that is, for the highest possible purpose to which language can be put.

During this century, too, English people began to think and write about their native language as a vehicle for literary creation. They discussed at great length such questions as the fitness of English to be used for poetry; the proper kind of vocabulary for a writer to use—whether 'old and homely' native terms, or words derived from Latin—they discoursed much, and often tediously, upon the principles of English prosody; they tried many experiments, some fortunate, such as those of Wyatt and Tusser, some dismal failures, such as those of Phaer or Stanyhurst, and some other 'painful furtherers of learning'; they thought much of prose style and played some strange pranks therewith; they tried hard to amend and fix English spelling, and practically succeeded in the latter effort; lastly, they examined and attempted to describe the sounds of English speech.

The accounts of English pronunciation which begin in this century open a new chapter in our investigations of the past history of our language, and one which from this time onward has to be taken into account. For the present writer it is a question open to discussion, though many will think this an impiety, whether this new source of information has not been rather a curse than a blessing to English Philology, and whether we have not been bamboozled for the last thirty or forty years by these early writers on English pronunciation, into all sorts of wrong ideas. But of this more later.

We have said that definite references exist to a standard of English speech, to varieties, one of which is the best, while the others are to be avoided; but this is not all, for it is distinctly suggested that there exist, and are recognized, not only Regional, but also Social varieties. And we are not left with mere statements of this fact; we have a long document, the Diary of Henry Machyn, which is of priceless value in that it enshrines, not a counterfeit presentment, such as we might find in comedies, of lower class speech, but the genuine thing, naturally and unconsciously set down by a man who is obviously putting his own English on paper. We are fortunate in possessing many familiar letters of the sixteenth century, which give a picture of colloquial speech so far as this is possible in a written document, but none is perhaps so individual, or so abundant in revelations of the habits of speech of the writer and his class, as Machyn's Diary. It is true that many, perhaps most of the occasional spellings which we find so instructive in the writings of the diarist, can be matched from the letters of this period of persons of far higher rank, but the most characteristic peculiarities occur nowhere else so frequently, and some are not found at all among persons of more refinement and breeding. At any rate, the cumulative effect is considerable, and leaves the impression of a distinct social dialect. We have plenty of material from which to establish a comparison—letters from Henry VIII, Edward VI, Queens Mary and Elizabeth; from great nobles such as Norfolk and Somerset; from statesmen like Cromwell and Burghley; ecclesiastics such as Wolsey, Latimer, Cranmer, Warham, Lee, and many others; from courtier scholars like More, Ascham, and Sir Thomas Smith; from great merchants and men of affairs like Gresham; from admirals and soldiers whose very names are enough to make any age illustrious, and whose deeds are among the chief glories of our race, such as Howard and Drake, Sydney and Raleigh. All these famous persons reveal in their letters certain individualities of origin, while conforming, in the main features, to the common well-bred English of the time. They all had opportunities, in varying degree it is true, of acquiring the Court form of English of their age, and many of their varieties are due, doubtless, to the different native dialects upon which the Court English was grafted. Machyn, however, is in a class apart; his English is almost as different from that of the Courtiers as is the dialect of Robert of Brunne from that of Trevisa.

To come to closer quarters, we may ask, What are the chief general characteristics of sixteenth-century English?

The first point to be mentioned is that Regional dialect disappears completely from the written language of the South and Midlands; both from Literature proper, and from private letters and documents. We shall look in vain in poetry for such distinctive Regional character as we saw in Bokenam in the preceding century, or in private letters, for even such slight traces of Regional influence as we found in Shillingford's letters. We are able at most to point here and there to a feature—generally connected with grammatical forms—which we may attribute to the writer's native county.

On the other hand, while the literary dialect is in a fair way to being fixed, and while in private documents which reflect more faithfully the colloquial conditions, and in works of literature, both prose and verse, where the language is more studied and deliberate, considerable, though by no means absolute, uniformity in the distribution of dialect elements is found, we discover a host of those revealing occasional spellings which, as we saw, were fairly common in the fifteenth-century documents.

Evidence of the sort which we exhibited in the previous chapter, for the occurrence of certain sound changes in the fifteenth century, is confirmed abundantly, and is much larger in quantity in the age of Henry VIII and Elizabeth. Almost every private letter, and many literary works, contain a certain number of spellings which throw light upon pronunciation, and it is evident that even at the Court such tendencies as that which added an 'excrescent' consonant at the end of words, e. g. *for the nonnest* ' nonce ', *orphant* ' orphan ', *vilde* ' vile ', and so on, were certainly current among all speakers, from Queen Elizabeth herself downwards. It is rather important to point out that the same variety of spellings, by which is meant spellings which throw light on actual pronunciation, the same kind of fluctuation in the distribution of dialect types, and the same diversity in grammatical forms are found in printed books, whether prose or poetry, and that in the works by the most accomplished writers, as are to be noted in private, familiar, and more or less hastily written letters. We might attribute these 'slips' in the latter class of documents to the carelessness of individual writers, but when the same kind of 'slip' occurs again and again in letters written by very different kinds of persons, we are bound to infer that these 'slips' in writing represent realities in uttered speech, and linguistic habits that were very widespread. When we further meet with the same peculiarities, both in spelling and in grammatical forms, again and again in printed books, we must be convinced that the literary language is not a phenomenon apart, having an existence independent of the spoken language, but that the former is in very deed identical with the latter, and reflects its various and changing character.

This intimate relation between the highest type of colloquial English and the English of literature cannot be too strongly insisted upon. The ' tongue which Shakespeare spake ' was the tongue which he wrote ; the makers of Elizabethan English as we know it in the imperishable literature of the period, were the men, illustrious and obscure, who were also making English history, that is, who were living and fighting ; sailing strange seas, and discovering new worlds ; ruffling at Court, or deliberating in the councils of Church and of the State ; conferring and negotiating abroad with princes and prelates, and often, at the last, going ' darkling down the torrent of their fate ', and dying joyfully and gaily, like Christian gentlemen, on the battle-field or 'the deck, which was their field of fame ', or, by some strange reverse of fortune, by a no less splendid death upon the scaffold or at the stake.

This unity of the colloquial language and the language of literature will be illustrated later on, but as immediate proof that features which we should now consider ' vulgarisms ', or too slipshod even for colloquial use, were in the sixteenth century current in Court English, and that they find their way into works of first-rate literary importance, we may mention that such features occur in Lord Berners' translation of Froissart, in Sir Thos. Elyot's *Gouernour*, in Bp. Latimer's Sermons before Edward VI, in Edward VI's First Prayer Book, in the works of Roger Ascham, in Lyly, both in his dramas and in *Euphues*, that model of propriety in language, and in the First Folio of Shakespeare. These are the works of only a few writers from among the many that might be mentioned, but between them they cover practically the whole of the sixteenth century, and the authors must all be assumed to have been conversant with the English of the Court. These writers were all scholars as well as courtiers, but they are no less prone to introduce into their books, colloquialisms of the type of *sarmont* and *orphant*, and many others, than are the less bookish admirals and men of business of the period to put these things into their private letters.

It is thus clear that the standards of refinement which in a later day forbade such forms to speech and writing alike, were unknown to some of the best scholars well acquainted, between them, with the standards of speech at every Court from Henry VIII to Elizabeth.

The English of the sixteenth century, both in the printed works and in private letters, still shows considerable dialectal individualism. The Standard, as we have said, is not yet completely fixed. While the more pronounced features of Regional dialect are absent, there remains considerable variety of usage among writers belonging approximately to the same social stratum. Since this variety is found both in published works of Literature and in private correspondence, we are entitled to argue that a rather large degree of latitude existed in the Standard Spoken English of the period, and that if we assume that the unstudied language of private letters gives a true picture of the actual speech of the writers, the variety in forms found in literary works is also an indication of the variety existing in speech, since the kind of variety found in Literary English is identical with that found in the private letters. When we are able to compare the private letters with the literary compositions of the same writer, as for instance is possible in the case of Queen Elizabeth herself, we find that the distinctive features are the same in both. This circumstance is a further proof of the identity of the English of Literature with the Spoken Standard of the Court. Considerable latitude of usage, we have said, is tolerated in both, and the same kind of latitude. We shall later study in more detail, the variety upon which we are insisting, but we may briefly indicate some of the points at once.

First, there are different types of pronunciation in the same words :— e.g. *bisie, besie*; *than* and *then*; *whan* and *when*; *geve* and *giv(e)*; *sowne* and *sound*; *bankette* and *banquet*; *fader* and *father*; *moder* and *mother*; *stop* and *stap*; *hott, hoate*, and *whot* 'hot'; which spellings show (1) a pronunciation similar to that of the present day, (2) one with a long vowel, (3) one with a short vowel but with an initial *w* or *wh*; *one* (pronounced as now in *on*-ly); *wone* (pronounced, as *one* is now, with an initial *w*-); *othe* and *wothe*; *other* and *wother*; *earth* and *yearth*. Finally, we may mention the remarkable variety in the distribution of -*er*- and -*ar*- forms in *hert* and *hart*, *service* and *sarvice*, *swerve* and *swarve*, *ferm* and *farm*, and all the other words of this group.

In the realm of accidence, we begin with Nouns. Weak Pls. occur by the side of the more usual Strong Pls. (and that in writers like Wilson and Ascham), e. g. *housen* for *houses*, *peason* for *peas*, *shoon* for *shoes*, *sisterne* by the side of the more usual *sisters*. In Possessives of words ending in -*f* we often find *v* before the suffix, as in the Pl., e. g. *wolves, wives*, by the side of forms with *f* as at present—*my wife's father*, &c. It is still permissible to use the old uninflected Possessive of Feminine Nouns :— *the Scotish Quene lettres* (Lord Burghley); *my ladye Elizabethe grace*, but *my ladye Maryes grace* (both in Latimer).

The Neuter Pronoun is still written *hit* as well as *it*. The Indefinite Article occurs without the final -*n* before vowels—*a opinion*, &c.

The 3rd Pers. Sing. Pres. of Verbs ends in -*s* in some writers, with considerable frequency, at a point in the century when others use it but rarely, and others not at all.

These are but a few samples of variety taken from a large number, but they are enough to establish our point.

It is evident that these differences of usage are more considerable in character than those at present tolerated in Received Standard Spoken English, while in written English, except in poetry, there is now practically no latitude of this kind at all.

If we consider the possible variations in pronunciation which would pass muster at the present day in Received Standard, we shall find that they are very few in number.   They consist chiefly in a few classes of words which admit of two types, such as [kɔf, kɔ̄f] 'cough', [puə, pō] 'poor', &c.

The deduction from the above is that in the sixteenth century the relation between Standard Spoken and Literary English was more intimate than at present, and that the greater allowable latitude of usage which existed in the former was reflected in the latter.   While we insist upon the existence of a standard of speech at least as early as Henry VIII, and probably earlier (see p. 5 above), it is not suggested that this had anything like the currency which Received Standard has at the present day, nor can the general diffusion of this among the higher classes be assumed much before the end of the eighteenth century.

In the sixteenth century there is good reason for thinking that the Standard was practically confined to those persons who frequented the Court, or who came directly or indirectly under the influence of Court speech.   The various Regional dialects, more or less modified doubtless by the habits in vogue at Court, as these filtered through the Universities, and some of the clergy, were still spoken by all classes in country districts. That many members of the country squire class still spoke Regional dialect well into the eighteenth century, and, in isolated instances, much later, is evident from various sources. (See, however, pp. 163, 166–7, below.) Puttenham, or whoever wrote *The Arte of English Poesie* (1580), recommends as the best type of English 'the vsual speach of the Court, and that of London and the shires lying about London within IX myles and not much aboue'. He remarks that 'Northern-men . . . whether they be noblemen or gentlemen, or of their best clarkes', use a type of English which is 'not so Courtly nor so currant as our Southerne English is'.   That is to say, the upper classes, and educated persons generally, in the provinces, do not speak Standard English, but their own Regional dialect.   It is recorded that Sir Walter Raleigh spoke with a strong Devonshire accent.

Already in the reign of Henry VIII people paid attention to the 'proper' pronunciation of English, and we find Palsgrave (1530 and 1532) (see p. 198, below) referring with disapproval to a current pronunciation of the old short ă, other than the 'true' one.   In a letter to 'his right honorable maister Mr. Thomas Crumwell chief Secretary vnto the Kings Maiestie', Henry Dowes, the tutor of Gregory Cromwell, reports concerning that young gentleman's education, and refers to a certain Mr. Southwell 'dailie heringe hime to reade sumwhatt in thenglishe tongue, and advertisenge hime of the naturell and true kynde of pronuntiacon thereof'.   Now this talk of 'true pronunciation' as distinct from some other kind, is a new thing in English, and implies a definite recognition of a Standard form.

Sir Thomas Elyot writes in his *Gouernour* :—

Hit shall be expedient that a noblemanes sonne in his infancie, haue with hym continually onely suche as may accustome hym by litle and litle to speake pure and elegant latin. Semblably the nourishes and other women aboute hym, if it be possible, to do the same; or, at the leste way that they speke none englisshe but that which is cleane, polite, perfectly and articulately pronounced, omittinge no lettre or sillable, as folisshe women oftentimes do of a wantonnesse, wherby diuers noble men and gentilmennes chyldren, (as I do at this daye knowe) haue attained corrupte and foule pronuntiation.

It is characteristic of Henry VIII and of his children that they loved learning and that their Courts were the resort of scholars. Henry, whose most absorbing interests were matrimony and theology, was himself no mean scholar. Writing in 1550, Ascham says of King Edward VI (I use Giles's translation of the Latin, see Ascham's *Works*, vol. i, pp. lxii and lxiii), 'Our illustrious King Edward surpasses all men, as well as his own years, and every one's expectations, in talent, industry, perseverance, and learning'. Of Princess Elizabeth, then sixteen years of age, he says in the same letter—'There are many honourable ladies now who surpass Thomas More's daughters in all kinds of learning, but among all of them the brightest star is my illustrious Lady Elizabeth the King's sister: ... she had me for her tutor in Greek and Latin for two years. ... She talks French and Italian as well as English; she has often talked with me readily and well in Latin, and moderately so in Greek. When she writes Greek and Latin, nothing is more beautiful than her handwriting', and so on. In view of Elizabeth's later tastes in dress, it is interesting to find Ascham saying, 'In adornment she is elegant rather than showy, and by her contempt of gold and head-dresses, she reminds one of Hippolite rather than of Phædra'. Ascham's account, in his *Scholemaster*, of his visit to Lady Jane Grey at Leicester is well known, but a briefer reference to this event occurs in a letter to Sturm in 1550. 'I found the noble damsel—Oh ye gods!—reading Plato's Phædo in Greek, and so thoroughly understanding it, that she caused me the greatest astonishment' (Giles, vol. i, p. lxxi). In the same letter he refers to another learned lady, Mildred, daughter of Antony Cook (or Coke) and wife of William Cecil, who, he says, 'understands and talks Greek as well as English'.

Harrison, in his *Description of England*, says of Elizabeth's Court: 'The stranger that entereth in the court of England upon the sudden, shall rather imagine himselfe to come into some publike schoole of the universities, where manie giue eare to one that readeth, than into a princes palace, if you conferre the same with those of other nations.' Holinshed, Vol. I, p. 196, Ed. of 1586.

It is remarkable what a number of those who under the Tudors held great offices of State, were employed in some more or less responsible position about the Court, or who were sent on embassies abroad, were also distinguished in learning and literature. The gentle, saintly, and learned Sir Thomas More (1478–1535), the author of *Utopia*, was a successful barrister, a member of Parliament; he served on various embassies abroad, was Speaker of the House of Commons, and Lord Chancellor of England. John Bourchier, second Baron Berners (1467–1533), who in his noble translation of Froissart approaches nearer than any other writer of his age to the grand style in prose, was a soldier, a diplomatist, and Chancellor of the Exchequer; he accompanied Henry at the Field of the Cloth of Gold. Sir Thomas Elyot (c. 1499–1546), author of the *Gouernour*, and friend of More, was Clerk to the Privy Council, M.P. for Cambridge, and was sent as ambassador to Charles V. Roger Ascham (1515–68), whose name is best remembered by his *Toxophilus*, a treatise on archery, and by the *Scholemaster*, after being for many years a Cambridge don, was appointed tutor to Princess Elizabeth, was secretary to the English Ambassador to Charles V, Latin secretary to Queen Mary, and later on secretary to Queen Elizabeth. Sir John Cheke (1514–57), who very literally 'taught Cambridge and King Edward Greek', since he was Professor of that language in the University, and tutor to Edward VI, was Clerk of the Privy Council and a Secretary of State. Thomas Wilson (1525–81), author of the *Arte of Rhetorique* and the *Rule of Reason*, a writer of pure and unaffected English prose, was M.P., served on several foreign missions, and was a Secretary of State. Sir Thomas Smith (1513–77), author, in Latin, of a treatise *De Recta et Emendata Linguae Anglicae Scriptione Dialogus*, and, in English, of an admirable account of the English Constitution, *De Republica Anglorum*, was Regius Professor of Civil Law at Cambridge, Vice-Chancellor of the University, and Provost of Eton, was employed on foreign missions, and was ambassador in France in 1562. He left several entertaining private letters concerning his experiences abroad. Lastly, in considering the roll of scholar-statesmen, we may recall that Francis Bacon, Lord Verulam (1561–1626), was M.P. for Liverpool and other boroughs, was Attorney-General, Lord Keeper, and Lord Chancellor of England.

But if the number of scholars and authors who took an active part in politics and the affairs of State is large, no less striking is the roll of those who, being of high birth, and courtiers, politicians, or soldiers by tradition and circumstances, also cultivated literature with enthusiasm and often with distinction. Of these it is sufficient to mention a few. Henry Howard, Earl of Surrey (c. 1517–47), one of the chief contributors to Tottel's Miscellany of *Songes and Sonnettes* (1557), the translator of Books II and III of the *Aeneid* into blank verse, which does not, it is true, strike a very high poetic note :—

> They whisted all, with fixed face attent,
> When prince Æneas from the royal seat
> Thus gan to speak: O Queen, it is thy will
> I should renew a woe cannot be told,

and so on. Surrey wrote many poems besides those in Tottel, including paraphrases of Scripture and love poems, but his chief claim to be remembered as an author rests upon his introduction (along with Wyatt) of the sonnet into English. Perhaps the sonnet of Surrey's best worth remembering is that beginning :—

> The soote season that bud and blome furth bringes.

Like the work of nearly all the poets of the late fifteenth and early sixteenth century many of Surrey's lines appear to halt through uncertainty of accentuation, and of the number of syllables. The above line, for instance, requires the accent to be placed upon the second syllable of *season*, and, in the same sonnet, the line—*The swift swalow pursueth the flyes smale*, requires a strong stress on the second syllable of *swalow*, needs that *pursueth* should have only two syllables, and that in *flyes* the flexional syllable (long lost in natural speech) should be pronounced.

Such apparent anomalies are no doubt due to the fact that poets were torn between the old M.E. tradition of Chaucer, which preserved the unstressed flexional endings as separate syllables and often accented words like *nature, sesoun,* after the French method, upon the second syllable, and the modern colloquial usage in which the English manner of accentuation, upon the first syllable, was rapidly becoming the exclusive method, while the endings *-ed, -es,* &c., except in certain specific circumstances, as at present had lost the vowel, and were no longer pronounced as separate syllables. There is reason to think that *-es,* the Possessive of Nouns, survived longer as a separate syllable than the same ending as a Plural (see pp. 314–15, 319, below).

This accomplished and gallant gentleman fell a victim to the jealousy of 'that majestic lord', Henry VIII. His romantic and unfortunate love for the fair Geraldine inspired Scott with one of his most moving ballads, while his genius, his valour, and his misfortunes called forth from the chivalrous poet that noble tribute which few now will care to challenge :—

> The gentle Surrey loved his lyre—
> Who has not heard of Surrey's fame?
> His was the hero's soul of fire,
> And his the bard's immortal name,
> And his was love, exalted high
> By all the glow of chivalry.

Sir Thomas Wyatt (1503–42), the reputed lover of Anne Boleyn, also contributed to Tottel many love poems. To him perhaps belongs, rather than to Surrey, the honour of having written actually the first English sonnet, but he will be longest remembered by the lovely little song *The louer complayneth the vnkindnes of his loue,* of which we may quote the best verses, that is, the first and the three last :—

> My lute awake performe the last
> Labour that thou and I shall waste;
> And end that I haue now begonne :
> And when this song is song and past :
> My lute be styll for I haue done.

> .   .   .   .

> May chance thee lie witherd and olde,
> In winter nightes that are so colde,
> Playning in vaine vnto the mone :
> Thy wishes then dare not be tolde.
> Care then who lest, for I haue done.

And then may chance thee to repent
The time that thou hast lost and spent
To cause thy louers sigh and swowne.
Then shalt thou know beaute but lent,
And wish and want as I haue done.

Now cease my lute this is the last
Labour that thou and I shall wast,
And ended is that we begonne.
Now is this song both song and past,
My lute be still for I haue done.

Thomas Sackville, Lord Buckhurst and first Earl of Dorset (1536–1608), a cousin of Anne Boleyn, and the ancestor of the Dukes of Dorset, among many other offices, was M.P. before being raised to the peerage, a privy councillor, an ambassador, a commissioner at State trials, and to him fell the duty of announcing the death sentence to Mary Queen of Scots. He planned a great work, *The Mirour for Magistrates*, the object of which was to show ' by examples passed in this Realme, with how greevous plagues Vices are punished in great Princes and Magistrates, and how frayle and unstable worldly prosperitie is found, where Fortune seemeth most highly to favour', of which, unfortunately, he only had leisure to write the Introduction, or, as he calls it, the *Induction*, and the Complaint of the Duke of Buckingham. The work shows genuine poetic feeling and a fine facility for verse, as may be judged from the single stanza here quoted :

And sorrowing I to see the summer flowers,
The lively green, the lusty leas forlorn,
The sturdy trees so shattered with the showers,
The fields so fade that flourish'd so beforn,
It taught me well, all earthly things be born
To die the death, for nought long time may last;
The summer's beauty yields to winter's blast.

Sackville's position in the history of English literature is chiefly due, however, to his being the part author of *Gorboduc*, the first English tragedy in blank verse, which was acted in 1561. Of this work it may be said that the last two acts, which critics attribute to Sackville, have considerably more poetic quality than the earlier ones by Thomas Norton ; the diction of the former is in the grand manner, and the ideas and images both noble and striking. The verse, however, though generally musical enough, has an air of strangeness, as of a first attempt, and rather suggests to the ear the effect of couplets with the rhymes left out.

Of all the brilliant and memorable figures which made illustrious the age of Elizabeth, none is more romantic and attaching than that of the accomplished, the gallant, the chivalrous Sir Philip Sidney, whose name, indeed, and the splendid qualities of character and genius of which it has become the symbol, would lend a special dignity to any age and any country.

Of all the writers of his class, traditions, and habitual occupations, his contribution to literature is, with the exception of Sir Walter Raleigh's, the most considerable in extent, and it is certainly among the most remarkable in quality. His *Defense of Poesie* is a classic, though, as Mr. Gosse excellently says, it ' labours under but one disadvantage, namely, that when it was composed in 1581, there was scarcely any poesy in England to be defended'.   His gigantic, and to us perhaps somewhat tedious, pageantries of poems, *Astrophel and Stella*, and those in the *Arcadia*, are nevertheless remarkable in the variety of their experiments in metre, and remain gorgeous, if somewhat unwieldy, relics of an age when even courtiers and captains took poetry seriously.   Sidney's poetical industry was untiring—he was indeed, as he says, ' admitted into the company of the paper-blurrers '—he attained a wonderful mastery of technique, and if none of his sonnets are among the best in the language, there is certainly no other writer, outside the great masters, who has produced so many of such a high degree of excellence.   But Sidney is, above all things, a great English gentleman—' I say that my chiefest honour is to be a Dudley '—and our immediate point is that being this, and all that it implied in his age, he loved poetry and practised it assiduously.   Were it only for the manner of his death it would be ' vain to praise, and useless to blame him '.

Nor had ' the noble and valorous Sir Walter Raleigh ', as Spenser calls him, a career less romantic and picturesque than Sidney's, though less happy in the manner of his death.   As a writer he was far more voluminous.   The son of a Devonshire gentleman, born about 1552, he was at Oriel College, sailed with his half-brother, the famous Sir Humphrey Gilbert, was at Court, in high favour with the Queen, from whom he obtained several grants of land, married Elizabeth Throckmorton, went in search of treasure in the New World and failed to find it, fought at Cadiz and at the Azores with distinction, was tried for high treason under James I, found guilty on the flimsiest evidence, sentenced to death with all the hideous circumstances associated at that time with such a sentence and such a crime ; was reprieved, and after living for thirteen years with his wife, in the Tower, was at last set free.   His insatiable spirit of adventure led him once more to make a voyage to Orinoco, lured by dreams of fabulous wealth to be found in the mines of El Dorado.   This expedition was equipped by Raleigh himself, who realized all his own and his wife's property for the purpose.   It was largely manned by gentlemen adventurers, most of whom were Sir Walter's kinsmen. Disaster by storm and sickness dogged his steps, and while he was ill from fever his captain, Kemis, to whom the command of the expedition passed, destroyed the Spanish settlement of San Tome, thus breaking Raleigh's solemn agreement with James to engage in no hostilities with the Spaniards.   In this assault, his eldest son ' having ', as he says, ' more desire of honor then of safety was slaine, with whome (to say the truth) all respect of the world hath taken end in me '.   After this the crews became demoralized and there was nothing for it but to return to England.   He was soon arrested ; he had failed to find the treasure, and he had, through his lieutenant's action, broken faith.   After spending a short period in the Tower, the once gay and splendid Raleigh died on the scaffold by virtue of his former sentence, in 1618.

Raleigh left some poems of great merit, though many have been lost ; among those which survive a few may be recalled : the fine sonnet beginning *Methought I saw the grave where Laura lay*, and the *Farewell*, a poem of thirteen verses, of which the first runs—

> Go, soul, the body's guest
> Upon a thankless errand;
> Fear not to touch the best;
> The truth shall be thy warrant.
> Go, since I needs must die,
> And give them all the lie.

Equally memorable is the short poem supposed to have been written on the night before his execution :—

> Even such is time that takes on trust
> Our youth, our joys, our all we have,
> And pays us but with age and dust;
> Who in the dark and silent grave,
> When we have wandered all our ways,
> Shuts up the story of our days!
> But from this earth, this grave, this dust,
> My God shall raise me up I trust.

These, if indeed they are by Raleigh, show the touch of a true poet and craftsman.

But Raleigh is chiefly known to us as a writer of prose, and of this he was a consummate master. Besides the ambitious *History of the World*, which occupies six large volumes in the Oxford Edition of Raleigh's works of 1829, Sir Walter wrote many other essays upon historical, political, constitutional, and geographical subjects, as well as a *Discourse upon the invention of ships*, and *Observations on the Navy and Sea Service*.

We cannot forbear giving a short example of his prose style. The magnificent passage ' O eloquent, just, and mighty Death !' which closes the *History of the World*, is commonly quoted and well known. We select, therefore, from that most fascinating of travellers' tales, the *Discovery of Guiana*, a passage in a very different key.

' That cassique that was a stranger had his wife staying at the port where we anchored; and in all my life I have seldom seen a better favoured woman : she was of good stature, with black eyes, fat of body, of an excellent countenence, her hair almost as long as herself, tied up again in pretty knots; and it seemed she stood not in that awe of her husband as the rest ; for she spake and discoursed, and drank among the gentlemen and captains, and was very pleasant, knowing her own comeliness, and taking great pride therein. I have seen a lady in England so like her, as but for the difference of colour I would have sworn might have been the same.'

Aubrey said of Raleigh that he was ' a tall, handsome, and bold man, but damnable proud '. The same authority states that he heard from Sir Thomas Malet, one of the justices of the King's Bench, who had known Sir Walter, ' that notwithstanding his so great mastership in style, and his conversation with the learnedest and politest persons, yet he spoke broad Devonshire to his dyeing day. His voice was small, as likewise were my schoolfellows his gr. nephews.'

Such were some of the figures that distinguished the Court of Elizabeth and her immediate predecessors. They have been dwelt upon here thus far because the intimate union of learning and literature with action, in the field, upon the high seas, or in the council chamber, is of vital importance for our present study. The Greek professor in the University is no musty pedant living immersed in books and remote from life. He stands before kings and is not ashamed ; he conducts delicate negotiations at his own and in foreign Courts. The professor of Civil Law knows at first hand the working of the Law which he expounds, he is in touch with living problems of the constitution, and sees history and legislation in the making. He must cultivate those graces of manner and speech which alone can commend learning to the truly discerning and polite. On the other hand, the courtier, and the statesman by profession, the gallant soldier, and the adventurous sea-rover, are not mere fops, cut-throats, or quarter-deck desperadoes. They can turn a sonnet as easily as a compliment, they discuss a trope as eagerly as a treaty, they play pranks with metres with as much zest as with the Spaniards ; the future of Poesie interests them as keenly as the fate of nations, and they handle a pen as deftly as they do the lance or the tiller. Literature is not the property of a tribe of helots living in obscure corners and speaking a strange jargon, but the common heritage and patrimony of those who are living and doing, and who speak a tongue that all men use. The scholar and the great writer appeal not merely to a few choice souls in garrets or in pothouses ; they know that the men of action, who are themselves writers, will hear them, understand their ' great language ' and cherish it ; for are not these same men of action also craftsmen and explorers, not in strange lands and seas only, but in prose and verse as well ?

Ascham can write to Sir William Cecil in 1548 : 'I hope you will devote some of your time to cultivate the English tongue, so that men might understand that even our language allows a man to write in it with beauty and eloquence.' To what purpose the writing of English was cultivated by several of Cecil's sort we know. It is not without significance that Ascham was reputed to be addicted to cock fighting, which he says is ' of all kinds of pastime, fit for a gentleman'. Here was the kind of man whom a gentleman might trust in graver matters !

Now it is not for nothing that matters stood thus between the men of letters and the courtiers and explorers in the age when Literary English was being made, or rather, let us say, when English speech was being put to new uses, and made to express in all its fullness the amazing life of a wonderful age, with all its fresh experiences, thoughts, and dreams.

If any one doubts whether the language of Elizabethan literature was actually identical with that of everyday life, or whether it was not rather an artful concoction, divorced from the real life of the age, let him, after reading something of the lives and opinions of a few of the great men we have briefly referred to, ask himself whether the picture of Ascham, Wilson, Sidney, or Raleigh posturing and mouthing like the Della Cruscans of a later age, is a conceivable one.

Better still, let him compare the colloquial language of the sixteenth century, as it is found in the private letters of men and women of all ranks and occupations, with that of the works of literature of the same period. The more the colloquial and literary types of the sixteenth century are studied side by side, the more clearly does the essential unity of the language appear.

When we consider the various kinds of eminence collected together at

Queen Elizabeth's Court, the mental and literary attainments of many of the foremost men, and the general standard of taste and refinement among the courtiers of that age, we shall assert that the English which they spoke was not merely reputed the best type, but that it actually was the best attainable. We shall not assent to the view that certain habits in this politest form of Elizabethan speech, the outcome of natural linguistic tendencies, which are different from those now prevalent among the best speakers, are 'slipshod', merely because a later age, wishing to be more 'correct', has discarded them. If the speech of the great men we have been considering was unaffected and natural, it certainly was not vulgar. If it be vulgar to say *whot* for *hot*, *stap* for *stop*, *offen* for *often*, *sarvice* for *service*, *venter* for *venture*; if it be slipshod to say *Wensday* for *Wednesday*, *beseechin* for *beseeching*, *stricly* for *strictly*, *sounded* for *swooned*, *attemps* for *attempts*, and so on; then it is certain that the Queen herself, and the greater part of her Court, must plead guilty to these imputations in some or all of the above instances. The absurdity of such a contention is manifest, and it will not be seriously made by those who are properly informed of the facts.

Before we examine in some detail the peculiarities in the writings of some typical authors of this age, there are one or two general questions which fall to be discussed.

We have seen that the language of the Court was recognized by Puttenham as the best type of spoken English, and that that type is also recommended for the use of writers. We have contended in the foregoing pages that the colloquial Court English was as a matter of fact used by writers, whether learnt from books or by actual personal experience and usage. The existence of a Standard, both in speaking and writing, and that the same Standard, has been assumed as established beyond cavil. This Standard was used, as far as possible, in writing, even by those who did not conform to it in speech. The more opportunities the writer had for being acquainted with Court English the nearer was the English of his literary works to that Standard. The individualism in spelling which still to a certain extent prevailed in the sixteenth century, enables us to collect from written works, to a far higher degree than at present, the individual habits of speech which the writer possessed. The result of an examination of the writings, both private and published, of this age, from this point of view, is that we see that there existed there a greater degree of variety in speech—both in pronunciation and in grammatical forms—than exists now. Such variety is found among persons of the same kind of education and social standing, possessing equal opportunities of hearing and using the Court dialect. This shows that Court English was by no means so uniform as present-day Received Standard, and, since the relation between a man's mode of speech and his manner of writing was extremely intimate, the language of literature also was still liable to variation. Such is a brief summary of what we have so far arrived at.

The question arises, How far are the apparent varieties the result of Regional, and how far of Social, speech habits? It is admitted that varieties of the former kind are not very common or numerous. But if they are due to social causes, may they not, in the printed works of the period at least, be the work of the printer? An interesting investigation would be to show how far the printer of this period followed, in the main at any rate, the author's manuscript, and how far he departed from it and introduced his own spelling. Perhaps some day, when research in these questions of the history of our native language is properly organized in this country, some one will carry out such an investigation among many others. In the meantime we can only argue from what we know.

It might be contended that while a polite and fastidious Court would tolerate a rustic mode of speech—as indeed it must have borne with Raleigh's Devonshire accent—it would reprobate and ostracize persons who spoke with the accent, or otherwise after the fashion, of a lower social stratum. It is one thing to listen to a gentleman using the dialect, or a modified form of it, from his native county; it is quite another thing, and far less bearable, to hear the eccentricities of the Custard Makers' wives, and Sunday Citizens of London Town. But is it not more likely therefore, it may be asked, that those varieties found in printed books, in so far as they are not of Regional origin, are in reality not those of the writers' own speech, when these were in a position to know how people spoke at Court, but mere vulgarisms of the printers? Are we justified in attributing to the writers many of the peculiarities of pronunciation, &c., that occur in printed works, and in drawing conclusions from them as to the speech of the author himself?

It certainly makes an enormous difference whether we are being let into the secrets of the habits of speech of Latimer, Wilson, and Ascham, or only into those of some unknown and humble compositor.

In this work it is assumed that we are entitled to take the printed books as reflecting the actual speech of the authors themselves, and that for the following reasons:

(1) The varieties referred to, while as a rule they do not suggest any specifically Regional origin, are not, so far as can be judged, of the nature of vulgarisms. For the most part they consist merely in differences of distribution of elements which we know to have existed originally in the dialect of London.

(2) If the varieties in the language of printed works were solely or chiefly the work of the printers, we should expect definite vulgarisms such as are found habitually used in Machyn's Diary.

(3) The same varieties are found in private letters of the period which were not printed at all for hundreds of years afterwards.

(4) The same, or similar, diversities in pronunciation may be inferred from the statements of writers upon English pronunciation such as Palsgrave, Salesbury, and Smith.

(5) The printers are unlikely to introduce, of themselves, any considerable novelties in spelling. They are conservative and conventional, and follow the main lines of the old scribal tradition. It is more likely that they would eliminate the 'incorrect' spellings of the authors' manuscript than introduce these themselves.

(6) The individualities found in the printed works, as in the private letters, are not all concerned with pronunciation, but include also differences in the use of grammatical forms. These the printer would hardly alter.

From these considerations, and also from the impression of consistency and genuineness produced by the perusal of a large number of sixteenth-century published books, an effect which it is very difficult to analyse, the present writer is convinced that we are justified in regarding the outstanding linguistic features in printed literature of this period as really reflecting the individualities of the authors, and not of the printers. If the language of books is less individual than that of private letters, it is because in writing a serious literary work, destined for the public, the author was less unrestrained and followed the conventional spelling of the day—rather an elastic one at the best, or the worst—more rigidly than in familiar correspondence.

Writers vary, even in their letters, in the degree and frequency of their departures from the normal spelling, and it is true, on the whole, that academic writers and ecclesiastics adhere more rigidly to a conventional, and therefore an unenlightening spelling than the pure man of action or the courtier. But even within these classes there are persons who are more precise than others. Thus the sermons of Latimer, though preached before the King, are much less orthodox, and therefore more interesting, in spelling, style, and thought, than those of John Fisher, Bishop of Rochester. Ascham is less conventional than More or Sir Thomas Smith; Wolsey, Cromwell, Cranmer, Burghley, and Bacon are more so in their letters than Henry VIII, Anne Boleyn, Admiral Lord Seymour, or Queen Elizabeth. The letters of women, as we saw in the fifteenth century, and shall see again in the seventeenth and eighteenth centuries, are far less carefully spelt as a rule than those of men, and tell us more concerning their actual mode of speech.

The next point is, granting that the occasional spellings really mean something, and that they really express the writers' own speech, how far we shall go in the inferences we draw in regard to this. It must be made clear that the phonetic spellings, which we advisedly call *occasional* spellings, are rarely consistently used by the same writer, even for the same word. Now if we find the spelling *sarvis*, &c., we may quite safely assume that the writer pronounced in the first syllable a vowel which, whatever its precise nature, was better expressed in that way than by the spelling *-er-*. But supposing, as often happens, the same writer also puts down *servis* in the same letter or document, are we to assume that he, or she, used two pronunciations of the same word? I think not, and should conclude that a single such departure from the traditional spelling of a word would show that this was the type of pronunciation employed by that writer. If not, and if the traditional spelling expressed his pronunciation best, why should he ever depart from it? A much more difficult question is this. Suppose a writer spells *sarvis*, *hard* 'heard', *dark*, *swarve*, *clark*, &c., each of them once, or many times, whence we conclude that, in those particular words, he certainly pronounced *-ar-*, but always *werk* 'work', *swerd* 'sword', *ferm* 'farm', *sermon*, never writing *-ar-* in these words, are we to extend the *-ar-* pronunciation to these and all the other words belonging to the old *-er-* group, and assume that this writer pronounced *-ar-* here as well, although he never happens to lapse from the traditional spelling in their case?

If London polite English had ever hitherto been a uniform dialect, or had become so by the sixteenth century, we should certainly answer this question in the affirmative. But we know that this was very far from being so. The axiom of philological method that in the same dialect, at a given time, the same sound or combination of sounds, under the same conditions, changes everywhere in the same direction, cannot be applied to such a dialect as Standard English without many reserves and qualifications. It is enough to point out that at the present time, although we pronounce -ar- in *clerk, hearth, heart*, &c., we do not do so in *earth, service, heard*, &c. We have here, as in so many other instances, a double usage within what was originally a single class of words. This duality may have existed, and almost certainly did exist in the sixteenth century in the *clerk, learn, heart* class, as it did in many other classes of words having originally the same sound. There is no doubt that by the end of the sixteenth century a very large proportion of words of the old -er- class were pronounced with -ar- by good speakers. On the other hand, this is probably one of the cases in which latitude was allowed, and it is perhaps safer to assume an -ar- pronunciation only for those words in which it is actually proved by occasional or consistent spellings. We may think it highly probable that a speaker said -ar- in many words in which he only writes -er-—indeed the rhymes in this and the succeeding centuries go far to prove that this was so, but in the absence of either spelling or rhyme it is perhaps temerarious to assert it as a fact for a given writer or speaker. We shall give later a list of all the words for which the -ar- pronunciation is proved, in one or other of these *two* ways, and it will be seen that almost every word of the class was so pronounced, at one time or another, by at least some speakers.

The principles which are advocated in regard to the interpretation of such occasional spellings as *sarvis*, &c., should be applied to all classes of words of which such spellings are found. If we content ourselves with saying that some undoubted speakers of Court or Standard English, at a given time, pronounced such and such words in this or that way, because their occasional spellings show this, we are safe, and are not going beyond what can be proved. But even this moderate statement involves the further conclusion that such isolated pronunciations, as they may appear to be, were at least tolerated among speakers of Standard, and that therefore they cannot have been mere eccentric individual vagaries. They must have been shared by a large number of speakers of the same social position, that is, they were current among these speakers, though not necessarily to the exclusion of other types of pronunciation. We have remarked above that even at the present time, when the degree of latitude in Received Standard is comparatively limited, we have two types of pronunciation equally current in certain cases, sometimes in isolated words, such as *girl*, when both [gɛəl] and [gᴧl] are equally 'good', the former being rather old-fashioned now, sometimes in a whole class of words, e. g. those which have an old short ŏ before *s, f, th*, where both [ɔ] and the lengthened [ɔ̄] are equally current—[lɔs—lɔ̄s, sɔft—sɔ̄ft, klɔþ—klɔ̄þ].

The sources of such divergence may be either Social or Regional dialect, or the coexistence at the same time of an older and a younger type of pronunciation within the same period.

In the above remarks we have stated the weight to be attached to the occasional spellings at a minimum, as it would be a mistake to urge evidence of this kind too far, or to attempt to construct too much upon it. It cannot be denied, however, that the testimony of these spellings is cumulative, and the effect of a considerable collection of them, drawn from all kinds of sources, is impressive, and gives a consistent picture of the average speech of the time, one which is supported by the statements of the more intelligible writers upon pronunciation, and by the known facts of English pronunciation in its later developments.

This is a convenient occasion to say something concerning the Orthoepists, as they are called, of this and later times. Since the pioneer work of Ellis and Sweet in the last century, writers upon the history of English have attached enormous weight to the statements of the writers upon English pronunciation from the sixteenth century downwards, and to within the last few years these statements, together with the evidence of rhymes, were almost the sole, certainly the principal, basis upon which conclusions as to the character of English pronunciation in past ages were built. The opinion of the majority of students of English would probably still approve this method. From this starting-point Ellis and Sweet had constructed a very definite picture of the sounds of our language in the past, and later investigators have worked on precisely the same lines. Quite recently, however, Zachrisson has appealed also to the testimony of the occasional spellings, with the result that the views handed on by the great pioneers have been to some extent modified. The works of the Orthoepists themselves have been reprinted and subjected to a fresh scrutiny and critical analysis. It is, however, true that hitherto writers upon the history of Modern English have relied mainly upon the Orthoepists, and have only used comparatively slight collections of actual forms taken from contemporary literature as a kind of secondary luxury. Now the view which we hold regarding the relative importance of the two sources of information is likely to vary according to the amount of first-hand information which we have of each or both.

After considerable study, on the one hand, of the writings of the old Orthoepists, of the exhaustive, and often very tedious, disquisitions which have been written upon them, and, on the other, of a large number of works of all kinds written during the fifteenth and following centuries, the present writer confesses that he now leans definitely to the view that the path of progress lies in the minute study of the letters and books written in the periods under consideration, rather than in that of reiterated torturing and weighing of the descriptions given by the writers on pronunciation. When we find that these writers invariably start from the 'letters' and proceed to discuss the 'powers' of these, that their descriptions of the sounds are, for the most part, entirely dominated by the relation, real or fancied, of these to the letters, and are almost always most vague and indefinite, so that, for instance, we can rarely be sure, when a writer speaks of a diphthong, whether he means simply a combination of two letters, or whether he is really thinking of a combination of two sounds, we are filled with something like despair of ever arriving at any clear ideas at all, if these writers are to be our principal guides.

When we turn from what these men have written to what other men have written about them, the effect is, if possible, even more dismal. The essential inadequacy of most of the old would-be describers of English sounds for their task is most painfully brought out by the extreme ambiguity which the commentators discover in their writings. The simplest fact of pronunciation is usually so darkly and mysteriously set forth, that the explanation is frequently far longer than the original statement ; the critic has to turn and twist this in many directions to make it mean anything definite, and often to perform prodigies of legerdemain to make it mean what he thinks it ought to mean. Then again, some critics are anxious to square all the contemporary statements regarding a particular vowel, so that they shall all mean the same thing, regardless of the fact that writers of the same period often appear to be describing quite different sounds in the same word. Other editors of, and writers upon, particular Orthoepists are so carried away by the supposed claim of their pet author to be authoritative, that they set up his particular bundle of ambiguities, or rather their own interpretation of them, as the standard for the period, although other contemporary writers, no less obscure, appear to say something directly opposed. As a rule, it is impossible to assert with confidence that such and such an old writer definitely says that such and such a vowel had a particular sound; all we can be sure of is that his editor or commentator thinks that he says so. The seeds of madness lie in all this.

I believe we shall have to change our views of the importance of the old writers, and put the study of the private letters and the books written and printed in the period which we are studying first, and that we should only apply to the writers on pronunciation after we have extracted all the information we can get from the former source. When we find the statements of the old grammarians in opposition (in so far as we understand them) to the plain facts, as revealed again and again by the occasional spellings, we shall, I believe, do well to disregard the former, and be guided by the latter.

No one who has studied the English of the sixteenth and seventeenth centuries in the texts of this period, rather than in the pages of the grammarians, will doubt that these writers have grievously misled those who trusted them so implicitly, with regard to the chronology of the vowel changes, while they leave us almost entirely in the lurch with regard to the pronunciation of vowels in unstressed syllables, and to that of many important consonant combinations.

We hasten to say that there is a great variety of merit, or demerit, among the old Orthoepists; some are fairly intelligent in their method, really seem to know the difference between sounds and letters, and to have some capacity for discriminating and describing the former ; some are almost worthless from these points of view; all are disappointing in some particular.

Nor is this to be wondered at. At the present time in England, after several generations of scientific Phonetics, the number of men who could give a complete and intelligible description of the sounds of our native language is extremely small. Every year books upon English Grammar are still published in which the accounts given of actual English pronunciation are useless to every one, from the complete ignorance of the writers regarding the nature, mode of production, the principles of classification, and transcription of sound.

It is not surprising that between three and four hundred years ago there were writers equally ignorant of the elements of phonetic description, nor that, given such ignorance, their efforts should have been failures as dismal as those of their modern fellow-craftsmen.

The most that the best of the old writers do, is to put us on the track of changes that have taken place, and are well established before their time, but they are nearly always reluctant to admit any great divergence between actual pronunciation and the supposed legitimate ' powers of the letters '—a phrase we get positively sick of in the seventeenth century. The result is that the descriptions are always some way behind the facts, or made to square with the traditional spelling so that they are quite misleading. Thus, although it is fairly certain that M.E. short *ă* had developed into its present sound in some parts of England before the end of the fifteenth century, and that the new sound was used among good speakers long before the end of the sixteenth century, it took the Orthoepists about a hundred years to find this out and to describe the sound as it really was. Again, while long *ā* (as in *bake*, &c.) was well on the way to its present sound before the beginning of the sixteenth century, Gill, in 1621, ridicules those who use the new sound as vulgar and affected innovators, maintaining that the real sound was still old long *ā*. Perhaps the most useful part of the work of most of the writers on pronunciation is the lists which they give of words having the same sound, which at least enable us to ascertain the distribution of the sound, even if they give us no very definite idea of what the sound was.

These remarks apply especially to sixteenth-century writers, and to those of the first quarter or so of the seventeenth. After that date the Orthoepists are more helpful, though they still leave much to be desired. See Ch. V on some later writers.

We shall now give a short account of the language of a few typical personages of the sixteenth century. We base our present observations for the most part upon published works, since these being more extensive than letters afford more copious material for a general survey of the language, although they may not be so fruitful in the occasional spellings. The account of Queen Elizabeth's language is based upon several collections of her letters, and upon her translations from the classics—a work of no great literary merit, however praiseworthy it may be as showing industry and a love of learning. The private letters of the sixteenth century will be referred to later in our systematic general survey of the development of sounds and grammatical forms from the fifteenth century onwards.

We begin here with **Lord Berners'** translation of Froissart, using Vol. I of Professor Ker's edition of this great work.

Pronunciation.

(*a*) **Vowels.** O.E. *ȳ* occurs with all three types :—*hylles, hyrdell, stirr* ' stir ', *shitte* ' shut '; *yvel* ' evil '; *businesse, buryed, brused* (long *ȳ*), *moche* ' much '; *besynes(se)* (very frequent), *sterre* ' stir '.

e for *i* is found in *jebet* ' gibbet ', *suspeciously, hedeouse* ' hideous ', *mengled* 'mingled'. M.E. -er- occurs both as -er- and -ar-. We give here only the more remarkable words, as the complete list will be given later (p. 217). With -er- :—clerkes, herte (also harte), swerd 'sword', ferr (and farr 'far', clergy; with -ar- :—harte (also herte), harde 'heard', farr (and ferr), wark, defarre 'defer', armyns 'ermines', darth 'dearth', swarved 'swerved'. The Southern form (fr. O.E. ǣ) occurs in drad P. P. 'dreaded', but spredde P. P. M.E. ă has apparently been fronted in renk 'rank' (twice). M.E. ē has been raised to i, as is shown by the occasional spellings achyved, relyve, belyved 'believed'.

M.E. o is unrounded in yander 'yonder'. The common sixteenth-century Busshoppe, with rounding after b, occurs. Earlier ĕ before ng becomes ĭ :—Ingland. The old short form survives in wyckes 'weeks', M.E. wike.

M.E. eu is monophthongized to ē before a following lip-consonant :— Beamond 'Beaumont', M.E. Beumont; Beachame. Initial e in erthe appears ye- in yerth, a common sixteenth-century spelling.

(b) Consonants. Addition of a final parasitic Cons. occurs in 'the quene kneld downed'. Loss of a final Cons. occurs in Beamon (by the side of Beamond); loss of l in an unstressed syllable occurs in hosteries.

(c) Unstressed Syllables. There are not so many spellings indicating the treatment of unstressed syllables as in many other works, but the following may be noted :—the diphthongs ai, ei, monophthongized in— battel (by the side of batayle), certenly (by the side of certeinly), appareled (by the side of aparailed), travell and traveled (by side of travailed with same meaning), rascalle (and rascaille), counsele (and counsaile), burgesses. The form mentayne 'maintain' shows weakening of the unstressed first syllable.

The old suffix -es in the Pl. of Nouns is often written -is—featis, changis, frendis, &c., sometimes -es—lordes, clerkes, and the vowel is often omitted—barouns, archers, &c. The Superl. suffix is sometimes written -yst—wekyst. In the P. P. of Wk. Vbs. both -yd and -ed occur, but the vowel may be omitted as at present in unharnest.

Old ui (= [y]) is unrounded as in bisket, bisquet 'biscuit'.

Examples of confusion of vowels, showing reduction in the unstressed syllable, are discomfeture, comen 'common', but commonly; astate, aspeciall, ascaped. y is very common in final syllables before all Cons.—helmyttes, opyn 'open' passim, sadyls.

Initially an unstressed vowel is lost in poyntment 'appointment', 'great rayne and a clypps'. Of occurs as a in men a warre, and the Auxil. have in wolde a bene.

The suffixes -ier, -eour become -er, -our respectively in fronters 'frontiers', barrers 'barriers', currers 'couriers', behauour 'behaviour'.

Inflexion of Nouns.

The suffix of the Pl. often loses its vowel when the Noun ends in -n or -r—barouns, strangers, susters.

On the variants -es and -is, see under Unstressed Syllables.

The Wk. Pls. yën and eyen 'eyes', kyen 'cows'.

Irregular :—brethern, womenne, chyldren.

Invariables :—xxiii Englisshe myle, a thousand horse = horsemen.

Pls. with voicing of *f*—*lyves, wyves,* but *wifes* is also found.

Possessives.—Note the construction—frendis of the erle of *Arundels.*

The following uninflected:—old Feminines—Mary *Maudlyn* day, our *lady* day ; when the second noun begins with *s-* —by the *father* syde.

Group Possessives :—*the kynge of Englandes homage, the lorde of Mannes quarrell, Sir Gaultier of Mannes fader, the kyng of Englandes doughter.* The older construction, *the kynges doughter of Englande,* also occurs.

Adjectives. The French Pl. in *-s* occurs in *letters patentes.*

Mutated Comparatives :—*lengar, strenger.*

Superlative suffix contracted after *s-* :—*outragyoust, ungracyoust.*

Comparative suffix preceded by *more* :—*more stronger, the more fressher.*

Superlative suffix preceded by *most* :—*moost neweste and secrettest, the moost outragyouste people, the moost ungracyoust of all.*

Adverbs :—*a foote, a horse backe* (*a =* earlier *on*).

Pronouns. The 3rd Pers. Pl. seems to have only the *th*- forms—*they, theyr, theym, them.* In the 2nd Pl. Berners always distinguishes between Nom. *ye* and Possess. and Dat. *you.* The Possess. of 2nd Pl. has *-s* in final position—the noble and gentyl kyng of *yours.* The Neuter Pron. is commonly *it,* but *hit* is also found.

The Def. Art. elides the vowel before words beginning with another vowel—*thentent, thother,* &c. &c.

Verbal Endings. The 3rd Pers. Sing. Pres. Indic. always ends in *-th.* The Pres. Pl. often has the Southern *-th* suffix :—other thynges *lyeth* at my hert, your knightes *abideth* for you to wasshe, what *weneth* the Frenchmen ?, their husbandes *payeth.* The P. P. of Strong Vbs. generally ends in *-en,* but *gotte, won, fought,* occur; the Pres. Part. ends in *-yng.*

The Strong Vbs. call for little remark. The following forms may be noted :—*gyve, gave, gyven* ; the Prets.—*strake, spake, brake, drave* (analogy of *gave,* &c.), *fyll* ' fell ' (as in Chaucer), though *fell* is commoner, *strave* ' strove ', *flang* ' flung ', *gatte.*

Auxiliaries. The Pl. of *be* is *ben, are, ar,* &c. *Will* is always *wol. Have* becomes *a* when unstressed :—ther might *a* ben sene ; the kyng wolde nat *a* consented.

Constructions and Phrases. The following may be noted :—I *can* you good thanke ; we knowe at this day, no persone in the worlde that we lovethe preferment *of,* so much as yours.

The old double negative is still used :—ther needeth *nat* to make *no* provisyon for their hoost.

Characteristics of the Language of Sir Thomas Elyot's ' Gouernour '.

Vowels.

M.E. *-er-* so written in *erthe, hertes, serue, ferre, lernyng, herbes, keruinge, herde* ' heard ', *derke, sterres* ' stars ', *ferme* (fr. Elyot's Will), *swerde.*

M.E. *er* appears as *-ar-* in *hartes, warres* ' wars ', *warke, stare* ' starling ', *darke, parson* ' person ' (Elyot's Will).

O.E. *y* appears as *e* in *ketchyn, stereth* 'stirs', *stere* Inf, *kendled* 'kindled', *euil*; the *u-* type is found in *suche, buyldynge, thursty, thurst*; the only *i-* form appears to be *iuel*.

O.E. *ǣ*[1] shows the Southern type (shortened) in *lasse* 'less', *praty* 'pretty', *radde* passim 'advised', &c., *dradde* Adj. and P. P.; the non-Southern type appears in *lesse, redde, drede* (Noun).

M.E. *i* written *e* in *sens* 'since'; Early M.E. *i* lengthened in open sylla-ble:—*weete* 'to know'; short *i* retained in *wike* 'week'.

The combination *-and-* appears as *-ond-* :—*londes* (Will), *hondes* (Will).

The Northern form of O.E. *ā* apparently occurs in *drane* 'drone'.

Before *-r* a glide was pronounced after a long vowel or diphthong as at present:—*hiare* 'hire'. The inverted spelling *mantion* 'mention' probably points to M.E. short *ǎ* having a fronted pronunciation as at present day.

Consonants.

Omission of Cons. occurs in :—*chylhode* 'childhood', *shud* 'should'. *ng* becomes *n* before *-th-* :—*strenthe* 'strength'.

Addition of final consonant in *fesaunt*.

Sound expressed by *gh* lost before *-t—lyte* 'light'. The same fact is proved by the spellings *dought* 'doubt', and *cloughtes* 'clouts', where no sound could have been intended to be expressed by *gh*.

Unvoicing of *b* before *t* is seen in *optaine* 'obtain'.

Unstressed Syllables.

Flexional suffixes constantly written *-i-* :—the Pls. *horsis, versis, princis, menacis, sickenessis*, &c.

Other endings :—*askidist* 'askedst', *causid* P.P., *haruist* 'harvest'.

The diphthong *ei* simplified—*palice* 'palace', M.E. *paleis*.

Hesitation, pointing to a 'neutral' vowel in the unstressed syllable, is seen in :—*writars* 'writers', *redar* 'reader', *Italions* 'Italians', *burgine* 'burgeon', *profest* 'provost' (this, however, is a M.E. spelling).

Loss of syllable is seen in *robbry* 'robbery'.

Nouns.

In words ending in *-f*, this often remains before the Plural suffix :—*wolfes, lyfes, ourselfes, wifes* (Will).

On the other hand, the Pl. of *hoof* is *hoeues*.

Weak Pls. *eien* 'eyes' (also *eies*), *All Soulen College* (Will), *shone* 'shoes'.

Irregular Pls. *chyldren, bretherne, bredern* (Will), *wemen* and *women*.

The old Neuter *thing* remains invariable—*to loue god of whome we haue all thinge*.

Adjectives.

The Adjective follows the Noun occasionally, as in French :—*beastes sauage, actes martiall, spirites vitall*.

The Adjective takes *-s* in Pl. in the legal phrase—*heires males* (Will).

Most is used as an Adjective in—*her mooste discomforte*.

Pronouns.

These are as at the present time, except that *hit* is still used occasionally, the Possess. Neuter is *his*; *ye* Nom., and *you* Acc. and Dat., are distinguished.

Verbal Endings.

The 3rd Pers. Pres. Sing. always ends in *-th*. The Pres. Pl. generally ends in *e*, that is, has no ending, but the Southern *-th* forms are not infrequent:—harts *lepeth*, people *takethe* comforte, after exploitures *hapneth* occasions, &c. The Sing. of the Vb. is used after *both—bothe the body and the soul is deformed*. In Strong Vbs. the *-n* of the P. P. ending seems almost invariably to be retained—*founden* (also *founde*), *yoten* 'poured', *comen*, *songen* 'sung', *holpen*, &c. The old E. Midland forms *chese* and *lese* 'choose, lose' are kept; the Pret. of the former is *chase*; that of *fight* is *faughte*, fr. the old Sing. Pret. type *fauht* (O.E. *feaht*, *fæht*), not from the old P. P. *fouhten-* type as at present. The archaic P. P. *yolden* 'yielded, payed', and the new *aboden* 'abode', instead of *-biden*, may be noted.

Among the forms of Auxiliaries we may recall *mought* instead of *might* (also used by Queen Elizabeth), the P. P. *kanned* in the sense of 'known', the Pret. *darte* of the Pret. Pres. *dare*. The form *shud* occurs as well as *shulde*.

The curious 'Ablative Absolute' construction of which I have two examples is worth mentioning:—*After a little good meates and drinkes taken*; *I toke her not my father liuynge*.

We pass now to the *Life of Cardinal Wolsey* by **George Cavendish** (1500–61), who from his long residence in Wolsey's household had every opportunity of being acquainted with the speech of the Court. Cavendish, who loved the Cardinal 'on this side of idolatry', has left a wonderful picture of the great prelate and statesman at the height of his power and splendour a glowing description of the magnificence of his personal surroundings and his princely hospitality, and a pathetic account of his fall and death. The following account of this interesting book is based upon the unmodernized reprint from the Kelmscot Press.

Vowels.

M.E. *er* is so spelt in *ferther*, *Herre* 'Harry', *ferre* 'far', *kervers* 'carvers', *sterre* (chamber), *ferme* 'farm', *herd* 'hard'. It is written *-ar-* in *warres*, *darknes*, *hard* 'heard' (more frequent than *herd*), *harold* 'herald', *marre*, *parells* 'perils'.

Southern *er* for O.E. *-eard*, &c., appears in (wood)*yerd*, *smert* 'smart'. O.E. *y* appears in all forms:—*myche*, *kychen*, *myrtle*; *such*, *busynes*, *busylie*; *stere* 'stir', *shet* 'shut'. The old combination *-and* or *-ond* has the latter form in *Eylond*, *londed*, *londyng*.

e for *i* occurs in open syllables:—in *suspecyon*, *prevye*, *shreven* P. P., *delygence*; in a close syllable:—in *sence* 'since'.

The following words, to judge by the spelling, show shortening of the vowel before two consonants in *Bridwell*, *Flet Street*, *backhowse* 'bakehouse': and in close syllables before *t*, in *strett* 'street', *botts* 'boats', *swett*. Among isolated forms may be noted *wyry* for 'wherry' (see similar form as regards vowel, in Latimer), *laft* 'left', *thether, whan, than*, 'when, then', *yearthely* 'earthly', a common form in the period (cf. the 1st and 2nd Prayer Books of Edward VI, &c.), and the interesting spelling *Guees* for *Guise*, which shows that *ee* stood for the same sound as at present. The spelling *strayngers* (very common) may either indicate a real diphthong surviving from M.E. before *-ng-* [ndž] or that *ay* and *a* both had the same sound, which is more probable.

Unstressed Syllables.

The inflexional endings have very commonly *-i-* :—*horssis; crossis; extendyth; commendyd, providyd; · hosyn, rysyn* 'risen', &c. *-ei, ai* become *e* or *i*:—*chapplens, councell, certyn, ther* 'their', *palice*. The 'murmur vowel' for *ei* is probably indicated by the spelling *curtosye*. Old *oi* appears as *-a-* in *turkkas* 'turquoise'. A pronunciation identical with that of the present day is indicated in *orrynge* 'orange'.

Unstressed *-a-* is written *i* in *ambassiter* ; French *u* is *i* or *e*, cf. *voluptious, somptious, sumptiously, commynicacioun, commen* Vb. 'commune'.

The endings *-en, -on, -in* are evidently levelled under a single sound to judge by the varying spellings—*opeyn* 'open', *tokyn* 'token', *cusshons, cusshens, latten* 'Latin', *waggans* 'wagons'. These spellings rather suggest a 'syllabic *-n*', as in present-day *button*, in all these words—that is, for all vowels + *n* finally.

Consonants.

gh before *t* had no longer any sound, or it could not have been written, as we have already seen in these or similar words, in *whight* 'white', *therabought, to wright* 'write'.

wh- had the sound of *w-* as at present in the South of England, and the spelling is confused in *wye* 'why', *where* 'wear'.

The 'fronted' or 'palatalized' type of O.E. *č* occurs in *archebyssnopriche, bisshopriche*.

French *-qu-* is pronounced *k* in *banketts*.

The metathesized form *axed* 'asked' is used.

The old form *Putnethe* occurs twice on the same page, but *Putney* two pages earlier.

The spelling *Pumfrett* 'Pontefract' shows a pronunciation which still survives, though perhaps now obsolescent.

Hankyng 'hanging' suggests a pronunciation still heard in provincial English.

l is lost before *t* in *vaughtyng* 'vaulting', which form also shows the '*gh*' had no sound.

k is lost in combination with other consonants in *Worsopp* 'Worksop'; *b* is lost after *l* in *tremlyng* 'trembling'.

On the other hand, *d* is already added after *-n* in *roundyng in the eare*, earlier *rowne-*.

Initial *h-* is omitted in the French-Latin word *armonye* 'harmony'. Initial *h-* is never written *wh-* (apparently) as by many writers of this period :—*hole* 'whole'.

Nouns.

Nouns ending in *-f* generally keep this before the Possessive suffix in the Singular :—*selfs.* Before the Pl. suffix *-f-* sometimes remains, as in *lyfs, beafes*; but sometimes becomes *v* :—*staves.* The *v*-forms sometimes occur in the uninflected cases—*love* ' loaf ', on hys *lyve.*

Weak Pls. :—*hosyn* ' hose ', *Allhallon day* (twice).

Invariable Pls. :—*xv foote thyke*; *vi of the beste horse.*

Irregular Pls. :—*childerne, brethern.*

Uninflected Possess. Sing. :—*Our lady mattens* (old Fem.); *my hart blode.*

Group Possessives :—*Kyng Herre the VIIIths sister*; *Ayenst the Kyng and my lords commyng*; *my lord of Shrewsburys servaunts*; *therle of Shrewsburyes* (absolute); but *the abbots of Westminster* (absolute).

Pronouns.

The Neuter Sing. 3rd Pers. is *hyt.* The 2nd Pers. *ye* and *you* are used indifferently for the Nom., especially in addressing one person.

The Def. Art. elides the vowel before a following vowel :—*therle*, &c.

Verbal Endings.

The 3rd Pers. Sing. Present is almost universally *-yth* or *-ith*, but *me semys* occurs.

The Pl. generally has no ending, but the Southern *-th* occurs in *them that hath.*

The Weak P. P. *pact* ' packed ' may be noted.

Among Strong Verbal forms we may note *geve* instead of *give*, P. P. *gevyn.* The M.E. Prets. *hild* ' held ', *fill* ' fell ', as in Chaucer, survive. The Prets. *spake* and *spoke, sang, strak* ' struck ', *stale* ' stole ', *drave*, and *shew* ' showed ' (analogy of *knew*) may be noted, and the P. P. *lyen* ' lain ' (as in the Prayer Book) and *shreven* ' shriven '.

Auxiliaries.

The only points which call for mention are :—the P. P. *byn*; *was* used in Pl., *walls whiche was*; *wol* ' will ' by the side of *wyll.*

We now pass to consider the language of a far better known writer, namely **Hugh Latimer** (*c.* 1491–1555), so far as this can be gauged accurately from the versions of his sermons that have come down to us. The style is much more colloquial, and more touched with provincialisms than the other works we have hitherto dealt with, and this albeit these sermons were preached before King Edward VI. Latimer was the son of a yeoman farmer in Leicestershire, who, as he tells us, ' had no landes of his owne, onely he had a farme of iii or iiii pound by the yere at the vttermost, and here vpon he tilled so much as kepte halfe a dosen men. He had a walke for a hundred shepe, and my mother mylked xxx kyne. . . . He kept me to schole, or elles I had not bene able to haue preached before the kinges maiestie nowe.' At the age of 14 Latimer went to Clare Hall, Cambridge, and graduated B.A. at 18, having been elected a Fellow of his College while still an undergraduate. He became M.A.

at 22, and at 24 (1514) was Professor of Greek in the University, being ordained priest the same year. In 1530 he preached before Henry VIII at Windsor, 'when his maiestie after ye sermon was done, did most familiarly taulke with me in the gallery'. When Cranmer became Archbishop of Canterbury in 1533, Latimer gained a powerful friend at Court; the following year he preached before the King every Wednesday in Lent, and in 1535 he was consecrated Bishop of Worcester. In 1539, however, unable to swallow the *Six Articles*, he resigned his See. After being imprisoned, and apparently only escaping death for heresy by the King's death, he was offered for a second time, but declined, the See of Worcester. During this and the following year he preached before King Edward at Whitehall and at 'Paules'. He retired to Lincolnshire in 1550, where he remained, preaching much, until, early in Mary's reign 'a pursiuant was sente downe into the countrey to call him vp'. As he passed through Smithfield he remarked that 'Smithefield had long groaned for him', but his death was destined for another place. In 1555 he was burnt at the stake in Oxford, as Foxe says 'upon the Northe syde of the Towne, in the Dytch over agaynst Baily College'. Such, in brief, was the life and 'dolorous death' of Bishop Latimer, whom some will venerate as a saint and apostle, and others detest as a wrong-headed and dangerous heretic, whose teaching was wellnigh fatal to the Catholic faith in the Church of England. His worst enemies, however, must admit his sincerity, and his cheerfulness and courage at the last; and few will deny that he possessed a copious flow of invective, and a ready, if a rude and coarse eloquence.

The following notes are based upon Arber's Reprints (1) of the Seven Sermons before Edward VI, and (2) from the Sermon known as 'the Ploughers'.

Vowels.

O. and Early M.E. $\bar{o}^1$, which, as we have seen, probably became [ū] in Late M.E., is frequently written *u* and *ou*:—*must, blud, shutyng*; *bloude, gould* 'gold', *boune* (N. Fr. *bōn*) 'boon'.

The *u* of *must* was probably short in the unstressed position, and that of *blud* had been shortened before a final consonant.

M.E. $\bar{o}^2$ initially is sometimes written *wo-*, and *hō* becomes *who-*:—*such a wone* 'such an one', *whomlye* 'homely', *whore, whoredome*; on the other hand, we also find *holsome* 'wholesome', *horynge*.

M.E. *-er-* is far more often so written, but there are some important *-ar-* forms:—*swaruing* 'swerving', *parson* 'clergyman', *harde* 'heard' (also *herd*), *clarke, maruel* (and *meruel*), *clargy* (and *cleargy*), *faruentlie* (and *feruentlie*) 'fervently'. On the other hand we have *hertes* 'hearts', *mercie, herken, sterue* 'starve', *swerd, sweard* 'sword', *learne, ferme* 'farm', *sermon, Personage* 'parsonage'.

O.E. *y* appears in all three forms, sometimes in the same word:—*sturred—sterryng—styrred* 'stir'; the words which so far as I have noted have only *u* are:—*busie, suche, burden, buyldynge*; those which have *i* or *y* are:—*synne, sinners, myntes, myntyng, fyrst, gilty, hyl* 'hill'. Both *listed* and *luste* 'list' Vb. occur. The latter may be influenced by the Noun *lust*.

M.E. *i* appears as *e*—in close syllables—*sence* (very common) 'since' (also *since*), *Chechester*; in open syllables—*preuie* 'privy', *preson* (oftener *pryson*), *thether* 'thither'.

M.E. *ē* is written *ye*, which may indicate an [ī] sound in :—*thyefe* 'thief', *fryendes*, *pryeste* 'priest'. The word *devil* is written both *deuyl* and *diuyl*, the latter indicating a pronunciation with short *i* which we know to have existed later.

The spelling *preaty* 'pretty' apparently stands for the Southern form.

i for *e* occurs in *opprision* 'oppression', *trimble* 'tremble', and *whirry* 'wherry'.

The spelling *clausset* 'closet' implies a lengthened vowel, and shows that *au* no longer expressed a diphthong. Diphthonging of *o* before *-ld*, which we know occurred, is expressed in *toulde*, *soulde*, *oulde*.

The consonantal *y-* is developed before initial *ē* in *yearth* 'earth', *yer* 'ere'.

A long vowel is suggested by the spellings *wourse* 'worse', *Loordes* (supper), *woorde* 'word'.

A short vowel is shown in *watter* 'water'.

Vowels in Unstressed Syllables.

The interesting form *unscripterlye* shows the treatment of *-ure* when unstressed, which is vouched for later by the writers on pronunciation and so often expressed by the spelling at this time, before, and after. The spelling *rightuous* may owe its *u* to *virtuous*. The endings *-es*, *-eth*, *-el*, *-en*, &c., are nearly always so written, but *deuil* 'devil' alternates with *deuel*, *euyl* with *euel*. Loss of an unstressed vowel occurs, initially, in *poticaries*, *leauen* 'eleven'; medially, in *Deanry*.

Consonants.

Omissions. *d* is lost before *-ns-* in (asshe) *Wensdaye*; after *n-* before *-sh-* in *frensheppe*; *p* after *m* before *t*, *temted*; *f* after *l* before *p*—*halpeny*.

Hoise 'hoist' has not yet acquired the final *-t*; *faut* 'fault' has not yet restored the *l* through the influence of a supposed etymology direct from Latin; the *l* is, however, inserted in *faulse*. *b* is not yet added in *detter* 'debtor'.

h- is lost in the unstressed syllable of *shepard*.

Addition of consonant. The only case noted in Latimer's Sermons is *myxt* 'mix' Imperat.

Entirely bogus spellings are *accoumpt* 'account' and *depntely* 'daintily'. Nearly as bad is *victalles*, where again a Latin etymology has introduced *c* where it was not pronounced.

Banquet, as so frequently at this period and much later, is spelt *banket*; the form *banketers* is also found.

Final *-t* is written *-th* in *comforth*.

Nouns.

A woman's name is sometimes inflected in the Possessive—*my Ladye Maryes grace*, sometimes uninflected according to the M.E. method— *my Ladye Elizabethe grace.*

Nouns ending in *f* sometimes change this to *v* before the Pl. suffix—*wyues, theaues*; sometimes retain it—*woulffes.*

The Pl. suffix is generally *-s, mi' betters,* or *-es, egges,* but the curious *wayeys* is also found. There is no reason to suppose that this suffix, however written, was syllabic, except under the same conditions as at present.

The word *newes* is used as a Pl.—*these be the newes, I fear they be true.*

Both elements are inflected in the Pl.—*Lordes Presidentes.*

In the phrase—*The Parliamente house are wyser,* &c., the collective Noun is treated as a Pl.

Pounde with a number before it is, as usual at this period, uninflected.

An interesting Group-Possessive occurs—*oure holye father of Romes eares.*

Adjectives.

The Comparative suffix is used where we should now use *more* with the Positive—*greuouser.*

The double Comp. *more diligentes* so common in the sixteenth century is found.

The old mutated Comp. *lenger* ' longer ' is used.

The old form *bedred* ' bedridden ' survives.

The Adj. in *-lye, byshoplye dutyes and orders*; *unscripterlye* may be noted.

The Adv. *vpsydowne* ' upside down ' shows a more primitive form than our own.

Pronouns.

The 1st Pers. Possessive seems to distinguish between *my* and *mi',* the latter shorter and unstressed.

The form *me* is used Reflexively—*one kneleth me downe.* The unstressed *a* is used for *he*—*here was a not gyltye.*

Ye and *you* are used indifferently in the Nom. Pl.

In the 3rd Pl. only the *th*-forms are used in all Cases.

The Absolute Possessive forms *theyres, heres* ' hers ' occur.

The Def. Art. is written both *the* and *ye,* the *y* standing for old *þ.*

The old Neuter survives in *the tother.*

Verbal Endings.

The most striking point in Latimer's grammar is the exceedingly frequent use of the *-s* forms of the 3rd Pers. Sing. Pres. of Vbs. I have noted about sixty-three examples in the Sermons. No one acquainted with the writings of the sixteenth century can fail to be struck by the frequency of these forms at this date. Perhaps it may be attributed to Latimer's residence in Lincolnshire; perhaps these forms were acquired by him at Cambridge.

The *-th*-forms also occur, and are perhaps rather more numerous than the others. The ending in this case in almost invariably *-eth.*

The Pl. Pres. generally has no ending, but the Southern *-th* occurs at least three times, and a few *-es* Pls. are also found, especially after *some*—*some that liues, there be some writers that saies, some sayes,* &c. The extraordinary form *we mustes* also occurs. Note also *is* with a Pl. subject—*greate reformacions is,* &c.

The 2nd Pers. Sing. is usually -*est*, but the Northern -*es* occurs :— *thou pilles, polles . . . oppresses.* A strange use is *you measurest*, with the Sing. Vb. in spite of the Pl. Pron.—here used of one person only. Note also the construction *thou which doth.*

In the P. P.'s of Strong Vbs. the distribution of -*en* endings is the same as at present.

Among other Strong forms we may note *chose* Inf. (not the older *chese*), *geue* by the side of *gyue*. Of Prets., *brake* and *bracke*, *spake* and *spak*, *quod* (he) and *quode*, *strooke* 'struck', *stacke* 'stuck', *wrot* and *wrote.*

Auxiliaries.

The Pl. Pres. of *be* is both *are* and *be.*

Doth seems to be used as an Auxiliary; otherwise *doeth.*

Will has a negative form *nill*—*wil thei, nill thei.*

The form *we mustes* is noted above.

Oughte is used as the Pret. of *owe*—as if *I oughte another man xx M. poundes.*

Worth is still used in the sense of *happen*—*what wyl worth ?*

Constructions and Phrases.

The following idiomatic phrases are worth noting—some of them strikingly modern in flavour, some remarkably colloquial for a bishop to use in a sermon preached before his sovereign.

He thought all cocke sure ; *when all came to all* = ' when all was said and done ' ; *the diuel and all* ; *Feyne and put case our sauyour Christe had committed al the sinnes of the worlde* ; *wo worth the O Deuyll* ; *another day* = ' some day ' ; *I here saye he redeth much Sayncte Ieromes workes and is wel sene in theim.*

A very ancient use of 'abide', in the sense of 'to go through, experience', is seen in *what terror and distresse abode he.* Notice the archaic use of *at* in—*the Byshoppe of Rome shoulde haue learned that at him.*

We turn now to another Cambridge man to whom we have already referred several times—**Roger Ascham.** Our survey is based upon Arber's Reprints of (*a*) *Toxophilus* (1545) and (*b*) *The Scholemaster,* posthumously published in 1563.

Vowels.

Ascham does not differ greatly from Latimer in his vowel spellings, and his spellings do not teach us very much with regard to the pronunciation.

The M.E. -*er*- words show the usual variety. The only -*ar*- form which we do not still keep is *hard* 'heard'. By the side of this, Ascham has also *herd*; further *hert* and *hart, sweord* and *sword.*

O.E. *y* appears to have the same forms and in the same words as at present.

The Southern form of O.E. $æ^1$ appears in *drad* 'dread', Adj.

In open syllables *i* appears as *e* in *preuie* and *weeke.* In a close syllable *i* is written *e* in *splettyd.*

K

The diphthonging of *ŏ* before *l* is expressed in the spellings *oulde. boulde, coulde* 'cold', *houldyng, bouling, roule* (Noun) It is doubtful whether this was still pronounced as a diphthong. The spelling *wount* 'accustomed' rather suggests that *ou* expresses length.

The diphthonging of *a* before *l* is occasionally expressed :—*taulke, caulme, faul* 'fall'.

M.E. *ē* is written *i, y* in *piuyshlye, lipe* 'leap', *style* 'steel'; but *e* becomes [*i*] before *nch* in *wrynchynge*.

Vowel quantity is often expressed by doubling the vowel, or writing *ou*, for long vowels :—*moost, woordes, woorke, boorde* 'board', also *bourde, thoumbe* 'thumb', *seeldomer* 'seldomer', *hoote* 'hot'.

Unstressed Syllables.

The flexional syllables are generally written *-es*, &c.

Both *ay* and *e* are written for *ai* when unstressed :—*battayle* and *battel, trauayle*. Possibly the *-ayl* spellings represent actually surviving variants with the stress on the second syllable. The form *maynteners* shows weak stress on the second syllable. *Persever* Vb. no doubt was accentuated on the second syllable, a mode of pronunciation which survived well into the eighteenth century at least.

French *-our-* becomes simply *-er-* in *unsauery*. Initially, unstressed syllables are sometimes lost as in *spence* for 'dispense', 'expenditure'. The common sixteenth-century form *emonges* 'among' is found in Ascham.

Note what would now be an illiterate form—*barbariousnes*, due to confusion of suffixes *-ious* and *-ous*.

Consonants.

Omissions. *l* is not written in *mouted* 'moulted', *Matravers*, family name, for *Maltravers, faules* 'faults'. *f* is lost between *l* and *p* in *halpeny*; *t* is lost finally after *-mp-, prompe* 'prompt'; *d* is lost after *-n* before *s, unhansome*. *b* is lost, finally, in *clame* 'climbed'.

Addition. *t* is developed finally, after *-f, grafte* Vb., earlier *graffe* 'engraft'; also finally after *s* in *amongest*, old form *amonges*, which also occurs; after older *-ks* (spelt *x*) *betwixt*.

The form *optaine* shows unvoicing of *b* before the following *-t-*.

d is still written in *moder* by the side of *mother*, in *wedder* by the side of *wether* 'weather'.

y is often written for old *þ* in *yat, ye*, also *that, the*.

Initial *wh-* for *h-* occurs in *wholie*, by the side of the Noun *hole* 'whole'. In *ones, onse* 'once' we have the only form; the *won-* spellings do not occur.

Nouns.

The Pronoun *his* constantly occurs after a Noun, instead of the Possessive suffix. It is always written *his*, never, apparently, *is*—*on a man his tiptoes, the kinge his wisdome, another his heeles, the king his foole.*

The suffix *-s* is omitted when the next word begins with *s-* :—*Robin Hood seruant, for his country sake, for conscience sake* ; also when the word in the Possessive case-relation ends in *-s* :—*horse feete.*

The Weak Pl. *housen* 'houses' is found, but *eyes* occurs instead of the older *eyne*, &c. The Pl. of *woman* is *wemen* and *woomen*. The Pl. of *child* has both *chyldren* and *chylderne*.

Yere is invariable in *fourtene yere olde.*

Adjectives and Adverbs.

The mutated Comparative *lenger* is used, but also *longer* and *stronger*. The Comp. *willinger* and the Superl. *formest* may be noted.

Throwlye occurs for 'thoroughly', and the Adverb *hedlynge* 'headlong' is interesting as preserving the old adverbial ending, seen also in our present *darkling*. The suffix was much commoner in the sixteenth century than it is now.

Pronouns.

You and *ye* are used indifferently in the Nom., both in addressing one or several persons. On one occasion *ye* is used as if for variety in a sentence in which *you* has already occurred three times.

The Masc. *he, hym* are used instead of *it*, of a bow.

The words *fewe* and *none* used as Pronouns take a Singular Verb—*fewe or none hath yet atteyned*, &c., unless *hath* here as a Pl., which is possible. (Cf. below, under Verbal Endings.)

Verbal Endings.

The 3rd Pers. Sing. Pres. generally ends in *-eth*, but Ascham has an unusually large number of *-s* endings, though not so many as Latimer. These often occur in the same sentence as the *-eth-*forms.

The Pl. Pers. generally has no ending, but some *-s* torms are found, e.g.:—*the ends haue nothyng to stop them, but whippes so far back*, &c. The *-s-*forms both in 3rd Sing. and in the Pl. may be due to Ascham's native Yorkshire dialect, or the former perhaps to Cambridge influence.

The Auxiliaries *doth* and *hath* are used fairly often with a Pl. subject—*as wild horses doth race; where one hath learned to singe, vi hath not.*

Weak P.P.'s, such as *mard* 'marred', *cockerde*, show the loss, as in present-day English, of the vowel of the suffix.

The P.P.'s of Strong Verbs have *-n* in those words where we now have the ending, otherwise apparently not, except in *gotten* and *foughten*.

Strong Verbs.

In the Pres. both *gyueth* and *geueth* are found, and both forms occur also in the P. P., where, however, the *gyu*-forms are overwhelmingly more frequent.

The Prets. *quod* (and *quoth*), *clame* 'climbed', *draue* 'drove', and the P. P.'s *gotten, holpen, foughten, clouen* may be noted.

The old (Eastern) form *leese* and *lease* 'lose' occurs in the Inf. and Pres.

Auxiliary Forms.

The chief points are that *be* is more frequent than *are* in the Pl., and that the P. P. form *be* is used by the side of the usual *ben, bene*.

The use of *is* with a Pl. subject must be due to the writer's native dialect:—*howe many kindes there is of it.*

Idioms and Constructions.

We may note the peculiar use of certain prepositions in the following :— *to shoote in a bow* (= with a bow); *to playe of instruments* (cf. French *jouer* or *toucher du piano*).

The idioms *as weake as water* and *winked at* (in the modern sense).

A curious phrase from the Modern point of view is *all man seeth it* = 'every man'. The expression *put case* 'supposing' is used by Ascham as by Latimer.

We next turn to another academic writer, also a Cambridge man, and contemporary and friend of Ascham—**Thomas Wilson,** author of the *Arte of Rhetorique,* from which the following forms are taken. This work was published in 1560, again in 1567, and in 1585.

Vowels.

M.E. *er* appears as *-ar-* with some frequency :—*farre, starres, swarue, darth* 'dearth', *farmer, clarkes,* but also *clerkes, verlet* 'varlet', *ierre* 'jar, discord', &c.

O.E. *y* seems to have the same distribution of the various forms as at present.

The common *e* for *i* occurs, apparently, only in *grenning* 'grinning'. In open syllables we find *liue, giue* instead of the *geue* or *yeue* forms so common at this period.

Woorke 'work' has evidently a long vowel.

Vowels in Unstressed Syllables.

One of the most interesting forms is *mannering* 'manuring', where the weakened vowel of the second syllable shows that Wilson accentuated the word on the first syllable.

The form *volupteous* is due either to the normal unrounding of French *u* in the suffix *-uous,* or to a substitution for this of *-eous,* as in *righteous.* The spelling *spanell* 'spaniel', the dog, shows an assimilation of French *-ni-* or *-nj-* (for *-gn-*) in *espagnol,* which still survives in uneducated speech in this word. A precisely similar pronunciation is the now vulgar *Dannel* for *Daniel,* which is recorded as 'correct' in the eighteenth century.

Wilson adheres to the old spelling of *-ail, -ain,* in *battail, baraine* 'barren'. On the other hand, *-oi-* is simplified in *turcasse* 'turquoise'.

Consonants.

wh- for initial *ho-* appears in *whoredom, wholy.*

An interesting assimilation of *-nf-* to *-mf-* with *-mph-* is seen in *imphants* 'infants'.

A final *-d* is added after *-n* in *gallands* 'gallons'.

The excrescent *-t* after *-f* which we saw in Ascham's form *grafte,* which we still retain, is not yet added in Wilson's *graffe* Vb. He writes *banqueting* as at present, and not with *-k* as so many of his contemporaries do.

Nouns.

Wilson uses the Weak Pls. *peason, sisterne* 'sisters', *bretherne, shone* shoes'. He has the old Possess. Sing. in *wiues* (*v* instead of *f* as at present). He uses Invariable Pls. after numbers—*this thirty winter, three 'housand pounde.*

Verbal Endings.

It is characteristic of Wilson's grammar that he uses the -*s*-endings in 3rd Pers. Pres. Sing. with great frequency, more often indeed than Ascham, especially in less solemn and stately passages. This peculiarity is also found in a letter of his of 1602 published in Ellis (2. 3. 201). It is true that towards the end of the sixteenth century these forms are fairly frequent generally, but the group of Cambridge men whose language we have been studying are distinctly ahead of most good writers in this respect. Wilson makes use of the Northern and N.E. Midland -*s* in the 2nd Pers. Sing. Pres.—*thou sleepes, places, waites,* &c., alongside of the -*est* form. After *some* we find -*s*—*some speakes, some spittes,* &c. (I have noted sixteen forms in -*s* after *some* on one page, 220.)

Strong Verbs.

The chief forms to note are:—Inf. *chase*; Prets. *forgot, begot, gotte, quoth, rid* (also *rode*), and the P.P.'s *ouerloden* and *stroken* 'struck'.

A typical writer of the later sixteenth century, who enjoyed among his contemporaries a fame which we may think disproportional to his merits, and who by his vogue and influence is of great historical importance, is **John Lyly.** We have only the most shadowy notions of the facts of his life. He must have been born about 1554, and Anthony à Wood says that he was a Kentish man born, and entered at Magdalen College, where, according to the Oxford Register, being then described as *plebeii filius*, he matriculated in 1571 at the age of seventeen. He took his M.A. in 1575, 'at which time', says Wood, 'as he was esteemed in the University a noted wit, so afterwards was he in the Court of Queen Elizabeth, where he was also reputed a rare poet, witty, comical, and facetious'. He obtained a post of some sort in Burghley's household, had plays acted at Court, and aspired to the post of Master of the Revels, in which ambition he was unsuccessful. In the latter part of his life he sat in the House of Commons for various boroughs. Lyly left at least eight plays, and a tract taking the side of the bishops in the Marprelate Controversy, but his fame and influence rest mainly, the former perhaps exclusively, at the present time upon the two works *Euphues Anatomy of Wit,* 1579, and *Euphues and his England,* 1580.

His relations with Burghley do not seem to have been altogether happy, and a rather servile and long-winded letter to the latter exists, in which, with much characteristic verbiage, Lyly appears to repudiate some sort of accusation brought against him. For some reason Lyly did not find favour with Elizabeth, whom he petitioned on at least two occasions, asking for reward, or, 'If your sacred Matie thinke me unworthy, and that after x yeares tempest, I must att the Court suffer shipwrack of my tyme, my wittes, my hopes, vouchsafe in yor neuer-erring judgment, some planck or rafter to wafte me into a country, where in my sadd and settled devocion I may, in euery corner of a thatcht cottage, write praiers instead of plaies', &c. 'I feare', he says, 'to comitt the error I discomende, tediousness.' And much more in the same strain. Possibly the Queen thought that he had committed this error; at any rate she seems to have taken no notice of this or of a later petition, and, as has been said, he received neither the office he coveted nor other preferment at her hands.

At the present time probably many will find the wit of *Euphues* laboured and far-fetched, its eloquence turgid and vapid, the moral reflections lacking in profundity, the dialogue unreal and stilted, the style with its elaborate antithesis and balance, its ceaseless flow of images drawn from a more than dubious Natural History, its ever-recurring and often intricate alliteration, insufferably tedious, the portrayal of human character unnatural, and the situations devoid of verisimilitude. It would be difficult to rebut any of these strictures, and yet there are passages here and there where the blemishes disappear for a moment, where the thought is filled with good sense, and in which the style attains real grace and freedom of movement. To say this is not, however, to admit the extravagant claims made for the author. Lyly brought to a greater pitch, and employed more systematically than his predecessors, a manner, the beginnings of which at its worst may be seen in Caxton, and which at its best exists already in Lord Berners. It is preposterous to assert that Lyly gave to English prose style any graces of which it was incapable before. Neither the illustrious translator of Froissart, nor Cranmer, or whoever composed the English of the incomparable prayers and exhortations of the two first Prayer Books (1549 and 1552), would have had anything to learn from the author of *Euphues*. But, though we may dissent from, we cannot afford to ignore the judgement of Lyly's contemporaries upon his work. As, for example, the encomium of Webbe (not perhaps a very discriminating critic of English Prose or Poetry), in his *Discourse of English Poetrie* (1586), where he says that 'Master Iohn Lilly hath deserued moste high commendations, as he which hath stept one steppe further therein then any either before or since he first began the wyttie discourse of his *Euphues*. Whose workes, surely in respecte of his singuler eloquence and braue composition of apt words and sentences, let the learned examine and make tryall thereof thorough all the partes of Rethoricke, in fitte phrases, in pithy sentences, in gallant tropes, in flowing speeche, in plaine sence, and surely in my iudgment, I thinke he wyll yeelde him that verdict, which Quintilian giueth of bothe the best Orators Demosthenes and Tully, that from the one, nothing may be taken away, to the other, nothing may be added' (D. of E. P., Arber's Ed., p. 46).

With Lyly the saying *le style c'est l'homme* seems completely verified. We find the same absurdities and affectations in his plays, even in his private letters, as in *Euphues*. We feel that in ordinary life he must have talked like that at last, and if he ever spoke in the House the country gentlemen must have writhed under him. We open the plays at random and we light on such a passage as this, in *Sapho and Phao*: 'Of acornes

comes oakes, of drops flouds, of sparkes flames, of atomies elements.
But alas it fareth with me as waspes, who feeding on serpents, make their
stings more venomous: for glutting myself on the face of Phao, I have
made my desire more desperate.   Into the neast of an Alcyon, no bird
can enter but the Alcyon; and into the hart of so great a ladie, can any
creepe but a great lord?'   That might have come straight out of *Euphues*.
And yet with all Lyly's absurdities in prose, it would be foolish to deny
that the man was a true poet who wrote such songs as 'Cupid and my
Campaspe', or that (also in *Campaspe*) in which occur the lines :—

> who is't now we heare
> None but the larke so shrill and cleare;
> How at heavens gates she claps her wings,
> The morne not waking till she sings,

or that in *Sapho and Phao* beginning :—

> O cruell Love! on thee I lay
> My curse, which shall strike blinde the day;
> Never may sleepe with velvet hand
> Charme thine eyes with sacred wand, &c.

Nor should we forget that Shakespeare, though he made fun of Lyly's
prose, condescended to copy his lyrics, while Polonius's advice to his son
is more than slightly reminiscent of *Euphues*.

We must now address ourselves to the more prosaic task of examining
in some detail the forms of English employed by this writer.   The following account is chiefly based on the two parts of *Euphues*, with some
additional forms from the Plays.

Vowels.

M.E. *er*.   The *ar* spellings are not very numerous, and several words
appear both with *er* or *ear*, and *ar* :—*hart* and *heart* (the phrase *neither
art nor heart* leaves no doubt of the pronunciation intended); *deserts* and
desarts ; *warre, farre, farther, harken, quarrellous* ; on the other hand,
vertue, swerue, clearkes.   The spelling *furre* 'far' is curious.

O.E. *y* has the three forms distributed as now, so far as they occur,
except *creple, creaple* 'cripple', which in view of the author's origin we
are tempted to regard as a survival of Kentish dialect, though the form
occurs in fourteenth-century London documents.

The spelling *e* for *i* only occurs in *sheuering* 'shivering'.   The *e* in
hether, hetherto 'hither', &c., is to be otherwise explained.   (Cf. p. 226,
&c.)

Instead of *e, a* appears in *dragges* 'dregs', and *hauenly* 'heavenly',
which may point to a front pronunciation of old *ă*.

M.E. *ō*[1] is written *ou* in *bloud* 'blood'.

The M.E. spelling -*aun*- is largely preserved—*aunswered, graunt,
chaungyd, glaunces, graundfather, daunger, straunge, graunge*.

The new diphthonging of *o* before *l* is expressed in *mould, souldiours,
rowle* 'roll'.

Vowel Lengthenings, &c.   These are shown in the following
spellings :—*woorth, woord, retourne, toossed* 'tossed', *foorth, woont* 'wont';
old length is preserved in *cloath, threede, threade, hoat* 'hot', *insteed(e)*.

Vowel Shortenings. *Hotte* 'hot', *beheaddest.* The following show shortenings after raising of *ē* to *ī* :—*sillye, thrid* 'thread' (N.), *diuell, deuilles* 'devil', M.E. *dĕvel.*

Unstressed Vowels. Confusion of original sound is shown in *destany, musition, Italionated, dyot* 'diet'.

Old *oi* is written *ey* in *torteyse,* also *tortuse* (in *Mother Bombie*). French *u* is written *e* in the second syllable of *venterous.*

Consonants.

Addition of a final *-d* after *-n* occurs in *sound*-ed 'swooned', *round*-ing 'whispering'; after *-r* in *visard*; of *t* after *-n* in *margant, margent* 'margin'; of *b* after *-m* in *lombe* 'loom'; of *p* after *-m* in *mushrompe.*

Loss of final consonant is seen in *yron Mowle, to clyme* 'climb', *strick*-ly.

Final *-d* is lost before an initial *d* in next word in *ole drudge* = 'old'.

Final *-t* is not yet added to the old *hoise* 'hoist' (cf. the P. P. *hoised*).

Initial *qu-* [kw] becomes *c* [k] before *o* in *from coting of ye scriptures* —'quoting'.

The older *banket* is found, by the side of *banqueted.*

Intrusive *-n-* is seen in *messanger.*

The artificial learned spellings *dampnable,* to *condempne, accompt, solempn* may be noted.

A few isolated archaisms are worth recording :—*retchless* 'reckless' (as in Article XVII of the Prayer Book, where it is spelt *wretchlessness*), *euets* 'newts', O.E. *efete,* still heard in provincial dialects, *chekin* 'chicken'.

Nouns.

Possessive Singulars without a suffix, when the Noun ends in *-s* :— *Appolos Musicke, Euphues feature.* The use of *his* after the Noun instead of the suffix—*Philautus his faith, Fidus his loue.* This usage is extended to the Fem., which takes *hir,* in *Juno hir bedde,* by the side of *Junos brauerie.*

The Plurals are, on the whole, as at present, but the Invariable *apple*— *to bring forth apple,* evidently in a collective sense, is noteworthy.

The word *newes* is used with a Singular Vb.—*Other newes here is none.*

The form *sheeve* 'sheaf' is derived from the Oblique case type.

Adjectives.

Double Comparatives, as is typical of this period, occur, e. g. :—*the more fitter, more swifter, more sweeter,* &c. The Elizabethans had no compunction in adding the Superlative suffix to words of three syllables— *delicatest.* The irregular Comparative *badder* occurs in a sentence where it is contrasted with *better.* In this case, *worse* would have spoilt the alliteration.

The old mutated *elder* is used as the ordinary Comparative of *old*—*You are too young . . . and were you elder,* &c.

Pronouns.

The forms of the Personal Pronouns are pretty much as at present, and only the following remarks fall to be made. *You* is used for all cases, both Sing. and Pl., but *thou, thee, thy* (*thine* before vowels) are used in affectionate address in the Sing. *Ye* also occurs in Nom. Pl.

The Possessive Sing. of the Neuter is *his*—*then shall learning haue his hire, whose bloud is in his chiefest heate*, &c.

The Indefinite Pron. *any* takes a Possessive suffix when used absolutely—*my fortune should be as ill as anies*. *One*, in the sense of 'one man', is also inflected—*ones loynes* = 'one man's'. The Indef. *one* is used as at present—*to cut ones meate*.

Verbal Endings.

The 3rd Pers. Sing. in *Euphues* hardly ever ends in -*s*, apparently, but nearly always in -*eth*, except the irregular forms *dares* (Pret. Pres.) and *giues*. The Pl. as a rule has no ending, that is, it represents the old Midland type, the final -*n* being lost. There is, however, at least one example of the retention of the latter—*they loaden*. I have noted two examples of the old Southern Pl.—'*pleasaunt sirroppes doth* chiefliest impart a delicate taste', and *whose backes seemeth*. In the Plays, while the 3rd Sing. in -*th* is the normal form, especially in the more solemn passages, -*s* is quite frequent in the songs and blank verse portions, for the sake of the metre, and in the more colloquial parts of *Mother Bombie*—e. g. *This happens pat*, &c. Plurals in -*s* also occur in the Plays, as in the passage quoted above from *Sapho and Phao*—*of acornes comes oakes*.

Strong Verbs.

These, on the whole, are as at present, but the following forms may be noted:—

The old Inf. *leese* 'lose', by the side of *loose*, and *to strick*, by the side of *strike*. The Prets. *stroke* 'struck', *wan* (and *wonne*), *quoth*, and *flang*. The Vb. *give* has only *give, given*, in Inf., Pres., and P. P., no *geue* forms. Among P. P.'s, *forlorne* (Adj.) occurs by the side of *lost*, the real P. P., *strooke, stroken*, and *stricken, striken*; *meaten* 'measured', and *melten* 'melted'.

The Auxiliaries call for no special remark, except to point out the use of *art* with *you* in the Sing.—*art not you* instead of *art not thou*. This is the same kind of tendency which later produces the construction *you was*, so common in the eighteenth century.

Constructions and Idioms.

We may note the use of *was* after *there* in Impersonal constructions—*there was all things necessary*. The Negative follows the Verb immediately in *I meane not to follow them*. The still-familiar expression *straightlaced* occurs, and the phrase *Philautus came in with his spoake* (i. e. in the conversation), equivalent to our 'put his oar in'. The expression *Euphues whom thou laydst by the wals* (= 'shelved', 'gave up') recalls at once our phrase *to go to the wall,* and the very old expression which occurs in O.E. poetry—e. g. *duguð eall gecrong—wlonc bi wealle* in the Wanderer.

We may fittingly conclude these brief studies of the language of typical writers and speakers of Court English during the sixteenth century with an account of the English of **Queen Elizabeth** herself. The materials for the following statement are drawn from various sources, of which the chief are letters of the Queen, from the third quarter of the century onwards, written to various people, and published in different collections (see Bibliography), and the volume of Translations made by the Queen in 1593, from classical authors, published by the Early English Text Society, under the quaint title of *Englishings.* A few early letters from Ellis's collection have also been used. In collecting forms to illustrate the Queen's English, I have avoided all letters not reprinted from the originals in her own handwriting ; and, as regards the 'Englishings', have taken forms only from the Metres of Boethius, and the translations of Plutarch and Horace which are all in Queen Elizabeth's own hand.

A very characteristic habit of the Queen's is the frequent use of *i* for M.E. *ē*, and this is seen in her letters as early as 1549. So persistent is this mode of spelling that any document purporting to be written by Elizabeth which shows no example of it might safely be rejected as spurious.

Vowels.

The -ar- spellings. These are very common in the Queen's writings, and are found already in the early letters. The following is a complete list of those I have noted from all sources :—*disarued, desarue, hartiest, hartely, hart, desart, sarued, the Cars* (the Kers of Fernyhurst), *swarue, justice-clarke, hard* 'heard ', *marcy, darkness, stars, wark* 'work' (also *work*), *defar* 'defer', *parson* 'person'. On the other hand, *-er-* spellings occur also, chiefly in the early letters :—*servant, serues, preserue, deserued, herde* 'heard'. The spelling *learning* is ambiguous.

O.E. ȳ. With *i* :—*litel, gilty, bisy, styrring.* The spelling *ivel* may come under this head, or it may be the Queen's way of writing the type *evil.*

With *u* we have *much, stur* 'stir ', *sturred put* 'stirred pit', *furst, busy, businis.*

Only one *e-* form seems to occur, and that is dubious in origin—*weshing* 'wishing', and should perhaps be placed in the following group.

e for i. The only forms are *bellowes* 'billows', *rechis* 'riches'. I am doubtful whether to include *weshing* here or to take it as representing the Kentish form of O.E. *wȳscan.*

Unrounding of M.E. ŏ.

The form *stap* occurs—*I pray you stap the mouthes.* It is interesting to find this form at this period. As noted above (p. 78 (St. Editha)) the unrounding of *o* is characteristic of the South-West, where it is found in the first quarter of the fifteenth century. These forms became current in fashionable speech in the seventeenth century, when they are ridiculed by Vanbrugh in the well-known character of Lord Foppington with his often-quoted cliché *stap my vitals*, and many other forms of the same class.   In Standard English a few of these forms have gained permanent footing, such as *strap* by the side of *strop*, *plat* (in Biblical language) by the side of the now usual *plot* (of land).   It seems at the first blush a plausible surmise that the gallant and accomplished Raleigh, with his broad Devon speech, may have helped to make such forms fashionable at Court.   In any case, this is one of the few examples of the influence of Regional dialect upon Standard Spoken English, dating from the Modern Period.   (See, however, p. 240, below.)

The Raising of M.E. ē¹.

We have already seen plenty of examples of the spelling *i* for *ē* from the sixteenth century onwards, and the writers on pronunciation make it clear that old [ē] was pronounced [ī] in Standard English as early as the first quarter of the fifteenth century.   It is desirable, however, to give fairly numerous examples from the writings of so important a speaker as the Queen, and, indeed, I know of no other writer in whose works so many of these spellings can be found.   The following are instructive :—

hiresay ' hear- ', *kiping*, *briding* ' breeding ', *fried* ' freed ', *besiche*, *spidye* ' speedy ', *hire* Inf. ' hear ', *dides* ' deeds ', *spich* ' speech ', *shipe* ' sheep ', &c.

All these represent M.E. tense [ē].   It should be noted that the same spelling also occurs in *spike* Vb. ' speak ', and *bequived* ' bequeathed ', where *i* stands for M.E. [ẹ̄] from O.E. *ĕ* lengthened in the open syllables.

The Queen is not perfectly consistent, however, for she also writes *deapest*, *seake* ' seek ', *beleaved* ' believed ', which all have M.E. [ẹ̄], and *sead* and *sede* ' seed ', which may represent either the Southern type with M.E. [ẹ̄] or the E. Midland type with [ē].

The spelling *shild* probably stands for [ʃīld], from the E. Midland M.E. *schēld*, and not for the Southern M.E. *schild*.   The spelling *whir* ' where ' establishes an [ī]-sound in this word, which is described later also by writers on pronunciation.   The explanation of this sound in this word is, doubtless, that it has been influenced by *here*, which has *ē¹*.

Monophthonging of M.E. Diphthong ai.

This, I think, is proved by the spelling *agane* ' again ' in a letter of 1553, by *ganesays*, *pant*, *panter* ' paint ', ' painter ', in the Translations, and by the ' inverted spellings ' *maid* Vb. ' made ', and *maike* Vb. ' make '.

The spellings *dainger*, *daingerous* to my mind point in the same direction and probably indicate a pronunciation with [ē].   The Queen also occasionally retains the M.E. spelling *daunger*.

Murmur Vowel between Long Vowel, or Diphthong and following -r.

This seems to be shown by such spellings as *I desiar* ' desire ', *fiars* ' fires ', *hiar* ' hear '.   Such spellings are not uncommon in the sixteenth century, and curiously enough *desiar* occurs in a letter written by the Queen's mother, Anne Boleyn.

Other Vowel Spellings.

We are not surprised to find a diphthongal spelling in *faule* 'fall
fauleth, and *stauke* ' stalk ', since we saw these spellings in the former
century. Whether this was still pronounced as a diphthong is very
doubtful. (See pp. 251–3.)

The spelling *ou* and *u* for O.E. and Early M.E. *ō*, as we shall
see, is found several centuries earlier (cf. p. 234). Queen Elizabeth has
several examples :—*bloud, floude, louke* ' look ', *boutes* 'boots', *boukes,
houke,* ' hook '. The form *must* is probably short, and arose in the
unstressed position.

We must not omit to mention the spelling *fortiune* with *iu* for the
earlier French *ū* [*ȳ*]. I regard this form as representing M.E. *fortūne*
with the original French accentuation, on the second syllable. The
other type, accented on the first syllable, had become *fortin* by the middle
of the fifteenth century.

Vowels in Unstressed Syllables.

The suffixes *-ed, -es, -est, -ness* are constantly written *-id, -is,* &c. :—
preventid, acquaintid, &c. ; *-ed* is rarer ;
scusis ' excuses ', *practisis* ;
expertist, largist, fullist, hottist, &c. ;
kindnʾs, wekenis, happinis, darkenis ; also *witnis* ;
bestoith, burnith.

The ending *-er* is often written *-ar,* implying probably the pronunciation [ər] :—*sistar, bettar, bordars, murdar.*

The ending *-en* is written *-in* in *heauin.*

Where we now have the ending *-iour, -or* is written, in *behavor.*

The M.E. diphthong *ei* is written *a* in *vilanous,* and *e* in *the* for ' they ',
a very common spelling with Queen Elizabeth.

The tendency to join a consonant after a weak syllable to the following
syllable, when this is stressed, is shown in *my none witte* = ' mine own '.

The vowel of the Superlative suffix is lost in *carefulst, thankfulst.*

The unstressed forms *the* and *ther* ' they, their ' are frequent in all
Elizabeth's writings.

Consonants.

Loss of Consonants. *t* is lost after another Cons. before *-s* in *attemps,
accidens* ; after *f* before *n* in *offen* ' often '.

b is lost between *m-* and *-l-* in *nimlest* ' nimblest '.

l is lost before *-k* in *stauke* ' stalk '.

Addition of Consonants. A parasitic *t* is developed finally in *in
middest* (cf. also *Amidz it*), and *for the nonest.*

The parasitic nasal is seen in *messanger,* earlier *messager.*

Other Consonant Changes. The nasal [ŋ] ' *ng* ' in the suffix *-ing*
occurs once written *-n*—*besichen* ' beseeching '. The same sound at the
end of a stressed syllable occurs twice written *-nk*—*brinkinge of me up, our
brinkers up.*

The old voiceless *w,* formerly written *hw,* and then *wh,* was apparently
not pronounced in the Queen's English, since she writes *wich* ' which ',

and evidently used the voiced sound in this and other words beginning
with this consonant, as all Southern speakers do at present, unless they
have been subjected to Scotch or Irish influence.

M.E. *ō²* (from O.E. *ā*) when initial is written *wo-* in *won, wons* 'one,
once', and *ho-* is written *who-* in *wholy* 'wholly'. The former is the
ancestor of the type now in use, and it is interesting to note that *won*
occurs also in a letter in the handwriting of Henry VIII, written in 1544,
which shows that this type was current in Court English at this period,
although the other type, pronounced as in *on-*ly, seems also to have
survived much later in good English (see pp. 306–7). The arbitrary
character of present-day spelling is shown by the fact that we write *one*
and pronounce [wan], while although we do not pronounce *wh-* in *whole*
we yet write it thus. Queen Elizabeth also writes *hole* by the side of the
wh- spelling.

To pronounce [v] for voiced '*-th-*' [ð] is to this day an individual
peculiarity which is heard here and there, and Queen Elizabeth apparently
had it, and betrays it in the spelling *bequived* for *bequeathed*.

The metathesized form of old *-sc-* occurs in *axed* 'asked'.

Flexional *-s*, both as a Pl. and as a Possessive ending, is often written
-z, generally after voiced consonants, as in *quarelz, equalz, Russelz*
(Possess.), *Godz tuition, lordz*, &c.

The spelling *-tz* for *-ts* is also commoner in the Letters and the Translations—*fitz* Vb., *hartz, dartz*.

The old (English) type with *y-* instead of the Scandinavian type with
g- survives in *foryetfullness*.

Nouns.

The traditional change of *-f-* to *-v-* between vowels still survives in
liues, a typical Possess. Sing. of this period.

A 'group-possessive' occurs in 'I shulde . . . long sithens have
appeased *my lorde of Bedfords mynde therin*' (1553).

Among noteworthy Pl. forms we may note *oxe—a hundred oxe*, and
thanke—'the two gentilmen I trust shal receaue your *thanke*'.

News is used as a Sing. in *This last newes*; as a Pl. in *how grate ful
such newes were*.

A curious construction with *sort* is seen in '*a few sort* of outlawes *fils*
up his traine'.

Adjectives.

The only point I have noted is the inflected Pl. in *clirristz days*
(clearest).

Personal Pronouns.

There is not much to note beyond the fact that the Queen never uses
thou, &c., in the Sing.—always *you(e)*, and that by the side of *yt* the old
spelling *hit* is extremely frequent—I have counted twenty-eight examples
in twenty-one letters, and the form is also found in the Translations.

The unstressed forms of the Pl. Pronouns of the 3rd Pers. have already
been mentioned.

The Indefinite Article.

It is worth noting that *a* before a word beginning with a vowel occurs three times in a letter of 1549—'*a encreasinge* of ther ivel tonges, *a bridinge* of *a ivel* name, so ivel *a opinion*'.

Verbal Endings.

The chief points of interest are the endings of the 3rd Pers. Sing. Present, and of the Pl. Present. Concerning the former it must be recorded that the ending -*s* is very common in the later letters, and in the Translations. In the latter, indeed, this is the most frequent form, the -*th* ending being comparatively rare. In the early letters the -*s*- forms also occur, but in nothing like the same proportion as in the later ones and the Translations.

The Auxiliaries *hath* and *doth* seem only to occur in this form, and hardly ever with -*s*, though I have noted *your Grace has*—in a letter of 1549.

As regards the Pres. Pl. we find, besides forms with no ending, others in both -*th* and -*s* : e. g. the (' = they ') ar most deceued that *trusteth* most in themselves ; the (they) *breakith*, &c. ; all our *subjectes lokes* after ; small *flies stiks* fast for wekenis ; your *commissionars telz* me ; sild (= seldom) *recouers kings* ther dominion ; as the *hunters rates* ther houndz, and *kipes*, &c., &c. See also pp. 339–41, below.

Strong Verbs.

There is little to note under this head except that although *geue* 'give' occurs, the usual type is *giue, gyue*. The P. P. is *geuen* and *giuen*, and the curious and archaic type *yeouen* is found in a letter of 1595.

We have now examined, in some detail, the English of some typical personages of the sixteenth century, who between them cover the whole century. They spring from various classes and were engaged in different pursuits, but all of them, from the circumstances of their birth, their fortunes, and their occupations were brought into contact, in varying degrees, with the Court, and with the highest and most distinguished society of their age ; all of them by virtue of their opportunities and their education were certainly acquainted with the best type of Spoken English of the day, and in spite of occasional lapses into a native form here and there, they may be taken as individually and collectively exhibiting the Standard English of daily life and of literature.

From our brief survey we learn the existence of a certain latitude in the choice of type, both in pronunciation and in the use of grammatical forms.

It seemed worth while to make, on this account, this study of the speech of individuals, which brings home to us how considerably greater then than now was the possible variety in the speech of persons of approximately the same social entourage.

We learn also from the occasional spellings cited above, many important and interesting facts concerning the development of sound change in English, and concerning the distribution of varieties due to dialect of one kind or another.

We now turn to consider the English of an entirely different social stratum from that whose language we have hitherto examined in this century. **Henry Machyn**, the Diarist, seems from his own words to have been a simple tradesman, possibly an undertaker, with a taste for pageants—especially for funerals (as was natural)—and for gossip. Of the great persons whom he mentions, he knew no more than their names and faces, scanned as they rode past him in some procession, and an occasional piece of gossip picked up, one is inclined to think, from some other spectator among the crowd.

Machyn's work is a priceless monument of the English of the Middle Class Londoner with no particular education or refinement. We shall find therein, naturally, much that is common to the speech of the higher orders, but also certain marked features which distinguish his English from theirs; certain things, also, which are definitely stated to be Cockneyisms at a later date, although they have now passed away; and other things which we know from personal experience, or from comparatively recently extinct tradition, to have been typical vulgarisms fifty or so years ago.

The English of Henry Machyn, Citizen and Merchant Taylor of London.

Vowels.

M.E. _er._ The following occur with *-ar-* :—*clarkes* (passim), *Harfford* (Hereford), *sarvand*, the yerle of *Darbe*, *fardyng* 'farthing', *harold*, *armyn* 'ermine', *hard* 'heard', *hart*, *sarmon*, *parson*, *Garnsey*, *farm*, *Barmsey* 'Bermondsey', *sward* 'sword'. The *-er*-spellings include the following :—*clerk, serten, Bernard castyll, servandes, serjants, lernyd,* (Cole)*herber.*

M.E. _i_ is written _e_ (a) in the following two-syllabled words, in open syllables :—*denner*, also *deener* 'dinner', *cete* 'city', *pressun* 'prison', *vetell* 'victuals', *pelers* 'pillars', *pete* 'pity', *wedew, wedow* 'widow', *jebett* 'gibbet', *leved* 'lived', *veker* 'vicar', *velyns* 'villains', *vesitars, consperacy, sterope.*

(b) In the following words of three or more syllables:—*leveray* 'livery', *pelere* 'pillory', *Necolas, prevelegys, menyster.*

(c) In the following the vowel is certainly short :—*deleverd* 'delivered', *chelderyn, Recherd, essue* 'issue', *Eslyngton* 'Islington', *prensepulles, selver, red = rid* 'rode', *bellets, hes* 'is', *ennes* of the cowrtt.

The list under group (a) is larger than in most if not all other London writers or writers of Literary English whose language we have considered; group (c) is considerable, and if, as is probable, we are entitled to put (b) under the same head, i. e. of short *ĭ* lowered to _e_, the list becomes very large. The list in group (a) probably illustrates the lengthening and lowering of *i-* in open syllables, which is characteristic of the Northern dialects of M.E. and is also found in E. Midland—Robt. of Brunne, &c.

O.E. _ў_ occurs in all three types, the distribution of which is not precisely as at present :—

(a) With *i* :—*myche* 'much', *ymberyng* days 'Ember days', *first, gylded* Vb., *rysses* 'rushes' (plant).

(b) With *u* :—*furst, buryall*.

(c) With *e* :—*bered* 'buried' (very frequent), *besiness, mere* 'merry', *Crepulgate, beldyd* 'built', *kechens*.

M.E. *ŏ* unrounded :—the *marow* 'morrow', *caffen* 'coffin', *Dasset* 'Dorset'.

M.E. *au* appears to be monophthongized :—*ontt* 'aunt', *a nobe = an aulb* 'alb', *commondyd* (M.E. *commaund-*), *hopene* 'halfpenny' (earlier *haulf-*), *agmentyd* 'augmented'. That *au* had already become [ɔ] is further made probable by the spelling *caumplet* 'complete', which shows that the writer could not have considered *au* to represent a diphthongal sound.

This [ɔ] resulting from earlier *au* appears also to have been unrounded in *drane* 'drawn', *straberries* 'strawberries', *agmentyd* 'augmented'. Note the spelling *sarter* 'salter', which shows monophthonging of *sault*, then *unrounding*, the loss of *l* before *t*, and the use of -*r*- after a vowel to express mere quantity.

The spelling *Crenmer* 'Cranmer' shows the fronting of M.E. *ă*. The spelling *prast* for 'pressed' points in the same direction.

y is written for M.E. *ē* in *Qwyne, prych, fryndes, spykyng, brykyng, brykefast*. By the side of *weke* 'week', *wike* is also found. The form is, however, ambiguous.

Early Modern *ŭ* from *ū* from M.E. *ō*, or from M.E. *ŭ*, is written *a* in *Chamley* 'Cholmondeley', *Samerset* 'Somerset', and suggests that the un-rounding of *ŭ* had already taken place. The form *Watton* for 'Wotton' appears to indicate that this change had come about, in the speech of Machyn, also after *w-*.

The old diphthong *ai* can hardly have retained its diphthongal pro-nunciation. Such spellings as *mayde* 'made', *stayffes* 'staves', show that this combination of letters could be used without any idea of a diphthongal value, and the word *mayor*, which formerly certainly had a diphthong, is found written *mere* as well as *mayre*.

The spelling *oy* for M.E. *ō²*, O.E. *ā*, is curious and occurs several times :—*cloyth* 'cloth', *boyth* 'both' (passim), *hoyth* 'oath'. Initially this vowel is still written in *one, oon* 'one', but the form *won* also occurs.

The Southern type, from an old *ǣ*, is preserved in *prate* 'pretty'.

The combination -*ench* appears as -*ynch* in *Kyngbynche* (twice).

The combination *wă-* becomes *wo-* in *wosse* 'wash'.

Vowel Shortenings.

These are evidently expressed by the doubling of the final consonant in the following words :—*gott* 'goat', *fottman* 'footman', *swett* 'sweat', also *swett* 'sweet', *grett* 'great', *heddes* 'heads', *mett* 'meet' (passim).

Vowel Lengthening.

This has already taken place in *gaard*, where the doubled vowel can have no other meaning. In this case, either the *r* has already been weakened, or the lengthening occurred earlier than the loss of *r*. It is pretty certain that *aa* here does not imply [*a*] but [*ǣ*].

Unstressed Syllables.

There is the evidence so common since the fifteenth century of the levelling of the vowels in unstressed syllables under an indeterminate sound which the writer found it hard to express :—

Roch*a*ster, Wynch*a*ster, but Lank*o*ster; Just*u*s a pesse, Cheyffe Just*u*s ; progr*a*sse, comp*e*ny, Crystynm*u*s, secret*e*ry, where the italicized letters probably all stand for [ə]. The family name *Seymour* is written *Semer* = [sĩmə(r)].

Initially where unstressed *ŭ* is written *a* in *apone* ' upon ', *o* is written in the same way in *apinions*, *e* in *aronyous* ' erroneous '.

The ending *-y* is often written *e*, e. g. *lade* ' lady ', *Darbe* ' Derby ', *pete* ' pity ', *galere* ' gallery '.

French *u* is written *e* in *mysseforten* ' misfortune ', *y* in *nevys* ' nephews ', *venterer* ' venturer ', also written *ventorer*.

Old long vowels are shortened in unstressed syllables—this is probably a survival of the normal M.E. shortening in *wyldfulle* = ' -fowl ', *greyhond* ' greyhound ', M.E. *-hŭnd*.

The diphthong *oi* is written *y* in *Gaskyn* ' Gascoigne ' ; *ai* is written *e* in *palles*, M.E. *pallais* or *palleis*.

Loss of Syllable.

Initial vowels are lost in *postyll* ' apostle ', *salt* ' assault '.

An unstressed syllable immediately following that with the chief stress is lost in *Barmsey*, i. e. *Beorhmundesēy* ' Bermondsey '.

The Consonants.

A peculiarity of frequent occurrence in Machyn is the confusion of *v-* and *w-*, so that the former is used for the latter and vice versa.

Examples of *w-* for *v-* :—*wacabondes* ' vagabonds ', *wergers*, *waluw* ' value ', *wue* ' view ', *welvet* ' velvet ', *wettelle* ' victuals ', *walans* ' valance ', *woyce* ' voice '.

Examples of *v-* for *w-* :—*voman*, *vomen*, *veyver* ' weaver ', *Volsake* ' Woolsack ', *Vestmynster*, *Vetyngton* ' Whittington ', *Vosseter* ' Worcester ', *Voderoff* (Pr. N.), also written *Woodroffe*.

Loss of Consonants.

(a) *Finally* :—*blyne* ' blind ', *Egype*.

(b) *Initially*, *w* before *o* = [ŭ]:—*Odam* for *Woodham*.

(c) *Medially, in combinations* :—*t* + *s* becomes *-s-* —*Wyssun* ' Whitsun ', *d* lost after *-l-* before *j* [dž]—*Oll Jury* = ' Old Jewry '.   *d* + *s* is lost :—*Wostreet* ' Woodstreet ', *Lumbarstrett* ; *ndf* becomes *-nf-* —*granefather* ; *-nds-* becomes *-ns-* —*granser* ; *-rnm* becomes *-rm-* —*Yrmongers*. The combination *-pb-* is simplified to *-b-* —*cubard* ' cupboard '; *-nkt-* becomes *-nt-* —*santtuary*.

Loss of -l- *before consonants* :—This occurs before *-n-* in *swone* P.P. ' swollen '; before *-m-* in *reme, ream* ' realm '; before *-k-* in *Northfoke* ; before *-p-* in *hopene* ' halfpenny '; before *-f* in *Raff* ' Ralph ' (this is perhaps

L

from a French form *Rauf*, as *sāfe* from *sauf*); before *g* [dž] in *sawgears* 'soldiers'.

Loss of -r *in combination with* -s:— *Woseter*, *Vosseter* 'Worcester', *Dasset* 'Dorset', *Masselsay* 'Marshalsea', *Cosseletts*.

Loss of -v- *between vowels* :—*Denshyre* 'Devonshire'. In an unstressed syllable, before another cons., -n- is lost in *sune elaw* 'son-in-law'.

Addition of Consonants.

Final -d- *after* -l :—*Sakefeld* for Sackville. This may, however, be partly suggested by the suffix -*field*.

Development of a parasitic -n- before [dž] is seen in *messenger*, *Selenger* from *Se(nt) Leger*.

The Misplacement of an Initial Aspirate.

This is dropped in the following words :—*alffe, alff* 'half', *alpeny* 'halfpenny', *Amton courte, elmet* 'helmet' (frequently), *arnesse* 'harness', *alters* 'halters', *ard* 'hard', *yt* 'hit' Vb., *Allallows, ede* 'head'. In *Cornnyll* 'Cornhill' the loss is normal in the unstressed element of a compound, and the same is true of *Lussam* for 'Lewisham'. *h* is improperly added initially in :—*hanswered, haskyd*, Sant Andrews *hundershaft, Halesander* 'Alexander', *harme* 'arm' (of the body), *harmes* (in heraldry), *here* 'ear', *hoathe, herth* 'earth', *hetten* 'eaten', *hevere* 'every', *Hambrose*. This addition, as in present-day vulgar speech, only occurs in stressed words ; thus we find *hat* for *at*, at the end of a sentence—*a grett dener as I have be hat*, and *has* for *as* when this stands in a stressed position at the beginning of a sentence.

The above is the largest list of 'dropped aspirates' in words of English, not Norman-French, origin which I have found in any document as early as this. The addition of *h*- is commoner, but nowhere, I believe, so frequent as in Machyn.

Initial *wh*- was evidently pronounced simply as *w*- by Machyn, as is shown by the spellings *wyped, wypyd* 'whipped', *wyche* 'which', *watt* 'what', *warff* 'wharf', and the inverted spelling *whent* for *went*.

Old -*gh*- = [χ] is written -*th*- in *Luthborow* 'Loughborough'.

Initial *th*- [þ] appears as *f*- in *frust* 'thrust', *Frogmorton* 'Throgmorton'.

Final *ng* in the suffix -*ing* is written -*yn* in *standyn—The Queen grace standyn in the galere*, also *syttyn, rydyn, syngyne* ; on the other hand we get *evyngsong* 'evensong', *ymberyng days = ymberen* 'Ember days'.

The combination -*rth*- [rð] is occasionally written -*rd*- —*fardyng* 'farthing'.

The initial lip-glide is expressed by *w*- in *won* 'one', by the side of *one, oon*. The phrase *good ons* occurs, which suggests our 'good 'uns'.

An initial front-glide before a front vowel occurs in *yerle* 'earl'. This may possibly be a Kentish form (cf. p. 41 (4)).

Voicing of Consonants.

This occurs finally (before the Pl. suffix) in *drynges* 'drinks'; medially before suffix -*yd* in *hundyd* 'hunted'; further as a combinative change before *-b* in *sagbottes* 'sackbuts'; medially, between vowels in *elevant* 'elephant'.

Nouns.

The Possessive Singular is fairly frequent without any suffix—e. g. *the Kyng grace, his brodur horse, my lord cardenall commyng, a hossear sune* 'hosier's son', *yn ys father stede.* Some of the above have a normal loss of *-s* before a word beginning in *s-*.

The following uninflected Possessives may be regarded as old Feminines:—*Lade Mare grace, my lady grasys,* &c., 'my lady's grace', &c., *the quen syster,* though in the last instance the loss of suffix may be due to the following *s-*. The use of *ys* instead of the regular Possessive suffix after a noun is seen in *the penter ys nam.*

The following Group Possessives are found, showing omission of the suffix:—*the bishop of London palles; the duke of Somerset dowther.*

The following instance occurs of Group Possessives in which *ys* 'his' is used instead of the Possessive suffix after the last noun:—*the nuw byshope of Lychffeld and Coventre ys wyff.*

The older construction instead of the Group Possessive occurs:—*master Godderyke sune the goldsmith.* The *-s* is omitted of *Godderyke* before following *s-*.

As regards Plurals, the only noteworthy points are the use of the invariables—*sturgeon* and *C gret horsse,* and a curious collection of names of animals:—*mottuns* 'sheep', *velles* 'calves', *swines, samons.* The voiceless *f* before the Pl. suffix occurs in *beyffes* 'beeves', and *wyeffes* 'wives'. Similarly we find *f* in the old Dat. Sing. *a-lyffe* 'alive' from *on life.*

Pronouns.

There is not much of note to record regarding the Pers. Pronouns. The weak form *ys* of Possess. Sing. 3rd Pers. Masc. is very frequent. In the 2nd Pers. Pl. *youe* seems the only form in the Nom. The form *hytt* 'it' is still found, but is rare. It does not seem to be determined by strong stress. *Yt* is the usual form. *Her* 'their' occurs at least once, cp. p. 328 below.

Emphatic Pronouns. *The yonge French Kyng has proclaymed ynseyllff Kyng of Skotland.* Is *yn-* written for *ym-*, or is it by any chance a late survival of the O.E. *hine,* rare already in Early M.E.?

She lepyd into a welle and drownyd yr seyllff.

Relative Pronouns. 'Who' is spelt *wo,* a curious form, as we should have expected *ho.* Can there have been a real pronunciation with *w-* at this period?

We find *as* used as a Relative :—*the goodlyest collars as ever youe saw.*

A fairly frequent construction with *the wyche,* followed by a Pers. Pron. or a Noun, recalls a modern Cockney vulgarism with *which* :—*the funeral of my lade Browne the wyche she ded* ('died') *in chyld-bed; the wyche he dwelt in Lumbarstrett; the wyche the Quen grace was ther.*

An interesting example of the omission of the Relative is found :—*This ij day of March was consecratyd at the byshope of London palles master Younge byshope of Yorke, was byshope of San Davids.*

Impersonal Pronoun. The Possess. of *one* is found in the form *one ys ere* 'one's ear'.

Indefinite Article.

The form without the nasal is sometimes used before a vowel :—*a arme, a orayson, a elevant* ('elephant').

Definite Article.

The forms *her thuder* 'her other', *her thodur ere cut*, &c., presumably stand for *the* with the elision of the vowel before a following vowel, which is very common at this period and much later. It is curious to find the Article used after a Possess. Pron.

Verbal Endings.

I have few examples of Machyn's form of the 3rd Pers. Pres. Sing. From the form of his work this part of the Verb would naturally be rare. But cf. specimen, and p. 333, below. There are, however, a few examples of Pres. Pls. in -*s* :—*comys, lys* 'lie'.

There is little to note concerning Auxiliary Verbs. *Ar* is used in Pres. Pl.; the P. P. is *be*, as well as *bene, byne*, and the shortened *byn*.

In unstressed positions weak forms of *have* without the aspirate occur : 'If my lord mer, and my lord Cortenay *ad* not ben ther'; and a shortened form of the Inf. occurs in 'he told them that he wold not *a* savyd', &c.

Do is used as now in negative sentences—'the chyld *dyd not* spyke.'

Strong Verbs.

The following forms are worth notice :—Preterites—*gayf* (where *y* apparently expresses length), *begane* (with long vowel on analogy of Pret. of *give*?), *I say* 'I saw' (corresponding to Chaucer's *sey*), *sluw* 'slew', *druw* 'drew' (apparently phonetic renderings of the normal descendants of the O.E. forms *slōg* and *drōg*), *red* 'rode' (from the P. P. type, with the characteristic lowering of *i* to *e*); the P. P.'s *gyffen, drane* (with monophthonging followed by unrounding from *draun*), *swone* 'swollen', *sene* 'seen', and the phonetically-written *syne*.

The word *choose* appears in two varieties—*chuysse* (Inf.) and *chusse*. It is probable that these both represent the same form with [ȳ], which must perhaps be regarded as a descendant of the Western type with [ȳ] spelt *u*. On the other hand, since *y* in Machyn's spelling seems to be used occasionally as a sign of length, these spellings may both stand for [tʃūz] from M.E. *chōsen*, O.E. *c(e)ósan*. The spelling *loysse* 'lose' may represent the ancestor of our present type with [ū] from old tense *ō*.

The great value of Machyn's Diary is that it lets us into more secrets of contemporary speech than does any other work of the period—indeed we have to go back a hundred years, to Gregory, to find a collection of spellings and forms which throw such light upon pronunciation. Machyn is obviously inferior to his predecessor both in social standing and in education. The latter fact has turned out to be of inestimable advantage to students of English, since the Diarist is marvellously emancipated from traditional spelling. The former circumstance makes him a priceless guide to the lower type of London English of his day. His lack of literary education, combined with the absence of views regarding elegance and refinement, make him a high authority upon the ways of natural unstudied speech in the sixteenth century.

Among the chief features of Machyn's Class dialect we may mention:—the large number of cases of lowering of $\breve{i}$ to $\breve{e}$, ; the cases of unrounding of short $\breve{o}$, which are rather in excess of those found in writers of higher standing; the misplacement, by omission and wrong insertion, of initial h-; the interchange of v- and w-; the excessive number of combinative changes in the consonants, which, although they may all be paralleled from the writings of persons of a higher class, do not occur in their written documents in such profusion as here ; the peculiar use of *which* noted above, and the use of *as* as a Relative Pronoun.

We conclude this chapter with a short specimen of Machyn's style.

p. 139, 1557. The xvj day of June my yong duke of Norfoke rod abrod and at Stamford-hylle my lord havying a dage hangyng on ys Sadylle bow, and by mysse-fortune dyd shutt yt, and [1] yt on of ys men that ryd afor, and so by myssforten ys horse dyd flyng and so he hangyd on by vn of ys sterope, and so thatt the horse knokyd ys brayns owt with flyngyng owt with ys leges.

p. 146, *last day of June.* The sam day the Kyng grace rod [2] on untyng into the forest and kyllyd a grett stage with gones.

The iiij of August was the masse of requiem for my lade prenses of Cleyff . . . and ther my lord abbott of Westmynster mad a godly sermon as ever was mad, and the byshope of London song masse in ys myter, (and after) masse my lord byshope and my lord abbott mytered dyd (cense) the corsse, and afterward she was caried to her tomb (where) she leys with a herse-cloth of gold the wych lyys (over her) ; and ther alle her hed offerers brake ther stayffes, her [3] hussears brake ther rodes, and all they cast them into her tombe; the wyche was covered her co(rrse) with blake, and all the lordes and lades and knyghtes and gentyllmen and gentill-vomen dyd offer, and after masse a grett (dener) at my lord abbots, and my lade of Wynchester was the cheyff (mourner) and my lord admeroll and my lord Dacre wher of ether syde of my lade of Wynchester and so they whent in order to dinner.

[1] hit.   [2] a hunting.   [3] ushers.

CHAPTER V

THE SEVENTEENTH AND EIGHTEENTH CENTURIES

'MEN of the renascence', says Mr. Swinburne, in his tract on Shakespeare, 'could no more be expected to talk like men of the middle ages—whether contemporaries of Dante, of Chaucer, or of Villon—than like men of our own age. Each century or so, if we accept the convenient and casual division of manners and of styles by the rough and ready reckoning of successive dates, has its own natural conventions of life and art, from which none can entirely escape but by servile affectation of an obsolete manner, or fatuous affectation of an unnatural style.'

The student of English, who has some vital feeling for the genius of English speech as it was in the age just following Chaucer, and in the age of Elizabeth, discovers, when he continues his studies into the seventeenth century, that he is gradually emerging as the century advances into a new world of language, and one more different from that which he is leaving behind him, than was this, at least to his perceptions, from those earlier periods through which his studies have led him. The ordinary reader has not time or occasion to saturate himself thoroughly in the style of the successive periods of Hoccleve and Lydgate and Skelton, of the Pastons and Celys; of More, Elyot, and Lord Berners; of Surrey, Wyatt, Latimer, and Fisher; of Sackville, Sidney, Spenser, and Raleigh; of Machyn, Ascham, Gabriel Harvey, Sir Thomas Smith, Lyly; of Bacon, Shakespeare, and Jonson. He is conscious, indeed, that where all is more or less remote and unfamiliar as regards turns of phrase, cadence, and the general movement of sentences, the style of the three last is nearer to him than that of the writers whose names come earlier in the list, but he feels that in numerous ways theirs is not the English of his own day. It is difficult, perhaps, to be fully alive to the gradual changes which are coming over the modes of expression during a couple of centuries, when everything is more or less strange. It is different as we proceed into the heart of the seventeenth century. We begin to feel that we are getting into our own time as we leave behind us the great writers who were born, and did most of their work, in the sixteenth century, and with Beaumont and Fletcher, Carew and Walton, we lose more and more the feeling that we are reading the 'old writers'. Putting aside Milton, whose 'soul was like a star and dwelt apart', and perhaps Sir Thomas Browne, whose style, in spite of its opulence and magnificence, never attains the easy familiarity of Suckling, we feel, when we read the prose of the men born during the first and second decades of the seventeenth century, and in some cases of those born in the nineties of the sixteenth, that all, though in varying degrees, speak like the people of our own age. This is specially true of Suckling (1609–42) and Cowley (1618–67).

After these men there can be no question that however much it may be possible to indicate here and there certain characteristic habits of style, tricks, mannerisms, or whatever we may call them, which adorn or disfigure the prose writings of a particular generation, we have reached our own English in very spirit and substance.

In order to bring home this gradual passage from something different to something which is the English of our own age in all its essentials, we must examine, side by side, a few passages from writers born between the middle of the sixteenth century and the end of the second decade of the next. We may take as a typical piece of late sixteenth-century prose a passage from *A View of the Present State of Ireland*, by Edmund Spenser (1552(?)-99).

'And yet the rebellion of Thomas Fitz Gerrald did well-nygh stretch itself into all partes of Ireland. But that, which was in the time of the government of the Lord Gray, was surely noe less generall then all those ; for there was no part free from the contagion, but all conspired in one to cast of theyr subjection to the crowne of England. Nevertheless, through the most wise and valiaunt handling of that right noble Lord, it gott not that head which the former evills found ; for in them the realme was left, like a shippe in a storme amiddest all the raging surges, unruled, and undirected of any : for they to whom she was comitted either faynted in theyr labour, or forsooke theyre charge. But he (like a most wise pilote) kept her course carefully, and held her moste strongly even agaynst those roring billowes, that he brought her safely out of all ; soe as long after, even by the space of twelve or thirtene yeares, she rode in peace, through his only paynes and excellent enduraunce, how ever envye list to bluster agaynst him.'

The next example is from Bacon's *Essay on Friendship*. Bacon was born in 1561 and died in 1626.

'How many things are there which a man cannot, with any face or comeliness, say or do himself ? A man cannot alledge his own merits with modesty much less extol them : a man cannot sometimes brook to supplicate or beg ; and a number of the like. But all these things are graceful in a friend's mouth, which are blushing in a man's own. So again, a man's person hath many proper relations, which he cannot put off. A man cannot speak to his son but as a father ; to his wife, but as a husband ; to his enemy but upon terms ; whereas a friend may speak as the case requires, and not as it sorteth with the person. But to enumerate these things were endless ; I have given the rule, where a man cannot fitly play his own part ; if he have not a friend he may quit the stage.'

The gentle Izaak Walton is a good representative of the seventeenth century. Born in 1593, six years before the death of Spenser, he lived well into the last quarter of the seventeenth century, dying in 1683. If his style lacks the brilliancy and sparkle that belong to the later generation which grew up and matured long before the end of his life, Walton is endeared to us by his genuine goodness of character, his love of the country, and the simplicity and sincerity of his writing. His failings, if they were such, certainly 'leaned to virtue's side'. Besides his enthusiasm, which we need not further refer to, for fishing, he was deeply attached to the Church of England, and had a distinct *penchant* for dignitaries. The following passage from the *Life of Sir Henry Wotton* exhibits the simple and unaffected graces of Walton's style :

'He (Sir Henry) returned out of Italy into England about the thirtieth year of his age, being then noted by many both for his person and comportment; for indeed he was of a choice shape, tall of stature and of a most persuasive behaviour; which was so mixed with sweet discourse and civilities, as gained him much love from all persons with whom he entered into an acquaintance. And whereas he was noted in his youth to have a sharp wit and apt to jest; that, by time, travel, and conversation, was so polished, and made so useful, that his company seemed to be one of the delights of mankind; insomuch as Robert Earl of Essex—then one of the Darlings of Fortune, and in greatest favour with Queen Elizabeth—invited him first into a friendship, and, after a knowledge of his great abilities, to be one of his Secretaries; the other being Mr. Henry Cuffe, sometime of Merton College in Oxford,—and there also the acquaintance of Sir Henry Wotton in his youth,—Mr. Cuffe being then a man of no common note in the University for his learning; nor after his removal from that place, for the great abilities of his mind, nor indeed for the fatalness of his end.'

We pass now to the prose of perhaps the greatest Englishman born during the seventeenth century, John Milton. When Milton was born, in 1608, Spenser had only been dead nine years, Shakespeare had still eight more years to live, Donne was a young man of 35, Marston and Fletcher were 33, and Beaumont nine years younger. Bacon was 47, Waller was a child of three. It is almost impious to say so, but it must be said that Milton's prose is not in the direct line of descent from the great writers his predecessors, nor do those of the following ages derive from him. In spite of its many splendours, and its massive weight, this style does not reflect the age, however much it may express the personality of Milton. It is magnificent and memorable, but it exists in solitary state, remote, and unrelated to the general current of English speech.

Against Prelatry, Book II (vol. i, p. 221):

'For although a Poet, soaring in the high Region of his Fancies, with his Garland and singing Robes about him, might, without apology, speak more of himself than I mean to do; yet for me sitting here below in the cool Element of Prose, a mortal thing among many Readers of no Empyreal Conceit, to venture and divulge unusual things of my self, I shall petition to the gentler sort, it may not be envy to me. I must say therefore, that after I had from my first years, by the ceaseless diligence and care of my Father, whom God recompence, been exercis'd to the Tongues, and some Sciences, as my Age would suffer, by sundry Masters and Teachers both at home and at the schools, it was found, that when ought was impos'd me by them that had the overlooking, or betak'n to of mine own choise in English, or other Tongue, prosing or versing, but chiefly this latter, the stile by certain vital Signs it had, was likely to live. But much latelier, in the privat Academies of Italy, whither I was favor'd to resort, perceiving that some Trifles which I had in memory, compos'd at under twenty or thereabout (for the manner is, that every one must give some proof of his wit and reading there) met with acceptance above what was lookt for, and other things which I had shifted in scarcity of Books and Conveniences to patch up amongst them, were receiv'd with written Encomiums, which the Italian is not forward to bestow on men of this side the Alps, I began thus far to assent both to them and divers of my friends here at home; and not less to an inward prompting which now grew daily upon me, that by labour and intent study, (which I take to be my portion in this Life) joyn'd with the strong propensity of Nature, I might perhaps leave something so written to after-times, as they should not willingly let it die.'

This is Milton speaking in prose, 'with his Garland and singing Robes about him'; it is not the speech of ordinary life, nor of ordinary people in any age. But even when Milton descends to a very different level and expresses such human feelings and passions as personal hatred, prejudice, and intolerance, his style is never that of the common man; like his own hero, he is never ' less than Archangel ruined '.

No less remarkable than Milton in possessing a prose style aloof from, and unrelated to, that which is typical of the age, is his near contemporary Sir Thomas Browne, from whom we quote three passages.

Religio Medici, Pt. II, Sec. 11 (Ed. of 1659):

'Now for my life, it is a miracle of thirty years which to relate, were not a history but a piece of Poetry, and would sound to common eares like a fable; for the world I count it not an Inne, but an Hospital, and a place, not to live, but to dye in. The world that I regard is my selfe, it is the Microcosme of mine own frame, that I cast mine eye on; for the other, I use it but like my Globe, and turne it round sometimes for my recreation. Men that looke upon my outside, perusing only my condition, and fortunes, doe erre in my altitude; for I am above Atlas his shoulders. The earth is a point not onely in respect of the heavens above us, but of that heavenly and celestiall part within us : that masse of flesh that circumscribes mee, limits not my minde; that surface that tels the heavens it hath an end, cannot perswade mee I have any; I take my circle to bee above three hundred and sixty, though the number of the Arte doe measure my body, it comprehendeth not my mind : whilst I study to find how I am a Microcosme or little world, I find my self something more than the great.'

From *Vulgar Errors*, Book III, chap. xxii :

'As for its possibility we shall not at present dispute; nor will we affirm that Iron ingested, receiveth in the stomack of the Oestridge no alteration at all; but if any such there be, we suspect this effect rather from some way of corrosion, then any of digestion; not any liquid reduction or tendance to chilification by the power of natural heat, but rather some attrition from an acide and vitriolous humidity in the stomack, which may absterse and shave the scorious parts thereof.'

From *Hydriotaphia*, chap. v :

'There is nothing strictly immortall, but immortality; whatever hath no beginning may be confident of no end. All others have a dependent being, and within the reach of destruction, which is the peculiar of that necessary essence that cannot destroy it self; And the highest strain of omnipotency to be so powerfully constituted as not to suffer even from the power of itself. But the sufficiency of Christian Immortality frustrates all earthly glory, and the quality of either state after death, makes a folly of posthumous memory. God who can onely destroy our souls, and hath assured our resurrection, either of our bodies or names hath directly promised no duration. Wherein there is so much chance that the boldest Expectants have found unhappy frustration; and to hold long subsistence, seems but to scape in oblivion. But man is a Noble Animal, splendid in ashes, and pompous in the grave, solemnizing Nativities and Deaths, with equall lustre, nor omitting Ceremonies of bravery, in the infamy of his nature.'

The first passage above quoted, and much of the work from which it comes, is the nearest approach which Sir Thomas Browne makes to a natural style in his great works themselves. The Epistles to Thomas

Le Gros, and to Nicholas Bacon, and the Preface, to the Reader, of *Religio Medici* are, on the whole, free from the author's peculiar mannerisms, and while they lack the qualities which distinguish the best writing of the age, are not very different from the general run of such productions.

Every element in this author's characteristic style is intensely individual: the vocabulary—a marvellous assemblage of costly incrustations—the word order, the whole structure and cadence of the sentence. The last chapter of *Hydriotaphia* is a veritable *tour de force*; it soars to an almost incredible pitch of sustained eloquence, which never falters nor declines in intensity and volume, from the opening to the closing words.

It is probable that whether Sir Thomas Browne's contemporaries enjoyed his style or not, it appeared to them nearly as bizarre as it does to us. It would be interesting to know, for instance, what Dryden, who was born about a quarter of a century later than Browne, and outlived him by eighteen years, thought of the style of *Hydriotaphia*.

We may now with advantage pass to Sir John Suckling and Cowley, both of whom are contrasted by Dryden with the writers of the former age—Shakespeare, Ben Jonson, Beaumont and Fletcher—as exhibiting the best qualities of his own, qualities to which the older writers had not yet attained. ‘Shakespeare's language is likewise a little obsolete’, says Dryden in *Essay of Dramatic Poesy* (p. 81), and again, ‘they’ (the writers of the former age) ‘can produce nothing so courtly writ, or which expresses so much the conversation of a gentleman, as Sir John Suckling; nothing so even, sweet, and flowing, as Mr. Waller; nothing so majestic, so correct, as Sir John Denham; nothing so elevated, so copious, and full of spirit, as Mr. Cowley’ (ibid., pp. 34–5).

We are not immediately concerned with the ultimate justness of this appraisement of relative literary values, but merely with the fact that Dryden wishes to emphasize the difference of language which separates the older writers from those of his own day. ‘That an alteration is lately made in ours (our language), or since the writers of the last age (in which I include Shakespeare, Fletcher, and Jonson), is manifest’ (*Dramatic Poetry of the Last Age*, p. 164). This will be manifest also to the reader who has studied the various specimens given above when he compares them with the short quotations from Dryden, and still more so when he considers longer passages of this great man. But, not to anticipate, let us first see how Sir John Suckling ‘expresses the conversation of a gentleman’. I take this to refer not merely to the dialogue of his plays, but to his writing as a whole, to the ease, the lack of stiffness, and the well-bred self-possession and naturalness which pervade all he wrote.

Here is one of his letters to ‘Aglaura’:

‘My dear Dear,—Think I have kissed your letter to nothing and now know not what to answer; or that, now I am answering, I am kissing you to nothing, and know not how to go on! For, you must pardon, I must hate all I send you here, because it expresses nothing in respect of what it leaves behind with me. And O! why should I write then? Why should I not come myself? Those tyrants, business, honour, and necessity, what have they to do with you and I? Why should we not do love's commands before theirs, whose sovereignty is but usurped upon us? Shall we not smell roses 'cause others do look on, or gather them 'cause there are prickles, and something that would hinder us? Dear, I fain would, and know no hindrance but what must come from you; and why should any come? Since 'tis not I but you, must be sensible how much time we lose, it being long time since I was not myself but yours' (Works, ii, pp. 197–8).

The following is in a very different strain, and is taken from the *Discourse of Religion* (Works, ii, pp. 245–6):

'The strangest, though most epidemical, disease of all religions has been an imagination men have had that the imposing painful and difficult things upon themselves was the best way to appease the Deity, grossly thinking the chief service and delight of the Creator to consist in the tortures and sufferings of the creature. How laden with changeable and unnecessary ceremonies the Jews were, their feasts, circumcisions, sacrifices, great Sabbaths and little Sabbaths, fasts, burials, indeed almost all worship sufficiently declare; and that the Mahometans are much more infected appears by . . . lancing themselves with knives, putting out their eyes upon the sight of their prophet's tomb, and the like. . . . Our religion teaches us to bear afflictions patiently when they fall upon us, but not to force them upon ourselves; for we believe the God we serve wise enough to choose his own service, and therefore presume not to add to His commands.'

It is hardly temerarious to date the beginning of typical seventeenth-century prose from Suckling.

In him we find, almost for the first time, the accents of that age which has given to succeeding generations the models of clarity, elegance, and urbanity. Dying in 1642, Suckling was 'taken away from the evil to come'; but if he was spared the mortification of seeing the triumph of the usurper and the martyrdom of the King, neither did he enjoy the frolics of the Restoration, nor know the later perfections of English speech in literature and in its colloquial forms.

From Suckling we naturally pass to Cowley, and consider a passage from an Essay.

Of my Self.

'It is a hard and nice Subject for a man to write of himself; it grates his own heart to say any thing of disparagement, and the Readers Ears to hear any thing of praise from him. There is no danger from me of offending him in this kind; neither my Mind, nor my Body, nor my Fortune, allow me any materials for that Vanity. It is sufficient, for my own contentment, that they have preserved me from being scandalous, or remarkable on the defective side. But besides that, I shall here speak of my self, only in relation to the subject of these precedent discourses, and shall be likelier thereby to fall into the contempt, than rise up to the estimation of most people. As far as my memory can return back into my past Life, before I knew, or was capable of guessing what the World, or Glories, or Business of it were, the natural affections of my Soul gave a secret bent of aversion from them, as some Plants are said to turn away from others, by an Antipathy imperceptible to themselves, and inscrutable to Mans understanding. Even when I was a very young Boy at School, instead of running about on Holydays, and playing with my Fellows, I was wont to steal from them and walk into the Fields, either alone with a Book, or with some one Companion, if I could find any of the same Temper. I was then too so much an Enemy to constraint, that my Masters could never prevail on me, by any perswasions, or encouragements, to learn without Book the common Rules of Grammar, in which they dispenced with me alone, because they found I made a shift to do the usual exercise out of my own reading and observation.'

With Cowley the new era is well on its way. This is no longer the diction of the 'last age'. It has all the grace of the seventeenth century in its middle period, none of the eccentricities of Browne, none of the soaring above human life and common modes of expression that is felt in the prose of Milton, none of the frigid didactics or haughty aloofness of Bacon. The style of Cowley's prose Essays has given to these works a permanence which their intrinsic interest alone would hardly have secured. It is familiar without overstepping the bounds of good manners, easy without lapsing into slovenliness, and it preserves stateliness without sacrificing intimacy. It is colloquial in the best sense. What Dr. Spratt affirms of his conversation is true of his writings—'In his Speech neither the pleasantness excluded gravity, nor was the sobriety of it inconsistent with delight.'

In Cowley are found neither the lofty eloquence of Dryden's noblest passages, nor the pointed brilliancy of Congreve. The former was alien to the altogether slighter character of the elder poet, while the latter belongs peculiarly to the Restoration.

And this brings us to Dryden, whose style in 'the other harmony of prose' we shall observe as he acts as our guide to the matter in hand—the development of English literary and colloquial style after the age of Elizabeth.

In the Essay on the *Dramatic Poetry of the Last Age* (Essays, vol. i, p. 174, &c.) Dryden says:

'I have always acknowledged the wit of our predecessors, with all the veneration which becomes me; but I am sure their wit was not that of gentlemen; there was ever somewhat that was ill-bred and clownish in it, and which confessed the conversation of the authors.

'And this leads me to the last and greatest advantage of our writing, which proceeds from *conversation*. In the age wherein these poets lived, there was less of gallantry than in ours; neither did they keep the best company of theirs. Their fortune has been much like that of Epicurus, in the retirement of his gardens; to live almost unknown, and to be celebrated after their decease. I cannot find that any of them had been conversant in courts, except Ben Jonson; and his genius lay not so much that way, as to make an improvement by it. Greatness was not then so easy of access, nor conversation so free, as now it is. I cannot, therefore, conceive it any insolence to affirm, that, by the knowledge and pattern of their wit who writ before us, and by the advantage of our own conversation, the discourse and raillery of our comedies excel what has been written by them.'

It is necessary to note that, as Mr. Ker points out in the Preface to his edition of the Essays, Dryden uses *Wit* in the larger sense of propriety of language, and also in the narrower and stricter sense of *sharpness of conceit*. In the above passage it appears to be used in the former sense.

Dryden here advances several important propositions. The dramatic writers his predecessors did exhibit in their plays the actual speech of their age—the style 'confessed the conversation of the authors'; but it was not the conversation of gentlemen, not the best example of the speech of their age therefore, but that of clownish and ill-bred persons;

the dramatic writing of his own age also expresses the 'conversation' of
the time, but now, being based upon a more refined and polished type
of this, 'the discourse and raillery of our comedies excel' those of his
predecessors.

Dryden proceeds :

'Now, if they ask me, whence it is that our conversation is so much
refined? I must freely, and without flattery, ascribe it to the Court; and
in it, particularly to the King, whose example gives a law to it. His own
misfortunes, and the nation's, afforded him an opportunity which is rarely
allowed to sovereign princes, I mean of travelling, and being conversant
in the most polished courts of Europe ; and thereby cultivating a spirit
which was formed by nature to receive the impressions of a gallant and
generous education. At his return, he found a nation lost as much in
barbarism as in rebellion; and as the excellency of his nature forgave
the one, so the excellency of his manners reformed the other. The
desire of imitating so great a pattern first awakened the dull and heavy
spirits of the English from their natural reservedness; loosened them
from their stiff forms of conversation, and made them easy and pliant to
each other in discourse. Thus, insensibly, our way of living became more
free ; and the fire of English wit, which was before stifled under a con-
strained melancholy way of breeding, began first to display its force, by
mixing the solidity of our nation with the air and gaiety of our neighbours.
This being granted to be true, it would be a wonder if the poets, whose
work is imitation, should be the only persons in three kingdoms who
should not receive advantage by it ; or if they should not more easily
imitate the wit and conversation of the present age than of the past.'

It results from the various remarks quoted from Dryden that he was
conscious of great differences between the speech of his own time as
reflected in literary works, and more particularly in dramatic literature, and
that of the Elizabethans. This difference Dryden holds to be greatly to
the advantage of his own contemporaries, and he attributes the improvement to the refinement and polish of the language of the Court under
Charles II. The 'stiff forms of conversation' had passed away.

Dryden's complaint against the older writers is in reality threefold :
their language is 'obsolete'; it was based upon bad models; it has
often a certain incorrectitude.

The obsolescence of these writers, in so far as it existed, is not a
reasonable ground of complaint, since it is inseparable from the normal
development of speech. The other two charges are to a great extent
part and parcel of the first. It is inadmissible that Shakespeare was not
acquainted with the best colloquial English of his time, or that when he
chose he could not make his characters speak like gentlemen. The
colloquial convention had changed greatly during the century or so
between Shakespeare and Dryden, and it is this difference between them
that Dryden mistakes for 'clownishness' in the older poets. In the same
way Dryden's contemporaries speak of the 'rude unpolished strain' of
Chaucer, and Dryden himself cannot praise this poet's verse more highly
than in comparing it to the 'rude music of a Scotch tune'.

As for the 'incorrectness', some of it no doubt, judged by the strictest
standards, had a real existence, but as Professor Sir Walter Raleigh says
of Shakespeare—'the syntax and framework of his sentences have all the

freedom of impulsive speech', and again—' He breaks through grammar only to get nearer to the heart of things.'

Some of the constructions which fall under Dryden's censure are perfectly normal in the sixteenth century, as, for instance, Ben Jonson's *Contain your spirit in more stricter bounds*, which is a very usual form of the Comparative among the Elizabethans, and continued in colloquial use after their day (cf. p. 326, below). But it is not from the consideration of isolated features of this kind that the essential character of the language of an age is to be apprehended. This is the result of innumerable factors—vocabulary, the particular associations attached to certain words, the order of these in the sentence, the balance and cadence of the sentence, the peculiar movement, one might almost say the speed of the utterance. The general impression of the typical seventeenth-century style at its best is one of rapidity, lightness, ease, suppleness, and grace. It is almost impossible to conceive that the dialogue which we find in Sir Thomas More's Life, in that of Wolsey's Life by Cavendish, or in *Euphues*, could have rattled and flashed along with the same swift inevitableness which is felt to belong to the dialogues of Dryden's best manner, to those of Otway, of Vanbrugh, or even of Mrs. Aphra Behn, and, above all, to those of Congreve (see examples on pp. 369, 397, &c.).

In this connexion it is interesting to recall the views propounded by Bacon in his Short Notes for Civil Conversation, which no doubt were shared by many in his day.

'It is necessary to use a stedfast countenance, not wavering with action, as in moving the head or hand too much, which sheweth a fantastical light, and fickle operation of the spirit. . . . Only it is sufficient with leisure to use a modest action in either.

In all kinds of speech, either pleasant, grave, severe or ordinary, it is convenient to speak leisurely, and rather drawlingly, than hastily; because hasty speech confounds the memory, and oftentimes, besides unseemliness, drives a man either to a non-plus or unseemly stammering, harping upon that which should follow; whereas a slow speech confirmeth the memory, addeth a conceit of wisdom to the hearers, besides a seemliness of speech and countenance.'

This passage appears to recommend a gesture and a manner of utterance as sober and slow-moving as the style in which the advice is couched. Precept and example are here become identical. These few sentences of Bacon have the atmosphere of his age, and certainly they neither lack anything of the leisureliness which he enjoins in conversation, nor err on the side of sprightliness of movement which would correspond to the 'wavering with action' in uttered speech.

If we put these and similar passages of this age side by side with others from the later seventeenth century, the difference between the Elizabethan and the post-Revolution sentences in what we have called the general mode of movement at once becomes apparent.

This characteristic movement will depend very largely upon the sentence structure, word order, and syntax; to some extent also upon accidence, and upon the general habits of pronunciation. It is the subtle fusion of all these factors which gives to the language of an age its special flavour, character, and atmosphere. Only the grosser and more obvious of the elements which compose the whole submit to our analysis. There are hosts of imponderables which no philological microscope can focus.

To the critics of Dryden's day there was only one test of supreme excellence in English style, and that was conformity to their own standards. What differed from these was suspect, and it was natural that, convinced that ' Well-placing of words for the sweetness of pronunciation was not known till Mr. Waller introduced it ', the men of the seventeenth century should feel, in reading diligently the works of Shakespeare and Fletcher, that a man who understood English would ' find in every page either some solecism of speech, or some notorious flaw in sense '. It is well to remember that Dryden, although he may try to justify his strictures by producing a series of examples of the supposed improprieties of the Elizabethans, is simply protesting against what is to him archaic and unfamiliar. However much we may be alive to the differences between the English of the age of Shakespeare and that of the age of Dryden, it is evident that Dryden himself and the men of his time felt these differences far more keenly. To be obsolete was to be inferior, and the charges of ' clownishness ', and the assertion that the ' wit ' of the earlier dramatic writers was ' ill-bred ', amount to no more than an insistence that the colloquial style, and with it the style of prose generally, had changed.

This is perhaps the proper place to reiterate what was insisted upon in general terms in the earlier chapters, that the literary and colloquial styles of any age are most intimately related.

The style of literary prose is alive and expressive, chiefly in so far as it is rooted in that of colloquial utterance. The general atmosphere of both is the same in any given age. It may be safely affirmed that a piece of prose which is genuinely typical of the period in which it is produced, no matter how highly-wrought and finished it may be, will not sound strange when read aloud and judged by the colloquial standards of its own day. Dryden attributes the improvement of dramatic literature in his day to the polishing of conversation since the Restoration. It may be said that dramatic style necessarily aims at reproducing conversation at its best, and that the relation between this genre of literature and the colloquial language is closer than that between the latter and any other form of writing. To recognize this is not to exclude the extension of the principle to other kinds of prose. We may make every possible allowance for differences which distinguish the various types of colloquial speech from each other, according to the occasion which calls them forth, and for those differences again which naturally divide the style of uttered speech from that of written prose, of whatever kind this may be, yet we must recognize that at a given period the language is everywhere one and the same—within the limits of the same dialect—and that written and uttered language, passing through the various gradations from the most familiar and colloquial to the most elevated and carefully finished, are all of a piece ; they all represent merely different ways of using the same instrument ; they breathe the same general spirit and atmosphere, and express, in divers tones, the same characteristic genius of the age to which they belong.

This is why the changing genius of a language such as English may be illustrated by means of literary prose. If this has changed, it is because the colloquial language has changed first. Everything which is true of one is true of the other, allowing for the different conditions under which conversation and writing are severally produced. Dryden's account of the English of his age, although this refers primarily to that of literature, is applicable also to the colloquial language.

The change in English style from the close of the age of Elizabeth to the Restoration has been illustrated above from the more polished and deliberate types of literary prose; the more specifically colloquial types will be displayed later on in their proper place, in the general survey of colloquial English.

Passing on to the next generation after Dryden we come naturally to Swift, whose various treatises on the English of his own day and that of the age immediately preceding this, are very instructive.

They consist (1) of a short article in the *Tatler* (No. 230, Sept. 28, 1710); (2) a burlesque entitled *A complete Collection of Genteel and Ingenious Conversation*, &c., known also by the shorter title of *Polite Conversations*; (3) *A Proposal for correcting, improving, and ascertaining the English Tongue*, In a letter to . . . the lord high treasurer of Great Britain. This is dated Feb. 22, 1711–12.

These three documents are all in the nature of an indictment of the fashionable English of the period, on various grounds :—that there is a great deal of deliberate affectation ; that this takes the form of ' corrupting ' the pronunciation—sometimes by leaving out vowels, so that awkward combinations of consonants are brought about—sometimes by dropping whole syllables and otherwise ' clipping ' words ; a further form of affectation is the use of what we should call ' slang ' words and phrases ; another is the persistent use of set words, tags, and phrases, so that conversation degenerates into a mere string of *clichés*. The most elaborate of these articles is the *Introduction* to the *Polite Conversations*, which describes, in a vein of irony, some of the chief features of fashionable pronunciation, as well as the various airs and graces of manner which distinguish the bearing of genteel persons in social intercourse. A much more serious document, though perhaps hardly more instructive, from the amount of light which it throws upon the actual habits of speech of the period, is the *Letter to the Lord Treasurer*. The great interest of this lies in the author's attempt to discover the causes of the corrupting tendencies which he censures, and to trace them to their different sources. Throughout these treatises Swift includes both writers and speakers under a common condemnation, referring specifically now to one, now to the other.

Perhaps the first point in Swift's *Letter to the Lord Treasurer* which will strike the reader who is familiar with Dryden's views concerning the English style of his own day compared with that of the Elizabethans, is the remarkable divergence between the views taken by these two great writers. Born in 1667, Swift was just a generation younger than Dryden. We have seen what Dryden thought of the Elizabethans as writers, and how superior to them he considered his own contemporaries.

In contrast to this we find Swift saying of the former—' The period, wherein the English tongue received most improvement, I take to commence with the beginning of Queen Elizabeth's reign, and to conclude with the great rebellion in forty-two.'   Now for Swift's opinion of the effect of the Restoration upon English style. 'During the usurpation, such an infusion of enthusiastic jargon prevailed in every writing, as was not shaken off in many years after. To this succeeded that licentiousness which entered with the restoration, and from infecting our religion and morals fell to corrupt our language; which last was not like to be much improved by those, who at that time made up the court of King Charles the Second; either such who had followed him in his banishment, or who had been altogether conversant in the dialect of those fanatic times; or young men who had been educated in the same country; so that the court, which used to be the standard of propriety and correctness of speech, was then, and I think hath ever since continued, the worst school in England for that accomplishment; and so will remain, till better care be taken in the education of our young nobility, that they may set out into the world with some foundation of literature, in order to qualify them for patterns of politeness.   The consequence of this defect in our writing may appear from plays, and other compositions written for entertainment within fifty years past; filled with a succession of affected phrases and new conceited words, either borrowed from the current style of the court, or from those, who under the character of men of wit and pleasure pretended to give the law.   Many of these refinements have already been long antiquated, and are now hardly intelligible, which is no wonder when they were the product only of ignorance and caprice.'

The function of the Court of Charles II then, in regard to English, was, from Swift's point of view, hardly that which Dryden attributed to it.

After the courtiers and 'dunces of figure', Swift passes to 'another set of men who have contributed very much to the spoiling of the English tongue; I mean the poets from the time of the restoration'.   The fault of these writers is alleged to be that they abbreviate words 'to fit them to the measure of their verses, and this they have frequently done so very injudiciously, as to form such harsh unharmonious sounds that none but a northern ear could endure: they have joined the most obdurate consonants without one intervening consonant, only to shorten a syllable....' It was maintained that words 'pronounced at length sounded faint and languid'.

'This was a pretence to take up the same custom in prose, so that most books we see nowadays are full of these manglings and abbreviations.'   Swift gives instances of the fault complained of—*drudg'd, disturb'd, rebuk'd, fledg'd*.   We may note in passing that the omission of the vowel of the suffix *-ed* had been in vogue for centuries, but if Swift is to be relied upon, there must have still been many in his day who pronounced the P. P. suffix in the above words as a separate syllable.

The next cause—'perhaps borrowed from the former'—which has 'contributed not a little to the maiming of our language, is a foolish opinion, advanced of late years that we ought to spell exactly as we speak'.   Swift naturally condemns phonetic spelling on various grounds. For us the most interesting of those alleged is that 'Not only the several towns and counties of England have a different way of pronouncing, but

M

even here in London they clip their words after one manner about court, another in the city, and a third in the suburbs'. If all these varieties were reduced to writing it ' would entirely confound orthography'.

The last source of ' corruption' mentioned by Swift is a certain school of young men from the Universities ' terribly possessed with a fear of pedantry', who from his description wish to be what we should call ' up to date'. ' They . . . come up to town, reckon all their errors for accomplishments, borrow the newest set of phrases; and if they take a pen into their hands, all the odd words they have picked up in a coffee-house, or at a gaming ordinary are produced as flowers of style, and their orthography refined to the utmost.' Such a ' strange race of wits', with their ' quaint fopperies' of manner and speech, exist in every age. Their mannerisms rarely pass beyond their immediate clique, and have no more permanence than foam on the river.

Swift's indictment appears at first sight rather a grave one. It is not altogether clear whether he objects more to certain habits of pronunciation, or to those tricks of spelling, certainly common in his day, which were supposed to represent those pronunciations. It is possible that Swift did not distinguish very clearly between sound and symbol, and included both under a common curse. When we remember the many peculiarities of pronunciation, eccentric as we should think them, which were prevalent during the seventeenth and eighteenth centuries, more particularly in the way of dropping consonants in various positions (see pp. 296, &c), we might suppose that Swift's criticism is directed against this mode of pronunciation, slovenly and slipshod as it would be considered at the present time. Some readers might be inclined to say, ' Here is Swift, a man of taste, refinement, and by no means unacquainted with the fashionable world of his day, but he censures the careless speech of his period. Is it fair to assume, in the face of Swift's strong disapprobation, that the best speakers really spoke in the manner suggested by the writers in the *Verney Memoirs* or the *Wentworth Papers*?' It may be well to inquire what it really is with which Swift finds fault. The few examples given in the Letter to the Lord Treasurer are really of no meaning, unless the strictures passed upon them refer primarily to the spelling. The *Tatler* article, however, gives a letter which is evidently intended to illustrate as many as possible of the ' late refinements crept into our language'. They do not amount to very much—*to ha' come*; *I'd ha bro't 'um*; *ha'nt don't* ' haven't done it'; *do't* ' do it'; *that's pozz*; *to g'imself airs*; *their phizz's*; *the hipps*; *promis't*; *upon Rep.* ' reputation'; *incog*; *mob*—instead of *mobile*—; *'tis*; *banter'd*, and a few more. Some of these, such as *ha*, *do't*, *that's*, &c., were already well-established forms, at least a century or a century and a half old.

The really new, or comparatively new, abbreviations are *rep, phizz, mob, pozz, plenipo*, &c. The number of these truncated words which appear already in the latter part of the seventeenth century was never very large, and most have now become obsolete, *mob* being the only one which has passed into permanent and universal use. *Pozz* has vanished, *rep* still lingered in the phrase *demirep* in the middle of the nineteenth century, *phizz* barely survives, as a half-facetious word which amuses no one and which few now employ.

We look in vain among Swift's examples for what were indeed the characteristic pronunciations from the sixteenth to late in the eighteenth century, for instances of the dropping of consonants in the middle and at the end of words. Why does Swift not mention *Lunnon, Wensday, Chrismas, greatis* (for *greatest*), *respeck, hounes* (for *hounds*)? How is it that the common habit of adding a *d* or *t* at the end of a word has escaped him? Why does he allow such pronunciations as *laft* (for *laugh*), *generald* (*general*), *varmint* (*vermin*), and a dozen more of the same kind to pass without notice? In Chapter VIII numerous instances are given of these and similar omissions and additions, and it will be observed that not a few are taken from the late seventeenth and early eighteenth centuries. It is inconceivable that Swift should not have heard these pronunciations, yet they do not fall under his lash. Why not? Because they were so widespread among the best speakers that to take exception to them would have been to fall foul of the English of all his contemporaries, his own included. Does not Swift himself rhyme *vermin* with *ferment*, thus implying either that he pronounced a *t* at the end of the former, or dropped one at the end of the latter? Let the reader glance at the lists on pp. 217–20, and he will probably come to the conclusion that these things were so common, so much part of the fabric of English pronunciation in Swift's day, that he did not notice them, indeed that he himself shared the universal habit of his age. In the long, satirical *Introduction* to the *Polite Conversations*, he refers again to *pozz* and *bam* (bamboozle) and shortenings of that class, as in the *Letter*, and further to *can't, han't, shan't, couldn't, isn't*, &c., where it is surely rather the spelling than the suggested pronunciation which is aimed at. He does, however, refer to four words whose pronunciation was different in his day from what it is in our own, and we must perhaps suppose, from the fact that these words are mentioned, that Swift did not himself pronounce them according to the manner usual to his contemporaries.

These words are *learnen* for *learning, jometry* for *geometry, vardi* for *verdict*, and *lard* for *lord*. On the various points involved see pp. 289, 303, 242, below. Probably *lard* was in any case going out of fashion.

Swift is not a purist in pronunciation ; at any rate he is not bent upon reforming the fixed habits of his time, however much he may dislike the mere passing fashions which he regards as ephemeral affectations. He sees on the one side a rather vulgar slanginess, and on the other an equally intolerable preciocity.

He is mainly concerned with propriety of vocabulary and diction, and he dislikes neologisms. It is evidently upon these grounds that Swift objects to the style of the dramatists of the Restoration. What he considers as 'a succession of affected phrases and new conceited words' was to Dryden the embodiment of all that is gay, gallant, and polite, as it was exhibited in the easy and elegant conversation of King Charles's Court. It is apparently this very identity between the diction of literature and that of life which is condemned by Swift, or if, theoretically, he would not deny the necessity of this, he at any rate disapproves of those very models of colloquial English which Dryden most admires. To this extent then, and in theory, if not in practice, Swift represents the view of the academic pedant, and Dryden that of the urbane man of the world.

If we consider the general character of the English of the average printed books after the first decade of the seventeenth century, compared with that of a similar class of work in the preceding century, we observe a far greater uniformity of spelling and of dialect generally. Only rarely do we find, here and there, those occasional spellings which we have seen occurring with surprising frequency in books of all kinds, down to the end of the reign of Elizabeth, and even, to some extent, for the first few years of the seventeenth century.

The spelling and accidence of literary English, especially when printed, have gradually become crystallized, deviations from the recognized standard are more and more rare, and those trifling variations from this which do occur are of no importance, as a rule, in throwing light upon the changes of language. What is true of printed literature is true, in a general way, and with certain important exceptions, of the English preserved in the letters of the period. Whereas in the former century we found that such writers as Sir Thomas Smith, Barnabe Googe, Ascham, Cranmer, Lyly, and so on, often employ very instructive spellings in their private correspondence, and that they retain certain dialectal features in the forms and accidence, such things are increasingly hard to find during the seventeenth century among persons of the same type. Thus if we examine the considerable collection of letters contained in Ellis's nine volumes, we find that whereas on almost every page of the sixteenth-century letters several forms of great interest occur, these are remarkably rare later on. Orthography and grammar are uniform and stereotyped, and more than this; the personages whose correspondence is presented to us, mostly highly educated officials, courtiers, and bishops, adhere with great consistency to the orthodox spelling.

On the other hand, a priceless collection of letters for our purpose exists in the [1] **Verney Memoirs,** which cover practically the last three quarters of the seventeenth century. These four volumes are an inexhaustible treasure-house of material for the study of seventeenth-century colloquial English. The letters are principally those of Sir Ralph Verney, his wife (and later of his children), his sisters and brothers, his uncle Dr. Denton, his aunts and cousins, besides many other persons among the intimate friends of the family. There are a few letters from humbler persons, bailiffs and other dependants, but the vast majority are from people of the same social standing, men and women belonging to the class of country gentry, some of them, as in the case of several of Sir Ralph's sisters, living pretty continuously in the country—at Claydon on the borders of Oxfordshire and Buckinghamshire—others, such as Lady Hobart, Mrs. Eure, Mrs. Sherard, and Dr. Denton, living principally in London. Dr. Denton, a member of an old Buckinghamshire county family, was a man of considerable cultivation who was educated at Oxford, where he studied medicine, and subsequently became a fashionable physician in London; his opinions concerning both health and

---

[1] Less important only because less numerous are the letters in the *Verney Papers* (*Letters and Papers of the Verney Family*, Ed. Bruce, Camden Soc. 1853) to which reference is often made below. These come down to 1639, with which date the later collection begins.

other grave problems of life were greatly prized by all his family and friends, including his close relatives, the Verneys.

A very large proportion of the letters in the Memoirs are from ladies, and it is from these that we obtain the greater number of those occasional departures from the conventional spelling which shed so much light upon current pronunciation. But these spellings are by no means confined to the letters of the ladies. Sir Ralph himself, his brothers, his sons, Dr. Denton, and Sir John Burgoyne, to mention no others, all now and then employ spellings of the same kind as those found in the letters of the female correspondents, and the indications given by these spellings, though less frequent, point in exactly the same direction as the spellings of the ladies, and suggest an identical pronunciation. Thus we are by no means justified in supposing that the ladies habitually used a more careless and slipshod mode of speech than the men of their family and class. If the Verney ladies spell phonetically, and in such a way as to imply what we should now call a careless and even illiterate pronunciation, this is because they read less than their men folk, and were less familiar with the orthodox spelling of printed books. To spell badly was not a ground of reproach in the seventeenth, nor even in the eighteenth, century. It is not a plausible suggestion that the ladies of a family spoke otherwise than their sons and brothers, and indeed the evidence is all against such a supposition. Regional dialect does not appear in the letters of these Buckinghamshire ladies and their friends, and the characteristic features revealed by the Verney Memoirs seem to be those of the English of the age as spoken among the upper classes. There seems to be no reason for supposing that the pronunciations recorded, and the easy-going grammar of the letters, were not those in general use. As one reads these Memoirs one has a very vivid impression of reality, and no amount of study of the purely literary works of the period on the one hand, or of the contemporary writers on English pronunciation on the other, can possibly give such an insight into the actual pronunciation and the familiar, unstudied diction of the seventeenth century, as is to be gained from a perusal of these documents, written on the whole, as we have said, by persons of the same class, but various in character, temperament, education, and the general circumstances of their lives. It might be said that the whole of the seventeenth-century colloquial English is here, in its various degrees of familiarity, and also of more studied utterance. The number of persons whose letters appear makes the collection truly representative of the age, and we can observe the differing modes of expression of three generations. Every mood finds expression, and almost every shade of temperament, and if none of the writers has the pen of a Sévigné or a Walpole, the correspondence holds us by its intense human interest, quite apart from its value for linguistic and social history. These letters are genuine human documents, in which living men and women tell the story of their lives in the natural diction of their age, and, we must repeat, in the actual pronunciation of their age. We are in an altogether more attractive world than that of the litigious Pastons and huckstering Celys, whose correspondence is nearest to that of the Verneys in point of linguistic interest. It is worth noting that the spellings into which the writers in the Verney Memoirs often drop unconsciously are in many cases identical with those employed by contemporary writers on pronunciation, such as Wallis and Cooper, in order to express the pronunciation they wish to describe.

Another collection of letters covering about the same period as the Verney Memoirs is the **Correspondence of Dr. Basire.** This volume contains chiefly the letters of the Reverend Doctor himself, and of other more or less eminent clergy, and these are of small value for the light which they throw upon the pronunciation, but the letters of Mrs. Basire —formerly a Miss Corbet of Shropshire—are as enlightening as those of the Buckinghamshire ladies. The pronunciation exhibited by these letters shows the same general character as that of the Verneys. A linguistic uniformity of this kind between, on the one hand, a group of persons chiefly belonging to Buckinghamshire, some of them residing in London, and on the other a lady of the same class belonging to Shropshire, but living most of her life in the North of England, goes far to confirm the impression regarding pronunciation which we gain from the Verney Memoirs; it also shows that in the latter part of the seventeenth century there was a Received Standard which had a very wide currency among people of a certain social standing. From the spontaneous deviations from the convention in spelling which occur in the letters of the Verneys and of Mrs. Basire, it would be possible to reconstruct the pronunciation of the period with considerable minuteness and no little certainty. The Standard thus reached is that which might be adopted were it desired to reproduce the pronunciation of the great Restoration dramatists. If it be thought that the modes of speech of the Verneys and Mrs. Basire are too careless and unstudied for the sparkling dialogue of the smart ladies and gentlemen of Congreve and Vanbrugh, it should be remembered that these characters are almost exact contemporaries of Sir Ralph and Lady Verney, of Lady Sussex and Dr. Denton; that all these personages, real and fictitious, belong to the same class; that, allowing for the literary polish and brilliancy imparted by the dramatists to the conversation of the latter, they all employ the same diction, grammar, and constructions.

Passing on to about a generation later than the last letters in the Verney Memoirs, &c., we find in the **Wentworth Papers,** documents no less important as illustrating the colloquial English of the Court circle during the first third of the eighteenth century. The best letters, from our present point of view, are those of old Lady Wentworth, who had been Woman of the Bedchamber to the Queen of James II, of her son Peter, and of her daughter-in-law Lady Strafford. There are many other letters in the collection which are of great value for the study of eighteenth-century English—as indeed is nearly everything which was written during the first three quarters of the century—but the above are the chief.

The general character of these letters closely resembles that of the Verney collection. They are intimate effusions from a mother to her son, from a wife to her husband, from one brother to another. The style of the three characters mentioned is absolutely unaffected and natural, and is clearly as close as it is possible for that of written documents to be to that of everyday life. The spelling, even of Peter Wentworth—the 'Querry', as he calls himself—is instructively remote from the conventional type, and shows that the pronunciation of the period was practically identical, in all essential features, with that suggested by the Verney correspondence. It is impossible to exaggerate the importance for our knowledge of seventeenth- and early eighteenth-century conversational English of the Verney and Wentworth letters. Those who have not made themselves familiar with these collections, or with others of a similar character, have missed the richest and most vital sources of information.

Both the Verney Memoirs and the *Wentworth Papers* are freely drawn on in the later chapters of this book, but it will not be out of place to bring together here a few of the priceless gems of spelling which the former volumes contain.

As full references are given later to page and volume, as well as to the writer, and the date, these are omitted here. The following forms are all taken from letters written between 1640 and 1688:

Vowel Spellings.

ar for *er* :—*sartinly, desarve, sarvant, sarve, presarve, divartion, larne* 'learn', *vartus* 'virtues', *yarn* 'earn', *marcy*, &c., &c.

M.E. *ẽ²* = [ē] :—*discrate* 'discreet', to *spake*.

ĕ for *ĭ* :—*stell, sperits, keten* 'kitten', *pell* 'pill', *fefty, pettyful, shelings, untel*, &c., &c.

a for *ŏ* or *au* shortened :—6 *a clake, becas* 'because' (also *bicos*), *faly* 'folly', *sassages* 'sausages'.

wo- for *wa-* :—*wore* 'war', *worning, whot* 'what', *woater, quorill, quollity woshing*, &c.

Confusion of M.E. ĩ and oi :—*byled* leg of mutton, *implyment* 'employment', *gine* 'join'.

Oblige written *oblege, obleging*, &c., several times.

Unstressed Vowels.

-est :—*gretist, sadist*.

-el :—*cruilty*.

-une, -ure :—*fortin, misfortin*, &c. ; *jointer, venter, futer*.

-age :—*corige* 'courage', *advantig, acknoliges*.

-on :—*pardenn, surgin* 'surgeon', *ribins, fashing* 'fashion'.

-day :—*Frydy, Mundy* (days of the week).

-oin, -oi(s) :—*Borgin* 'Burgoyne', *Shammee gloves*.

Consonantal Spellings.

-in for *-ing* :—*seein, missin, comin, shillins, disablegin*.

w- for *wh-* :—*any ware, wig* 'whig'.

shu- for *su-* :—*shuite* (of clothes), *shewted* 'suited', *shewer* 'sure'.

Loss of -r- :—*quater* 'quarter', 'no *father* than Oxford', *doset* 'Dorset', *fust* 'first', *passons* 'persons', *wood* 'word'.

Loss of other consonants :—*friten* (P.P.), *diomons, gretis* (Superl.), *Wensday, granmother, Papeses* 'Papists', *respeck, crismus, nex, hounes* 'hounds'.

(Mrs. Basire has *Lonan* 'London', with which cf. *Lunnon* referred to in eighteenth century. See p. 303.)

Addition of consonants :—*lemonds* 'lemons', *night gownd, clendlynes, schollards, mickelmust* 'Michaelmas', *hold year* 'whole', *homb* 'home'.

These spellings speak for themselves, and the few examples here given, out of hundreds equally enlightening, are sufficient to illustrate the importance for the student of seventeenth-century pronunciation of extending his inquiries to naturally-written documents, and of not trusting to the professional orthoepist alone.

A few examples may be added from the Verney Memoirs of peculiarities of Accidence.

The suffix -*s* is often used with plural subject in the Pres. Indic.— '*My Lady and Sir tomos remembers* their sarvices to you and Mrs. Gardiner'; *is* also used with Pl. subject:—' all hopes of peace *is* now taken awaye'.

The Auxiliary *have* shortened to *a* :—' It would *a* greved there harts to *a* sene ', &c.

Speake, rit, and *right* ('wrote'), *sate,* are used in the Pret. ; *spok, took, choose, lyen, eat, loaden,* as Past Participles.

Confusion between the Nom. and Objective of Pronouns :—*between you and I* ; *Sis*(ter) *Peg and me got an opportunity*. *His* used instead of Possess. suffix—*My lord Parsons his sonne.*

Adjectives are used where we should use Adverbs :—*he is reasonable well agane* (Lady Verney); *the weather has been wonderful stormie* (Sir Edm. Verney).

The general question of the survival of Regional dialect among the upper classes has already been touched upon (pp. 102, 103, 112, 163). A few words may, however, be added with special reference to the seventeenth and eighteenth centuries. This is particularly necessary as the well-known passage in which Macaulay deals with the speech of the country gentry of the seventeenth century, does not give an altogether accurate idea of the facts, nor put them in their proper perspective in the general picture of the history of English. We have shown that the rustic Verneys and Mrs. Basire did not write in such a way as to suggest that they spoke a local dialect, but rather that their speech was the Standard English of their day. This is true of all the correspondents whose letters appear in the Verney Memoirs. It is probable that a minute examination of these letters would reveal certain rusticities, and it is inconceivable that such should not have occurred, here and there, in the speech of the Verney ladies and their brothers. But that they all spoke a Regional broad dialect is quite inadmissible. Macaulay's picture of the speech and manners of the country squire of the seventeenth century is apparently constructed partly upon the testimony of the Restoration Comedies, and more especially from the portrait of Squire Western. His mention of Somersetshire and Yorkshire reveals Fielding and Vanbrugh as his chief sources, and they are very good ones. It is certain that in the remoter shires many country gentlemen spoke their Regional dialect well into the eighteenth century. Many did, but not all. By the side of Squire Western we have his neighbour, Mr. Allworthy, and for the matter of that, Tom Jones himself, whose education was purely local until he was fully grown, when he went to London. The dialect-speaking, swearing, drinking country gentleman of the Squire Western type had plenty of opportunity of hearing the more polite forms of English, and could probably use them when he chose, without much difficulty. After all, we do not gather that his woman-kind spoke the rustic dialect, so that even in his own household the other type was constantly heard. When he went to town, the rustic squire was certainly a butt for the wags and bloods about the Court—the seventeenth-century comedies offer plenty of examples of this—but his little oddities of speech and manner did not cut him off from others, of exactly his own class, indeed often of his own family, whose acquaintance with the town was of longer duration and older date than his own. Thus his angles were soon rounded off.

It must not be forgotten that the fashionable circles of the seventeenth and eighteenth centuries were made up of persons, some greater, some smaller, but all ultimately of this very class which Macaulay describes indiscriminately as boors, drunkards, and clowns. All of the fine ladies and gentlemen of the Court, from the days of Charles II to those of Anne, spent some portion at least of each year on their estates : they might affect to jeer at rustic speech, but they were not unfamiliar with it, and its accents doubtless often mingled with their own, as they lapsed in unguarded moments into the speech of their native county. It is just this constant touch with country pursuits and rustic dialect which distinguished, and still distinguishes, the upper classes from the middle-class dwellers in the towns. As was said above (p. 112), it was possible to speak with a rustic accent and still be a gentleman ; it was not allowable to speak like a ' Sunday citizen ' or a ' comfit maker's wife '. In any attempt to realize the conditions under which Received Standard has developed, these considerations must not be forgotten. If many country gentlemen, even in their own homes, spoke what was in all essentials the language of the Court, so also there were many courtiers and gallants who when they spoke the latter form of English, must have retained certain features of their native Regional dialect, and these passed muster as accepted and permissible variants in the speech of a gentleman, some of them, perhaps, in time, becoming more or less universal. In 1772 Dr. Johnson said that if people watched him narrowly, and he did not watch himself, they would find him out to be of a particular county. He added—' In the same manner, Dunning (afterwards Lord Ashburton) may be found out to be a Devonshire man ', cp. *Life*, Oxford Ed., ii. 159.

It is not wholly fanciful to connect the free and easy pronunciation and grammar which are characteristic of fashionable English down to the middle of the eighteenth century, with the intimate relation with the country and with Regional speech which existed among the ruling classes. The reaction to which reference is made later begins, and progresses at first, chiefly among the learned middle class whose touch with country life and rustic speech was of the slightest.

It is desirable to say something concerning the professional writers on pronunciation of this period. They are so numerous that it is necessary to make a selection of some of the most typical and informing. The best of these writers, especially those from the middle of the seventeenth century onwards, are far more intelligible than the grammarians of the sixteenth century. With most of the latter we not only have the very greatest difficulty in understanding what sounds they are trying to describe, but when by chance we do make out some meaning we cannot escape the gravest doubts that the information conveyed is very wide of the truth. The great difficulty with all these writers, supposing that some definite conception can be gathered from their statements, is to decide how far their accounts are reliable, and to what extent the type of pronunciation described may be accepted as the Received Standard of the period. On the one hand are the pedants and purists like Gill and, to some extent, Butler and Cooper, and on the other the writers whom we are inclined to suspect of Regional or Class modification, such as Daines and Jones. The safest test to apply is that of the evidence derived from the Verneys, Mrs. Basire, and the Wentworths. Pronunciations which recur in these sources, but which are nevertheless characterized as vulgar, careless, or barbarous, by the grammarians, may safely be accepted as belonging to the Received Standard of the day.

Provided we are armed with a touchstone in the form of material supplied by our correspondents, it is true that some small pieces of information can generally be extracted from nearly any of the professional writers, even from such unsatisfactory authorities as Gill or Bullokar ; but it more often happens that a large collection of occasional spellings from contemporary letters will render reference to the former superfluous.

In the English Grammar prefixed to his Dictionary, Dr. Johnson complains that ' most of the writers on English grammar ', in dealing with pronunciation, 'have often established the jargon of the lowest people as the model of speech '. This is hardly applicable to the seventeenth-century writers such as Butler, Wallis, and Cooper, with whose works Dr. Johnson was well acquainted, and one must suppose that he had in his mind, perhaps, such early eighteenth-century writers as Jones and Baker. It is the peculiar merit of these men, as we shall see, that they do actually describe, not an ideal form of speech, but one which we know from other sources to have been that in actual use.

We shall consider in due course Dr. Johnson's general views regarding English pronunciation, and may now mention in chronological order a few of the earlier writers, all of whom are his inferiors in learning, as they usually are in judgement also.

*Gill, the author of *Logonomia* (1621), was High Master of St. Paul's School, ' a very ingeniose person ', says Aubrey, ' as may appear by his writings. Notwithstanding he had moodes and humours as particularly his whipping-fitts.' Aubrey tells a ludicrous story to illustrate Gill's zeal with the rod, and quotes a lampoon upon the subject which shows the estimation in which he was held, on this account at least. He was among the numerous would-be reformers of spelling, and has left a number of texts in his notation. His brief remarks on English pronunciation are so wide of the mark, and his notation, based upon his conception of how English ought to be pronounced, gives a picture so wildly remote from what we are compelled by other evidence to consider as the true one, that in spite of his great reputation as flogger of little boys little or nothing is to be gained from detailed consideration of his book. The chief interest lies in his strongly expressed prejudices against the prevailing habits of pronunciation of his day, and his abuse of certain classes of speakers as affected and effeminate ' mopseys '. Forms of pronunciation which had certainly been long in use by the end of Queen Elizabeth's reign are denounced by Gill as affected. Thus he even

* See Appendix I.

pretends that M.E. *ā* was still a back vowel [ā], and that *ai* was still a diphthong.

He expresses the greatest contempt for those who pronounced 'I pray you give your scholars leave to play' as [əi prē ju gī jə(r) skalə(r)z līv tə plē], which, on the whole, was the way in which most decent speakers pronounced at that time (except that not all said [līv, skalə(r) gī]) instead of [əi prai jū giv jūr skolarz lēv tū plai], which probably none but yokels had said for a hundred years or more. The chief information is to be derived from his exhibition of certain types of pronunciation for the purpose of pillorying them. Altogether, Gill seems to be a cantankerous and rather ridiculous person, who, if he lived up to his theories, must have spoken a detestable English.

A more agreeable man, and a rather more informing writer, is **Charles Butler**, born in Buckinghamshire in 1560. He was educated at Magdalen College, Oxford, was a schoolmaster at Basingstoke, and Rector of Laurence Wotton in 1594. He lived till 1647. He published his *English Grammar* in 1634. Butler uses a special notation of no particular merit and very little phonetic value. His chief aim is to be consistent in spelling. His intentions were good, and some of his remarks upon the relation of spelling to sound are not uninteresting, but he lacked both the special training which might have fitted him for his task, and the intelligence to supply its lack. Thus his book remains a barren, vague, and unsatisfactory account of English speech. Commenting on the uncertainty of English spelling in his day, Butler remarks that one of the causes of this is that 'in many words wee ar fallen from the old pronunciation, and therefore soom write them (i. e. words) according to the nu sound and soom (for antiquitis sake) do keep the old writing'. Again—'Wee hav in our language many syllables which having gotten a nu pronunciation, doo yet retain their old orthographi, so that their letters doo not now rightly express their sound . . . the which errour if we will correct . . . the question will be whether we should conform our writing to the nu sound ; or reform our sound and return to the old '.

'For solution of which doubt, it is meet that when wee have generally, or in the most civil parts (as the Universities and Citties) forsaken the old pronunciation, then wee conform our writing to the nue sound, and write as wee speak, deede, neede, sleepe, hart, change, strange, angel, danger (for chainge &c.) not dede, nede, sleap, hert, or heart (which is woors) chaunge, straunge &c. as they ar yet sounded in the North, and were not long since written in the book of Homilies (imprinted 1562) and where the olde sound is left only by soom, and in soom places ; that there we reform the vowel sound and speake as wee write : first, third, bird, dear, ear, hear, heard : not furst, thurd, burd, deer, eer, heer, hard.'

We are not told more precisely than this just what we should like to know, what the old sounds and the new sounds severally and respectively were. We must suppose that Butler intends to recommend [dīd, nīd, slīp, hært, tʃēndʒ], &c., in the first group. Incidentally, we may note that these pronunciations had been fairly widespread, if not universal, for about 150 years at least. As regards the second group, it is difficult to imagine what he is driving at ; *furst* represents an originally different dialectal type from *first*; *thurd*, *burd* represent a later pronunciation than that expressed by *i*; every one said [hīər, dīər], certainly not [hēr, dēr], and most, probably, said [ēr] if not [ɪr, iər] for *ear*. '*Hard*' [hærd], where we now write *heard* and say [hᴀd], was apparently the commonest type from early in the sixteenth century to the end of the seventeenth at least. These passages illustrate well the invincible futility of Butler and his kind. They have a gift for selecting the worst possible examples to illustrate their meaning, and their statements are generally confused. Butler is quite incapable of giving an intelligible account of the character of a vowel sound, and it is impossible to be sure what he means when he talks of diphthongs. The following are a few of his most definite and specific statements, taken from the *Index of words like and unlike* :— '*Errand* a message commonly pronounced arrand;—*Devil* or rather *deevil*, not *divel* as some far fetching it from *diabolus* would have it— *deevil* comes from *eevil*;—For *enough* we commonly say *enuf*, as for *laugh*, *daughter* soom say *laf*, *dafter*, for *cough* all say *coff*;—*ere*, *erst*, not *yer*, *yerst*;—*Ew* not *yew* ovis femella, as *iw* not *yiw* taxus, though *y* be vulgarly sounded in them both' (p. 70).

John Wallis published in 1653 his *Grammatica Linguae Anglicanae*, a work which was many times reprinted for more than a century, and from which many later writers pilfered right and left.

The 'learned and sagacious Wallis', as Dr. Johnson calls him, was born in 1616 at Ashford in Kent, of which his father was incumbent. He was educated at a school near Tenterden, kept by a Scot, at Felstead School, Essex, and Emmanuel College, Cambridge. He held two livings in London, and was elected, in 1649, Savilian Professor of Geometry at Oxford, where he died in 1703.

Wallis has considerable merits as an observer of sounds, he has good powers of discrimination, nor is he led astray by the spelling like all the sixteenth-century grammarians, and Bullokar, Gill, and Butler in the seventeenth.

He makes several interesting observations. He perceives that the sound expressed in English by *au* or *aw* is a kind of *o*-sound, which, although long, differs otherwise but little from ' short *o* '. Thus he gives *fall—folly*, *hall*, *haul—holly*, *call—collar*, *laws—losse*, *cause—cost*, *aw'd— odd*, *saw'd—sod*, as longs and shorts of the same sound.

Again, he recognizes the existence of a short ' obscure ' sound which he identifies with the French '*e* feminine', and which is heard in the word *liberty*—presumably in the second syllable. This must be [ə].

Wallis further notes the existence of another, similar, but slightly different ' obscure ' sound, which the French have long in the last syllable of *sacrificateur*. This sound is expressed in English by short *ŭ* in *turn*, *burn*, *dull*, *cut*. This sound is also heard in English among those v·¹ o pronounce rather negligently, in words in which *o* or *ou* is written, ⸺ in *come*, *some*, *done*, *company*, *country*, *couple*, *covet*, *love*, &c: Although the identification with French *-eur* is inaccurate, it is sufficiently near to allow us to understand that Wallis is referring to a vowel approximately the same as our [a]. The pronunciation indicated of *turn*, *burn* is apparently that heard in the present-day Scotch pronunciation of these words. It is not quite clear from Wallis's account whether our [ᴀ] had yet developed. He says that an obscure sound occurs in *vertue*, and identifies it with the former of the two obscure vowels mentioned. We should expect the vowel in the first syllable of this word to be identified with that in *turn* and *burn*.

Another great merit of Wallis is that he includes the M.E. short *ă* in *bat*, *ban*, *Sam*, &c., among 'palatal' vowels, and definitely ranges it, as what we should call a front vowel, with M.E. *ā* in *pale*, *same*, *bane*, *bare*, &c., and with the sounds in *still*, *steel*, *set*, *seat*, &c.

It is rather remarkable that so acute an observer as Wallis should think it worth while to say that *au*, *aw* rightly pronounced, consists of a combination of short English *a* and *w*, when in the next sentence he notes that 'nowadays it is mostly pronounced simply like the thick German *á*, the sound of this being prolonged, and that of *w* nearly suppressed'. This description implies [ɔ] with perhaps a faint diphthongal effect, produced by a very slight additional rounding of the lips before the end of the vowel.

By far the most reliable phonetician among the seventeenth-century writers is **Cooper**, whose *Grammatica Anglicana* was published in 1685. Cooper was born in Herts., went up to Cambridge in 1672, took orders, and became Head Master of Bishop Stortford School in Herts. He died in 1698. Cooper tries, in his book, to describe the actual pronunciation, and the facts of articulation which underlie it, giving an account of the speech organs and their activities. He distinguishes, as none of his predecessors except Wallis do, between sound and letter.

Cooper not only regards *ă* as a front vowel, but describes it as being formed 'by the middle (that is what we call the '*front*') of the tongue, slightly raised towards the hollow of the palate'. This leaves no doubt that he is describing [æ], and that he thoroughly understood the character of the sound, and the way in which it was formed. He notes that this same sound occurs in *cast*, *past*, only lengthened, which implies [kæst, pæst]. Strangely enough, he says that the vowel in *pass* is short. He gives later on a list of words with the short and long vowel. Those containing [æ] are :—*bar*, *blab*, *cap*, *car*, *cat*, *dash*, *flash*, *gasp*, *grand*, *land*, *mash*, *pat*, *tar*, *quality*. [ǣ] is heard in :—*barge*, *blast*, *asking*, *carp*, *dart*, *flasket*, *gasp*, *grant*, *larch*, *mask*, *path*, *tart*. He distinguishes thus the vowels in *can*, *cast*, as respectively long and short of the same sound. From this he separates the sound in *cane*, *wane*, *age*, as containing in reality 'long *e*', 'falsely called long *ā*'. Thus *ken* contains the short, and *cane* the long of the same sound. His description of this vowel is '*e* formatur a lingua magis elevata et expansa quam in *a* proprius ad extremitatem, unde concavum palati minus redditur et sonus maior acutus ut in *ken*'.

A noteworthy feature of Cooper's pronunciation is his account of a diphthongal pronunciation of M.E. *ā* in certain words—*name* and *tale*. He says : '*u* gutturalis interseritur post *a* ut in *name* quasi scriberetur *na-um* dissyllabum. . . . *Tale* pronunciatur quasi scriberetur *ta-ul*.' There is no doubt as to what Cooper means by 'guttural *u*', since he says elsewhere that this vowel, which occurs in *nut*, &c., is like 'the groans of a man afflicted with sickness or pain', which might serve as a description for [ʌ, a] or [ə].

It is quite certain, therefore, that Cooper, as regards *name*, *tale*, is describing a pronunciation approximating to [nēəm, tēəl]. The description is so circumstantial that it is impossible to doubt its occurrence within Cooper's own experience, perhaps in his own usage. In any case, we have no reason to regard such pronunciations, at any period, as other than provincialisms.

The question of the probable pronunciation of M.E. *ā* and *ē²* in Cooper's day is fully discussed later on (pp. 194–6, 209–12), and it is sufficient here to note that his description appears to refer to the sound [ē] rather than to [ē], although, for several reasons, duly set forth below, the latter sound seems the more probable. Differences due to mere tenseness of the tongue have been properly described only comparatively recently, and Cooper would find it difficult to distinguish between [ē, ē], or to describe the former otherwise than by comparing it to the short vowel in *ken*, &c., of which he might quite naturally suppose it to be merely the lengthened form. Had the English of his day possessed both the tense and the slack mid-front vowels, he would doubtless have perceived the difference, but if, as seems certain, only one of these vowels existed, it was almost impossible for him to let us know without ambiguity which it was. It is much that Cooper distinguishes different degrees of height of the tongue, and between back and front activities.

Cooper must be commended for endeavouring to face facts in actual speech, even although it was rather disconcerting for a man of his age to admit too great a disparity between spelling and pronunciation. Thus, although he says that 'the sound in *bait, caitiff, eight, ay* consists of a combination of the vowel sound in *cast* (previously described as [æ]) followed by '*ee*', while that in *praise, height, weight, convey* is a diphthong composed of the *a* in *cane* ([ē] according to his description) placed before *i*, he admits, at least for the latter group, that in familiar conversation people 'speaking negligently' pronounce the simple *a* in *cane*. As will be seen below (p. 248), the evidence of the occasional spellings, in letters and other unstudied writings, is against the assumption of a diphthongal pronunciation for old *ai, ei*.

Cooper has some interesting indications of the pronunciation of unstressed syllables, the correctness of which is confirmed from other sources. Thus he says that *picture* is pronounced like *pick'ther*, that is, [pɪktə], and he gives a long list of words ending in *-ure* in which this is pronounced [ə] and not [jə] as at present. Of these, *figure* [figə] is as now, but not so *rapture, rupture, sculpture, structure, torture, scripture, future*, &c., &c. [skrɪptə, tortə] are proved by the occasional spellings to have been the sixteenth- and seventeenth-century forms. (See on this, pp. 277–8, below.)

We now pass to certain classified lists of Cooper's which are important from several points of view.

The first is a collection of pairs or larger groups of words which, according to our author, 'have the same pronunciation but a different sense, and mode of writing'. This collection includes :—*are—air—ere—heir; ant—aunt; coat—quote; comming—cummin; coughing—coffin; jerkin—jerking; flea—flay; fir—fur—far; heart—hart; hard—heard—herd; i'le* (I will)—*isle—oil; leaper—leper; line—loin; meat—mete; a notion—an ocean; own—one; order—ordure; pastor—pasture; rare—*

rear Vb.; *raisin—reason*; *season—seisin*; *spider—spi'd-her*; *tire—ty* (tie)-*her*.

We may note, among the above, the pronunciation [eər] for *are* (cf. p. 357, below); [ɔ(r)də(r)] (cf. p. 299, below); the pronunciation of -*ing* as -*in* (cf. p. 289, below); -*on* = -*in* in *reason, season* (cf. p. 276, below).

The next list we shall mention is one in which the pairs are said to have '*nearly*'—affinem—the same sound. This probably means that the sound was really identical, but that Cooper, for some reason, was not quite prepared to admit it:—*Eaton—eten*; *Martial—Marshal*; *Nash—gnash*; *Noah's—nose*; *Rome—room*; *Walter—water*; *carrying—carrion*; *craven—craving*; *doer—door*; *pulls—pulse*; *saphire—safer*; *shire—shear*; *sex—sects*; *stricter—stricture*; *throat—throw't*.

We come next to a list of forms which belong to a 'barbarous dialect', and are therefore, according to Cooper, to be avoided, although many of these spellings, or others which imply the same pronunciation, are to be found in the letters of the Verneys or of Lady Wentworth. The most interesting are:—*Bushop*; *Chorles* 'Charles' (cp. Mrs. Basire, p. 205, below); *eend* 'end'; *fut* 'foot' (= [fat], cp. *sutt* in the Verney Memoirs, p. 237, below); *gove* 'gave'; *hild* 'held' (cf. p. 354); *leece* 'lice', *meece* 'mice' (S.E. or S.E. Midl.); *ommost* 'almost'; *wuts* 'oats', *hwutter* 'hotter' (cf. p. 307); *ap to* 'up'; *stomp* 'stamp'; *sarvice* (cf. p. 219); *tunder* 'tinder'; *yerb* 'herb', *yerth* 'earth' (cf. p. 308); *yeuseles*; *yeusary*. With regard to the two last, it is doubtful which pronunciation they are intended to suggest. If [jūslɨs], &c., why not have written *yousless*? If not this then is it [jy̆s-]? If the former was condemned by Cooper, did he still adhere to the latter pronunciation? Or is he condemning [jy̆s-], which must have been very archaic by his time? (Cf. p. 243.)

Finally, a few examples from the comparatively small list of pronunciations which, Cooper says, are used 'for the sake of ease', concerning the propriety of which he offers no comment.

Bellis 'bellows'; *dander* 'dandruff'; *axtre* 'axeltree'; *ent* 'isn't'; *git* 'get'; *hundurd*; *hankercher*; *reddish* 'raddish'; *sez* 'says'; *shure* 'sure', *shugar*; *squourge* 'scourge' (cf. p. 307); *vittles*; *wusted*.

So we take leave of Cooper, a competent and conscientious observer, with very few fads. His work is by far the best of its kind we have met so far, or shall meet, perhaps down to Ellis and Sweet. It is true that he can tell us very little that we cannot learn for ourselves from the Verneys and Wentworths, but his statements unquestionably confirm many of the conclusions which we are inclined to draw from the occasional spellings of these writers. If in some cases Cooper is at variance with this testimony, this must be put down partly to a want of familiarity with the speech usage of the circles in which Sir Ralph Verney and his family moved, partly to the natural tendency of a writer on pronunciation at that period to describe an ideally 'correct' form of English. From this, the besetting sin of the schoolmaster and the professional grammarian in all ages, Cooper is, on the whole, commendably free. We must not forget to recognize that we owe to him the knowledge, or at least the accepted view, that M.E. *ă* when lengthened in the Mod. period before -*st* and -*th*, &c., as in *past*, *path*, &c., was still pronounced [æ] in the third quarter of the seventeenth century. (See pp. 203-5, on this lengthening.)

We now come to **Dr. Jones**, author of the *Practical Phonographer*, published first in 1701, whose unprejudiced attitude to his subject, and the very copious examples which he gives to illustrate his rules for the relation of sound and symbol, render his book very valuable. Jones was born in 1645 at Pentyrch in Glamorganshire, and died in 1709, so that he represents the English of the latter half of the seventeenth century. He is older than Cooper, rather younger than Sir Ralph Verney and most of his sisters, and older than old Lady Wentworth. So far as we can judge, the pronunciation which Jones describes is not at all archaic, and his account of the distribution of vowel sounds and of the various treatment of the consonants agrees with the prevailing habit down at least to the end of the first quarter of the eighteenth century. We know but little, to judge from Ekwall's account in his very carefully annotated edition of the *Phonographer*, of the details of Jones's life and of his social experience. He was educated at Jesus College, Oxford, studied medicine, and became a qualified physician. Later in his life he was Chancellor of the Diocese of Llandaff. A minute observer, he is yet in no way comparable to Cooper as a phonetician, and does not attempt to describe how sounds are formed. A sub-title of his book is ' The New Art of Spelling words by the Sound thereof, and of sounding them by the Sight thereof, Applied to the English Tongue '. He also professes to set forth 'English Speech . . . as it is commonly used in England (particularly in London, the Universities or at Court) '.

Jones's work is at once an elaborate spelling-book, and one that gives indications of the pronunciation. It proceeds by means of question and answer—thus :—' When is the sound of *a* written *wa* ? ' ' When it may be sounded *-ward* &c. in the End of words.' The examples include *athwart, backward, coward, eastward, Edward, forward, inward, Northward, Windward,* &c., &c. This evidently implies that Jones regarded [bækəd, ɪstəd, ɛdəd, forəd, inəd], &c., as the normal and usual pronunciation, but at the same time recognized a pronunciation with [w]. He often gives additional information on words which are not covered by the question, as when he adds, after the above list, the statement that *somewhat* is sounded *som'at* (= [samət]).

Jones's habit of recording alternative pronunciations is meritorious, and if his statements in this respect are reliable, we may perhaps draw the inference that a reaction had begun against the extreme negligence and independence from the written form, which characterized fashionable pronunciation from the sixteenth century to far into the eighteenth. We must not, however, push this too far, since, as we have seen, Swift, who is censorious enough in certain respects, does not touch upon the main features which would now be considered as monstrous blemishes in speech.

We shall return to this point later on.

There are few writers of the sort from whom so much may be learnt as from Jones, and this is owing to his very remarkable freedom from bias in favour of ' correctness ', and the thoroughness with which he compiles his lists. He very rarely censures, and when he does so he merely

notes that such and such a word is 'abusively sounded' in such a way—
as when he tells us that *appetite* is 'abusively sounded *appety*'.

A few examples may be given of the kind of information, generally
quite definite, which may be gathered from Jones.

(1) Among a list of words in which Jones says that *l* is not sounded,
in many of which we still omit this sound, the following occur, in all of
which we have now 'restored' *l*:—*St. Albans, Talbot, falchion, falcon,
almanac, almost, Falmouth, falter, Walter* (p. 30).

(2) The sound of *ee* (that is [ī]) written *i* in *oblige* = [oblīdž].

(3) Jones gives a very much longer list than Cooper of words ending
in *-ture*, in which, as he says, *-ure* is sounded *-er*. Among these are
adventure, conjecture, departure, failure, gesture, jointure, mixture, nature,
&c., &c. (p. 52). The list includes also all those words mentioned by
Cooper.

(4) 'Some sound *daughter, bought, naught, taught, nought* &c. with
an *f*, saying *daufter, boft* &c.' (pp. 54, 55). The *au* in *daufter* is prob-.
ably suggested by the orthodox spelling; there is no lack of examples of
dafter among the letter-writers (cf. p. 288).

(5) 'The sound of *o* written *au*, when it may be sounded *au*', as in—
*Auburn, auction, audience, August, aunt, austere, because, daunt, fault,
fraud, jaundice, Pauls, sausage, vault.* 'Which may be sounded as with
an *o*' (p. 79). Here clearly two possible sounds [ɔ̄, ɔ̆] are indicated.
While most of the words in the list, and all are not included here, are
now pronounced with [ɔ̄], several of them are almost universally pronounced [ɔ], such as [bĭkɔz, sɔsĭdž], while [ɔ] may be heard from some
speakers in *fault, vault.*

(6) 'The sound of *o* written *wo* where it may be sounded *wo*.' Jones's
list is a long one, and although it is certain that good speakers did omit
the *w*- consonant in some of the words as late as the forties of last
century (cf. p. 297), one wonders whether, even in Jones's day, its
omission in other words in the list was not due to Regional dialect
influence. This is the list:—*forswore, swole, swol'n, swop, sword, swore,
wolf, Wolverhampton, worm, worn, worry, Wolverton, woman, womb,
wonder, wont, word, work, worse, worship, worth, worthy, woven, would,
wound.* 'Which are', says Jones, p. 82, 'especially those of two
or more syllables, sounded as beginning with *o*.' (Cf. also p. 296,
below.)

The next book which we may consider is an unpretentious little work
by **William Baker**—*Rules for True Spelling and Writing English*
(2nd Ed.), Bristol, 1724. The author gives an instructive list of 'Words
that are commonly pronounced very different from what they are
written'. The grammar of this title does not inspire confidence in the
general cultivation of the author, but most of the pronunciations he
indicates are confirmed by the evidence of the letter-writers in the
Wentworth Papers, or by the Verneys.

Some useful light is shed upon the pronunciation of unstressed syllables.
The tendency to reduce *-on* to *-in* (cf. pp. 275–6, below) is recognized
in the forms *sturgin, dungin, flaggin, carrin, cooshin*, for 'sturgeon,
dungeon, flagon, carrion, cushion'. *Stomick* is given as the pronunciation
of 'stomach', *Izic* for 'Isaac'; *spannel, Dannel* for 'spaniel, Daniel';

N

janders for 'jaundice'; *hankercher* for 'handkerchief'; *mastee* for 'mastiff', as in Jones.

As regards consonantal pronunciations, *Egip, poscrip* occur with the loss of final -*t*; the disappearance of *r* before -*s* is shown in *nus* 'nurse', *pus* 'purse', *Usly* 'Ursula', *thusty* 'thirsty', *sasnet* 'sarsanet'. The proper names *Birmingham, Dorothy, Margaret, Katherine* are spelt *Brumminjum, Dorraty, Marget, Katturn.* Among other individual forms are *sparagras, slafter* 'slaughter', *conster* 'construe', and *crowner* 'coroner'.

We are told that *i* is not sounded in *venison*, and that *medicine* is pronounced *medson.* G- is not sounded in *gnat, gnaw*, nor *k*- in *knead, knee, knife*, &c.; 'Words terminated in -*re* sound -*ur* as *Acquire, aspire, fire, hire*', &c., &c.

This pronunciation [*aiə*], &c., probably existed early in the sixteenth century at any rate (cf. p. 300, below). The few examples show how informing some of these simple treatises by unknown writers may be, compared with the pretentious works of an earlier day written by men incomparably more learned, such as Sir William Smith, Richard Mulcaster, Bullokar, and Gill.

During the eighteenth century the teaching of English pronunciation was a common means of livelihood; innumerable quacks flourished, and many of them published small manuals on their art. Their practice lay, no doubt, largely among the richer tradesmen's families in London, who, while they were able, so far as mere wealth could permit this, to cut some figure in the polite world, were afraid of rendering themselves ridiculous by their lack of breeding and their ignorance of the English spoken in fashionable circles. Dr. Johnson, as usual, has a pithy remark upon the rich retired shopkeepers who in his day were pushing their way in Society. 'They have lost', said he, 'the civility of the tradesman, but have not acquired the manners of a gentleman.'

Smollett, in chap. xiv of *Roderick Random*, gives an account of one of the quack teachers of pronunciation, a Scotchman in this instance, and the picture is probably not overdrawn. The following is the young Scottish surgeon's impression :

'This gentleman who had come from Scotland three or four years before, kept a school in town, where he taught the Latin, French, and Italian languages; but what he chiefly professed was the pronunciation of the English tongue, after a method more speedy and uncommon than any practised heretofore; and indeed, if his scholars spoke like their master, the latter part of his undertaking was certainly performed to a tittle; for although I could easily understand every word of what I had heard hitherto since I entered England, three parts in four of his dialect were as unintelligible to me as if he had spoken in Arabic or Irish.'

Unfortunately very few examples are given of this worthy's pronunciation, and these not particularly enlightening :—*caal* for 'call'; *I vaw to Gad*; and *hawze* for 'house'. It would be interesting to know what this Scotchman made of the English diphthong in *vow, house*, a sound quite new to him. Vanbrugh spells Lord Foppington's pronunciation of the English diphthong as *au*, so it is just possible that an affected pronunciation [ɔ] existed.

We have seen that the writers on pronunciation of the sixteenth century and those of the next, before Wallis, are chiefly concerned, not to give a true picture of English speech as it actually existed, but to concoct a more or less fanciful form of language based largely upon their own conception of what English *ought* to be, a conception mainly determined by the supposed 'powers of the letters'. The result of these efforts at restoring 'true' pronunciation was nil. The writers' descriptions were so wildly remote from reality that no one paid any attention to them. Natural tendencies appear to have continued unchecked in the speech of all classes, and a vague ideal of 'correctness' was the last factor which determined what was fashionable and polite. This was settled rather by the convention of the moment in the Court and among the superior classes. These tendencies and their results are recognized by Cooper and Jones, especially by the latter, and, as has been said, their statements agree wonderfully, on the whole, with the truth so far as we can gather it from the unstudied familiar letters of the day.

From the middle of the eighteenth century or thereabouts, there are signs of a reaction against what came to be considered too great a laxity. This reaction is represented, and was probably influenced to some extent, by Lord Chesterfield in the great world, and still more considerably by Dr. Johnson in the world of letters. It does not follow that these two extremes would agree completely, either in theory or practice. Lord Chesterfield's attitude to 'correctness', in speech no less than in manners, has already been illustrated by quotations (cf. pp. 19–23). That of **Dr. Johnson** is well defined in the general remarks on pronunciation in the Grammar prefixed to his great Dictionary (1755). The vital passages are these :—' Most of the writers of English Grammars have given long tables of words pronounced otherwise than they are written, and seem not sufficiently to have considered that of English, as of all living tongues, there is a double pronunciation, one cursory and colloquial, the other regular and solemn. The cursory pronunciation is always vague and uncertain, being made different in different mouths, by negligence, unskilfulness and affectation. The solemn pronunciation, though by no means immutable and permanent, is yet always less remote from the orthography, and less liable to capricious innovation. They have however generally formed their tables according to the cursory speech of those with whom they happened to converse; and concluding that the whole nation combines to vitiate language in one manner, have often established the jargon of the lowest people, as the model of speech.'

' For pronunciation the best general rule is, to consider those the most elegant speakers who deviate least from the written words.'

The new trend in English pronunciation then, which Dr. Johnson favoured, and which with his enormous influence and prestige as a scholar, and a dictator in what was correct, he was able to impose upon his own circle, and upon others far outside it, was in the direction of the 'regular and solemn' rather than of the 'cursory and colloquial'. We shall probably not be far wrong in placing the serious beginning of this reaction in the period in which these words were written. The age of Swift and Pope apparently did not regard 'deviation from the orthography' in pronunciation as a lapse from politeness, or from the speech of the 'best companies'. We have seen that Swift's attacks on the English of his day are directed against quite other features; he neither pillories in his *Polite Conversations* the typical laxity of his period in this respect, nor scruples himself to take advantage of the prevailing usage in his rhymes.

Pope has plenty of rhymes which show that he must have pronounced very much as did Lady Wentworth, and so we may believe did the 'Chiefs out of War and Statesmen out of Place' who resorted to the poet's villa at 'Twittenam'. If Lady Mary Wortley Montagu, in her letters, does not spell like Lady Wentworth, with whom by the way she was perfectly acquainted, it is not that she spoke differently from this lady and her other contemporaries, but simply that she was a more bookish person and was better informed as to the conventional orthography. She has such rhymes as *please—stays, fate—deceit, theft—gift, coquet—wit.*

As to the age before this, that of Charles and James II, a society which is doubtless faithfully depicted in the comedies of Congreve, Wycherley, Vanbrugh, and Mrs. Aphra Behn, a generation which laughed 'à gorge déployée' at such pranks as that narrated in Grammont's Memoirs, of my Lady Muskerry at the ball, when the frolicsome Duke of Buckingham ran about squeaking like a new-born infant, and inquiring among the maids of honour for a nurse for my young Lord Muskerry—'vastly pleasant burn me'—such a world as this was not likely to spare time from more diverting pursuits to 'correct' its speech after the model of the 'true spelling'.

The great Dictionary of Johnson was greeted with some enthusiasm, though in a bantering tone, by Lord Chesterfield in Nos. 100 and 101 of *The World.* 'I hereby declare', says the writer, 'that I make a total surrender of all my rights and privileges in the English Language, as a freeborn British subject to the said Mr. Johnson, during the term of his dictatorship.'

Lord Chesterfield has some remarks upon the prevailing uncertainty, in the spelling of private persons, down to that time, which are of some importance. 'We have', he says, 'at present two very different orthographies, the pedantic, and the polite; the one founded upon certain dry crabbed rules of Etymology and grammar, the other upon the justness and delicacy of the ear. I am thoroughly persuaded that Mr. Johnson will endeavour to establish the former; and I perfectly agree with him, provided it can be quickly brought about. Spelling as well as music, is better performed by book, than merely by the ear, which may be variously affected by the same sounds. I therefore most earnestly recommend to my fair countrywomen, and their faithful or faithless servants, the fine gentlemen of this realm, to surrender, as well for their own private as for public utility, all their natural rights and privileges of misspelling, which they have so long enjoyed, and so vigorously exerted. I have really known very fatal consequences attend that loose and uncertain practice of auricular orthography.'

It may be noted that Lord Chesterfield does not condemn the current pronunciation itself, but only the habit of expressing it in irregular spelling. It is improbable that his Lordship would have endorsed Dr. Johnson's definition of the 'most elegant speakers' without considerable qualifications and reservations.

A younger contemporary of Johnson's was James Elphinston, whose life covers the last three quarters of the eighteenth century and extends into the nineteenth. Elphinston was born in Edinburgh in 1721, the son of an Anglican clergyman, and was educated at the High School and at the University in that city. He lived chiefly in Scotland until he was 32, when he went to London. Here he taught school for about twenty-five years, and then returned to Scotland in 1778. He lectured upon the English language in Edinburgh and Glasgow and returned to London in the following year. Thence he removed to Hertfordshire in 1792, but returned to London—Hammersmith—in 1795, where he spent the remaining fourteen years of his life. Elphinston appears to have been in every way an excellent man, and to have occupied a respectable position in society. He was a friend of Dr. Johnson, who said of him, 'his inner part is good, but his outward part is mighty awkward'. The latter part of this estimate, as we know, agrees fairly accurately with Lord Chesterfield's portrait of the Doctor himself. In spite of the little peculiarities of his 'outward part', however, Elphinston was a very superior type of man to the Scotch teacher of English pronunciation described by Smollett. He was an accomplished French scholar and published a poetical translation of Racine's *La Religion*, which received the approbation of Edward Young.

He also translated the *Fables* of Fénelon and Bossuet's *View of Universal History*, made an Anthology of English Verse, and wrote some original poems and a translation of Martial's Epigrams.

Of this last, Garrick said that it was 'the most extraordinary of all translations ever attempted'; Beattie that it was 'a whole quarto of nonsense and gibberish'; while Burns thought it worth while to devote an Epigram to it:

O thou whom Poesy abhors
Whom Prose has turned out of doors,
Heard'st thou yon groan?—Proceed no further!
'Twas laurell'd Martial calling 'Murther!'

The translation of Martial's Satire given in full by Müller displays neither wit nor felicity of phrasing and versification. We see that Elphinston, although possessed of very indifferent literary gifts, was at least a man of commendable industry and varied activities.

They are not exhausted by the above enumeration, which is given as a factor in our estimate of the author's qualifications for the task which concerns us here, of describing the English pronunciation of his day.

This subject is dealt with by Elphinston in a series of works written between 1756 and 1790. Of these the most important is *The Principles of the English Language, or English Grammar*, which appeared in 1765. The gist of the whole collection is given by Müller in his book *Englische Lautlehre nach James Elphinston*, 1914.

The first thing which occurs to us with regard to Elphinston is that he was a Scot, not in itself a drawback in the ordinary affairs of life, but a fact which produces some misgivings in connexion with one who is to act as a guide to English speech in the second half of the eighteenth century. We should expect to find that a Scotsman who, like Elphinston, came to England for the first time when he was over thirty, would

have his Scottish habits of speech pretty firmly rooted, that he would be
censorious of Southern English, and would be often inclined to put down
as vulgarisms some of the most widespread features of good speech in the
South. This is certainly true of Elphinston's attitude to English.
Further, because the London type is the only Southern type he really
knows, he is naturally inclined to regard as vulgarisms peculiar to London
English, many things which were by no means confined to London, and
which, moreover, were not vulgar at all. Even at the present time
a learned Scot who is unfamiliar with Southern English is very apt to
look with great disapproval at what is alien to his own speech habit,
and to regard agreement with the latter as the test of correctness and
elegance.

It is very difficult for a stranger to appreciate the nice shades between
different Class dialects, and just as Elphinston sets down as improprieties
of speech pronunciations which were habitual among good speakers, so
he also credits 'Manny Ladies, Gentlemen and oddhers' with the misplacement of initial *h*-, and observes concerning a 'yong Lady'—'So
hamiabel howevver iz dhis yong Lady, dhat, widh her fine *air*, sweet *hies*,
quic *hears*, dellicate *harms*, above all her tender *art* she wood giuv anny
man a *ankering* to *halter iz* condiscion', &c., &c. Which is supposed to
represent the lady's pronunciation.

In a translation of one of Martial's Epigrams Elphinston professes to
illustrate the characteristics of London English. The interchange of *w*
and *v*—(*ve* for *we*, *wulgar* for *vulgar*, &c.)—is at least as old as the
fifteenth century, and was probably not confined to London, even in the
latter part of the eighteenth. *Wite* for *white*, *wen* for *when*, &c., is characteristic of the whole South of England, and has been so for centuries; it has
nothing to do with Class dialect, and apparently never had. *Larn'd*
for *learned* in the eighteenth century was certainly not a vulgarism, nor in
any sense a Regional peculiarity. *Sence* for *since*, *ef* for *if*, &c., were common enough in the seventeenth and early eighteenth centuries, in circles such
as Elphinston in all probability never aspired, even if he desired, to enter.
It is, however, possible that such forms were going out of fashion in
Elphinston's time. *Feller* [felə] for *fellow* was certainly Pope's pronunciation, and as it is still a perfectly good and natural form in colloquial
speech, it is improbable that it was a vulgarism at the time the translation
was written.

Many of the other supposed inelegancies satirized by Elphinston, such
as *we was*, *come* as a Pret., *came* and *began* as P. P.'s, and so on, are
'mistakes' of accidence, which have no local habitat, but may occur
anywhere. Many well-bred seventeenth- and early eighteenth-century
speakers would have used such forms.

Present Pls. in -*s* were common in the sixteenth and seventeenth
centuries, and are not infrequent in the Wentworth correspondence. On
the whole, Elphinston's statements as to what is vulgar and characteristic
of London English may be received with the greatest scepticism, and
should never be accepted unless they are confirmed from other sources.
His works are nevertheless useful in establishing the existence, in his
day, of such and such forms and pronunciations. We must hesitate before
accepting the author's estimate of their 'correctness', or the reverse, in

the speech usage of the time.   At the same time, while we may exercise
due caution in believing all Elphinston's statements as to what is or is
not ' good ' English, especially when we know that a quarter of a century
before him, at any rate, standards were quite different from what he represents them in his own time, it is certainly probable that standards had
actually changed, or were changing as has been said, in the time of
Elphinston and Dr. Johnson, though probably not as much as both
of them would have liked, nor as much as Elphinston's statements suggest.   As the knowledge and practice of a fixed spelling gain ground
among the better sort of speakers it becomes increasingly difficult to
check the statements of the writers on pronunciation, and experience has
shown that their evidence on points of fact is frequently unreliable, and
that what these gentlemen put down as an actual Pronunciation may be
no more than an unrealized ideal of their own construction.

The last of the tribe whom we shall mention here is John Walker.
This writer formerly enjoyed a great reputation, and his pronouncing
Dictionary was reprinted again and again, and indeed probably forms
the basis of more than one of the cheap dictionaries at the present time.
Walker was born at Colney Hatch—which had not then its present
associations—in 1732. His family seem to have occupied a very humble
position, and Walker left school early and was put to trade. He did
not stick to this very long, but went on the stage, married a comic
actress, Miss Myners, and is said to have achieved some success in the
characters of Cato and Brutus. He left the stage in 1768, and set up
a school in Kensington, but gave this up after two years.

He now began to give lectures on elocution, and had a great success,
especially in Scotland and Ireland. According to the account of him
given in the *Dictionary of Nat. Biogr.*, Walker was invited by some
of the Heads of Houses in Oxford to give private lectures on his subject
at the University. He was acquainted with, and enjoyed the patronage
of, Burke and Johnson. Boswell records a rather dull conversation
between Walker and Johnson. He said he had only taught one clergyman to read, ' and he is the best reader I ever heard, not by my teaching,
but by his own natural talents '. To which Dr. Johnson replied, ' Were
he the best reader in the world, I would not have it told he was taught '.
Amongst other remarks, Walker observed that ' the art (of oratory) is to
read strong though low '.

Fanny Burney, in her Diary, under the date of Jan. 13, 1783, mentions
meeting Walker at dinner. All she has to say of ' Mr. Walker the
lecturer' is that ' though modest in science, he is vulgar in conversation '.
This may refer merely to the subject-matter, or the general bearing of
the speaker, but it does not of itself inspire confidence in Walker as
a guide to propriety in speech. Besides his Dictionary, Walker produced a *Rhyming Dictionary, Elements of Elocution,* and a *Rhetorical
Grammar.* The latter first appeared in 1785, and went into many
editions. It is difficult, from the meagre facts given in the *Dictionary
of Nat. Biogr.*, to judge what opportunities Walker had for becoming
acquainted with the politest forms of English, but we must suppose that
he made the most of his chances for observing the conversation of Burke
and Johnson, and of such other members of their circle as he came

across. It is only fair to say that, in spite of his early training on the stage and his profession of teacher of elocution—one wonders what sort of people sought his aid—Walker does not appear to inculcate an artificial and pedantic pronunciation. On the contrary, his remarks are generally sober, sensible, and, so far as we can test them, accurate. The style of pronunciation which he recommends seems to be a perfectly natural and easy one, and the *Rhetorical Grammar* is probably a much safer guide than the works of Elphinston. He is also a fairly minute observer, and a faithful chronicler. Thus he notes with approval the ' liquid *k,* and *g'* in *sky, kind, guide, card,* &c., that is [skja*i*, kja*i*nd, gja*i*d, kj*ā*d], &c., a pronunciation which lingered on amongst old people far into the last century. (See p. 310, below.)

He says that ' polite speakers always pronounce *educate* as though written *edjucate, virtue* as *vertchew'.*   These pronunciations are the usual ones at the present day, [ɛdj*u*keit, v*ā*tj*ŭ*] being quite recent. A still older form of the first of these words was [ɛd*i*keit] (cf. treatment of unstressed Fr. *u,* p. 265). Walker has some interesting remarks on *Indian, odious, insidious,* &c. He says, in continuation of the sentence quoted above—' if the general ear were not *corrupted* by being *corrected,* we should hear *Indian* pronounced *Injian, odious ojeous,* and *insidious insidjeous . . .* but the speaker ought to avoid sinking the *i* and reducing *Indian* into two syllables as if written *In-jan, odious* as *o-jus, insidious* as *insid-jus.* The *i* ought to be heard distinctly like *e* in these words as if written and divided *In-je-an, o-je-us ',* &c. Of all this it may be said that it is very greatly to Walker's credit that, although a teacher of elocution, he is able to talk of the ear being ' corrupted by being corrected '. Again, while the phonetic descriptions, and the notation employed to express the pronunciation, are those of a man totally untrained and unskilled in scientific phonetics, they yet leave no kind of doubt as to the pronunciation referred to. Lastly, while we no longer say ' *ojus* ', &c., it is well known to many still living that good speakers born early in the last century used these and similar forms, and it is rather strange that Walker should have thought it necessary to warn his readers against *Injun, ojus* [*i*ndžən, oudžəs], pronunciations which most good speakers in his day must have employed, and to insist upon ' the *i* ' being heard distinctly.

Walker shows his superiority to Elphinston in not regarding as a vulgarism the ' sinking of the *h'* in *while, where,* &c., although he regards it as ' tending greatly to impoverish pronunciation ', and also as apt to produce confusion of meaning. Such a view is perhaps excusable in an elocutionist. An interesting observation on the part of Walker is that *r* has disappeared, ' particularly in London ', in *bar, bard, card,* &c., which are pronounced as *baa,* &c. What is perhaps even more remarkable is that he does not find fault with this, but merely notes that *r* ought to be strongly pronounced initially, but that in *bar, bard,* &c., it must be nearly as soft as in London. Incidentally, we may note that the disappearance of ' *r* ' in these words probably implies, by this time, [*ā*] as the vowel, and not [æ].

With regard to the interchange of *w* and *v* (*vind* for *wind,* and *weal* for *veal,* &c.), Walker records that this occurs ' among the inhabitants of London, and those not always of the lower order '.

His statements touching the final consonant in the suffix -*ing* are largely borne out by our information from other sources, although he is inclined to limit the pronunciation -*in* to verbs whose root-syllable already contained '*ng*', such as *fling*, &c. See on this point pp. 289-90, below.

Walker has some sound observations concerning the vowels in unstressed words, such as pronouns and prepositions. Thus he says that *you* is pronounced *ye* in such a sentence as 'he had no right to tell you' (= [tɛl ī]), and that *my* is pronounced '*me*' in 'my pen is as bad as my paper'—[mĭ pɛn, mĭ pēpə], both of which forms of reduction are perfectly in accord with the habits of eighteenth-century English.

Walker also recognized the reduced forms of *of*, *for*, *from*, *by*, which he writes *uv*, *fur* [əv, fə], &c., as distinct from '*ov*, *four*', &c. On the other hand, '*to* must always preserve its true sound as if written *two*, at least when we are reading, however much it may be suffered to approach to *te* (= [tə]) when we are speaking'.

The value and truth of Walker's account of the pronunciation of the latter part of the eighteenth century can best be tested by checking it, on the one hand with the various sources of information prior to his day, the private letters, the testimony of rhymes, and the statements of the earlier grammarians, and on the other, with what we know of the pronunciation after his time, especially what could be learnt from the speech of old people, mostly now dead, who were born early in the nineteenth century, and from the recollections of these persons concerning forms of speech still current in their youth among a yet older generation.

Walker emerges very creditably from the test, and he must be placed among the most reliable and informing writers of his class, that is, with Wallis, Cooper, and Jones. He is a good and enlightened representative of the reaction already referred to, against the laxity of speech of the earlier generations. His tendency is towards a moderate 'correctness', and an approximation to the supposed pronunciation implied by the now fixed orthography, but he does not set out to 'reform' English speech by destroying everything that is traditional and habitual. He appeals constantly to the habits of 'our most elegant speakers', that is, to a real type of existing English, and he must be held to mirror the usage of his day among refined and learned, and, though to a less extent perhaps, among fashionable speakers, with considerable fidelity. Since Walker's day, the 'correcting' process has gone much farther and has unquestionably obliterated, in the speech of the general average of educated persons, the results of many tendencies which had existed for centuries. The process, as is shown in various places throughout this book, involves both isolated words and whole categories.

At any and every period, no doubt, there may be found among speakers of Received Standard those who are purists and those who are careless and negligent speakers, giving full rein to the natural tendencies which make for change in pronunciation. If the seventeenth century had its Gill, the eighteenth had its Elphinston and many others of the same sort, while the nineteenth had its Dean Alford, to mention but one amid innumerable 'reformers'. But while no one seems to have paid any attention to Gill, among those who set the standard of polite English, from the middle of the eighteenth century onward, the general ideals expressed by Dr. Johnson in the passage quoted on p. 177 have gained an ever-increasing assent. It is this gradual but undoubted triumph of the learned class, within which may be included the real scholars of whom Johnson is the type and chief, down to the humble and ignorant teacher of elocution filled with false and extravagant theories of 'correctness', which is claimed as exemplifying the influence of Class dialect on the development of Received Standard (see also pp. 18–20). This influence is by no means confined to the introduction of 'Spelling pronunciation', but includes also the introduction of other types, naturally developed, among different social strata. It is not always easy to distinguish between these two classes of forms. The present-day pronunciation of *nature*, &c., instead of [nētə] may belong to one or the other (cf. p. 265). The same applies to the pronunciation of *gold*. It is certain that the two forms [gōld, gūld] coexisted, and that the rise of each can be explained by natural processes, but it is by no means certain that the final selection of [gould] as the 'correct' form was not determined by its apparent agreement with the spelling.

During the lifetime of many who are still of middle age, numerous old pronunciations have been given up by large sections of the community, while other sections adhere to them most obstinately. There are still many who consider as very offensive vulgarisms the modern pronunciations of *waistcoat, often, forehead, landscape, handkerchief*, as [weistkout, ɔftən, fōhɛd, lændzskeip, hændkə ʃif] instead of [wɛskət, ɔfn, forid, lænzkip, hæŋkətʃif], and there are perhaps as many more who use all these pronunciations habitually without a single qualm. Whatever may be the resistance of the present generation of middle-aged or elderly people to these innovations, it seems probable that they will appear as natural to our grandchildren or great-grandchildren as the now universally-received forms of *gold, servant, oblige, nature, London, Edward*, &c., do to us.

It must be reiterated that all the 'reforms' in pronunciation and grammar which have passed into general currency in colloquial English during the last century and a half, have come from below, and not from above, in the first instance, so far as we can discover. This fact will be variously received and interpreted according to the peculiar social bias of the reader. One interpretation at any rate has been suggested in Chap. I, pp. 20–23, above.

The reaction against the happy-go-lucky pronunciation and grammar of the Restoration, and of the early eighteenth century, is accompanied by a certain bias towards formality and stiffness which is traceable in the poetry and the literary prose, and, as we may well believe from the evidence before us, in the conversational style also, of the later eighteenth and early nineteenth century. It is a tendency towards the 'regular and solemn' and away from the 'cursory and colloquial'.

Pope and his generation still kept the sparkle, along with the ease of the seventeenth century. The later writers often lose the brilliancy of their predecessors, if they preserve the ease and grace of movement. Gray, and Walpole, and Goldsmith perhaps combine both qualities to a higher degree than many of their contemporaries. If we put a passage of the *Deserted Village* alongside one from Pope, taken almost at random, the different genius of the two ages is as perceptible as when we compare Congreve's dialogue with that of *She Stoops to Conquer*. It may be said, probably with justice, that the younger writer surpasses the older ones in tenderness, humanity, and real feeling for nature, possibly in humour, and that he is their equal in his mastery of a supple and intimate style, free from literary affectation.   But the swift thrust of Congreve's rapier, the epigrammatic finality of Pope's couplet, are no longer there.

What the later age lost in keenness and glitter it may be said to have gained in sincerity and solidity.   There were, however, not wanting, even among the contemporaries of Pope, those who foreshadowed the style and spirit of a younger day.   The sweetness, naturalness, simplicity, and shrewd gaiety of Addison, Pope's senior by sixteen years, are perhaps nearer to the spirit of Goldsmith than to that of the age immediately following the Restoration ; while the sober decorum of Richardson, born only a year later than Pope, with his leisurely narrative and rather stiff and pompous dialogue, exhibits the correctitude of Middle Class propriety in speech and conduct.   The formality of the conversations in *Pamela*, which to us is almost ludicrous, is typical of a habit of mind and mode of expression which were gaining ground among our people, and held them for three-quarters of a century.   Allowing for differences of genius, wit, and of social setting, it may be said that the recorded conversations of Johnson are on the same note, and we catch echoes of this spirit in the utterances, both trivial and serious, of Mr. and Mrs. Segrave.

The later eighteenth century and the early nineteenth seem to have favoured a very serious turn of mind which expressed itself in a formal and solemn style.   It is easy to find exceptions to this, as in the Diary and letters of the sprightly Fanny Burney, or the captivating letters of Cowper in his happier moments, or the irresistible mirth of Sheridan, but are not these in many ways less representative of their age than, let us say, Wesley's *Journal*, and *Sandford and Merton*?   Miss Austen has left a gallery of imperishable portraits of human beings, drawn from the life if any ever were.   But the conversation of her characters, even of those whose parts are most extolled, is singularly lacking in brilliancy, humour, pointedness, or charm of any kind.   The charm, the humour, the magic lie in the author's handling of these rather second-rate though generally well-bred people, in whose conversation, which hardly ever rises above the commonplace, and in whose self-centred lives, she contrives to interest us amazingly.   We have here the representation of actual life and dialogue as the author knew it.   There can be no doubt that this is the real thing, and that people really spoke like this in the closing years of the eighteenth century.   Perhaps no books were ever written which embody the spirit and idiom of an age so faithfully as Miss Austen's novels.   All the little pomposities and reticences, the polite formulas, the unconscious vulgarisms, the well-bred insincerities, are here displayed.   It is not Miss Austen who is speaking, it is the men and women of her day, each perfectly distinct, a complete and consistent human being.   The characters reveal themselves naturally and inevitably in their conversation, with hardly any commentary by their creator, who rarely troubles to pass a personal judgement upon them, or to see that they are very good—or otherwise as the case may be.

We shall not go far wrong in supposing that the Bennets, the D'Arcys, and the Wodehouses, &c., pronounced their English very much according to the principles laid down by Mr. Walker in describing the utterance of ' our most polite speakers '.

They undoubtedly pronounced '*kyard, gyearl, ojus, Injun*', to use Walker's own rough and ready notation, and almost certainly said '*comin', goin', singin', shillin''* ; some of them, Lady Catherine de Burgh in particular, probably said '*Eddard*', '*tay*', '*chaney*', '*ooman*' ' woman ', '*neighb'rood*', '*lanskip*', '*Lunnon*', '*cheer*' for ' chair ', and possibly '*goold*', '*obleege*', and '*sarvant*'. Many still living have heard the last echoes of these things in the mouths of their parents and grandparents. We can remember old ladies and gentlemen who spoke in this way in our childhood, and whose conversation still preserved the decorums of the former age, its quaint mixture of eighteenth-century survivals, with the new ' correct ' forms of their youth. Unfortunately most of these are now ' fallen asleep '.

In this very imperfect account of the character and general tendencies of English speech during something like two centuries, a few important problems are touched on, and many more are omitted altogether from our survey.

This period offers ample scope for investigation. It is no exaggeration to say that a proper history of the English of each of these centuries has still to be written.

We want minute studies of such documents as the Verney Letters and the Wentworth Papers, and also of other similar letters and diaries of the same period, and if possible, of more recent collections covering the period from about 1740 to the first quarter of the nineteenth century. Apart from these, the well-spelt letters and diaries of such writers as Fanny Burney should be carefully examined for the sake of the colloquial and grammatical usage which they reveal, and much may be learnt incidentally from casual remarks scattered through biographies and memoirs (cf., for example, instances quoted, pp. 203, 215, 272, &c., from Leigh Hunt's *Autobiography* and Tuckwell's *Reminiscences of Oxford*). Many works which few scholars would think of investigating specially for such a purpose, contain priceless, if isolated, pieces of information as to the speech habits of our immediate ancestors. This is why the dutiful and painful philologist, who 'goes through' large numbers of the orthodox ' sources ', may often miss some of the best things, unless he happens also to be widely read in English Literature. It is much to be regretted that during the last twenty or thirty years a series of observations into the speech of old people speaking the best English of the first half of the last century was not made in a systematic way. These old people, both by their own actual usage, and by their recollections of that of their own elders, could have shed a very valuable light on much that is now obscure. The present writer had the advantage of knowing, during his boyhood and early manhood, a considerable number of excellent speakers who were born between 1800 and 1830, and although he remembers accurately certain points of interest from the speech and recollections of this generation, these are unfortunately all too few. It is remarkable that while the English of illiterate elderly peasants has often been examined, with the view of recording for posterity the rugged accents of the agricultural community, and even of the inhabitants of slum villages in colliery and industrial districts, it has not been thought worth while to preserve the passing fashions of speech of the courtly and polite of a former day, and those whose good fortune it was to be in a position to record these at first hand have neglected their opportunity.

Among the general problems still to be solved may be mentioned:— the precise extent and character of both Regional and Class dialect influence upon Received Standard during the seventeenth and eighteenth centuries; the divorce of prose style from the colloquial language of the day which may appear in any language from time to time, and which research might possibly show occurred among the latest Elizabethans and their immediate successors, and again towards the end of the eighteenth century; the precise linguistic results, if any, of the Civil Wars upon our language, whether in conducing to laxity of pronunciation and grammar, or in modifying the diction of conversation or of literature; the beginnings of the reaction in favour of the 'regular and solemn' style of pronunciation and grammar, and the progress of this movement in colloquial and literary English down, roughly, to the Early Victorian period; the rise of bogus pronunciations, based purely on the spelling, among persons who were ignorant of the best traditional usage; the gradual process by which many of these obtained currency among the better classes. It would be desirable to run these monstrosities to earth, when it would probably appear that many had their origin with the class of ignorant teachers of pronunciation referred to by Smollett.

Among special questions, it would be satisfactory to know with certainty approximately when the modern [$\bar{a}$] sound in *path, last*, &c., developed out of [$æ$] and became generally current in Received Standard.

The whole question of unstressed vowels is a virgin field for the young investigator. A small beginning is made in Chap. VII, below, towards a systematic collection of material upon which conclusions may be based. What was the attitude of the more sober 'reformers' like Dr. Johnson in this matter? Is it probable that he applied his principle of conforming pronunciation to orthography to the vowels of unstressed syllables? If so, how far did he and 'those associated with him' go in this respect? If we may judge from his younger contemporary Walker, that generation probably did not pronounce *fortune, future*, &c., as '*fortin*', '*futer*', like the Verneys, the Wentworths, Cooper, and Jones; but did they attempt to 'restore' all unstressed vowels to the extent to which Mr. Bridges would like us all to do at the present day? Perhaps Mr. Bridges can tell us. So far as the evidence now available carries us, it looks as if nearly the whole movement towards 'full' vowels in unstressed syllables is an absolutely modern conceit, based entirely upon spelling. To this there are certain exceptions, such as the *-ure, -une* words whose present-day pronunciation may be explained as a purely phonetic development from a different type from that which produced '*fortin*', '*futer*', &c., and again, the interchange of [-ən] and *-in*, [-ət] and *-it* in *ribbon, faggot*, &c., appears to represent two different speech-usages. (See pp. 276–8.)

But all these and many other points await investigation.

It would be an interesting inquiry how far the falling off in the quality of prose style among the generality of writers after the third quarter of the eighteenth century is related to social developments. An East Indian Director is said to have told Charles Lamb (of all men!) that the style the Company most appreciated was the humdrum, thus doubtless voicing the literary ideals of the rising class of bankers, brokers, and nabobs whose point of view was largely to dominate English taste for several generations. Horace Walpole lived and wrote on nearly to the end of the century, but his spirit, his gaiety, and the sprightliness of his style belong in reality to the early eighteenth century. Even Macaulay was unable to rate him at his true value. The letters of Gray are probably better appreciated to-day than in the age which immediately followed his death. The peculiar quality of Sheridan's wit and raillery is assuredly nearer to Congreve in spirit than to Hook and Jerrold.

But this is not the place to pursue a subject which is the business of the critic of Literature. If an appeal is made to pure Literature, in discussing the changing spirit and atmosphere of Colloquial English, it is because of the principle so often propounded here, that the style of Literature is rooted in the life and conversation of the age. From these sources alone can prose renew its life from generation to generation. When Literary prose style loses touch with the spoken language it becomes lifeless and unexpressive, powerless to ' strike the ear, the heart, or the fancy ', remote alike from human feeling and from the speech of man because it has never known real life and movement.

CHAPTER VI

THE HISTORY OF ENGLISH PRONUNCIATION IN THE MODERN PERIOD

I. The Vowels in Stressed Syllables.

In the foregoing chapters we have taken a series of rapid surveys of the English of the Modern Period, not only of the pronunciation, but of other aspects also, century by century, from the fifteenth century onwards.

In the following portions of this book it will be our business to attempt to work into a continuous account the facts of development exhibited by our language throughout the whole period with which we are dealing. Of the various aspects with which we shall concern ourselves, pronunciation is one of the most important, the one perhaps which demands the greatest amassing and sifting of detail in the elucidation of fact; it is also the one which involves most care in the construction of a reasonable theory in the interpretation of the facts.

It has been already said that the convenient practice of dividing English, chronologically, into Old, Middle, and Modern English is apt to be misleading, and to give the impression that our language has changed by a series of sudden bounds. Still more danger is there in conveying such a wrong view when we divide our treatment of the language, as has been done in this book, into centuries. It is therefore desirable to renew the warning previously given, and to re-state our conception of the History of English as a process of continuous development and change. If the previous chapters, which aimed at discovering what is characteristic of the language of each of a series of centuries, have led the reader to think too much of English as broken up into a number of brief, clear-cut, and distinct periods of development, in each of which a new set of tendencies and impulses arises, the following chapters may possibly act as a corrective.

The student who constructs his picture of the unfolding of English chiefly from the long series of documents of all kinds, in which the language of each age is enshrined, is not likely to be misled into what one may call the spasmodic view of its history. To him the gradual and insensible passage from one phase of development to another is so manifest that he finds it ever more difficult to draw the line between period and period, and he becomes increasingly sceptical of the propriety of attempting to define the limits of each. But it is one thing to be conscious of the continual onward sweep of evolution, and quite another to be able to convey the sense of this. The realization of this linguistic development comes slowly, from the prolonged study of a mass of individual facts and details, all of which contribute something to the picture which exists in the student's mind. In the present state of our knowledge, it is difficult to see how we are to bring home to the reader this sense of perpetual and continuous development, otherwise than by presenting him with a considerable quantity of detail, together with certain generalizations based upon this.

Let it never be forgotten that in tracing, by means of the sources of knowledge at our disposal, the history of a language, we have not and cannot have all the links in the chain of development. We know—approximately—the starting-point, and we know what is the outcome at the present time. But of the intervening stages, many are missing altogether, while at the precise character of too many others we can but guess.

For instance, if we are tracing the change of M.E. $\bar{a}$ in *name* into its present form, while we can easily construct theoretically the various stages of development, it is impossible to say exactly at what period each of them is reached. Supposing that already in the first half of the fifteenth century we find M.E. $\bar{a}$ written e, what precise value are we to attach to this symbol in this period? How far has the sound gone towards its present pronunciation? And so with all the other vowels; we have divers hints of changes—from peculiar spellings, from rhymes, from statements of grammarians—and we must piece all these scraps of information together, compare, and check one with another, but when all is said and done, there are more lacunae in our picture than some scholars like to admit.

In former days, when those great figures of English Philology Ellis and Sweet were in their prime, these men, and others who followed limpingly in their footsteps, believed it to be possible to construct, almost entirely from the accounts given by the Orthoepists, a fairly exact chronological table of vowel changes, and to say with confidence, such and such was the shade of sound in the sixteenth century, this or that other shade in the seventeenth, yet another in the eighteenth, and so on. As I have already indicated above, I cannot find any such sure foundation in the statements of the old writers upon which Ellis and Sweet relied, and when I compare these statements with the testimony of the other kinds of evidence, I become more than ever distrustful of the results which were formerly accepted so confidently, less inclined to be dogmatic as to the chronology of vowel changes. For one thing, quite recently, many scholars have been led to put back the beginnings of the modern vowel system, anything from one to two hundred years earlier than the date to which Ellis and Sweet assigned the rise of this. If this is justified, then it follows, since the formerly-received chronology was almost entirely based upon the testimony of the old grammarians, that these have misled us, and that much of the system of minute chronology derived from them crumbles. A single instance will suffice. Sweet, trusting to the Orthoepists, believed that far into the sixteenth century, and among some speakers well into the seventeenth century, M.E. $\bar{a}$ in *name*, *take*, &c., retained its old sound $[\bar{a}]$. But we know now that as early as the first half of the fifteenth century this sound must have been completely fronted, and that before the end of the sixteenth it rhymed with the M.E. $\bar{e}$ in *seat*, &c.   Now this entirely knocks the bottom out of the delightfully simple old tables such as :—

M.E.	16th c.	17th c.	18th c.
$\bar{a}$	[ǣ]	[ḗ]	[ē]

which satisfied most of us down to within the last few years, and if I had to be tied down to a definite statement on the chronology of this sound I should be inclined to construct, from the facts at my disposal, some such table as :—

M.E. (13th and early 14th c.)	late 14th c.	15th c.	16th, 17th, and 18th cc.
$\bar{a}$	[ǣ]	[ḗ]	[ē] (among some speakers [ī])

But I should know that this was rather a dangerous table to make, because at least two and perhaps more of the stages which are here neatly packed into separate periods, certainly coexisted in the same period, and overlapped into the periods before and after that to which they are assigned.

And this brings me back to the point which I set out to emphasize, namely, that a clear-cut and precise chronology is impossible in linguistic history, since, as was said earlier in this book, the periods overlap as do the generations of speakers.   From this point of view it is obvious that some men must have been born in the M.E. period and have died in the Modern Period, just as they may be born in one century and die in another.   Thus while Chaucer himself no doubt always spoke what must still be called M.E., he must have heard, before he died, younger speakers who were at least on the verge of Early Modern.   He may himself always have pronounced [māk(ə)], and probably he did so, but it is, I think, certain that he must have heard the younger generation say [mæk], possibly with disapproval as strong as that with which the present Poet Laureate hears the unstressed vowel in [ɔksfəd] and so on. But whereas the vowel above indicated in *make*, was a novelty in Chaucer's old age, the unstressed vowels of which his illustrious successor complains have been in pretty common use for five hundred years or so. While then, in dealing with each sound change, we naturally ask—When did it start? and attempt to answer the question, it is absurd to suppose that our answer, however carefully considered, is absolutely exact.   We can give the earliest evidence known to us of a modification of the old usage, and of a move in the new direction, but we must never forget that there may be older evidence which our industry has failed so far to discover, and that a sound change is nearly always considerably older than the earliest documentary evidence of its existence.   Further, although we may be able to say that a sound change in a certain direction has begun, and is well under way by a given period, we can rarely say with certainty exactly how far it has gone.   Any effort to do this must be tentative, and is based upon reasoning from all sorts of collateral evidence.   (Compare, in illustration of this, the attempt to fix approximately the various stages of development of M.E. $\bar{a}$ on pp. 195, &c., below, together with the inferences drawn from the history of other vowels.)

In tracing the history of the English vowels I have followed the usual

o

practice, and an excellent one it is, when dealing with the later periods of the language, of starting from the M.E. vowel system.

But the term Middle English covers a long period which begins, roughly, towards the beginning of the eleventh century and extends, according to the view taken, down to about 1400, or twenty or thirty years later. It is not to be supposed that English pronunciation stood still, even within a single dialect, all this time. Even if we adopt the further divisions—Transition, Early M.E., M.E. Central Period, and Late M.E.—the limits of each of these will depend upon the feature which we take as the test. Thus while we have no *direct* evidence, from areas more southerly than Lincolnshire, before about 1420, of the alteration towards its present pronunciation of the *ā*-sound which arose—in English words—about the middle of the thirteenth century, and which we call 'M.E. *ā*', we have unmistakable indications that one of the O.E. *ō*-sounds—as in O.E. *mōna* 'moon'—had moved on far towards, even if it had already reached, its present sound, perhaps 100 to 125 years earlier, and this in the South-East.

Therefore when we speak of 'M.E.' sounds, we do not always refer to one and the same period. In the case of the vowel last mentioned, M.E. *ō* (which is also O.E. *ō*, and further occurs in words borrowed from Norman French), this sound was certainly no longer pronounced in the old way, but had become almost, if not quite, [ū] probably early in the fourteenth century, and in some dialects, perhaps, much earlier.

With these qualifications of our terminology we may pass to some general observations on what is sometimes called 'the Great Vowel Shift'. From what has been said above the reader will be on his guard against supposing that the phenomena of which we treat in this chapter are new and sudden departures of the Modern Period. He will consider that the pronunciation which the old vowel sounds have now acquired is the result of a slow and gradual process, and of tendencies which undoubtedly existed in English long before the various periods at which the changes can be shown severally to have come about.

If we compare the M.E. vowels in stressed syllables with the corresponding sounds in the same words at the present day, it appears that all the old diphthongs, all the old long vowels, and some of the short vowels, have acquired a totally different pronunciation. But if we compare the two lists of actual sounds, the M.E. vowels and diphthongs, and those of the present day, we notice that, as far as we can judge, the contents of each list are not so very different. M.E. had, amongst others, the simple sounds [ā, ū, ī, ō], and the diphthongs [ai, au], and so has the English which we speak. But they do not occur in the same words now as then. Where M.E. had *ā* as in *nāme* we have the diphthong [ei]; where M.E. pronounced [ū] as in *hus*, *hous*, we pronounce [au]; in the words in which [ī] occurred in M.E., e.g. *wīf*, &c., we now pronounce [ai]; and corresponding to M.E. [ō] as in *boon* 'bone' we now have [ou]. Again, we do not retain the diphthongs [ai, au] in our pronunciation of *rain* and *cause*, but have substituted for them [ei, ō] in these and other words. On the other hand, our [ā] as in *path*, our [ū] in *moon*, our [i] in *queen*, our [ō] in *saw*, are not survivals of the M.E. sounds, but have developed out of sounds entirely different.

Thus the new sounds never caught up the old sounds which, so far as we can tell, were identical with them, except in the case of M.E. *ā* and M.E. *ē* = [ē̞], on which see pp. 194, &c., 209, &c., below. This fact has an important chronological bearing. It means that supposing we are able to ascertain, for instance, that not later than a given year, O.E. *ō* in *mōna*, &c., had reached the [ū] stage, it follows that the O.E. *ū* in *hūs* had, before that stage was reached, been so far altered in pronunciation, that it was quite unlike the new sound which had developed in the word *moon*, and although this word and other words containing O.E. *ō* now have the same vowel sound that once existed in *hūs* and other words containing O.E. *ū*, there never was a time at which *moon* and *house* were pronounced with the same vowel. For if this had been so, they would be pronounced with the same vowel now. When once two originally different sounds become levelled, as often happens in the course of their history, under one and the same sound, the history of the sound in both is henceforth one and the same. We see an instance of this in the vowel [a], which occurs in the words *nut*, *blood*, and *judge*. In the first of these words the O.E. and M.E. sound was [ŭ], in the second it was [ō], and in the last it was French [y]. The present sound developed probably in the sixteenth century, and its immediate predecessor was [ŭ]. This means that some time before the rise of [a] the three originally different sounds [ŭ, ō, y] had all, under certain circumstances, been levelled under one single sound [ŭ]. This sound, no matter what its antecedents may have been, was unrounded at a given point, and gradually developed into the present vowel [a]. In such a case as this, it is evident that whatever the period at which the unrounding of old [ŭ] occurred, the various other processes whereby old [ō, y] became [ŭ] must have already taken place.

To return to our former line of argument concerning sounds originally different which remain different, this is often of the greatest use in determining at least the relative chronology of sound changes. With regard to the history of old *ō*, it has been already mentioned that this sound had apparently become [ū] as early as the first half of the fourteenth century. We must therefore assume that certain disturbances had arisen prior to that date in the old [ū] sound. Now, although this latter has now become the diphthong [*au*], it does not by any means follow that anything like the present form had been reached before old *ō* had become [ū]. All that we can say is that something had happened to *ū*, that it had started upon that series of changes which was to result in our present diphthong. The same line of argument may be applied to all other vowels whose pronunciation has changed from what it formerly was, and which have either themselves taken the place of other vowels which have also become something quite different, or have had their old places taken by other vowels.

The old *ī* in *wīf*, *līf*, *bīte*, &c., has been diphthongized to [*ai*], but a new [ī] sound has developed—in *seek*, *green*, *feet*, &c.—from an old [ē]. It is instructive to consider the histories of these two original vowels in relation to each other. It is evident that the old [ī] must have changed into something different before the new [ī] in *feet*, *green*, &c., was fully developed. The old and the new [ī] never had the same sound at the same time. In this instance we have evidence of about the same age, on the one hand, that old *ī* had become a diphthong, and on the other, that old [ē] had become [i] (cf. pp. 205–7). It seems certain that at least as early as 1420 [ī] had become a diphthong (cf. p. 223), but how far it had gone towards its present sound is another question. In this connexion we must consider also the history of the old diphthong *ai*, which later on became [ē]. The development of all three sounds took place in such a manner that the new [ē] from *ai* never caught up old *ē̆*; this latter, while it was clearly on the move towards [ī], never caught up old *ī*; and this, though it subsequently became [*ai*], never overlapped with the old diphthong, since if it had done so it would have gone still farther and become monophthongized again to [ē]. Incidentally, it may be pointed out that all this illustrates the fact that in all languages certain tendencies arise, at a given moment, which change certain sounds. in a particular direction. Then the tendency, for the time being at any rate, dies out, so that when, perhaps shortly after the beginning of the process which changed the original sound ·has set in, the same sound arises from some different source, the tendency has spent itself and this sound remains unaltered, it may be for centuries.

The consideration of the history of several sounds during the same period, such as has been briefly attempted above, is of value sometimes in checking the statements of the Orthoepists. Thus, when some of these seem to tell us, in the sixteenth century, that old *ī* is still pronounced [ī], while at the same time they admit that old *ē̆* is pronounced [ī], we know that either they are deceiving themselves, and would mislead us if we trusted them, or that we must have misinterpreted their statements.

The Vowels in Detail.

M.E. *ā̆.*

This vowel must have been definitely fronted by the beginning of the fifteenth century. This is proved by rhymes in the first quarter of the century and by spellings which occur during the first half.

The earliest spellings I have found which indicate fronting are in R. of Brunne's Handlyng Sinne, Lincs. 1303, where *meke* 'make' Inf. occurs line 1618, and *mekest* 3906. It would be rash, at present, to generalize too much from these N.E. Midland forms.

In the Siege of Rouen (*c.* 1420) we have the rhyme *cāre—were*, and Bokenam writes *credyll*, S. Cecil. 80, for earlier *crādel* 'cradle', and *bare*,[1] Pr. 149, for M.E. *bēre* O.E. *bǣr* 'bier'. This use of the symbol *a* to express what can only have been a front vowel [ē̄], or in Suffolk more probably [ē] in the latter word, is as convincing as is the use of the letter *e* to express the sound usually written *a*. The Treasurer of Calais, in 1421, in a letter among the collection of letters of Marg. of Anjou and Bishop Bekinton, p. 16, writes *er* 'are'. If this represents the strong M.E. form *āre* it is a case in point, but it may possibly represent the weakened form in unstressed positions which in M.E. was *ăre*. In this case it might be evidence of the fronting of M.E. *ă̄.*

Since the evidence shows that the old diphthong *ai* had been monophthongized and fronted in the fifteenth century (see treatment of *ai, ei*, p. 248), the use of the symbol *ai* for old *ā̆* is a further evidence of fronting,

---

* See Appendix II.

[1] The forms *meke* and *mekes* fr. Handlyng Sinne should be struck out. They stand for M.E. *mēke* 'meek', not from *māke*. Bokenam's *bāre* is M.E. *bāre* adj., and not for *bēre*.

and also of the fact that M.E. *ā* and *ai*, *ei* had all been levelled under
one sound. In the account of the State of Ireland (State Papers,
Hen. VIII, Part III, p. 18) *save* is written *saive*; the Coventry Leet Book,
under date 1421, p. 24, writes *maid* 'made', M.E. *māde*; *waiter mylne* is
thus written in a Leics. Will of 1533 (Sir J. Digby), cf. Lincs. Dioc.
Docs., p. 142. 9. The Cely Papers have *ceme* M.E. *cāme* 'came',
p. 46, and Zachrisson has noted *teke* M.E. *tāke* 'take', and *fēder* M.E.
fāder 'father', in the Paston Letters of the fifteenth century. I have also
noted *yeate* 'gate' in Shillingford's Letters, p. 10. Now *ea* is a regular
L.M.E. and Early Mod. method of expressing the sounds [ē̩] or [ē].
So far as I know it rarely expresses any other sound, certainly never any
sound like [ā]. Possibly, however, *yeate* represents M.E. *yēte*, rather than
yāte, in which case the form is not to our purpose here. Jul. Berners
constantly writes *aege* 'age', M.E. *āge*, and the same spelling occurs in
Bishop Fisher's Sermons, p. 306. This spelling seems to show that *a* was
not felt as a suitable symbol for the sound as it then was. Rede me, &c.
(1528) rhymes *declare—theare* 46, *spare—wheare* 76, *declare—weare* Vb.
122. French writers on English pronunciation from 1529 onwards liken
the English sound of *ā* to French *é* and *ai*, that is [ē̩]. English grammarians and orthoepists are ambiguous upon the nature of this as of
most other vowels (though both Palsgrave and Ben Jonson hint at the
existence of a sound other than [ă̡]), and it is not until the first quarter
of the seventeenth century that we find, in Gill's Logonomia, the fronted
sound referred to, but then only with contemptuous disapproval, as of an
effeminate and affected pronunciation. Gill would apparently have us
believe that he himself said [ā]. It is more important to arrive, if
possible, at the current pronunciation of his time, and for this we shall be
guided by other evidence.

Since the fronting is so definitely established comparatively early in
the fifteenth century, and for Lincolnshire much earlier still, as we see
from a consideration of the spellings of, and rhymes with, old *ā*, taken
together with the facts and arguments given below (pp. 196, 211)
concerning the development of the old diphthong *ai*, it is reasonable
to suppose that the fronting of *ā* had begun, even in London, at least
as early as Chaucer's day. The first stage was probably [æ], and this,
we may conjecture, lasted into the beginning of the fifteenth century.
From the moment that *ā* and *ai* are levelled under a single sound, that is
by the end of the first quarter of the century, it is most probable that the
stage [ē̩] had been reached. The next change consists in making the
slack vowel into tense [ē], and we may believe that this has come to pass
from the moment that we find the old *ā*-words rhyming with those containing M.E. *ē²* [ē̩], which became [ē] towards the end of the fifteenth
century (see p. 209, below). The period could be fixed with fair
accuracy by a careful examination of the rhymes from the first half of the
sixteenth century or so down to the middle of the seventeenth, before the
first of which dates, I believe, the change took place. To take a concrete
example, the question is how early are *hate* and *heat*, or *mate* and *meat*,
pronounced precisely alike; how early does *heat* rhyme with *mate*, *make*
with *speak*, &c.? We have seen that already in the fifteenth century
care and *were* rhymed, but the [ē̩] sound was retained before *r*

so that we must find examples of rhymes before other consonants. The identity of *mate* and *meat* is proved in 1685 (see p. 210), but how much earlier can it be established? It is pretty certain that the old $[\bar{e}]$ became $[\bar{e}]$, otherwise than before *r*, as soon as, or at least soon after, M.E. $\bar{e}^1 [\bar{e}]$ had been raised to $[\bar{\imath}]$ (cf. pp. 209–10). At this point it was, or just before old $[\bar{e}]$ had become $[\bar{e}]$, that the new $[\bar{e}]$ from $\bar{a}$ caught it up. We must note here, though the point will be discussed later, that the fact that we now pronounce $[\bar{\imath}]$ in *heat* and other words from M.E. $\bar{e}^2$, whereas in the seventeenth and eighteenth centuries the Received pronunciation, on the whole, favours $[\bar{e}]$ in these words, does not imply a sound change whereby $[\bar{e}]$ has become $[\bar{\imath}]$ since the eighteenth century, but merely indicates one of the many instances of the adoption of a different and already existing type of pronunciation as the normal standard.

Had there really been a late sound change of the kind suggested, it is clear that it must have involved all the old $\bar{a}$-words as well as the $\bar{e}^2$-words. That is to say, we should now pronounce *heat* and *meat* with the same vowel as *hate* and *mate*, as was the habit in certain circles in the seventeenth and eighteenth centuries.

As early examples of the apparent identity of old $\bar{a}$ with old $\bar{e}^2$, we may cite Lord Buckhurst's rhyme *speake—make*, Complaint, p. 154; Spenser's rhymes *states—seates*, Heavenlie Beautie, *estate* and *late* with *retrate* (sic) 'retreat', F. Q. 1. 8. 12; Shakespeare's rhyme *nature—defeature*, V. and A. 734–6; and Mrs. Isham's spelling *discrate* for *discreet* in 1655, Verney Mem. iii, p. 235. It appears from a careful comparison of the statements and equations of Wallis and Cooper that they intend to imply that in their day, the three original M.E. sounds $\bar{a}$, *ai*, and $\bar{e}^2$ had all been levelled under what they call 'long *e*'. The precise character of this sound is open to discussion. I believe it to be tense $[\bar{e}]$, but having here brought the history of $\bar{a}$ down to the point at which it is levelled under a vowel in which it converges with two other originally different sounds, I reserve the arguments in support of the view just stated until the treatment of M E. $\bar{e}^2$; cf. pp. 209, &c., below.

The present-day diphthong into which old $\bar{a}$ has developed (in *make*, &c.) is first noted by Batchelor, *Orthoepical Analysis*, pp. 53–4, 1809.

M.E. ă in the Modern Period.

In Received Standard English the present pronunciation of M.E. short ă, in all words where this sound was unaffected by any combinative change, either in Late M.E. or at some subsequent period, is $[æ]$. Examples:—*mad, man, cat, rag, wax*, &c., &c. The Late M.E. -ăr from -*er* (cf. pp. 212–22) became $[-ær]$, for the subsequent history of which see pp. 203–5, below. The problems are when and in what dialect did the new sound first develop, and when did it become the received pronunciation in Standard English? The process is one of fronting, and if we assume that M.E. ă was a *mid-back* vowel, also of lowering. The lowering may have accompanied the fronting, or $[a]$ might become first $[ɛ]$, and then have been lowered. The difficulty of the second hypothesis is that a general tendency to lower all $[ɛ]$ sounds would have necessarily involved also original M.E. ĕ in *tell, bed*, &c.

The dialectal and chronological problems are not altogether easy of solution. The earliest (sixteenth century) writers on pronunciation, especially the native-born grammarians, give us very little help, their remarks being extremely ambiguous. And this is not to be wondered at when we reflect that the modern English sound is, even to-day, very rare among the languages of the world, that it is by no means universal in the English dialects, whether Regional or Social, at the present time, and that, for those speakers who have not used it from childhood, it is apparently one of the most difficult vowels to acquire, difficult to recognize and discriminate, and difficult to analyse and describe. It is a matter of very common experience that English speakers who have studied and perhaps spoken a foreign language for years, in which no sound at all resembling the genuine English [æ] occurs, continue, when pronouncing this foreign tongue, to substitute their native sound for the foreign [a] without the slightest misgiving, and without entertaining any doubt as to the complete identity of the two sounds. I have also known persons who, without having had any systematic training in phonetics, had yet given much intelligent attention to phonetic questions, who maintained stoutly that English [æ] was not a front vowel at all, but a back vowel, closely associated with [a], and this although they themselves undoubtedly pronounced the normal front sound.

From these considerations I am impelled, when the sixteenth- and seventeenth-century English writers on pronunciation identify the English ă with the sound usually expressed by this symbol in continental languages, and give no hint of the existence of another sound, to disregard their testimony as proving nothing at all—not even that the new sound did not exist in their own pronunciation. When it further appears that a writer has no phonetic knowledge, no grasp of foreign sounds, but is completely under the spell of the 'letters' and their supposed mysterious 'powers', it seems mere waste of time to spend it in trying to make definite sense out of his vague nonsense.

Our best chance of help from the grammarians is in the works of foreigners who, having no prejudices in favour of one sound more than another, have no hesitation, if they are acute enough to observe a difference between the English pronunciation of a 'letter' and their own, in pointing it out.

The occasional spellings which are often so enlightening shed some faint light on our problem, in that we find a few examples, even in the fifteenth century, of e written for a. Many of the words in which this spelling occurs may be otherwise explained than by the assumption of a genuine development of a front pronunciation from old ă. It is true that e is an unsatisfactory spelling for [æ], but supposing that a writer feels that the vowel in cat is front (he does not of course call it 'front' to himself), what symbol can he use to express this except e? But spellings of this kind which are not patient of some other explanation—e. g. as representing a M.E. (S.E.) ĕ-type, and not an ă-type at all—are very few and far between.

Lastly, there is the testimony of rhyme, which in the present instance can serve us but little, since there can be no genuine rhymes with [æ] except in words which are derived from ă, and it therefore proves nothing that words originally containing [a] and spelt *a* are rhymed together, for the rhyme would be equally good before and after the change of sound, which would affect all words of this class equally. The nearest approach we get to any enlightenment from this source are rare rhymes of *ă* with *ĕ*. This is comprehensible if the former sound had been fronted to [ɛ], but not if it was still a back vowel.

The information, such as it is, from the various sources is the following :

During the fifteenth century we have a few examples of *e* written instead of *a* in different parts of the country :—in St. Editha (*c.* 1420) the rhyme *was—cress* ' cross ' occurs twice, lines 1543, 1548. *Cress* is written for *crass*(*e*), which is found in line 1387. That the writer of St. Editha unrounded *o* is shown by this form and by *starme* ' storm ' 939, which rhymes with *harm*. It would appear from the spelling *cress* that he had also fronted *ă* ; *sedness*, Palladius, 10. 255 ; ibid., *eddres* ' adders ', 34. 935 ; *wex* ' wax ', 38. 1023 ; *wesshe* ' wash ', 40. 1105. Wm. Paston, the judge, has —*I heve* ' have ' (perhaps long) ; Duke of Buckingham—*thenking* ' thanking ', 1442–55, Paston Letters, 1. 61 ; Bokenam—*venyschyd*, Agn. 603 ; *wecheman*, Agn. 295 ; Marg. Paston—*seck* ' sack ', ii. 179 ; *pollexis* ' -axes ', ii. 215 ; *welch* ' watch ' (Vb.), ii. 362 ; Shillingford—*Sheftesbury*, 5 ; *hendes* ' hands ', 46 ; Gregory—*becheler*, 203 ; *jesper*, 209 ; *fethem*, 213 ; *cheryte* ' charity ', 232 ; Rewle of Sustr. Men.—*wexe* (Vb.), 107. 24 ; *chesiple* ' chasuble ' 91. 4. In the sixteenth century I have noted *es for*, Rec. Cath. of Ar., L. and P. ii. 405. 1501 ; *bend* ' band ', Bp. Knight (1512), p. 191 (twice) ; *renk* ' rank ', Lord Berners, i. 295 (twice) ; *axemyne*, in the Letter of Thos. Pery to Mr. R. Vane (Ellis 2. 2), p. 142 ; and the same writer has *exemynyde*, pp. 142 and 145 ; *Jenewery*, 149, *cheryte*, 156. Machyn writes *Crenmer*, 57, and *cherete*, 131. Wm. Faunte, Alleyne Papers—' if you *hed* him ', p. 32, 159–, where *hed* is stressed. Mrs. Basire writes *settisfie* 135 (1654), *Frencis* 139 (1655), *sednes* 140 (1656).

The inverted spellings (*a* for *e*) occur in *Wanysday* ' Wednesday ', Gregory, 97 and 229 ; *massynger*, 124, and *massage*, 223, in the same writer ; *zastyrday* ' yesterday ' (z = M.E. ʒ) 1. 81 ; and *massynger*, 1. 110, Marg. Paston ; while in the sixteenth century Sir T. Elyot writes *mantion*, 2. 316 ; and Machyn *prast* for ' pressed ', 127. We are perhaps entitled to assume that when a writer puts *a* for *e*, he attributes a front pronunciation to the former symbol. Of the first group above (*e* for *a*), it might be contended that the forms from Palladius (Essex) represent not M.E. *a* at all, but the old S.E. type with *e*, though this particular explanation does not apply to *wesshe*. *Heve* for *have* may possibly be an unstressed form. Shillingford's *Sheftesbury* may be from an O.E. South-Western form with *scĕft-* for earlier *scĕaft-*. On the other hand, the whole collection may be perfectly genuine, in which case it would be established that as early as the fifteenth century *a* had been fronted in Essex, Suffolk, and possibly in London, though Gregory, as we have seen (p. 64), was by birth a Suffolk man. None of the English writers on pronunciation of the sixteenth century appear to throw any light, except Palsgrave (1530), who hints at the existence of a pronunciation other than [a] :—French *a* is sounded ' suche as we vse with vs, where the best englysshe is spoken '. Some of the French writers on English assert that

English *a* is pronounced like *e* ('at least in Latin', Tory, 1529); '*e* almost as brode as ye pronounce your *a* in englysshe' (Wes. 1532). Unfortunately, we do not know whether this refers only to long *ā* or to *ă* as well.

Shakespeare rhymes *scratch—wretch* in Venus and Adonis (Vietor, Shakespeare Pron., p. 208), and *neck—back* in V. & A. 593 (Horn, N.E. Gr., § 40) Publ. Pprs. 6, *beck* 'back', 1485. Diehl (Eng. Schreibung und Ausspr.) mentions a few more occasional spellings—*stren* 'strand', 1554 Machyn, 72 ; *ectes* 'acts', 1598 Henslowe's Diary, 137, l. 13.

The statements of the grammarians down to the second half of the seventeenth century are nearly as useless for our purpose as those of their predecessors in the former century.

Butler (1634) only tells us that *ă* and *ā* differ 'in quantity and sound'. This might mean that *ă* was still unfronted, while *ā* was fronted, or that *ă* = [æ] and *ā* = [ɛ̄ē]. Ben Jonson, however (Gr. 1640, but written twenty years or so earlier), notes a difference between French *à* and the English vowel in *art, act, apple.* He says : '*A* with us in most words is pronounced lesse than the French *à*.' This is, perhaps, intended to refer to a fronted vowel.

Wallis (1653) has the grace to distinguish between 'guttural' and 'palatal' vowels, and among the latter he includes English *a*, both long and short, which he also denominates '*exile*', that is 'thin, meagre'. If these terms mean anything when applied to vowel sounds they must mean that the sound thus described is a front sound. We know, fortunately, from other sources that M.E. *ā* was undoubtedly fronted long before the time at which Wallis wrote (cf. pp. 194–6, above, concerning M.E. *ā*), and therefore this author's equation of the vowels in the pairs—*sam—same, lamb—lame, bat—bate,* &c., as simply long and short forms of the same sound makes it pretty certain that the short vowel was [æ].

Cooper (1685) is the first serious phonetician, and the most accurate observer we have hitherto met. He describes English *a* and says, 'formatur a medio linguae ad concavum palati paululum elevato, in *can, pass a* corripitur ; in *cast, past* producitur'. This is quite unambiguous and can only mean [æ], and the analysis is identical with that which the best modern phoneticians have made of the sound, described by Bell and Sweet as the low front. Cooper's list of words containing the short vowel is :—*bar, blab, cap, cat, car, dash, flash, gard, grand, land, mash, hat, tar, quality.* It will be seen that this includes words where *a* occurs before *-r*, and the word *quality* which we do not now pronounce with [æ]. The explanation of this will appear later (cf. pp. 201–3).

We need not pursue any farther the winding mazes of the grammarians in their descriptions of this sound, since it is clear that our present-day vowel is now fully recognized and adequately described. We may note in passing that Bachelor (1819) warns his readers against a prevalent vulgarism in the pronunciation of *a*. He says (p. 22) : 'Refinement should be kept within very moderate bounds with respect to this letter, as the real exchange of *a* for *e* is the result of ignorance or affectation, by means of which certain words will cease to be distinguished in pronunciation.' He illustrates his meaning by a list of words showing how one vowel is passing towards the pronunciation of the other. Thus *had* is becoming like *head, lad* like *led, man* like *men,* and so on.   'The broadest provincial tone', he adds, 'seems to make a far nearer approach to propriety than the exchange of the (= these) sounds. . . . It cannot be foreseen whether the fickle goddess of fashion will not one day authorise such an alteration.' She has not done so yet. We catch echoes of this vulgarism, springing, no doubt, from a desire for a bogus elegance, in the satires of Dickens and Thackeray, and we may still hear '*head*' instead of *had* from a few would-be refined vulgarians, as well as from certain sections of Cockney speakers.

We may now attempt a constructive theory of the course of events, which are somewhat imperfectly reflected by the facts which have so far been collected.

It seems probable that the fronting of M.E. *ă* began in the S.E. counties, notably in Essex, in the beginning of the fifteenth century, and that it spread during the first half of the century to Suffolk, and possibly to Norfolk. Only gradually did the tendency spread to London, and at first only among the proletariat or the middle classes. The forms in Gregory's Chronicle, if we take them as establishing that he had the fronted pronunciation, may be due largely to his Suffolk origin. The fronting was very gradual, so that *a* was not felt as an incongruous symbol for the sound. When we find *e*-spellings, or rhymes of *ă*-words with those containing *e*, we may reasonably assume that the vowel implied was fully front. From the lower and middle classes in London the new pronunciation passed during the sixteenth century to the upper classes, and even into the English of the Court.

Among the latter sections of the community the fronted sound may quite possibly have been at first an affectation adopted from some feeling that it was more refined than the 'broader' [*a*]. This seems likely in view of the fact that even to-day, outside Received Standard and the dialects of the Eastern Counties (as far as Bedfordshire and Cambridge-shire?), the sound is practically unknown in natural Regional and Class dialects. In any case, it was in all likelihood universal among fashionable speakers by the end of the sixteenth century. If the professed writers on English pronunciation are so slow to recognize and admit the existence of [æ], this is due partly to their inadequate observation and incapacity for phonetic analysis, partly to their dislike of new departures in pronunciation, and their reluctance to admit these, especially when there was no traditional symbol ready to their hand to express the new sound. It was comparatively easy to admit the new [ǣ or ē] from old *ā* because it was possible to liken the sound to French or Italian or Latin *ē*. Also a long vowel is always easier to recognize and describe than a short one. It was hardly possible to give any idea of [æ] without some knowledge of the functions of the tongue in the production of vowels, such as Cooper and, to some extent, Wallis possessed. It seems likely that many old-fashioned speakers, even at Court, preserved the old sound well into the seventeenth century.

If Shillingford's *hendes* really implies a front pronunciation of the vowel, he must have picked up the sound during his trip to London together with many other features of his English which are foreign to his native dialect (cf. pp. 65 and 81 above). It is hardly possible that [æ] should have existed in Devonshire in the fifteenth century, seeing that it is foreign even now to the dialect of that county. The form can hardly be of Scandinavian origin—in Devonshire! If we take St. Editha's *cress* = *crass* seriously, this was probably a foreign importation. While at the present time most English provincial dialects show more or less well-marked advancing or fronting of old *a*, except in the North, none would seem to have developed a full front vowel. Even the considerably advanced [ă] of many of the forms of Modified Standard, especially as heard in large towns, is probably not a survival of the native Regional, but due to the influence of Received Standard. In the would-be refined English of certain classes in Edinburgh and Glasgow, vigorous efforts to attain an 'English accent' have resulted in a front sound indeed, but in [ɛ] instead of [æ].

M.E. *al* becomes *aul*.

In Late M.E. *ă* followed by *-l* is diphthongized to *au*. This happens only in stressed syllables, and only when these end in a consonant. There are many examples in the fifteenth and sixteenth centuries of the spelling *aul* or *awl*. It is doubtful whether these spellings, at any rate by the end of the fifteenth century, do not express a sound very like our present sound [ɔ] in *hall, ball, all, salt*, rather than the diphthong.

The development of [*au*] to [ɔ] is discussed below (pp. 251–3).

A few examples will suffice to illustrate the *au*-spellings.

Gregory, *Saulysbury*, 102 (this must have been pronounced [saulzbĭrĭ] with no vowel following the *-l*); Cely Papers, *Tawbot* 'Talbot', 46, *fawkyner*, 81, *aull* 'all', *cawlyd*, 74, *schawl* be. The last word must be the strong or stressed form. Our present-day *shall* [ʃæl] is derived from the undiphthongized unstressed form, which is far commoner.

Thos. Pery (1539), *saume* 'psalm', Ellis ii. 2. 152; Sir Thos. Seymour, *cawlle*, St. Pprs. Hen. VIII, i, p. 773 (1544); Sir Thos. Smith, *hawle*, Ellis ii. 3. 15 (1572–6); Q. Elizabeth, *faule*, Letters, 48, *fauleth*, Transl. 2; *stauke* 'stalk', Trans. 26.

It is unnecessary to multiply examples, as these may be found scattered about in most fifteenth- and sixteenth-century letters.

Wherever, in present-day English, the combination *-al-* is pronounced [ɔl], or when the *l* is no longer pronounced, as in *talk, stalk,* &c., [ɔ], we may be sure that this vowel is derived from the earlier diphthong *au*. The change of this into [ɔ] has been so regular that *au, aw* are regarded in English as the natural symbols to express this vowel sound.

See p. 251, &c, below, for the history of *au*.

M.E. *ă* in the Modern Period after *w-, wh-, qu-, squ-*.

At the present time we pronounce a rounded vowel [o] in *wand, wash, what, quantity, squash*, &c. If we assume that the preceding [w, w̥] rounded M.E. *ă* before fronting to [æ] had taken place, the change in sound is easy to understand. In this case the change was earlier than that of [a] to [æ] (cf. pp. 196–200). If we place this in the fifteenth century in the South-East and in the following century in London English, the rounding after *w*, &c., must be earlier still. This would put the development of the rounded vowel in this position rather earlier than the meagre evidence of occasional spellings would lead us to suppose. The Celys write *wosse*, *whos*, &c., for *was* several times, and the same form occurs in Cr. of Duke of York a Knight of the Bath, p. 390; but this is not absolutely convincing, since the Auxiliary is usually unstressed, and the spelling may represent the reduced vowel. The first convincing spelling with which I am acquainted is *wosse* 'wash'[1] Machyn, p. 230. In William Watson's Teares of France (1593) occurs the very bad rhyme *songs—swans*, which seems to imply a rounded vowel in the latter word. After that there is nothing until the seventeenth century, when Sir R. Gresham in Verney Papers, p. 106, writes *Whoddon* for *Whadden* in 1622. The grammarian Daines (1640) says that *au* is pronounced in *quart*, *wart*, *swart*, and *thwart*. This implies the sound [ɔ] with the lengthening of *o* before *r*. The Verney Memoirs from 1642 onwards furnish numerous examples of *o*-spellings of *a* after *w-*, &c., and Cooper in 1685 gives *war*, *warm*, *warder*, *watch*, *water*, *wattle*,*wrath as containing either the short vowel in *of*, or the long vowel in *off* respectively.

Already in the fourteenth century I have noted a few instances of *o* for *a* after *w-*, but always before *-l*, so that one is led to suppose that the latter consonant exercised some influence. The examples are :—*swolwe-bridde*, Earliest Eng. Pr. Psalter (1350), p. 180; *swolʒ* 'swallow' (N.), Allit. Poems, Patience, 250; *swolʒed* (Pret.), Patience, 363, 1268. Chaucer in the House of Fame, 1035, rhymes *swallow* (Vb.) with *holowe*.

The list of *o*-spellings in the letters of the excellent Verney ladies is a fairly long one. *Whot* 'what', V. Memoirs, iv. 87, 1662; *wos* 'was', 1642, ii. 67, 70, 71; *wore* 'war', 1644, i. 201; *worr*, 1688, iv. 449; *worning*, 1646, ii. 356; *woshing* 'washing', 1661, iv. 21; *woching* 'watching', iii. 433; *Worik* 'Warwick', 1658, iii. 416; *quorill* 'quarrel', 1674, iv. 226; *quollity* 'quality', 1683, iv. 273; *quollyfications*, 1685, iv. 275; *squobs* 'squabs', 1664, iv. 72.

Woater 'water', 1688, iv. 449, though representing the rounding of M.E. *ā*, may be included here.

Cooper indicates a rounded vowel [o] in *was*, *wasp*, *wan*.

The words *waft*, *quaff*, usually pronounced [wǎft, kwǎf], though some speakers say [wɔft, wɔ̄ft, kwɔ̄f], have in the former case escaped the rounding. Unless this be a spelling pronunciation, which is unlikely, since *wa-* for most Englishmen stands for [wɔ, wɔ̄], these forms must represent a type in which M.E. *wǎ-* became [wæ]. The subsequent change in this vowel before *-ft* is dealt with on p. 204, below.

The Pret. *swam* [swæm] instead of [swom] may be explained by the analogy of *began* and other Prets. of this class.

By the side of the rounded forms whose existence is fully established among the best speakers, by the above evidence, for the seventeenth century, Mulcaster, 1582, puts *warde*, *wharf*, *dwarf*, *warn*, *wasp* into the same list as *cast*, *far*, *clasp*, *grasp*, &c., as regards the vowel, *Elementarie*, 127, and some seventeenth-century and eighteenth-century grammarians seem to suggest the existence of unrounded forms such as [wæz, swæn, kwælĭtĭ, kwæntĭtĭ], which again are either spelling pronunciations or dialectal variants. It looks as if we must assume the existence of a speech community among which *wǎ-* became simply [wæ] and not [wɔ], whose habits of speech have left some slight traces. It is certain, in spite of the

---

[1] But note now *wosshyng*, Stonor Papers, i. 92 (1466).
* See Appendix II for Milton's spelling *wrauth*.

Verney forms, that many eighteenth-century speakers said [kwælɪtɪ and kwæntɪtɪ]. This is asserted by the writers on pronunciation, and is confirmed by a statement made to me by a lady who died recently, aged eighty-six, that nearly eighty years before, a great-aunt of hers, then very old, corrected my informant for saying [kwɔlɪtɪ, kwɔntɪtɪ], asserting that these were vulgar pronunciations. Further, in Leigh Hunt's *Autobiography*, p. 180, it is recorded that John Kemble the actor (1757–1823) always said [kwælɪtɪ].

The rounding does not normally occur in Received Standard English when *wa-*, *qua-*, *wha-* are followed by *g* or *k*. Hence we pronounce [æ] in *wag*, *whack*, *wax*, *quack*, *quagmire*. The Danish writer Bertram (1753), whose observations are generally accurate, states, however, that a rounded vowel was heard in *quagmire*, and [kwɔg-] may still be heard.

If the seventeenth- and eighteenth-century unrounded forms of such words as *wash*, *swan*, *wasp* were not spelling pronunciations, that is, if *wa-* really developed into [wæ-] and subsequently became [wo], then we must assume that the initial *w*, while not hindering the early fronting of the vowel, later unfronted it again before rounding. This would be a later process than that which, among a different set of speakers, rounded M.E. *a* direct, before fronting took place.

The poets of the sixteenth and seventeenth centuries (e. g. Surrey, Wyatt, Sackville, Spenser, Shakespeare, Habington, Donne, and Herrick) do not, so far as I have got evidence, rhyme *wa-* with *o*, but with *a* —e. g. *want* rhymes with *grant*, *pant*, &c., *was* with *grass*. Pope rhymes *rewards—cards*, Moral Essays, Epistle ii. 243. These rhymes would still be held perfectly sound, being traditional, and also appealing to the eye. These reasons would explain their occurrence at an earlier date, even if those who used them pronounced [wɔnt, wɔz], &c. Such rhymes prove nothing one way or the other. The absence of the rhymes *wa-—o* may be due to the dislike already alluded to, to rhyme in antagonism to the conventional spelling.

M.E. *ă* before *s*, *f*, *th* [s, f, þ]; also before *r* and *r* + consonant.

The words *path*, *bath; pass*, *glass; chaff*, *after; hard*, *far*, &c., may serve as types of what has happened to the old short vowel before the above-mentioned consonants. In Received Standard, instead of a short vowel [ǣ] we have a long [ā]. In the various Regional and Class dialects, different developments occur, such as [glas, glæs, glǣs], &c.; these, however, do not concern us here, except in as much as they may represent survivals of the stages through which the Received Standard forms have passed in their time. Two things, then, have happened to the vowel in Early Modern [pæþ, glæs, tʃæf]: it has been lengthened, and it has been retracted, from a front to a back vowel.

The generally received view is that M.E. *path*, &c., became [pæþ], whenever the fronting took place; that this was then lengthened to [pǣþ] in the seventeenth century, whence [pāþ] developed in the course of the eighteenth. In the same way *hărd* became [hærd, hǣrd, hā(r)d]. There is little fault to find with this, except as regards the approximate period of lengthening. This took place, in all probability, much earlier than is usually supposed.

We shall see (p. 257) that *ŏ* is lengthened in Warwickshire as early as

1420, when we find *crooft* for *croft* (Coventry Leet); also that the spelling *marster* for *master* occurs in the Cely Papers. This last form has been adduced to prove that *r* could have had no consonantal sound at this period before *-s*, but it also shows that the preceding vowel was long, in fact that *ă* was already lengthened before *-s* + consonant. There is no reason for supposing that lengthening of *ă* took place earlier before *-s* than before [f, þ], or that the vowel *ŏ* was lengthened earlier before *f* than *ă* was. If we draw what seems the natural inference from these facts we shall have to assume that, at any rate by the end of the fifteenth century, the vowel in *path*, *glass*, *chaff* was already long. Did this lengthening occur before or after the fronting of *ă*? Are we to assume for the six-teenth century [pāþ, glās, tʃāf], or [pǣþ, glǣs, tʃǣf]?

The question seems open to discussion, and it may be well to argue it out. Let us assume that M.E. *băþ* 'bath' was lengthened direct in the fifteenth century, before the fronting of *ă*, to *bāþ*. In this case what was its position with regard to the verb *bāthe*, which had a long *ā* in M.E.? Either this latter vowel had already been fronted, or it had not. If not, then *bāþ* and *bāð* must have had the same vowel, and this, as we have seen, was fronted in the fifteenth century and subsequently became [ē]. The same fate would, therefore, have overtaken the same vowel in both words, with the result that there would have been no distinction in vowel sound at the present time between *bath* and *bathe*. But there *is* a distinction. Let us assume, then, that when *băþ* became *bāþ*, the old *ā* in [bāð] was already fronted and had thus got far ahead of the new *ā*. This assumption necessitates the further one that at a later period a fresh tendency arose to front *ā*. But this assumption is not justified, apparently, by facts. We are compelled, therefore, to assume that *băþ* did not become *bāþ* direct, but that the vowel had already been fronted before the lengthening took place, so that the development was [băþ, bǣþ, bǣþ]. This offers no difficulty, since we know that [bǣþ] did exist (from the testimony of the seventeenth-century Orthoepists), and the only question which arises is, *when* did it come into existence? If it be held, as it still is by some, that M.E. *ā* had only reached the [æ] stage by the sixteenth century, this would certainly be a difficulty, but we have established already (pp. 195-6) at least a very strong probability that by that period [ē], or still more probably [ē], had already been reached by the old *ā*, so that, if that be so, the difficulty is removed.

Incidentally it may be remarked that such a rhyme as *past—waste*, which occurs in Shakespeare's sonnet, 'When to the sessions of sweet silent thought', is intelligible if we assume that the vowels in both words were long—[pǣst—wēst]—but hardly so if we are to suppose [pǎst—wēst] or even [wēst].

As regards the change from [pǣst, bǣþ, æftə(r)] to [pāst], &c., it is difficult to be sure of the approximate date of the change. The state-ments of the eighteenth-century authorities are very unsatisfactory. The chief argument against assuming a very early (say late seventeenth or early eighteenth century) retraction to [ā] is the fact that this vowel seems to have been difficult for Englishmen at that time. Why, if the sound was a common one in our language, did it always become [ɔ], written *aw* or *au*, in foreign words when borrowed into English?

We find *spaw* for *Spa* in the Verney Memoirs, ii. 23 (1641); iv. 120
(1665), and the habit survives in the spelling and pronunciation of
Cawnpore, Punjaub, brandy pawnee, and in the pronunciation [kɔbʊl]
for *Cabul,* really [pandžăᵗᵇ, pānɪ, kābʊl], &c. The old-fashioned and
now vulgar pronunciation [vɔz] for *vase* illustrates the same point. The
word in this form must have been borrowed when [ā] was unknown in
English. Our present-day pronunciation [vāz] is the result of a comparatively recent approximation to the French sound.

Before *r, a* becomes *-o* in some dialects; cf. for instance *Charlbury,*
Oxon., locally called [tʃɔlbrɪ]. There was in the nineteenth century
a hyper-fashionable or vulgar by-form [tʃɔlz] of *Charles.* This used to be
facetiously written 'Chawles'. The prototype of this form seems to occur
in Mrs. Basire's *chorls,* 141 (1655). Cp. also Cooper, p. 173, above.
The form is difficult to account for unless [ā] had already developed
from [æ].

The Vowel in *half, laugh, dance, &c.*

If we assume that our pronunciation of these words goes back to
a late M.E. *hăf, lăf, dănce* which became [hæf—hǣf—hāf], &c., there is
no difficulty concerning them, nor one or two other words, such as *calf.*
If, on the other hand, we insist on deriving our present forms from Early
Modern forms with the diphthong *au—haulf, caulf, lauf, daunse,* &c.—as
some scholars do, then we are put to all sorts of shifts to explain the
present-day [ā] instead of [ɔ]. That diphthongized forms *haulf, caulf*
existed, no one doubts, but it is suggested that undiphthongized forms
also existed, and that from these our present received pronunciation is
derived. As regards *laugh, laughter,* there is no proof that [lauftər], &c.,
ever existed. In words of this kind there were two types, one in which
the final [χ] became [f], and in this type *au* did not develop; but there
was another type in which final [χ] or this sound before *t* did not
become [f] but retained its back character and then disappeared. In
this type *au* did develop, and afterwards, quite normally, became [ɔ].
Our forms *laugh, laughter* (in spite of the spelling which really belongs
to the second type), and the earlier forms, so much in vogue right into
the eighteenth century, *slafter, dafter,* are derived from the first type. On
the other hand, the received pronunciation of *slaughter, daughter* with
[ɔ] is derived from the second type. See p. 288, below, for early
examples of the spellings *laffe,* &c., and p. 297 for *haf* 'half'.

M.E. *ē¹* in the Modern Period.

By common consent, the long tense *ē* of M.E., no matter what its origin,
was raised to [ī] in the Early Modern period. Apart from present-day
vulgar English of big towns, the new vowel sound has been preserved.
In the degraded forms referred to, there appears to be a tendency to
diphthongize [ɪ] to something like [əi]. This tendency generally goes
with a drawling habit of speech which seems incompatible with the
preservation of any long vowel as a pure sound. The same speakers
who pronounce [həi, bəi, məi] for *he, be, me,* &c., also diphthongize the
vowel in *boot,* &c. (cf. 235, below).

The first indications we get of the change of [ē] to [ĭ] are given by the occasional spellings of persons who write *i, y* instead of *e*. These spellings, so far as my knowledge goes, begin before the end of the first quarter of the fifteenth century. They are fairly frequent during the fifteenth and sixteenth centuries, and are found even in the seventeenth century. The following examples will suffice:

Siege of Rouen, *c.* 1420—*hyre* 'hear', l. 23, *hyrde* 'heard', 29. Bokenam (1443)—*besychyn*, S. Marg. 925; Shillingford (1447–50) *mykely*, *myte* 'meet', 6, *hire* 'hear', 9, *dyme* 'deem', 13, *myve* 'move', 60, from M.E. *mēve, meeve, pryving, pryved*, 57, 'proving', &c., from M.E. *prēve*. Shillingford's *wyke* 'week', 59, may = [wĭk], or it may represent an old form *wĭke* without lengthening. *Sike* 'sick', 64, may be either M.E. *sēke*, or an early shortening.

Gregory (1450–70)—*hire* 'hear', passim, *dyre* ' dear', 116, *stypylle* ' steeple ', 149, *slyvys*, 160, ' sleeves '; the spelling *schyppe*, 162, ' sheep', no doubt expresses a shortening of the vowel after it had been raised to [ĭ]. Margaret Paston (1440–70)—*thir*, 2. 142, 'there, in which', *hyrafter* ' here-', 2. 178, *agryed*, 2. 179, *priste* ' priest', 2. 179, *symed* 'seemed', 2. 186, *spyde* ' speed', 2. 188, *syying*, 2. 192, *dymeth*, 2. 193, *shype* 'sheep', 2. 196, *kype*, 2. 197, *wypyng* ' weeping', 2. 226. Creation of Knight of the Bath (1494)—*sien* 'seen', 390, *indied*, 391, Letters and Papers, vol. i. Hymn to B.V.M. (before 1500)—*wi, Quin* ' queen', *tri* ' tree', *wiri* ' weary', *si* ' see '.

Anne Boleyn in 1528 writes *besyche*, Ellis 1. 1. 306 and 307, and so does Thos. Pery in 1539, Ellis 2. 2. 148. The spelling *Mons. de Guees* for *Guise* in Cavendish's Life of Wolsey, p. 76, makes it quite clear what value the symbol *ee* had for the writer. Ascham has *style* ' steel', Toxophilus, 112, and *piuyshlye*, Tox. 83 and 84; Roper's Life of Sir Thos. More, *liver* ' rather', xxviii. 16 (1556). As has been pointed out already, p. 136, Queen Elizabeth in her letters and in her Translations makes very frequent use of this spelling. The following list is rather fuller than that given above, and includes references. From letters to James VI (1582–1602):—*agreed*, p. 11, *hire*say (Noun), 17, *grivous*, 19, *ivel*, 20, *kiping*, 23, *fried* ' freed', 23, *nideful* ' need-', 27, *kipe* ' keep', 53, *besiche* ' beseech', 53, *spidye* ' speedy', 53, *hire* (Inf.), 61; from Ellis:—*briding* ' breed-', 1. 2. 157 (1549), *dides* ' deeds', 1. 2. 147, *hire*, 1. 2. 146. In the *Translations*, among other forms, we find *whir* ' where', p. 146. The habit of these spellings, then, is observable in the Queen's writings from her girlhood to the end of her life. It is unnecessary to prolong the list farther, and still less necessary to refer to the early Orthoepists, who for once seem all to agree, and all to be describing the real facts. It may be useful to observe that when the late sixteenth- and the seventeenth-century writers on pronunciation speak of the sound of ' *ee* ', they invariably mean [ĭ].

How early did the sound change take place? Since we have evidence of it in spelling as early as 1420 or thereabouts, it is probable that the present sound was fully developed in pronunciation considerably, perhaps fifty years, earlier. A thorough search through the late fourteenth-century texts might reveal examples of *i, y* spellings in these. It is probable that M.E. *ẽ* was pronounced very tense, and slightly raised, like the vowel in

Danish *se* 'see', which to English ears is almost indistinguishable from [sī]. This point is reached before the full high position of the tongue is attained. It might, of course, be argued that the fifteenth-century spellings indicate only a very tense and very high [ē], and that the full [ī] sound is only reached in the following century. The exact chronology of minute degrees of sound change is not obtainable with absolute certainty, but the facts and inferences based upon them with regard to the history of M.E. *ē*³ [ē] (see pp. 209–13) all make, in my opinion, in favour of the view here taken, that [ī] was probably fully developed from *ē*¹ before the end of the fourteenth century.

So far as my present knowledge goes, I see no reason for claiming any particular Regional dialect as the starting-point of the change, nor any Class dialect as the medium through which it passed into the English spoken in London, and ultimately into Received Standard. The sound change appears common to the speech of all areas and classes.

The Vowel in *evil*, &c.

We have now briefly to consider a group of words containing M.E. *ē*¹ of Late M.E. origin.

There are a few words in Received Standard English at the present day which have [ī] spelt *e* or *ee*, about which there has been some discussion. The chief words are *evil*, *beetle*, *weevil*, and *week*, the last three of which all have original *ĭ* in O.E. In some dialects *bitul*, *wifol*, *wicu* appear as *beotul*, *weofol*, *weocu*. In M.E. these become *bētel*, *wēvel*, *wēke* respectively, the *ē* being due to monophthonging of *eo* to *e*, and the lengthening of this in open syllables in M.E. Until recently these M.E. forms were accepted as the ancestors of the present-day forms. *Evil*, O.E. *yfel*, was regarded as the descendant of the Kentish type, O.E. *efel*, M.E. *ēvel*. It has been pointed out, however, that M.E. lengthened *ē* was slack, and would not produce [ī] in the Earliest Modern, but at best [ē]. It is pretty generally accepted now that in certain dialectal areas—not yet very precisely defined—O.E. *ĭ* in open syllables was lengthened in M.E., and lowered to a tense [ē] which would account perfectly well for the Modern forms of the above words. *Evil* is regarded not as a 'Kentish' form, but as an E. Midland form from *ivel*, the vowel of which was lengthened to tense *ē* in later M.E. (See on this question my *Short Hist. of Eng.*, §§ 174 and 229, Note 1, and references there given.)

In present-day Standard English we usually retain the short forms of words with O.E. and M.E. *ĭ*, as in *live, give, written, shriven, little, to wit, privy, city, pity, stick* Vb., &c., &c. As we shall see, however, the long forms with [ī] were far commoner during the first four centuries of the Modern period than at present. 'Peety' [pīti] for *pity* was occasionally heard till quite recently, and 'leetle' [lītl] is still used facetiously in the sense of 'very little'. There is some difficulty in distinguishing among the early spellings with *e*, those which really represent the long vowel, from those which are the lowered form of the short *ĭ*, discussed pp. 226–9, &c. In the case of some words such as *live, give*, we know in other ways that the pronunciation [līv, gīv] was current; in other cases the spelling *ea* or *ee* sometimes reveals the length. It is certainly possible that all three pronunciations [līv, lev, līv, gīv, gev, gīv], &c., coexisted.

P

The dialectal distribution of the late M.E. *ē*-forms from earlier *ĭ* needs much more investigation than it has hitherto received.   At any rate, the view that the lengthening (to *ē*) of *ĭ* in open syllables was a purely Northern process must be given up.   It undoubtedly involved a considerable area of the E. Midlands, and may even have spread South, and, to some extent, Westwards.

The following examples, in so far as they contain a long vowel and are rightly classified here, must be regarded as having M.E. *ē¹*, which was raised to [ī] very early, in these as in other words.

Lydgate—*wedewe*, &c.; Coventry Leet (1421)—*previe*, 131; Hen. V (Letters of Marg. of Anjou, &c.)—*yeuen* P.P., 21 (this may, however, be M.E. *ē²*); Wm. Paston—*abedyn* P. P., 1. 30; Bokenam—*pete* 'pity', Pr. 41, *sekyr*, Pr. 70, *wretyn*, Pr. Marg. 41, *weteth*, Pr. Marg. 228, *presoun*, Pr. Marg. 289, *iebet*, Marg. 428, and Christ. 366, *bedel*, Pr. Marg. 349 (may represent either M.E. *bĭdel*, or S.E. type *bedel* with lengthening), *wedowe*, Ann. 578, *shrevyn*, Elev. Thous. Virg. 415, *quekyn* Inf., Cecil. 782, 793, 796, *leuin* Pres. Pl., Lucie 296; Gregory—*preson*, 65, 81, *levyd* 'lived', 106, *wete* 'wit' Vb., *levyn* Inf., 130, *wedowe*, 164, *petefullyste*, 199, *rever* 'river', 207; Shillingford—*weket*, 101; Exeter Tailors' Guild—*weke*, 319, *wekett*, 322, *geven*, 315 (perhaps M.E. *ē²*, fr. O.E. *geofen*), *dener*, 315 (both long and short forms of *e* occur in this word, cf. Machyn; *dēner* being a case of the lengthened forms we are considering, *dĕner* of the lowering treated on pp. 226–9); Ord. of Worcester—*geve*, 388; Shillingford—*prevyly*, 61, *prevy seal*, 63; Marg. Paston—*levyn* 'live' Inf., *petous*, ii. 26, *preson*, ii. 84 (*indeferently*, i. 178, and *levery*, ii. 192, &c., are doubtful); Short Eng. Chron.—*presone*, 74, *prevely*, 75; Cr. of Knt. of Bath—*shreven* P. P., 390, *gentilwemen*, 393; Caxton—*to wete* 'wit', Jason, 58. 13, *wreten* 'written', 15. 24; Sir Robt. Wingfield (1513)—*gevyn* P. P., Ellis 2. 1. 212; Bury Wills—*wedow*, 78, *dener*, 74, *wedowed* '-hood', 75 (1482), *leve* 'live', 111 (1509); Lord Berners—*suspeciously* (?), 1. 71, *jebet*, 1. 36; Sir Thos. Elyot—*weete* Inf., 1. 51; Will of R. Bradley (Leics. 1533), L. D. D.—*levyng*, 161. 19, *geue*, 161. 27; Will of R. Astbrooke (Bucks. 1534), L. D. D.—*I geue*, 168. 11; Sir Thos. Seymour, St. Pprs. Hen. VIII 1 (1544)—*rever*, 776; Thos. Lever's Serm.—*forgeuenesse*, 50; Machyn—*deener*, 138, *cete* 'city', 10, presuns, 18, *Prevesell* 'Privy Seal', 37, *pete*, 43, *wedew*, 49, *leved*, 67, veker 'vicar', 80; Gabr. Harvey's Letters—*steekid*, 2, *steek* 'stick', 34; Verney Memoirs —*letel*, M. Faulkiner, ii. 55 (1642), *leetle*, ii. 355 (1645) and 384 (1648), *reaver* 'river', Lady Hobart, iv. 137 (1666), *pety*, Lady Hobart, ibid. 138.

In the eighteenth century Lady Wentworth has—*leved* 'lived', Wentw. Pprs. 64, 116, *levin* and *leving* 'living', 54, *pety*, 39, *geven* P. P., 40, 56, 64, *lever* 'liver', 42, *wemen* 'women', 113.

We see that these forms were both fairly numerous and widespread formerly, and it is remarkable that nearly all should have been eliminated from Received Standard and Literary English.

It is highly probable that many more of these forms, in documents of the fifteenth, sixteenth, and seventeenth centuries are concealed under the spelling *i*, in which case it is impossible to distinguish them from the unlengthened forms.   Thus such a spelling as *give* may well represent either of the two forms [gĭv, gīv].

M.E. $\bar{e}^2 = [\bar{\varepsilon}]$.

This sound, which remained during the whole M.E. period, and for some time afterwards, quite distinct from $\bar{e}^1 = [\bar{e}]$ (see pp. 205-7), has various origins (for which see pp. 29, 30; 33-4, above). With the exception of the words *break, great, steak*, all words originally containing this sound, unless shortening or other combinative influences have supervened (see p. 212), have in present-day Received Standard developed the vowel [ī], so that the old $[\bar{\varepsilon}]$ is now completely levelled under old $[\bar{e}]$. Examples of words containing M.E. $\bar{e}^2$ are :—*meat, eat, breathe, speak, steal; heat, teach, heath, deal* (Vb.); *clean; leap, heap, east;* also the French words *feast, beast, veal,* &c., &c.

For the shortening of this vowel see p. 254.

When $\bar{e}^1$ was raised to [ī] (cf. pp. 205-7), $\bar{e}^2$ at first remained unaltered. At this point M.E. $\bar{a}$ and M.E. *ai*, which, as we have seen (pp. 194-6), had by this time both been levelled under a single sound, caught up $\bar{e}^2$, and thus the three originally distinct vowels were all represented by the single sound $[\bar{\varepsilon}]$, which was tending more and more to become tense.

Between this stage and the present sound the intermediate stage $[\bar{e}]$ must certainly be assumed. When was this stage of a fully tense vowel reached?

It seems likely that soon after M.E. $\bar{e}^1$ became [ī], $\bar{e}^2$ would take its place as a mid-front-tense vowel; the tendency of Modern English being, on the whole, to make long vowels tense and to reserve slack quality for short vowels. We shall probably be within the mark if we place the development of the new tense $\bar{e}$ at least as early as the first quarter of the fifteenth century. This view is confirmed by the fact that in Gregory's Chronicle (1450-70) M.E. *hēlen* 'conceal', fr. O.E. *hĕlan*, is written *hylyn* (p. 146), where the M.E. vowel was certainly $[\bar{\varepsilon}]$.

This is evidence that among certain sections of the community, at any rate, this new $\bar{e}$ had already been raised to [ī]. Again, in the virulent Protestant tract *Rede me and be not wrothe* (1528) the rhyme *cleane—bene* 'been' occurs. Now the latter word can only have had [ī] at this time, since it contains M.E. $\bar{e}^1$.

During the sixteenth century we find scattered spellings of this vowel with *i*, e. g. Machyn—*prych* 'preach', p. 13, &c., *brykyng* 'breaking', 109, *bryke-fast*, 199, *spykyng* 'speaking', 35; Ascham has *lipe* 'leap', Toxophilus, p. 89; Gabriel Harvey, Letters, 1573-80, has *birive*, p. 53; Q. Elizabeth has *bequived* 'bequeathed', Transl. 140 (M.E. *quĕþe*, O.E. *cwĕþan*), besides *spike* Vb. The Queen also has *spich*, but this no doubt represents the non-Southern form with $\bar{e}^1$. Skelton rhymes *stepe—lepe*, Ph. Sparowe, 114-15; Surrey rhymes *grene—clene* (Tottel, p. 3). Spenser rhymes *seas—these* in Heavenly Beautie, and *streeme—seeme* in Prothalamion, *cleene* with *beene* P. P., *sheene* (Adj.) and *seene*, F. Q. 2. 1. 10; Shakespeare rhymes *teach thee—beseech thee*, V. & A. 404 and 406; but all of these poets have, more commonly, rhymes which suggest the $[\bar{e}]$ pronunciation (cf. p. 211). The grammarian Gill, in Logonomia (1621), mentions with contempt what he considers affected, effeminate pronunciations with [ī] of *leave* and *meat*, which he writes *liv, mit*. Thus the comparatively early raising to [ī] and therefore a still earlier 'tensening' of M.E. $\bar{e}^2$ are completely established.

But this is not the whole story. It is evident from rhymes and from the statements of writers on pronunciation that [spīk] for *speak* and so on was not the only, nor indeed the prevalent, type in Received Standard during the sixteenth and seventeenth centuries. Another pronunciation. with [ē], in words of this class is recorded, and this seems to have been the more usual during this period. We must assume, therefore, that the [ē] from earlier [ę̄] was differentiated among different classes of speakers—whether in a Regional or a Class dialect I am unable at present to say—into two types, one of which retained the old [ē], while the other gradually raised this to [ī]. It is unnecessary to discuss at length the often contradictory and never very clear statements of the English and French writers as to the precise quality of sixteenth and seventeenth-century English 'long *ē*', but so much at least seems certain, that they refer to a mid and not a high vowel. We have come to the conclusion that this was tense and not slack, quite apart from their statements. If these were accepted literally they would generally tend to show that the vowel was slack. Even Cooper (1685) equates the quality of 'long *e*' with that of the short in *ken*. On the other hand, Wallis (1653), and Sherwood in Cotgrave's Dictionary (1672), state that English 'long *e*' has the sound of French *é*, that is, a *tense* sound.

If these men are right, then Cooper is wrong, and it is not extraordinary that, good phonetician as he is on the whole, he should not have realized that there was a difference of *quality* as well as *quantity* between the vowels in *sell—sail, tell—tale* respectively, these being, amongst others, the examples he gives of 'long' and 'short *e*'. Cooper shows clearly that he did not appreciate the distinction of tense and slack, since he gives the pair *win—wean* [*i—*ɪ] as differing only in the length of the vowel.

However, passing from this point, we may note that Cooper gives a longish list of words containing 'long *e*', words, that is, with '*ea* pro *e* longa', which includes the following :—*beacon, bead, beam, lean* (Vb. and Adj.), *beat, bequeath, bleach, breach, break, deal, dream, Easter, eat, great, heal, cheap, heap, heat, heath. heathen, leaf, leap, clean, leave, mead* (the drink), *meal, meat, sea, seat, sheaf, sheath, speak, squeak, steal, stream, sweat, teach, weak, wean* (Vb.), *bean, wheat* ; also the words of French origin :—*appeal, beast, cease, cheat, conceal, cream, creature, deceave, defeat, disease, ease, extream, feast, impeach, preach, queasie, repeat, reveal, treat, veal.* This is a pretty satisfactory list of words which had [ē] in M.E., and it is perfectly certain, in my opinion, that in Cooper's pronunciation all these had the sound [ē]. I am quite unable to see the force of the arguments of Jones, the recent editor of Cooper, and of Zachrisson, who seek, apparently, to prove that Cooper intended to suggest that all these words were pronounced with [ī]. He definitely places them under *ea*; immediately above comes a list of words like *behead, bread*, &c., in which he says '*Ea* ponitur pro *e* brevis', and our list, as stated, is headed '*ea* pro *e* longa'. Of '*E*' he says, 'Vera huiusce soni productio scribitur per *a* absque à longum falso denominatur ut in *cane, wane, age*'. Further, in a list of words pronounced alike though written differently, 'Voces quae eandem habent pronunciationem', &c., Cooper includes *meat—mate.* Surely if this means anything it means what we have already tried to establish, that M.E. *ā* and M.E. *ę̄* had both the same sound in the seventeenth century, if not much earlier, and further, if we can ever learn anything from the Orthoepists, we may learn that this sound was a *mid* and not a *high* vowel. Shakespeare rhymes *sea* with *play*,&c.(see p.248); Spenser, *seates—states,* Heavenly Beautie, *retrate* (sic)—*late,* F. Q. I. 8. 12; Habington—*sea* with *pray*, Castara, 134, with *play,* 89, with *away,* 91, and so on; *Thames—streames,* ibid. 21; and Suckling—*cleane* with *Seine* in 'I came from England into France'. Donne—but these rhymes are not quite conclusive—rhymes *meat* with *great, breake* with *weake* (Auct. of the World).

Such a spelling as 'to *spake* to her' (1693), C. Stewkley in Verney Mem., iv. 464, leaves no doubt as to the type of pronunciation intended.[1]

Cooper's list, then, is invaluable, and may be considered reliable as showing that words of the class we are now considering were still commonly pronounced according to a different type from that now in vogue in Received Standard English, although our present type was certainly already in existence, as we have proved above, and had existed before the end of the fifteenth century. Cooper himself seems to have known both pronunciations of *wean*. It is rather strange that the evidences of the [ē] pronunciation of the old [ɛ̄] words should be so comparatively rare as they are. This may be due partly to the dislike of the more fastidious poets for rhyming together words which are spelt with different vowel symbols although the sounds are identical, so great a hold has spelling on the literary imagination, partly also perhaps to the fact that the [ī] type may have gained ground more rapidly in fashionable speech during the eighteenth century than we suppose. Still, such rhymes as *great—cheat, sea—survey, gate—eat* (Pope), *dreame—name* and *speake— mistake* (Swift, An Apology), *shade—mead* (Pope, Windsor Forest, 135–6 (1713)), *please—stays, ease—days, fate—deceit* (Lady M. Wortley), &c., occur far into the eighteenth century. A thorough investigation of these rhymes from the early sixteenth to the end of the eighteenth century would be a laborious but repaying piece of work. In dealing with M.E. *ā,* p. 104, above, I have shown the existence of the rhyme M.E. *ā* with M.E. *ệ*² before *r*, as early as *c.* 1420.

This is the proper place to emphasize the fact that our modern usage with [ī] in *heat, meat,* &c., is not in the nature of a sound change as some writers seem to suggest, but is merely the result of the abandonment of one type of pronunciation and the adoption of another, a phenomenon which, as we know, is of the commonest occurrence in the history of Received Standard Colloquial English.

Had such a sound change taken place between the seventeenth century and the present day it must have involved all the words which had *ā* and *ai* in M.E., and *made, maid,* and *mead* would all have been pronounced alike. It is possible that a tendency to make M.E. *ā* and *ai* into [ī] did actually exist in some Regional dialects, and, if Gill is to be believed, some affected speakers of Standard English in his day actually said [kīpn] for *capon.*

This tendency, however, must have been confined to a small and obscure community, and it has not affected Received Standard. It is not comparable in importance to the tendency to raise M.E. *ệ*² to [ī], and in the community among whom this latter process was carried out, it is evident that this must have started before the descendants of the old *ā* and *ai* had developed into the full [ē] sound. Incidentally, this shows how early must have been the 'tensening' of *ē²*. To make the matter more concrete for those unused to this kind of discussion, we may say that in the dialect from which is derived the present pronunciation of *mead*, this word must have been approaching that pronunciation before *made* and *maid* had reached the [mēd] stage and while they were both pronounced [mēd].

The three words *break, steak, great* may be simply survivals of the type represented in Cooper's list, in which they all occur.

On the other hand, *great* has been explained on the analogy of the old Comp. *grĕtter*, which was fairly common in the fifteenth century (cf. p. 325). The shortened form preserved [ĕ], and the quality of this vowel may, it is said, have influenced that of the Positive by preventing so great a differentiation between the two forms as would exist between [grīt—grətə]. This explanation now appears to me improbable. *Break* and *steak* have been supposed to be loan forms from a South-West dialect. But the South-West dialects have had extremely little influence upon Received Standard, in spite of Drake and Raleigh. Besides, while this might be a plausible explanation for the sixteenth century, the problem does not arise till the late seventeenth or eighteenth century in this case.

It is simpler to regard all three forms as survivals of the older type. As a matter of fact these words were pretty widely pronounced with [ī] in the eighteenth-century Received Standard, and *break* is still [brīk] in Irish English and in many Regional dialects.

Dr. Johnson said that Lord Chesterfield told him that *great* should be pronounced so as to rhyme with *state*, while Sir William Yonge sent him word that it should rhyme with *seat*, and that 'none but an Irishman would pronounce it *grait*'. (See Boswell's *Life of J.*, Oxford Ed., ii, p. 161.)

The Change of -*er*- to -*ar*-.

A number of words in Mod. Engl. which formerly had -*er*- are now pronounced with [ā], and this irrespective of the fact that some are still written -*er*-, e.g. *clerk*, others -*ear*-, e.g. *heart*, while others are written -*ar*-, e.g. *hart, starve, far, carve, star*, and so on. On the other hand, a larger number of words which formerly had -*er*- in the spelling retain this spelling, as *clergy, mercy, person, swerve*, &c., or are written -*ear*-, as *learn, early, search*, and are pronounced [ʌ]. We have here the survivals of two types, differentiated in Late M.E. from one original type— one type which preserved -*er*- unaltered, until by a series of changes this vowel developed into present-day [ʌ], the other type in which M.E. -*er*- became -*ar*-. This has normally become present-day [ā] when the *r* is followed by a consonant as in *starve*, or is final, as in *star*, but has remained short and is fronted to [æ] when another vowel follows the -*r*-, as in *tarry*.

Our task now is to trace the rise and history of the M.E. -*ar*- type, and to give some account of its distribution in the Mod. Period.

The phonetic process is most probably one of simple retraction of [ɛ] to [a] before -*r*-, but it is conceivable that the series of changes was [ɛr—ær—ar]; that is to say, the sound represented by *e* in M.E. may first have been lowered and then retracted. The difficulty of the problem lies in the fact that at no period, and in no early writer after the appearance of the -*ar*- spellings, is either type used with perfect consistency, the same writer often spelling the same word in both ways. Nor is it easy to see why in a certain number of words the -*ar*- spelling should gradually have become fixed, thus helping to fix the pronunciation, while in others again in which -*er*- or -*ear*- is written, the pronunciation should preserve the other type, nor further why yet a third group has preserved the -*er*- spelling, and are pronounced according to this type. It is difficult enough to reach a satisfactory solution of the difficulties even when the facts are known with some fullness; it is quite impossible to do so when the facts are imperfectly known. The following account, though incomplete, is less so than those which have appeared hitherto.

From an examination of the list of words which have been found written -*ar*- from the fifteenth to the eighteenth century, it seems impossible to formulate any law to account for the change in terms of combinative phonetic conditions, since almost every word formerly containing -*er*- in a stressed syllable is found at one time or another to have been written -*ar*-, and therefore, presumably, to have been pronounced according to this type among some groups of speakers. The nearest approach to any combinative influence which might be suspected is that of lip consonants, which present some slight appearance of having predisposed to the -*ar*- type when they stand before, and perhaps also after, the combination. I consider this, however, very doubtful, and it leaves much unaccounted for.

It seems more probable that dialect is at the bottom of the difference, dialect of a Regional character to start with—though, as we shall see, this is hard enough to determine—which, however, was later on rather social than Regional.

The Chronological Facts.

The -*ar*- forms are very rare in any text before the beginning of the fifteenth century. I cannot profess to give an exhaustive account of the conditions in M.E. until my M.E. Grammar is much farther advanced than at present, and I only give the results of my investigations on M.E. vowels so far for what they are worth. I have not yet examined Pl. N.'s in respect of our present point. The earliest example of -*ar*- for -*er*- which I have is *darc* in St. Juliana, line 30 (Prose), MS. Royal, *c.* 1250. The Eastern and South-Eastern texts are slightly more fruitful, and I have noted *sarmon* and *sarmoun* in Will. of Shoreham's Poems (*c.* 1320), 4. 1212, 56. 1562, 50. 1411, 100. 67, and *harkne*, 141. 330, in the same writer. From the Norfolk Guilds of 1389 I have noted *parsones and prestes*, p. 23, *garlond*, 117, and *farthing*, 122 (five times). Chaucer has only *fart*, *harre* 'hinge' (rh. with *knarre*, Prol. C. T. 550), *tarie* 'tarry' (Vb.), and *harrie*.

When we come to the fifteenth century we find that the larger number of the -*ar*- forms occur in S.E. and E. Midland texts, and they are not common here until well on in the century. Palladius on Husbandry (Colchester, *c.* 1420) has only *barn* and *barley*; Bokenam has very few of these forms, and they appear in the Suffolk Wills apparently only from 1463 onwards; it is perhaps only a coincidence that Marg. Paston, also belonging to Suffolk, has hardly any of these forms before 1461, and that before that date she writes her own maiden name *Berney*, after 1461 *Barney*. The Essex family of Celys have a larger number of *-ar-* forms in their letters in the late seventies and eighties of the century than is found prevailing in any other collection of documents. The writers of this century who belong to the more Westerly parts of the country have practically no *-ar-* forms. This is true of the Life of St. Editha, Bishop Pecok, Shillingford's letters, and the Exeter Guild documents. In the last mentioned, however, *tarmes* is a remarkable exception.

Turning to London documents, the *-ar-* forms here are very rare before the middle of the century, though scattered instances will be found in the list. It is not until the second half of the century that we find any considerable number, and it is significant that we find most of all in the Chronicle of Lord Mayor Gregory, who was a Suffolk man by birth. Caxton has very few *-ar-* forms, and they are very rare in the official documents down to the end of the century.

In the following century the *-ar-* spellings are more frequent, and most writers, of all classes, have a certain number. The examples quoted below are from documents of all kinds, including private letters, and works published in the sixteenth century. It will be noted that in some words, e.g. *clerk, heard, serve*, &c., *swerve, war*, these spellings are fairly widespread. It will be found, I believe, that the writers who use these spellings most frequently are Bishop Latimer, Machyn, and Queen Elizabeth. The evidence seems to point to the probability that before the end of the sixteenth century the *-ar-* pronunciation was far more common, that is, it included a much larger list of words, than at present. For the seventeenth century our best evidence is derived from the Verney Papers and the Verney Memoirs. These collections of letters put us in possession of the habits of speech of all the members of a very numerous family, and of a large circle of their friends (see remarks on these documents, pp. 162–3). We find not only the Verney ladies, but many of their male relatives and friends writing *-ar-* in words where we now pronounce the other type. It would be absurd to deny that the writers of these letters spoke typical upper-class English of their period, and we are led to the conclusion that *sarvent, vartue*, and so on, really represent the pronunciation in vogue at this time. If these spellings are more common in the ladies' letters than in those of the men, we must, I think, put this down to the fact that the former read fewer books than the latter, and were less influenced by the spelling which was rapidly becoming stereotyped by the printers. Many people doubtless used the *-ar-* forms who wrote *-er-*; cf. Ch. Butler in his Gr., p. 3—'We write *person* though we say *parson*.' Lady Wentworth, whose letters contain a large number of these spellings, although her letters continue down to 1711, must be held to represent the English of the Court during the last quarter of the seventeenth century. She therefore continues our record of this type of English for thirty years or so after the Verneys. Those whose views on the history of pronunciation are derived mainly from the statements of writers on pronunciation, will be glad to find that Jones (1701)—one of the best of his kind—includes *mercy, heard*, and *verdict* in his rather brief list of words in which '*e* is sounded as *a*', p. 24. Apart from the evidence of the Verneys, several of Lord Rochester's rhymes point in the same direction, and in supplement of Lady Wentworth's spellings we have several rhymes and spellings of Swift, which tell the same tale, and make it certain that down to about the middle of the eighteenth century the [*ā*] pronunciation, or its immediate ancestor, obtained very largely in a number of words which are now pronounced according to the -*er*- type.

Later in this century, Elphinston, a Scotchman who lived for many years in England and moved in decent society, puts down *larn'd* as a London Vulgarism in 1783, though we have reason to believe that the word was normally so pronounced by the best speakers of an earlier generation. Elphinstone is not absolutely above suspicion, since as a professional authority on pronunciation he was bound to uphold a theoretically 'correct' pronunciation, while he would be inclined to preserve a certain number of Scotticisms and Scottish prejudices against certain types of English pronunciation.

Apparently, by the end of the eighteenth century the distribution of [*ā, ă*] among the old -*er*- words was, on the whole, the same as our own, though doubtless the older usage lingered here and there, among good old-fashioned speakers, much later. According to Leigh Hunt's *Auto-biography*, i, p. 180, the actor John Kemble (1757–1823) pronounced -*ar*- in *virtue*. Leigh Hunt regarded this as an eccentricity. It is evident that the -*ar*- pronunciations were declining from the middle of the eighteenth century, since Fielding singles out *sarvis, sartain, parson* 'person' for ridicule by putting them into the mouths or the letters of vulgar persons. This pronunciation evidently died out in some words earlier than in others, and the usage varied among speakers of the same breeding, at the same period. Thus it is curious that in spite of the testimony of the Verneys, and the habit of John Kemble 150 years or so later, Vanbrugh appears to discredit the pronunciation *vartue* by attributing it to a peculiarly dingy and dubious character, Mrs. Amlet in *The Confederacy* (1705). Seventy years later Goldsmith puts *varment* into the mouth of Tony Lumpkin. As a rule, when a comic writer departs from ordinary spelling in depicting the speech of one of his characters, he intends to suggest a pronunciation which is out of the ordinary, though there is always the possibility that he is deceiving himself; as when a writer at the present time attempts to express the pronunciation of a vulgar person by writing '*orf*' for *off*, '*wen*' for *when*, '*chewsdy*' for *Tuesday*, thereby expressing nothing different from the normal pronunciation. Swift's spellings *vardy* for *verdict* and *varsal* for *universal* in *Polite Conversations* may have represented fashionable pronunciations of his day, of which he disapproved. The reality of the vowel in the former is confirmed by Jones. Swift himself evidently said '*clargy*', and *varment*. (See these forms in the lists.)

To sum up, we may say that the -*ar*- pronunciations appear to have been almost universal for at least two and a half centuries, among the politest speakers, and that the use of this type was gradually discontinued from about the middle of the eighteenth century in a large number of words.

Why was this? The most natural explanation seems to be that it was chiefly due to the influence of a different social stratum, which had either preserved the -er- type traditionally, or deliberately adopted it on account of the spelling, from a desire for correctness. The question naturally arises, Why should the spelling of the printers of -ar- in certain words, and -er- or -ear- in others, have gradually crystallized? The practice cannot have reposed altogether, or mainly, upon that of the Late M.E. professional scribes, since the -ar- forms were not nearly sufficiently well established in their time to make their usage consistent, and as we have seen the -ar- spellings are rare, and very scattered in M.E. texts. It would seem that the early printers were a law unto themselves, for had they followed the scribes in this respect, as they did in most others, they must have printed no -ar- forms at all.

We must suppose then that the distribution of -er- and -ar- spellings in the printed books of the fifteenth and sixteenth centuries had a certain phonetic basis. The very inconsistency in usage seems to show that the printers did to a certain extent reproduce their authors' own spelling (see discussion of this point, pp. 112–13). And if the early writers, as we know is the case from numbers of autograph letters and other documents, wrote sometimes -er- sometimes -ar-, this must have represented a conflict between traditional and phonetic spelling on the one hand, or, on the other, a different pronunciation in different words. How did this fluctuation arise? Clearly only from a mingling of the habits of two different dialects.

Dialectal Origin of the -ar- Forms.

Looking at all the facts so far as they are known to me, and set forth in the preceding pages and the following lists, I am inclined to assume that the change of -er- to -ar- began in Kent early in the fourteenth century, and spread thence to Essex, to Suffolk, and to Norfolk. During the fourteenth century the new forms began to filter into London speech very gradually from Kent or Essex, or from both. They were rare in the speech of the upper classes at first, but gradually gained ground, probably through the speech of the lower strata of society, during the fifteenth century, possibly also through the direct influence of merchants from the Eastern Counties who acquired wealth and position like Gregory.

During the sixteenth century these South-Eastern forms became fashionable, and were much used by Queen Elizabeth herself. Incidentally, we may call attention to the occurrence of *desarve* in a letter of Anne Boleyn, and the same form in a letter of her daughter about twenty years later. In the former case the form may be due to native Eastern dialect, while Queen Elizabeth was simply following the increasingly fashionable tendency. As a matter of fact, the -ar- forms are more frequent in the Queen's later letters and her translations than in those written in her girlhood.

According to the view here taken, the -ar- forms were originally from a Regional dialect, then passed into the London Class dialect of the lower orders, whence they spread upwards.

The precise distribution of -er- and -ar- forms would thus be as impossible to account for as that of the three forms *i, e, u* from O.E. *y*.

The second list of -er- spellings shows how comparatively late many of these persisted, even in words where -ar- spellings and pronunciations have long been absolutely fixed, and which one might therefore suppose to have been among the earliest words to be adopted in the -ar- type.

To my mind this shows that, even in these cases, difference of pronunciation persisted for a long period.

List of Words which formerly had -er-, but which appear occasionally written -ar- from the fifteenth to the eighteenth centuries.

Bark Vb. *barcke*, Lever's Sermons, 115, 1550.

Barley. *barley*, Pallad. on Husbandry 1420; Bury Wills 1467.

Barn. *barnes*, Pallad. on Husbandry 1420; *barnys*, Bury Wills 98, 1504; Sir Thos. Elyot's Gouernour 1531; Ascham.

Carve. Engl. Conq. of Ireland (MS. Trinity 1425); *karue*, p. 1423; *carue*, Shakespeare 1st Fol. Loves L. L.

Clergy. *clargy*, Gregory's Chron. 1450–70; Rede me and be not wrothe 1528; Latimer's Sermons; Thos. Lever's Serm. 1550; Swift rhymes *clergy—charge ye*.

Clerk. *clarke*, &c., Linc. Will 1451 (Linc. Dioc. Docs.); Rede me, &c., 1528; Skelton, Magnificence; Cavendish, L. of Wolsey 1577; Latimer; *clarklie*, G?briel Harvey 1578–80; *-clark*, Q. Elizabeth; Machyn 1550–63; Thos. Wilson, A. of Rhet. 1585.

Certain. *sartayne, cartayne*, Gregory 111, 176; *sartten, sarten*, Cely P. 64, 139, 140, &c., 1475–88; *unsartin*, Mrs. Pulteney, Verney P. 199, 1639; *sartinly*, Lady Sussex 1641, Verney Mem. ii.·1, 82, 83; *carten*, Mrs. Basire, 140, 1655; E. of Rochester rhymes *certain—Martin*; *sartain*, Wentworth P. 48 (Lady W.), 1705; and Fielding in Tom Jones, where it is said by Landlady of an Inn, and is written by Mrs. Honour, a lady's-maid.

Confirm. *confarmes* (Luce Sheppard), Verney Mem. iii. 75, 1651.

Concern. *consarned*, Pen. V. in Verney Mem. ii. 195, 1642.

Dark. Skelton rhymes with *clarke*, Magnif. 485 (†1529); *dark*, Fisher, Bp. of Rochester's Serm. (fl. 1459–1535); Lord Berners's Froissart; Sir Thos. Elyot's Gouernour 1531; *darknes*, Q. Elizabeth.

Dearth. *darth*, Lord Berners 1520, i. 344, 415; Lever's Serm., p. 84, 1550; Thos. Wilson, A. of Rhet. 1560, &c.

Defer. *defarre*, Lord Berners, i. 100; *defar*, Q. Elizabeth 1572 (letters).

Divert. *divartid*, Cary V. in Verney Mem. iv. 276, 1686; *divartion*, ibid. iv. 275.

Early. E. of Rochester rhymes *early* with *Farley*, Epistle fr. B. to E.

Errand. Gabr. Harvey, *arrand*, Letter Bk. 1573–80.

Earn. *yarne*, Edm. V. Verney Mem. iv. 193, 1675.

Ermine. *armyns*, Lord Berners 1523; *armyn*, Machyn 1550–3.

Far. *farre*, &c., Lord Berners; Sir Thos. Elyot; Bp. Fisher; Ascham; Wilson; Lyly.

Farther. Bury Wills 1535; Latimer; Bp. Fisher; Lord Burghley; *farder*, Ascham; Lyly, *farther*.

Farm. *farme*, Machyn; Lever's Sermons, *farmes, farmer* three times.

Fervent. *faruentlye*, Latimer.

Farthing. *fardyng*, Machyn 1550–63.

Guerdon. *guardon*, Bokenam, S. Agn., 701, 1443; Shakespeare 1st Fol. Loves L. L., four times.

Heard (Pret. and P. P.). *herde* rhymes *farde*, Siege of Rouen *c.* 1420; *harde*, Marg. Paston, P. Letters ii. 124, 1463; ibid. ii. 241, 1465; Cely Papers 77; Skelton, Magnif.; Sir R. Wingfield 1513, Ellis 2. 1. 212; Lord Berners; Cranmer, Letters (Ellis 1. 2. 33) 1533; Sir T. Elyot; Lever's Serm.; Latimer; *hard*, Machyn 1550–63; Gabr. Harvey, Letter Bk. 1573–80; Lord Burghley, Letters, Bardon P., and Ellis 1. 3. 12; Cavendish, L. of Wolsey; Ascham; Ch. Butler, Gr. 1634; Verney Mem., passim—Cary V. ii. 70, 1642; Lady V. ii. 268, 1647; Pen. Denton, ibid. iii. 228, 1655, &c., &c.; Lady W. in Wentworth Papers, 51, 1706, &c.; Jones, Practical Phonogr. 1701.

Heart. Hoccleve, Reg. of Pr. 1412; rhymes *smarte*, Siege of Rouen *c.* 1420; M. Paston, Letters ii. 365, 1469; Fortescue 1470 (?); Anne Boleyn 1528, Letter in Ellis 1528; Skelton, Magnif.; Thos. Pery, Ellis 2. 2. 149, 1539; Sir T. More; Thos. Lever; *hartly*, J. Mason, Ellis 2. 2. 54. 1535; *hartie*, Cranmer, Letter 1533; Bp. Fisher; *hartes*, Ascham; Lord Berners; Sir T. Elyot; *hartily*, Lord Burghley; Ascham; *hartiest, hartily, hart*, Q. Elizabeth; Lyly; Ch. Butler, Gr. 1634; Cooper 1685; Jones, Practical Phonogr. 1701.

Hart. *hart*, Lord Berners 1520; Machyn, *hartes ede* = head.

Harbour. *harborowe*, Sir Thos. Seymour 1544, Letter in State Papers, Hen. VIII, i. 775.

Hark—hearken. *harke*, Thos. Lever 1550; *harken*, Lyly 1579–80; Ch. Butler, Gr. 1634, *ea* in *hearken* = *a*.

Harvest. Ascham.

Hearth. Chapman, *harth*; Mons. D'Olive, Wks. i. 239 (1606); Cooper 1685.

Herald. *harold*, Machyn 1553–60.

Hereford. *Arfford, Harrford*, Machyn 1550–3.

Hurdle [fr. S.E. form M.E. *herdel*]. *hardel*, Palsgrave's Esclarcissement 1530; *hardels*, Dives Pragmaticus 1563; *hardell*, Bury Wills 1569; Levins, Manipulus 1570.

Herbage. *tharbage* 'the herbage', Letters and Pprs., i. 80, 1483.

Infer. *enferre* Vb. rhymes *debar*, Skelton's Magnif. 60.

Learn. *learne* rhymes *warne*, Rede me and be not wrothe, p. 123, 1528; *larne*, Henry V in Verney Mem. iii. 368, 1647; Luce Sheppard, ibid. iii. 98, 1652; Swift rhymes *learn* with *darn* in 'A Panegyric'; Elphinston, 1783, regards *larn* as a London vulgarism.

Mar Vb. *marre* rhymes *barre*, Rede me, &c., 1528; *marre*, Cavendish, L. of Wolsey 1577.

Mercy. *marcy*, Siege of Rouen *c.* 1420; *marcyfully*, Bokenam, S. Ann. 665, 1443; *marcy*, Gregory's Chron.; *Marcie* (girl's name), Gabr. Harvey 1578–80; *marcy*, Q. Elizabeth; *marzy*, Lady Sussex, Verney Mem. ii. 151, 1642; Lady V, ibid. ii. 296, 1647; Mrs. Basire, *marci*, 135, 1654; *marcey*, Mall Verney, ibid. iv. 214, 1655; Jones, Practical Phonogr. 24, 1701.

Marvel, &c. *marvylyously*, Cely Papers.
Merton College. *Marten Colege*, Rich. Layton (afterwards Dean of York) in Letter, Ellis 2. 1. 60, 1535.
Peril. *paryl*, Ordinances of Worcester 374, 1467; *parill*, Caxton's Jason 1477; *paryll*, Lord Berners, 1. 288; *parillouse*, ibid. 1. 31; *parells*, Cavendish, L. of Wolsey 1577.
Person. *parson*, Marg. Paston; State of Ireland, St. Papers Hen. VIII, iii. 15, 1515; Thos. Pery, Letter, in Ellis 2. 2. 147, 1539; Lord Berners; Sir T. Elyot's Will; *parsonages*, ibid.; *parson*='person', Machyn; Q. Elizabeth; 'We write *person*, though we say *parson*', Butler's Gr. 1634, p. 3; Lady Sussex in Verney Mem. ii. 88, 1641; Dr. Denton, ibid. iii. 461, 1660; Lady Wentworth in W. Papers, 94, 96, 1709; occurs in a letter by Mrs. Honour, a lady's-maid, in Tom Jones.
Parson. *parson*, Latimer's Serm.; Machyn.
Prefer. Rede me, &c., *prefarre*; E. of Rochester rhymes *preferred—Blackguard* in Nell Gwynne.
Search. *sarche*, State of Ireland, St. Pprs. Hen. VIII, iii. 15, 1515.
Serjeant. *sargent*, Gregory's Chron. 81, 1450–70; *sarjant*, Dick Hals (cousin of Verneys) in Verney Mem. iv. 310, 1674.
Sermon. *sarmon*, Bury Wills, p. 17, 1463; Gregory's Chron. 203; Machyn; *sarment*, Lady W. in Wentworth Papers 221, 1711.
Serve. *sarvyd*, Cely Papers 44; to *sarve*, Ld. Adm. Sir Thos. Seymour 1544, St. Pprs. Hen. VIII, i. 778; *sarue, sarved*, Q. Elizabeth; *sarve*, Lord Barrymore, Verney Mem. ii. 53, 1642; Magdalen Faulkiner, ibid. ii. 56, 1642; Lady Hobart, ibid. iv. 127, 1665; Lady Wentworth, W. Pprs. p. 77, 1709; *sarving*, ibid., p. 118, 1710; Prior rhymes *served—carved*, The Ladie.
Servant. *sarvant*, Sir T. Seymour, St. P. Hen. VIII, 1. 776, 1544; *sarvand*, Machyn; *sarvant*, Q. Elizabeth; *sarvante*, Sir J. Hotham 1560, Ellis 2. 2. 325; Sir E. Sydenham, Verney Mem. ii. 102, 1642; Lady V., ibid. ii. 257, 1647; Sir R. Burgoyne, ibid. iii. 51, 1652; Lady Wentworth in W. Papers, passim, 1705–11.
Service. *sarvyse*, Gregory's Chron. 222, 1450–70; Cooper, 1685, designates *sarvyse* as belonging to a 'barbarous dialect'; *sarvice*, Verney Papers ii. 120, 1642; ii. 68, 1642; ii. 70, 1642; Lady Wentworth, W. Pprs. p. 95, 1709; *sarvis* is written by Mrs. Honour, a lady's-maid, in Tom Jones.
Deserve. *desarve*, Cely Pprs. 63. 1475–88; Anne Boleyn, Letter, Ellis 1. 1. 305, 1528; *disarued*, Q. Elizabeth 1546; E. of Rochester rhymes *deserving—starving*, 'Bath Intrigues'; *desarve*, Lady Sussex, Verney Mem. ii. 83, 1641; Lady V., ibid. ii. 347 (twice), 1647; Lady Wentworth, W. Pprs. 118, 1710.
Desert. *desart*, Q. Elizabeth; Shakespeare rhymes *deserts—parts*, Sonnet xvii.
Preserve. *presarve*, Lord Barrymore, Verney Mem. ii. 53, 1642; Mrs. Isham, ibid. iv. 118, 1665.
Quarrel. Q. Elizabeth; Lyly.
Smart. *smart*, Siege of Rouen c. 1420; *smarting*, Caxton, Jason 1477.

Star. *starre*, Gregory's Chron. 80, 1450–70; Sir Thos. More, Letters in Ellis i. 1 and 2; Wilson, A. of Rhet. 52, 1585; Q. Elizabeth.

Starling. *starlyng*, Cely Papers 1473–88; *stare*, Sir Thos. Elyot 1539.

Start. *astarte* rhymes *harte*, Hoccleve, Reg. of Pr. 1412.

Starve. *starue*, Wilson, A. of Rhet. 61.

Swerve. *swarue*, Skelton, Magnif. 1529; *swarved*, Lord Berners, i. 376, 1523; *swaruing*, Latimer's Serm.; *swarue*, Wilson, A. of Rhet. 53; Q. Elizabeth; Gill, Logomonia 1621; Daines, Orthoep. Angl. 51, 1640.

Tarry Vb. *tarying*, Bokenam, Agn. 476, 1443; *taryed*, Lord Berners.

Term. *tarmes*, Exeter Taylors' Guild 317, 1466; Cary V. in Verney Mem. iii. 431, 1657.

Universal. 'the *varsal* world', 'Miss' in Swift's Polite Conversation.

Virtue. *vartus* (Pl.), Lady Hobart in Verney Mem. iv. 57, 1664; *vartuous*, Vanbrugh's Confederacy (said by Mrs. Amlet), Act III. Sc. 1, p. 174, 1705.

Verdict. Jones, Practical Phonogr. 1701, includes this word among those pronounced with *ar*; one of the fashionable speakers in Swift's Polite Convers. says *vardy*.

Vermin. *varment*, Thos. Pery, Letter, Ellis 2. 2. 145, 1539; *varmin*, Mrs. Eure, Verney Mem. ii. 86. 1642; *vermin* rhymes *garment* in Swift's poem 'The Problem'; *varment*, said by Tony Lumpkin in Goldsmith's *She Stoops to Conquer*, Act v, 1773.

War. *warre*, &c., Sir J. Fortescue 1471–6; Gregory's Chronicle 1450–70; Caxton, Jason 1477; Bp. Knight of Bath and Wells 1512; St. of Ireland, St. Pprs. Hen. VIII 1515; Sir Thos. More; Lord Berners 1523; Sir Thos. Elyot 1531; Lever's Serm. 1550; Cavendish, L. of Wolsey 1577; Ascham; Lyly.

Work. *workys*, Siege of Rouen 1420; *warkys*, Bokenam, Christ. 887, 1443; Exeter Taylors' Guild *awarke* Adv., 1466; *wark*, Lord Berners i. 82; *awarke* Adv. i. 161; *wark*, Skelton, Magnif.; Lincolnshire Inventory, Linc. Dioc. Docs. 1527; *warke*, Sir Thos. Elyot; Q. Elizabeth (Trans.); *worke* (Letters).

Proper Names.

Barney. This, the maiden name of Marg. Paston, is always written *Berney* by her down to 1461; from then onwards generally with *a*.

Berkley. *Barkeley*, Gregory's Chron.; *Barkly*, Bp. Knight of Bath and Wells 1512; Lord Berners; Shakespeare, First Fol., Pt. I, Hen. IV, Act I, Sc. iii.

Bermondsey. *Barmondsay*, Creation of Duke of York a Knight of Garter, L. and P. i; *Barmsey*, Machyn 303.

Dunfermline. *Dunfarlin*, Sir J. Temple, Verney Mem. ii. 249.

Derby. *Darby*, Rede me, &c., 59, 1528; the yerle of *Darbe*, Machyn; *Darby*, Tom Verney in Verney Mem. iii. 174, 1659.

Guernsey. *Garnesey,* Machyn 271; *Garnsea,* Sir Ralph Verney in Verney Mem. iv. 289, 1658; Baker, Rules for True Spelling, &c., 1724, says that this name is pronounced *Garnzee.*

Herbert. Included by Jones, Pract. Phonogr. 1701, among words where -*er*- is pronounced -*ar*-.

Jerningham. *Jarnyngham,* Marg. Paston ii. 29.

Jersey. Lady Wentworth in Wentw. Papers, Lord *Jarzys* (Possess.) 84; *Garzy* 55; *Jarzy* 149.

Ker of Fernihurst (family name). Written *Car* by Q. Elizabeth.

Verney. This name occurs, with very few exceptions, in this form throughout the Camden volume of Papers, and the four volumes of Memoirs, in which nearly all the letters are by members or near connexions of the family. The only exceptions I have noted are— *Varny,* Lady Sussex, ii. 82, 1641; Sir R. Burgoyne, ii. 166, 1641; Susan Verney, same date, ii. 167, 170; Lady Hobart (a Denton), iv. 285, 1657, and iv. 49, 1662. The family now call themselves *Verney* [vānɪ].

List of words which now have [ā] in pronunciation whether spelt -*er*-, -*ear*-, or -*ar*-, but which occur spelt -*er*- in the fifteenth and sixteenth centuries.

Barley. *Barley,* Lord Lovel's Will 1455, Linc. Dioc. Docs. Pl. Name now *Barley.* The first element is O.E. *bere, barley.*

Barn. *berne,* Palladius *c.* 1420; *bernys,* Marg. Paston; *berne,* Bury Wills 21, 1463; ibid. 94, 1501; ibid. 100 *bern,* 103 *beern* 1504.

Carve Vb. *kerver,* Short Eng. Chron. 1465; *kervyr,* Gregory; *kerved, kervyr,* Cr. D. of York 1495; *kerued, keruinge,* Sir Thos. Elyot; *kervers,* Cavendish, L. of Wolsey 1577.

Clerk. *clerkis,* Bp. Pecok *c.* 1449; *clerk,* Lord Lovel's Will 1455; *clerkes,* Marg. Paston; Lord Berners; *clerk,* Machyn.

Dark. *derk,* Shillingford Papers 1447–50; Bp. Pecok; Bk. of Quintessence 1460–70; *derke,* Caxton, Jason 1477; Gregory's Chron.; Jul. Berners, Fysshynge 1496; *derkness,* Lever's Sermons 1550.

Far. *ferre,* Pallad. *c.* 1420; *fer,* Hoccleve, Reg. of Pr. 1412; Bp. Pecok; Rewle of Sustris Men. *c.* 1450; *ferre,* Sir J. Fortescue; *afer,* Shillingford 1447–50; *ferre,* Bury Wills 20, 1463; *fer,* Exeter Taylors' Guild 1466; *ferre,* Caxton, Jason 1477; *ferr,* Lord Berners; *ferre,* Sir T. Elyot.

Farther, &c. *ferther,* Pallad.; *ferdyr,* Marg. Beaufort (1443–1509), Ellis i. 1; Bp. Pecok; *ferther,* Shillingford; *ferthermore, ferthest,* Marg. Paston; *ferther,* Gregory; *ferthest,* Caxton, Jason 1477; *ferther,* Skelton †1529; *ferther,* Sir T. More.

Farthing. *ferthing,* Bury Wills 1463, p. 15.

Farm, &c. *fermed,* Bp. Pecok; *fee-ferme,* Lord Lovel's Will 1455; *ffee ffermys,* Sir J. Fortescue; *ferme,* Shillingford; *ferme, fermor,* Marg. Paston; *ferme,* Gregory; Bury Wills, many times from 1467–80; Sir Thos. Elyot; Lever's Sermons (*ferme,* four times); *ferme,* Latimer; Cavendish, L. of Wolsey.

Harvest. *hervest,* Pallad. *c.* 1420.

Heart. *herte, hertely,* Judge Paston 1425–30; Bp. Pecok; Shillingford; *herte,* Gregory; Marg. Paston; Marg. Beaufort (letters); *hertes,* Fortescue; Caxton; Jul. Berners; *hert, hertiest,* Bp. Knight of Bath and Wells 1512; Dean Layton of York 1535; Lord Berners; Bp. Fisher of Rochester; *hertes, herted,* Latimer; *hert,* Ascham; *heart,* Lyly.

Harbour. *Colde Herborowe,* Gregory; *Cole herber,* Machyn.

Hark. *herke,* Skelton †1529; Lever's Sermons 1550.

Hearken. *herkened,* Latimer.

Jar 'discord'. *ierre,* Wilson's A. of Rhet. 166.

Marvel. *mervilyous,* Cely P.; *mervelous,* Bp. Knight 1512.

Parson, &c. *person,* Gregory; *person, personage* 'parsonage', Lever's Sermons 1550; *personage,* Latimer.

Partridge. *pertrych,* Jul. Berners.

Serjeant. *serjeants,* Machyn.

Smart. *smertli,* Bp. Pecok 1449.

Star. *sterre,* Bp. Pecok; *sterres,* Gregory; *sterris,* Bk. of Quintessence 1460–70; *sterres,* Caxton, Jason 1477; Sir T. Elyot; Bp. Fisher.

Starve. *sterue,* Hoccleve, Reg. of Pr. 1412; Pallad. 1420; Latimer; Cavendish, L. of Wolsey; *sterue,* Shakespeare, First Fol., Hen. IV, Pt. I, Act I, Sc. iii.

Start. *stert,* a Lincs. Inventory, 1527, Lincs. Dioc. Docs.

Tarry. *terryed,* Marg. Paston.

ĕ becomes *i* by a combinative change.

Before certain consonants or combinations of consonants there was an early tendency to raise *e* to *i*. The traces of this have almost faded from Received Standard at the present time, except in a few words where the change is recorded by the spelling, e. g. *wing* from M.E. *weng,* O.N. *veng-,* string, M.E. *strenge*; and in *England,* English, where the old spelling remains.

In Early Modern, and even in the seventeenth and eighteenth centuries, a certain number of spellings with *i* are found, chiefly before *-n* + consonant, but also before *-s,* and, more rarely, before *-l.*

England occurs with the spelling *Ing-* fairly often, quite apart from Northern texts, already in M.E., and *Ing-, Yng-* forms are scattered throughout fifteenth- and sixteenth-century texts. A few references are:— Gregory 63; Fortescue 113; Wm. Paston (the Judge) I. 29; Cr. Duke of York 414; Inventory of J. Asserly, Linc. Dioc. Docs.; Letter of Thos. Pery, Ellis 2. 2. 146 (1539); Letter of J. Mason, Ellis 2. 2. 56 (1523); Lord Berners, passim; &c., &c.

The Short English Chron. 1465 still writes *bowes strenges,* 73.

Before *-nch*:—Gregory, *Kynges Bynche,* 194; also Short English Chron. 68, &c., and Machyn 195 (twice); Ascham has *wrynchynge,* Tox. 145.

Before *-n* + *d, t, s*:—*Gintlemen,* Laneham's Letter 40, 1575; *repint,* M. Faulkiner, Verney Mem. ii. 56 (1645); *atinding,* Doll Leake, ibid. iv. 113 (1665); *rintes* 'rents', Lady Sussex, ibid. ii. 84 (1642); *sincible,* Peter Wentworth, Wentw. Papers 211 (1711).

Before *-s*:—Latimer, *opprision,* Serm. on Ploughers 22; Q. Elizabeth, *opprissing*, Transl. 26; Lady Sussex, *requist*, Verney Mem. ii. 121 · Cary Verney, *bist* 'best', ibid. ii. 70.

Before *-l*:—Fortescue, *rebillion* 129 (twice), *rebyllion* 130, Cary Verney, *will* 'well', Mem. ii. 63, *till* 'tell', ii. 70; Mrs. Basire, *will* 'well', 134 (1654).

Cary Verney, who seems fond of the *i*- forms, also has *lit* for *let*.

M.E. *i* in the Modern Period. *

The present-day development is the well-marked diphthong [*ai*]. The first stage in the process was most probably [ī*i*], that is, the latter part of the old long vowel was made slack. We must consider this stage as already diphthongal. The next stage was probably a further differentiation between the first and second elements of the diphthong, the former being lowered to [ĕ]. The subsequent career of the diphthong may well have been [ɛi—æi—ai]. A point of importance is that at one stage the diphthong became identical with that developed out of old *oi*. This identity is still preserved in some Regional dialects—e.g. that of Oxfordshire, where the sound in both *line* and *loin* appears to be something approaching [ai]. The rhymes of the seventeenth and eighteenth centuries tend to show that the identity still survived, and it seems to have existed as early as the fifteenth century (see history of *oi*[1], p. 250, also 324, below). The fact of this one-time identity to some extent affects the views we shall take concerning the precise path followed between the starting-point and the present stage. The stage [ei] may be represented by the occasional spellings with *ey*, *ei* in the fifteenth century. These spellings are not particularly common—I have noted more in St. Editha (*c.* 1420) than in any other text—and although they occur here and there as late as the seventeenth century, it seems clear from other evidence that they do not always express the same diphthong. The scattered spellings I have found are—St. Editha—*y-leyche* 'like', 399; *neynthe* 'ninth', 668; *leyʒt* 'light', 904; *weyʒt* 'wight', 960; *feyre* 'fire', 1294; *myelde* 'mild', 1408, 2833; *seyʒt*, 1517; *bleynte* 'blind', 2731; *bleynde*, 2822; *bleynasse*, 2937; *feynde* Inf. 3254. *Meynde* 'mind', 3858, rhymes with *hende* 'end', and therefore probably represents the form *mēnde*, rather than *minde*. Marg. Paston has *abeyd* Inf. 'bide', ii. 26. The Hymn to the Virgin, in Welsh spelling (*c.* 1500), writes *meichti, breicht, seicht, geiding, abeid, deifyrs* 'divers', *ei* 'I'. Sir Thos. Seymour has *Eylle of Wyght*, and *trey* 'try', St. Pprs. Hen. VIII. i. 780 (1544); Machyn writes *feyre* 'fire', 41; and *meiʒt* occurs in a letter of John Hotham of Scarborough, Ellis 2. 2. 325, 1570.

In the Verney Memoirs we have *obleiged*, Sir R. V., ii. 358 (1647), *obleige*, M. Eure, iii. 336 (1657). The English and French Orthoepists of the sixteenth century generally describe English *i* as consisting of *e* and *i*, though Smith and Bullokar appear to regard it as a single long vowel, a view which we cannot take seriously. In the seventeenth century, Butler (1634) and Howel and Sherwood, independently, in Cotgrave's Dictionary (1672) all say that the sound is the diphthong *ei*. By this time, probably [æi] is intended, and we may suppose that the same type of pronunciation is referred to as that used by the writers of the occasional spellings *ei*, *ey* just quoted.

---

* See Appendix II for variant of *high, height*.

There is no difficulty in assuming that such a diphthong as [ei] could become [ai]. We find the M.E. diphthongs *ei* and *ai* levelled under a single diphthong, apparently [ai] in the M.E. period, and at the present time London Cockneys have made the early nineteenth-century diphthong [ei] (cf. p. 196) into something approaching to [ai], although the former remains in Received Standard.

On the other hand, during the same period throughout which the *ei* spellings are found for old [ī], other spellings are found which seem to establish the existence of another type of pronunciation of this, identical with that of the old diphthong *oi*.

St. Editha has the spelling *anynted* 'anointed', 376; Gregory writes *dystryde* for 'destroyed', p. 59, *pyson* for 'poison', p. 161; in the Cely Papers, p. 69, we have *vayage* 'voyage', where the first syllable may, it is true, represent either *ī* or *oy* in M.E. Shakespeare in V. and A., 1115–16, rhymes *groin* with *swine*; the rhyme *tryall—disloyal* occurs in Marston's *Insatiate Countess* (1613), Act iv; Lady Sussex in 1639 writes *kainde*, V. Pprs. 2 06; in the Verney Memoirs the following spellings may be noted:— *gine* 'join', Cary Stewkley, vol. iii, p. 433 (1656); *byled* leg of mutton, Dr. Denton iv. 227 (1670); *implyment* 'employment', C. Stewkley, iv. 276 (1686); Mrs. Basire writes *regis* 'rejoice', Corresp. 137 (1654). In 1712 we find *voiolence*, Wentworth Papers, p. 280. The spelling *joyst* for original *jiste* is found in 1494, and *boyle* (on the body) from *bile*, in 1529 (cf. Jespersen, *New Eng. Gr.*, p. 320). To Jespersen's early examples of *oy* for *ī* we may add *defoyled*, Mnk. of Ev. 59, 1482, *Obroyn* 'O'Brien', St. of Irel. St. Pprs. Hen. VIII, iii. 9, and *defoylynge* in *Rede me and be not wrothe* (1528), *St. Goyles*, Lady Gardiner, Later V. Letters i, 73 (1700).

The spelling *ruight* 'right', Cely Papers, 46, 158, &c., clearly expresses a diphthongal pronunciation, possibly [ai], at any rate it could hardly have represented the same pronunciation as that expressed by the spelling *ei*. These spellings can only mean one thing, namely, that those who used them pronounced old *ī* and old *oi* in exactly the same way. What was the probable character of the diphthong thus expressed? Certainly not [oi], but very possibly a sound not unlike [ai] now heard in Oxfordshire for both old *ī* and old *oi*. The spelling *vayage* cited above from Cely Papers points to the first element being already unrounded, in fact, to either [ai] or [ai], and this is not necessarily contradicted by *ruight* from the same source. A curious spelling, *loay* 'lie', used by Cary Stewkley in 1656, Verney Mem. iii. 434, shows that this lady did not regard *o* in diphthongal combinations as expressing a rounded vowel.

But the testimony of the writers on pronunciation also confirms the identity of pronunciation of *ī* and *oi* already proved by the occasional spellings cited. Thus Wallis (1653) says that 'long *i*' is composed of 'feminine *e*' followed by *i*. He has previously described 'feminine *e*' (of the French) as an 'obscure sound', which is heard in English when 'short *e*' immediately precedes -*r*-, the examples given being *liberty*, *vertue*. It is impossible to be sure whether Wallis means [ə] or [a]. That he is either trying to describe one or other of these sounds, or that he is confusing them and making one description apply to both, is pretty certain. At any rate, the first element is not a front vowel and not

a round vowel. Cooper, thirty years later, is more explicit. He says
that there is a diphthong composed of the sound *u* in *cut* + *i*, which is expressed in English sometimes by *i* as in *wine, wind, blind*, &c., and
sometimes by *oi* as in *injoin, joint, jointure, broil*, &c. Concerning the
sound of *u* in *cut* he tells us (1) that it is different from the vowel in *bull*,
and (2) that it is made in the throat and resembles the groans of a man
afflicted with illness or pain. The English pronounce this short sound
almost everywhere, as in *nut*, even in Latin, except when the preceding
consonant is labial as in *pull*. He gives a very precise analysis of the way
the sound is made, saying that guttural *u* is formed if when pronouncing
long *o* the lips are retracted into an oblong form. This appears to be
another way of saying that the sound is ʻunrounded *ō*ʼ, which is precisely
the analysis we now make of the English vowel [a] in *cut*, &c.—ʻmid-
back-(tense)ʼ.

From this combined evidence of occasional spellings and the statements
of grammarians, it appears (1) that from the fifteenth to well into the
seventeenth century old *ī* was pronounced by many speakers as a
diphthong of which the first element was a front vowel, the diphthong
thus being either [e*i*, e*ɪ*] or [æ*i*]; (2) that during the same period other
speakers pronounced old *ī* and old *oi* with one and the same diphthongal
combination; (3) that, at any rate from the seventeenth centu.y onwards,
the first element of the diphthong was either [ə] or [a], most probably
the latter, giving the diphthong [a*ɪ*]. The transition from this to the
present-day sound consists merely in making the first element slack.

It seems thus to be established that there were, in the fifteenth, sixteenth, and seventeenth centuries, two types of pronunciation for this *ī*,
as for so many other sounds in English. Two questions arise, namely,
by what process did old *ī* pass into the [ai] type, and from which type is
our present pronunciation descended?

The most probable answer to the first question appears to me to be
that the [ai] type branched off from the other at the [e*i*] stage, and that
the process was one of simple retraction from a mid-front to a mid-back-
tense vowel. We may illustrate the development of the two types by
a simple diagram.

$$\text{M.E. } [\bar{\imath}] \; < \; i^i \; < \; e^i \; \begin{cases} e^i \\ a^i \end{cases} \begin{array}{l} \text{Type A.} \\ \text{Type B.} \end{array}$$

It seems to me that it is impossible to reconcile the undoubted existence of the two pronunciations [e*i*, ai] at the same time, as proved by the
evidence, without some such theory.

As regards the second question, it may be said that either type could
become [a*i*]. Possibly both types had this development, so that they
were finally reunited thus:—

$$[i^i \; < \; e^i \; \left\langle \begin{array}{c} \text{Type A.} \\ e^i \; < \; \alpha^i \\ \text{Type B.} \\ a^i \; - \; a^i \end{array} \right\rangle \; < \; a^i]$$

On the other hand, A may have died out altogether in Received
Standard, leaving the field entirely to B. Or it may have survived only

in provincial dialects, and in some of these its descendants may still linger, offering more or less strange variants from the Standard, and constituting a characteristic feature of rustic speech. This is a question for the ' dialectologists' to solve.

The word *oblige* was commonly pronounced with [ī] during the seventeenth and eighteenth centuries. In the Verney Memoirs, Lady Verney writes *obleged*, ii. 305 (1647), Lady Gaudy ends a letter '*your obleged humble sarvant Vere Gaudy*', iii. 224 (1650), and Sir Richard Browne refers to '*your most obleginge letter*', iii. 111 (1653) ; Lady Hobart has *disablegin*, iv. 55 (1664), *obleg*, 139 (1666). On the other hand, Sir Ralph Verney writes *obleiged*, ii. 305 (1647), and Mary Eure *obleige*, iii. 336 (1657), and Mrs. Basire's spelling *ableiage*, Corresp. 141 (1655), certainly suggests [ai]. Pope, as is well known, rhymes *obliged* with *beseiged*, and Jones (Practical Orthographer, 1701) says that *oblige* contains the sound of ' *ee* '.

As may be inferred from the above spellings of Sir R. Verney and Mrs. Eure, the word was also pronounced with a diphthongal sound [ai] as now, even in their day. The old [ī] pronunciation survived among some speakers far into the nineteenth century, and according to *The Bookman*, May 1907 (cit. Jespersen, Mod. Eng. Gr., 8. 33), Wilkie Collins retained this mode. It has been said that the dying out, even during the eighteenth century, of the old pronunciation is due to the influence of Lord Chesterfield, who, it is alleged, warned his son against [ī] in this word. This statement seems to have been repeated without verifying the facts, or at least without considering the meaning of words, among others by myself in my [1]*Short Hist. of Engl.*, § 254, Note. I cannot excuse the statement, nor indeed even explain how I came to make it, since I was acquainted with the passage in which Lord Chesterfield refers to the word. His words are these :—' The Vulgar man . . . even his pronunciation of proper words carries the mark of the beast along with it. He calls the earth *yearth* ; he is *obleiged* not obliged to you.' The plain meaning of this, written 1749, Letter 195, in my Edition, is that [oblaidžd] is the vulgar pronunciation, and some other—presumably [oblīdžd]—the polite pronunciation.

Lord Chesterfield has been made to say exactly the reverse of what he intended, and a theory which is not even consonant with the facts has been based upon a misinterpretation of his words.

We must suppose that [oblaidž] is derived from a M.E. form with *ī*, while [oblīdž] owes its second vowel to late French influence.

Lowering of *ī* to *ĕ*.

In documents of all kinds, public and private, during the fifteenth century and in the successive centuries until the eighteenth, there are numerous examples of *e* written for original *ī*. It cannot be doubted that these spellings reflect an actual tendency in pronunciation, since late in the eighteenth century Edmonston censures ' *tell* ' for ' *till* ', and ' *sense* ' for ' *since* ', &c., as London vulgarisms. Whatever may have been the history of the introduction of these forms in London and Court English,

---

[1] Altered in 1927 Edition.

there is no doubt that from the middle of the sixteenth century or so, down to the first third of the eighteenth century at any rate, they were current in circles whose speech, however much we may now take exception to this or that feature, was certainly not the vulgar speech of the day.

Among the various forms with *e* instead of *i* that occur scattered through the documents during the four centuries with which we are concerned, there are some in which the quantity is doubtful, and we hesitate whether to class them under our present heading or under that of *ĭ*, which became *ē* in open syllables in the M.E. period. (See pp. 207–8, above.)

But even if it is certain that the quantity is short, e. g. in *knet* 'knit', some doubt may arise whether we have to do with *ĕ* lowered from *ĭ*, or whether we have the survival of an old dialectal type with the 'Kentish' or South-Eastern vowel, from O.E. *ў*.

We have already seen (p. 30. (3)) how this vowel became *ĭ* in E. Midland, but *e* in the South-Eastern dialects, and that the London dialect of M.E. has many examples of the latter type (cf. pp. 41. (3), 53). Thus *knet*, or for the matter of that, the present *knell*, which both contain a development of O.E. *y*, might be explained either from the South-Eastern type, or as the E. Midland *ĭ*-type with the lowering which we are considering.

As regards the antiquity and dialectal origin of the change of *ĭ* to *ĕ*, a minute and far-reaching examination of the M.E. sources would be necessary to arrive at very definite conclusions, and at present I am only able to indicate that apparent examples—e. g. *gresly* 'grisly', *merour*— are found in Robt. of Brunne's Handlyng Sinne, and *Lenne* for *Lynne* several times in the Norfolk Guilds. In the fifteenth century, so far as my observation goes, forms with *e* are more frequent in definitely E. Midland or Essex writers such as Palladius, Marg. Paston, Bokenam, the Celys, or in writers who came from Norfolk and Suffolk such as Lydgate and Gregory, than in documents written by Westerners, or in the pure London dialect.

In the following century the forms are found more frequently than earlier, in documents which exhibit no Regional features, but are more common in Machyn's Diary than in any other work of the period with which I am acquainted.

From the by no means complete material at present at my disposal I draw, tentatively, the conclusion that the tendency to lower *ĭ* to *ĕ* arose in the E. Midlands, probably in the northern part of the area, and that it gradually extended southwards and found a footing in the dialects of Norfolk, Suffolk, and Essex. How far westwards the tendency spread I am at present unable to say, though the Oxfordshire Oseney Register (1460) and a Bucks. Will of 1534 show some traces of it. During the fifteenth century a certain number of forms showing this change penetrated into the London dialect, perhaps from Essex, and they gained an increasing currency first, probably, among the lower orders of the population.

It would be unwise to press too far the view that the *e*-forms in London English belong to a lower Class dialect, although Machyn, as has been said, has more of them than any of his contemporaries. since they are found in fair numbers in letters of Sir Thos. Seymour (1544), and later in Queen Elizabeth's Letters and Translations. I have noted the following examples :—

Fifteenth Century

Definitely E. Midland and South-Eastern writers.

Palladius rhymes *children—eldron* 26. 713, and *myrour—terrour* 36. 976; Marg. Paston has *well* 'will' 1. 83, *Beshopys* 1. 236, *hese* 'his' 1. 245, 1. 355, *Welyam* 1. 438, *vetayll* 1. 371, *Trenyte* 1. 43, 355, &c., 'Trinity'. *Chene* 'chin', 1. 69, has perhaps a long vowel, and *wech*, ii. 217, might be otherwise explained. Bokenam has *smet* P. P. Marg. 431, *sneuelyng* Marg. 482, *contenuely* Ann. 465, *flekeryngs* Fth. 232, *menstralsy* Marg. 743, *merour* Pr. Marg. 166; Bury Wills 1463, *merours* 21; Cely Pprs. have *fet* 'fit' (Noun) 77, 1504, and *cheldren*, 47; *beche* 'bitch' 74, *sen* 'since' 41, *fenyshe* 47, *sweffte* 48, *wendow* 82, *scheppe* 'ship' 70, *deshes* 182, *smethe* 'smith'. The Will of Sir Thos. Cumberworth, Lincs. 1451, has *peler* 'pillar', L. D. D. 51. 2.

Writers who on the whole write London English, but who were born in Suffolk.

Lydgate has *merours, glemeryng*; Gregory *schelyngys* 79, *pejon* 'pigeon' 80, *lemyted* 123, *pelory* 183; *denyr* is doubtful and may have either *ĕ* or *ē* (cf. Machyn's forms, below). The three-syllabled words just quoted have almost certainly a short *ĕ*.

Other writers—fifteenth and following centuries.

The Western writers—Shillingford and Bp. Pecok—and the Ordinances of Worcester and the Exeter Tailors' Guild, appear not to use these forms. The last mentioned has *es* 'is', and *hes* 'his', p. 314, but these are both unstressed. Fortescue, however, has *contenually* 147, *lemited* 128, *deficulte* 144, 147, 149 (probably *ĕ*), *inconsederably* 143 (probably *ĕ*, cf. Lady Wentworth's forms, below), and the rather doubtful *wech* 'which' 118, &c., by the side of usual *wich*. Short Engl. Chron. has *Beshoppes* 55, Caxton *shellyngs* 'shillings' Dial. in Fr. and Engl. 16. 6. *Sech* 'such', *knetted* Jas. 174. 31, and *besines* Jas. 96. 31, are most probably to be reckoned as 'Kentish' forms.

Skelton has *gletteryng*, Magnyf. 855; Will of R. Astbroke (Bucks. 1534), *cheldryn*, L. D. D. 169. 3; Lord Berners' Froissart, *mengled* 1. 379, *hedeous* 1. 230; Sir Thos. Elyot's Gouernour, *sens* 'since' 1. 197, 208, 221; Sir Thos. Seymour 1544, St. Pprs. Hen. VIII, vol. i, *fesshermen* 784, *Premrose* 790, *weteleres* 778, *Beshope* 777, *begennyng* 776, *fenyshed* 776, *shepe* 'ship' passim (vowel probably short, cf. spelling in Cely Pprs.); Bp. Latimer, *sence* 'since', Serm. of Ploughers 24 and 25, Sev. Serm. 119, Chichester ibid. 120, *mestris* 166 (may be intermediate form from *mastres?*), *thether* 166; Ascham, *splettyd*, Tox. 109; Q. Elizabeth, *bellowes* 'billows' Letters to J. VI, 29, *weshing* ibid. 4 (might be 'Kentish', but this is improbable), *rechis* Transl. 49; Euphues, *hether* 60, *hetherto* 83; *sheuering* 161 (probably short?); Machyn, *pelere* 'pillory' 14, *pelorie* 22, *vetell* 20, *deleverd* 23, *chelderyn* 24, *pelers* 'pillars' 27 (twice), *Rechard* 38, *sent Necolas* 42, *sennet* 'signet' 51, *essue* 'issue' 71, *menyster* 79, *velyns* 'villains' 82, *Eslyngton* 89, *prensepalles* 90 (Noun), *selver* 90 (might be fr. O.E. *ĕŏ* if in a Western text, but not here), *red* 'rid' Pret. of *ride* 167, *vesetars, veseturs*

206, 207, *bellets* 211, *denner* 2, &c., &c., also *deener* 138, *leveray* 'livery' passim, *prevelegys* 61, *ennes of the cowrt* 131, *consperacy* 104, *hes* 'is' 139, *sterope* 'stirrup' 139.

The following are found in Verney Memoirs :—M. Falkiner, *fefty*, ii. 52, *strept* 'stripped' 52, *pettyful* 52, *cheldren* 53, *sence* 'since' 55, *melch* 'milch' 55, *resestance* 56, *mesry* 'misery' 56, *stell* 'still' 52 (all 1642); Sir R. Verney, *untel* ii. 24; Anne Lee, *shelings* ii. 235 (1646); Lady V., *untel* ii. 249 (1646); Mall Verney, *sence* ii. 379 (1647); Lady Elmes, *thenck* 'think' ii. 381 (1647), *consedowring* 381 ; Lady Hobart, *bet* 'bit', *pell* 'pill' iv. 53 (1664); Doll Leake, *peted* 'pitted' iv. 51 (1664).

Lady Sussex's *speriets* 'spirits', ii. 102, has probably a short vowel, since [sper*i*ts] still survives as a vulgarism. Mr. H. Blaxton, Corresp. of Dr. Basire, has to *vesit* 35, 1638, and *contenew* 36, and Mrs. Basire herself has *sens* 'since' 108, *presnor* 108, *relegos* ibid., *ret* for 'rit' 'wrote' 109, all 1651; *cheldren* 135, 1654. Aubrey writes—'he would *sett* up very late at nights', Lives, i. 150, Clark's Ed.

In the next century the *e*-spellings are pretty numerous in Wentworth Pprs.—Lady W. has *tel* 'till' 84, *hender* 'hinder' Vb. 95, *setting* 'sitting' 107, *veseting* day 39 ; *consperacy* 40, *delever* 40, *contenew* 40, *condedder* 41, *senc* 'since' 50, *spelling* 51, *sesterns* 'cisterns' 65, *beger, begest* 'bigger, biggest' 129, *well* (unstressed) 'will' 129; Peter Wentworth has *hetherto* 435 ; Lord Wentworth (a child) has *sesters* 'sisters' 461.

Lady Mary Wortley Montagu rhymes *wit* with *coquet*, and *gift* with *theft*, which may imply a pronunciation [wɛt, gɛft].

These examples, though less copious than could be desired, are sufficient to establish the wide currency which the -*e*-forms once enjoyed. That they have so completely died out of Received Standard English must be put down to the increasing tendency, to which attention has so often been called, to approximate pronunciation to the spelling.

The *i* in Bishop.

It is perhaps worth noting that from the fifteenth to the beginning of the eighteenth century this word is fairly often spelt *bushop, busshop*, &c.

I have noted the following instances:—Marg. Paston, *Archebusshop* ii. 372, 373 ; Lord Berners, Froissart 1. 28; Archbp. Cranmer, *Busshope* (at least nineteen times in a letter of 1537), Ellis 3. 3. 23, &c. ; Ascham, Scholem. 127; Roper's Life of Sir Thos. More, *Bushopps* xlv. 14 ; Dr. Denton in Verney Memoirs iv. 430, 1688; Cooper (1685) includes *Bushop* among the pronunciations to be avoided as belonging to a 'barbarous dialect'; Jones (1701) notes that the word is 'sounded *Booshop* by some'.

With all this evidence we are bound to take the early spellings as meaning something. It looks rather as if the *i* had been rounded to [y] through the influence of the initial *b*-, and this vowel then retracted, along with the other [y] sounds, to [ŭ]. It is impossible to say whether this underwent unrounding, or whether it was preserved after *b*. It is possible that some speakers said [baʃəp], while others said [bŭʃəp]. Jones's spelling rather suggests the latter pronunciation. In any case, in spite of

Cooper, the pronunciation was not always a vulgarism; witness Cranmer, who ought certainly to have known the best pronunciation of the word.

It is strange that this word should be apparently the only instance of the rounding of *i* after *b*.

M.E. *ū* in the Modern Period.

This vowel has been diphthongized to [*au*]. Typical examples are— *house, mouse, how, bow* (Vb.), *cow, shroud,* &c., &c. All these words had [ū] in Old and Middle English, written at first *u,* and later, after the French fashion, *ou* or *ow.* Thus while no change has taken place in the spelling, the change in pronunciation has been considerable. The actual process probably began, as in the case of M.E. *ī,* by a differentiation of the first and latter parts of the long vowel into tense and slack respectively, a condition which may be expressed as [ŭᵘ]. The first element in this homogeneous diphthong was then lowered to [o], and this was subsequently unrounded, which resulted in a diphthong approximately the same as that in use to-day in Received Standard. The whole series would thus be :—[ū—ŭᵘ—o*u*—a*u*—*au*]. At the present time there are several varieties of pronunciation of the old *ū.* In the dialects of the *North no diphthongization has taken place,¹ and ' house ' is still pronounced [hūs], with a single vowel, although various sounds, all of an ū-like character, are heard in different areas. In some parts of Yorkshire, on the other hand, diphthongization apparently took place, but the second element of the diphthong was lost, and the remaining vowel lengthened, so that instead of [ha*us*] we get [(h)*as*]. Again, in some parts of Lancashire the development seems to have been [ha*us,* hæ*us*—(h)ɛ*us*—ɛ"s— ēs], the last being actually in use. In Middle-Class London Cockney the first element of the diphthong has been fronted, and a typical mark of the beast, as Lord Chesterfield would call it, in certain circles, is the pronunciation [hæ*us*].

When did the beginning of the diphthongization take place? My own collections of spellings throw no light upon the question, but Zachrisson (*Pronunciation of English Vowels,* p. 79) has brought forward a few spellings with *au, aw,* for old *ū,* during the fifteenth and sixteenth centuries, collected some by himself, some by others. Of these the most convincing seem to me *abaught* ' about ', *faunde, withaught,* from Paston Letters; *aur* ' our ', Cely Papers, 20; Register of Godstow, *sauth* ' south ', *faul* (cit. ' More ', and no reference except to a German Dissertation which I have not seen); Henslow's Diary, *hause* ' house ' (from Diehl). With regard to some of these spellings it has been maintained that the writers merely wrote *au* ' by mistake ' for *ou,* and that they are not phonetic at all, and therefore cast no light upon the matter in hand. Who shall pretend to decide with absolute certainty the meaning of these spellings, unless it be some foreign philologist who is, naturally, infallible? It must be admitted on the one hand, that if the sound was still [ū] *au* would be the very worst way of expressing it, and on the other, that these occasional spellings do not inspire quite the same confidence as do some others of the kind, and this from their extreme rarity. I have found none in the thousands of documents I have looked through, and have even

---

* See Appendix II.

¹ While the Mod. Dialects of Nth. England and of Scotland have not developed [*au*] for old *ū,* Orton points out that some degree of diphthonging has in fact occurred in a few of them. Thus [dŏ*un,* (h)ŏ*us,* kŏ*u*], &c., &c., for O.E. dŭn, hŭs, cŭ, in Byers Green, Durh.

overlooked, owing to slowness of vision, the few that there were in some of the documents which I did examine.   It may be asked, Why should these tell-tale spellings (if indeed they be such in this case) be so rare in respect of old *ū*, when in the case of some other vowels we find them so frequently?   The answer, I think, is not far to seek.   The traditional spelling *ou*, if taken literally to mean *o* + *u*, was by no means a bad representation of the pronunciation of the diphthong as it probably was during perhaps the greater part of the sixteenth century.   In fact, Salesbury (1547) and Hart (1569) appear to describe the sound as made up of these two elements.   The other English grammarians of this century are so obscure on this vowel that it is mere waste of time to try to wring some meaning out of their accounts.   The French grammarian Mason (1622) transcribes *how* as *haow*, which certainly suggests a pronunciation not far removed from our own.   Diphthongs are always difficult to analyse exactly.

Wallis, in 1653, describes the sound in *house, mouse, out, our, owl, foul, sow,* &c., thus : ' obscuriori sono efferuntur; sono nempe composito ex *ò* vel *u* obscuris, et *w*.'   Cooper (1685) says : ' composita ex *u* gutturali et *oo* labiali, sonatur.'   Both of these descriptions indicate approximately [a*u*] or [ə*u*], that is to say a diphthong differing from our own, if at all, only by a difference of tenseness in the first element.   It may well be, however, that Wallis and Cooper are really referring to a diphthong to all intents and purposes identical with that now in use.

It is doubtful whether any further torturing of the other sixteenth- and seventeenth-century French grammarians, not mentioned above, will bring us any nearer the truth with regard to the history of this sound.   As for the early spellings in *au*, supposing they *do* mean something, how shall we interpret them?   If we take Salesbury and Hart seriously at all, it is reasonable to believe what they tell us, when for once they are intelligible and even plausible, and not to attempt to make their perfectly definite statements mean something quite different from what they appear to mean.   But to believe Salesbury and Hart is to assume that in the sixteenth century, at least in the form of English which they are describing, the first element of the diphthong was rounded.   In this case, either the fifteenth- and sixteenth-century writers who occasionally wrote *au* were using a very unsuggestive mode of expression, or they were representing a different pronunciation altogether—one more like that suggested by the French writer who transliterates *aou* forty or fifty years later.   It is quite possible that some speakers pronounced [*au*] while others still said [*ou*], the first element in the latter case being perhaps only slightly rounded.   It must be remembered that the diphthonging of old *ū* must have begun very early—before old *ō*[1] had developed into *ū*, and this, as we shall see (pp. 234–5), was probably completed during the fourteenth century at latest.   From the moment, therefore, that old *ō*[1] has become [ɑ] we may be sure that old *ū* has started on that career of change which subsequently brought it to its present sound.   But the process was not necessarily equally rapid in all areas, or among all sections of speakers.   It is extremely probable that a full-blown [*au*] had arisen— perhaps in the Eastern parts of the country—during the fifteenth century. When we remember how many of the Modern sound changes first appear in the South-East or E. Midland dialects, it will perhaps not seem to be without significance that the earliest—in fact, the larger number—of the spellings with *au* are found in the letters of the Pastons and Celys.

It is absurd to dogmatize where, at the best, intelligent speculation must take the place of certainty.

Unrounding of M.E. *ŭ*.

M.E. *ŭ*, which had originally the pronunciation of a short (probably tense) [u], underwent in the Modern period a process of unrounding and then of lowering, whereby the present peculiar sound, so characteristic of English, was reached.

The short *ŭ* thus affected had four distinct origins, only one of which we are perhaps really entitled to describe as M.E. *ŭ*. The latter, which we may call (1), was undoubtedly the sound in such words as *buck, run, hunt, suck, summer*, &c., &c. In addition to this, earliest Modern *ŭ* sprang (2) from original English *ü*, O.E. *y̆*, where this survived, as in *bundle, thrush, cudgel*, &c.; (3) from M.E. *ü* of French origin, as in *judge, just, study, public*, &c., &c.; (4) from the new *ŭ* derived from earlier *ō¹*, as in *blood, flood, glove, done*, &c. (cf. pp. 236–7 on this last group).

Since the unrounding process involves the three later groups, it is evident that it is later than the retraction of earlier [y̆] to [ŭ], later than the development of the new [ū] from *ō¹*, and later than the shortening of this new sound. In 1528, *vnjust* rhymes with *must*, Rede me, &c., p. 105.

As to the approximate date of the development of *ŭ* from [y] we have no precise evidence, but we know that *ō¹* had become [ū] already in the fourteenth century (see pp. 234–5), and we shall see there is good reason for believing that the shortening had taken place at any rate by the middle of the fifteenth century, if not earlier. We are therefore free to assume that the process whereby short *ŭ* was unrounded began any time after the latter date.

From the direct statements of Wallis and Cooper, quoted above, p. 224–5, it appears that the sound had attained to all intents and purposes its present stage by the third quarter of the seventeenth century. If that is so, the unrounding must have begun some time before. In 1580 a French writer states that the *u* in *upon* sounds like the French *o*, and in 1620 another French writer, Mason, says that French *o* is heard in *hungrie*, while yet another in 1625 identifies the vowel in *up, butter, sunder*, &c., with French *o*. Now there are several vowels in present-day French expressed by *o*, of which that in *homme, bonne*, has a very distinct acoustic resemblance to the English sound in *but*, &c., especially to untrained and uncritical ears. In fact, in a French Grammar which I used as a boy, it was definitely stated that *bonne* is pronounced like the English word *bun*! This theory is still held by many Englishmen, apparently, and they put it into practice in pronouncing French.

Therefore, if in the late sixteenth and early seventeenth centuries the English sound in *butter* was pretty much what it is now, the French writers who described it as being like the French *o* were not wider of the mark than the Englishmen above referred to, at the present time, nor than present-day French writers who write *tôb* for *tub*. The most reasonable inference is that as early as 1580 the old *ŭ* had reached a stage of pronunciation not very different from that of our own time.

The occasional spellings, which we have found so helpful in indicating the pronunciation of other vowels, are less frequent in the present instance than in some other cases, but they are none the less convincing.

In the chapter on the vowels in unstressed syllables it will be seen that in this position *u* and *o* are not infrequently written *a*, in the fifteenth century, a spelling which certainly expresses our unrounded vowel. Whatever the precise sound, therefore, a vowel, the result of unrounding *u* and *o*, was already in existence in the language, if only in unstressed syllables. But there are fortunately a few instances of spellings with *a*, for *ŭ*, in stressed syllables also, from the middle of the fifteenth century. The following are all that I have found :—*gannes*[1] ' guns ', Marg. Paston, ii. 372 (twice); *sadanly* 'suddenly', Sir John Fortescue, p. 126; *camyth* 'cometh', Cely Papers 146, and *warsse, wars* ' worse ', Cely Papers 159; *Samersett*, Machyn 182; *Chamley* 'Cholmondely', Machyn 38. Zachrisson (*Eng. Vowels*, and *Contributions*, p. 319) has all of these except the form from Fortescue, and *warrse*, &c., from Cely Papers, but he also adds *farniture* and *Saveraigne*. I regard all these forms as establishing beyond a doubt that those who wrote them pronounced an unrounded vowel in place of the old *ŭ* in the words given. (It is possible that Machyn's *Watton* = *Wotton* [watən]? should also be included with the above examples.)

The precise nature of the vowel may be uncertain, but it certainly was no longer *ŭ*; the process of unrounding has begun, and that is all we are concerned with.

I regard Cooper's account, given about 200 years later than the Celys and Sir John Fortescue, as an accurate description of our present sound in Received Standard ; the French writers, respectively sixty, and a hundred years, earlier than Cooper, are evidently describing a sound which is not very far from our present one, and the fifteenth-century writers, by their spellings, clearly indicate a vowel which is no longer *ŭ*.

The confusion which we find in the sixteenth and seventeenth centuries between [a, ə, ʌ] I regard as perfectly natural. Many people at the present day are unable to distinguish between the two former, and consider the last as merely a lengthening of one or both of these.

If the above view is accepted, it follows that we must regard the early shortenings *bludde, sutt*, &c., instanced on pp. 236-7, below, as containing the sound [a] or at least a stage in the development of this sound, that is, an unrounded vowel.

It will be noted that in words containing genuine M.E. *ŭ*, the unrounding does not always take place, or rather, perhaps, a new rounding has sometimes taken place, when a lip consonant immediately precedes the *ŭ* as in *bull, pull, put, push*, &c.[2] On the other hand, this is not invariable, for we have the unrounded vowel in *pulse, bud, but, butter, Puck, pug, mug, mud*. It is therefore probable that we have here a duality due to difference of dialect, perhaps of Social rather than Regional character. We may remark that the Frenchman's example *upon* is unfortunate, since *u* here is unstressed, and we have several examples

---

[1] Fifteenth-century spellings with *a* for M.E. *u* are suspect. Zachrisson has shown that Marg. Paston's spelling is certainly *gonnes*, not ' gannes ' in the MS. The first vowel in Cely P. *comyth* may be *a*, which it much resembles. See *Engl. Pron. at Shakespeare's Time*, pp. 125-30.

[2] The first vowel in the name Bolingbroke probably belongs to this group. The following forms from the Wentworth Papers show the contemporary pronunciation, the tradition of which is now largely lost :—*Bullingbrook*, Peter Wentworth, pp. 293 (1712), 398, twice, (1714); Lady *Bullinbroke*, Lady Strafford, p. 499 (1734); My lord *Bullingbrook*, Benjamin Bathurst, p. 528 (1738).

(cf. p. 278) of the spelling *apon*, which I regard as illustrating unrounding in an unstressed position. If he had mentioned *up*, he would have been right. Probably, however, like many of his countrymen to-day, he pronounced [ápɔn].

It will be observed that before original *r*, which has now disappeared in pronunciation, [a] has been lengthened, and altered in character. Originally, *purse, hurt, word, worse*, &c., were pronounced [pars, hart, ward, wars] as in Scotch. As the *r* was weakened, the vowel was gradually lengthened and passed into the present-day [ʌ̄]. Already in the seventeenth century, Wallis identifies the vowel in *turn* and *burn* as being like *eur* in French *serviteur*. This makes it probable that [ʌ̄] was already pronounced. Many Englishmen to-day believe that *cur* and *cœur* are identical in pronunciation, and, indeed, although the articulation of the two sounds is absolutely different, the inherent pitch of both is very close, and the acoustic effect is very similar to a more or less superficial observer.

M.E. *ō*[1] [ō] in the Modern Period.

In the fourteenth century there is evidence from widely separated areas of England that old tense *ō* had either developed completely its present sound [ū], or progressed far in this direction. While as a rule the most careful scribes still write *gode* or *goode*, &c., for O.E. *gōd* 'good', others, more enterprising, occasionally adopt the spelling *goude*, &c., or *gude*. The former is the ordinary spelling for the sound [ū] from the middle of the thirteenth century. I have come across a fair sprinkling of these spellings for *ō*[1] in the fourteenth and early fifteenth century. Thus R. of Brunne's Handlyng Sinne, 1303, has *þe touþer* 'other' 406, *doun*, O.E. *dōn* 'do', *mysdoun* rhymes *enchesoun* 1101; William of Shoreham (Kent, 1320) has *roude* 25. 685, O.E. *rōd* 'rood', *douþ* 'doth', O.E *dōþ*, Pl. Pres., 53. 1471, *bloude* 'blood', O.E. *blōd*, *goud* 'good', O.E. *gōd* 60. 1701, &c., &c., *loukeþ* 'looketh', O.E. *lōceþ* 75. 2142, *touke* 94. 256 'took', O.E. *tōc*, and so on; the Feudal Aids of 1370 or so have *Boucland*, O.E. *Bōc-*, *Lollebrouk*, O.E. *-brōc*, *Curypoule*, O.E. *-pōl* 'pool', *Caresbrouc, Cokepoule*, &c., which are Pl. N.'s which occur in documents dealing with Dorsetshire, Somersetshire, and Hampshire; Alliterative Poems (Cheshire or Lancs. *c.* 1350) write *goud*, Patience 336, Pearl 33 (twice), &c.; St. Editha (Wilts. *c.* 1420) has *gowde* 'good' 1472, *brouk* 'brook' 1363; Bokenam (Suffolk, 1441) not infrequently writes *u—suthly* 'soothly', St. Agn. 524, &c., *forsuk*, O.E. *-sōk*, St. Faith, 68, *stude* 'stood', St. Eliz. 206, and so on. One of the commonest words to be written otherwise than with *ō* is earlier *mōste* 'must', often written *must, mwst* during the fifteenth century. This may not really be a case in point at all, as it may represent the unstressed form and stand for some sound quite other than [ū]. The spelling at any rate is found in Palladius (1420), Rewle Sustr. Men. (*c.* 1450), Bp. Pecok (1449), Marg. Paston, passim, and Cely Papers, and Monk of Evesham (1482) to mention no more. As we know, this has become the Received Spelling, and it is one of the few cases where old *ō* is now spelt otherwise than *o* or *oo*. Marg. Paston also writes *Munday*; London Records (1419, cit. Morsbach) have *gud*; Cely Papers have *gud* and *tuk*.[1]

---

[1] The spelling *roonge* (M.E. *rungen*), P.P. Hist. S. Barthol. Ch. (c. 1400) seems to imply [rŭnge]. If this is so we must conclude that *oo* stands for [ŭ] at that time as now.

The *ou*- or *ow*- and *u*-spellings in words of this class persist through-out the sixteenth century in private letters and in published books; the *u*-spellings are less common. The former are found amongst other places in a letter of Thos. Pery, Ellis 2. 2 (*mounth* 'month'); Rede me, &c., has *shues* 'shoes' 81, 82, *must* rhymes *vnjust* 105; in Edward VI's First P. B. (*floude*, &c.); Latimer's Sermons (*bloud, gould, shutyng*); Machyn (*sune* 'soon', *bludshed*, &c.); Ascham, *bowne* 'boon', *lowse*; Fisher, Bp. of Rochester's Sermons; Sir Thos. Smith, De Republ. (*bloud*); Queen Elizabeth's Letters (*houke* 'hook'); John Alleyne, *dueth* 'doth', Alleyne Papers 16, 159–; &c., &c. Such spellings as *blud*, in Ascham, Fisher, &c., may indicate the shortening of the vowel, on which see below, p. 236, &c. On the other hand, Latimer's *shutyng* 'shooting', Serm. 161, and Ascham's 'it *buted* not', Toxoph. 81, almost certainly represent the long vowel.

Few will doubt that *ou* in the words from the fifteenth century onwards implies [ū]; how much sooner the sound was fully developed, and when the new sound was first pronounced exactly as in present-day Received Standard, is more questionable. The spellings just illustrated from writings from the South and Midlands, or from the London dialect, have nothing to do with such spellings as *gude, guid*, &c., in the Northern texts of the four-teenth century and later. In the North, old *ō* pursued quite a different path of development from that which it followed farther South, and the rhymes of fourteenth-century Northern texts show an approximation to the sound of French *ū* [ȳ], e. g. *stude—fortitude*, &c.

Even the sixteenth-century grammarians agree in describing [ū] as the vowel heard in words containing old *ō*[1].

As regards the phonetic process it seems certain that it resembled that now in progress in Swedish in *bo* 'live', &c., where the old long *ō* is strongly over-rounded, so that to unaccustomed ears it sounds rather like some kind of [ū]. The full development of the latter sound, however, demands also the raising of the back of the tongue from a mid to a high position. It is quite possible that the early fourteenth-century *ou*-spellings in English may indicate only that the over-rounded stage is reached, and that the sound pronounced at that time was the same as the Swedish vowel just referred to.

If all words containing old long *ō*[1] were pronounced with [ū] at the present time, the history of this sound would offer no difficulties. The fact, however, is that we note a threefold development of the sound in present-day English.

(1) Words which have [ū]:—*rood, spoon, moon, food, fool*.

(2) Words which have [ŭ]:—*good, stood, hood, hook, book, shook, forsook, look*.

(3) Words which have [a]:—*flood, blood, glove, done, month, brother, mother, other*.

In class (1) the Early Mod. or Late M.E. vowel has remained unaltered; in (2) it has been comparatively recently shortened; in (3) it was shortened much earlier, and underwent a further change. This change also involved original M.E. (or O.E.) short [ŭ], so that at the time when it came about, the latter sound and original *ō*[1] in certain words were pronounced exactly alike. In other words, at a certain period, short [ŭ], whatever its origin, began to alter in the direction of [a]. This question has been treated above under $\ddot{u}$, pp. 232–4 ; it is our business here to inquire what information is available (a) of the early shortening of the new [ū] which gave us class (3), and (b) of the late shortening which gave us class (2).

Early Shortening of [ū] from $\bar{o}^1$.

I assume that when, in M.E. and later, the consonant following a vowel is doubled, this implies that the preceding vowel was short. When in texts which express long $\bar{u}$, whether original or derived, by the process we have just discussed, from original $\bar{o}^1$ in some words by *ou*, we find *u* written in other words even when the following consonant is not doubled, it is probable that we are justified in assuming that this represents a short vowel, since, except in the North, *u* was not commonly used for a long vowel, apart from French $\bar{u}$, which had quite a different sound from [ū]. The conditions under which old long vowels were shortened in M.E. have often been formulated (cp. my *Short Hist.* §§ 175, 176, 177), but the shortenings of the kind we are considering belong to a different category from any of those mentioned. If on the strength of *blood* and *flood* we assume that the *-d* exercised the shortening influence, this appears to be contradicted by *rood* and *stood*, for although we pronounce a short vowel in the latter at the present time, the fact that the short vowel here is [ŭ] and not [a] shows that it did not undergo the early shortening of [ū], otherwise it would have shared the fate of *flood* and *blood*. Again, why was the vowel in *done* shortened but not that in *moon* and *spoon* ?

I believe it to be impossible to formulate the precise combinative conditions under which these forms were produced, and am inclined to think that the explanation of the three pronunciations of old $\bar{o}^1$, or at any rate the existence of the [a] pronunciations, must be explained by assuming a mixture of dialect, probably of Social origin. This becomes more probable when we consider that while the group of words with [a] in Received Standard is now quite fixed, the distribution of these forms has varied according to the usage of different periods, and a greater latitude seems to have existed formerly in this respect.

The earliest shortened form of the new $\ddot{u}$ which I have found is *sunner* ' sooner', R. of Brunne's Handlyng Sinne, l. 386 (Lincs. 1301). This is a remarkable form as showing how early the attainment of the new pronunciation was in this dialect. The shortening may be explained as due to the same process which has shortened the vowel in *done*, in which case it implies a Positive *sŭn* ' soon ' and is a very early instance of the process, or on the other hand it may be due to the analogy of other Comparatives which shortened the vowel, when the word ended in a consonant, before the suffix *-re*. This is an early M.E. shortening. Palladius (Essex *c.* 1420) has *sonner* ' sooner', 83. 615, which may represent the old M.E. Comp. when the shortening of $\bar{o}$ before it had become [ū] would produce $\ddot{o}$, or it may represent the new form *sunner* as in R. of Brunne, the old spelling with *o* being retained as elsewhere in Palladius. Machyn's *fottman* 126 probably stands for a M.E. shortening before [ū] developed, but may be identical with Bp. Fisher's form *futt* below. St. Editha (Wilts. *c.* 1420) has *flodde* ' flood' rhyming with *gode*, and in view of the present pronunciation of the former word I am inclined to accept the spelling here, as standing for [flŭd]. We know that this dialect had already developed the new [ū] from $\bar{o}^1$, cf. p. 234. In the will of Sir Thos. Cumberworth,

Lincs. 1451, Lincs. Dioc. Docs., the spellings *gud*, 46. 29, *utherwise*, 56. 15, occur, but these may be Northern spellings.[1] In the sixteenth century Berners, Froissart, has *fludde*, i. 221, 241, 291 (three times); Edward VI's First P. B. has *fluddes* and *bludde*; Spenser, On the State of Ireland, has *flude*; Bp. Fisher has *blud* and *bloud* in his Sermons; Gabriel Harvey in his Letters has *blud* 32, *futt* 'foot' 121, and in a poem, *whudd* 'hood' rhyming with *budd*, Letter Bk., p. 125. In Sackville's Induction (1563) *undone* and *done* rhyme with *run*, 119. Marston has *hudwinkt*, What You Will, Act 1, Sc. i (1607). In 1621 Gill (Logonomia) gives the following as containing short *ŭ* :—*blood, glove, good, brother, done, does* (Vb.), *mother, other*. Butler (1634) gives *gud, blud* as short. Sir Edm. Verney in 1639 writes *bludd, bluddynose*, Verney Papers 212. Daines (1640) mentions the pronunciation *swut* = [swut or ?swat], but says it is 'better written and pronounced *soot*' = [sūt]. Wallis (1653) mentions *done* as having 'obscure *o*' = [a]. In 1653 Wil. Roades, the Verneys' bailiff, writes *tuck* 'took', Verney Mem. iii. 275. Cooper (1685) gives *flood, hood, other, soot, stood*, as having labial *o* shortened, which according to his terminology = *ŭ*, which again he defines as being the sound of *oo* shortened, that is [ŭ]. Cooper also has *fut* 'foot' as a 'barbarous' form. Does this mean [fat] or [fūt]? At any rate it is represented also by Bp. Fisher's form *futt* given above, and would be [fat] at the present time. Sir R. Verney writes *sutt* 'soot', Verney Mem. iv. 358, 1686 (= [sŭt or sat]?). Jones (1701) has a list with [ŭ] which corresponds to our present usage :—*book, brook, cook, foot, forsook, good, hood, look, soot, stood, took*. The one word in this list which we should not now include is *forsooth*. Jones's list of words with [a] is *another, mother, brother*. He appears to recognize both [ŭ or ū] as well as [a] in *foot, forsooth, good, hood, look, -sook, stood, took*. He further says that the sound of *ŭ* is written *ou* 'when it may be so sounded' as in *floud, bloud*, which seems to imply the pronunciations [flad, blad; flŭd, blŭd].

In the *Gr. of the Engl. Tongue*, 1713, attributed to Steele, *brother, mother* are said to contain an 'obscure sound like *u* short' = [a], and the same sound is said to occur in *flood, blood*. Bertram (1753), the writer of an Engl. Gr. for Danes, in Danish, and an excellent observer, gives *book, look*, and other words ending in *k*, and also *hood* and *foot* as containing the sound of Danish *ŭ*, while *blood, flood, soot* are said to contain Dan. *o*, e.g. *blodd*, &c. This clearly means the sound that is now [a].

From the above brief account it seems to be established that the new [ū] was shortened by the first quarter of the fifteenth century at any rate, if we disregard the somewhat doubtful evidence from Robt. of Brunne, or if we accept it, more than a century earlier. Until there is more evidence forthcoming of the development of the new [ū] at this early period, it is safer not to build too much upon this. At the same time it may be pointed out that the *ou*-spellings in this text for old *ō*[1] may well dispel the suspicion which some might attach to the *u* in *sunner*, if this stood alone. In that case it might be said that the Lincs. dialect was influenced by the Northern English. But since, so far as I know, the

---

[1] Further fifteenth-century examples of the early shortening are :—*gud*, Lord Moleyns, Past. Letters, i. 80 (1449) ; *mut*, O.E. *mōt*, Past. Letters, iii. 25, Marg. Paston (1471) ; *gudde*, Stonor Papers, ii. 81 (1479). This agrees with Gill and Butler, who include *good* among the shorts. This must = [gad] in seventeenth century. Milton writes *floud*, Com. 831, but *flood* in Com. 930, where it rhymes with *mud*.

Northern *u*-spellings for *ō*[1] which express the sound [ȳ] are not found as
early as 1303, since in any case Northern texts do not write *ou* for old *ō*,
and since Handlyng Sinne is quite definitely E. Midland (though of
a N. Midland type certainly) in dialectal character and not Northern, we
may, I think, take the *ou*-spellings in this text seriously as representing
an E. Midland sound change, especially as the rhyme *slowe—vowe*
[slū(e)—vū(e)] occurs lines 1887–8.

Probably further investigation of fourteenth-century texts would show
that during the first half of this century old *ō*[1] became, in the Eastern
dialects, from Lincolnshire to Kent and Essex, a sound approximating
to if it not quite attained the character of [ū].   From thence it passed
into the London dialect.   We ought probably to regard the spelling *must*
in fourteenth-century texts as representing the unstressed form, with
a vowel shortened after the [ū]-stage had been reached.

In any case, the forms with short [ŭ] are the ancestors, so far as they
survive, of those with [a] of a later date.   The question of the unrounding of [ŭ] has been discussed in its proper place (cf. pp. 232–4, above).

In the meantime we are left in doubt by the statements of the grammarians down to the middle of the seventeenth century as to which of
the forms which they describe as having 'short *ŭ*' really had [ŭ], and
which had [a] or its immediate ancestor.   They appear to correspond
very largely with our [a] type, and include the words most commonly
indicated as short by the occasional spellings.   So long as we are not
sure of the existence of [a] we cannot say with certainty whether the
forms with 'short *ŭ*' are the descendants of those which had [ŭ] in the
fifteenth century, and are the ancestors of our [a] type, or whether they
are the beginnings of the second or later shortening which has produced our [ŭ] in *cook*, &c.   It does not follow even when once the
[a] forms had come into existence in some dialects, that they were used in
the best type of London and Court speech.   The shortened forms from
which they came probably came in slowly and sporadically, and it is
certain that many speakers still said [flūd] long after others said [flŭd],
and may have continued to do so after the latter had gone on to the next
stage [flad].

The Later Shortening of New [ŭ].

While Wallis and Cooper undoubtedly recognize the three types
[ū, ŭ, a] in the class of words we are considering, by far the larger
number of words, according to them, have one or other of the two former
vowels.   This being so, and bearing in mind what was said in the last
paragraph of the preceding section, we may be inclined to assume that
the forms with short [ŭ] which these writers mention, are really rather
survivals of the early shortening, which in this dialect underwent no
unrounding because they were only adopted *after* original short *ŭ* had
been unrounded, than the ancestors of our present type of words like
hood, cook, &c.   This view becomes more probable when we consider
that words such as *foot, stood, good*, and *look*, all of which at the present
time show the late shortening, occur in the lists of Wallis and Cooper
among those with [ū].   This is even more strongly emphasized if we
compare Gill's list of shorts already given above (which all correspond to

our [a] type) with his list of longs, which include both of our other types
—[ū and ŭ]. Gill's list of words with long [ū] is :—*soot, soon, moon,
book, shook, forsook, look, brook, hook, food, foot, brood, stood, goose, smooth,
tooth, doth.*

When we come to Jones the case is different.   As has been said, his
account points to a considerable variety of usage in the pronunciation of
the same words.   Evidently the [a] type has become much more widespread than in the periods which Wallis and Cooper describe, and his list
of words with [ŭ] is, as has been shown above, pretty much the same as
our own.

On the above grounds I am therefore inclined to put the late or
second shortening of [ū] as late as the end of the seventeenth or the
beginning of the eighteenth century.

Henceforth the chief interest lies in the distribution of the several
types of pronunciation among the different words.   There is no further
question of sound change.   The whole question is a very difficult one,
and I see no solution to it except on the lines already suggested, of the
influence of Social or Class dialect.

At the present time the distribution of the types in the various Modified Standards still differs more or less considerably from the usage of
Received Standard.   The only variations of usage in the latter appear to
be in *groom*, and to some slight extent in *soon*, in which words [ū, ŭ] are
both possible.   Within my own memory some old-fashioned speakers of
Received Standard still said [sat] instead of the now universally received
[sŭt].

ROME*AND GOLD.

The present pronunciation of *Rome*, instead of the historically normal
[rūm], is comparatively recent and is due to the influence of the French
or Italian pronunciation of the name, perhaps also to the spelling.
Cooper, Jones, and Steele all give [rūm] as the normal pronunciation.
In some verses on Sir J. Davenant, by Sir J. Menis (1641), cit. Aubrey,
Lives, i. 206, *Rome* rhymes with *groome*.

The present-day pronunciation of *gold* goes back to a M.E. short form
gŏld, which may be derived from an adjectival *gŏldne*, or from such
a compound as *gŏldsmith*, &c.

The normal O.E. and M.E. forms of the noun had a long vowel, and
would yield a Modern [gūld].   This type was in use among some
persons who lived far into the nineteenth century, though by that time it
was doubtless old-fashioned.   An old lady who died in 1855, aged over
80, a very near relative of my own, always, so I have heard from her
children, said [gūld].   It was a very usual though by no means the only
pronunciation in the seventeenth and eighteenth centuries among good
speakers.   It is indicated probably by the spelling *gould*, Latimer, Serm.
7 and 26, G. Harvey's Letters, p. 86, and it is recognized by Elphinstone.

On the other hand, the ancestor of the present-day type is referred to
by the grammarians of the seventeenth and eighteenth centuries.   In
Rede me, &c., *gold* rhymes with *cold—sold*.   In Alphabet Anglois (1621)
gaould is supposed to represent, for French speakers, the pronunciation
of the English word.

For *ō¹-* < *wō*, and *hō-* < *whō*, &c., cf. p. 308, below.

* See Appendix II.

The Unrounding of M.E. ŏ in the Modern Period.

During the fifteenth century, especially in documents written by men from the West Country, but not here alone, we find *a* written for M.E. ŏ. In the sixteenth century a certain number of these spellings are found in London English, a few in Machyn, and one in Queen Elizabeth's letters. In the following century the *a*-spellings occur occasionally in the Verney Papers, and the habit of unrounding ŏ, by this time evidently a fashionable affectation, is pilloried by Vanbrugh in *The Relapse* in the well-known character of Lord Foppington. Early in the eighteenth century Lady Wentworth and her son Peter each have, so far as I have observed, one of these spellings.

This unrounding is at the present day heard chiefly in the South-West of England, but at least as far East and North as Oxfordshire. It has been suggested that Raleigh and Drake—both Devon men, the former, as we have seen (p. 109), speaking with a Devon accent all his life—made this pronunciation fashionable and current in the Court English of their day. This may be so, but the largest number of *a*-forms in any one writer in the sixteenth century are found in Machyn, who was not likely to reflect fashionable habits of Court speech, and who wrote at a time when Drake was still a boy, and Raleigh a baby, the former having been born, according to the *Dict. of Nat. Biogr.*, about 1540, the latter about 1552. Evidently then, the habit was current among the inferior orders of the metropolis long before either of the two heroes were in a position to exert any influence upon London English. It is certainly possible that at a later date the courtiers may have adopted Raleigh's pronunciation of words containing ŏ, though it does not seem very likely that the haughty Queen would follow another's lead in matters of this kind. As the following examples show, traces of the *a*-spellings are found also in Palladius and Margaret Paston. If the pronunciation were in vogue also in the South-East and South-East Midland, it is comprehensible that it should penetrate into London speech, along with many other features from these areas.

At any rate, wherever the habit came from, there is no doubt that it existed, and that it rose in the linguistic world. It has even left a few traces at the present time, notably in *Gad*, a weakened blasphemy, and in *strap* by the side of the unrounded *strop*. We have now restored the rounded vowel in *plot* (of ground), where the Authorized Version has *plat*.

These are the examples I have noted :—

Palladius, *strape* 'strap', 92. 870; St. Editha, *starme* 'storm', rhymes 'harm', 932, *crasse* 'cross', 1387; Shillingford, *aftetymes*, 53, 'oft-'; Marg. Paston, *last* 'lost' Pret. Subj., ii. 373; Lord Berners, *yander* 'yonder', Froissart, I. 205; Machyn, C. *hars* 'horse', 12, the *marrow* 'morrow', 47, *Dasset* 'Dorset', 48, 57, *caffen* 'coffin', 120; Q. Elizabeth, 'I pray you *stap* the mouthes', Letters, 64. This last word will cause a thrill of pleasure to those who know Lord Foppington's celebrated '*stap* my vitals'. Lady Hungerford has *swarn* 'sworn' p.p., Letters, p. 256 (c. 1569). A certain number of these forms occur in the Verney Memoirs :—*becas* 'because', Lady Sussex, ii. 77 (1642), cf. also the shortened form *becos*, Cary Verney, ii. 68, from which *becas* is derived; *faly* 'folly', Mall V., ii. 380 (1647); *sassages*, Dr. Denton, ii. 318 (1648); 6 *a clake* 'o'clock', Luce Sheppard, iii. 78 (twice, 1652); Sir *A*rlandoe Bridgmen, Lady

Rochester, iii. 434 (1656). Mrs. Basire prays for *Prence Gearge* in 1655, Corresp. 139. To these should probably be added *naty* 'naughty', Lady Sussex, ii. 154, and *dater* (see p. 305). These forms presuppose probably the unrounding of a shortened vowel from [ɔ̄]. On the other hand, the vowel in both may still be long, and in that case we must assume that it was pronounced as [ǣ]. In Marston's *Eastward Hoe* occurs the rhyme *after—daughter*, Act v, Sc. i, and here we must suppose an earlier form '*dŏfter*'.

Lord Foppington, already referred to, has—*stap, Tam, Gad, pasitively, harse, plats, bax*, &c. Lady Wentworth writes *Anslow* for 'Onslow', p. 67 (1708), and *beyand*, 127 (1710).[1]

This habit must have been fairly widespread in the seventeenth century, since it survives to-day in the English of America.

The fact that several French writers on English pronunciation from the third quarter of the sixteenth century onwards find a resemblance between English ŏ and French ă certainly suggests that the former was commonly pronounced with but slight rounding. Bellot (1580) says that the English vowel is almost like French *a*. *L'Alphabet Anglois* (1625) says 'O se prononce souvent A. come *Thomas, short*, qu'il fauct prononcer *thames, chart*'. Mauger, *Grammaire Angloise* (1679), says of *o*—'Quand il est lié à *m, n, r, t, d, g, p, st, ss, sk*, il se prononce comme notre *a*—*from* lisez *fram*, anon—*anan*, nor—*nar*, not—*nat*, God—*Gad*, lodge—*ladge, frost—frast*.

It is, I think, impossible not to believe that there is a connexion between these statements, and the above spellings, taken from documents written by English people during the same period. It does not much matter whether these Frenchmen got their ideas of English pronunciation from lower-class speakers or from the ultra-fashionable. They cannot be misleading us altogether, for their statements agree so well with the testimony of the occasional spellings and other known facts. An interesting and I think a valuable light is thrown by these French writers upon the probable character of the vowel sound implied by the spelling *a* in the English documents. It cannot have been [æ], the sound of the ordinary English 'short ă', because these Frenchmen, or some of them, have fixed this as a front vowel—'quasi comme le premier *e* du verbe *être*' (Gr. Angl.); 'comme *e* Latin ... *master* lisez *mester, man* lisez *men*' (Mauger). Since *lodge*, &c., are described as having a sound rather like French *a*, we must suppose that the French writers heard a back vowel for the English short ŏ, and that vowel I take to have been approximately a more or less slightly unrounded form of ŏ (i. e. mid-back, or perhaps low-back with slight rounding). This is, I believe, pretty nearly the sound now heard in America and in many South-Western English dialects. The Frenchmen's description is the nearest they could get to such a sound, since even if they had perceived, as they apparently did, that the vowel was not precisely the French *a*, not being phoneticians they would be unable to fix upon the essential factor—the slight rounding—which differentiated the English vowel from their native sound.

[1] Spenser rhymes *stormes* with *harmes—armes*, F.Q., 68. 47 ; Shakespeare, *dally—folly*, Lucr. 554–56 ; Dryden, *noddle—addle*, Prol. to Don Sebast., 44–5; Gill (1621) writes *skalers* for the pronunciation of the 'Mopsae'; Cooper (1685) says *volley* and *value* are sounded alike. (See -*y* for -*u*, p. 277.)

On rhymes showing unrounding of *o*, see Gavin Bone, *Times Lit. Suppl.*, March 21st, 1929.

When the unrounding was complete, as it subsequently became in the politer forms of English, the resulting vowel was advanced (fronted) and levelled under the ordinary English [æ], the old sound of short *ă* having long disappeared. This is what has happened in *Gad* and *strap*.

During the eighteenth century the old fully rounded vowel was restored, partly from the spelling, by purists, partly by the influence of a large body of speakers who still preserved it unaltered. We must remember that Lady Wentworth is to be regarded as a fashionable speaker of the late seventeenth century, although her letters were written in the opening decade of the eighteenth.

If proof is needed that the French writers sometimes *do* intend a slightly rounded vowel when they refer to French *a*, it is, I think, found in Mauger's statement that the *a* in *water* is pronounced like French *a*. There is little doubt that the vowel of *water* was rounded by the time at which Mauger writes, and even if it were already [ɔ] as now, this has always been a most baffling sound for French people to apprehend. If Mauger had been referring to the other pronunciation of the word he would not have hesitated to write it *wĕter* for French speakers.

M.E. *ŭ* from French *ū* [ȳ]; and M.E. *ēu*; *eu* [ēu]; *īu*; become [jū].

The sounds have all been levelled in present-day English under the combination [jū], which after [r, dž, tʃ] and sometimes after *l*- becomes [ū]; e. g. *due, duke*; *knew, grew*; *dew, few*; *Tuesday, steward*; *blue, true, fruit*, &c., &c. The O.E. *ȳ*, where it survives in the single word *bruise* (cf. p. 34. (3)), has the same history. The questions involved are (1) when did the levelling take place, (2) what was the path of development towards the present sound, and (3) how long did the old sound of French *ŭ* [ȳ] survive, and when, on the other hand, did the present sound appear? The answer to the first is, during if not before the fifteenth century; to the third, that the old [ȳ] still existed, apparently, among some speakers in the sixteenth century, possibly later, but it is no less (and no more) certain that in the sixteenth century many speakers clearly pronounced the present sound.

As to the process, the three diphthongs probably became [iȳ] (ēu and ēu, having first been levelled under the former sound), while old long *ŭ* also became [iȳ] or [jȳ]. This stage was apparently reached in the fifteenth century. Then the second element was retracted, giving [jū], which is the present sound. Shillingford's spelling *knywe* [knjy] 'knew', 14, M.E. *knĕw*, shows the change in the first element of this diphthong. All words which now contain this combination derive it from one of the above sources. From the fifteenth century, we find in occasional spellings *u*, *eu*, *ew*, &c., written indifferently for the old diphthongs and French *ŭ*.

Examples of this are:—St. Editha, *blwe* = *ue* [bljy] for M.E. *blĕw* Pret.; *hue* and *slew*, Robt. the Devil, 922; here the first word is M.E. *hĕu* from the O.E. Pret. *hēow* 'hewed'; *greu* 'grew' (O.E. *grēow*) rhymes with *vertu*, Bokenam, Pr. Marg. 159, and with *isew, pursew*, Bokenam, Ann. 261; *Bewford* 'Beaufort', Gregory, 219; *nyew* 'new', Rewle Sustr. Men. 96. 25; Cely Papers have several examples of French *ŭ* written *ew—sewer* 'sure', 77, *Dewke* 'Duke', 112, *dew* 'due', 112, *continew*, 78, *indewer*, 27; Q. Elizabeth writes *fortiune*, which doubtless represents the type *fortúne* with an accentuated second syllable, Letters, 27; Gabriel Harvey has *blue* 'blew', Letters, 144, and *nu* 'new', ibid. 14; Mrs. Sherard, Verney Mem. iv. 16 (1661), writes *fortewen* and *fortewn*, representing the same type as Q. Elizabeth's, *fortewen* R. Cely (1480), p. 50. Nan Denton has *shued* 'showed' (M.E. *schēwed* O.E. *scēaw-*), Verney Mem. iv. 107, 1663; Mrs. Sherard has *hewmor* 'humour', Verney Mem. ii. 392, 1648. What vowel sound is expressed by *ew, iu, u,* &c. ?

Those who appeal primarily to the Orthoepists sometimes get very dubious answers; at other times, in the sixteenth and seventeenth centuries, some authorities state as definitely as they are able that the English sound is [*i*ū, jū], while others, with equal definiteness, maintain that it is [ȳ, jȳ]. The present-day writers who put these old writers on the rack, in the endeavour to wrest their secrets from them, generally take sides in this question. One school backs the accuracy of observation and general veracity of the—quite numerous—body of old writers, going down far into the seventeenth century, who appear to assert that [ȳ, jȳ] is the sound; the other school is much perturbed by this attitude and stakes its credit on [ū, jū]. Apparently it must have been one thing or the other. An enormous amount of learning and ingenuity has been expended by both sides. Personally I am not at all convinced that either side has the whole truth. Did the sound [ȳ] exist at all in English after, say, the middle of the sixteenth century? It practically resolves itself into whether the old grammarians can be trusted when they say that French *ū* in *sure* was identical with the English sound in the same word. Did they really know what the French sound was? When they appear to be describing [ȳ] are they not in fact attempting to describe something quite different? Are there not plenty of Englishmen at the present day who believe, for instance, that French *pu* and English *pew* are identical in every respect? It is absolutely certain that there are many such, and I think equally certain that there must have been many in the reign of Queen Elizabeth who would have been unable to distinguish the sound of these two words, even if the difference had existed, still less to describe it. But is it not probable that there were some Englishmen in the sixteenth and seventeenth centuries who could distinguish between [jū] on the one hand, and [ȳ, jȳ] on the other? I think that such men existed, and I therefore believe the strong body of testimony which asserts that what we may call the French sound did still exist in English well into the seventeenth century. But I think it is equally well established that there were other speakers who did not habitually pronounce this sound, who in fact were probably unable to pronounce it. *

I know several highly educated, not to say learned, Cockney speakers at the present time, who, if they were to give a descriptive analysis of their 'long *ū*'-sound, would with perfect accuracy give a totally different account from that which I should give of my own sound in *boot*, but not different from that which I should give of theirs. I can imagine that if the students of Historical English Grammar in the year 2200 should dig up our books from the British Museum, the fiercest war may rage among them, unless they realize that both schools are perfectly right,

---

* Appendix IV deals further with this subject.

but were describing two quite different sounds. They might say, X. is a fairly reliable authority on the whole for the pronunciation of his period, but he has gone off the lines here, and was evidently under the impression that the sound in *boot* was almost identical with that in German *hut* (hat). But here are the "London writers" Smith, Brown, and Robinson, who all agree that the sound in *boot*, at the beginning of the twentieth century, was a diphthong, and that the second element was not, as X. asserts, the full, high back-tense-round, but a back vowel very much advanced and partially unrounded.'. A still more disastrous attempt of the future grammarian would be to try to square the two descriptions as referring to one and the same sound, and to check one against the other, with the result that both parties would be credited with something quite different from what either had, quite rightly, described, and an utterly wrong statement would emerge from the muddle.

I am certainly not inclined to repose blind faith in the old grammarians, even in the best of them, but if I were convinced that all of those who appear to describe the sound [ȳ] were entirely wrong, or that they were in reality describing quite a different sound, I should certainly despair of ever learning anything from these old writers.

As for the approximate period at which [jū] first appeared, from old [jȳ], &c., I do not know when to place it, but I think there can be no doubt concerning the interpretation of the following spellings:—*youes* vb. ' use ', Lady Hungerford, Letters, p. 254 (*c.* 1569) ; *youse*, ' use ', A. Boorde (*c.* 1535), Ellis Letters III, ii, 303 ; *yousefull*, Mary Verney's Will, Verney Mem. ii. 17, 1639 ; *youst* 'used', Mall Verney, ibid. ii. 380, 1647 ; *youseg* ' usage', ibid. iii. 214, 1655 ; *youmore* 'humour', Wentw. Papers 320 ; *youmored*, ibid. 107, 320 ; *buity* 'beauty', ibid. 94, and *Buforde* 'Beaufort', 118, 119, 130. Mrs. Basire writes *ashoure* 'assure', 112 (1653), *quewre*, *quewored* 'cure, cured', 112 (1653); I take these spellings to indicate [əʃūə(r), kjūə(r)], &c. The spelling *yewthe* 'youth' in a letter of Richard Layton to Lord Cromwell, Ellis 2. 2. 60, 1535, is ambiguous, as the origin of the present vowel in this word is doubtful. The above spelling may either. point to an early identity in sound with the M.E. *ŭ*, *ēu*, &c., and suggest *ġȳġþ* as the original type, or if we take the present form to be from a Northern *ū*-type, it points to *ew*, &c., being a symbol for [jū] as early as 1535.

M.E. *ŭ* (O.E. *ȳ*).

It has been clearly stated (pp. 30. (3), 34. (3), 41. (3), &c.) that O.E. *ȳ* already in the O.E. period was differentiated into *e* in Kentish and South-Eastern, while the old sound remained elsewhere apart from combinative unrounding before front consonants in the South-Western dialects. In M.E. both types *e* and *y* (the latter written *u* from the twelfth century onwards) are found, but a new type with complete unrounding to *i* is characteristic of the North and of the E. Midlands, and apparently also of certain areas in the South-West.

The London dialect, as we have seen (pp. 9, 53, 57, &c.), has all three types in currency from an early period, the E. Midland gaining in frequency as time goes on. The history of the three types falls under that of the vowels *i*, *e*, and *ŭ* respectively. We are concerned primarily here with *ŭ*, whose history may be briefly summed up. It was retracted to *ŭ*, at any rate before the period in which this was unrounded, and it shared the common fate of all short *ŭ*-sounds no matter what their origin. Thus we have today [a] in *rush* (the plant), *thrush, shut, dull, bundle, blush, drudge, clutch, cudgel, burden, hurdle*, and probably *much* and *such* should be included here. The same sound in French words, *judge, just*, &c., had the same history. Cp. p. 232.

Busy and *Bury* appear from their spelling to belong to this type, but the former is pronounced [bɪzi] according to the E. Midland type, and the latter [berɪ] according to the South-Eastern. We noted considerable fluctuation in the distribution of the various types in the literary English of the fourteenth century and later (pp. 53, 57, &c.), but by the end of the fifteenth century the London usage was, on the whole, pretty much as at present, and even provincial documents show the influence of the speech of the Metropolis in their distribution of these forms. On the other hand, certain fluctuations continue during this and the following century, which show that a certain latitude still existed. The following lists, which do not profess to be complete, will give some idea of the principal deviations from our present distribution in Early Modern. I have not enumerated the forms, generally more numerous, which agree with our present usage.

I begin with some of the provincial texts, which are roughly classified into Eastern (including Suffolk and Essex) and Western (including South-Western and South-West Midland).

Eastern Group.

Palladius, *burstels* 'bristles', 27. 724, *cornel* 'kernel', 56. 332, *curnels*, 98. 1032; *besily*, 11. 28, *werst* 'worst', 14. 356, *wermes* 'worms', 32. 783; *rysshe* 'rush', the plant, 4. 69.

Bokenam, *thrust* 'thirst', Chr. 444; *mech* 'much', Pr. 97, *besy*, passim, *berthe* 'birth', Pr. Marg. 131, *werst*, Chr. 1015, *kechyn*, Eliz. 899; Marg. Paston, *hyrdillys* 'hurdles', ii. 84, *swich* 'such', passim; *beye* 'buy', i. 224, *meche*, i. 69, *werse*, ii. 61, 65, *seche*, ii. 130. 9.

Western Group.

Fortescue, though a Devonian, can hardly count as a provincial writer; his forms agree on the whole with our own, except for *furst* 'first', *sturred* 'stirred'.

St. Editha, *putte* 'pit', l. 4169; Shillingford has *myche* 'much', 4, *yuell* 'evil', 13, *myry, myryly*, 16, *shitte* P.P., 'shut', and *y shitte*, 88; *furst, stured, luste* Vb., 'list', 90; *werche* 'work' Vb., O.E. *wyrċan, ferst* 'first', 55, *yshette*, 86; Reg. of Oseney, *mynchons* 'monks' O.E. *mynċen, Medehulle*, 26, *buturhulle*, 26, *brugge*, 27 and 49; Exeter Tailors' Guild, *furst*, 318; Ord. of Worcs., *putts* 'pits', *brugge*, 374; Coventry Leet, *to wurche*, 1. 33; Pecok's Repressor, *yuel*, 1. 3, *rische* 'rush', 1. 166; Reg. of Godstow, *werste*, 55, *unschette* Inf., 'unshut, open'; *beried* agrees with our pronunciation, but not with our spelling.

I now pass to the non-dialectal sources.

Hoccleve has *thursteth*, but otherwise seems to agree with our present usage; Lydgate, who has certain East Country tendencies, has *sterid, besynesse, felthe* 'filth', *furst*; Rewle Sustr. Men., *gerddlis, schet* P. P., 91. 36, *schette* 'shut', 91. 38, *besily*, 93. 3; Gregory, who it must be remembered was born in Suffolk, has *lyfte* 'left hand', 86. 139, *syche*, 131, *schytte* Pret., 'shut', 159; *steryd*, 85, *Yelde* halle, 101; Caxton, *shitte* Pret., 'shut', Jason, 48; *knetted*, 174. 31, *shette* 92. 13, *seche* 'such', 96. 16, *besines*, 96. 21; *burthe*, 4. 16; Bk. of Quint., *yulis* 'evils', 10, *sich* 'such', 13, *mich* 'much', 3, *biriede*, 2, *sterrid*, 11; Skelton, Magnyf., agrees, apparently, with our present usage; Cr. Knt. of Bath, *furst*, 389, *lift* 'left hand', 391; Bp. Knight (1512), *mych*, Ellis 2. 1. 190; Rede m?, &c., *knett* P. P., 21; Sir Thos. More, *mych*, Ellis 1. 1. 197; Thos. Pery (1539), *bessy*, Ellis 2. 2. 140; John Mason (1535), *mych*, Ellis 2. 2. 54, *sich*, ibid.; Lord Berners, *hyrdell* 'hurdle', 1. 38, *shitte* 'shut' P. P., 1. 155, *yvell*, 1. 200; *besynesse*, 1. 25, 96, &c., *stere* Vb., 1. 136, &c.; Adm. Sir Edw. Howard, *steryd*, Ellis 2. 1. 214; Sir Thos. Elyot, *ketchyn*, 1. 71, *stereth*, 1. 145, *sterynge* 'stirring', 1. 149, *stere* Inf., 208, *kendled*, 2. 51; *thursty* 'thirsty', 1. 189, *thurste*, 2. 155; Bp. Fisher, *sturre*, 372; Latimer, *sterryng*, 204; *sturred*, 46, *sturrs*, 471; Machyn, *mych*, 2, *ymberyng* days 'Ember', 4, *rysses* 'rushes' (the plant); *bered* 'buried', 1, 2, &c., &c., *besiness*, 4, *Crepulgatt*, 125, *belded* 'built', 174, &c:., *kechens*, 203; *furst*, 2; Cavendish, *myche*, 9; *stere* 'stir', 52, *shett* 'shut', 242; Sir Thos. Smith, *suich*, 'such', Letters, Ellis 2. 3. 16; *furst*, ibid. 2. 3. 19; Ascham, *rishe*, Scholem. 54; Q. Elizabeth, *ivel* 'evil', Letters to James VI, 20, 65, *bisy*, Tr. 73; *stur*, Letters, 23; *weshing* 'wishing', Letters, 4; Euphues, *creeple*, *creple* 'cripple', 131 (but cf. p. 247, below). Milton writes *terfe* in his autograph MS. in Com. 280 and Lyc. 139.

It is unnecessary to pursue the subject farther. Throughout the sixteenth century we find that these forms correspond exactly to our own usage, and the above exceptions are comparatively insignificant by the side of the overwhelmingly larger number of forms which call for no mention at all. It should be pointed out that a certain proportion of the *e*-spellings may in reality represent the lowering of *i* to *e* according to the account given on pp. 207–8, 22⁶–9, above.

M.E. *ŭ* from O.E. *ȳ*.

The long vowel was treated in O.E. and M.E. in the same way as the short, and the three types *ū, ē, ī* also exist. In Modern Standard English, however, the *ī*-type is the only one which survives with the exception of the single word *bruise*, O.E. *brȳsan*, and the English origin of this is disputed, it being alleged that *bruise* is derived from Old French *bruser*, which, however, is itself a loan-word.

Some East Country dialects still preserve a few *ē*-forms—e. g. *meece* 'mice', *leece* 'lice'. Otherwise the descendants of the M.E. *ī*-type hold the field. The development of this vowel has been that of all other M.E. *ī*-sounds, namely, that it has been diphthongized to [ai] (cf. pp. 223–6, above).

Words of this origin are—*hide* Vb. and Noun, *hive* (for bees), *bride*, *kind*, de-*file*, *fire*, *mind*.

All these had *ȳ* in O.E.

The dialectal distribution of the various types *ū, ē, ī* in M.E. appears to have been pretty much the same as that of the corresponding short vowels—*ī* in the North and in the E. Midlands; *ē* in the South-East and part of the E. Midlands, perhaps as far north as Lincs.; *ŭ* in the South,

South-West, and West Midlands.   In the South-East both *ū* and *ē* seem
to have been current.   The E. Midland *i*-type seems to have gained
ground in areas where it did not originally belong, earlier, and more
rapidly than in the case of the short vowel, and the *ē*-type is next in
frequency, *ū* being less widespread outside the South-West and West-
Central Midlands.   In the London dialect all three types were in use in
M.E., *i* and *ē* being the commonest, but the latter was gradually eliminated and is, I think, not found in Literary English much after the middle
of the sixteenth century.   The long *ū* is often written *ui* or *uy* in M.E.
and later.

I give a few examples of survival of other types than that which we now
use, during the fifteenth and sixteenth centuries.

Provincial Sources.

East Country.   Palladius, *brēsed* 'bruised', 25. 679; Bokenam, *feer*
'fire', Agn. 537, &c., also *fyre*, Chr. 629, rhymes with *chere*, *mende*
'mind', Ann. 389; Marg. Paston, *mende*, ii. 362.

West and South-West.   Reg. of Oseney, *beeldid* 'built', 56, Ordinances of Worcs., *fuyre* 'fire', 371, 372, *huydes* 'skins', 374.

London Sources and Literary English.

Hoccleve, *thēmel* 'thimble', Reg. of Pr. 682; Lydgate, *fuyre* 'fire',
unkende; Skelton has no disagreement with present-day usage in those
words which survive, but the interesting archaism *lylher* 'bad', O.E. *lȳðer*,
may be noted; *fyre* 'fire' rhyming *byre* 'beer', Rede me, &c., is a phonetic
spelling for the M.E. *feer* type; cp. also Bokenam's rhymes above; Dives
Pragmaticus (1563), *heeves* 'hives'.

I have included *crepul*, *cre(e)ple* (see above, under Machyn and
Euphues) under short *ū* because I take it to be from O.E. *crȳpel* from
crupil. It might, however, be from Pr. O.E. *crūpil*, in which case
these forms should come here.

In the same way there is a difficulty about *build*.   The vowel in O.E.
byldan was originally short, but lengthening generally takes place in late
O.E. before -*ld*. On the other hand, our own present-day form is clearly
derived from an unlengthened form. The lengthened form, however,
seems certain in *beeldid* (Reg. of Oseney). Machyn's *beldyd*, 174, might
be either long or short.

M.E. *ai*, *ei* in the Modern Period.

These diphthongs, originally different, were pretty generally levelled
under one in M.E. at latest by the fourteenth century.   In different dialects
this single sound may have tended towards either [*ai*] or [*ei*].   By the
first quarter of the fifteenth century the sound, whatever it was, had
evidently been very widely monophthongized, and the single vowel thence
resulting was a front vowel, either [ǣ] or [ē].   This levelling is proved
by the occasional spellings *a*, *ea* for former *ai*, *ei*, and further by the fact
that *ai*, *ey* are sometimes written for old *ā*.   That the sound into which
both *ai* and *ā* had developed was a front vowel is shown by rhymes in
which old *ā* is coupled with old *ē* (cf. discussion of the history of
ā, pp. 194-6, above), and by the fact that *ey* is sometimes used for old
ē = [ē or ē̄], and that *ea* which is written for old *ai* never does nor could
stand for anything but a front vowel.

The history of *ai, ei* should be considered in connexion with that of old *ā*, since from the moment that they have converged into a single sound, whatever is true of the one is true of the other.*

To show the levelling of the diphthong with old *ā* and that the same symbols are used to express both, the following appear to me conclusive:—

(1) *ai, ei*, written *a*:—*sa* 'say', Mary Beaufort (1443–1509), letter in Ellis 1. 1. 47; Duke of Buckingham (1442–5), *fethfull*, Past. Letters (1442–5) 1. 62; *panes* 'pains', 1528, Anne Boleyn, Ellis 1. 1. 306; *agane*, 1553, Q. Elizabeth, letter in Ellis 2. 2. 213; 1642, *pade* 'paid', Lady Sussex, Verney Mem. ii; *wate* 'wait', ibid. 103; *pra* 'pray', Cary V., Verney Mem.

(2) Old *ā* written *ai*:—1421, *maid* P. P., Cov. Leet 1. 24; 1529, *trayvell*, Lord Berners 1. 222; 1533, *waiter* 'water', Will of Sir J. Digby (Leicestershire), Linc. Dioc. Docs. 142. 9; 1539, Letter of Thos. Pery, Ellis 2. 2, *spayke*, 141; *bayde* 'bade', 146; *laydinge*, 142; *tayking*, 146; *mayde* 'made', 142; Q. Elizabeth, *maik*, Transl. 148; *maid*, ibid. 143; 1550–60, *stayffes* 'staves' M.E. *stāves*, Machyn 51, *mayde* 'made', ibid. 53; 1642, *saifly*, R. Verney, Verney Mem. ii. 137; *shairer*, Ed. V., ibid. 141; *brayke*, Pret., Stonor Pprs. ii, 64 (1478).

(3) Rhymes:—Donne *are—dispair*, Heroical Epistle, 21, 22; *are—aire* 'air', ibid. 41, 42; *faire—compare*, ibid. 15, 16; Lord Rochester, *are—dispair—declare—fair* in 'Insulting Beauty you misspend'; *Playr's—cares* in poem entitled 'The Rehearsal'. Shakespeare, in the song 'Orpheus with his lute' (Hen. VIII, Act III, Sc. i), rhymes *play* with *sea*.

The evidence that *ai, ei* had become a front vowel as early as the fifteenth century is that in St. Editha (*c.* 1420) we find *deythe* for *death*, 445; *meyte*, 1001, for *meate*, M.E. *mēte*; *eyer*, 2908, for *ere*, M.E. *ēr* O.E. *ǣr*; *eysterday* for *Easterday*, 3104, 3105, and that Shillingford writes *feale* for *fail*, p. 19. Q. Elizabeth in Transl., p. 100, writes *cheane* for *chain*. Sir Thos. Elyot's *waiker* 'weaker', Gouernour 1. 173, and Bp. Fisher's *weyke* 'weak', Serm., p. 312, may represent a traditional spelling of the Scand. *veik*—though this seems to me extremely unlikely. If these forms represent the normal M.E. *wēke* then they are good illustrations of our point.

(For proofs that M.E. *ā* had been fronted by 1420 or so, see under that heading, pp. 194–6.)

As early as 1303 Robert of Brunne, in Handlyng Synne (Lincs.), writes *deyl*, 826, for M.E. *dēl* 'part', and *weyl* for *wēl* 'well', but it may be thought that this represents the Northern method of expressing length. In the North, O.E. *ā* as well as M.E. *ā* were undoubtedly fronted in the fourteenth century, and the sound is often expressed by *ai, ei*, but this does not concern us here.

, At the present day the old diphthong is preserved in some dialects, for instance in that of Oxfordshire; the normal forms for *rain, way*, and even for *fair* being [rain, wai, fair (or vair)]. This has nothing to do with the Modern Cockney pronunciation, which is quite recent, but is an interesting survival. It is probably to this type that Sir Thos. Smith and Gill allude as the 'rustic' pronunciation, a 'fat' sound. Unfortunately these writers appear, together with others of their kind and period, to assert

* See Appendix II.

that a diphthongic pronunciation [*ai*] was also the educated habit, the first element, however, being less 'fat'. The French writers of the sixteenth century who deal with our pronunciation often observe accurately, and they give an intelligible account of the facts when they identify the sound of English *ai* with French *é* and *ai*. It is unnecessary to follow in detail the ambiguous or misleading statements of the English grammarians on the point. They may be read, together with those of the French, most industriously collected and ingeniously discussed by Zachrisson, Engl. Vowels, pp. 124 &c., 190 &c. As an example of the sort of help we get from them we may quote one passage from Mulcaster's *Elementarie* (1582):

'*Ai* is the mans diphthong and soundeth full, *ei* the womans and soundeth finish in the same both sense and use—a woman is deintie and feinteth soon, the man fainteth not because he is nothing daintie ', p. 119. Gill, *Logonomia*, p. 33 (reprint), asserts that [*ai*] is the proper pronunciation, and that to substitute [ē] for this is an affected mode of speech.

Charles Butler, in 1634, says—' The right sound of *ai* . . . is the sound of the two letters whereof (it is) made. . . . But *ai* in imitation of the French is sometime corruptly sounded like *e* as in *may, nay, play, pray, say, stay, fray*.'

Cooper says that in *bait, caitiff, praise* the diphthong consists of the sound of *a* in *can*, joined to that of *i* pronounced *ee*. This would presumably mean [æi]. *ei, ey* in *height, weight, convey*, may be pronounced as regards the first element with either *e* in *ken* or *a* in *cane*, which would suggest either [ei or ēi]. But as if to show what nonsense all these refinements are, he winds up with what is clearly the simple truth—' plerumque autem in colloquio familiari, neglegenter loquentes pronunciant *ai* prout *a* simplicem in *cane* '. Which one may perhaps interpret to mean that everybody who spoke naturally pronounced a single long front vowel in words where *ai, ei* were written, but that some rather pedantic speakers, misled by the spelling, and wishing to be very 'correct', still said [æi or ei] in these words. It must not be taken as certain that any of the above-mentioned grammarians really pronounced a true diphthong, in spite of their theories. Later on, under the heading of '*a* exilis ', that is, the development of old long *ā*, Cooper gives a list of *ai* words which have the same sound as *a* in *cane*, e. g. *bain—bane, main —mane, hail—hale, maid—made, tail—tale*, &c., &c.

In addition to the various arguments which have been already adduced, to show the early monophthongization of this diphthong, there is the fact that from the fifteenth to the seventeenth centuries inclusive a pronunciation [ei] existed for M.E. *ī*, present-day [*ai*]. (See on this point, p. 223, &c., above.) If we are to assume that M.E. *ai, ei* were still pronounced as diphthongs in the seventeenth century we shall, I think, land ourselves in inextricable confusion. *

M.E. *oi* in the Modern Period.

It has been shown above, p. 224, in dealing with M.E. *ī*, that early in the Modern Period the new diphthong derived from the latter was identical in pronunciation with M.E. *oi*, and that this diphthong was

* See Appendix II.

probably [ai], at any rate in the sixteenth and seventeenth centuries. The accounts given by the grammarians of the seventeenth century regarding the pronunciation of old *oi* suggest that there was more than one pronunciation. While, as stated on pp. 224–5, they confirm the conclusions drawn from other evidence as to the identity of *ī* and *oi*, the sound thus described is mentioned under the treatment of *ī*, and additional information regarding the pronunciation of *oi* is often given under that diphthong itself. Mulcaster on pp. 117 and 118 of his *Elementarie* (1582) distinguishes clearly two pronunciations of *oi* : one 'sounding vpon the *o*' as in *boie, enioie, ioy, anoy, toy*, and another 'which soundeth vpon the *u*', or again, 'which seme to haue an *u*' as in *anoint, appoint, foil*. This would appear to imply a spelling-pronunciation [ɔi], here illustrated by the larger number of words, by the side of another pronunciation [ai]. Thus Wallis says that in *noise, boys, toys, oil* (1) the sound is *o* 'open, clear but short' +*y*; that some pronounce either (2) *ū* as the first element in certain words, or (3) '*ŭ* obscure'. He illustrates two types of pronunciation—*toil, oil*, or *tūyl, ūyl*. Cooper groups together (1) *wine, blind, wind, injoin, broil, ointment*, &c., as having the same diphthong, namely, the sound in *cut* followed by *i*. This agrees with the Wallis's sound described in (3) above and denotes [ai]. (2) Cooper gives *joy, coy, coif* as containing a diphthong consisting of the *o* of *loss* followed by *i*. This agrees with Wallis's (1) and refers to [oi]. (3) Cooper says that in *boil, moil, point, poison* the sound is *u* in *full*, or *o* in *fole* (= 'fool'?), followed by *i*, but that except in these words this diphthong, 'apud nos non pronunciatur'. This apparently refers to a pronunciation [ui] or [ūi] and corresponds to Wallis's (2).

These three pronunciations may be easily accounted for. The old sound seems to have been more like [ui] than [oi] just before its transformation. The first element appears to have been unrounded, and to have been lowered to [a], just like old short *ŭ* (cf. p. 232). This was the diphthong that was levelled with that produced from old *ī* (p. 224). This unrounding, however, did not take place after lip-consonants, hence [buil, muil], &c. (Cooper's type (3)). This retention of the rounded first element after lip-consonants was not universal, however (cf. Dr. Denton's *byled* 'boiled' [ai], p. 224).

The [oi] pronunciation indicated by Mulcaster, Wallis, and Cooper represents probably an artificially 'restored' pronunciation due to the spelling, and this is the Received pronunciation at the present time. The [oi] pronunciation occurred among some speakers in both [ui] and [ai] words, since in another place Cooper indicates it as possible for *join, toil*, &c., as well as for *boil, poison*, &c. The 'restoring' tendency has been carried too far in *boil* 'inflamed swelling' (M.E. *bīle*), and in *joist* (*jīste*). Jespersen (*N. Engl. Gr.*, p. 320) thinks that the spelling of these words cannot be explained in this way because *joyst* occurs as early as 1495, and *boyle* in 1525. But these early spellings do not necessarily prove that [oi] was pronounced in these words, but merely that old *ī* and old *oi* already had a common pronunciation, so that they were written indifferently to express the same sound. See also p. 224.

The curious spelling *junant* 'joining' is found in Shillingford, p. 86, &c., who also writes *joynant*, p. 89, and Gregory, a few years later, writes

cunys for 'coins', p. 185. This may mark the change of the first
element to [ŭ], but it is not a satisfactory method of expressing [ŭi].

Jones (1701), p. 113, says that the sound of *u* is written *o* in *boil, coil,
coin, foil, moil, voyage*, &c. It is rather doubtful whether he means to
imply the pronunciation [uɪ] or [aɪ], but as he includes in the list words
without a diphthong, in which [a] was certainly the vowel intended, such
as *mother, door, work*, &c., it is pretty evident that he intends to express
the pronunciation [aɪ].

In Baker's *Rules for True Spelling and Writing English*, among a list
of 'words commonly pronounced very different from what they are
written', we find the pronunciation of *coin* expressed as *quine*.

The twofold pronunciation [oɪ, aɪ] is recognized in *Growth of the
English Tongue*, published by Brightland, 1712 (or 1714?), attributed to
Steele. In *boil, toil, oil* the first element is said to be 'sometimes obscure
u' (= [a]). But—'I grant by the pronunciation of some men open (*o*)
is used in these words'.

The frequent rhymes such as *join—line* which occur in the eighteenth
century (in Pope and other writers) show that the 'unrestored' pronunciation of *oi*, which identified it with 'long *i*', was not an offence against
the taste of the fastidious. The final adoption of [aɪ, aɪ] as the Received
pronunciation was a slow process, and by some arbitrary standard in
some words the restored pronunciation was fixed while others were excluded. This is seen by the remark of Kendrick (1773) quoted by
Jespersen (*New Engl. Gr.*, p. 329), that it is an affectation to pronounce
boil, join otherwise than as *bile, jine*, and yet it is 'a vicious custom in
conversation' to use this sound [aɪ] in *oil, toil*, which thereby 'are
frequently pronounced exactly like *isle, tile*'.

In Received Standard at the present time there is, so far as I know, no
exception to the [oɪ] pronunciation. One rather remarkable exception
to this rule used to, and probably still does, occur in the Place Name
Foynes, in the County Limerick. Twenty-five years ago, when I lived
there, the local peasantry and farmers, and the middle classes of Limerick
City, pronounced it [foɪnz], but the neighbouring gentry, including the
landlord himself, all called the place [faɪnz].

The type [uɪ] seems to have vanished after the seventeenth century.

The testimony of rhymes during the sixteenth and seventeenth
centuries also confirms the evidence of the occasional spellings and of
the grammarians as to the identity of *oi* and *ī* in the pronunciation of
those times. A few examples will suffice:—Spenser, *guile—assoyle*,
Prothalam.; Shakespeare, R. of L., *swine—groin*, 1115–16; Suckling,
in the poem 'There never yet was woman made', rhymes *find—joined*;
Habington, *shin'd—joynd*, Castara, 83.

On the development of a lip-glide after a consonant, before *oi*, leading
to '*twoil*', &c., see p. 310, below.

The M.E. Diphthong *au* in the Modern Period.

The diphthong *au*, which, besides its development from *-al-* as
described above (p. 201), had various origins in M.E., has long been
monophthongized to [ɔ̄]. It is not difficult to determine in which words

the diphthong formerly occurred, as the old spelling *au* or *aw* is generally kept, apart from the cases of later development before *-l*, and here the spelling is preserved in *caul, haul,* &c.

Examples are—*draw, hawk, law, saw, gnaw, slaughter, cause, taunt, haunch,* &c.

The process of change followed was probably [*au, ou,* ō͞ᵘ, ɔ͞ᵘ, ɔ̄], that is to say, the first element of the diphthong underwent rounding through the influence of the second element; the former became longer and more important, and the latter proportionally weaker until it disappeared altogether.

It is naturally impossible to fix the precise period at which complete monophthongization took place, but it is reasonable to suppose that the [oᵘ, ɔᵘ] stage had been passed before old *ū* had become [ou] (see pp. 230–1), otherwise these two diphthongs, which must have been closely alike in sound, would have been levelled under a single form, and would have shared an identical fate. It is evident, however, that this did not happen. On the contrary, the period in which speakers tended to get rid of the second element of such a diphthong as [ɔ͞ᵘ] and to turn this into something which has become [ɔ̄] must have preceded that during which the speakers preserved this or a very similar diphthong (from old *ū*), and gradually unrounded the first element, thus producing approximately [*au*]. There is nothing to prevent us supposing that *ū* had become [ou] or even [au] early in the sixteenth century; on the contrary, this is highly probable (see pp. 231–2). The older [ou] from *au* may therefore have been monophthongized in the preceding century.

The occasional spellings in early documents which are enlightening are of two kinds: (1) those which write *ou* or *o* for older *au*, showing either that the first element was rounded or that, in addition, the second element had been lost; (2) those in which *au* or *aw* is used to express a sound which we know could never have been diphthongic.

I see no reason to distrust the obvious testimony of some of the forms adduced by Zachrisson, *Engl. Vowels*, E. St. 53, pp. 313 and 314—e. g. *stolkes* 'stalks', Cely Papers (this form, however, is of doubtful identity); *oll*, 1505, *defolte, ofull* 'awful', after 1500, which are given as from ' Suffolk Records ', without further reference than to ' Binzel 49 '; further, *olso* from Sir Thos. More, *c.* 1535. Among my own collections are these from Machyn :—*hopene* ' halfpenny', *solmon* 'salmon', 170, *ontt* 'aunt', 64, (all these are mentioned by Z.); further, from Machyn—*a nobe* 62, ' an alb' = [ɔ̄b] from *aulb*. Surrey has the spelling *tought* 'taught' rhyming with *ywrought*, cf. Tottel, p. 7, Compl. of a Louer. &c., 11 and 12; and Thos. Sackville rhymes *wrought—caught*, Compl. of Duke of Buckingham, 125, also *draught—thought—fraught*, ibid., 127. Of spellings belonging to the second class may be mentioned *saufte* ' soft ', cit. Zachrisson as being from Tyndale, 1525; I have noted also *caumplet* 'complete', Machyn, p. 12, which has not escaped the eagle eye of Dr. Zachrisson, and *clausset* 'closet' in Latimer, *Seven Serm.*, p. 38. A much earlier spelling which has not yet been mentioned in this connexion, but which may well be a case in point, is *y-fole* 'fallen', St. Editha, 522. These spellings satisfy me that the writers no longer pronounced the old *au* as a diphthong, but rather as a single vowel, not very different from that we now use. The French grammarians of the seventeenth century insist that the sound in English *awe* resembles or is identical with French *a* long. If this refers to a sound like that now heard in French *âpre, pâte*, the description is as near to that of [ɔ̄] as a Frenchman could be expected to get. At the present time French provincial speakers pronounce the vowel in *pâte*, &c., very low with a slight rounding, so that the sound is not far removed from our [ɔ̄]. It is instructive to compare with the Frenchman's statement the spelling *Spaw* of Sir R. Verney, Verney Mem. ii. 23 (1641), for *Spa*, and of Lady Elmes, iv. 120 (1665).

Other interesting spellings from the Memoirs in the present connexion are—*Sent Obornes* ' St. Albans ', Lady Sussex, ii. 81 (1642); *sossy* 'saucy', Pen. Verney, ii. 78 (1642); *cose* 'cause', M. Faulkiner, ii. 56 (1642); *smol* ' small ', Betty Adams (née Verney), iv. 131 (1665).

Mrs. Basire (Corresp. of Dr. Basire) writes—*sow* 'saw', 108 (1651), *doter* 'daughter', 112 (1653), *colling* ' calling ', 135 (1654), also *fool* ' fall ', 134, at the same date.

Otway writes *Gaud* for *God* in *Soldier's Fortune*, Act v, Sc. i (1681), which certainly implies the now vulgar pronunciation [gɔ̄d], a pronunciation also exhibited by Pope in the lines :—

> Slave to no sect, who takes no private road
> But looks through Nature, up to Nature's God.
> *Essay on Man*, Epistle iv, 320,

and more unmistakably in :—

> Persist, by all divine in man unawed,
> But learn, ye dunces ! not to scorn your God.
> *Dunciaa*, 223-4.

Lengthenings and Shortenings of Vowels in the Modern Period.*

This whole question is beset by various difficulties. Lengthening and shortening of vowels has occurred at various periods during the history of English, sometimes under conditions which are clear and can be formulated without hesitation, since the results are found with regularity, and the apparent exceptions can be explained by a specific analogy, sometimes under conditions which are more or less obscure, since the lengthening or shortening is apparently intermittent, being present in some words, but absent in others in which the phonetic conditions seem to be identical. A further difficulty, when the quantity itself is sufficiently clear from the spelling, is to be sure whether this or that particular quantity is attributable to a M.E. change or to one of later date. This difficulty arose in discussing the various developments of M.E. *ō*¹ in the Modern Period. (Cf. pp. 236–9, above.)

The handling of these various problems needs caution, since many of them cannot be settled without reference to other sound changes, and a certain view respecting one may involve much else besides.

Thus it would seem that the lengthening of M.E. *ŏ* as in *lost, croft* [lɔ̄st, crɔ̄ft] must be later than the change of M.E. *ō*² from a slack to a tense sound, so that whatever approximate date we may fix for the former we

* See Appendix II.

are bound to admit that by that time the new tense $\bar{o}$ must have been already in existence, since if this were not so, and if the lengthened M.E. $\check{o}$ had caught up M.E. $\bar{o}^2$ before this had become tense, then the process of 'tensening' must have overtaken both together and we should now pronounce *lost*, to rhyme with *boast*, and there would be no distinction in pronunciation between *cost* and *coast*.

We may get some guidance as to the approximate period of these Early Modern shortenings if we examine their effect on vowels whose quality changed during Late M.E. or very Early Modern.

Both M.E. $\bar{e}^1$ [ē] and later M.E. $\bar{e}^2$ [ē], as we know, have become [ī]. Now in *sick*, *silly*, *rick* (of hay), *riddle*, *breeches* = [britʃiz], and the now vulgar *divvle* 'devil' we have a vowel produced by the shortening of M.E. $\bar{e}^1$ after it had become [i].

On the other hand, in *head, dead, breath, sweat,* &c., we have a shortened form of M.E. $\bar{e}^2$. In no case, so far as I know, have we [i] as the result of the shortening of this vowel. We have no reason to suppose that this shortening process, in one and the same dialect, affected one vowel earlier than the other. If the shortening of both was synchronous, then it is evident that this took place not earlier than the period when $\bar{e}^1$ became [ī], and not later than that during which $\bar{e}^2$ was still a mid-vowel, although it may have become tense.

We have seen (p. 206, above) that the raising of $\bar{e}^1$ to [ī] was possibly a Late M.E. process—it was certainly a very Early Modern change—and we have seen further (p. 209) that $\bar{e}^2$ became tense very soon afterwards; that in some dialects at least it, too, became [ī] before very long. This argument would place the shortening period at least as early as the fifteenth century, and sure enough we have some fifteenth-century spellings which indicate a shortening of $\bar{e}^1$ and that the change to [ī] had already taken place. I take Gregory's *schyppe* 'sheep', 162, and Marg. Paston's *kypt* 'kept', ii. 179, from the new formation *kēpt*, as quite conclusive. Marg. Paston has also *kype*, and *keeped* is a form found as late as Lady Wentworth. Shillingford has *sike* 'sick', 64, and Rewle Sustr. Men. has the same spelling, 89. 19, but it may be said with reason that it is not absolutely certain that a short vowel is intended here. Coming to the next century, Lord Berners has *wyckes* 'weeks', 1. 219, and Latimer has the unambiguous *braincicke*, Seven Serm., 28. Lord Berners's form might be from M.E. *wĭke*, but this is not nearly so common as *wēke* or *wōke*, &c., in the South. *Silie* is found, Ascham, Scholem. 110, and *sillye*, Euph. 260. Sir Thos. Smith, Republ., has *divils*, 18, corresponding to the pronunciation '*divle*', now common in Ireland, fr. M.E. *dēvil*, Early Modern [dīvil]. Thos. Lever has *diuilysh*, Serm. 45.

Another important shortening is that of M.E. $\bar{o}^1$ after it had become [ū]. The effects of this process are heard in the pronunciation of *blood, flood, must, glove, month, mother,* &c. We have seen that the change of $\bar{o}^1$ to [ū] was accomplished in some dialects as early as the fourteenth century (cf. p. 234, above). The shortening was therefore later than this. On the other hand, it cannot have been later than the other, isolative change, whereby all short *ŭ*-sounds were unrounded to a vowel which subsequently became [a]. But this change, in spite of the silence of the grammarians until well on in the seventeenth century, we have reason to think had at least begun in the fifteenth century, even in stressed syllables. (Cf. p. 233, above.)

Therefore the shortening of the vowel in [blūd], &c., must have occurred early in this century. Thus we are led to place the shortening of the three vowels we have discussed at approximately the same period. (See pp. 236–8 for examples of early shortening of $\bar{o}^1$ and discussion of probabilities in regard to this vowel.)

In fixing the shortening of these three vowels at such an early date, it is not asserted that all speakers of all types of English had carried out these changes by the end of the fifteenth century. On the contrary, it is quite certain that this was not the case, otherwise we should have a far larger number of words involved; indeed, all words of each class, that is to say, wherever $\bar{e}^1$, $\bar{e}^2$, and $\bar{o}^1$ stood before d, v, th (voiced or voiceless), and so on. The comparatively small number of words involved, and the impossibility of formulating the conditions under which the shortening took place, show that we have here, not a change of universal scope, but one which obtained in a Regional or Class dialect. From this certain forms have passed in Received Standard, but they have not always been the same forms.

What we have tried to establish is the approximate date at which shortened forms, from which certain forms now current in Received Standard are derived, were in existence. The fact that this or that seventeenth-century grammarian maintains that a certain form, which is now short, was pronounced long in his time does not upset the inference drawn above. In the first place the grammarian may be misleading us as to the facts, and even if he is not, this simply means that he is describing a different type, the possible existence of which is not denied. Thus it does not disturb us if we are told that in the seventeenth century the vowel in *foot* was long.

We suspect that already in the fifteenth century a shortened form of this word was in existence, but we know that this would have produced [fat] in the seventeenth century, a form which still survives at the present time, and that side by side with this there was also a form [fūt] with unshortened vowel which is no doubt the ancestor of our [fŭt].

The following are a few examples of old longs (other than those already illustrated), or possible longs, which may apparently be regarded as shortened in the forms given. Some of them are M.E. shortenings which we have now lost, preferring the alternative, unshortened forms; others we still use.

S. of Rouen—*horsheddę*; Pallad.—*woddes* 'woods', rhymes *goode is*, 93. 1169 (this may be either the old short *wŭde* retained or a shortening of *wōde*; the rhyming word in either case must be an early example of the shortening of the new *ū*), *hottest*, 64. 275, *watter* 'water', 62. 33 (from inflected *wătres*, &c.), *sonner*, 83. 615 (M.E. shortening; on analogy of Comparative), *channge*, 86. 708.

Lord Berners—*loffe* 'loaf', 1. 52, *roffes* 'roofs' (M.E. shortening ?), *fludde*, 1. 221 (shortening of new [ū] fr. $\bar{o}^1$), *bottes* 'boats', 1. 228, *rodde* 'rode', 1. 350 (M.E. shortenings ?), *Arch presst*, 1. 399 (M.E. shortening); Elyot—*hedde*, 2. 242, *yocke* 'yoke' (unlengthened form fr. Old Nom.); Sir Thos. More—*cummen*, Ellis i. 1. 299 (1533, retention of old

s

ŭ or shortening of ū from ō?); Latimer—*watter*, 86 ; Edw. VI First
P.B.—*cummeth*; Machyn—*mett* 'meat', passim, *swett* ' sweat', 71, 'sweet',
136, 310, *heddes* 'heads' 138; Cavendish, L. of Wolsey—*strett* 'street',
3 (M.E. shortening), *Flet* Street, 12 ; *bak howsse* 'bakehouse', 24
(M.E. shortening before *k + h*), *botts* ' boats', 150, *swett*; Ascham—
yocke of oxen, Tox. 73 (unlengthened Nom.); Euphues—*hotte*, 41,
beheaddest, 316 ; Lord Burghley—*whott* ' hot', Ellis ii. 3. 99 (1582);
Spenser—*craddle* ' cradle' (M.E. absence of lengthening fr. inflected
cases before *d + l*); Shakespeare, First Fol.—*smot* P. P., M. N. D.;
Gabr. Harvey, Letters—bride*grumme*, 136 (shortening of ū fr. ō¹), *blud*,
22, *futt*, 121 (shortening of new ū fr. ō¹), *hedd*, 68, *halliday* (M.E.
shortening of ā in first syll. of three syll. word), *boddies*, 22 (M.E. absence
of lengthening fr. *bŏdyes*, before *d + y*); W. Roades, the Verneys'
steward—*tuck* 'took', V. Mem. ii. 275 (1656), Sir R. Verney—*sutt*,
Mem. iv. 358 (1686).   The two last forms are almost certainly early
shortenings of the new ū fr. ō¹, comparable to *fludde*, *blud*, *futt*, in Lord
Berners and Harvey.   These would give rise to present-day [flad, blad,
sat, fat], the two first being the forms in normal usage now, the two last
having disappeared from Standard usage.   (Cf. also pp. 236–9, on the
early and later shortening of new [ū].)

There is, however, evidence that by the side of the shortened or short
forms whose existence seems to be established by the spellings quoted,
there were in existence at the same time, among other speakers, or perhaps
among the same speakers, forms which maintained the length of the vowel.

It is sometimes taught that vowels were shortened, or not lengthened
in open syllables, in M.E. before the O.E. suffix -*iǧ*, *body* being given as an
example.   The fact is the O.E. *bŏdiǧ* became normally *bōdy* in M.E. in the
Nom., but not in the inflected cases—*bodyes*, &c.—where the combination
-*dy*- preserved the short vowel.   The Standard pronunciation of *body* is
derived from the inflected type.   On the other hand, the Nom. type, with
lengthening, is seen in the Coventry Leet *boodies*, *boody*, 26, and in
Gregory's *boodys*, 111.

The unshortened form of *head*, as in M.E., is seen in Lord Berners's
beheeddyd, 1. 34, of *pretty* in Latimer's *preaty*, 85, of *hot* in *hoate*, 293, &c.,
of *thread* in Euphues, *threed*, 157.   Gabriel Harvey has *moonie*, 59,
' money', and *coover*, 63.   Lengthening before *r* + consonant is seen in
teerm ' term', Bk. of Quint., 24, in *foorde*, Euphues, 276, and in Gabriel
Harvey's *leerne*, 138 ; in *woorse*, *woorde*, *woorke*, *woorthie*, &c., in the
First Prayer Book ; and many other instances occur.

In M.E. doublets arose, as we have seen in the forms *bŏdy*—*bōdy*,
owing to the different treatment of vowels in open and close syllables.
Words like *băk* 'back' retained the short vowel in the Nom., but
lengthened it in inflected forms, so that the Pl. would normally be *bākes*.
Either or both types might be generalized for the whole declension.   In
Modern English we have often the type with the lengthened vowel, as in
dale, fr. M.E. *dāle*, *yoke*, fr. *yōke*, &c., by the side of the Nom. *dăl* and *yock*.
On the other hand, we have *back*, *black*, &c., unlengthened.   Traces
remain in Early Modern of long forms which we have now lost.   Thus,
Palladius has *saak* ' sack', 90. 814, and *on his bāke*, rhyming with *tāke*,
stook ' stock'.   Elyot has *blāke* 'black', rhyming with *quāke*, i. 47.

Perhaps the variants which we have noted in *head, sweat,* &c., should be explained in this way. For reasons already apparent from the discussion above and on pp. 235–6, &c., this principle cannot be extended to the differences in the sixteenth and seventeenth centuries between *blüdd,* &c., and *bloud,* &c.

The lengthening of the vowel in *God,* referred to on p. 253, above, is an Early Modern rather than a M.E. process. Pope's rhyme of this word with *road,* however, may conceivably reflect a M.E. lengthening in the inflected cases.

A very important group of vowel lengthenings took place in the Modern period before the sounds [f, s, þ, ð]—*f, s, th*—and before these consonants followed by another consonant. It is this lengthening which has given us *after, laughter* [āftə, lāftə], &c. (see pp. 203–5, above). It is probable that the lengthened vowel in *cost, cough, froth* [kɔ̄st, kɔ̄f, frɔ̄þ], &c., belongs to the same period, and the now old-fashioned pronunciation [mɔ̄þ] for *moth,* instead of [mɔþ]. These lengthenings, as has been said, are by no means universal, even among speakers of Received Standard. In Coventry Leet *crooft* occurs 43 (1422), and again 46 and 47 (1443), and *geestes* 'guests', p. 29. I have not noted other examples until we come to Euphues, in which work we find *moathes,* 34, *toossed* 'tossed', 208; *clausset,* Latimer, *Seven Serm.,* 38; Lady Verney writes *moathes,* V. Mem. ii. 270 (1647).

Now it would seem from the above, that before the middle of the fifteenth century vowels were lengthened before *ft* and *st,* in the dialect of Warwickshire at any rate.

If *e* and *o* were lengthened, why not *ă* too? Cely Papers have *marster* 'master', which, while it shows that *r* could not have been pronounced before *s,* also shows that the vowel was long. *Rede me,* &c., rhymes *after—carter,* 119–20. Are we to assume that this lengthened vowel was [ā], or [æ]? From what has been said above (pp. 196–201), we shall assume the latter if we think that M.E. *ă* had already been fronted. If we reject this evidence and assume that the lengthened vowel was [ā] we shall find it difficult to fit in the subsequent development with that of old *ā* (cf. pp. 195–6, above).

Are we to assume that old *ă* had been lengthened before the end of the fifteenth century—among those speakers who were affected by it—in the whole group of words where *ă* stands before *s, f, th,* that is, in *path, father, bath, grass, fast, chaff, laughter,* &c., &c.?

As a matter of fact Palladius has *graas,* 4. 69, and *on his baathe,* 40. 1080. Are these forms to be derived from the inflected forms, M.E. *grāse, bāþe,* or are they lengthened by the same process which, as we have seen, had shortly after this time certainly produced *crooft, geestes, mäster,* and which, as we know, assuredly did at some time produce lengthened vowels in all these words?

The question is far too difficult, and involves too many others to be settled hastily. The whole question of Modern lengthenings and shortenings requires special investigation, which at present is lacking. Having indicated some of the problems and possibilities we leave the matter unresolved for the present.

CHAPTER VII

THE VOWELS OF UNSTRESSED SYLLABLES

For the student who wishes to acquire some knowledge of the treatment of vowels in syllables devoid of stress during the Modern Period, it is a great advantage that the early writers on English pronunciation have avoided the question altogether. We are thus spared the labour of reading through, and comparing, a number of statements which, to judge by other parts of the work of these writers, would not have been very enlightening. We are even more grateful for the absence of endless discussions and explanations by more recent authorities of what the earlier writers meant or did not mean. Speaking generally, we may say that it is not until the eighteenth century that we find direct accounts of the pronunciation of unstressed vowels, and by that time we are in a position to know from other sources many at least of the principal facts. The eighteenth-century writers often describe the unstressed syllables by means of a rough and ready but quite intelligible phonetic spelling, and these transcriptions frequently establish, for the period in which they were made, pronunciations which we know had been in existence for centuries before.

The present chapter deals with the subject as from the fifteenth century. I have not attempted to follow the weakenings of vowels back into the M.E. period. My collection of material from M.E. sources, although not inconsiderable, is not yet by any means adequate for generalizations of value to be based upon it. Many of the phenomena here exhibited are no doubt much older than the fifteenth century. This is notably true of the weakening of the inflexional endings -ed, -es, -eþ, -en to -id, -is, &c.

From the material contained in the following pages one may venture to formulate one or two statements of a general character.

(1) At least as early as the middle of the fifteenth century vowels in unstressed syllables were shortened, reduced, or confused, very much as in Colloquial English at the present time.

(2) This may be inferred from numerous occasional spellings which reveal either (a) a sound of an undefined character, different from that expressed by the traditional spelling, which the writer is undecided how to express, or (b) a definite sound different from that expressed by the traditional spelling.

(3) The spellings which indicate a reduction of the unstressed vowel are not used consistently by any writers, except in the case of such suffixes as -is, -id, &c., and even here the consistency is only relative.

(4) While a violent and definite departure from the traditional spelling, whether sporadic or habitual, must be taken to imply some change in

pronunciation, the adherence to the conventional spelling does not necessarily imply that no change has taken place. (N.B. The examples given illustrate, as a rule, only departures from the older spelling.)

(5) Varieties in spelling may express only indecision on the part of a writer in transcribing a sound (cf. (2), above); but they may also indicate the existence of more than one type of pronunciation.

(6) Different types of pronunciation in the same vowel may represent (*a*) the results of different conditions of stress in the same word, or (*b*) they may be due to different tendencies which coexisted among different classes of speakers.

(7) Examples of indecision in transcribing a vowel sound are:— -*el*, transcribed in Cely Papers in four different ways in the same word, e. g. *stapell, stapyll, stapal, stapul*. Here possibly -*ell* and -*yll* represent approximately one and the same type of pronunciation, and -*al*, -*ul* another. The same confusion is found in the spelling of the unstressed ending -*er*. It is evident that already in the fifteenth century the vowels in -*er*, -*ar*, -*or*, -*ur*, -*our* were all levelled under one sound—[ər] or syllabic *r*.

(8) Examples of varieties due to different conditions of stress are :— *certin* from M.E. *cértein* : *certayne*, &c., from M.E. *certéin*; *battel* from M.E. *báttaille* : and *battayl* from M.E. *battáille* ; *forten, fortin* from M.E. *fórtune* : *fortune*, present-day [fɔːʃən], from M.E. *fortúne*; *aventer* from M.E. *avénture* : *aventure* from M.E. *aventúre*; &c., &c.

(9) Examples of varieties due to different tendencies are :—*sesyn, reasyn* compared with *sesoun, resoun*, &c. This difference of treatment of -*on* in unstressed syllables is still heard to-day, when some speakers pronounce *pigeon* [pɪdžɪn], others [pɪdžən]. The type represented above by *sesyn*, &c., has almost died out in Received Standard, although formerly the chief type, and has given place to that represented by *resoun*, &c., now [rīzn]. *Pigeon* is perhaps the only word still commonly pronounced with [ɪn], and this pronunciation is considered by many as old-fashioned.

(10) The differences which exist between the pronunciation of unstressed vowels at the present time, and that indicated by the spellings as existing in former centuries, are chiefly due to the adoption in recent times of a different type (cf. remarks on unstressed -*on* in (9), above), and not to new developments in changes of sound. These have hardly occurred since the late sixteenth century. Some of the pronunciations of to-day are due to the influence of the written form, and the recent efforts in some quarters to ' restore' the full forms of vowels in stressless positions, cf. the spelling-pronunciation [pɔːpoiz] instead of the historical [pɔːpɪs] of the one type, or [pɔːpəs] of the other. The distribution of the different types among the various words in which the same original vowel occurs in an unstressed position, as well as the selection of the unstressed vowels in certain words for ' restoration', while in others the ancient historical reduced form is still pronounced, are matters, as it would seem, of arbitrary chance and the fashion of the moment.

I now pass on to give a brief summary of the actual changes which resulted from the weakening of vowels in unstressed syllables. so far as these can be gathered from the material, far from adequate, although not altogether contemptible, which I have collected and classified.

I may say here that, so far as I can see, the results are the same, provided a vowel is unstressed, no matter where it stands in relation to the principal stress of the word or breath-group in which it occurs. The nature of the surrounding consonants probably exerts some influence, but the present material does not suffice for formulating the conditions or nature of such influence, except in respect of vowels before -*l*, -*n*, and -*r*.

Front Vowels are raised: *a* = [æ] becomes *e* [ɛ]; this *e* levelled later under original *e* which becomes *i*.

Rounded Vowels
are unrounded
{ *u* and *o* probably levelled under the same sound, (written *a*) = [a] which becomes [ə].
French *u* [y] becomes [i, *i*]; the result of this unrounding written *i* and *e*.

Diphthongs
{ *oi* becomes *i* [*i*], written *e*, *i*.
ai (*ei*) (which had become [e]) result in a front vowel written *e* or *i*, probably = [*i*].
au, *ou*, monophthongized to [o,o] which is unrounded to [a] written *a*; this often fronted to a vowel written *e* or *i* (*y*).

There appear to be two quite different tendencies at work from early in the Modern period among different sections of speakers. One group tends to level all weak vowels under some front vowel, written *i* or *e*; the other to level all weak vowels under the 'obscure' vowel [ə] or some such sound, written variously *a*, *o*, *u*. It is probably safe to infer that the symbols for old back or back-rounded vowels, *a*, *o*, *u*, generally imply some sound corresponding to [ə] at the present time, and that the symbols for front vowels—*i*, *e*—imply the kind of vowel now heard in the second syllable of *ladies*, here written [*i*], although it may have been the high-flat-slack vowel [*ï*].

The two tendencies above referred to are specially observable in the treatment of vowels before -*n* and -*l*. One tendency results in developing and preserving the 'clear' vowel, so that we get [*i*n, *i*l] for earlier -*en*, -*el*, and even for -*on* (cf. (9), above, and pp. 271–2, 274–5, below). The other tendency results in [ən, əl], which are further weakened to syllabic *n* and *l* respectively as present-day *button*, *beaten*, *cradle*, *rebel* (Noun), &c. We know both from practical experience and from the records of the past of the existence of both these types, [*i*n, *i*l] and [n, l].

As regards the treatment of vowels in unstressed syllables before -*r*, although -*yr*, -*ir* are common spellings for old -*er*, it seems very doubtful whether the genius of the English language ever tolerated such a combination as [-*i*r] in actual speech, at least finally. On the other hand such spellings as *fadr*, *remembr*, both fifteenth century, suggest that a syllabic [r] was pronounced. The various spellings *or*, *er*, *yr*, *ur*, *ar* for the same syllable *er* seem to imply a vowel which it was difficult to identify, probably [a, ə]. The 'murmur' vowel [ə] probably developed quite early before -*r*, and [ər] was later reduced to syllabic [r]. This in its turn was weakened and gave place to the present [ə]. We have apparently no confirmatory evidence from any living form of English of the existence of an [*i*r] type, and the records of the past are ambiguous.

After these general remarks I now pass to consider, as briefly as possible, the details which are exhibited in the lists. The latter are for the most part so arranged as to show the prevailing tendencies, so far as these may be inferred by the particular kind of departure from the conventional spelling in each century. I have tried to avoid needless subdivision, but a certain amount, especially under the heading -a and -*e* in unstressed syllables, seemed necessary and unavoidable.

THE UNSTRESSED VOWELS IN DETAIL.

e *in Unstressed Syllables.*

(N.B. The reader of the following brief comments may refer, if he please, to the lists, pp. 267–82, upon which the views here set forth are based.)

The Suffixes.

-ed. The suffix -*ed* in weak Prets. and P.P.'s appears as -*id* very commonly in all kinds of texts throughout the fifteenth and sixteenth centuries. The Adjective *wretched* appears with -*id* as early as 1451. Even St. Editha, alongside of the Western -*ud*, has not a few -*id* endings in Prets. and P.P.'s. This form -*ud* is no doubt the ancestor of the present-day provincial or vulgar [əd]. It is evident that the [id] form, now universal in polite speech, was established very early. Coote's warning against -*id* proves the existence of the pronunciation in his day, although such proof is quite superfluous. His statement that the pronunciation is Scottish is sheer nonsense. He might as well have said that it was Devonshire, and Norfolk, and London, and so on.

-eth. The present pronunciation of this suffix [iþ], which only survives in Liturgical and Biblical language or in Poetry, was established in the fifteenth century in a wide circle and over a large area.

-es. The present-day pronunciation [iz] was established beyond dispute from the fifteenth century onwards. The old Western -*us* represents doubtless the type [əz], which still exists as a provincialism and vulgarism.

-est. The [-ist] type was evidently as widespread during and since the fifteenth century as among good speakers to-day. The spelling *intrust* in the Verney Memoirs is the ancestor of present-day [intrəst], which is provincial. The more polite forms are [int(ə)rist, intrest]. Every other form in the list might stand for the present pronunciation, including Sir T. Elyot's *haruist.*

-er. The early forms of -*er* as an ending point to at least two types, [ər] and syllabic *r.* Is it possible that the -*yr*-spellings represent the ancestor of the present-day vulgar pronunciation with a tense vowel? Lady Sussex's spelling *misirable* stands, if we may draw any conclusion from -*ir*-, for a type no longer heard. The present-day possibilities are either [mizərəbl] or [mizrəbl].

-en, -em. The spellings suggest three types of pronunciation:— [in, ən], and syllabic [n]. All three types exist in present-day polite English, variously distributed. Of these [ən, n] are perhaps the commonest. Still, most good speakers preserve [in] in—*woollen, kitchen, chicken, women, linen, Latin, rosin,* &c. = [wulin, kitʃin, tʃikin, wimin, lĭnĭn, rɔzɪn]. On the other hand we have [ən] or syllabic *n* in—*golden, earthen, wooden, even, often, sudden, children, heaven*, and in P. P.'s in *-en*, such as *forgotten*.

-em, as in *solemn* and *'em*, is now usually [əm]. Note Sir R. Verney's *solome*, which doubtless expresses this pronunciation.

-el. The early spellings show a preponderance of *-yl* forms, with a few *-ul* = [əl], and Sir Thos. More's *Russll* = syllabic *l*. This is the prevailing type at the present day, after consonants, whether in words like *evil, devil, fossil*, where [ɪl] is also heard, or in those spelt *-le*. It is probable that many speakers who wrote *-yl* in earlier centuries often pronounced [əl, l].

After a vowel the best usage on the whole now favours [ɪl], as in *cruel* (cf. also forms from Verney Memoirs in lists, *fuel, towel, vowel*).

Other Suffixes and Endings containing -e-.

-less. Now always [lɪs] in Received Standard. This pronunciation is established in the fifteenth century by Marg. Paston's spelling *harmlys*. The provincial [ləs] and the spelling-pronunciation [les] may often be heard.

-ness. Present-day [nɪs]. I have not noted any spellings with *-nis* earlier than Queen Elizabeth, who makes frequent use of them.

[ɪs] is also the normal pronunciation of *-ess*, as in *mistress*, &c.

-chester. The spelling *Rochister* of the Wentworth Papers, 1710, agrees with present-day usage in this and other similar names—*Chichester* [tʃɪtʃɪstə], *Manchester* [mæntʃɪstə], &c.

-le(d)ge. *Knowledge, college* are pronounced [nɔlɪdʒ, kɔlɪdʒ] at the present time. This pronunciation of the weak vowel in the former word dates at least from the fifteenth century, that of the latter word I have not found recorded earlier than Gabriel Harvey. The 1482 spelling *collage* of the Bury Wills corresponds to the present-day provincial [kɔlədʒ].

-et. This ending is pronounced [ɪ] after consonants, in *covet, helmet, bullet, blanket*, &c., but [ə] in *diet*. These conditions are expressed by the sixteenth-century spellings given in the lists.

e-. Unstressed *e-* followed by strong stress is now usually pronounced [ɪ], as in *estate, escape, elect, erroneous*, &c. = [ɪsteɪt, ɪskeɪp, ɪlekt, ɪrounjəs], &c. The spellings—fairly numerous in the fifteenth and sixteenth centuries —*ascape, astate*, &c., apparently imply a pronunciation with [ə].

-a- in Unstressed Syllables.

The early spellings, and even the late spellings of the seventeenth and eighteenth centuries show a more widespread tendency to weaken *a* to [ɪ] than at present prevails in Received Standard. Many of the spellings, from each of the centuries, represent pronunciations which it is true still obtain in English, but only in Regional or Class dialects. The mere fact that *a* is weakened to a sound written *i* or *e* is not in itself surprising, when we consider that one of the sounds for which *a* stood was, in the fifteenth century, in many areas, especially in the E. Midlands and South-East, in process of being fronted. This process may well have begun earlier in unstressed positions. It is most probable that an antecedent stage to the front vowel, written *e*, or more often *i*, was [æ]. This was apparently raised to a sound intermediate between [ɛ, *i*], and from this stage the differentiation into a full [*i*] on the one hand, or [ə] on the other, took place. Received Standard has now adopted the [ə] type in most of the cases illustrated in the lists. Attention may be drawn to the spelling *Up-* for *Ap-* quoted from Capgrave. This form shows that *u* in unstressed syllables was already unrounded, and that the symbol expresses [a] or [ə] when used for a vowel in this position.

I note first the points of agreement in type between the early spellings and present-day usage. Both agree in having [ə] in the following:—*as* when unstressed in sentence ; cf. *os* in Cely Pprs. ; *-mass* in *Christmas*, &c., cf. Machyn's form in *-mus*, and Lady Sussex's *crismus* in 1639 ; in *-as*, *Thomas*, &c., cf. Cary Verney's *tomos* in 1642 ; *-an*, *musician*, &c., cf. *musition*, *Italionated* in Euphues ; *-ac* as in *stomach*, cf. Gabr. Harvey's *stummock*.

Present-day usage agrees with the early spellings in having [*i*] for unstressed *-a-* :—

-ange, *messenger* (M.E. *messager*), cf. fifteenth-century form *messynger* ; -ac, in *obstacle*, *character* = [ɔbztikl, kæriktə], cf. *obsticle*, Verney Mem. 1647, and *carecter*, Wentw. Pprs. ; -age in *cottage*, *courage*, *marriage*, *advantage*, *message*, &c. = [kotidž, kæridž, mæridž, ədvāntidž], cf. Lever's *cotingers* which implies **cotige*, Lady Sussex's *corige*, Cranmer's and Roper's *marriges*, &c., and Mrs. Sherard's *advantig*. The pronunciation [aizik] still survives, indeed it is my own, but probably [aizək] (from the spelling) is now more usual. Note Baker's *Izic* for *Isaac*. Many speakers, including present writer, pronounce [dɔŋkistə], with which compare *Donkister* in Verney Mem. 1665. I also say [æmbæsidə], cf. Cavendish's *ambassiter*, though many now pronounce [æmbæsədə]. As regards -ate, we say [praivit tʃɔkəlit], &c., cf. *pryvit chockolet* in Wentw. Pprs.

Present-day usage favours [ə] for old *-a-*, in the following words and their likes, where earlier spellings have *i* :—

as, in unstressed positions = [əz], but cf. *es* in the fifteenth and sixteenth centuries ; -an = [ən] in *company*, *-land*, *-man*, but cf. Machyn's *company*, Lady Sussex's *compiny*, and *inglende*, and Lady Rochester's *Bridgemen*, where we have [kampəni, inglənd, bridžmən].

-as in *purchase*, *Thomas* = [pātʃəs, toməs] with which compare Gabr. Harvey's *purchise*, and Lady Sussex's *tomis*. I remember hearing [pātʃis] in my boyhood from excellent speakers who preserved the habits of an earlier generation.

-ac as in *stomach* = [stamək], but cf. Anne Lee's *stomichers* in Verney Mem., and Baker's spelling *stomick*. I have heard the latter word so pronounced by very old speakers whose speech was merely old-fashioned though it contained no vulgarisms. At the present time [stamik] survives chiefly in lower-class speech. In *almanac* we have 'restored' [æk] in final syllable. I have heard [ɔlminik], cf. form in Cely Pprs.

-ant :—we now say [infənt] with which cf. C. Stewkley's *infints* in Verney Mem. ; -ark in *Southwark*, now = [saðək], but cf. Baker's *Southwick*, probably = [saðik].

The spellings -*er* for -*ar* probably show no more than that -*er* and -*ar* were levelled under one form [ə(r)].

The only example where [e] is suggested for *a* where we now pronounce [ɪ] is *passongers* (earlier *passager*) in Cely Papers.

Initial *a*- followed by the strongest stress, which is now always [ə], as in *annoyed, anoint*, &c., was apparently sometimes weakened to [ɛ] or [ɪ] (?) in the fifteenth and sixteenth centuries. Cf. *enoyd, enointed*, &c., p. 275, below.

o *in Unstressed Syllables.*

The early spellings indicate (1) that *o* when unstressed was unrounded, and (2) that in a large number of words, chiefly, though not exclusively, before -*n*, and -*t* in the same syllable, this unrounded vowel was fronted. The simple unrounding is expressed in the fifteenth-century spellings— *dysabey, sa* (= 'so'), *abedyenses, Byshap*, &c., and in the sixteenth century *men a warre, apinions, tenne a clocke*, &c., &c. This vowel, which was either [a] or [ə], has survived at the present time when we still say [əklɔk, mæn ə wɔ, dɪsəbeɪ, bɪʃəp], though a rounded vowel is generally pronounced in *obey*, and often in *opinion* and *obedience*.

More interesting, and remarkable, are the fairly numerous forms of the fifteenth to the eighteenth century, in which a front vowel is clearly intended, although we now pronounce [ə] in Received Standard.

Taking first the words in which -*on* occurs finally, we find a considerable number of spellings of the fifteenth, sixteenth, seventeenth, and eighteenth centuries which point unmistakably to a front vowel, generally written -*yn, -in*, but also occasionally -*en*. Of this class the only ones which retain the old pronunciation in Received Standard at the present time are *pigeon, widgeon*, and even in these the usual [ən] is probably now more common. Several other words, however, retain [ɪn] in vulgar speech, e. g. *wagon, ribbon, cushion*, &c., though the schools are fast eliminating these old forms from the language altogether. As a boy I knew several old people whose English was the Received Standard of the beginning of last century, who pronounced [ɪn] in *luncheon, puncheon, cushion, surgeon, dungeon*, to my clear recollection, and possibly in other words also which I never heard from them, or which I have now forgotten. I remember noticing at the time the difference between these old people and myself in respect of the words just mentioned. I notice that Baker gives *inin* as the pronunciation of *onion*. Whether this was not a vulgarism already in his day it is impossible to say, but it apparently represents a pronunciation [aɪnɪn] which I know is used at the present moment by at least one man, a labourer, in Oxfordshire. At an earlier period of my life I remember hearing [rɪbɪnz, pădɪn, pădɪŋ] from domestics. Passing to words of other classes, I am inclined to believe that I have heard [prɔvɪst] comparatively recently, but I am unable to indicate the position of the speaker.

Faggot is still pronounced [fægɪt] by some vulgar speakers (cf. Lady Hobart's *fagets*, 1663), and *carrots* is [kærɪts] in the same circles.

Unstressed -*o*- in the middle of words is now either [ə] or [ŏ], e. g. *accommodate*, &c., but cf. Lady Sussex's *acomidasyon* and *sorifull*. In the last word 'sorry' may have influenced the form, now [sɔrouful].

Unrounding of Unstressed u and ou = ū.

The unrounding of this vowel perhaps took place earlier in weak than in stressed syllables. It can hardly be doubted that in such spellings as *apon, sapose, anethe,* a vowel without lip-rounding is indicated. Unstressed *o* and *u* were levelled under a single vowel, which ultimately became [ə]. So far as I know, there is no evidence to show that *u* in unstressed syllables was fronted after being unrounded. The spellings *faver, semer* (Seymour), &c., of the fifteenth and sixteenth centuries merely indicate that *ᴸour* together with *ᴸer* had become [ə(r)].

Unrounding of French u = [ÿ] in Unstressed Syllables.

This process is a simple one, and its results are repeatedly traceable in the collection of spellings given below from documents of the fifteenth, sixteenth, seventeenth, and eighteenth centuries. On the forms in -*ir* (*feutir* 'future', &c.) and in -*in* (*fortin* 'fortune'), see remarks below, pp. 277–8, at the end of the lists.

The present-day types [fɔtʃən, ventʃə, vælju, repjuteiʃn], &c., which have taken the place of the old forms [fɔtɪn, ventə, væli, repitēʃn], &c., demand a few words. It is possible to explain all these new forms as due to the influence of the spelling, but I am inclined to agree with Jespersen that this cannot be the explanation in all cases. I have already propounded an explanation of the double forms (Short Hist. of English, § 265, and in Mod. Lang. Teaching, June 1915) which still appears to me to be sound. It is briefly this. The only normal forms developed when there was no stress on the -*u*, are those in *i*, or its subsequent developments [ər] and sometimes [ən], by the side of [ɪn]. Forms such as [fɔtʃən, ventʃə, vælju], &c., are due to a different type of accentuation, in which *u* was not, as a matter of fact, unstressed at all, but fully stressed— *fortúne, valú, aventúre,* under which circumstances French *u* became *iu* [jŭ] in Early Modern English, as in *duke, virtue* (from *vertúe*), &c., &c. This type coexisted with the other, possibly into the early sixteenth century. At any rate its descendants, so far as the vowel is concerned, survived, and, after *fortune* had already become *fortin, fortúne* survived in the form *fortiune,* although by the beginning of the sixteenth century, if not earlier, this type, too, had very likely been assimilated to the commoner (English) mode of accentuation, so that it was pronounced *fórtiune.* The combination -*ti* became [tʃ] (cf. p. 293, below); hence we got [fórtjŭn, fórtʃŭn, fórtʃən]. This theory, which is based on known facts, explains the present-day pronunciation of all the words of this class. The adoption of this type wholesale in Received Standard may well have been encouraged by the fact that it seemed to agree better with the traditional spelling. In some words analogy helped, e. g. *reputation* on the pattern of *repúte.*

While it so happens that I have found a fair number of spellings which show the unrounding of French *u*, it stands to reason that in the vast majority of cases the traditional spelling is preserved. This has no value for our purpose, since many who pronounced '*fortin*' from habit and training continued to write *fortune,* &c., and while we may be certain as to which type is intended when the former spelling is used, we cannot tell whether the latter really implies that the writer pronounced the word with the accent on the final syllable, and therefore also pronounced the vowel in that syllable as [jū] or not.

There are, however, among the forms collected in the lists a few whose spelling, while departing from the tradition, seems to imply a type of pronunciation derived from the accentuation of the final syllable. Such are Queen Elizabeth's *fortiune*, Lady Verney's *pictuer*, Mrs. Eure's *cretuers*, and Mrs. Sherard's *fortewen*. I regard these spellings as definitely expressing [jū] in the final syllable, or at least the type of pronunciation derived from this. It is probable that Queen Elizabeth, and still more so that the Verney ladies, already pronounced [ſo(r)tʃən, pɪktʃə(r)z, krīt ʃə(r)z], that is to say that they used the same type, and pronounced it in the same way, as we do now.

On the other hand, if any importance is to be attached to the statements of the grammarians, it seems certain that during the seventeenth and eighteenth centuries [pɪktə, krītə], &c., were chiefly in vogue. It is enough, however, if we can establish the coexistence of the other type in the sixteenth and seventeenth centuries, as this would go far to prove that our modern pronunciation is not wholly new and inspired by the spelling, but rather that it is the survival, now in universal use, of a type which has always existed alongside of that which has now been discarded.

The forms *volupteous*, Wilson and Cavendish; *verteous, vertious*, Roper and Lady Wentworth; *sumptious*, &c., Cavendish, may owe their *e* or *i* to confusion of the suffixes *-uous, -ious*, and *-eous*. That can neither be definitely proved nor disproved. It is quite certain, however, that *vertious* is a perfectly normal development—*vertúe* becomes [vāt ʃu], *vértuous* becomes [vertɪəs].

Lady Wentworth's *yousyal* 'usual' [jūzɪəl] seems an excellent example of the unrounding process.

The process also affects French unstressed *u* when final, and this is well illustrated by Machyn's *newys* 'nephews', and by Lady Sussex's *valy* 'value' (Vb.), and Lady Wentworth's *vallyed*. It is wonderful what education has done for us nowadays; *nevy* 'nephew' hardly survives outside the pages of comic writers, and *vally*, I suppose, is now never heard, and has ceased even to be a traditional vulgarism.

The Diphthongs.

ai, or **ei** (= *ai*). When this diphthong stood before *l*, *n*, as in *travail*, *battail, counseil, certain, villain*, &c., it was first reduced to [*i*], giving *-il*, *-in*, and these combinations either remain or are further weakened to syllabic [l, n] or to [əl, ən] respectively. Thus we say either [kaunsl] or [kaunsɪl] and either [sātn] or [sātɪn]. On the other hand the early spelling *battle* has left no choice in pronunciation even to the most fastidious.' We have differentiated *travail* at the present time in spelling, pronunciation, and meaning, *travel* and *travail* being now felt as quite independent. The pronunciation of *travail* as [træveɪl], while partly due to the spelling, may also be accounted for by assuming that it represents the form which would naturally occur in the verb when this was followed by an inflexional syllable, with the accent on the second syllable—*traváille* (N.). The form so accentuated would survive the weakening undergone by *trávaille*. Later on the accent was shifted back to the first syllable without further altering the now unstressed vowel.

Before other consonants the unstressed syllable is [*i*] in Received Standard, [ə] in other forms, cf. [pælis̄, pæləs]̄.

oi. Not much comment is needed beyond pointing out that we have now 'restored' the diphthong *oi* in nearly all words except *chamois* leather, and the family name *Jarvis* (from *Jervoise*).

It is satisfactory to find *shammee gloves* in Sir Ralph Verney's letter of 1685.

We learn from Spenser's spelling how the name of the author of the *Steele Glasse* was pronounced by his contemporaries. The form *Gaskin* still survives as a name by the side of the more usual *Gascoigne*, pronounced [gæskoin].

Our present pronunciation of *turquoise* [tākwōz, tākwɔiz] is shown to be quite recent. The only possible lineal descendant of Milton's *turkis* would be [tʌkis̄].

The early forms of this word, as well as that of *tortoise*, show the two tendencies which are found in nearly all unstressed syllables in English— towards [*is̄*] and towards [əs]. The present-day usage favours [əs] in *porpoise* and *tortoise*, but we may note Gregory's *porpys*, and the two types *tortes* and *tortus* in the Verney Memoirs. We may regard [tōtoiz, pōpoiz] as mere schoolmaster's pronunciations. It is possible that *tortes, &c.*, should be placed in the list illustrating the unrounding of French *u*, as there is a M.E. *tortuce*, cf. Jespersen 9. 332. The form quoted from *Euphues* at any rate shows that the ending might equally well have been *-ois*. There may have been two forms, one in *-uce* and one in *-ois*. The early spellings might represent the reduction of either of these.

Note. This process is apparently identical with that assumed to have taken place in Primitive Aryan, whereby *ei*, *oi* appear as *i* in the 'Reduced Grade', cf. Gk. οιδ- and ιδ- corresponding to Gothic *wait*, *wit-* from **woid-*, **wid-*.

The Pronunciation of the Vowels in Unstressed Syllables.

Examples of Occasional Departures from Traditional Spelling.

FLEXIONAL SYLLABLES.

15th Century.

-ed (Pret. and P. P.), &c.

St. Editha (**1420**). clepud P.P., 50; dwellyd, 46 (corrected from *dwelt*), scomfytyd, 67; y-cronyd, 60.

Archbp. Chichele (**1418**). assentyd, Ellis i. 1. 5.

Card. Beaufort (*c.* 1420). belovid, Ellis, Letter, i. 1. 8.

7th Lord Lovel's Will (**1455**). beeldid 'built', Linc. Dioc. Docs., pp. 76. 37, 77. 23.

Bp. Pecok. feelid, schewid, strengthid, hurtid, 1. 110.

Sir T. Cumberworth's Will (Lincs. 1451). L. D. D., wrechid, 45. 6; accordid, 46. 4; offendid, 46. 13.

Sir J. Fortescue. keepid, callid, 109, tredit 'treated', 109.

Marg. Paston. gid*i*t, ii. 241; pardonyd P. P., i. 115; -*yd*, the usual form of this suffix.

Gregory's Chronicle. i-callyde, 61, i-halowyde, 65.

Capgrave (Chronicle). punch*i*d, 291.

Rewle of Sustris Menouresses (c. 1450). bilouid, 81. 1, encresid, 81. 7, blessid, 81. 12, &c., &c.

Bury Wills, 1480. blessid, fotyd, 23, steryd, 15, &c., &c.

Cely Papers (Essex, 1475–88). -*yd* by far commoner than -*ed*, e. g. depertyd, 31; blessyd, 33; whelbelovyd, 34; mendyt, 35; alectyd, 162; derectyd, 274.

-red.

Bokenam. hundryd, 980.

16th Century.

Admiral Sir Edw. Howard (1513). steryd, Ellis i. 1. 214.

Dr. Knight (Bp. of Bath and Wells), 1512, to Wolsey. -*id*, -*yd* more frequent than -*ed*.

Sir Thos. Elyot (Gouernour). causid P. P. 2. 51 (generally -*ed*).

Sir Rauf Verney's Will (1525). aduis*i*d, bequeth*i*d.

Anne Boleyn (1528). preservyd, Ellis i. 1. 306.

R. Pace to Wolsey (Ellis 3. 1; 16 Hen. VIII). contentidde, 195.

Berners' Froissart (1523–5). (Generally -*ed*), also -*id*, -*yd*.

Cavendish (Life of Wolsey). providyd, commandyd, &c. (also -*ed*).

Latimer (Sermons). Generally -*ed*.

Thos. Lever's Sermons (1550). Nearly always -*ed*.

Gabriel Harvey (Letter Book, 1573–80). offendid, 13, persuad*i*d, 13, reiectid 'rejected', 14, &c., &c.

Q. Elizabeth (Letters; Transl.). Generally -*id*; -*ed* rarer; preventid, acquaintid, L. 3.

Sir Thos. Smith (Letters ; De Republ. Angl.). -*id*, -*yd* frequent, but -*ed* more usual.

Euphues. Very conventional in spelling, unstressed syllable always -*ed*.

Ascham. Generally -*ed*, auoyded, &c., sometimes syllable dropped— mar*d*e.

Puttenham. -*ed*, count*e*d, &c.

17th Century.

Coote, English Schoolmaster, 1627. 'Take heed that you put not (*id*) for (*ed*) as *unitid* for *united* which is Scottish ', p. 27.

FLEXIONAL SYLLABLES.

M.E. -eþ = -ith.   *15th Century.*

1420 *Palladius.* wexith, 51. 193 (Pl.).

1425–30 *Paston Letters.* namyth, i. 19; afferm*i*th, semyth, ibid. (all fr. Letter of Wm. P., judge).

1443 *Coventry Leet Book.* holdithe, 47, streechith, 50, holdyth, 50, &c., &c.

1443 *Bokenam.* always *-yth.*
1447–50 *Shillingford's Letters.* menyth, p. 12.
1447 *Bp. Pecok's Repressor.* him likith, 1. 113.
　　Marg. Paston. sendyth, faryth, &c.
1450 *R. of Sustris Menouresses.* þey etith, 111. 17; redith, 116. 17
　　and 20; singiþ, 110. 9.
1455 *Will of 7th Lord Lovel.* folowith, Linc. Dioc. Docs. 72–4.
147– *Sir J. Fortescue.* makyth, 109; praisith, 110.
1470, &c. *Cely Papers.* camyth, 146.
1480 *Bury Wills.* foluith, 16, longith, 16, stretchith (Pl.), 20.
1494 *Cr. of Dk. of York Knt. of Bath.* Letters and Papers, endentith,
　　1. 388, purposith. justithe, 389, gevyth (Pl.), 398.
1496 *Jul. Berners, Treatyse of Fysshynge.* folowyth, makyth.

16th Century.

1513 *Sir R. Wingfield to Hen. VIII.* dwellith, Ellis, Letters, ii. 1.
　　167, holdith, ibid.
1525 *R. Pace to Wolsey.* makyth, Ellis, Letters iii. 1. 196.
1533 *Sir J. Digby's Will* (Leic.). apperith, Linc. Dioc. Docs. 142. 34.
1560 *Cavendish, L. of Wolsey.* extendyth, 14, tornyth, assuryth, 15,
　　&c., &c.
1573–80 *Letter Bk. of Gabriel Harvey.* askith, 16.
　　Q. Elizabeth (*Letters to J. VI*). bestoith; burnith, Transl. 13.

-es. ### 15th Century.

c. 1420 *Siege of Rouen.* clerkys.
1420 *St. Editha.* monnys, 8; goddis (Possess.), 1056; thingus, 7;
　　myჳtus (Pl.), 2.
1443 *Cov. Leet.* mannys, 51, croftys, 47, fellys, 49.
1450 *Rew. Sustr. Men.* massis, 110. 16; versis, 111. 7.
1455 *Lord Lovel's Will.* chargis, Linc. Dioc. Docs. 77. 31.
147– *Cely Papers.* *-ys* far outnumbers other forms.

16th Century.

1512 *Dr. Knight* (Chaplain to Hen. VIII). fortressis, Ellis ii. 1. 193.
　　16 Hen. VIII, *R. Pace to Wolsey.* Hostagis, Ellis iii. 1. 195;
　　causis, ibid. 196.
1530 *Sir Thos. More* (Letter). promessis, Ellis i. 1. 209.
1530 *Sir T. Elyot's Gouernour.* princis, 1. 44; horsis, 1. 63; sicke-
　　nessis, 1. 169; placis, 1. 45, &c., &c.
1532 *Cranmer.* bargis, Ellis i. 2. 36.
1533 *Leic. Will.* hallowys, Linc. Dioc. Docs. 161. 10.
1560 *Cavendish, L. of Wolsey.* horsis, -ys, 7; crossis, 35.
　　Q. Elizabeth. scusis, Letters, 109; practisis, ibid. 60.

17th Century.

1629 *Mrs. Wiseman.* necis (Pl.), Verney Papers 144.
1642 *Mrs. Eure* in Verney Mem. ii. justisis, p. 86 (1642); taxis 91;
　　Mrs. Isham, ibid., purssis; Pen. Verney, expensis, 354 (1644).

18th Century.

1705-11 Lady Wentworth. Jarsis, St. Jamsis, 47 (Possess.) ; glassis,
111 ; oringis (Pl.), 107 ; freezis, 111.

-est in Unstressed Syllables.

= 2nd Pers. Pres. of Vbs. and Superl. Suffix, &c.

-est.   15th Century.

Bokenam (1443). clepyst (Vb.), Pref. Marg. 281.
Bp. Pecok (1449). studiedist, enhauncidist.
Northants Will (1450). In Linc. Dioc. Docs., grettist.
Gregory's Chron. (1450–70). eldystè, 101.
Cr. of Dk. of York a Knt. of Garter (Letters and Papers ii), 1490,
   fairyst (Superl.), p. 389.
Will of Richard Welby (Lincs., 1465), L. D. D. eldist, 123. 2.

16th Century.

Anne Boleyn (1528). humblyst, Ellis i. 1. 305.
Lord Berners' Froissart (1529). wekyst, 1. 161.
Sir T. Elyot's Gouernour (1533). kepist, 2. 76 ; askidist, 2. 76 ;
   haruist, 2. 256.
Gabriel Harvey (*Letter Bk.*, 1578–80). dearist, 13 ; deadist, 12 ;
   surist, 14 ; hardist, 14 ; haruist, 14 ; honist, 14, &c., &c.
Q. Elizabeth (*Letters* and Transl.). expertist, L. 29 ; largist, 50 ;
   fullist, Transl. 4 ; hottist, Transl. 97.

17th Century.

Anne Poyntz, Alleyne Pprs. honyst, 31 (1605).
Verney Memoirs, vol. ii. *eldist*, Marg. V.'s Will, 18 (1639) ; *gretist*,
   Cary V., 71 (1642) ; *sadist*. ibid. ; *greatist*, 121, Lady Sussex ; also
   intrust 'interest', M. V.'s Will, p. 18.
Mrs. Basire. greatist, 140 (1658).

18th Century.

Wentworth Papers (1705–39). dearist, passim ; modist 'modest',
   113.

-er.   15th Century.

Bokenam. aftyr, Pr. 54, &c. ; phylosophyr, Pr. 54 ; mynystyr, Marg.
   978 ; lengur, Ann. 438 ; wondurful, Ann. 641.
Marg. Paston. fadr, i. 544 ; massangr, ii. 390 ; remembr, ii. 419.
Bury Wills. ovyr, 15 ; fadir, modir, 29 ; powdyr, 15 ; anothir, 17 ;
   aftir, 17 ; bettyr, 20 ; tymbyr, 20, &c., &c. ; also preyours 'prayers',
   21 (1463) ; soupar 'supper', 21.
Gregory's Chron. ovyr.
Fortescue. remembr, 123, 124 ; vndr, 135 ; but also aftir, undir,
   passim.

Caxton (Jason).   murdre, 12. 35, 36; watre, 78. 5; vndre, 96. 21; writars, 3. 22; helpars, 13. 31.

Cely Papers.   bettyr, 6; nwmbyr, 33; ovyr, 6; dowttyr, 105; remembyr, 28; lettyrs, 33; mannor 'manner', 69; annsor, 78; sumor, 9; octobor, 21; dynar, 76; manar, 17; wryngar, 7; finar, 30; answare, 8; brocur, 24.

16th Century.

Q. Elizabeth.   sistar, Ellis i. 2. 163–4 (1549); bettar, Letters to James VI, 13; murdar, ibid. 19.

17th Century.

In middle of word:—misirable, Lady Sussex, Verney Mem. ii. 88.

-en and -en + Cons.   *15th Century.*

St. Editha.   y-writon P. P., 367; lokedone, 285, throngedone, 461 mournedone, 461, burydone, 462; prayden, 287, putten, 1880, deden, 1888, &c.

Bokenam.   oftyn, Pr. 205; Inf. in -yn.

Marg. Paston.   eronds, i. 201; Infinitives:—askyn, i. 49; heryn, i. 67; getyn, i. 68; tellyn, i. 68; sellyn, i. 69; Pres. Pl.:—owyn, i. 68; Pret. Pl.:—ze badeyn, i. 69; zedyn, i. 70 (z = z); haddyn, i. 110.

Bury Wills.   gravyn, 15; euyn, 19 (Adv.); wretyn, 19; opynly, 18; erthin, 22.   (Also *-en* forms.)

Shillingford.   aunsion, 10.

Pecok.   thousind, 1. 215.

Rewle Sustr. Men.   opunli, 100. 22; opynli, 110. 30; songoun P. P., 105. 7.

Sir T. Cumberworth's Will (Lincs., 1451), L. D. D.   opyn, 45. 8; kechyn, 49. 12, 24.

Fortescue.   writun, 130, gotun, 137.

Cely Papers.   wryttyn P. P., 35; gevyn, 26; hosyn (N.), 28; lynyn (N.), 200; happon, 30; hofton 'often', 81.

Cr. Duke of York.   evyn, 389, brokyn (P. P.), 395.

-ent.   *Cely Papers*.   carpyntter, 180.

16th Century.

Lord Admiral Sir Edw. Howard to Hen. VIII (1513).   burdon, Ellis ii. 1. 216.

State of Ireland (St. Pprs., Hen. VIII. 1 (1515)).   *waypyn* 'weapon', 18.

Lord Berners' Froissart.   havyn, 1. 33; opyn, passim.

Inventory of J. Asserley (Lincs., 1527), L. D. D.   wholyn 'woollen', 135. 18; kytchyn, 135. 30.

Sir Thos. More's Letters.   Ellis i. 2; hevyn, 52.

Thos. Lever's Sermons.   chikynnes, 56.

T

Cavendish, L. of Wolsey. opyn, 15; tokyn, 19; hosyn, 88; rysyn, 116; Latten 'Latin', 71.
Gabr. Harvey (Letters). chickins, 31; tokins, 150.
Q. Elizabeth. heauin 'heaven', Transl. 61.

17th Century.[1]

Cary Verney. takin (P. P.), V. Mem. ii. 70 (1642).
Mrs. Isham. childrin, V. Mem. ii. 220 (1645); suddnly, ibid. 200 (1644).
Mrs. Eure. wimin (Pl.), V. Mem. ii. 86 (1642).
-em. *Sir R. Verney.* solome, V. Mem. ii. 67 (1642).

18th Century.

Lady Strafford. kitching, Wentw. Pprs. 540.

19th Century.

John Kemble said sentimint, innocint, conshince according to Leigh Hunt, *Autobiogr.* i, p. 180.

-el. ### 15th Century.

Bokenam. appyltre, Ann. 441; lytyl, Pr. 55, &c.
Marg. Paston. tempill, i. 81; unkyll, i. 202.
Bury Wills. litil, 20; bokyll, 16; nobil, 17; candylstikke, 19; pepill, 19; sympil, 21; stepyll, 19; ladyll, 23; tharchangill, 62.
Rewle Sustr. Men. dobel, 107. 25, dubbil, 107. 12, double, 107. 18.
Will of Sir T. Cumberworth (Lincs., 1451) L. D. D. stabul, 50. 4.
Will of Richard Moulton (Lincs., 1465) L. D. D. stabull, 124. 37.
Caxton (Jason). sadyl, 7. 34; sadle (Inf.), 11. 29; litil, 13. 22, &c.; nobole, 12. 1, noble, 12. 4, &c.
Cely Papers. myddyll, 34; saddyl, 34; stapyll, 5; craddyll, 157; medell, 11; stapell, 6; fardel, 71; stapal, 4; stapul, 77.

16th Century.

Skelton's Magnyfycence. startyl, sparkyl, 741; dyvyls, 944; devyll, 941.
Inventory of J. Asserley (Lincs., 1527). tabyl, L. D. D. 135. 28.
Sir Thos. More (Letters, Ellis i. 1). Sir John Russll, 205.
Machyn. postyll 'apostle'; castyl 'castle', 11.
Sir Thos. Smith (1583). evangill, Rep. 123.

17th Century.

Doll Leake. cruilty, V. Mem. ii. 213 (1644).

-e in Unstressed Syllables.
15th Century.

-less. 1465. *Marg. Paston.* harmlys, ii. 226.
-mest. 1447-50. *Shillingford.* utmyst.

---

[1] For discussion of *-en, -on* reduced to syllabic *-n*, see Appendix III, p. 401, &c.

16th Century.

-ness. *Q. Elizabeth.* kindn*i*s, Letters 40; wekenis, L. 41; happin*i*s, L. 50, &c., &c.; darken*i*s, Transl. 4; businis, Transl. 126.

17th Century.

-ess. *Shakespeare,* First Fol. mistr*i*s, passim.
Habington's Castara (1630–40). mistris, 51, &c.
-ness. *Doll Leake.* bisnis, Verney Mem. iv. 114 (1665).

18th Century.

-ester. 1710. *Wentworth Papers.* Ld. Roch*i*ster, p. 118.
-ess. 1701. *Jones.* mistri*s*s, p. 62. *Lady Wentworth.* dutchiss, W. Pprs. 45.

15th Century.

-lege (*-leche*) and original -lege.
Marg. Paston. knowlych, ii. 185.
Bury Wills. collage, 66 (1480).
Shillingford. knowliche, 67.
-et. *Cely Papers.* markyt, 17.

-et.   *16th Century.*
Lord Berners' Froissart. helmyttes, i. 362.
Thos. Lever's Sermons. couitous, 84.
Euphues. dyot 'diet', 276.
Gabr. Harvey. interprit, Letters 15.
-lege. *Gabr. Harvey* (*Letters*). collidg, 54.

-ledge (earlier *-leche*).   *17th Century.*
Betty Verney. acknowliges, Verney Mem. iv. 21 (1661).
-et. *Lady Lambton.* interpritt, Basire Corresp. 80 (1649).

18th Century.

-et. *Wentworth Papers.* bullits, 81; *blanckitt,* 62.
Initial e*t*. as*t*ate 'estate', Bokenam, Pr. Marg. 877; Fortescue, 143; Gregory, 132; Elyot, passim; Berners, passim; *alectyd,* Cely Pprs. 162; *ascuse* 'excuse', Cely Pprs. 9; *ascapyn* 'escape', Bokenam, Marg. 877; *ascaped,* Lord Berners, i. 72; *aronyous* 'erroneous', Machyn, 81.

-a+consonants.   *15th Century.*

-ac. Will. Paston, Jun. *stomechere,* Paston Letters, iii. 237 (1478); *Cely Papers.* almyneke, 156.
as *Cely Papers.* os 'as', i. 30; *Cr. Duke of York.* ys = as—for as moche *ys* (= 'as') at so noble feast, &c., 389.

-ave. John Russe. Seynt *Oleffes*, Paston Letters, ii. 112 (1462).
-age (-ange). *Siege of Rouen, mesyngers,* 31. *Gregory, messyngere,* 124; *longege* 'language', 214.
    Cely Papers. passongers, 153.
    State of Ireland (St. Pprs. Henry VIII, iii). *messyngers,* 14.
    Will of R. Astbroke (Bucks., 1534). *messynger* (Pers. N.), L. D. D.
    169. 21.
ap². *Capgrave's Chron. Uphowel,* 96 (= Ap-).
-a-. *Bury Wills. testement,* 15. 43 (1463).

-ar-.   *16th Century.*

    Archbp. Cranmer (Letters). particulerly, Ellis i. 2. 172 (1549).
    Lyly, Euphues. perticulers, 234.
    Machyn. secretery, 10.
    Spenser, Pres. State of Ireland. schollers, 626. 2.
-a-. *Cavendish, L. of Wolsey. ambassiter,* 7.
-aster. *Machyn. Lancoster,* 244.
-mas. *Machyn. Cryustynmus.* 122.
-an-. *Machyn. compeny,* 303.
    Euphues. musition, 213, *Italionated,* 314.
-ac. *Gabr. Harvey's Letters. stummock.* 14.
as, -as. *es = as,* Sir Thos. More's Letters, Ellis ii. 1 ; *such entreprises es shold if they mought,* &c., 289.
    Gabr. Harvey's Letters. purchisse Vb., 67.

                  17th Century.
-ant. *infints.* C. Stewkley, V. Mem. iii. 433 (1656).
-man. *Bridgemen.* Lady Rochester, V. Mem. iii. 466 (1660).
-an-. *compiny.* Lady Sussex, V. Mem. ii. 133 ; *inglende,* Lady Sussex,
    V. Mem. ii. 88 (1642).
-aster. *Donkister.* Verney Mem. iv. 121 ; Lady Elmes (1665).
-ac-. *stomichers,* Anne Lee, V. Mem. ii. 235 (1646); *obsticle,* Sir R.
    Verney, Mem. ii. 357 (1647); *carictor,* C. Stewkley, Mem. iv. 226.
-mas. *crismus,* Lady Sussex, Verney Pprs. 205 (1639); *mickelmust,*
    M. Falkiner, V. Mem. ii. 52 (1642); Doll Leake, *crismus,* V. Mem.
    iii. 287 (1656).
-as-. Sir *tomis* Chike, Lady Sussex, Verney Mem. ii. 153 (1643);
    Sir *tomos,* Cary Verney, V. Mem. ii. 68 (1642).
-a-. contrydicting, ibid.

                  18th Century.
-ac-. *stomick, Izic =* Isaac, Baker, Rules for True Spelling (1724);
    carecter, Wentw. Pprs. 50.
-ark. *Southwick* for Southwark, Baker (1724).
-ave. (St.) *Olive = St. Olave,* Jones (1701), p. 59.
-able. 'Sounded abusively', *-ible* in *Constable, Dunstable,* Jones, p. 59.
-ate. *pryvit,* Lady Wentworth, Wentw. Pprs. 94 (1709), *chockolet,* Lady
    Strafford, Wentw. Pprs. 213 (1711).
-dale. *Dugdel's Baronage,* Peter Wentworth, Wentw. Pprs. 88 (1709).

-age. *16th Century.*

Archbp. Cranmer, Letters. marieges, Ellis i. 2. 36 (1533).
Roper's L. of More (1556). marriges, xliv. 10.
Thos. Lever's Sermons. cotingers, 82.
John Alleyne. Alleyne Pprs., marrige, 15, incurrich 'encourage', 16
(159–?); Ph. Henslow in Alleyne Memoirs, *spenege* spinach, 28
(c. 1593).

17th Century.

Vicaridge, Agreement for purchase of the Manor of Dulwich, Alleyne
Memoirs, 191 (1605).
corige 'courage', Lady Sussex, ii. 38 (1641), *disadfantige, mesege;*
advantig, Mrs. Sherard, iii. 317 (1657) (all in Verney Memoirs);
vicaridge, Dr. Basire, 303 (1673).
Saucidg and *cabbidg* are mentioned by Cooper.
Milton writes *passinger* in Trin. Coll. MS. Comus 39.

Initial a͛. *15th and 16th Centuries.*

Cely Papers, *enoyd* 'annoyed', 106; Elyot, enointed, 2. 235; Ascham,
emonges, Tox. 37.

o *in Unstressed Syllables.*

ᴸon. *15th Century.*

St. Editha. caren 'carrion', 4328.
Marg. Paston. sesyn 'season', v. 1. 201.
Gregory's Chron. Devynshyre, 216; -un-, Aryndelle, 101.
Cely Papers. questyans, 153; ressenabull, 74; rekenyng, 34;
resenably, 14.
-o͛. *Marg. Paston.* dysabey, i. 252; sa mých, ii. 308.
Cely Papers. abedyensses, 69.
-og. *Caxton.* genelagye, Jason, 336, 38.
o͛. *Short Engl. Chron.* (1465, Cam. Soc.). tawárd, 62.
ᴸost. *Marg. Paston.* provest, ii. 187 (perhaps survival of Early Engl.
form).
ᴸop. *Bokenam.* bysshape, Elev. Thous. Virg. 108, 110.

16th Century.

-on. *Dr. Knight* (Chaplain to Hen. VIII). reasyn 'reason' (1512),
Ellis ii. 1. 203.
Sir Thos. Elyot (1528). burgine Vb., 'bud', Gouern. 1. 30.
Rede me, &c. (1529). mutten 'mutton'.
Richard Layton to Lord Cromwell (1538). Martn Colege (= Merton),
Ellis ii. 2. 60.
Thos. Pery (1539). commyshin, Ellis ii. 2. 140.
Cavendish, L. of Wolsey. waggans, 88.
Bishop Latimer. dungen, Seven Serms. (1549), 119.
Lady Hungerford (1569). prysin, 255; passiane, ibid. 256.
Gabriel Harvey's Letter Bk. (1573–80). duggin 'dudgeon', 29;
to reckin, 16.
Edm. Spenser. scutchin, F. Q., Bk. iii. 7. 30.

John Alleyne, Alleyne Pprs. (159–?).   *posshene* 'portion', 16; *fashenges*, 'fashions', 16.
Sir Thos. Smith (1583).   recken, Republ. 76.
of. *Lord Berners' Froissart.*   men *a* warre, 1. 156.
Machyn's Diary.   justus *a* pesse, 122.
Gabr. Harvey's Letters.   seaven a clocke, 72; tenne a clocke, 129.
-ord.   *Inventory of J. Asserley* (Lincs., 1527) L. D. D.   Cobberdes, 136. 1.
o-.   *Bishop Latimer, Seven Sermons* (1549).   riatous, 51.
-ost.   *Elyot's Will.*   provest, 311.
o*ᴸ*.   *Machyn.*   apinions, 81.

17th Century.

-on.   *Chapman's All Fooles.*   fashin'd 'fashioned' (1605).
Verney Memoirs.
    parden, Mall V., ii. 381 (1647); surgin 'surgeon', Pen. V., iii. 201 (1657), ribins, Doll Leake, iv. 66 (1664); fashing, Mrs. Edm. V., iv. 71 (1664); prisiner, Sir R. V., ii. 122.   Lady Verney has the inverted spelling *reasons* for raisins, ii. 285 (1647).
o-.   sorifull, Lady Sussex, ii. 121.
-o*ᴸ*.   acomidasyon, Lady Sussex, ii. 153; and Mrs. Basire, *oppertunity*, 104 (1651), *abay* 'obey', ibid. 135 (1654); Sir *A*rlandoe Bridgmen, Lady Rochester, iii. 466 (1660).
*o*ot.   fagets, Lady Hobart, iv. 46 (1663); Pigit (Piggot), Pen. V., Lady Gardiner, iv. 327 (1685); Charr*e*t (?), Edm. V., iv. 397 (1687).

17th and early 18th Century.

Preposition *on* unstressed.
She sent a man a purpos, Lady B. Harley, 29 (1638); *a* (= on) Satterday, Later V. Letters, i, 48 (1696).
o purpos, Lady Wentworth Papers, 46 (1705); *abroad a Munday*, ibid. 41 (1705).

18th Century.

-on.   Jones, 1701.   'Sound of *e* written *io* in *carrion, clarion, contagion, cushion, fashion, lunchion, opinion*', p. 45.   *Truncheon = trunsheen*, p. 102.
    Peter Wentworth.   *beckinged* 'beckoned', W. Pprs. 108 (1710); Lady Wentworth, *Comten* 'Compton', W. Pprs. 98 (1709); Baker, 1724, *sturgin, dungin* 'dungeon', *punchin* 'puncheon', *flaggin* 'flagon', *cooshin, carrin* 'carrion', *inin* 'onion'.
-ot.   Jones.   chariot, p. 45; *somewhat* sounded *som'at* (= [samət]), Jones, p. 26.
-oard.   *cubberd*, Jones, 33.

Early Forms of Cushion.

It is doubtful how far the forms of this word which end in *-in* are to be regarded as weakenings from *-on-*.   Both endings may have been in use from an early period.
    Bury Wills (1463)—*kusshownes, cusshonys*, 23; Sir Thos. Elyot's Will—*cusshyns*, 311; Thos. Pery—*kwsching*, Letter, Ellis ii. 2. 50, 1539; Cavendish, Life of Wolsey—*cusshons*, 16, *cusshens*, 65; Knaresborough Wills—*qwhissinges*, 29 (30 Hen. VIII); Wm. Baker (1725)—*cooshin.*

French u *in Unstressed Syllables.*

15th Century.

-ur. to paster, St. Ed. 3767 (*c.* 1420); moist*e*r, Palladius (1420) 29,
773; aventer, Cely Papers 5, the venter, C. P. 6.

-ule. sedell, ' schedule ', (three times), E. of Oxford, Paston Letters i,
161 (1450).

-un. commyne, Shillingford Papers (1447–50); comynlaw, Shillingford
40; com*y*ned togeder, 12, comyners, comeners, Gregory's Chron.
64.

-ut. savecondyte, C. P. 45 (-condute, ibid. 163); condytte, Gregory
71 ('conduit'); byskitt, C. P. 182; myn*i*te 'note'. Statement
concerning Edm. de la Pole (1501), Letters and Papers i. 147.

-us. letuse, Bk. of Quint. 22.

-u*ʹ*. rep*e*tation, Marg. Paston, P. L. ii. 340; contymacy, Gregory.

-u-. arg*a*ment, Shillingford 10.

16th Century.

-un. comyne (Vb.) (1503), Negotiations of Ambassadors, Letters and
Papers i. 205, &c., &c.; comyngcasion, Wolsey to Hen. VIII, L.
and P. i. 446; mysseforten, Machyn's Diary 139 (*c.* 1550).

Also :—*fortiune,* Q. Elizabeth, Lttrs. to J. VI. 27.

-ur. unscript*e*rlye, Latimer's Sermons, Arber, 7. 48; jointer, E. of
Bath, Ellis, Letters ii. 2. 157; vent*e*rous, vent*o*rer, Machyn 67, 161;
jointer, Roper's L. of Sir T. More (1556), xliii. 18; venterous,
Euphues, Arber, 39; mann*e*ring (the ground), Wilson, Arte of Rhet.,
Oxford Ed. 53; tortering, Shakespeare (First Fol.), Titus Andron.;
John Alleyne, gointer 'jointure', Alleyne Pprs. 16 (1593?).

-uous. vert*e*ous, Roper's L. of More (1556), vi. 29; volupteous, Wilson
73; voluptious, Cavendish, L. of Wolsey 116; sumptiously, 3;
sumptious, ibid. 25; tortious, Spenser, F. Q., Bk. vii. 7. 14.

-u-. newys 'nephews', Machyn 302; mon*i*ment, Spenser, Globe Ed.,
F. Q., Bk. ii. 7. 5; cit. Elyot's Gouernour ii. 375, Wks., vol. v, p. 51.

17th Century.

-ur. *Verney Memoirs.* ventarous, Cary Verney, ii. 70 (1642); joint*e*r,
Mrs. Isham, ii. 74 (1642); venter (Noun), Mrs. I., ii. 203 (1643);
ventir, Lady Warwick, iii. 313 (1657); feutir, Mrs. Sherard, iii. 324
(1657); futer, Lady Hobart, iv. 66 (1664). Milton writes *venter*
(vb.), Trin. MS. Com. 228 (1637). Cooper says *picture* = *pick't her,*
and the pairs *stricture* and *stricter, ordure* and *order, gesture* and
jester are sounded alike.

Also :—picktuer, Lady V.'s Will, ii. 18 (1639); cretuers, Mrs. Eure, ii.
96; lesuer, Lady Sussex, ii. 31 (1641).

-une. misfortin, Cary V., ii. 70 (1642); fortine, Mrs. Isham, ii. 220
(1645); fortin, Pen. V., ii. 353 (1644); unfort*i*nate, Cary V., iii. 439
(1659); fourt*i*n, Lady Hobart, iv. 56 (1664); fort*i*ne, fort*i*ng,
Mrs. Isham, iv. 108 (1663).

Also :—fortewen, fortewn, Mrs. Sherard, iv. 16 (1661).

-u-. mirac*i*lous, Edm. V., iv. 233 (1677); contin*i*al, W. Roades
(Steward), iii. 234 (1655).

u*ʹ*. m*e*nishone, ii. 56, ' munition '.

-u. valy (Vb.), Lady Sussex, ii. 87 (1642), 'to value'; *neuie* 'nephew'
Mrs. Basire, 142 (1655); a *nagy* ' ague ', Mrs. Isham, Verney Mem.
i. 288 (1639). Cooper (1685) says *volley* and *value* are sounded
alike (= [væli]).

18th Century.

-u-.   *Lady Wentworth.* *vertious, vallyed,* Wentw. Pprs. 52 ; *yousyal,* 84, ' usual ', ibid. 84.

-une.   *Goldsmith,* ' She Stoops to Conquer ', Act II.   Tony Lumpkin : ' If I'm a man, let me have my *fortin.*'

-ure.   *Jones* (1701).   ' " *er* " written *-ure* when it may be sounded *-ur* better than *-er* ', p. 52, as in debent*ure,* acc*u*rate, sat*u*rate ; ' when it may be sounded *-er* ', advent*ure,* az*ure,* cens*ure,* conject*ure,* cinct*ure,* conj*ure,* cult*ure,* depart*ure,* fail*ure.*

Wentw. Pprs.   creetors, 475 (Capt. Powell) ; *torter,* 64, *picturs,* 63.

Fr. u = [y] is unrounded already in the fifteenth century in unstressed syllables, and written *i* or *e.*   The inverted spelling *profutez* ' profits ' in Lord Lovel's Will, 1455, L. D. D. 73. 21, shows that in unstressed syllables *u* was pronounced like *i.*   Before *-r* this short front vowel probably becomes [ə] pretty early in common speech, as is suggested by Machyn's vent*o*rer, and later by Cary Verney's vent*a*ros.

The seventeenth-century vent*i*r, feut*i*r are probably not indicative of a pronunciation with *i,* any more than is *-ir, -yr* for earlier *-er,* which is so common in the fifteenth century and later.   Before *-n* the front vowel was probably preserved, though there was doubtless a tendency in certain speakers to reduce *-in* to [ən] or simply to [n].   See remarks on pp. 264–5 on the fondness for the [in] types generally, down to the eighteenth century and beyond.

Back Vowels in Unstressed Syllables.

u^. *apon,* Shillingford 6 ; Fortescue 123 ; Gregory 107, 238, 259 ; Cely Pprs. 14, 47 (twice), 203 ; Machyn 12.

^un ; un^.   *Swythan* ' Swithun ', St. Editha 188 ; *anethe* ' hardly ' (O.E. *unēþes*), Bokenam, Marg. 971 ; *Aryndelle,* Gregory 101.

-mouth J. Paston Jun., *Yermeth,* Paston Letters ii, 100 (1462).

^our.   Gregory, *faverynge,* 134 ; Cely Pprs., *faverabull,* 137 ; Ascham, *unsauery,* Tox. 76 ; Machyn, *Semer,* 27 (= Seymour) ; Mall Verney, *faver,* V. Mem. ii. 381 (1647).

^ous.   Ph. Henslow, *greavesly,* Alleyne Memoirs 28, *c.* 1593; *disadvantages,* Lady B. Harley, 30 (1639); *tegis,* Mall Verney, V. Mems. ii, 381 (1647): Jones (1701) writes *contages.*

-aw, -ow.   Bokenam, *felas,* Agn. 377, 395 ; Cely Pprs., *feleschyppe,* 120, *felyschepe,* 5, *fellyschyp,* 6.

Shortening of Vowels in Final Unstressed Syllables.

-ite.   Shakespeare (First Fol.).   *Muscouits* (rhymes *witts*), L. Lbr's Lost ; Lady Wentworth, *infenitt.*

ile.   Cavendish, Life of Wolsey, *fertill,* 11 ; Shakesp. (First Fol.), *stirrill* ' sterile ', First Pt., Hen. IV, 4. 1.

-meal.   Dr. Denton, *oatmell* ' oatmeal ', Verney Mem. iii. 209 (1657) ; Wm. Baker, Rules for True Spelling, &c. (1723) also gives the pronunciation of this word as *otmell,* in this case apparently implying also a shortening of the vowel in the first syllable.

night.   Cary Stewkley, *senet,* Verney Mem. iii. 434 (1656); *fortnet,* Mrs. Basire 132 (1654); (Roger) L'Estrange his Appeal, *that day sennet* ' se'nnight ', 56 (1681).

-ū. Marg. Paston often writes *zu* 'you' in unstressed positions—e. g.
i. 67 ; otherwise generally *zow, yow*, &c. This may express the
shortened form in a weak position.

M.E. **ai, ei** *in Unstressed Syllables.*

15th Century.

ᴸein, ᴸain. *St. Editha.* vyleny, 2. 384.
   Shillingford (1447–50). certyn, 53.
   Marg. Paston. meynten, ii. 83.
-ainᴸ, einᴸ. *Shillingford.* synt Stevyn, 9 ; sent Paull, 11.
   Gregory's Chron. (1450). Syn Lénarde, 61 ; Syn Jóhn, 94 ; men-
   táyne, 86.
   Cely Papers. bargen, 40.
   Letters and Papers, ii. certen, 59 ; abstynence (?).
ᴸei. *Shillingford.* curtessy, 20.
   Cely Papers. Calis ' Calais ', 200.
ᴸail, ᴸeil. *St. Editha.* coúnselle, 3 ; consyler, 725; bátelle, 35 ;
   vítel.
   Shillingford. counselle, 18.
   Sir J. Fortescue (1470). véssells, 123, vítalles, 132 (also **vessáilles**,
   123).
   Capgrave's Chron. councelle, 171.
ᴸeir. *Gregory's Chron.* devyr, 152.
ᴸai. *Cely Papers.* Thursda, 12.

-ail. *16th Century.*
   Lord Berners' Froissart. báttel, 1. 121, batelles, 1. 19 ; counsell (N.),
      1. 34 ; véssell, 1. 36, ráscalle, 1. 50 ; trávell, 1. 222 ; trayvell (N.),
      1. 222, traveled (P. P.), 1. 222 ; appáreled, 1. 43 (also batáyle, 1.
      121) ; vitaylle, 1. 33 ; aparailed, 1. 30 ; counsaile (Vb. and N.),
      1. 28.
   Ascham. báttell, Tox. 76 (also battáyle, Tox. 73).
   Sir Thos. Smith, Rep. Angl. councels, 15 ; battell, 15, 63.
   Cavendish, L. of Wolsey. councel, 5 ; *travelled* ' worked ', 57 ; travel
      (present-day sense), 62.
-ain, -ein. *Lord Berners' Froissart.* certenly, 1. 194; capten, 1. 255.
   Thos. Lever's Sermons. bargens, p. 96; citizins, 101.
   Roper's Life of Sir T. More (1566). certyne, vi. 35; Ann Bullen,
      xx. 7.
   Ascham. máynteners.
   Sir Thos. Smith. villens, Rep. Angl. 130; forren, Rep. Angl. 59.
   Cavendish, Life of Wolsey. chappelens, 25 ; certyn, 90 (also chapeleyn,
      4).
   Q. Elizabeth. vilanous, Letters 53 ; Transl. 14.
-ais, -eis. *Lord Berners' Froissart.* curtesy, 1. 30 ; burgesses, 1. 205,
      &c., &c. ; unharnest, 1. 46.
   Sir Thos. Smith. Rep. Angl. 128, courtisie.
   Cavendish, Life of Wolsey. palice, 77 ; Calice (Place N.), 67.

-ai, -ei. *Gabriel Harvey's Letter Bk.* Mund*y* (day of week), 40; ther
'their', 23.

Q. Elizabeth. the 'they', usual form.

17th Century.

-ain, -ein. *Verney Memoirs*, vol. ii. sartinly, Lady Sussex, 82 (1642);
captin, Lady Sussex, 103; chapl*e*n, Lady Sussex, 152. Vol. iii.
villin, Pen. Denton, 228 (1655).

-ail. *Aubrey's Lives.* travills, ii. 15. (A letter from Isaac Walton
said to be in his handwriting.)

-air, -eir. Vol. ii. the 'they', Lady Sussex, 81 (1642); ther 'their',
Sir J. Leeke, 48 (1641).

-ai, -ei. Vol. ii. Frid*y*, Lady Sussex, 156 (1642); Mund*y*, Mall V.
380 (1647).

Summary.

The diphthongs *ai* and *ei*, already in M.E. probably, levelled under
[æi] or [ɛi] in stressed syllables, are simplified in unstressed syllables to
a simple front vowel, probably [i], written sometimes *e*, sometimes *i*, at
least as early as the first half of the fifteenth century.

Before *l* and *n* the spelling is also generally *e* or *i*, the latter becoming
increasingly more frequent in course of time. Certain speakers seem to
tend to [ə] expressed by *a*, cf. vit*a*lles (Sir J. Fortescue); rasc*a*lle (Lord
Berners); vil*a*nous (Q. Elizabeth). Present-day usage leans, on the
whole, to [ə] or syllabic *l* in [vitlz, bætl], &c., but keeps [i] before *n* [vilin,
kæptin], &c.

Finally, we find *a* = [ə] in Cely Papers—Thursd*a*—but more frequently [i], as at present—written *y* by Gabriel Harvey and the ladies of
the Verney family.

In the unstressed prefix *saint* = [sn] or [sən] we get apparently the
type corresponding to the Early Modern *an* in vil*a*n-ous [vilən-əs], the
old forms *syn* [sin], &c., only surviving in St. John, St. Clair (or Sinclair),
St. Leger as family names [sindžən], &c., where the stressing of the first
syllable is clearly more recent than the unstressed forms in which [sin]
arose.

Machin has *selenger*, and must have stressed the first syllable, since the
intrusive -*n*- (cf. mess*e*nger, &c.) is only found in unstressed syllables.

See p. 329 for weak forms of old *they, theym, theyr.*

M.E. oi *in Unstressed Syllables.*

15th Century.

-ois. *Gregory's Chron.* Camyse 'Camoys', 178; porpys 'porpoise',
141.

Bury Wills (1501). toorkes 'turquoise', 91.

-oir. *Will of Joan Raleghe* (Oxf., 1455). my maner of Ilvenden,
L. D. D. 68. 14.

Will of Lord Lovel (Oxf., 1455). manoirs, L. D. D. 74. 9; manourys,
ibid. 73. 1.

16th Century.

-ois. *Cavendish, L. of Wolsey.* turkkas ' turquoise ', **167.**
Thos. Wilson (1560). turcasse, 206.
Euphues. torteyse, 61.
-oin. *Machyn's Diary.* *Gaskyn,* 292 ; Spenser, Glose to Shep. Cal.,
Nov., ' Mr. George *Gaskin,* a wittie gentleman, and the very chefe
of our late rymers '.

17th Century.

-oin. *Verney Memoirs,* vol. ii. Borgin (Burgoyne), Cary V., 71 (1642).
-ois. Vol. ii. torteshell, Lady V., 315 (1648).
Vol. iii. tortus shell, Mrs. Spencer, 50 (1652).
Vol. iv. Shammee Gloves, Sir R. V., 327 (1685) ; Mrs. Aphra Behn—
Lucky Chance (1686), 2. 1, has *shammy* breeches.
Milton's Comus, Sabrina's Song. turkis.
Sir Thos. Browne, Vulgar Errors. porposes, bk. iii, ch. 26.
Marston's Eastward Ho. porpice.

Confusion of **·eous, ·ous ; -iour. -our, &c. ; ·ier, -er.**

Cely Papers. marvylyusly, 165.
Jul. Berners. laborous.
Sir T. Elyot. laborousely, 2. 275.
Latimer's Serm. rightuous, 181.
Ascham. barbariousnes, Tox. 28.
Shakespeare, First Fol. *ieallious,* Merry Wives, iv. 5.
Lady Hobart. serus ' serious ', Verney Mem. iv. 41 (1663) ; Sir
R. L'Estrange, *stupendious,* Dissenters Sayings, pt. 2. 56 (1682).
Wentworth Pprs. *covetious,* 102, *mischevyous,* 174.
Reg. for Council of the Nth. mysbehavors, Lttrs. and Pprs., i. 57
(1484).
Lord Berners' Froissart. behavour, 1. 69.
Sir T. Elyot. hauour ' good behaviour ', 2. 409.
Q. Elizabeth. behavor, Lttrs. to J. VI, 28.
We may note that Lady Wentworth's *mischevyous* [mistʃiviəs] is now one
of the worst possible vulgarisms, and *covetious* would run it pretty close.
Much has been written on the confusion of these suffixes, cf. Jespersen,
Mod. Engl. Gr. 9. 82, &c., and Müller, *Engl. Lautlehre nach James
Elphinston,* §§ 208–12.
Lord Berners' Froissart. *fronters,* 1. 72, 1. 125 ; *barrers,* 1. 129 ;
currers, 1. 137.

Loss of Vowel.

Initial weak syllable.
St. Editha—scomfytyd, 67 ; *Pecok—pistle* ; Cely Pprs.—*pwoyntment,*
71 ; Lord Berners—*poyntment,* 1. 215 ; *a great rayne and a clyps,* 1.
297 ; Latimer—*poticaries,* 86, leauen ' eleven ', 102 ; Ascham—
spence ' expenditure ' ; Machyn—*postyll* ' apostle ', *salt* ' assault ',
282 ; Q. Elizabeth—*scusis* ' excuses '.
Lady Hobárt. '*amel* ' enamel ', Verney Mem. iii. 25 (1650).
Peter Wentworth. Querry ' equerry ' (now generally [ekwəri]),
Wentw. Pprs. 409, 433, 443 (twice).

Loss of -i *before* -sh *followed by suffix.*
Bokenam—embelshyn 'embellish', Ann. 341 ; Capgrave's Chron.—*banchid* 'banished', 187, *punchid* 'punished', 29.

Loss of vowel (-i-) *in superl. suffix.*
Siege of Rouen—ryalste 'royalest', 27 ; Lord Berners—*the moost outragioust people*, i. 311 ; Q. Elizabeth—*carefulst*, Lttrs. 48, *thankfulst*, ibid. 66 ; Otway—*ungratefull'st*, Friendship in Love.

Loss of vowel immediately after chief stress, before -n.
Cely Papers. *reknyng*, 145.

Loss of -e-, &c., *before* -r + *vowel.*
Marg. Paston—*Margretys*, i. 236 ; Elyot—*robry*, Gou. i. 273, ii. 86 ; Latimer—*Deanry*, 67 ; Lever's Sermons—*robry*, 27, *brybry*, 34 ; Gabr. Harvey's Lttrs.—*trechrously*, 73.

Loss of vowel (-i?) *before* -n.
Gabr. Harvey's Lttrs.—*reasnable*, 13 ; Edw. Alleyn—*parsnage*, Alleyne Pprs., p. xiii (1610).

(a) *Loss of vowel after and before another cons.* ; (b) *also after* -r *and before a vowel, with shifting of stress.*
(a) Bokenam—*spyrtys* 'spirits', Pr. Marg. 48 ; Capgrave—*barnes* 'barons', 171 (twice).
(b) Latimer—*shriues* 'sheriffs', 154.

Loss of vowel following first, stressed syllable, between consonants.
S. of Rouen—*enmys*, 24 ; *singler*, Cov. Leet 72 (1424) ; Marg. Paston—*fantsy*, ii. 83 ; Gregory, *cytsyn* 'citizen', 64 ; Doll Leake—*bisnis*, Verney Mem. iv. 113 (1665) ; Wm. Baker, Rules for True Spelling (1724)—*medson* 'medicine', *venzin* 'venison'.

Loss of vowel immediately after stressed syllable, before weak vowel or (h-).
Gregory. *unt hym* (unto), 218.

Loss of -i- *after front vowel.*
Marg. Paston. *payt* 'pay it', i. 256.

Other losses after stressed syllable.
Marg. Paston. *yts* 'it is', ii. 386.

Loss of syllable in the middle of words.
Machyn. *Barmsey* 'Bermondsey', *Chamley* 'Cholmondeley'.

CHAPTER VIII

CHANGES IN CONSONANTAL SOUNDS

THE consonantal changes which we have now to consider are remarkable in that while the results were undoubtedly characteristic of English speech for several centuries, a very large number of those pronunciations, the existence of which can be proved by occasional spellings oft-times repeated, by rhymes and by the statements of the grammarians, have, during the last hundred years or so, been eliminated from polite speech, and survive only in Provincial or Vulgar forms of English. Such are the added -d in *gownd*, or -t in *sermont*, &c. Others, again, survive in what is rapidly becoming archaic usage, although, like 'the dropping of the *g*' in *shillin*', &c., they are still widespread among large classes of the best speakers, no less than among the worst. Yet other tendencies in the pronunciation of consonantal combinations are repudiated altogether by purists as slipshod, while many persons who slip into them quite naturally in rapid speech would disavow any such habits if questioned upon the subject. To this class belongs the dropping of *t* in *mostly, roast beef*, &c.

If we could recall speakers from the seventeenth and eighteenth centuries it is probable that what would strike us most would be the pranks that even the most refined and well-bred persons would play with the consonants. From this point of view the English of these periods would appear to us with our modern standards as a mixture of rusticity, slipshodness, and vulgarity. It is, I think, impossible to doubt that speakers who, from their education or their social experience, or both, must have been among the most irreproachable of their time, who could and did mingle with the great world, really did speak in what we should now consider a most reprehensible manner. The testimony from all sources is too strong to be ignored. We might disbelieve, or hesitate as to the interpretation of any one authority, if unsupported by other evidence, but when all tell the same tale, when we find Pope rhyming *neglects* with *sex*, the Verney ladies and Lady Wentworth writing *respeck, prospeck, strick*, and so on, and the writers on pronunciation before, after, and contemporary with these personages deliberately stating that final *t* is omitted in a long list of words which includes the above, then we must admit that if all this is not conclusive evidence on the point, it will be impossible ever to get any reliable information regarding the modes of speech of past ages.

But the case for taking these various indications seriously becomes stronger when we discover that the existence of many of these, to us, peculiar pronunciations is established by occasional spellings reaching far back to the fifteenth century, and beyond that into the M.E. period itself.

In fact the more persistently the records of English speech are studied, the more it becomes apparent that the same general tendencies of change which are even to-day in force have been active for centuries. This is nowhere truer than of consonantal changes, but it holds good also of the treatment of vowels in unstressed positions, and, to some extent also, of the isolative changes in vowels in stressed syllables.

It has been pointed out earlier in this book that down to far on in the eighteenth century the natural tendencies were allowed more or less unrestricted play, and this among speakers of the Received Standard of the period no less than among the more uneducated. Purists, as we know, existed, who protested against this or that usage, but few listened to them. Standards of refinement were certainly recognized, there were fashionable tricks which had a vogue and died away, vulgarisms and rusticities were unquestionably clearly perceived, and laughed at by those who had the entrance to the *beau monde* and were conversant with its usages. But the standards of this class of speakers were not those of the self-constituted authorities on 'correctness' who abound from the seventeenth century onwards. Habits of speech which provoked the mirth of the former because they were not those of persons of quality and fashion, were not, in most cases, the kind of 'errors' which came under the lash of the purists. It is characteristic of those who set out to instruct the public at large how they ought to pronounce, that they almost invariably fix as subject for their censure, among other things it is true, upon those very features in the natural speech of their time which are most deeply rooted in traditional habit and destined to remain as bases for the language of the future. This is true of Gill in the first quarter of the seventeenth century, to some extent of Cooper in the last quarter of the same century, of Swift early in the following century, and of Elphinston towards the end of the eighteenth century. With all respect be it said, it is true of Mr. Bridges in his heroic if unavailing onslaughts upon the present treatment in ordinary English of the vowels of unstressed syllables, grounded as this is upon tendencies which have prevailed in our language from its earliest history.

Among all the writers on pronunciation during the eighteenth century, Jones, in the Expert Orthographer, 1701, appears to be one of the least censorious. He records unblushingly, and without hostile comment, omissions and additions of consonants which we know from other sources, indeed, were habitual, but which it must have made some of his colleagues in the art of English speech extremely angry to see set down in this cool matter-of-fact way. Jones's business is primarily to teach English spelling, but his method of introducing each rule with the words 'When is the sound of such and such a letter written in such and such a way?' enables him to shed an amount of light upon the genuine pronunciation of his time which greatly exceeds that thrown by most other books of the kind before and for a long time after him. Now nearly all Jones's statements are shown to be true to fact by the enlightening spellings of the Verney family and of Lady Wentworth, to say nothing of the rhymes of good poets, but they must have appeared very outrageous to those whose main object was to get as far away as possible from realities, and to construct a fantastic form of English from the spelling.

But if the protests of the purists passed unheeded among 'the wits of either Charles's days' and those of James II, Anne, and the first two Georges, it cannot be denied that the grammarians came to their own at last—up to a point. The process of 'improvement', so far as one can see, but it is absurd to attempt great preciseness in these matters, began roughly in the third quarter of the eighteenth century, and has gained in force and volume ever since.

But if the triumph of the pedagogue is thus unquestionable, the success, as has been suggested repeatedly in this book, must be set down rather to social causes than to a sudden capacity on the part of the Orthoepist to persuade those to whom he had so long preached in vain. It was assuredly not the Verneys and Wentworths, the Lady Hobarts, or 'my sister Carburer' who first adopted the new-fangled English. These and their like, and long may they flourish, have hardly done so completely at the present time. It was the new men and their families, who were winning a place in the great world and in public affairs, who would be attracted by the refinements offered by the new and 'correct' system of pronunciation which they learnt from their masters of rhetoric, or from their University tutors. That this new, wealthy, and often highly cultivated class should gradually have imposed upon society at large the gentilities of the academy of deportment, and have been able to insist with success upon *gown* instead of '*gownd*', *strict* instead of '*strick*', *vermin* instead of '*varmint*', *richest* instead of '*richis*', and so on, would have seemed incredible to Lady Wentworth and her friends. But so it has come about. Possibly the relations of Dr. Johnson and Mrs. Piozzi are types of the process at its best, and one may suppose that the great man would not hesitate to correct what he took to be improprieties of speech in his circle, and that pronunciations which received his sanction would rapidly gain currency far and wide. In fact, it is not wholly fanciful to attribute in no small measure to the personal prestige of Johnson, a prestige of a very peculiar kind, more powerful perhaps than that possessed by any purely learned man before or since, the very marked reaction in favour of a certain type of 'correctness' in speech which set in about this time, and which has continued ever since to make fresh inroads upon established tradition. But even so mighty a force as Samuel Johnson required suitable social conditions in which to exert his influence.

The gradual penetration of those circles of society whose speech constitutes the Received Standard with something approaching the ideals of elegance and correctness maintained by the purists has been a slow process, and though each generation probably sees something of the old usage given up, there are many strongholds of ancient habits which still resist the encroachments of innovation. '*Ed'ard*', '*husban'*', '*edjikate*', '*Injun*', '*ooman*', '*masty*' (mastiff), '*pagin*' (pageant), and the like, have gone, but [grɪnɪdž, nɔrɪdž, ɔfn, lɪtrəlʃə, bousən], and many others, survive from the wreckage. These natural and historic forms are growing steadily less, and every 'advance' in education sweeps more of them away. It will be interesting to see what fresh pranks the rising generation will play, and with what new refinements they will adorn our language.

As regards the dialectal origin of the consonantal changes, it is difficult to assign any specific Regional starting-point to most of them. It seems probable that the loss or assimilation of consonants in groups, the dropping of final consonants, the development of parasitic consonants between certain combinations, and so on, belong to the universal tendencies of English speech.   We find evidence of all these changes East, West, and Centre in the dialects of the South and Midlands, in the fifteenth century. An examination of the early forms of Place Names would certainly reveal earlier examples of these and other processes than any given below, and might also enable us to say in which areas they were most prevalent. Other changes, such as the loss of initial *w-* before rounded vowels, the development of *w-* before certain other rounded vowels, the development of initial *y-* [j] before certain front vowels, might be localized with more precision were our knowledge of the distribution of Regional dialect features during the Late M.E. and Early Modern periods more complete than it is at present.

Whatever be the area whence these various consonant changes started, nearly all of them are found fairly early in the London dialect, and later in Received Standard.

For the sake of clearness it has seemed best to deal with the various phenomena in groups, according to the general nature of the process involved, rather than by taking every consonant separately and discussing everything that may happen to it.

The following general classification of consonant changes includes under its several heads most of the chief points that demand attention.

A. *Isolative Changes without either Loss or Addition.*

(1) *-h* becomes *-f-* ; (a) final, (b) in combination, *-ht.*
(2) *-ng* becomes *-n*, i. e. [ŋ] becomes [n].
(3) *th* [þ] becomes *f*, and [ð] becomes *v*, initially, medially, or finally.
(4) *-s-* becomes *-sh*, i. e. [s] becomes [ʃ], medially and finally.
(5) Interchange of *w-* and *v-*, and of *v-* and *w-*.

B. *Combinative Changes involving neither Loss nor Addition.*

(1) *ty*, i. e. [tj] becomes [tʃ] initially and medially.
(2) [sj] becomes [ʃ] initially and medially.
(3) [dj] becomes [dž] initially and medially.
(4) [zj] becomes [ž] medially.
(5) Assimilation of -nf- to -mf-.

C. *Loss of Consonants.*

(1) Loss of initial *h-*: (a) stressed, (b) in unstressed syllables.
(2) Loss of *w-* : (a) in stressed, (b) in unstressed syllables.
(3) Loss of *-l-* before certain consonants, immediately following.
(4) Loss of *r* : (a) medially before a following consonant, (b) finally.
(5) Loss of consonants, especially of *d, t,* when final, immediately preceded by another consonant.

(6) Loss of consonants between vowels, or after a consonant before a following vowel.

(7) Loss of back or front-open-voiceless consonant, written *h* or *gh* (a) finally, (b) in combination with *-t* (written *-ght*).

(8) Loss of final *-f*.

(9) Loss of *n* before other consonants, in unstressed syllables.

D. *Addition of Consonants.*

(1) Of *w-* before rounded vowels.

(2) Of *y-* [j] before front vowels.

(3) Of [j] after *k-*, *g-* before front or originally front vowels.

(4) Of *d*, medially in combination *-nl-* : of *b* in combination *-ml-*.

(5) Of *-d-* or *-t-* finally after *-r*, *-n*, *-l*, *-s*, *-f*.

(6) Of *h-* initially before vowels.

E. *Voicing of Voiceless Consonants.*

(1) Of initial *wh-* = [w̥].

(2) Of other consonants : (a) initially, (b) medially ; (1) between vowels, (2) after a voiced consonant before a vowel.

F. *Unvoicing of Voiced Consonants.*

It will be observed that the terminology employed in the above system of classification is not in all cases strictly accurate from the phonetic point of view. Thus *h-* the aspirate is not a consonant, but a ' rough breathing ', or stressed-breath-on-glide. Again, when *gown* is pronounced *gownd* there is in reality no 'addition' of a consonant at the end ; all that happens is that denasalization takes place before the tongue-position of *-n-* is dissolved. The effect to the ear is that a new and different consonant is added to the *-n* ; but from the phonetic point of view there is a diminution, not a renewal of activity. Similarly, we talk popularly of ' dropping ' a final consonant when *husban'* instead of *husband* is pronounced. As a matter of fact, all that happens in the former case is that nasalization continues to the end of the articulation. With this warning there can, I think, be no danger in adopting for the sake of convenience a popular terminology which regards the acoustic effect upon the listener, rather than the actual activities of the speaker.

A. Isolative Changes without either Loss or Addition.

M.E. -(g)h *becomes* [-f].

M.E. *h*, *gh* (back-open-voiceless cons.), at the end of a syllable, or before *-t*, either disappears altogether in the South or becomes *-f*. For the disappearance see p. 305.

The change to *f* is the result of a strong lip-modifying (' labializing ') tendency, which at last was so pronounced that the back consonant which it accompanied was gradually weakened and finally lost altogether, leaving presumably a lip-open consonant, which generally tends to become the lip-teeth [f]. In some dialects the latter sound was probably developed in M.E. It cannot have been fully formed in London English much before the fifteenth century or it would have been perpetuated in the spelling of some words at least. The following examples in some cases show -*f* in some forms which in present-day Received Standard have lost the consonant completely. Some of the examples are from documents which may show Regional usage differing from that of the London Standard of the period. The spelling *Edyngburth* 'Edinburgh', in Berners' Froissart 1. 85, shows that the old sound still preserved in the North was unfamiliar to him.

Spellings with -*f* are :—*thorf* 'through', M. Paston ii. 197, 1465; *troff* 'trough', 1553, R. Bradley's Will (Leics.), Linc. Dioc. Docs. 164. 14; to *laffe*, Letter of Barnabe Googe, Arber, p. 12, 1563; *laffe* rhymes *distaffe*, Gabr. Harvey's Letter Bk. 117, 1573–80; *troffe* rhymes *skoffe*, ibid. ; 'hold their hips and *loffe*, Shakesp., First Fol., 1621, Midsummer N. D. 1. i; 'and *coffing* drowns the parson's saw', L. L. Lost (Song at end of Play); also *chuffes*, First Pt., Hen. IV, Act II, Sc. ii ; Butler, 1634, '*laugh, cough, tough, enough* commonly sound like *laf, cof, tuf, enuf* '; 'I *laft* at him', Mall V., Verney Mem. ii. 379, 1647; Cooper, 1685, notes -*f* in *rough, trough,* and that *enough* as a 'numeral' is 'pronounced, and better written *enow*'.

It seems clear from the above that -*f* was pronounced, from early in the sixteenth century, in those words of this class in which we now use the sound. (For the vowel sound and the spelling of *laugh* cf. p. 205.) No doubt other words were included by some speakers. It is probable that *thof* for *though*, which Fielding puts into the mouth of Mrs. Honour, Sophia Western's waiting-woman in *Tom Jones* (1748), was at that time provincial or vulgar.

-ht- *becomes* ft.

The curious spelling *unsoffethe* 'unsought', Gregory's Chron. 192, 1450–70, is undoubtedly put for ' *unsoft* '. The rhyme *manslaughter— laughter* in Roister Doister, 1553, is ambiguous.

Marston rhymes *after—daughter*, Eastward Hoe, v. i, 1604; the Verney Papers have *dafter*(*e*), 1629, Mrs. Wiseman, p. 143 ; Butler, 1634, '*daughter* commonly sounded *dafter* '; Verney Mem.—*dafter*, ii. 203, Mrs. Isham, 1645, do. iii. 315 (three times), 1657, and again, iii. 232, 1655; Jones, 1701—'some sound *daughter, bought, naught, taught, nought*, &c., as with an *f*, saying *daufter, boft* ', &c., pp. 54 and 55. It is hard to say how far Jones is to be trusted not to include provincialisms or vulgarisms among his pronunciations. Mrs. Honour, the waiting-woman in *Tom Jones*, writes *soft* 'sought' in a letter. Probably by Fielding's time, at any rate, many of the -*ft* pronunciations given by Jones were becoming antiquated among the best speakers. To judge from the statements of the grammarian. and the evidence of the occasional spellings, it certainly looks as though throughout the seventeenth century the usage was not definitely fixed as regards the distribution of the various types, so that *dater, daughter, dafter* [dātər, dōtər, dǣftər, slǣtər, slōtər, slǣftər, bɔft, bōt], &c., were all in use.

There is no assignable reason beyond the fortunes of apparently arbitrary selection from among the various types why we should say [slɔ̄tə] on the one hand, and [lāftə] on the other.

Substitution of -th [þ] for -gh = [χ] or [ɟ].

We sometimes get a substitution of [þ] for the old voiceless back or front open consonants, where these still survive among an older generation, or occur in words introduced from another dialect. I take the spelling *Edyngburth* 'Edinburgh', Berners' Froissart 1. 85, and Machyn's *Luthborow* 'Loughborough', 309, to be examples of such a substitution, and likewise Peter Wentworth's *Usquebath* 'Usquebaugh', W. Pprs. 196, 1711; Jones's *sith* for *sigh* must also be a survival of such an imitative pronunciation. The same is true of the modern pronunciation [kiþlī'] for *Keighley*, Yorks., the younger generation of the district no longer using the old sound, and finding it more convenient to adopt one which can be mastered by speakers from farther south.

Substitution of [-n] for [ŋ], popularly known as 'dropping the **g**' in the Suffix -ing.

Such pronunciations as *huntin'*, *shillin'*, &c., which for some reason are considered as a subject of jest in certain circles, while in others they are censured, are of considerable antiquity, as the examples which follow will show. The substitution of '*n*' for '*ng*' [ŋ] in Present Participles and Verbal Nouns was at one time apparently almost universal in every type of English speech. At the present time this habit obtains in practically all Regional dialects of the South and South Midlands, and among large sections of speakers of Received Standard English. Apparently in the twenties of the last century a strong reaction set in in favour of the more 'correct' pronunciation, as it was considered, and what was in reality an innovation, based upon the spelling, was so far successful that the [ŋ] pronunciation ('with -*ng*') has now a vogue among the educated at least as wide as the more conservative one with -*n*.

It is probable that a special search would reveal far more numerous and earlier forms of the -*n* spellings than those I have noted.

Norf. Guilds (1389), *holdyn*, 63, *drynkyn*, 59, 66, 1389; Marg. Paston, *wrytyn* (N.), i. 49, 1443, *gidyn* (N.), ii. 74, *dyvysen* (N.), ii. 92, *hangyn* (Part.), ii. 124; Agn. Paston, *walkyn*, Past. Lttrs. i. 114, 1450; Gregory, 1450-70, *blasyn* sterre 'comet', 80, *hayryn* 'herring', 169; Guild of Tailors, Exeter, *hyndryn*, 317, 1466; Sir Richard Gresham, 1520, *hanggyns*, Ellis iii. 1. 234, 235; Machyn, 1550-, *syttyn*, 33, *rydyn*, 183, *standyn*, 191, *syngyne*, 281; Q. Elizabeth, *besichen*, Letter to James VI, 60.

The following are taken from Verney Memoirs:—*seein*, *missin*, ii. 63, *bein*, 70, *comin*, 71, *plondarin*, 71, all written by Cary Verney, 1642; *I may go a beggin*, a *beggen*, Mrs. Isham, ii. 207, 220, 1645; *shillins*, Doll Smith, iii. 409, 1657; *disoblegin*, Lady Hobart, iv. 55, 1664; *lodgens*, Lady Elmes, iv. 121, 1665, *lodgins*, Lady Hobart, iv. 126, 1665.

Cooper, 1685, includes among words having the same sound though differently spelt, *coming—cummin, coughing—coffin, jerkin—jerking*; Lord Rochester, 1647–80, rhymes *farthing*—bear-*garden* [færdən], in 'Against Disturbers of the Pit'.

Lady Wentworth has *takin, dynin*-room, 47, *lodgins*, 45, *levin* 'living', 54, *Feeldin*, 58, *approachin*, 66, *buildin*, 84, *Haystins*, 56, *devertin* tricks, 57, *prancin* along, 57, *ingagin*, 60, *digin* 'digging', 61, *fardin*, 99, want of *dungin* 'dunging', 111, *mornin*, 113, *stockins*, 126, *writins*, 275, the Anthem for the *Thanksgivin*, 321. Swift in the Introd. to *Polite Conversations* puts *learnen* among the words 'as pronounced by the chief patterns of politeness at Court, at Levees', &c., to which he objects. Pope, 1713, rhymes *gardens—farthings*, Epigr. to Lord Radnor, where the latter word is doubtless pronounced as by Lord Rochester and Lady Wentworth. Walker, Rhet. Gr., 3rd ed., 1801, hedges a good deal. He says that he can assert that the best speakers do not invariably pronounce -*ing* to rhyme with *king*, but rather as *in*. He recommends -*in* in the Present Participles of words like *sing, fling, ring*, but prefers -*ing* in others. ' Our best speakers universally pronounce *singin, bringin, flingin*.' After saying ' What a trifling omission is *g* after *n* ', he goes on : ' Trifling as it is, it savours too much of vulgarity to omit -*g* in any words except the -*ing*-type. *Writing, reading, speaking* are certainly preferable to *writin, readin, speakin*, wherever the language has the least degree of solemnity.' Walker is here trying to run with the hare and hunt with the hounds.

-ng *written for* -n.

The pronunciation implied by this spelling may be heard occasionally at the present time, sometimes from those speakers who 'leave out the -*g*' in the ending -*ing*. A few scattered spellings of this kind, one from the fifteenth and others from the sixteenth century onwards, may be recorded.

Lupinge 'lupin', the plant, Palladius 46. 60 ; *kusshing* 'cushion', Thos. Pery, 1539, Ellis ii. 2. 150 ; *slouinglie*, Latimer 55, ' slovenly'; *evyng* song, Machyn, 119, &c., &c.; J. Alleyne, Alleyne Papers 16, 159–?, *fachenges* 'fashions'; *chicking* 'chicken', Sir R. Verney, Verney Mem. iii. 115, 1653 ; *forting* 'fortune', otherwise *fortin*, cf. p. 277 ; *lining* 'linen', Lady Hobart, iii. 305, 1657 ; Mrs. Isham, ibid. iv. 108, 1663 ; *chapling* 'chaplain', Cary Stewkley (Verney), ibid. iv. 35, 1662 ; *fashing* 'fashion', Mrs. Edm., ibid. iv. 71, 1664; *childering* 'children', Pen. Denton, ibid. iv. 469, 1692. Lady Wentworth, early in the following century, writes ' Lady *Evling* Pirpoynt', and her daughter-in-law Lady Strafford, *kitching*, W. Papers 540, her son Peter, *beckinged* 'beckoned', 108, 1710.

It is difficult to say how far some of these are not inverted spellings implying that -*ng* has for the writer the same value as -*n*, and how far, on the other hand, they represent genuine pronunciations with [ŋ]. Such pronunciations undoubtedly do exist.

-nk = [-ŋk-] *for* -ng- [ŋ(g)].

Among very vulgar speakers—not in London alone—we sometimes hear ' *nothink* ' for *nothing* at the present time. Cavendish, L. of Wolsey, 1557, writes *hankyng*, p. 97, and Q. Elizabeth, in 1548, '*brinkinge* of me up', and ' our *brinkers* up', Ellis i. 2. 154.

This pronunciation is referred to by Elphinston, 1787, who remarks ' a common Londoner talks of *anny think else*, or *anny thing kelse*', and again, 'English vulgarity will utter *anny think* (dhat iz, *thingk*)'.

Assimilation of [ŋ] *to* [n] *before point-consonants*—d, t, th.

Shillingford has *leynth* ' length ', 85 ; Elyot's Gouernour has *strenthe*, 237 ; Milton in his autograph MS writes *strenth*, Com. 416, and again Com. 418, but he has written *g* above the line in the latter. *Strenth* occurs also in Verney Mem. ii. 106. Lady Sussex (1641), and *kaindom* ib. ii. 90. Elphinston regards *lenth*, *strenth* as ' the Scottish shiboleth ', and Walker as ' the sure mark of provincial pronunciation'.

Change of th [þ] *to* f; [ð] *to* v.

The results of these changes are heard sporadically at the present time. It is doubtful whether such pronunciations as [tïf, frī], &c., for *teeth*, *three*, &c., are characteristic of any Regional dialect as a whole. They appear to belong rather to individuals here and there, and they seem to occur more frequently in the speech of the lower strata of London speakers than else-where, though they may survive as uncorrected faults of childhood among individuals in all classes and belonging to any region. I have not found any very early examples, but the following are of some interest.

Finally, Bk. of Quint., *erf* = 'earth', 18, 1460–70; Gregory has *Lambeffe* for *Lambeth*, 229; initially, Machyn has *frust* for *thrust*, 21, and *Frogmorton* for *Throgmorton*; medially, Q. Elizabeth, *bequived* ' be-queathed', Transl. 149; and finally, John Alleyne, Alleyne Papers, *helfe*, 15 and 16 (159–?), and Middleton, Chaste Maid in Cheapside, has ' neither *kiff* nor kin', Act IV, Sc. i (1630); Mrs. Isham has *lofte* for *loathe*, Verney Mem. ii. 220, 1645. In the last instance the -*t* is a typical addition, cf. p. 309, and does not concern us for the moment.

Elphinston, in 1787, refers to ' the tendency of the low English to *Redriph* and *loph* instead of *Rotherhithe* and *loath*', cf. Müller, § 252. Readers of Cowper's correspondence are familiar with his pet name ' *Mrs. Frog*' for Mrs. Throgmorton, which shows that a pronunciation of the name similar to that used by Machyn still existed.

Lady Wentworth writes *threvoles* for *frivolous*, 127, which rather sug-gests that she pronounced ' *th*' as '*f*'.

Final and medial s *becomes* ' sh ' = [ʃ].

This isolative change does not appear to be widespread, but I include it because I find that I have a few early examples noted among my collec-tions, and it is referred to as a vulgarism by Elphinston in the eighteenth century. This fact makes it probable that the early forms mean some-thing, and are not mere scribal vagaries.

The following are the examples I have noted :—R. of Brunne, Handlyng Sinne, 1302, *reioshe* 'rejoice', 2032, *vasshelage*, 4610; Bokenam, 1443, *vertush*, Ann. 248, *mossh* 'moss', Ann. 360, *reioysshyng* 'rejoicing', Agn. 401, *dysshese* 'disease', Agn. 614 ; Engl. Register of Oseney, 1460, *blesshyng*, p. 13; M. Paston, a powter *vesshell*, ii. 75, 1461; Caxton, *kysshed* ' kissed', Jason 85. 35; Machyn has *the prynche of Spaine*, 51, 52,

66; Henslow's Diary (1598), *Henshlow*, 213; Sir J. Leake, Verney Mem., *burgishes* 'burgesses', ii. 218, 1645; Lady Lambton, *hushband*, Basire Corresp. 79 (1649); Mrs. Basire, *parshalles*, 111 (1653); 'touch'd a gall'd beast till he *winch'd*', Congreve's Old Batchelor, Act v, Sc. xiii (1693).

Elphinston notes the vulgar *cutlash, nonplush, frontishpiece, Poarchmouth*. In the last word the change is probably combinative; an earlier example of this 'vulgarism' is *Porchmouth*, Sir T. Seymour, St. Pprs. Hen. VIII, i. pp. 775, 776 (twice), 1544; the same spelling is used by C. Verney, V. Mem. iv. 136, 1665; J. Verney, 244, 1679; A. Nicholas, p. 265, and N. N. 266, 1680.

Those who are familiar with *Martin Chuzzlewit* will remember Mrs. Gamp's vagaries in respect of substituting '*sh*' for '*s*'.

Interchange of v- *and* w- ; v- *for* w-, *and* w- *for* v-.

This was formerly a London vulgarism, but is now apparently extinct in the Cockney dialect. Personally, I never actually heard these pronunciations, so well known to the readers of Dickens, Thackeray, and of the earlier numbers of *Punch*. My time for observing such points begins in the late seventies or early eighties of the last century, and I never remember noticing this particular feature in actual genuine speech, though I remember quite well, as a boy, hearing middle-aged people say *weal* for *veal* and *vich* for *which*, jocularly, as though in imitation of some actual type of speech with which they were familiar. I used to wonder why these people introduced this peculiarity in jest, and whose pronunciation it was supposed to imitate. I have since come to the conclusion that my boyhood's friends must have heard these pronunciations in their youth— say from twenty to thirty years before my time, which would bring us back to the forties and fifties of last century. Another possibility is that the generation to whom I am referring did not as a matter of actual personal experience hear this interchange of *v*- and *w*-, but that they took them over from Dickens.

The forms which I have noted are the following, though I have come across many others from the fifteenth century onwards :—Palladius, 1420, *vyves* 'wives', 25. 669; Bokenam, 1441, *valkynge*, Ann, 540, *veye*, Ann, 565; *avayte* 'await', Marg. Paston, ii. 249. 1465; Lord Lovel's Will, *vyne* 'wine', L. D. D. 17. 12, Oxf., 1455; Prynce of *Valys*, Gregory, 1450–70, 192; Reception of Cath. of Ar., 1501, *vele* 'weal', 415; Machyn, the Cockney Diarist, has *vomen*, 56, 59, &c., *Volsake* 'Woolsack', 91, *veyver* 'weaver', 83, *Vestmynster*, 86, *Velyngton* 'Whittington', 96, *voman*, 98, *Vosseter* 'Worcester', 102, *Voderoffe*, otherwise *Woodroffe*, 303.

Elphinston notes the habit of confusing *v* and *w* among Londoners, but, while disapproving, does not assert that it is confined to vulgar speakers only; Walker regards the practice as 'a blemish of the first magnitude', but says that it occurs among the inhabitants of London, 'not those always of the low order'.

I have noted the following early examples of *w*- for original *v*- :— St. Editha, *wex* 'vex', 47, *awowe* 'avow', 864; Bokenam, *wenger* 'avenger', Ann. 476, *wyce* 'vice', Fth. 42; Marg. Paston, *wochsaf*, i. 49, i. 354; Gregory, *wery* 'very', 192; Cely Papers, *were* 'very', 50, *whalew* 'value', 73, *Wyllars* 'Villiers', 76; Machyn, *welvet* 'velvet', 6, 11, 12, 19, &c., *walance* 'vallance', *woyce* 'voice', 58, *wetelle* 'victuals', *wacabondes*, 69, *wergers*, 141, *waluw*, 186, *wue* 'view', 293.

B. Combinative Changes without Loss or Addition.

-si-, -ti-, *that is* [-si-, -sj-], *also* **su** = [sjū], *become* '**sh**' [ʃ].

The examples date from the middle of the fifteenth century.   Marg. Paston—*sesschyonys* 'sessions', i. 178, 1450, *conschens* 'conscience', ii. 364, 366, 1469; Cely Papers—*prosesschchon*, 113, *pertyschon* 'partition', 57, *partyshon*, 133, *fessychens*, 23, *restytuschon*, 152, *oblygaschons*, 114, *commyngaschon*, 5, *derecschons*, 137; Letters and Papers i—*huisshers* 'ushers', 136. 1501; Admiral Sir Thos. Seymour—*instrocshens*, St. Pprs., Hen. VIII, 1. 779. 1544; Thos. Pery to Mr. R. Vane—*commyshin*, Ellis ii. 2. 140. 1539; Gabr. Harvey's Letters—*ishu* 'issue', 13. 1573–80; Q. Elizabeth, Letters to James VI (1582–1602)—*alteraçon*, 2, *expectaçon*, 3, *execuçon*, 3; Marston, What you Will, 1607—*caprichious*, Act v, Sc. i.   The following are all from the Verney Memoirs :—*indiscreshons, disposishons*, Mall V., ii. 380. 1647; *suspishiously*, Lady V., ii. 245. 1646; *condishume* 'condition', Mrs. Isham ii. 206; *menishone*, M. Faulkiner, ii. 56; *fondashon*, Lady Sydenham, ii. 101; *mentshoned* 'mentioned', Lady Sydenham, ii. 162; *hobblegashons*, ibid. ii. 125, 'obligations'; *adishon*, Mary V., iii. 28. 1650; *condishon*, Mall V. (Sir Ralph's sister), iii. 213. 1655; *possestion*, Cary Stewkley (Verney), iii. 434. 1656; *pashens*, Lady Hobart iv. 56. 1664.   Cooper, 1685, notes that *ci, ce, ti* have the sound of *sh* in *antient, artificial, conscience, magician, ocean, Egyptian, essential, pacience*, &c.   Jones, 1701, says that *ocean* is pronounced *oshan*, and *sh* also in *issue*.   Lady Wentworth writes :— Queen of *Prushee*, 63, *exprestions*, 50, *pation* 'passion', 49, *fation* 'fashion', 169, *Prutia*, 118, *Prution* (Lady Strafford), 243.   Baker, in True Spelling, says that *dictionary* is pronounced *dixnery*.   This last form indicates a pronunciation now extinct so far as I know.   The above examples are quite sufficient to establish the early development of the present-day pronunciation.

Initial **su-** = [sjū] *becomes* -'**shu·**' = [ʃu].

[1] The earliest examples of *sh*- spellings, initially, which I can record, date only from the late sixteenth and middle seventeenth centuries.   The first is found in the Alleyne Papers—*sheute* 'suit', J. Alleyne, 159–, p. 16; the next are from the Verney Memoirs :—*shur* 'sure', Cary V., ii. 71. 1642; *shuer*, Lady Sydenham, ii. 101; *shuite* (of clothes), Luce Sheppard, iii. 1653; *shewer*, Mrs. Sherard, iii. 324. 1657; *shewtid* 'suited', ibid. iii. 325. 1657.   Mrs. Basire writes *ashoure*, 112 (1653), *shut* 'suit', 132 (1654).   Cooper mentions the pronunciations *shure, shugar*, 'facilitatis causa'.   Jones says that *sh*- is pronounced in *assume, assure, censure, consume, ensue, insure, sue, suet, sugar.*

The careful pronunciation 'according to the spelling' has been restored now in some of the above, such as *suit, suet, consume*, &c.

---

[1] Note now, however, *persheue* 'pursue', Warden Rawlins of Merton Bp. Fox's Letters, p. 81 (1515 or –16).

-di- [dj] *becomes* [dž].

Present-day usage varies considerably as to the pronunciation of this combination in different words. Thus, while *soldier, grandeur* are pretty generally pronounced [souldžə, grændžə] we do not, for the most part, say [imidžıt, indžən, idžət, oudžəs] for *immediate, Indian, idiot, odious*. The 'careful' artificial pronunciation of these and other words which is now generally affected is, however, quite recent.

I am only able to offer comparatively few spellings, and only one of these earlier than the seventeenth century—Machyn's *sawgears* 'soldiers', 302—to prove the [dž] pronunciation. The Verney Memoir furnish the following:—*teges* 'tedious', Mall V., ii. 381. 1647 ; *sogers* 'soldiers', Lady Sussex, ii. 105, 153. 1642.

Jones, 1701, says that *contagious, soldier, Indian*, are pronounced *contages, soger, Injan*. Lady Wentworth writes *sogar* 'soldier', 113, *emedgetly* 'immediately'. Bertram, 1753, transliterates (for Danes) *soldier, Indian, could you, had you*, as *soldsjer, indsjan, kudsju, hædsju*. The last two examples are interesting as showing the same colloquial pronunciation of final -*d*, followed by *y* [j] in the next word of a sentence, as we now employ—[kŭdžu, hædžu].

Walker, Rhet. Gr., 3rd ed., 1801, says that polite speakers always pronounce *edjucate, verchew, verdjure*, and that they ought also to say *ojeous, insidjeous, Injean*. John Kemble, according to Leigh Hunt, Autobiogr. i. 180, said '*ojus*', '*hijjus*', '*perfijjus*'.

[zj] *becomes* [ž].

This occurs chiefly in such words as *pleasure, measure*, where, originally, *u* was pronounced [jù], and in *hosier, brasier*, &c., though in the latter group probably [houziə, breiziə], &c., are more common. Cary Verney, Mem. ii. 62. 1642, writes *pleshar, plesshur*, and Jones says that '*sh* '—here, clearly [ž]—is pronounced in *measure, leisure, brasier, glasier, hosier*.

-nf- *becomes* -mf-, -kn- *becomes* -tn-.

The assimilation of the point -*n*- to *m* before a following lip-consonant is a natural one, and may be heard even at the present time from persons who are not careful speakers, in rapid utterance. Thus, one may occasionally hear 'all *om* board', 'he's *im* bed', &c.

The following examples are worth noting as showing the tendency at work in the middle of words:—*imphants* 'infants', Wilson, A. of Rhet. 52. ; Lady Wentworth writes *comfution* 'confusion', W. Pprs. 113. 1710; *Twittenham* 'Twickenham' is found in Verney Mem. iv. 417. 1687; Lady Wentworth writes *Twitnam*, W. Pprs. 49. 1705, and this form is common in the eighteenth century, and often found in Pope's poems and letters; Lady W. writes Lord *Bartly* for *Berkley*, 174. 1711.

C. Loss of Consonants.
Loss of the Initial Aspirate.

In discussing this question we must distinguish between *h*- in stressed syllables and in unstressed, and further between words of pure English origin and those from French or Norman French. It is doubtful whether the latter were pronounced with an initial aspirate originally. As regards words of English origin, it is only in respect of stressed syllables that the question of ' dropping the *h*·' arises. In unstressed syllables, e. g. the second element of compounds, and words such as Pronouns and Auxiliaries, which more often occur in unstressed positions in the sentence, the loss of *h*· is very early, and at least as early as the thirteenth century is frequently shown by the spelling to have taken place in Pronouns (*madim* for *made him*) in the second elements of compounds (*-ham* and *-um*, &c., often confused in early forms of Pl. N.s). The question, then, is when did the tendency arise to pronounce *'ill* for *hill*, or *'ome* for *home*, &c., when these and other words occur as independent words in the sentence ? Norman scribes are very erratic in their use of *h*· in copying English manuscripts, and we therefore cannot attach much importance to thirteenth- or even to early fourteenth-century omissions of the letter which occur here and there. The forms in Norf. G.'s (1389), *alf a pound*, 80, and *alpenny*, 98, seem genuine. I have found comparatively few examples in the fifteenth century of spellings without *h*·; even the Celys, although they write *h*· where it is not wanted, do not omit it so far as I have noted. An unmistakable ' dropping' seems to be *owsold* ' household', in the Will of Sir T. Cumberworth, Linc. Dioc. Docs. 1451; Margaret Paston has *astely*, ii. 143. 1463. She also writes *eraftyr* ' hereafter ', i. 530. 1460, but as she does not write *ere* for *here*, the loss of *h*· in the former word is probably to be set down to lack of stress. The form *erefter* also occurs in a letter of Q. Mary of Scotland (daughter of Hen. VII), in 1503, Ellis i. 1. 42, and the same letter contains the spelling *oulde* for *hold*, a genuine instance of ' dropping the *h* '. Fifty years later, the Cockney Machyn has a fine crop of *h*-less forms :—*ede* ' head', 29, *alff* ' half', 13, 19, *ard*, 107, *yt* ' hit', 139, *alpeny*, 7, *Amton courte*, 9, *elmet* ' helmet', *Allalows* ' All Hallows', 61.

Cooper does not include the loss of initial *h*· among his traits of ' barbarous dialect'.

I have not noted any examples in the Verney Mem. except *ombel* ' humble', Cary V., ii. 63, and *yumer* ' humour', where the absence of the *h*· in pronunciation was normal; Lady Wentworth also writes *Umble*, W. Pprs. 47, for *Humble*, a family name, doubtless on the analogy of the Adjective, and *youmore*, 320, *youmored*, 105, 320. The restoration of an aspirate in the last word is a trick of yesterday, and I never observed it until a few years ago, and then only among speakers who thought of every word before they uttered it. Note *Ospittals*, eighteenth century V. Letters i, 105 (1700).

Mrs. Honour, in Tom Jones, writes :—' mite not *ave* ever happened'; ' that *as* always *ad* ', the last word being the only one *s*'ressed, except *at ome*. This phrase is still pronounced [ətoum] by excellent speakers, and *atóm* is found as early as Layamon, *c*. 1200.

In the letter written by Mr. Jackson's fiancée in Roderick Random, chap. xvi, there is not a single *h*· left out, although several are wrongly introduced, neither is there any in the letter written by Mr. Jonathan Wild to Letitia in Fielding's Life of that gentleman.

Later in the century Elphinston, 1787, notes that ' many Ladies, Gentlemen and others have totally discarded' initial *h*· in places where it ought to be used; Walker, 1801, also draws attention to the habit, which he attributes chiefly to Londoners, and Batchelor does the same.

The above evidence is too slight to found much upon, but so far as it goes, and its negative character is of some value, it would appear that the present-day vulgarism was not widespread much before the end of the eighteenth century. The gap in the evidence between Machyn and two hundred years later is remarkable. The practice, which apparently did exist in Machyn's day in London, must have been confined to a limited class. The evidence, from the spelling, for the wrongful addition of *h*- is, as we shall see, far more copious.

It may be remarked that the habit of omitting initial *h*- is common to all Regional dialects except those of the North.[1] In Modified Standard also, this was very widespread when I was a boy, even people, below a certain rank in society, who were fairly well 'educated' being very shaky in this respect. This state of things has been very noticeably altered in the last few decades, presumably by the efforts of the schools.

Loss of w.

Initially before rounded vowels.

Alice Crane (cousin of the Pastons) signs herself to Marg. Paston, 'Youre pore bede *oman* and cosyn', Past. Lttrs. i. 343 (1455).

Machyn writes *Odam* for *Woodham*, 80.

Jones, 1701, says 'the sound of *o*- written *wo*- when it may be sounded *wo*-' in *wolf, Wolverhampton, worry, womb, woman, wonder, work, word, worse, worthy, woven, would, wound*. *Woad*, he says, is pronounced *ode*. Mrs. Honour, Sophia Western's waiting-woman, writes *uman* 'woman' in a letter.

Tuckwell, Reminiscences of Oxford, records that Dr. Pusey's mother, Lady Lucy Pusey, who died well over 90 in 1859, always said '*ooman*' for *woman*.

w- *lost after a consonant before rounded vowels.*

Agnes Paston—*sor* 'swore', Past. Lttrs. i. 219 (1451); John Alleyne, Alleyne Pprs. 15, has *sord* 'sword' (159–?); *sowlen* 'swollen', Thos. Watson, Teares of Fancie, Sonnet 35. 1593; Daines, 1640, says *w* is scarcely pronounced at all in *swound* 'swoon', and but moderately in *sword, swore*, 51; Sir R. Verney writes *sourd* 'sword', V. Mem. ii. 32, 84 (twice), 164 (twice), 1641; Cary Stewkley, V. Mem. iv. 341. 1685, writes *sord*; Cooper, 1685, says '*w* quiescit' in *sword, sworn*; Vanbrugh writes *gud soons* = *God's wounds*, Journey to London, 1726; Baker, 1724, gives the pronunciation of *swoon* as *sound*; Cooper, 1685, says that *quote* is pronounced like *coat*; Jones gives *sord, solen, sorn*, &c., as the normal pronunciations.

Qu- = [kw] becomes *k*-:—'*coting* of ye scriptures', Euph. 320; Jones says *k*- for *qu* in *banquet, conquer, liquid, quote, quoth*.

Loss of -w- before an unstressed vowel.

This must be very old, cp. *uppard*, Trinity Homilies, p. 111 (*c.* 1200). *Hammard* 'homeward' occurs several times in S. Editha.

Except in Pl. N.s *Harwich, Greenwich*, &c., -*w*- has usually been 'restored', from the spelling, in this position—e. g. *Edward, forward*.

---

[1] Retention of *h*- in Northern dialects. Mr. Harold Orton informs me that the statement requires qualification; *h*- is lost in the speech of Lorton (Cumb.) and Hackness (Yorks.). In Penrith and Byers Green (Durh.) forms with and without *h*- occur.

Mrs. Basire writes *forard*, Corresp. 137 (1654); Mrs. Alphra Behn writes *aukard*, Sir Patient Fancy, Act II, Sc. i; *awkard* is also found in Mountfort's Greenwich Park, Act 5. Sc. 2, 1691; Lady Lucy Pusey, according to Tuckwell, still called her famous son *Ed'ard*.

Loss of -l- before Consonants.

At the present time *-l-* is no longer pronounced in normal speech before lip-consonants, as in *calf, half, balm, calm*, &c., nor before back-consonants, as in *walk, stalk, folk*, &c.   Before other consonants it is, on the whole, retained, e. g. *mall, salt*, &c.

The evidence for the loss of this consonant, so far as my experience at present goes, begins in the fifteenth century.[1] The loss of the sound itself is doubtless older than the earliest spellings which omit the letter.

Bp. Bekinton, 1442, has *behaf* 'behalf', p. 86; Short Engl. Chron., 1465, *Fakonbrige*, p. 70; Gregory, 1450–70, *sepukyr*, 233; Cely Papers, 1475, &c.:—*fawkyner*, 81, *Tawbot* 'Talbot', 46, *Pamar*, 15, *soudears, soudyears* 'soldiers', 146; *fawkener*, Jul. Berners, 1496; Ascham, *moutea* 'moulted', Tox. 26; Gabr. Harvey, Letters, *Mamsey*, 144; Mulcaster, Elementarie, p. 128, enumerates as examples the following words in which *l* is not pronounced:—*calm, balm, talk, walk, chalk, calf, calues, salues*, 'as though *cawm, bawm*', &c.   Q. Elizabeth, Transl. 20, 1593, writes *stauke* (N.); Machyn writes *hopene* 'halfpenny', *swone* 'swollen', 226, *Northfoke*, 149 (three times), *sawgears* 'soldiers', 302; Surrey, †1547, rhymes *bemoan—swolne*, Tottel's Misc. 28, thus justifying Machyn's spelling.

From Verney Memoirs come:—*sogers*, Lady Sussex, ii. 105, 153, *Sent-arbornes* 'St. Albans', Lady Sussex, ii. 104, my lorde *fakeland*, Lady Sussex, ii. 104, *hop* 'holp', Pret., W. Roades (Steward), iii. 274, 1656, *Norfuck*, Edm. Verney, iii. 282, 1656, *Mamsbury*, Lady Bridgeman, iii, 1660. Cooper, 1685, notes that there is no *l* in *Holborn*; Jones, 1701, says that *l* is lost in *Bristol* (*Bristow* being the old type, and showing really no *loss* of *l*), *folk, Cholmondeley, Holborn, Holms, holp, holpen* (= 'hope, hopen'), *Leopold, Lincoln, Norfolk, Suffolk, soldier, yolk*.   Lady Wentworth writes *sogars, sougar*, 113.   Jones, 1701, besides the ordinary words without *-l* mentions *Mulgrave*, pronounced *Moograve*.

[*] The pronunciation of *should* and *would* without *-l-* may be due to absence of stress in the sentence.   I have noted the following early examples:—*shudd*, Elyot's Gouernour 70, 1531, *shudd*, Gabr. Harvey, Letters, 3, *shud*, Cary Verney, Verney Mem. ii. 71 (twice), 1642, *wode* 'would', Lady Sussex, ibid. iii. 103, *wood*, W. Roades, ibid. iii. 275; Isaac Walton, in Aubrey's Lives ii. 15; *sha't* is written for *shalt*, Congreve's Way of the World, Act I, Sc. ix (1700).

At the present time *soldier* is no longer pronounced without *l*, though I knew an old cavalry officer, now dead, born about 1817, who always said· [sōdžə], and the same old gentleman also pronounced *falcon* as [fɔkən], and spoke of having followed the sport of [fɔkənri'] in his youth. The 'restoration' of *l* in these words is a modern refinement.   *Swone* of Surrey and Machyn, two extremes of the social scale, has passed into the limbo of forgotten pronunciations, and I have not found the form in the following centuries, though it may well have existed.

I have noted two interesting examples of the loss of *l* in unstressed

---

[1] A much earlier example occurs in Ayenbite (1340), *haf* 'behalf', p. 190 in E.E.T.S. Edition.   Another example is found in 1483—the *fyrst haf yere*, Regist. Annal. Coll. Mert., p. 64.

[*] See Appendix IV.

syllables before following consonants:—*sepukyr*, Gregory 283, and *hosteries* 'hostelries', Lord Berners, i. 77. Aubrey writes *Marybon* 'Marylebone', Lives, i. 67.

R.

The chief interest for our present purpose concerning this consonant lies in the conditions under which the sound is lost or retained.

The quality of the sound itself varies in different dialects. In Received Standard, at any rate in the South, the sound has a very weak consonantal character—that of a weakly articulated point-open consonant, generally voiced, but unvoiced after another voiceless consonant, e. g. in *fright*, *pride*, &c. = [fṛait, pṛaid]; in the true Regional dialects of the South— from East to West—it is, or was until quite latterly, an inverted point-open, rather more strongly consonantal than in Received Standard; in Northumberland, and among isolated individuals all over the country, a back -*r*, with slight trilling of the uvula, is heard; in Scotland the sound is a strong point-trill.

The conditions under which the sound is retained or lost in Received Standard are the following:—*it is retained*: initially, and when preceded by another consonant, before vowels—*run, grass*; in the middle of words between vowels—*starry, hearing*, &c.; and, though this is not always true of the speech of the younger generation, at the end of words when the next word begins with a vowel and there is no pause in the sentence between the words—*for ever, over all, her ear*, &c.

R is lost:—in the middle of a word before all other consonants—*hard*, *horse, bird* = [hād, hɔ͞s, bād], &c., &c.; at the end of words unless the next word in the sentence begins with a vowel.

There is evidence that *r* was lost in the South, before consonants, at least as early as the fifteenth century, and it will be noted that so far as the occasional spellings, and, very rarely, the rhymes, throw light, it is lost earliest before -*s*, -*sh*.

The following is the evidence I have collected, covering the period from the fifteenth to the eighteenth centuries inclusive. Bokenam (1441) rhymes *adust—wurst*, St. Lucy 60 and 61; in the Will of J. Buckland, 1450, cf. Linc. Dioc. Docs., p. 41. 15, the spelling *Red wosted qwisshens* occurs; Cely Papers has [1]*passell* 'parcel', pp. 31, 178, and the word *master* is written *marster*, p. 156, and *farther* for *father*, p. 83; Gregory has *mosselle*, 234, 'morsel'; *church* rhymes with *such*, Rede me, &c., 39, (1528); *skaselye* 'scarcely', Robinson's transl. of Sir T. More's Utopia (1556), *skasely*, Sir T. Seymour (1544), State Papers, Hen. VIII, vol. i, p. 781; Machyn (1550-2) writes *Wosseter*, 46, *Dasset* 'Dorset', 48, 57; *Masselsay* 'Marshalsea', 255, &c.; Surrey, in Tottel's Misc., rhymes *furst— dust, first—must*; Roper (†1578), in his Life of Sir T. More, writes *farther* for *father* (this work not published till 1626 in Paris); *dryardes* 'dryads' occurs, p. 14, in Laneham's Lttr. (1575); John Alleyne, *posshene* 'portion', Alleyne Papers, 16, 159–?; Sir Edm. Verney (the Standard Bearer) writes *Fotescue* and *Fottescue* 'Fortescue' (1635-6), Verney Papers, p. 170; the Verney Memoirs have the following spellings:—from vol. ii : *quater* 'quarter', M. Faulkner, 54 (1642), *doset* 'Dorset', Lady Sussex (1642), 102, *Senetabornes* 'St. Albans', where clearly no *r* was pro-

---

[1] *Wusshuppe* occurs in Stonor Prs. ii, 111 (1480).

nounced, Lady Sussex, 155 (1642), *passons* ' persons '. Mrs. Isham, 203
(1642), ' my sister *Alpotts* '¹= 'Alport's ', Lady V., 245 (1646), *wood*
' word ', Mall V., 380 (1647), *fust* ' first ', Mrs. Isham, 200, 208 (1642);
vol. iii : *Pasterne* = ' Paston', Sir R. V., 244 (1655), ' no *father* then
Oxford ', Sir R. V., 292 (1656); vol. iv: *quater*, Doll Leake, 113
(1665), *drawers* = ' draws ', Dick Hals, 307 (1674). Cooper (1685) says
that *wusted* represents the pronunciation of *worsted*. Jones (1701) indicates
the pronunciation minus *r* in *Woster, hash, mash* for ' harsh ', ' marsh '.
Lady Wentworth (1705–11) writes *Gath*, 63, 271, for the name of the
physician *Garth*, and other correspondents write *Albemal* Street, 274,
extrodinary, 321, *Dotchester*, 153, *Author* = 'Arthur', 77, 398, 399,
Duke of *Molbery*, 113, &c.   The spelling *Dowerger* = ' Dowager ', 464,
shows that the symbol *r* might be written without being pronounced.
Baker, in *Rules for True Spelling*, &c., 1724, says that *nurse, purse, thirsty,
Ursula, sarsanet* are pronounced *nus, pus, thusty,*² *Usly, sasnet.*   Jespersen
quotes German writers on English pronunciation of 1718 and 1748, who
assert that *r* is not pronounced in *mart, parlour, partridge, thirsty,* but
says that Walker in 1775 is the first Englishman ' to admit the muteness
of -*r* '.   In Bertram's Royal English-Danish Grammar, 1753, *r* is said to
be ' mute ' in *Marlborough, harsh, purse.*   Batchelor, 1809, speaking of
the vowel in *burn*, says it is difficult to ascertain what portion of the sound
belongs to *r*, as the vowel appears before -*r* to be only slightly different
from that of *u* in *nostrum.*   In other words, the vowel is lengthened and
the *r*-sound has disappeared.

In the more rustic forms of English, *r* before consonants retained a more
or less strong consonantal quality longer than in the East.   This is
indicated by such a spelling as *morun* ' morn ', Shillingford, p. 6, and
baron ' barn ', in the Will of R. Astbroke (Bucks.), Linc. Dioc. Docs.
167. 35 (1534).   At the end of the fifteenth century, Cr. Duke of York has
sundery, 389, and *therell* ' the earl ', 392.³   To summarize the above evidence, it would appear that the weakening and disappearance of *r* before
another consonant, especially, at first, before [s, ʃ], had taken place by the
middle of the fifteenth century at any rate in Essex and Suffolk; that
a hundred years later London speakers of the humbler sort (Machyn), as
well as more highly placed and better educated persons in various walks
of life, pronounced the sound but slightly, if at all; that the tendency is
more and more marked, not only before [s, ʃ], but before other consonants also, until by the middle of the next century it seems that the
pronunciation among the upper classes (the Verneys and their relatives)
was very much the same as at present.   The later evidence, from the
eighteenth century onwards, confirms this view.

It will be observed that the eighteenth-century pronunciations [nas,
pas], &c., which are clearly foreshadowed in the rhymes of Bokenam, and
later of Surrey, the Verneys, &c., have been ousted by another type [pãs,
nãs, &c.], in which the *r* was not lost until after lengthening had taken
place.   The modern semi-humorous vulgarisms, written *cuss, bust* for
curse, burst, represent the older type.   The lack of confirmation from the
fifteenth- and sixteenth-century Orthoepists of the loss of *r* before consonants has no significance, since many people at the present time are

---

¹ The rhyme *after—carter* in Rede me, &c., 119, must represent [ǣtǝ—kǣtǝ], and at
least shows that *r* was not pronounced in the latter word.

² The spelling *Ussly* actually occurs in a letter of Mrs. Adams, Later V.
Letters (1701), vol. i, 107.   On the same page *my three fust* (children) is written
in a letter of Lady Gardiner.

³ Note also *harem* ' harm ', and *teram* ' term ', Lady Hungerford, pp. 255,
256 (1570).

unable to realize that they no longer pronounce -*r*- in this position, being obsessed by the spelling.

Note.—The spelling *dace*, the name of the fish, shows that *r* must have been lost early before -*s*; Dame Jul. Berners, however (1496), still has *darse* in Wynkyn de Worde's print of her *Treatyse of Fysshynge*.

Loss of Final -r.

I have very little early evidence regarding this, but have noted the spelling *Harflew* in Bp. Pecok's *Repressor* (1449), i. 258, and in Shakespeare's *Hen. V*, First Fol., ii. i; Lady Wentworth's spellings, *Operer*, 66, *Bavarior*, 90, Lord *Carburer* = Carbery, must express the sound [ə] in the final syllable, and indicate that an -*r* in this position expressed no consonantal sound.

The vowel murmur [ə], developed from the suffixes -*er*, -*or*, &c., as in *better* [bɛtə], may probably be regarded as a simple weakening of a syllabic -*r*, which is still heard in provincial dialects. There are occasional spellings in which the termination is written without a vowel:—*remembr*, Sir J. Fortescue, 124, 125, *undr*, ibid. 135, and Dr. Knight's *modre*, 1512, Ellis ii. 1, probably indicate [rɪmɛmbr, undr, mūdr] respectively.

Development of Murmur-vowel after Long Vowel + r.

After old long vowels and diphthongs formerly followed by -*r* we have now [ə], the long vowel being partially shortened—thus *bear, hear, fire* become [bɛə, hiə, faiə]. It was formerly supposed that, as in the instances just considered, the murmur-vowel was merely a weakening of -*r*. There is reason, however, to suppose that [ə] developed between the vowel or diphthong and the following -*r*, before the loss of the latter.

The following sixteenth-century spellings appear to prove this:—Anne Boleyn (1528), *I desyerd, desyer, requyer*, all on p. 306, Ellis i. 1; Sir Thos. Elyot, *hiare* 'to hire', Vb., i. 113; Will of Sir J. Digby (1533), Leic., Linc. Dioc. Docs. 147. 16, *desyoring*; Gabriel Harvey's Letters (1572–80), *devower*, 128, *fyer* 'fire', 130, *youers* 'yours', 139; Countess of Shrewsbury, Letter, Ellis ii. 2. 66, *duaring* (1581); Q. Elizabeth, *I desiar*, Letters to James VI, 13, and Transl. 122, *hiar* 'hear', Tr. 76, *fiars* 'fires', Transl. 76. Of these possibly *hiar* might be questioned, the *ia* might be put for *ea*, but the others, I think, quite certainly point to [aiər, ūər, ɔuər]. I have not pursued the investigation farther, and can only offer one example of such a spelling in the seventeenth century, *desiar*, Cary Verney, in Verney Mem. ii. 68 (1642). Dr. Watts, *True Riches*, has the couplet—

> Or she sits at Fancy's *door*
> Calling shapes and shadows *to her*

where it is evident the rhyme is [dūə—tūə]. Baker, 1724, *Rules for True Spelling*, says words ending -*re* are pronounced as though with -*ur*, *fire, hire, mire*, &c. = [faiə], &c.

Metathesis of r.

In Received Standard we use many metathesized forms, such as *wright* O.E. *wyrhta*, *through* O.E. *þurh*, *wrought* O.E. *worhte*, *third* O.E. *þridda*.

The metathesized forms are probably E. Midland (Norfolk and Suffolk) in origin, to judge by M.E. In the fifteenth and sixteenth centuries other metathesized forms besides those heard to-day were in use, thus Marg. Paston has *drust* ' durst ', ii. 191; Cr. of Duke of York a Knight of the Garter, *wrothey*, ' worthy ', 399; Peter Wentworth, *crub'd* ' curbed ', W. Papers 236, 1712; *gurge* ' grudge ' occurs in 1515, State of Ireland, State Papers, Hen. VIII, i, p. 23; *brust* ' burst ', G. Harvey's Letters 33, 1573–80; Queen Elizabeth, *shirlest* ' shrillest ', Transl. 46.

On the other hand, *thorf* ' through ' is written by Marg. Paston, ii. 197; ' a silke *gridyll* ', Will of Sir T. Comberworth (Lincs.), Linc. Dioc. Docs. 50. 6, and *strike* ' stirk ', ibid. 50. 5 (1451), and *thrid* in Rewle of Sust. Men. 107. 36, and *Kyrstemes* ' Christmas ' in Cely Papers 22 (1479).

Cooper notes that ' *r* is sounded after *o* ' in *apron, citron, environ, gridiron, iron, saffron*, ' as though written *apurn*, &c.' He also notes the very common sixteenth- and seventeenth-century form *hunderd as being pronounced ' *facilitatis causa* '. Baker, *Rules for True Spelling* (1724), transcribes *apron* as *apurn*, *Katherine* as *Katturn*, *saffron* as *saffurn*. The Wentworth Papers have *Kathern*, Lady Strafford, 305 (1712), *childern*, Peter W., 68 (1709), *Chirstmas* [kɑ̄stməs], Lord Wentworth (a child), 462 (1730).

With regard to the general question of the loss of *r* medially, before consonants, and finally, a curious passion for eye-rhymes long obtained among poets, and to some extent still exists.

To describe such rhymes as *higher—Thalia* or *morning—dawning* as *Cockney rhymes* is foolish and inaccurate. The former is made by Keats, the latter by so fastidious a poet and gentleman as Mr. Swinburne. This prejudice is gradually dying out among poets. If this or that poet still dislikes and avoids such rhymes, perfect though they be according to normal educated English pronunciation, simply on account of the *r* in the spelling, that is his affair and his readers need not complain. If they are objected to on the ground that the rhyme is not perfect, and that it is only in vulgar ˉpronunciation that -*r*- is not heard in *morn*, &c., this is not consonant with fact.

Loss or Assimilation of Various Consonants in Combination.

Loss of **d** *before and after other cons.*

Hoccleve—*freenly*, Reg. of Pr. 2064; St. Editha, 1420—*bleynasse* ' blindness ', 2937, *pounse* ' pounds ', 213; Shillingford, 1447–50—*Wensday*, 51, *myssomer* yeven, 65; Marg. Paston—*Quesontyde* ' Whitsun ', i. 43. 1440, *Wensday*, ii. 201. 1465; Cely Papers—*hosbanry*, 43; Gregory, 1450–70—*Wanysday*, 96; Elyot—*chylhode*, Gouernour, Pr. cxcii; Latimer—*Wensdaye*, Ploughers 30, *frensheppe*, 128; Machyn, 1550—*granefather*, 274, *granser*, 169, *Wostrett* ' Wood Street ', 242, *Wyssunmonday*, 158; Lever's Sermons—*frynshyp*, 110; Shakesp., R. of L., rhymes *hounds—downs*, 677–8; John Alleyne, Alleyne Pprs.—*stane, stannes still, hunes* ' hands ', 16 (159–); Verney Pprs.—*Wensday*, Sir Edm. V., 229, 242. 1639; *grannam* ' grandam ', Dr. Denton, 242. 1639; Verney Mem.—*Wenesday*, Lady Sussex, ii. 123, also Dr. Denton, iii. 207. 1656, and *Wensday*, Cary Stewkley (Verney), iv. 136. 1665; *hinmost*, Dr. Denton, iv. 227. 1674;

---

* See Appendix IV.

Lord Rochester (died 1680), rhymes *wounds—lampoons*, Rehearsal; Vanbrugh, in *Journey to London*, 1726, makes Lady Arabella say gud *soons = wounds*; Jones, 1701—*Wensday*, and omits *d* in *intends, commands*, &c., 'men being apt to pass over *d* in silence between *-n-* and another consonant'; Lady Wentworth writes *Wensday* twice, 49, *hansomly, Clousley* for *Cloudsley*; Baker, 1724, notes absence of *d* in *hansone*. Jones also says that *d* is not pronounced in *landlord, landlady, friendly, handmaid, candle, chandler, dandle, handle, kindle, fondle*, and other words in *-ndl-*; further, in *children* (= [tʃɪlrən]).

The pronunciation of *London* as [lanən], which persisted among polite speakers far into the nineteenth century, deserves a few words. The process was probably [landn—lann—lanən]—the assimilation of *-d-* when flanked by *n*. The earliest examples I have found are from Mrs. Basire, who writes *Lonan*, pp. 133, 135, 137 (1654), and *Lonant*, 147 (1656). Gray, in a letter to Horace Walpole (July 11, 1757), says 'if you will be vulgar and pronounce it Lunnun . . . I can't help it'.

Elphinston, in his works from 1765 to 1787, says 'we generally hear Lunnon'.

I am now able to cite a still earlier example of this type. Gill, Logonom. (1621) 14. 2, writes *Lunun* for the pronunciation which he attributes to 'postmen'—*tabellarii*.

Loss of **-t-** *before and after other consonants.*

St. Editha—*fonstone* = 'font-stone'; Marg. Paston—*morgage*, i. 69. 1448; Machyn—*Brenfford* 'Brentford', 57; Q. Elizabeth—*attemps*, Lttrs. to J. VI, 23, *accidens*, ibid. 23, *offen* 'often', 39; Edw. Alleyne has *wascote*, Alleyne Mem. 26. 1593; Verney Pprs.—*wascott* 'waistcoat', Mrs. Poultney, 261. 1639; *Chrismas*, Lady Sussex, 205. 1639; Verney Mem.—*crismus*, Doll Leake, iii. 287. 1656; *Coven Garden*, Cary V., ii. 64. 1642; Sir Philip Warwick, Memoires of Charles I—*busling* 'bustling', p. 141. 1701; Lady Wentworth—*Crismass*, 66. 1708, *Wesminstor*, 62, *crisned*, 62, *Taufs* = 'Tofts', the singer, 66; *Shasbury* = *Shaftsbury*, 59, 198. Jones notes loss of *-t-* in the pronunciation of *Christmas, costly, ghastly, ghostly, Eastcheap, lastly, beastly, breastplate, gristle, bristle, whistle*, &c.; *listless, mostly, roast beef, waistband, wristband, christen, fasten, glisten*, &c., and further in *colt's foot, maltster, saltpetre, saltcellar, Wiltshire.*

Most of the above pronunciations may still be heard in rapid unstudied speech; to some, such as the omission of *t* in *mostly, roast beef*, &c., purists might object. It is interesting to note that Q. Elizabeth pronounced *often* without a *t*, as do good speakers at the present time. The pronunciation [ɔftn, ɔ̃ftn], now not infrequently heard, is a new-fangled innovation.

Loss of **b** *between other consonants; also between another consonant and a vowel.*

I have only noted a few examples of this :—*assemlyd*, Cely Pprs. 145; *tremlyng*, Cavendish, L. of Wolsey 234. 1557; *nimlest* 'nimblest', Q. Elizabeth, Lttrs. to J. VI, 29. *Camerwell* occurs in a memo. of sale of a house, Alleyne Mem. 83. 1607.

Machyn has *Cammerell* 'Camberwell', 300. The loss of *-w-* before an unstressed syllable is normal (see p. 296). *Lameth* 'Lambeth' occurs in a letter of Cranmer, 1534 (see p. 304, below). This particular form may well be mentioned here.

Loss of -n + *consonant.*

Westmyster, Gregory's Chron. 142, and passim, 1450–70; *Westmester*, Short Engl. Chron., passim, 1465; *Westmester*, Cr. Knt. of Bath, L. and Pprs. i. 388. 1493; *Wasmester*, Mrs. Basire, 140 (1655); both Jones, 1701, and Baker, 1724, indicate *Westmuster* as the pronunciation.

Milton writes *goverment* in autograph MS., Com. 25.

Loss of -n- *after a vowel followed by a consonant.*

Son y lawe 'son-in-law', Marg. Paston, ii. 195; *Sune elaw*, Machyn, 303.

mallicholie (twice), Shakespeare, L. L. L., Act iv, Sc. iii, said by Berowne.

Loss of Final Consonants.

The omission of final consonants, especially -*t*, -*d* after another consonant, but also occasionally after vowels, and, to a less extent, of other final consonants, seems to have been a common practice among all classes far into the eighteenth century.   Most of these final consonants have now been restored in the usage of educated speech.

Apart from combinative treatment, in which respect our natural rapid speech does not greatly differ from that of earlier centuries, in dropping final consonants before another word beginning with a consonant— [rousbīf, bīsli], &c.—the loss of -*b* after -*m*- (*lamb*, &c.) is the principal survival of the tendency to eliminate final consonants, once so widespread.

Loss of -d.

blyn 'blind', Norf. Guilds 35. 1389; 'God of Hevene *sene* ȝou', &c. = 'send', Constable of Dynevor Castle, temp. Hen. IV, Ellis ii. 1. 16; *husbon*, Marg. Paston i. 42, *hunder*, do. ii. 201; my *Lor*, Cely Pprs. 63; *Edwar* the iiij, Gregory 223; *rebowne* 'rebound', Rede me, &c.; *blyne* 'blind', Machyn, 105, *cole* harber 'cold-', do. 74; yron *Mowle* 'mould', Euphues 152, *ole* drudge 'old', ibid. 317; Verney Mem.—*friten* P. P., ii. 53. 1642; Cooper gives *thouzn* as the pronunciation of *thousand*; Lady Wentworth has *poun* 'pound', 62, *thousan*, 55, *Sunderlin* 'Sunderland', 118, *own* 'owned', 93; her son Peter writes (1710) *Richmon*, *scaffels* 'scaffold', 110, *Northumberlain*, 418; Jones notes 'the sound of *n*, written -*nd*, when it may be sounded in *almond, beyond, Desmond, despond, diamond* (cf. Lady W.'s *dyomons*, 57), *Edmond, Ostend, Raymond, riband, Richmond, waistband, wristband, scaffold, Oswald*', &c. Baker, 1724, says that *almond* is pronounced *almun*.

Loss of -t.

Seynt Johan þe babtis, Norf. Guilds 27. 1389; *nex*, Marg. Paston, ii. 82, &c.; *excep*, Cely Pprs. 58, *nex*, ibid. 68; *Braban*, Gregory's Chron. 80; *uprigh*, Reception of Cath. of Aragon, Lttrs. and Pprs. ii. 415. 1503; *Beamon* 'Beaumont', Lord Berners, I. 21. 1520; *Egype*, Machyn, 262; *prompe*, Ascham, Tox. 26 and 39; *stricklier*, W. Norris, Alleyne Pprs. 35. 1608; Verney Pprs.—*respecks*, Mr. Wiseman, 143. 1629; *respeck*, Mrs. Isham, 262. Verney Mem. have the following :—*gretis* (Superl.), Lady Sussex, ii. 123, *Papeses* 'Papists', Mrs. Isham, iii. 230. 1655, *honis* 'honest', Lady Hobart, iv. 52. 1664; *Mundy nex*, Mall V., ii. 380. 1647; *nex*, Lady Rochester (Sussex), iii. 467. 1660; *respeck*,

Lady Hobart, iii. 305. 1657; the *res* of our neighbours, Mrs. Basire, 110. 1651.

According to Jones, 1701, *-t* is omitted at the end of *rapt, script, abrupt, bankrupt, corrupt, manuscript*; *distinct, strict, direct, afflict, reflect, respect, sect*, &c., &c. He gives the pronunciation of *pageant* as *pagin*, or *pageen*.

Lady Wentworth—*prospeck*, 62; Peter W.—*strick* 'strict', 255; Lady W.—*richis* 'richest', Lord *Dyzer* 'Dysart', *tex* 'text', Lady W. **221**. 1711; Baker, 1724—*Egip, poscrip, ballas* 'ballast'; Pope rhymes *sex—neglects*, Epilogue to the Satires, Dial. I, 15–16. 1738.

Elphinston says that *t* cannot be clearly heard in *distinct*, but has not quite disappeared in *distinctly*.

Loss of final -t.

kerchys 'kerchiefs', Bokenam, St. Cecil. 862. 1441; *kersche* and *nekkerchys*, M. Paston, ii. 342. 1469; *Sant Towleys* 'St. Olaves', Machyn, 118; *masties* 'mastiffs', G. Harvey's Lttrs. 18. 1573–80; Marston— *handkerchers*, Ant. and Mell., Pt. ii, Act ii, Sc. i, 1602; *masty*, Middleton's Trick to Catch the Old One, i. 4 (1608); *handkerchers*, Lady Brill. Harley, 1641; Lady Sussex—*baly*, Verney Mem. ii. 156. 1642; Baker, 1724—*handkercher, mastee* 'mastiff'; Jones, 1701—*mastee, bailee, hussee*, or *hussy* 'housewife'.

Loss of final -b.

We no longer pronounce *-b* in *comb, lamb, jamb*, &c., nor in inflected forms of these words before a vowel, such as *combing, lambing*, &c. On the other hand, we have restored the *b* in *Lambeth*, originally *Lambhēþ* with the South-Eastern or Kentish form of O.E. *hȳþ*, a landing-place or wharf. As early as 1418 Archbishop Chichele writes *Lamhyth*, Ellis i. 1. 5; and in 1534 a letter from Archbishop Cranmer, though not, unfortunately, preserved in his own handwriting, contains the form *Lameth*, Ellis iii. 2. 319; *lameskynnes* occurs in Rewle of Sustr. Men., 1450. 49; to *clyme* 'climb', Euphues, 185. 1580.

lamme, Gabr. Harvey's Lttrs. 135, *lamskin*, ibid. 14. 1573–80; to *come* it = 'comb', Pen. Verney, V. Mem. ii. 177. 1642.

Cooper, 1685, notes that *-b* is lost in *climb, dumb, lamb, limb, thumb, tomb, womb*.

In *limb* and *thumb* the *b* is unhistorical, the O.E. forms being *lim, þūma*. The explanation of the spelling in these two words may possibly be that the final *-b* was once pronounced, having been developed according to the tendencies illustrated on p. 309, below.

Loss of Consonants between Vowels, or after Consonants before a following Vowel.

Loss of open consonants.

St. Editha, 1420—*senty* 'seventy', 414, *swene* = *sweven* 'dream', 906, *godmores* 'godmothers', 2215, *pament* 'pavement', 2027; Caxton, Jason—*pament*, 166. 27. 1477; Machyn—*Denshyre*, 39, *Lussam* 'Lewisham'; Marston—*I marle* 'marvel', E. Hoe 3. 2. 1605; Jones gives *Dantry* as the pronunciation of *Daventry*; Cary Stewkley—*senet* 'seven nights, se'nnight', Verney Mem. iv. 434. 1656; Aubrey, Lives (1669–96), has *Shrineham* 'Shrivenham' Berks., ii. 47, Clark's Ed.

Loss of d *between vowels.*

The form *la'ship* for *ladyship* occurs in Congreve's Way of the World, Act III, Sc. iv, said by a mincing waiting-woman, and in Tom Jones, said by Mrs. Honour, Sophia Western's waiting-woman.   As this is the only evidence I can produce for this form, it is probably to be regarded as a vulgarism.

Loss of h + t.

We must distinguish between the treatment ot the combination -*ht*—
(*a*) when preceded by original front vowels, e. g. in *night, light,* &c., and
(*b*) when preceded by back vowels, e. g. in *daughter, bought,* &c.

In the former case the sound represented by -*h*- disappeared in Southern English at least as early as the fifteenth century, in spite of the statements of some of the seventeenth-century Orthoepists ; in the latter case there were two developments—(1) total disappearance of the consonant before -*t*, and (2) a change to the sound -*f*-.   The latter development is treated above, p. 288.

The disappearance of the consonant is shown in the occasional spellings, both by the omission of the letter -*h*- in words where it belongs historically, and by the introduction of -*h*- or -*gh*- in words where no sound ever existed between the vowel and the following -*t*— *wright* for ' write ', *abought* for ' about '.

(a) *Loss of* h *before* t *when preceded by a front vowel.*

Curiously enough, the earliest proofs I have found of the disappearance of the consonant—here a front-open-voiceless [j]—in the combination -*ight*, consist of the introduction of the consonantal symbols where they do not historically belong.   In the following list the two types of spelling are enumerated indiscriminately, in chronological order, since they both go to establish the same thing.

Marg. Paston—*wright* ' write ', ii. 29, 1461, &c., &c., also E. of Surrey, Letter to Wolsey, St. Pprs. Hen. VIII, pt. ii. 39, 1520, Sir Thos. More, Ellis i. 1. 199 ; *quight*, Rede me, &c., 1528 ; *lyte* ' light ', Elyot's Gouernour 2. 355 ; *whight* ' white ', Cavendish, L. of Wolsey, 23, 1557 ; *baight* ' bate ', Whetstone's Remembr. of Gascoine, Steele Glasse, p. 24, 1577 ; *weight* rhymes *fate*, Habington's Castara 134, *height* rhymes *state*, ibid. 96, 1634 ; Henry Verney—to *wryght*, Verney Pprs. 190, 1637 ; Spenser constantly writes *quight, bight* ' bite ', &c., and rhymes *fight*, &c., indifferently with *white*, &c., or with *quite*, &c.

(b) *Loss of* -h- + t *when preceded by a back vowel.*

My evidence for this is earlier than for (a).   Already in the thirteenth century *broute* ' brought ' is found in Laȝamon, and *naut* ' naught ' in Hali Meidenhed, 1225, *dowter* ' daughter ' in Songs and Carols, 1400, while the spelling *foghte* ' foot ' is found in W. of Shoreham.

Marg. Paston has *kawt* ' caught ', i. 110, 1450, *abowght* ' about ', ii. 29, 1461, *ought* ' out ', ii. 341, 1469, *abaught*, ii. 362, 1499 ; *dowttyr*, Cely Papers 105 ;   Henry VIII writes *abought* in 1515, Ellis i. 1. 126 ; Elyot's Gouernour—*dought* ' doubt ', 1. 35, *cloughts*, 1. 247 ; Gabr. Harvey—*droute* ' drought ', Lttrs. 72, and *thoat* ' thought ', ibid. 15 ; J. Alleyn, Alleyn Pprs,—*dater, datter*, p. 15, 159— ; Anne Denton, Verney Mem. iii. 73—*dater* ' daughter ', 1650 ; Wm. Roades, V. Mem.

iii. 274—*slater* 'slaughter', 1656. Mrs. Basire has *doter* 'daughter', 112 (1653).

D. Addition of Consonants.

Development of w- initially before M.E. ō².

The word *one* and its old Gen. the Adv. *once* [wan], &c., are curiosities in Received Standard, being the only forms of their kind. The normal development of O.E. *ān* is heard in *on*-ly and al-*one*, and it is evident that the corresponding form of *one* [ōn] was in use in the Standard English of the seventeenth century, alongside the other type, that from which our present form is derived. The pronunciation [wan] or its equivalent, at any rate a pronunciation with initial *w*-, seems to be the sole form now in use in stressed positions in the various rustic dialects apart from those of the North, which are [ēn, jen], &c. In some it is, no doubt, indigenous, in most it must have been borrowed from Received Standard.

The development of the form [wan] is not altogether easy to follow. It is certain, however, that it owes its main feature—the initial '*w*-'—to what is called a strong rounded on-glide, which in time became a definite independent lip-back consonant. It is strange that this word should be the sole survivor of its type in Received Standard, strange also that it is not recognized in the official spelling. The first point may strike us as yet more remarkable when we call to mind the words *only* and *alone*, which, though almost completely isolated from their parent by form and meaning, were formerly closely associated with it by both of these ties; the second is the more astonishing when we note that a very similar tendency which overtook *ō²* preceded by *h*- (in *holy, hot*), &c., actually has been recorded in the orthodox system of spelling in the words *whole*, *whore*, although no trace of any lip consonant (*w*) survives in any form of Standard English, in any words of this class. But although at the present time there is only one word which retains the *w*-type which began originally with *ō*-, and none originally beginning with *hō*-, we shall see that down well into the seventeenth century at least, other words, as one would expect, also show this type of pronunciation, so far as can be judged by the occasional spellings.

We may well ask where our solitary [wan] came from, and to a great extent Echo answers—where? From what Regional dialect the tendency arose we cannot say at present.

The earliest spelling of the *wone* form I have found so far is in St. Editha (Wilts.), and other instances of the *w*- spellings in this and other words will be found below from other fifteenth-century texts of Westerly origin. But do we seek to draw any conclusions from this, behold the Cely Papers, in the same century, written for the most part by Essex people, also furnish examples. Still it is true that most of my fifteenth-century examples are from texts written in the West of England, and we may make what we can of that fact. If we turn to the facts of the Modern dialects, as they are recorded in Wright's Engl. Dial. Gr., they do not, I think, point to anything definite—the *w*-forms of words like *oats*, &c., seem to be peppered about, more or less at random, among the Regional dialects. This, like so many other problems of its kind, will never be settled by limiting our investigation to the Modern dialects. Not until we know much more than is known at present of the details of the distribution of dialectal peculiarities in the M.E. period and in the fifteenth century will these questions be solved.

The words of which I have found spellings with *w-* before original initial *ō* are M.E. *oon* ' one ', *oonly* ' only ', *ōthe* ' oath ' ; while those with an initial *h-* of which I have found *wh-* spellings are *hool* ' whole ', *hoom* ' home ', *hoot* ' hot '. I put them into two separate lists.

Forms with w- of ' one ', &c., ' oath ', &c.

St. Editha, 1420—*won* ' one ', 1835, 2302, 3086, 3103 ; *wonlyche*, 3529, *wothe*, 2100 ; Audelay's Poems, 1426—*won*, p. 38 ; Exeter Tailors' Guild, 1466—*won*, 322, *woth*, 322 ; Cely Pprs., 1475—*whon*, 33, *whone*, 24, ' one ' (the Celys often write *wh-* for *w-*, cf. p. 313) ; Cely Pprs.— *wolde* ' old ', 22, 1479 ; Henry VIII, Letters, Ellis i. 1—*won*, p. 126, 1515, and *won, woon*, i. 2. 130, 1544 ; Thos. Pery, Letters—*wone*, Ellis ii. 2. 140, 143, 1549 ; Latimer's Sermons—*such a wone*, 5, 7, 32 ; Machyn, 1550-63—*won*, 125.; Q. Elizabeth, Transl.—*won*, 74, *wons*, 4, 1593 ; W. Faunte, Alleyn Pprs.—*shuch a on* (= *w-*), p. 32, 159- ; Verney Mem. —*a meane wan*, Sir R. V. ii. 76, 1642 ; *won's* ' one's ', Lady Sydenham, II. 100, 1642 ; Wentw. Pprs., Lady Strafford—*won*, 213, 214, 1711, 280, 1712. Cooper, 1685, includes *wuts* ' oats ' among his list of dialectal forms.

Forms with whō, &c., for old hō-.

St. Editha—*wholle* ' whole ', 3368 ; Bp. Bekinton, 1442—*whome* ' home ', Lttrs., p. 80 ; Syr Degrevaunt—*whome*, l. 929 ; Sir J. Fortescue—*whome*, 153 ; Rede̅ me, &c., 1528—*whore, whoredom*, passim, *whoate*, 51, ' hot ', *whole, wholy*, 61, *wholines*, 85, 86, *wholy* ' holy ', 116, &c. ; Latimer's Serm.—*whomlye*, 134, *whore, whoredom*, 160 ; Lever's Serm.—*whot* ' hot ', 126, 1550 ; Ascham, Scholemaster—*wholie* ' wholly ', 92, 1563-8 ; Lord Burghley, Letters—*whott* ' hot ', Ellis ii. 3. 99, 1582 ; Sir Thos. Smith, Rep. Angl.—*whot*, 70, 1565; Peele, Edw. I, Malone Soc. —*whot*, 2389, *whote*, 1212, 1591 ; Q. Elizabeth, Lttrs. J. VI—*wholy*, 27, 1593 ; Spenser—*whott*, F. Q., Bk. ii, Cant. v. 18 ; Mulcaster, 1583— ' mere ignorance writeth so unwarielie *whole* for *hole* which (ought) to begin with *h-* ', Elementarie, p. 155 ; Henry Verney, V. Mem. ii. 355, 356, writes *whome* ' home ', 1647.

Cooper, 1685, notes *hwutter* ' hotter ' as belonging to ' barbarous dialect ' and to be avoided.

The Combination sō² becomes swō ; scou- [skū] becomes [skwū-].

Bp. Pecok's Repressor, 1449, has the form *swope* ' soap ', 1. 127. This must be regarded as a purely Regional form of a type which apparently never got a footing in the London dialect or in Common Literary English. Pecok's English is decidedly Western in type, in so far as it departs from the London form.

Cooper records the pronunciation *squrge* ' scourge ', ' facilitatis causa '.

Survival of [ōn] for one.

Note the older type in rhymes :— Sackville *one-stone, mone* ' moan ' ; Shakespeare with *bone* and *gone* ; Cowley with *grown* ; Lady Winchilsea with *alone*, and Dryden with *thrown*. Mrs. Eure, Verney Papers (1639), p. 230, has the inverted spelling *my one* ' own '. Cooper (1685) says *one* and *own* are alike. Wallis (1653) gives ' *ô rotundum* ' in *one*, as in *pole*, *boat*, *oat*. Writing Scholar's Companion (1690) says *wun* is vulgar.

ō¹- *initially becomes* **wō** [wŭ] ; hō¹- *becomes* **whō** [whŭ-].

Whatever may be the case in Regional dialects, the instances are rare in the London dialect and Literary English. I have noted *wother* 'other', Rede me, &c., 1528, 22, 27, 32, &c. ; also in a letter from Thos. Pery, Ellis ii. 2. 146, 1539.

Under this heading may be mentioned *Wolster* ' Ulster ', St. of Ireland, St. Pprs. Hen. VIII, p. 7, 1515.

In Gabriel Harvey's Lttr. Bk. 'hood' is written *whudd*, p. 125. I remember, as a boy, hearing a domestic pronounce ' Red Riding *Wood* ' = *Hood*. In Chapman's Mons. d'Olive, Wks. i. 246, *whoote* occurs for ' hoot ', 1606 ; *knightwood*, Lady Brill. Harley, 114 (1641) ; *falsewood*, ' falsehood '. Peter W. (1712), Wentworth P., p. 235.

Development of **y** [j] *initially before Front Vowels.*

A certain number of words occur written with *y*- in various writers, between the fifteenth and eighteenth centuries inclusive. I do not propose to deal with M.E. forms here. This feature is perhaps more characteristic of the Western dialects, but traces of it are found in Cely Papers, and it penetrates into the London dialect and the Received Standard of the sixteenth and following centuries. One form—*yearth*—as will be seen from the particulars below, is very persistent, and may perhaps be regarded as a Kentish or South-Eastern form originally—cf. M.E. (Kentish) *yerthe*, &c., where *ye* represents the old diphthong *eo*. I have noted the following examples of *y*- forms :—

St. Editha—ȝende ' end ', l. 1846 ; Coventry Leet Bk., 1430, ȝeuery ' every ', p. 131 ; Bokenam—*yorth* ' earth ' ; Shillingford—*yerly* ' early ', 16, *yeuen* ' even ', 16, *yese* 'ease ', 40 ; Cely Papers—*yelles* ' ells ' ; Recept. Cath. of Ar., 1501—*yest* ' east ', Lttrs. and Pprs. i. 394 ; Thos. Pery—*yending*, Ellis ii. 2. 140, 1539 ; Latimer's Serm.—*yere* ' ere ', 56, *yearth* ' earth ', 52 ; Edw. VI, First P. B.—*yer* ' ere ', Joh. viii, *yearth*, Venite, Te Deum, &c., &c. ; Machyn has *yerl* ' earl ' frequently throughout his Diary ; Lever's Serm., 1550—*yearthe*, 43, *yearthly*, 61 ; Butler, 1634, warns against *yer* ' ere ' and *yerst* ' erst ' ; Mall Verney—*yearnestly*, V. Mem. ii. 381, 1647 ; Mrs. Isham—*yeare* ' ear ', V. Mem. iv. 118. 1665 ; Cooper, 1685, puts *yerb* ' herb ' and *yearth* under his forms which illustrate ' Barbarous Dialect ', ; *a holl in her yeare*, Lady Gardiner, Later V. Letters i. 44 (1699); in 1749 (Letter 195), Lord Chesterfield mentions *yearth* as an example of the pronunciation of the Vulgar Man, which ' carries the mark of the beast along with it ' ; Goldsmith, in the Essay ' Of Various Clubs ', Busybody, 1759, makes a Club member tell a story of what a noble Lord said to him—' There 's no man on the face of the *yearth* ', &c.; young Squire Malford, in Humphrey Clinker, 1771, writes *yearl* ' earl ' (in italics) in a letter, evidently indicating a contemporary pronunciation which he did not use himself; Elphinston, 1787, mentions *yearth* and *yerb* as current both in Scotland and England, though not in good usage.

It is evident that some of these forms were once fairly widespread, and that not only in provincial usage. At the present time, the only one which still survives among good speakers is *year* for *ear*, and that is fast becoming archaic, and is heard less and less.

Addition of Consonants.

Finally, especially after -r, -n, -m, -l, -s, -f.

Palladius, 1420—*Spaniald* 'Spaniard' for *Spanyol*, 75. 409 ; St.
Editha—*Jaylardes*, 2923, *to past away*; Bury Wills—*wochsaft*, 17 ;
Capgrave's Chron.—*lynand* 'linen', 108, *ylde*, 257 ; Sir J. Paston—*ilde*
'aisle'; Marg. Paston—*wyld* 'will', i. 83, *combe* Vb. Inf., iv. 78 ;
Short Engl. Chron., 1465—*Lymoste*, 65, 'Limehouse'; Gregory's
Chron., 1450-70—*loste*, 215, *patent* 'paten', 86 ; Cely Pprs.—*Clifte*
'Cleave' Pl. N. Glos. 161 ; Cr. of Knt. of Bath—*felde*, 397 ; R. Pace to
Card. Wolsey—*synst*, Ellis iii. 1. 199 ; Lord Berners' Froissart—*kneled
downed*, i. 25 ; St. of Irel., St. Pprs. Hen. VIII, iii—*whylde* 'while',
p. 18, 1513 ; Thos. Pery—*varment* 'vermin', Ellis ii. 2. 148, *sermonte*
'sermon', 154 ; Machyn, 1550-63—*Sakefeld* 'Sackville', 153 ; Gabr.
Harvey, Lttrs., 1573-80—*surgiant* 'surgeon', 23 ; Ascham, Tox.—
grafte Vb., earlier *graffe*, p. 56 ; Wilson, Arte of Rhet.—*gallands*
'gallons', 155 ; Euphues—*visard*, 319, *lombe* 'loom', 293, *margent*, 270,
mushrompe, 62 ; E. of Shrewsbury—*orphant*, Ellis ii. 3. 60, 1582 ;
Q. Elizabeth, Lttrs. to J. VI—*for the nonest* 'nonce', 91. 1593 ; Marston,
Anton. and Mell., Pt. 2, Act II, Sc. iv—*orphant*, 1602 ; Shakespeare,
First Fol.—*vilde* 'vile', Mids. N. Dr. i. i, Merry W. iv. v, Hen. IV, Pt. 1, 3,
&c., &c.; *vildely*, Second Pt., Hen. IV, I. ii, II. ii ; Spenser—*vylde*, F. Q.,
Bk. vi, Cant. i. 1, and it rhymes *milde*, Bk. iii, Cant. viii. 34, &c. ; Donne
(1573-1631) rhymes *vilde* 'vile'—*child*, Elegie xiii. 7 and 8 ; Verney
Mem. have :—*schollards*, Sir R. V. ii. 21, 1641 ; *micklemust*, M. Faulkiner,
ii. 52, 1642 ; *generald* 'General', ii. 91, 1642 ; Mrs. Eure ; the *hold*
yeare 'whole', Pen. Denton, iii. 229, 1655 ; *lofte* 'loathe', Mrs. Isham, ii.
220, 1645 ; *lemonds*, Luce Sheppard, iv. 29, 1662 ; night *gownd*, Cary
Stewkley, iv. 442, 1688 ; *homb* 'home', Cary Stewkley, iv. 35, 1663 ;
Butler, Hudibras, Pt. i, 919-20, rhymes *wound—swound* 'swoon', 1664 ;
Swift rhymes *ferment—vermin*, The Problem ; Jones, 1701, seems to
take *clift* as the normal form, but says it may be written *cliff*; Wentw.
Pprs., Peter W.—'made the house *laught*', &c., 111, 1710, 'not *saft*
('safe') for me', 103, ibid., *sarment*, P. W. 221, 1711, and 321, Lady W.,
1713, *gownds*, 284, Lady Strafford, 1712 ; *lost* of time, P. W. 200, 1711 ;
—'were *liked* (like) to have obtained', P. W. 104, 1710 ; Lord Harvey,
Mem. of Reign of George II, often writes *Hulst* for Sir Edward *Hulse*,
cf. iii. 302, 315, 316 ; Elphinston puts down *sermont*, *drownd* (Inf.),
gownd, *scollard*, *wonst* 'once', as vulgarisms ; Pegge, 1814, regards as
London vulgarisms *verment*, *serment*, *nyst*, *margent*.

Addition of Parasitic Consonants between Groups of Consonants.

Already in the middle of the thirteenth century we find *dempt* 'deemed',
Gen. and Ex. 2038, *drempte* dremes, ibid. 2049. Later examples are :—
sumptyme 'sometime', St. Ed. 14 ; Cely Pprs.—*Montgwmbre* 'Montgomery', 80, *rembnant*, 75 ; St. of Ireland, St. Pprs. Hen. VIII, iii—
Lymbryk, p. 8, 1513 ; Archbp. Cranmer—*combly* 'comely', Ellis i. 2. 37,
1533 ; Thos. Lever, Serm.—*Humbles* = Homilies, 65, 1550 Gabr.
Harvey, Letters, 1573-80—*maltconceived* 'malconceived', p. 67 ; Verney
Mem.—*clendlynes*, Lady Hobart, iii. 78, 1644 ; Peter Wentworth—*Duke
of Hambleton* = 'Hamilton', Wentw. Pprs. 238, 1712.

Introduction of -w- (a lip-glide) between Consonant and following Rounded Vowel.

St. Editha has *twoile*, 2274, 2277; Cely Pprs. have *apwoyntyd*, 116, *pwoyntement*, 71; Bury Wills, *gwory*, 84 (1501); Butler, 1634, gives pronunciation *bwoĕ* for 'boy'; Wallis, 1653, says that after *p* and *b*, before *o, w* is pronounced, but not by all speakers, nor in all words—*pwot* 'pot', *bwoil* 'boil', *bwoy* 'boy'.

Lady Wentworth writes *twilete* 'toilette' = [twɔilʌt], perhaps in imitation of French pronunciation.

Development of front-glide between g-, k-, and following Front Vowel.

This may be expressed by Lady Hobart's spelling *gearl* = [gjɛrl]?, V. Mem. iv. 54, 1644, but I give the form tentatively.

Wallis, 1653, says that *can, get, begin* are pronounced *cyan, gyet, begyin*.

Elphinston affirms that *kyind, gyide*, and the introduction of '*y*' before the vowel in *sky, can, card, skirt, guard*, &c., are essential to a polite pronunciation. Walker, 1801, is very definite about the introduction of a 'fluent, liquid sound after *k, c*, or *g* hard before *a* and *i*, which gives a smooth and elegant sound to . . . and which distinguishes the polite conversation of London from that of every other part of the island'. Walker expresses the pronunciation referred to by the spellings *ke-ind, ke-ard, rege-ard*. The words 'which require the liquid sound' are :—*sky, kind, guide, gird, girt, girl, guise, guile, card, cart, cap, carpenter, carnal, cartridge, guard, regard*.

I used to hear the pronunciations [kjād, gjādn], &c., as a boy, from a very near relation of mine, a most fastidious speaker, a lady born in 1802, who died in 1886. (Note in *card*, &c., the glide developed while *a* still represented a front vowel; in *kind*, &c., it must have developed at some stage such as [kæind < kjæind].)

Aspiration of Initial Vowels, popularly called 'putting in an h'.

The 'incorrect' aspiration of initial vowels, one of the commonest of vulgarisms, appears to be confined not merely to stressed words or syllables, but chiefly to those which have extra-strong stress in the sentence. It is rarely heard before words that are weakly stressed. The habit seems always to have been considered a vulgarism, and the few examples I have recorded are nearly all from provincial sources, or from the writings of persons who otherwise show signs of defective education and vulgar habits of speech. Norf. Guilds have *herthe* 'earth', 35, *a garland of hoke leaves*, 117, &c. Another considerable number of instances occur in St. Editha (1420). These are :—*houʒt* 'out', 54, *Hyryssche* 'Irish', 48, *heyndynge* 'ending', 1, *hende*, 515, *herlyche* 'early', 270, *hynon* 'eyes', 1892, *hevelle* 'evil', 32, 34, *Hyronesyde* 'Ironside', 3279, *harme* 'arm', 4129. Bokenam has *herand* 'errand', Marg. 1081, and *hangyr* 'anger', Ag. 485. The Will of Sir T. Cumberworth, Lincs., 1451, has *haske* Vb., Linc. Dioc. Docs. 49.13; Gregory's Chron., *hasche* (the tree), 200; Cely Papers, *howlde* 'old', 48; Marg. Paston, *howyn* 'own', i. 438, *hour* 'our', i. 439, *howeth* 'oweth', ii. 26, 461, *haskyd*, ii. 26, *hondyrstonde*, ii. 32, *the hone* 'the one', ii. 62, *hewers* 'ewers', ii. 75, *herand*, ii. 215. Machyn furnishes more examples than any other source, and has one excellent instance of the *h-* occurring in a strongly stressed word at the end of a sentence— 'a gret dener as I haue be *hat*' 'at', p. 2, which might be said at the present time by a certain kind of speaker, *has*, 139, *hundershaft*, 116, *harme* (of the body), 85, *haskyd*, 205, *hanswered*, 242, *hetten* 'eaten', 16, *hoyth* 'oath', 25, *herth* 'earth', 6, *here* 'ear', 40, *Hambrose*, 48. John Alleyn has *hernest* 'earnest', Alleyn Papers 16, 159–.

Lady Sydenham writes *hobblegashons* 'obligations', Verney Mem. ii. 125.

The evidence, such as it is, does not point to this habit being very widespread before the eighteenth century. The grammarians of the sixteenth, seventeenth, and early eighteenth centuries do not utter warnings against it, and the fact that it is not found in the English of Ireland or America also suggests that it gained currency rather late. Smollett, in *Roderick Random*, ch. xvi, makes Mr. Jackson's fiancée—'a charming creature—writes like an angel'—introduce *h-* in her letters in *hopjack* 'object', *heys* 'eyes', *harrows* 'arrows', *harms* 'arms', which shows that when this book was written in 1771 the practice was a recognized and common vulgarism.

E.   Voicing of Voiceless Consonants.

Voicing of Initial **wh-**, *i.e.* [w̥ < w]. *Popularly called* '*leaving out the* h'.

At the present time in the Received Standard as spoken in the South and Midlands, and in the Regional dialects of these areas, no distinction is made between *whine* and *wine*, between *which* and *witch*, *while* and *Wight*, &c. The only exceptions are those speakers who have been subjected to Scotch or Irish influence, or who have deliberately chosen to depart from the normal practice for their own private satisfaction.

In the South and West we find *w*-spellings, instead of *wh-* or *hw*, from an early period in M.E. In the fourteenth and fifteenth centuries, *which*, *white*, &c., are the usual spellings in the London documents, though in 1494 we find *wich*, 388, *wen*, 391, *werof*, 388, in Cr. Knt. of Bath. We may, I think, dismiss the form *wich* as having probably arisen in positions of weak stress as a Relative Pronoun, but the others seem to illustrate the voicing. The form *wich* is very common in letters, wills, and other private and public documents in this and the following century, and it is suspicious because it is so often the only spelling of its kind. For instance, Marg. Paston writes *wich*(*e*), but otherwise *wh-*, and even *qu-*, a spelling which must have penetrated from the N.E. Midlands or lower Northern area, where it is usual, and was probably intended to express a particularly strong form of the voiceless consonant. *Wete* 'wheat' occurs in Will of J. Buckland, Northants, 1450, L. D. D. 42. 13. The Celys, in Essex, might have been expected to pronounce '*wite*', &c., but such spellings seem not to occur in their letters, though *wh-* for original *w-* is frequent, and is indeed one of the features of these documents. The evidence is slight so far as the fifteenth century is concerned.

In the next century Machyn has *wyped* 'whipped', 8, *warff* 'wharf', 13, and the inverted spelling *whent* is common. In Cavendish, L. of Wolsey,

I have noted *wyght* 'white', 148, *wye* 'why', 157, and the inverted *whear* for *wear*, 154. In the Verney Papers I have noted only *wich* (1629) without *h*; in the Verney Memoirs, which begin in the forties of the seventeenth century, we have any*ware*, Mary Gardiner, ii. 334, 1644, and *wig* 'whig', Edm. V., iv. 267, 1683. It is remarkable, if the habit of voicing was well established, that such independent spellers as the Verney family should not have recorded it oftener. It should be said that all the seventeenth-century writers on pronunciation assert that '*h*' is pronounced in *wh*-, a French writer (Alphabet Anglois, 1625) giving *houitch* as the pronunciation of *which*. Wallis, 1653, Howel, 1662, and Cooper, 1685, to mention no more, all declare, in various ways, that *wh* is pronounced *hw*, &c. Lady Wentworth in 1709, W. Papers 99, writes *wig* 'whig'. Elphinston, in his various writings from 1765–87, admits, while he deplores, the complete 'disappearance of *h*' in *whale, what,* &c. Dr. Johnson in 1765 still believes that he 'hears the *h*'. Walker notes with regret the London use of *w*- for *wh*-. It would appear from the above that the voicing of *wh*- was not unknown in the fifteenth century, and that this became more and more widespread, though for a long time not universal in London and the surrounding counties. There were perhaps always, as now, a certain number of speakers who prided themselves on 'pronouncing the *h*'. Milton in his autograph MS. writes *weele*, Lyc. 31, *wispers*, Lyc. 130, and *wistle*, Com. 346. In the last word he has corrected to *wh*-. It looks as though Milton used the voiced sound, and wrote *w*- without thinking, to express this.

Voicing of Voiceless Consonants ; Medially: between Vowels ; between a Vowel and a Consonant ; Finally.

Some of the examples of voicing between vowels persist to the present day among some speakers. The forms are arranged chronologically without sub-classification.

St. Editha, 1420, *crebulle* 'cripple', 432, 4347, *fedryd* 'fettered', 2301, *hondynge* 'hunting', 447, 4453, *drongon* 'they drank', 520, *thyngeth* 'seems' for *thynketh, thongedon* 'thanked' Pl., 461, *thonged*, 4372, *y thenge* 'I think', 3247, *dronge* 'drank', 1642, *shalde* 'shalt', 532, *servaunde*, 2342, 'servant', *y-graundyd* 'granted', 809, *peyndynge* 'painting', 1780, *peyndud* 'painted', 1781, &c., *Egberde*, 201, *parde* 'part', 517 (rhymes *whoderwarde*), *comforde* Pret., 1537, *Dorsed* 'Dorset', 2549 ; Bury Wills, 1463, *jebardy*, 163, 164, 165 ; Sir J. Fortescue, *treded* 'treated', 109, 145, *entreded*, 135 ; Bk. of Quintessence, *Jubiter*, 8, 18 (twice); Gregory's Chron., 1450–70, *radyfyde* 'ratified', 64, *depudyd*, 131, *dalmadyke*, 166, priest's dalmatic; Cely Papers, *jeberdy*, 163, *jebardy*, 164, 165 ; Letters and Papers, i, 1494, *juberte*, 397, *endendith* 'indenteth', 388 ; Caxton, Jason 7, *Jubyter* ; Bury Wills, *cobard*, 98, 1504 ; Rede me, &c., 122, 1528, *Constantinoble* ; Sir Thos. More, *Jubardy*, Letters, Ellis ii. 1. 289 ; Linc. Dioc. Docs., Will of J. Asserley, 1527, *cobberdes* 'cupboards', 13. 61; ibid., Will of R. Bradley, Leics., 1533, *coberd*, 161. 15 ; Bp. Fisher's Sermons, 1550, *Constantinoble*, 335 ; Machyn, 1550–63, *sagbottes* 'sackbuts', 78, *hundyd*, 292, *elevant*, 137, *cubard*, 206, *drynges* 'drinks', 208 ; J. Alleyn, *comford*, Alleyn Papers, 16 ; Verney Papers, *debutye*, Sir R. V., p. 56; *Dullege* 'Dulwich' is written by Ch. Massye, Alleyn Mem. 109, 1613 ; Verney Mem. :—*prodistants*, Lady Sussex, ii. 88, 1642, *combeanion*, Pen. V., ii. 129, *coberd*, Lady Sussex, ii. 162, *medigate* 'mitigate', iii. 317, Mrs. Sherard, 1657 ; *I thang God*, Cary Stewkley (Verney), iii. 437, 1656,

Debity, Mrs. Isham, iv. 33, 1662; *temberall*, Mrs. Basire, 141 (1655), *comford*, 134 (1655). Cooper, 1685, says that *s* in *casement* = *z*; Jones, 1701, says '*b* and *p* being like in sound, and *b* the easier and sweeter *p* does sometimes take the sound of *b*, as in—*Baptism, capable, culpable, passport* (= 'pass-board')! *Cupid, Deputy, Gospel, Jasper, Jupiter, napkin*'. Jones also notes '*Cubbard, nevew, Steven*, and *provesy*' = *prophecy*.

Lady Wentworth writes *prodistant* 'protestant', W. Papers 50, 1705; Peter W., *cenzure*, 100, 1710, and Lady Strafford, *prodistation*, 208, 1712. In the comic letter of Mr. Jackson's fiancée in Roderick Random, ch. xvi, the lady writes *Cubit* for 'Cupid'. Elphinston mentions the pronunciations *proddestant, padrole, pardner* as London vulgarisms. Mr. Bernard Shaw, in John Bull's Other Island, makes one of his Irish characters say '*prodestant*', but I doubt whether the *d* in this word is confined to Irish speakers of English. I hasten to add that Mr. Shaw does not assert that it is.

F. Unvoicing of Consonants.

A certain number of instances of unvoicing occur scattered through the texts I have examined. Some of these appear to be of the nature of dissimilative changes, to use an unsatisfactory term, due perhaps to an unconscious attempt at distinctness; others may be due to some obscure analogy, while others are altogether inexplicable, unless they may be set down as Regional peculiarities. Some of these changes might appear hardly worth recording, but in some cases the same voiceless form appears in widely separate sources, and is therefore probably genuine; other isolated examples are recorded in the hope that future investigations may reveal more of them and throw light on their origin.

Unvoicing of Initial Consonant (at beginning of word, and at beginning of stressed syllable).

Fochsave 'vouchsafe', Gregory 110; *felwette* 'velvet', ibid. 208; *file* 'vile', Lady Sussex, Verney Mem. ii. 107; *disadfantige*, ibid. 108; full of *fanity*, ibid. 85, 1642; *Fox hall* 'Vauxhall', J. Verney, Verney Mem. iv. 357, 1685.

Unvoicing of Final Consonant.

St. Editha :—*y clepyt*, 44 (two syllables), *clepyt*, 43 (two syllables), *encreset*, 190, *scarmysshute* (Pret.), 282; *aspyet* 'espied' P. P., 554; *twelffe* 'twelve', 624; *ayschette* 'asked', 872; *hulte* (Pret.) 'held', 1277, &c.; *byche* 'to buy*' = *bigge*, 1305, 1397; *y-tolte* (Pret.) 'told', 1830; *feynte* 'fiend', 2145; *bleynte* 'blind' Adj., 2731; Gregory, *Wardroper*, 196; Letters and Papers, ii. 72, Keper of the gret *Warderop*, 1485; *incurrich*, Alleyne Pprs. 16, 1591; Mrs. Elmes, Verney Mem., twenty *thousent* etc., ii. 82. 1641; Lady Strafford, *Wardrope*, W. Papers, 314, 319, 1713; Peter Wentworth, *becken't* 'beckoned', W. Papers, 431, 1714; *senting*, 202, 1711.

Medial Unvoicing.

Ambassiter, Cavendish, L. of Wolsey, p. 7, probably owes *t* to the influence of the preceding *s*; *optayne*, 'obtain', Fortescue 144, Ascham, Tox. 103, is a combinative change before *-t*; *puplishe*, Letters and Papers, ii. 388, may be due to the analogy of *puple*, a common spelling of *people*; *nefew*, Doll Leake, Verney Mem. iv. 291, 1655, is probably a spelling-pronunciation in origin, here popularly expressed; it may still be heard.

CHAPTER IX

NOTES ON INFLEXIONS

I

NOUNS.

Possessive Case of Nouns.

IN fourteenth-century London English the ordinary suffix, as written by the professional scribes, is *-es*. In Feminines this suffix is sometimes omitted, cf. Chaucer's In hope to stonden in his *Ladye* grace, &c.

During the fifteenth century the suffix *-es* tends to be written more and more as *-ys*, *-is*, both in private letters and official and literary documents. This is observable not only in Eastern texts but also in London documents. See on this point, p. 269, above. More or less rustic productions of the West, such as St. Editha, often write *-us*. The *-ys*-forms, however, while characteristic of Eastern texts from an early date in M.E., are very common everywhere in the fifteenth century.

Since the vowel is often omitted, even in M.E., it appears that the suffix ceased normally to be pronounced as a separate syllable—except, as now, after *-s*, *-ch*, &c.—in Colloquial English by the beginning of the fifteenth century. On the other hand there were circumstances which tended to restore a syllabic pronunciation of the suffix, as *-is* $= [iz]$, well on into, perhaps to the end of, the century, and in poetry an occasional syllabic pronunciation is revealed by the rhyme and metre for two hundred years longer.

The main points to be considered here are the confusion of the old Possessive suffix with the Possessive Pronoun *ys*, the weak or unstressed form of *hys*, *his*; the omission of the suffix *-ys*, *-s*, &c., in any form; the various constructions in the inflexion of groups of words—e.g. *the King of England's son*, &c.

Confusion of Possessive Suffix with the Possessive Pronoun Masculine.

From the moment that on the one hand the Pronoun *his* had lost the aspirate in unstressed positions, and on the other the Possess. suffix had become *-is*, *-ys*, there could be no distinction in pronunciation between a Noun inflected with the latter suffix and the same Noun followed by the weakened form of *his*. Thus confusion arose, and is revealed by the detachment of the suffix *-ys* from the Noun to which it belongs, and then by the spelling of this latter *hys* or *his*. *The kyng hys sonne*, &c., was felt as a definite construction and therefore so written. While this came to exactly the same as *the kyngys sonne*, the two constructions were doubtless recognized as distinct by the more careful speakers and writers.

On the other hand the less critical scribes were often doubtful whether to write the suffix *-ys* joined on to the Noun or whether to detach it, and in this case whether to write *ys* as they and every one else pronounced, or *hys* to show that they knew what it meant. The result of the new construction was that what was meant as a genuine inflected Possessive, e. g. *kyngys*, &c., retained the vowel in pronunciation long after this had normally disappeared in such words. Thus as late as Shakespeare's *L. L. Lost*, we find, ' To shew his teeth as white as Whal*es* bone ', Act IV. It is probable that this occurred also in colloquial speech, helped also by the analogy of Possessives like *Jamesys*. But after all, the construction with *his*, and the Noun with the old inflexion, were absolutely indistinguishable in pronunciation, and most speakers, possibly well into the seventeenth century, would have been hard put to it to say exactly which they intended.

We find traces of the construction with *his* as early as *Genesis and Exodus* (*c.* 1250), where the suffix is already separated, though joined to the Noun by a hyphen—*adame-is sune*, 493, *ðat dune-is siðen* ' the sides of the hill ', 1295. This text is noteworthy for constantly writing the weak forms of the Pers. Prons. without *h-*.

Again, in the fourteenth century this construction is found, e. g. in Trevisa (*c.* 1387), *to play with a chyld hys brouch*. From the early fifteenth century onwards the construction is common, and it will be remarked that *ys* is used indifferently after Masculine and Feminine Nouns :—

St. Editha :—*Wortynger is tyme*, 51, *seynt Dunstone his lore*, 751 ; Shillingford :—*seynt Luke is dey*, 5, *Calston is fayre*, 5, *my lord of Exceire is tenants*, 14 ; Marg. Paston :—*Harlesdon ys name*, ii. 191, *the knyt hys sonne*, ii. 240, *my moder ys sake*, ii. 364 ; Gregory's Chron. :—*Seynt Edmonde ys Bury*, 91, *the quene ys modyr*, 232, *no schoo apon no man ys fote*, 238, *my Lorde of Warwycke ys brother*, 230 ; Register of Oseney, *oure lord þe pope-is commaundments*, 61 ; Cely Papers :—*Margaret ys doughter*, 117 ; Earl of Desmond (Lttr. to Henry VII, *c.* 1489–93), *therle of Ormond is deppute* (Lttrs. and Pprs., i, p. 382 ; Thos. Lord Dacre, 1521 :—*her Grace is requeste*, Ellis ii. 1. 282 ; Archbp. Cranmer, 1536 :—*the Busshop of Rome his power*, Ellis ii. 3. 27, *the Busshoppe of Rome his lawes*, Ellis iii. 3. 25 ; Machyn :—*one ys ere* ' one his ear ', 64, *the penter ys nam*, 105, *the Bishop of London and Coventre ys wiff*, 229 ; Ascham, Toxophilus :—*on a man his tiptoes*, 47, *the Kinge his wisdome*, 38, *an other his heeles*, 47, *the Kinge his foole*, 50 ; Euphues :—*Philantus his faith*, 57, *Fidus his loue*, 277. Such phrases as *for Jesus Christ his sake* are familiar in the Prayer Book. Sir Thos. Smith, Republ. Angl., 1583, has *the daulphin of Fraunce his power*, 19. A few examples from the seventeenth century must suffice to illustrate the survival of this construction. Dr. Denton has *Dr. Read his treatise on wounds*, Verney Pprs., 1639 ; Edmund Verney, Verney Mem. ii, p. 130, has *my lord Parsons his sonne*, 1641, and Sir Ralph V. has *St. James his House*, Verney Mem. iii. 236, 1655. In these cases *his* may be written as the most satisfactory way of inflecting words ending in *-s* and to avoid *Parsonses*, *Jameses*. Lady Wentworth has *the Princ his* *buirying*, but makes no difficulty about writing *St. Jamsis*, 47. Lady Plyant in Congreve's *Double Dealer*, 1693, says, 'I am in such a twitter to read Mr. Careless his letter', Act IV, Sc. iii.

When this construction was well established and recognized as containing the Pron. *his*, the process was extended to the Fem. and the Pl. We get *Juno hir bedde*, Euphues, 86; *Mrs. Francis her mariage*, Lady Verney, Verney Mem. ii. 378, 1647; and *you should translate Canterbury and Chillingworth their books into French*, Dr. Denton, Verney Mem. ii. 222, 1645.

The Omission of the Possessive Suffix in Nouns.

In M.E. the suffix *-es*, *-ys*, &c., is used commonly to inflect Nouns of all genders, but is sometimes omitted. This occurs most frequently in the M.E. period—(*a*) after names ending in *-s*, such as *Moses*; (*b*) in old Feminines like *ladye*, where the *-e* is a survival of a Fem. Genitive suffix; (*c*) as a survival of old Weak Nouns whose Gen. ended in *-an*, M.E. *-en*, but which have lost the *-n* of the ending; (*d*) occasionally in old Nouns ending in *-r*, *brother*, *fader*, &c., which originally had no *-es* suffix.

All these cases of flexionless Possessives occur in the Modern period, and there are certain additional categories which arise, viz. there is an extension of class (*a*) to words like *hors*(*e*), and there are other instances of omission which cannot be brought under any of the above classes. We may summarize the classes of flexionless Possessives as follows:—

The suffix is often omitted—(*a*) in words ending in *-s*, where we now preserve it as a full syllable [*iz*]; (*b*) before a word beginning with *s*-; (*c*) in old Feminines, of which we have now only a few survivals in stereotyped phrases—*Lady Chapel*, &c.; (*d*) in groups, when we should inflect the last word of the group—the duke of Somerset dowther (which see below); (*e*) in old *-r* words—*father*, *brother*, &c.; (*f*) in other words where no special reason can be assigned.

It must be understood that in nearly all the above classes the inflected forms are more frequent, but the examples of omissions are sufficiently numerous to deserve recording. Some of the examples might be classified under more than one head.

(*a*) *Omission of Possessive Suffix in Words ending in -s.*

Siege of Rouen (*c.* 1420), *hors quarter, horse hedde*, 18; Marg. Paston, *my lord of Clarance man*, ii. 372 (this might fall under (*d*)); Machyn, *sant James parke*, 166; Ascham, *horse feete*, Tox. 157, *for conscience sake*, Scholem. 68; Webbe, 1586, *Achilles Tombe*, 24, *a horse necke*, 85; Lord Burghley, 1586, *ther Mastriss crymes*, Bardon Pprs. 43.

[*Note.* After [dž], where we either pronounce [*iz*], or omit the suffix altogether, as in *bridge head, College gate*, Pecok writes *-is*—*collegis gate*.]

(*b*) *Omission of Suffix before Words beginning with s-.*

St. Editha, *his sowle sake*, 382, *for synne sake*, 813; *my housbond sowle*, Will of J. Buckland, Northants, 1450, L. D. D. 43. 9; *my wyff soule*, Will of Sir T. Cumberworth, L. D. D. 53. 28, 1451; Ascham, *Robin Hoode seruant*, Tox. 44, *for earnest matter sake*, Tox. 44, *for his country sake*, Tox. 94, *for his pleasure sake*, ibid. 94, *for maner sake*, Sch. 68; Lady

Mary Gray (daughter of Duke of Suffolk), *for god sake*, Ellis ii. 2. 310, 1566; David Rogers to Burghley, *the younge kinge stomacke*, Ellis ii. 3. 147, 1588; Will of Ralph Wooton, Bucks., 1533, *my ffather and mother soules*, Linc. Dioc. Docs. 159. 20; Machyn, *the quen syster*, 63, *a hossear sune*, 121, *master Godderyke sune*, 258, *in ys father stede*, 258 (pernaps under (*e*)); Sir R. L'Estrange, *for Brevity sake*, A Whipp, a Whipp, 1662.

(c) *Omission of Suffix at the end of Old Feminine Nouns.*

St. Editha, *seynt Wultrude soule*, 3068; Bp. Pecok, *modir tunge*, i. 159; Shillingford, *oure lady belle*, 94; Gregory, *Mary Mawdelyn Evyn*, 103; Lord Berners, *our lady day*, i. 105, *Mary Maudlyn day*, i. 70 ; Sir J. Paston, *Ewhelme my Lady Suffolk Place in Oxenforthe schyre*, iii. 33 ; Bp. Latimer, *My Ladye Elizabethe grace*, 117; Machyn, *the quyn grace*, 167, *my Lade Elsabeth grace*, 167, *Lade Mare grace*, 30 (three times), &c., &c.; Lord Burghley, 1586, *the Scotish Quene letter*, Bardon Pprs. 46; D. Rogers to Burghley, *the Scottis Quene cryme*, ibid., p. 47. Machyn's construction *my lade grasys*, &c., 37, is normal in omitting the suffix of the first Noun, but as the second Noun is inflected the first might in any case tend to be uninflected in this sentence. Cavendish, L. of Wolsey, *our Lady mattens*; Edmund Verney, *our Lady Day last*, Verney Mem. iv. 404, 1688 = 'Our Lady's Day'. (It may be mentioned that in E. Midland Fem. Nouns took the *-s* suffix in the Possess. very early; cf. *þes cwenes canceler* 'this queen's', Laud Chron. 1123, written about 1154.)

(d) *Omission of Suffix in Group Construction.*

Marg. Paston, *my lorde of Clarance man* (should possibly come under (*a*) as already indicated); Machyn, *bishop of London palles*, 204, *the duke of Somerset dowther*, 253 ; Sir R. Verney, *my Lord of Essex Army*, Verney Mem. ii. 122, 1641.

(e) *Omission of Suffix in old Words ending in* -r.

St. Editha :—*his fader wyffe*, 238, *fader gulte*, 2491 ; Marg. Paston :— *hyr broder advice*, ii. 26. The construction, cited under (*b*), above, may also be explained under the present heading—*my ffather and mother soules*, 1533; Machyn:—*hys brodur horse*, 22, *in ys father stede*, 258, already cited under (*b*) may equally well belong to the present category ; the same may be said of Lord Berners' *by the father syde*, i. 181 ; 'the *father* good will', John Alleyn, Alleyn Pprs. 15, 159–.

(f) *Omission of Suffix in other cases.*

St. Editha :—[1] *heuene kynge*, 395, may perhaps be due to the analogy of an old Weak N.—O.E. *heofon* itself is occasionally weak in L.O.E., and this may well be due to the analogy of *eorþe*; Will of J. Buckland, 1450, Northants, *Richard Clavell wyff*, L. D. D. 44. 7; Will of R. Astbroke, Bucks, 1534, *the sayde Willyam Astbroke chyldren*, L. D. D. 169. 2 ; Lord Hastings, *c.* 1470, *my brother Roaf assent and agrement*, Paston Lttrs. iii. 108; Cr. of Duke of York—*Henry Wynslow horse*, 399, 1494; Machyn—*the kyng grace*, 77, *my lord cardenall commyng*, 77, *the bucher wyff*, 8, *a shreyff wyff*, 22, *a prest wyff*, 32. Thos. Lord Sackville :—*the Cardinall use*, Letter, Appendix to Wks., p. xxxiii. Thos. Lever's Sermons:—*the harte bloud*, 125 ; this may be a survival of the old Weak Gen. *herten*—*herte*, it is

---

[1] This construction is common in Middle English.

also an old Fem.; Cavendish also has *my hart blode*, 251. Lady Wentworth writes *my sister Batthurst offer*, 43, and Peter Wentworth, *a parson widdoe*, 85. Lady B. Harley, 2 (1625), *his grandfather loue*.

The Inflexion of Groups.

Such constructions as *the King of England's power, the Bishop of Worcester's palace*, and so on, are thoroughly established in the best colloquial and literary usage, and in the former there is practically no limit to the length of the group which the genius of the language permits to be inflected as a whole, by the addition of the suffix to the last element. While the evidence shows that this construction was used in the fifteenth century, there appears to have been, for a long time, a feeling that it was inelegant, and various devices are employed to avoid it. The usual M.E. type of construction is well represented by the title of the well-known song—*The Bailiff's daughter of Islington*, and this form survives here and there; for instance, Gregory writes *the dukys doughter of Northefolke*, 140; Lord Berners:—*the kynges doughter of Englande*, i. 319; even when two nouns are in apposition, as in *Lord Neville's wife*, the inflexion of the second in this order is sometimes avoided; thus Gregory writes *the Lordys wyffe Nevyle*, 140, and Machyn—*Master Godderyke sune the goldsmith*, 258, instead of — *Godderyke the goldsmiths sune*. A curious construction occurs in a letter of Henry V, 1418—*a man of the Ducs of Orliance*, Ellis i. 1. 1.

Another slight modification is to write *-is* or *his* instead of the ordinary Possess. suffix—e. g. *my lord of Excetre is tenantis*, Shillingford, 44 (cf. p. 315, above). In Cavendish, Life of Wolsey, *the abbots of Westminster*, 199, is used absolutely. Lastly, the suffix is sometimes omitted altogether, although the word-order is the same as though it were present. This has already been illustrated under (*d*) above. The following early examples of group inflexion are confined to cases where the suffix occurs joined to the last word of the group which it inflects.

St. Editha—*þe erle of Wyltones wyf*, 139; Cr. of Duke of York—*Sett in like maner as therle of Suffolkis*, 396; Recep. of Cath. of Ar.—*the Archebishoppe of Cantreburys barge, the Abbot of Westmynsters barge*, 405; St. of Irel. (St. Pprs. Hen. VIII, iii)—*the Erle of Kyldares sonnes*, p. 24, 1515; Bulmer (Lttr.)—*my Lorde of Richemoundes Affairs, my Lorde of Richmounds landes*, Ellis iii. 2. 122, 124, 1527; Latimer—*Ladye Maryes grace*, Serm. 117, *our holye father of Romes eares*, 107; Machyn—*my lord of Canterberes plasse*, 49; Q. Elizabeth (Letter, 1553)—*my Lorde of Bedfords mynde*, Ellis ii. 2. 211; Lord Berners—*the Kynge of Englandes homage*, i. 78, *the Lorde of Mannes quarrell*, i. 254, *Sir Gaultier of Mannes fader*, i. 254 *the Kyng of Englandes doughter*, i. 319; Cavendish, L. of Wolsey—*Kyng Herre the VIIIths sister*, 72, *ayenst the kyng and my lords commyng*, 81, *my Lord of Shrewsburyes servaunts*, 215; Sir Thos. Smith, Republ. Angl.—*King Richarde the secondes time*, 141, *King Henrie the eights time*, 104, *King Henrie the thirds time*, 123; in T. S.'s Letters—*the duke de Montpenciers son*, Ellis ii. 3. 13. A hundred years later we find in Aubrey's Lives—' *He* (Bp. Wilkins) *was one of Seth Lord Bishop of Sarum's most intimate friends*', ii. 301.

Strong Plurals: in -*es*, -*s*, &c.

The great majority of nouns in English take an -*s*- suffix in the Plural. The old so-called *strong* suffix is generally written -*es* by good scribes in London documents of Chaucer's day. Throughout the fifteenth century, however, the form -*ys* or -*is*, originally apparently chiefly characteristic of Eastern texts, becomes more and more common, not only in documents of all kinds written in the Eastern counties, but also in those from more westerly areas. Before the end of this century -*ys* is frequently written in London official and other documents. At the present time the vowel of the suffix is lost except after words ending in -*s*, -*sh*, -*dge*, and in these cases the Plural ending in Received Standard is [iz], so that although we write *fishes, asses, causes, bridges*, we pronounce [fiʃiz, āsiz, kɔziz, bridžiz]. There can be no doubt that this pronunciation of this suffix is the direct descendant of the forms written -*ys*, &c., in the fifteenth century, and it is, to my mind, quite certain that not only in Received Standard but in many Regional dialects this pronunciation has obtained for not much less than 500 years. Some years ago the question was raised whether this present-day pronunciation, and the fact that Caxton often writes -*ys* in the Plural, were not proofs that Literary English and Standard Spoken English were both influenced by what was called the 'Oxford type' of English, that is, by a more westerly type, as opposed to the usual East Midland character which, on the whole, dominates the Literary and the Spoken language. Here was indeed a very pretty mare's nest, which apparently arose chiefly because it was noticed that Bishop Pecok, in his Repressor (1449) and other works, makes copious use of the -*ys* form. Where the bishop got his suffix is another story, but it is quite certain that it is more characteristic of the East than of the West. In the latter area a very common form of the ending is -*us*, but even so definitely Regional a dialect as that of St. Editha (Wilts.), written about thirty years before the Repressor, often uses -*ys*, which form was rapidly becoming common both East and West. It is rather doubtful how far we can take the spelling -*ys*, -*es*, &c., seriously in the fifteenth century as representing a syllable, except after words ending in the consonants above mentioned. We may be certain, however, that it was at least pronounced as a syllable in those cases where we now so pronounce it, and if we find *causis* written, it is reasonable to suppose that a pronunciation identical with our own, so far as the suffix is concerned, is intended. It is probable that -*ys* was pronounced as a syllable in poetry long after it was lost in colloquial speech, as we still pronounce Prets. and P. P.'s in -*ed* [id]. Cf. Hoccleve's rhyme— *werkys—derk is*, Reg. of Pr. 277, 278; and Spenser's 'Then her embracing twixt her *armes* twaine', F.Q. Bk. VI. xii. 19. In the London area -*es* was the traditional spelling, and when the scribes depart from this it must mean something. If a scribe often, or even usually, writes -*es*, but occasionally -*ys*, we are, I think, justified in believing that in the former case he is merely following tradition, but that in the latter he is recording the usual pronunciation. In the sixteenth century it is certain that the vowel of the suffix was only pronounced where we now pronounce it, and while -*es* had, strangely enough, become the orthodox printers' spelling, more

Y

and more adhered to by educated writers, there are enough divergencies from the convention, and just in those words where the vowel of the suffix *was* pronounced, to show what the pronunciation was in such cases. It is immaterial that most writers use the spelling *-es* ; that was natural, and tells us nothing as to the pronunciation.　　What is significant is that so many also write *-ys*.

In the fifteenth century, among Western writers who have forms in *-ys* are St. Editha, Bishop Pecok, Shillingford, and we may, if we please, include Fortescue, although his dialect has very few Regional characteristics.　　Among the specifically Eastern writers we have Palladius, the Bury Wills, the Pastons, the Celys, and the Suffolk Londoner, Gregory. This list pretty well disposes of the 'Oxford' myth.　　Coming to less markedly provincial documents, all the more or less official records in Letters and Papers, vol. i, occasionally write *-ys* ; so do the Book of Quintessence, Capgrave, Caxton, and the Rewle of Sustr. Men.　　Caxton's *expensis*, and the Rewle's *versis, messis*, are significant.

Passing to the sixteenth century, a very large number of books and private letters, &c., write *-ys*.　　I mention a few of these sources, quoting only forms in which the vowel of the suffix was unquestionably pronounced, although many other instances of the spelling occur.　　In printed books the form *-es* becomes more and more fixed as the century goes on ; the occasional departures, both here and in private documents, are therefore the more noteworthy.

The form *-ys* occurs in all the following :—Elyot's Gouernour—*horsis, placis, versis, sickenessis* ; Pace, Letter in Ellis ii. 1. 1513—*hostagis, causis* ; Lord Berners—*chargis* ; Cranmer (Letters)—*bargis* ; Cavendish, Life of Wolsey—*horsis, crossis* ; Q. Elizabeth—*practisis, scusis* ; Machyn—*horsis, branchys, torchys* ; Gabr. Harvey's Lttrs.—*causis, coursis*.

The various writers in Verney Papers and Verney Mem. sometimes write *-is*—e. g. Mrs. Pulteney, *richis*, 1639.　　Lady Wentworth writes *glassis, horsis, oringis*, &c.　　(On this suffix see also pp. 269–70.) For the extension of the *-es* Pl. suffix to words of other types cf. p. 322.

Weak Plurals : in -*en*.

This class of Pls., once very large, has shrunk in present-day English almost to the vanishing point, the only survivor being *oxen*.　*Brethren* and *children* fall under the Irregulars, which see pp. 323–4, below.

In M.E. a considerable extension of the *-en* suffix took place, notably in the dialects of the South and South-East, but to some extent also in the Midlands.　　See a brief account of the M.E. conditions in my *Short Hist. of English*, § 112.　　A fairly large number of Weak Pls. still survive in the fifteenth and sixteenth centuries, and they are not confined to provincial writers, though these have the larger share of them.　　The following list shows the principal Plurals of this type, with references to the writers, or works in which they are found.　　At the present time, *primrosen, housen* may be heard in provincial dialects, and I have even heard *foxen* from an old woman in a Berkshire village.

Honden, Hondon ' hands ', St. Editha.

fon ' foes ', St. Editha.

knen ' knees ', St. Editha.

appullon 'apples ', St. Editha.

eyen, &c., ' eyes ' :—*hynon*, St. Editha ; *eghen, eyon*, Palladius ; *yeen*, S. of Rouen ; *iȝen*, Pecok ; *yȝen*, Sustr. Men. ; *eyen*, Caxton ; *yen, eyen*, Lord Berners ; *iyen*, Lord Buckhurst.

treen 'trees ', Pallad. ; Lord Buckhurst, Induction, 2, rhymes *green*—*been*.

oxen, Pallad., Pecok, Gregory, &c., &c. ; *exon*, Palladius.

eldron ' parents ', Pall.

fleen ' fleas ', Pall.

cleen ' claws ', Pall.

streen ' straws ', Pall.

kyn(e), &c., ' cows ', Pecok, *kyn* ; Gregory, *kyne* ; Caxton, *kyen, kene* ; Lord Berners, *kyen* ; Latimer, *kyne*.

bothen ' booths ', Shillingford, 12.

shon ' shoes ', Marg. Paston, ii. 125 ; Gregory, *shone* ; Caxton ; Wilson ; Elyot ; Gabr. Harvey, Lttrs.

All Sowlen (College), Elyot's Will, i. 310 ; R. Layton, 1535, Ellis ii. 2. 60—*All Sowllen College*.

Al Sawlyn (day), Shillingford, 17.

Al Halwyn, &c., Shillingford, 16, *Al Halwynyeuen* ; Sustr. Men. 86. 19. 109. 8—*alle Halwyn* ; Ord. of Worcester—*alle halowen day*, 397, 1467 ; Lttrs. and Pprs. i. 55—*Alhalowentyde* (Instr. to Northumb.), 1483 ; Cavendish, L. of Wolsey—*Allhalonday*, 222, *Hallhalonday*, 223.

Housen ' houses ', Bury Wills—*almesse howsyn*, 112 (1509) ; Ascham, Toxophilus, i. 121.

Hosyn ' hose ', Caxton ; Cavendish, L. of Wolsey, 88.

Horson ' horses ', Cely Papers, 67.

Peason ' pease ', Wilson, 53 ; Gabr. Harvey, Lttrs. 124.

Ewen ' ewes ', W. of J. Buckland, Linc. Dioc. Docs. 42. 143 (North-ants, 1450).

Aischen ' ashes ', Bk. of Quint. 8, &c. ; Hoccleve—*ashen*, Reg. of Pr. 287.

Invariables: Nouns without Suffix in Plural.

This class is represented in present-day English by *sheep, deer*, and these words belonged in O.E. to a large class of Neuters, which, being long monosyllables, had no suffix in the Nom. and Acc. Pl. Many of these words preserved this characteristic in M.E., some practically uni-versally, some occasionally, in certain dialects, but more were swept into the large class of Pls. in -*es*. With this type, however, were commonly associated, in Middle and Modern English, words expressing number, weight, measure, time, and mass, also certain names of animals. Of the words thus uninflected in the Pl. some were original uninflected Neuters, while others belonged to other classes. *Sheep, deer*, and *swine* may be omitted from the list, as these forms are universal and still survive. We may, however, note in passing that Machyn has several remarkable Pls. in -*s*, including *velles* ' veals ', 11, *swines*, 11, and one or two others recorded elsewhere (p. 322).

Year. Fortescue—*vii yere*; Shillingford, 68, 69; Caxton—*syxe score yere*, Jason, 52. 36; Sir Thos. Smith—*xxj yere old*, Rep. 120; Edm. Verney—*2 yeere*, V. Mem. ii. 134, 1641.

Winter. Wilson—*thirtie winter*, 186.

Foot. Pallad.—*seven fote*; Shillingford—*ix fote long*, 85; Gregory; Cavendish, L. of Wolsey—*xv foote thyke*, 8.

Finger. Pallad.—*sex fyngre thicke.*

Fathom. Gregory—*iiij fethem.*

Mile. Lord Berners—*xxiii Englisshe myle*, i. 491.

Mark. Fortescue—*an c. marke.*

Pound. Wilson—*three thousand pounde*; Latimer—*L pounde*; Lady Wentworth—*three hundred thousand pound.*

Shilling. Lady Wentworth—*ten shilling a pound, fifty shilling a chaldren*, 62.

Sturgeon. Machyn, 11.

Lamb. Will of W. Wolhede, Bucks., 1533—*ij lambe*, L. D. D. 153. 16.

Horse. Shillingford, 5, Cr. Duke of York; Lord Berners—*a thousand horse* (= soldiers here), i. 77; Cavendish, L. of Wolsey—*vi of the beste horse*, 285.

Apple. Euphues—*to bring forth apple*, 113. No doubt used collectively.

Thing. Gregory—*alle thinge*; Lord Berners—*to love god of whome we have all thinge*, ii. 190.

Thank. Q. Elizabeth—*the two gentilmen I trust shal receave your thanke*, Lttrs. to J. VI, 65.

Lady Wentworth has *this twoe last poste*, and *ten wax candle*. The former word perhaps owes its uninflected form to the consonantal combination—possibly Lady W. even pronounced it without the final -*t* (cf. p. 303)—the latter may be used collectively, referring to a bundle or group of candles.

A curious instance of an uninflected Pl. after the word *pair* is *a payre of coberd* 'cupboards', in the Will of R. Bradley, Leicestershire, 1533, L. D. D. 161. 75.

Exceptional Plurals in -*s*.

I have noted the following exceptional use of the -*s* suffix:—

hosys (instead of *hosen, hosyn*), Will of Sir Thos. Cumberworth, Lincs., 1451, L. D. D. 51. 23; *fotes* 'feet', Palladius, 8. 200; Machyn—*mottuns* 'sheep' (cf. also Pope—)*velles* 'calves', 11, *swines*, 11, *samons*, 11, *ees* 'eyes', 204. This form is usually weak. Sir Edm. Verney, in 1639, actually writes *in spight of our teeths*, Verney Pprs. 244.

The word *riches*, now taken as a Pl. (having no Sing.), is in reality the French *richesse*. Bp. Pecok inflects it regularly in the Pl.—*ricchessis*, i. 296, 297.

The Change of *f* to *v* before the Suffix of the Possessive and of the Plural.

At the present time we do not make this change in the Possess. Sing., except in the phrases *calve's head, calve's foot*, but say *calf's, wife's, wolf's*,

&c. On the other hand, we pronounce the voiced ending, and express it in the spelling, in the Plurals, *loaves, wives, wolves, calves*, &c., and usage varies in *roofs*, while in the Pl. of *hoof*, *hooves* is felt as archaic and more suited to poetry (cf. Lady of Shalott) than to colloquial speech. There is no historical reason for the distinction between the Possess. Sing. and the Plural. In O.E. voiceless open consonants (*s, f, þ*) were voiced between vowels, so that normally all inflected cases, Sing. and Pl., of the above words would have -*v*-, which in the Possess. Sing. and in the Pl. would produce the forms [wŭlvz, kāvz, waivz], &c., when the vowel of the suffix disappeared, and left -*vs* in contiguity. Our usage now has generalized the *f* for the whole Singular and *v* for the Plural, apart from those words where the Singular type has been extended to the Plural as well.

This is convenient and provides descriptive grammarians with their rule that 'words ending in -*f* form their Plural in -*ves*'. The habit was by no means fixed, however, in the fifteenth and sixteenth centuries, and the examples show that some speakers generalized *f* everywhere, both Sing. and Pl., while others adhered to the ancient practice of voicing the *f* in the Possess. Sing. and in the Plural alike. A few examples will suffice to show how unsettled was the usage.

Plurals in -f(e)s.

Lord Berners, *wifes*, i. 352 (but *lyves*, i. 356, *wyves*, i. 404); Elyot, *wolfes*, i. 22, *lyfes*, i. 110, our *selfes*, i. 138; Machyn, *beyffes* 'beeves', 11, *wyeffes*, 74; Machyn also writes *a-lyffe* 'alive', 75; Cavendish, *lyfs*, 56, *selfs*, passim, *beafes*, 97; Ph. Henslow, *wifes*, Alleyn Mem. 29, 1593; Lady Verney, *wifes*, Verney Mem. ii. 271, 1647.

On the other hand, the voiced type is the more usual, and Shillingford includes under it the French word *strife*, of which he has a Pl. form *stryves*, 98.

Possessive Singular in -v(e)s.

Marg. Paston, *wyvis*, ii. 365; Wilson, *wiues*, 56, 206; Q. Elizabeth, *your liues peril* (Sing.), Lttrs. to James VI, 71; Euphues, *wolues*, 322; Shakespeare (First Fol.), *wiues*, Merry Wives, iv. 5. The form *of lyue* in Lord Lovel's Will, 1455, L. D. D. 8. 4, 14, may be considered either as the survival of an inflected form (after *of*), or at least as based on the analogy of the inflected forms.

Irregular Plurals.

Under this head we include *children, brethren*, and several other Pls. of the same kind which are still found in Early Modern.

Children is remarkable for having both the Pl. -*r*- suffix—O.E. *cildru*, M.E. *childre*—and the weak Pl. suffix -*en*. *Brethren* has a mutated vowel in the base and the weak Pl. suffix. Several other words, mostly old Neuters, show in M.E. a Pl. suffix -*ren*, that is a combination of the old -*ru* suffix, with the addition of -*en*. Such are O.E. *lamb*—*lambru*, M.E. *lambre, lambren*; O.E. *calf*—*calfru*, M.E. *calfre, calfren*; O.E. *æg* 'egg', Pl. *ægru*, M.E. *eire, eiren*.

The group of words expressing family relationships, O.E. *fæder, mōdor, brōþor, s(w)ustor, dohtor*, all favour Pl. forms in -*en* in the South in M.E. The weak *sustren* survives, as we shall see, well into the sixteenth century.

A few examples are given to illustrate the variety of usage with regard to some of these Pls. in the fifteenth and sixteenth centuries.

M.E. *eyren*, &c., 'eggs'; Palladius, *eyron*; Rewle Sustr. Men., *eyrin*, 86. 31; Bk. of Quint., *eyrin*, 4; Caxton, in the well-known Preface to the Aeneid, uses *eyren* to illustrate that this archaic form was still in use, but the London innkeeper in the story did not understand what was wanted until *eggys* were asked for. Gregory has *eggys*.

Sistren, &c. St. Editha, *sustren*; Rewle Sustr. Men. *sustryn, -in,* 105. 27, &c. (*sustris* is the more frequent form); Pecok, *sistren*; Wilson, *sisterne.*

Brethren. St. Editha, *britheren*; Pecok, *bretheryn*; Gregory, *bretheryn*; Fortescue, *brotheryn*, 137; Elyot, *brethern*, Gou. 100, *bredern*, E.'s Will, 313; Berners, *bretherne*; Latimer, *bretherne*; Machyn, *bredurne*; Wilson, *bretherne*; Cavendish, *bretherne.*

Children. Childeren, childeryn, St. Editha, Pecok, Fortescue, &c.; Machyn, Euphues, *chylderne, childerne;* Elyot's Will, *childre,* which is a survival of the O.E. and M.E. forms; Coverdale has a Gen. Pl. *childers,* and Edw. VI First P. B. has *childers children* in the Marriage Service. The spelling *childre* doubtless stands for [tʃildr].

The rather rare Pl. *deytron* 'daughters' occurs in St. Editha. This shows mutation of the vowel (M.E. *dehter*), and the Wk. *-en.*

II

ADJECTIVES.

The inflexion of Adjectives, as regards case, has disappeared by the beg'nning of the fifteenth century, or, if it survives in poetry here and there for the sake of the metre, it must be regarded as archaic.

A belated Genitive Pl. occurs in the phrase *God our aller Creatour* from a letter of Richard III to James III of Scotland, Lttrs. and Pprs. i, p. 53, where *aller* represents M.E. *allre,* sometimes written *alder,* O.E. *allra.*

French Plurals.

The addition of *-s* to the Pl. of Adjectives, on the French model, which is rare in M.E., though there are a few instances in Chaucer (cf. *Short Hist. of Eng.,* § 319). In the fifteenth century I have found a not inconsiderable number of these Plurals, chiefly in legal and official documents. Some of the following are certainly more or less technical (legal) phrases, and are presumably taken straight from French legal documents. Others, again, are not to be explained in this way. Apparently the usage was extended from the legal clichés by certain writers, with a view to special elegance and correctness. It will be observed that the inflected Adj. usually follows the Noun, as in French, though this is not always the case. We may, I think, regard these *-s* Plurals as the result of a literary whim. They can hardly have had a real existence in uttered speech. The cases I have noted are:—

Palladius, *children clennes,* 9. 229; Shillingford, *letters patentz,* 77, 131 (legal documents); Will of Sir Thos. Cumberworth (Lincs., 1451), *prestes seculers,* Linc. Dioc. Docs. 53. 35; Rewle Sustr. Men., *Ministris prouinciallis*, 117. 36, *gode maneris and honestes*, 101. 14, *certaines wommen*, 101. 12, *greuousis trespassis*, 101. 24, *deuowtes handmaydenes*, 98. 1, *ii of the most demures and wise sistris*, 90. 26, *ii sistris vise, sad, and vertuouses of the Couent*, 92. 13, *massis conuentuales*, 110. 16, *at þe secunde euynsonges of festis doublis*, 114. 14, *festis simplis or lasse be þo festis which be nat dowbles*, 113. 33, *festis half doubles*, 110. 5; Sir John Fortescue, *Lordes of the lande both spirituellis and temporelles*, 145, *privatis personis*, 147; E. of Salisbury, 'the kings moste *noblez lettrez*', Past. Lttrs. i. 421 (1458); Reg. of Godstow, *diuinis seruices*, 18; Caxton, yong *children masles*, Jason 86. 3; Instructions to Lord Montjoie, *Lordes spirituelx and temporelx*, Lttrs. and Pprs. i. 12 (1483); Cr. of Knight of Bath, *lettres missives*, Lttrs. and Pprs. 388, *justes* ('jousts') *roiaulx*, 397; Will of Lord Lovel, *heires males*, Linc. Dioc. Docs. 82. 24, 27 (1455); Irish Documents, *Lordes spirituels and temporels*, Lttrs. and Pprs. i. 379 and 381 (*c.* 1489–93); Lord Berners, *letters patents*, i. 81; Sir Thos. Elyot's Will, *heires males*, 314. Note that while E. has such constructions as *beastes sauage*, i. 22, *actes martial*, 37, *spirites vitall*, 169, &c., he omits the *-s* except in the instance cited. Queen Elizabeth has *clirristz days* 'clearest', Transl. 19.[1]

The Forms of the Comparative and Superlative.

This is the main centre of interest, so far as Adjectives are concerned, in the Modern Period. The chief points to be considered are: (1) comparatives with vowel shortened by a M.E. process before the suffix *-re*, when the Positive ends in a consonant; this shortened vowel is sometimes extended by analogy to the Superlative, where it could not normally develop, and even to the Positive; (2) the survival of Comp. and Superl. forms with mutated vowel; (3) the pleonastic use of *more* and *most* before Adj. already inflected respectively with the Comp. or Superl. suffixes; (4) certain irregularities consisting either in the use of an entirely new form, cf. *badder* under 4, below, or in the addition of the Comparative or Superlative suffixes to words which we should not now thus inflect, preferring rather to prefix *more, most*.

Survival of Comparatives with Shortened Vowels.

Gretter 'greater', Palladius, Shillingford, 11; Fortescue, 122; Gregory, 277; Caxton, Jason 16. 33. The Superl. form *grettist* (*-est*) is found in Fortescue, 119, &c.; Gregory, 115; Jul. Berners and Machyn. The Positive *grett(e)* occurs in Fortescue, 121; Gregory, 83; Machyn, passim.

Depper 'deeper', Palladius, 52. 239; *sonner* 'sooner', Pall. 83. 115; *swetter* 'sweeter', Pall. 84. 644; *swettist*, in Pecok, i. 67.

Uttrist, Pecok; Caxton, Jason 71. 11. The positive of this word is in reality a Comparative—O.E. *úte*, with a Comp. suffix added.

Survivals of Mutated Comparatives and Superlatives.

The only surviving members of this class at the present time are *elder, eldest*, which are no longer used, as formerly, as the Comp. and Superl. of *old*, but in a special way, applied only to the members of a family, society, or group.

---

[1] The following additional examples of Pl. Adj: may be noted, all from Paston Letters—*certeins notables and resonables causes*, Will. Paston i, 30 (1430); *diverses persones*, Dalling's Petition, i, 36 (1434).

Pecok has *eeldir daies* 'former days', i. 107; Palladius, *elder* 'older', 28. 760; *elder* as an ordinary Comp. of *old* occurs in 1579 in 'E. K.'s' Epistle Dedicatory to the Shepherds' Calendar; and a little later in Euphues, 208—'You are too young, and were you *elder* . . .' In Congreve's *Way of the World* (1700) the phrase occurs, 'I suppose this Deed may bear an *elder* Date than what', &c., Act v, Sc. xiii.

Of the other words formerly mutated in Comparison, *long* and *strong* appear to be the only survivors in the fifteenth and sixteenth centuries, unless we include Gregory's *grytter*, 227 (O.E. *grētra*), but this is much more probably to be explained otherwise (p. 212).

The Comp. *strenger* is found in Pecok, i. 46; Jul. Berners (Adv., the Adjective is *stronger*); Lord Berners, i. 84. The Superl. *strengest* I have found in Caxton, Jason 70. 7 and 26. *Lenger* is found, Marg. Paston, i. 176; Sustr. Men. 93. 29; Gregory, 233; Lord Berners, i. 310 (-*ar*, Adv.); Latimer, 72; Lord Edw. Howard, Ellis ii. 1. 215 (1513); Ascham, Tox. 64; Gabr. Harvey, Lttrs. 20. *Lengest* I have noted, Palladius, 88. 772; Pecok, i. 133; Marg. Paston, i. 250.

Use of More and Most before Comparative and Superlative Forms.

Every one knows Shakespeare's '*most unkindest* cut of all', Jul. Caesar, Act iii, Sc. ii. The following are a few examples from works written before and up to Shakespeare's time.

Comparatives:—*more better*, Gregory, 200; Monk of Evesham (1482), *more worthior* 47, *more surer* 56, *more gladder* 101; *more larger*, Jul. Berners; *more gretter*, Caxton, Jason 63. 30; *more stronger*, Lord Berners, i. 59, *the more fresher*, ibid. i. 295; *more diligenter*, Latimer, 53; *the more fitter*, Euphues, 87, *more swifter*, ibid. 152.

Superlatives:—*þe most streytest*, Shillingford, 9; *the most best wyse*, ibid. 18; *the most gentellyst*, Gregory, 200, *most parfytyste*, ibid. 230; *most strengest*, Caxton, Jason 70. 7; *mooste byttyrste*, Mnk. of Ev. 43; *moost hardest*, Jul. Berners; *moost nerest* and *secrettest*, Lord Berners, i. 27, *moost outragyoust people*, ibid. i. 211, *moost ungracyoust of all*.

Dryden, in his Essay on the Dramatic Poetry of the Last Age, says:—'I think few of our present writers would have left behind them such a line as this—"*Contain your spirits in more stricter bounds*". But that gross way of two comparatives was then ordinary, and, therefore, more pardonable in Jonson.'[1]

Various Peculiarities and Irregularities of Comparison.

The most remarkable 'irregularity' in Comparison which I have found is perhaps *badder*, in Lyly's Euphues of all books. The passage in which it occurs is worth quoting for various reasons. It is typically Euphuistic in character, it is interesting as giving Lyly's opinion concerning a famous seat of learning, and the context seems to explain why the author took such a liberty with English grammar.

The passage occurs in the message 'To my verie good friends the Gentlemen Schollers of Oxford', at the end of the first part of Euphues.

'The Estritch that taketh the greatest pride in her feathers, picketh

---

[1] Note 'you would have dealt *more civiller* with', &c., Nick Arris (1657), V. Mem. iii. 398.

some of the worst out, and burneth them: there is no tree but hath some blast, no countenance but hath some blemish, and shall Oxford then be blamelesse? I wish it were so, but I cannot think it is so. But as it is it may be better, and were it badder, it is not the worst.'

'I thinke there are fewe Uniuersities that haue lesse faultes then Oxford, many that haue more, none but haue some', p. 208.

Lyly could not resist the alliteration and assonance of *better* and *badder*.

Pecok preserves *rathir* with its original force as the Comparative of *rath* 'early', and contrasts it with *latir*, i. 94. Lord Berners has the old Superl. *ferrist* 'farthest', the vowel of which has mutation. Elyot uses *moost* in the old Adjectival sense of '*greatest*'—*hir moost discomforte*, 2. 147. Latimer uses -*lye* as a living Adjectival suffix—*byshoplye duties and wordes*, 25, *unscripterlye*, 48. Far into the seventeenth century many words which we should not now inflect appear with the Comp. and Superl. suffixes. I give only a very few examples among many. *Openist*, Pecok, i. 77; *greuouser*, Latimer, 191; *willinger*, Ascham, Scholem. 23; *delicatest*, Euphues, 35; *naturalest*, Sir Thos. Smith, Rep. 22; *pacienter*, Gabr. Harvey's Lttrs. 137; *ungratefull'st*, Otway's Friendship in Love. A few more Superlative suffixes to words of this kind will be found on p. 282 to illustrate the loss of the vowel.

III

PERSONAL PRONOUNS.

The Personal Pronouns in the Plural.

The Old English Personal Pronouns *hie, heora, heom* appear in M.E. in the South and a great part of the Midlands as *hi, here, hem*, &c. In the London dialect these forms are gradually ousted by the forms, of Scandinavian origin, *þey, þeir, þeim*, &c., which get into this dialect from the North through the East Midlands.

The Nom. *hii* is the first to go, and is not found after the time of Davie. Chaucer, his contemporaries, and followers invariably write *þei, þey, thei, they*, &c. Some provincial works like St. Editha still preserve the archaic *hee, hoe*. There is nothing more to be said about the strong forms of the Nom. after the first quarter of the fourteenth century.

The weak forms will be discussed later.

The next of the *h-* forms to disappear is *her(e)*, and I know no examples of it after the third quarter of the fifteenth century, except in the Nut-brown Maid, c. 1500, and in Surrey. The *th-* forms do not appear in the London dialect before the fifteenth century, and they seem to come in rather reluctantly and very gradually during this century, generally accompanied by the older forms. Except, however, as occasional, probably deliberate, archaisms, the old Possess. *her* may be said to disappear from literature by the end of the fifteenth century.

The history of *hem* is rather curious. It survives in constant use among nearly all writers during the fifteenth century, often alongside the *th-* form. I have not noted any sixteenth-century example of it in the comparatively numerous documents I have examined, until quite at the end of the century. It reappears, however, in Marston and

Chapman early in the seventeenth century, and in the form *'em* occurs, though sparingly, in the Verney Mem. towards the end of the seventeenth century, where the apostrophe shows that already it was thought to be a weakened form of *them*. During the eighteenth century *'em* becomes fairly frequent in printed books, and it is in common use to-day as [əm]. It is rather difficult to explain the absence of such forms as *hem* or *em* in the sixteenth century, since the frequency at a later period seems to show that, at any rate, the weak form without the aspirate must have survived throughout. The explanation must be that *em*, though commonly used, was felt, as now, to be merely a form of *them*.

Survivals of here, *&c.*

Hoccleve, *here, hir* ; Lydgate, *her, here.*

St. Editha, *hure, here*; Audelay, *here*; Bokenam, *hyr, here* (and *ther*); Constable of Dynevor Castle, *her, har* ; Bp. Pecok, *her*; Sir J. Fortescue, *her* (occasionally, usually *thair*); Marg. Paston, *her*, passim (and *ther*); Rewle Sustr. Men., *her, here* ; Bk. of Quintessence, *her* (and *þer*); Ord. of Worcester, *hur* (and *ther*); Engl. Reg. of Godstow, *her* (and more rarely *their*) ; Engl. Reg. of Oseney, *here* (and *there, þere*); Gregory, *her, hir, here* (and *there* rarely); Caxton, Jason, *her* (rarely, generally *their*) ; Nut-brown Maid, *her*, line 6.

I have noted one certain example of *her* 'their' in Surrey's poems, Tottel, p. 24. Other cases are very doubtful. An undoubted example of *her* in late colloquial use is pointed out by Mr. Orton of Merton College, in Machyn 141,—'and after to *her* plasse, and they, &c.'

Mr. Henry Bradley, however, in *Shakespeare's England* mentions the following undoubted examples of *her*: Hen. VI, Pt. I, i. i. 83 ; Othello, III. iii. 66 ; Troilus, I. iii. 118. The first occurs in all the Folios, the second in all Quartos and Folios, the third in F¹. See perhaps also F.Q. V. 7, 10.

All later works which I have examined have the *th-* forms only.

Survivals of hem, *&c.*

It would probably be correct to say that down to the end of the first quarter of the fifteenth century most texts, except those of the Northern and North-East Midlands, use *hem* only. After that date *th-* forms appear very widely alongside the others, though many still have no examples of the latter.

Audelay, St. Editha. Wm. Paston (the Judge, 1425–30), Hoccleve (has, however, *themselfe* in Minor Poems), Lydgate, Myrc, Bk. of Quint., Bp. Pecok, Const. of Dynevor, Rewle Sustr. Men., J. Buckland's Will (Northants, 1450), appear to have no *th-* forms ; the following have *hem* by the side of less frequent *th-* forms:—Siege of Rouen, Hen. V. (in Letter, 1421), Shillingford, Fortescue, Marg. Paston (the Bp. of Exeter's letter in St. Pprs. has only *hem*), Lord Lovel's Will, 1450, Ordinances of Worcester, Engl. Registers of Godstow and Oseney Abbeys, Gregory, with whom *th-* forms are rare, and who has the weak form *em*—*ax of em that felde the strokys*, 236, and Caxton. '*Hem* occurs in Ben Jonson's Every Man in his Humour, 1598 ; Marston's Eastward Hoe, 1604 ; 'Goe Dame, conduct *-am* in', Chapman's All Fooles, 1605, p. 136 ; *'em* is in frequent use in the colloquial dialogue of the later seventeenth-

century comedies, and occurs occasionally in the letters of the Verney
family towards the end of the century—e. g. John V., Mem. iv. 349, 1685,
and Nancy Nicholas, iv. 428 (three times), 1688.   It is common in
serious poetry and prose in the eighteenth century.   Milton's own MS.
has *I saw 'em under a greene mantling vine*. Com. 294.   Note that this
form became so widespread in the early eighteenth-century speech that
Swift complains that ' young readers in our churches in the *prayer for
the Royal Family*, say *endue'um, enrich'um, prosper'um*, and *bring'um*.
Tatler, No. 230 (1710).   It may be noted that Milton actually puts the
apostrophe thus : *saw' em*.

Unstressed Forms of the Plural Pronouns.

The full stressed forms of these are, originally, generally *þei, þay, thei,
thai*; *þeir, þair, their, thair*; *þeim, þaim, theim, thaim*, &c.

The only one of these that certainly survives in pronunciation is *they*;
their [ðɛə] is doubtful, though it may very possibly represent old *their*;
them is certainly derived from the old weak form.

From the fifteenth century onwards spellings such as *the, ther, tham,
them* are found fairly frequently, and these are weak forms, which show
the normal monophthonging of *ei, ai* in unstressed positions.   (On this
point see further particulars, pp. 279–80.)

We have now lost the old *the*, which would have become [ðɛ, ði], and
we use the old strong form in all positions, though this no doubt sometimes undergoes a slight reduction when unstressed.

The old weak form *ther* survives in the form [ðə], which is now rather
falling into desuetude.   The old weak *them* survives as a strong form,
being used in stressed positions—'They have forgotten me, but I have
not forgotten *them*.'   From this we have formed a new weak form [ðəm],
which we habitually use in unstressed positions.

Examples of weak the.

This is the least frequent of the weakened forms, but it occurs in
Shillingford, e. g. p. 62, Gregory, and frequently in the letters of Queen
Elizabeth.   *The are all*, &c., Lady Sussex, V. Mem. ɪɪ, 81 and 82 (1642);
thy, Mrs. Basire, 109 (1651) and 135 (1654).

Examples of weakened ther (thyr).*

Marg. Paston, *ther*; Bk. of Quint., *þer*; Gregory, *there* (rarely);
Ordinances of Worcester; State of Ireland (St. Pprs., 1515), *ther*;
Skelton's Magnyficence, *thyr*; Q. Elizabeth (in Lttrs. and in Transl.),
ther; Cavendish, L. of Wolsey, *ther*.   Most of these writers generally use
their or *thair*, &c.

Strong and Weak Forms of them.

Already in the fifteenth century several texts write *them* only, and this
may be due to the influence of *hem*, which also occurs in these documents.
On the other hand, the spellings *theim, theym* are found far into the sixteenth century.

Hoccleve has hardly any *th-* forms, but *themselfe* in Minor Poems;
Sir J. Fortescue has *thaim, them*; Shillingford, *tham*; Ord. of Worcester,
them; Lord Lovel's Will, *theym*; Marg. Paston, *them*; Gregory, *them*;
Cr. of Duke of York, *thaym, them*; State of Ireland (St. Pprs., 1515),
them; Skelton, *them*; Rede me, &c., *theym*, passim; J. Mason (Letter,
Ellis iii. 2), *them*; Sir Thos. More (Letter, 1523), *theym* more frequently

---

* See Appendix V.

than *them* ; Lord Berners, *theym*, *them* ; Elyot, *theym*, *them* ; Latimer, *theym*, *them* ; Cavendish, L. of Wolsey, *theym* and *them* ; Euphues, *them*.

You *and* Ye.

Down to the middle of the sixteenth century writers generally distinguish between Nom. *ye* and Acc. Dat. *you*. The Pl. forms already in M.E. are used in respectful address to a single person.

While, for instance, Sir Thos. More and Lord Berners distinguish between *ye* and *you*, Bp. Latimer, Ascham, Cavendish, and Euphues use both forms indifferently for the Nom. Q. Elizabeth appears to employ *you* alone for Nom. and oblique cases, Sing. and Pl. On the whole, in the sixteenth century, while *you* is common as a Nom., *ye* is much rarer as an Acc. or Dat.

Ye is sometimes introduced merely for variety, cf. Ascham—'*you* that be shoters, I pray *you*, what mean *you* when *ye* take ', &c., Tox. 101.

In the seventeenth century *you* is far commoner than *ye* in Nom., though the latter is not infrequent. Sir Edmund Verney, in 1642, uses *ye* after a preposition—*any of ye*, V. Mem. ii. 136.

A distinction was formerly made between *thou*, *thee*, and *you*, in the sense that the former was used by superiors, or seniors in addressing their inferiors or juniors, and in the familiar and affectionate speech of parents addressing their children.

Sir Thos. More's son-in-law, Roper, in his Life of that famous man, represents him as addressing the writer—' Sonne Roper '—as *thou*, *thee*, but himself as using *you* in speaking to Sir Thomas More.

The Weak a for he.

This form scarcely survives at present except in the archaic literary *quotha*.

Ha and *a* are fairly common in M.E. in texts of the South-West and South-West Midlands—e. g. *quoðha*, St. Juliana (MS. Royal); *a* is used by Trevisa as a Neuter or Masculine; other Southern texts use *ha* as a Pl. Nom. The Constable of Dynevor Castle (temp. Hen. IV) uses *a* both for *he* and *they*, Ellis ii. 1. 16; Latimer, Sermons, writes ' here was *a* not gyltie ', 153.

Henry Verney writes, in 1644—' *a* dyed one newersday *a* is tomorrow caryed to his own church ', V. Mem. ii. 204, and in 1647—' *a* proves by fits very bad ', Mem. ii. 361.

hit *and* it.

The old spelling *hit*, *hyt*, persists nearly to the end of the sixteenth century, although the weak *it* is found as early as the twelfth century in E. Midland, and in the London dialect in the poems of Davie (*c*. 1327). *Hit* or *hyt* is still the only spelling in many sixteenth-century documents, while in others *yt*, &c., preponderates, and in others again *hit* or *hyt* is the more frequent. Sir Thos. Elyot has *hit* more frequently than *it* in his Will, but the conditions are reversed in the Gouernour; Machyn uses *hyt* but rarely; Queen Elizabeth writes *hit* with very great frequency in her Letters and Translations alike, *yt* being only occasionally used.

It can hardly be doubted that in the fifteenth and sixteenth centuries the aspirate was lost in unstressed positions, and the spelling *h*- was an archaism. At the same time it is possible that some speakers still pronounced *hit* when the word was stressed. Since the other Personal Pronouns which began with *h-* all had both strong and weak forms, there is no reason why the old strong form of the Neuter Pronoun should not also have been retained. By the end of the century, apparently, the *h-* form had disappeared from ordinary colloquial English.

The Possessive Neuter its.

I have found no trace of the present-day *its* during the sixteenth century, my earliest reference being in Charles Butler's English Grammar of 1634, p. 40. As Butler was born in 1560, it seems probable that *its* was in use in his youth, since it is unlikely that he would incorporate, without comment, a form which was a recent innovation.

At the same time, the form was evidently felt as a colloquialism at the beginning of the century, for it is avoided in the Authorized Version. Queen Elizabeth uses *his* of ' the matters ' (Letters to J. VI, 3), Euphues has *his* referring to ' learning '. Shakespeare does not use *its*.

Ascham, we may note, uses *he, hym,* speaking of a bow, Tox., p. 116. The earliest reference in O.E.D. is 1598. Charles Butler's Gr. (1634) gives *its* without any comment.

Milton writes *his—Now the spell has lost his hold.* Com. 919.

The Forms hir and her.

The old form of the oblique cases of the Fem. Pronoun is represented by the M.E. and Early Modern *hir, hyr,* and these forms persist until towards the end of the sixteenth century. Latimer, Ascham, Euphues, and Lord Burghley in his letters, all have *hir* and *hyr,* and these on the whole are the more usual forms in letters and printed books throughout the greater part of the century, though in many *her* is found also. The spelling *her,* which may represent a lowering of the vowel in unstressed positions, before *-r,* a process which may have been helped by the analogy of the Nom. *he* in those M.E. dialects which employed this form for *she,* is found very commonly in M.E. by the side of *hir,* but the more careful scribes distinguish between the Possess., &c., Fem., and the Possess. Pl., keeping *her* for the latter and *hir,* &c., for the former. In the fifteenth century Hoccleve has *hir* only ; *her* is found in the London official documents, in the Rewle Sustr. Men., which text often distinguishes the cases—*her,* Acc., *here,* Possess. and Dat.—in Lydgate's Poems, Lord Lovel's Will, Marg. Paston—*herr, here, hers,* by the side of *hyr.* Caxton has both forms. Cely Pprs., Gregory, the Will of Sir Thos. Cumberworth, Lincs., 1451, all have *hir, hyr.* Sir J. Fortescue has *huyr.* Hen. VIII, in a letter of 1515, writes *har,* Acc. and Possess., a survival of a M.E. unstressed form often found in the South-Eastern dialect.

Edward VI, First P. B., seems to have *her* only. *Hir* is still very common in the Verney Memoirs ; see especially the letters of Sir Ralph. The weak form without the *h-* is rather rare ; however, *hoselder* 'houselled her' occurs in St. Editha, and *carryer* ' carry her ' in Verney Mem., Henry V., Mem. ii. 366, 1647.

Indiscriminate use of I and me.

It is not uncommon at the present time to hear *I* used instead of *me* after a Verb or Preposition, as though the speaker wished to avoid the latter form. ' What have they to do with you and I ? ' writes Sir John

Suckling in a letter to Aglaura, Wks., ii, p. 198.   The phrase *between you and I* is used by Tom Verney, V. Mem. iii. 173, 1657, and by Lady Hobart, V. Mem. iv. 57, 1664 ; *It must all light upon Heartfree and I* is said by Belinda in Vanbrugh's Provok't Wife, Wks. vol. ii, 363.

In 1734 Lady Strafford writes *Lady Anne Harvey invited my love and I,* Wentw. Pprs. 499.

A habit more characteristic than the above, of illiterate speakers, is the use of *me* as a Nom.   Susan Verney writes, in 1645, *Sis peg and me got an opportunity,* &c.

Miss Austen makes that rather underbred young woman, Miss Lucy Steele, say *Anne and me are to go there later,* Sense and Sensibility, i, ch. 24.

IV

The Articles.

Survival of M.E. *thoo.*

The form *thoo, þō,* &c., originally the Pl. of the Def. Article, O.E. *þā,* survives into the sixteenth century, generally, it is true, with a rather more definite Demonstrative sense than belongs to the Article, sometimes with the full force of the Demonstr. *those.*   See my *Short Hist. of Engl.,* § 287, for details of the late M.E. use of *þō.*

Pecok appears to use the form practically as the Pl. of the Art. in *tho writingis, tho deedis to be doon,* Repr. 1. 23 ; *alle tho whiche,* ibid., is more definitely Demonstrative.   The form occurs in the Bk. of Quintessence, *bo men,* in the Will of J. Buckland, in Rewle Sustr. Men. (*þoo*), in Gregory—*one of thoo,* 140, *thoo that,* 233, and in Caxton.

The latest example I have found of *thoo* is in a list of ships of Hen. VIII's time, 1513, in the sense of *those,* Ellis ii. 1. 218.

Indefinite Article.

The stressed M.E. form *oo* survives in Gregory—*oo place,* 153.

A instead of *an* is sometimes used before vowels—*a Englyssche squyer,* Gregory, 184 ; *a increasing, a ivel name,* Q. Elizabeth in a letter, Ellis i. 2. 157, 1549.

V

Verbal Endings.

Ending of the 3rd Pers. Singular Pres. Indicative.

In M.E. the Southern dialects have universally *-eþ* and *-iþ.*   The E. Midland has almost exclusively the *-þ, -th* ending, except, very occasionally, *-es, -is,* and then chiefly in rhymes.   W. Midland has the *-s* ending far more frequently.   Chaucer seems to have *-es* only once, and then in a rhyme.

In the fifteenth century the *-th* forms (*-yth, -ith, -eth*) very largely hold their own in the South, the E. Midlands, and in the London dialect, with occasional outcrops of sporadic *-s* forms.

Thus, the essentially provincial and usually archaic St. Editha, while generally preserving *-eth* as the usual form, writes also *comys*, 617, he *louys*, 2028. The E. Midland Bokenam has only *-yth*, &c., with the rarest exception, and even some of the Lincolnshire Wills of the fifteenth century write *-ith* as the usual type, with rarer *-eth*, but *-es* very rarely indeed, though Sir T. Cumberworth's Will has several *-s* forms, and apparently no *-th*, L. D. D. 45. It is noteworthy that in a Will of 1465 *ligges* occurs, apparently as the only form of its kind. This appears to be a lapse into dialect as regards the form of the word (*lig* = ' lie '), with a Northern suffix retained to avoid the incongruity of *liggeth*.

Wm. Paston, the judge, has only *-yth*. Marg. Paston has few, if any, forms of ending other than *-yth*; Palladius has *-eþ*, Pecok only *-ith*; Fortescue, and Shillingford, and Ord. of Worcester, *-yth*, *-ith*, with occasional *-eth*; the Wills from Bucks., Oxfordshire, and Northants only *-yth*, *-eth*. Cely Papers have *-yth* as a rule, though the younger members of the family often use *-es*, *-ys* as well.

Passing to London English, the fifteenth-century official documents have an overwhelmingly large proportion of *-ith* forms, with a trifling number of *-s* forms, which might be counted on the fingers of one hand. Other prose documents which show no particular Regional influence generally agree with this, but poetical writers, for purposes of metre or rhyme, begin to use forms in *-s*. Thus, while Lydgate (a Suffolk man) has in his poems frequent forms in *-es*, and Siege of Rouen has *puttys*, 32, *askysse*, 33, Capgrave, according to Dibelius, has only one such form, and the Bk. of Quintessence and the Rewle of Sustr. Men. have *-ith*, *-iþ* only.

In the sixteenth century, apart from poetry, *-ith*, &c., is practically universal in literary prose, official documents, and in private letters, until well into the third quarter of the century. To this the Sermons of Bp. Latimer, preached in 1549, form an exception, but it must be remembered that we possess these only in the form in which they were printed thirty years or so later, and it is possible that we owe some of the peculiarities to the editor or the printer.

At the same time, Latimer's language shows certain traces of provincialism in other directions, and the *-s* forms may be perfectly genuine and characteristic of the bishop's dialect. At any rate, I have noted about sixty-three examples in Arber's Reprint of the Sermons, side by side with many *-eth* forms. In Thos. Lever's Sermons (1550) there are a few *-s* forms, though the first of these seems to occur on p. 65, where it is put into the mouth of what the preacher calls ' rude lobbes of the country ', who are supposed to say: ' he minisheth Gods servants, he *slubbers* up his service who cannot reade the humbles.' The 3rd Sing. Pres. is very rare in any form in Machyn's Diary, but he *lys* occurs, pp. 181, 204, *leys*, *lyys*, 146, *gyffes*, 147. Gabriel Harvey uses *-s* forms in his letters occasionally, especially in the more familiar letters—*smels*, 18, *hopes*, *heares*, 23. When writing to the Master of his College he uses only *-ith* forms. Cavendish, Life of Wolsey, has very few *-s* forms, *-ith*, *-yth* being nearly universal, but I have noted *me semys*, p. 60. Ascham has at least twenty examples of *-s* in Toxophilus, of which *endures*, 39, occurs in a metrical line, and *leaues*, 91, also in a verse. Sir Thos. Smith nearly always writes *-eth* in Republ., but *gettes*, ibid., p. 67. Queen Elizabeth, in her later letters (to James VI) and in the Translations writes -*s*, by the side of -*eth*, &c., very frequently. In the latter, -*s* is much commoner than -*th*. The -*s* forms are not so frequent in those letters in Ellis written when the Queen was a girl, but *methinkes* occurs in 1572, Ellis i. 2. 263. The Auxiliaries *doth* and *hath* are nearly always so written in all the Queen's writings.   In Wilson's Arte of Rhetorique -*eth* and -*s* forms are both frequent, the latter occurring more commonly than in Ascham, especially in the less stately and solemn passages. In the Letters of Lord Burghley (Ellis, and Bardon Papers), so far as I can see, and in Euphues, none but -*th* forms are found.   Bacon, in his Essays, seems invariably to use the -*th* ending.

From the beginning of the seventeenth century the 3rd Singular Present nearly always ends in -*s* in all kinds of prose writing except in the stateliest and most lofty.   Evidently the translators of the Authorized Version of the Bible regarded -*s* as belonging only to familiar speech, but the exclusive use of -*eth* here, and in every edition of the Prayer Book, may be partly due to the tradition set by the earlier Biblical translations and the early editions of the Prayer Book respectively.   Except in liturgical prose, then, -*eth* becomes more and more uncommon after the beginning of the seventeenth century; it is the survival of this and not the recurrence of -*s* which is henceforth noteworthy.   The -*th* forms are common in Sir Thomas Browne, but his style is not typical of his age.

The letters in the Verney Memoirs contain a few examples of -*eth* which show that this survived even in familiar and colloquial language down to the middle of the century.

Tom Verney writes *telleth*, Mem. ii. 156, 1646; Lady Verney, *expresseth*, ii. 246, 1646; Sir Ralph has 'on (= one) *looseth* his time, the other spends his money', ii. 247, 1646, and 'my Lady Browne *telleth* me ', iii. 70, 1650. In Tom Jones, Fielding makes Parson Supple, the hypocritical chaplain, say ' You behold, Sir, how he waxeth wroth at your abode here ', vol. i, p. 312, First Ed.

The -*s* forms are usually ascribed to Northern influence, but this cannot conceivably have been exerted directly, and one naturally turns to the East Midland dialects, which so often were the undoubted medium whereby Northern forms have reached London English, as the probable channel in this case also.   In this instance, however, the forms are almost as rare in the fifteenth century in the works of writers from Suffolk, Norfolk, and even from Lincolnshire, as they are in the documents of London and of the South generally.   It must be mentioned, however, that Norf. Guild Returns, 1389, have numerous -*s* forms in the documents of the Guild of St. Thomas of Canterbury, but elsewhere -*ith*. It is true, also, that Lydgate of Bury has -*s* forms in abundance, and it is possible that in other E. Midland documents, especially the official writings such as the Suffolk and some Lincolnshire Wills of the fifteenth century, the writers deliberately avoided these forms and assimilated their usage to that still prevailing in London, although the forms may have been in the normal colloquial usage of these areas.   This, however, would not apply to Bokenam, who shows few if any traces of specific London influence.   It is perhaps rather a far-fetched assumption that the E. Midland writers of the fifteenth century conceal their normal speech habit in this respect, while all the time the very peculiarity which does not emerge in their writings was in existence and was gradually influencing London speech. Again, it is significant that some of the earliest -s forms are found in St. Editha, and few will attribute Northern influence to this Wiltshire text. Some other explanation must be sought. They are also not infrequent in the letters of the younger Celys (Essex) in third quarter of fifteenth century, and they are here clearly a colloquial feature. It has been suggested that the -s forms of the 3rd Sing. passed into prose literature from the poetical writings, and from prose literature to colloquial speech. This now appears to me highly improbable. It is true that the exigencies of rhyme and metre make it convenient to substitute the forms in -s for those in -ith in verse. By this means a syllable is got rid of, and the possibilities of rhyme enormously increased. Thus, at a time when -s is comparatively rare in prose writings of any sort— that is, down to the middle of the sixteenth century—the ending often appears in poetry. But it is hard to believe that what was destined to become the only form in the colloquial language should have come into that form of English primarily from poetry. It is more likely that the use of the -s forms in poetry is quite independent of their introduction into colloquial English. The use of those forms made by Ascham and Queen Elizabeth strikes one as reflecting a prevalent habit of ordinary speech. We might suspect Northern influence in the case of Ascham, a Yorkshireman, but not in the Queen and her contemporaries generally. The avoidance of them—in Euphues—by the highly correct Lyly is not consistent with a purely literary origin. Had he regarded these forms as primarily poetical, why should he not have employed them in his essentially artificial dialogue? On the other hand, if Lyly regarded the -s ending as an innovation, associated with familiar colloquial speech, he was just the man to set his face against them in writing such a work as Euphues. The -s forms in Machyn are certainly the result of colloquial usage, as this writer is not the man to take his grammar from the poets, nor, indeed, from literature of any sort.

It is more in accordance with what we know of the relations of the Spoken language to the language of Literature to suppose that the feature we are considering passed, in the first instance, into everyday usage, quite independently of the poets, and thence into the prose style of literature. It is evident that the number of persons who read poetry must at any time be very small in comparison with the population as a whole; and poetical diction, in so far as it differs from that of ordinary life, can exercise but a slight influence upon the colloquial language at large. If the -s forms of the 3rd Sing. Present gained currency primarily from poetical and then from prose literature, it would be difficult to explain how, in a comparatively short time, they attained such universality of usage, and also, allowing for the weight of tradition in favour of the older form, why they should have been felt as too colloquial to be admitted at all into Liturgical English in any form, and into the Authorized Version.

But all this is purely negative, and does not account for the appearance of the forms and their gradual complete acceptance in a dialect area to which they were originally quite alien.

z

We are placed in this dilemma, that the only apparent possible inter-
mediary between the North and London and the South, by which
a dialectal peculiarity could pass, is the E. Midland area, whereas this
particular characteristic does not appear to be especially widespread in
the E. Midland dialects, or among such writers as might be expected to
show direct influence from these dialects in the fifteenth and sixteenth
centuries—e. g. Bokenam, Gregory, Capgrave, Bury Wills, some of the
Lincs. Wills, Marg. Paston.

From this dilemma the theory which saddles the poets ultimately with
giving currency to the -s forms in the Spoken language, if it can be
accepted, offers an easy escape. If, in spite of the improbabilities which
have been urged against it, this view commends itself to the reader, he
will have no further difficulty. It is possible, however, that the starting-
point of the -s forms has nothing to do with Regional influence, but that
the extremely common Auxiliary *is* may have provided the model. I am
inclined to think that this is the true explanation of the 3rd Pers. Pres. in
-s in the Spoken dialect of London and the South, and in the English of
Literature.

A few remarks upon the use of these forms by the poets down to the
first half of the sixteenth century will not be out of place.

The -s forms were a great boon to writers of verse, both in supplying
rhymes, and metrically, in providing a form with a syllable less than
the -eth form of the same verb.

Thus poets often make use of these forms both in rhyme and in the
middle of lines. As regards the fifteenth century, while Lydgate often
employs these forms, Hoccleve does not, and Stephen Hawes appears to
make but moderate use of them. Skelton, who was born in 1460, and
may therefore be regarded as belonging to the late fifteenth century from
a linguistic point of view, makes frequent use of the -s endings (-is, -ys,
-es, -s) in such a rough coarse satire as ' Why come ye nat to Courte?',
but generally writes -th in his more delicate work, such as Phyllyp Sparowe ;
in Magnyficence he has usually -eth, but also *she lokys*, 925, *he ne reckys*,
1168, rhymes *spekys*, 2nd Pers. S.

It has already been mentioned that the Wilts. writer of St. Editha has
a few -s forms, while the Suffolk writer Bokenam has practically none.

The Earl of Surrey has many of these endings, the sonnet *The Swete
sesoun* alone having *springes, bringes, singes, flinges, slinges, minges* all
rhyming, besides *decayes*, and they occur with fair frequency in all his
love poems and in the translation of the Aeneid. Sir Thomas Wyatt the
Elder has a great many in his Satires. Lord Buckhurst, in the Induction, has twenty -s forms in the seventy-nine seven-line verses.

The only -th endings are *hath*, four times, *doth, doeth*, three times,
and *ceasseth*, once. *Hath* and *doth* survive long after -s has become
universal in English, but so far as the metre is concerned it is evident that
has would do just as well, and the same is true of *does*. The spelling *doeth*,
which occurs in verse 69 of the Induction, is monosyllabic—' mine iyes. . . .
That fylde with teares as *doeth* the spryngyng well.' The form *ceasseth*,
verse 40, is metrically of the same value as *ceases*, which might,
therefore, have been used had the poet wished. All the -s forms in
the poem are necessary for the metre, and in the only cases where

there was any option Lord Buckhurst has written -*th* in preference
to -*s*. All these facts, taken together with the arguments stated earlier,
seem to me to confirm the view that the -*s* ending was of colloquial, not
of literary origin, in Standard English, and that it arose in various areas
in the South, not through external Regional influence but as a result of
a natural and widespread analogy. The ending may have had currency
first among the humbler classes (cf. the Celys and Machyn), and its usage
for convenience in poetry may have hastened its acceptance in the colloquial speech of the better classes.

Forms of the 3rd Pers. Present Singular without Inflexion.

At the present time such forms may occasionally be heard from vulgar
and uneducated speakers. I noticed, some years ago in Essex, that such
phrases as ' he *come* every day to see me', ' he always *take* sugar in his
tea ', and so on, were very common.

In earlier times these flexionless 3rd Singulars were used by far more
distinguished persons. The origin of the omission is presumably the
analogy of the 1st Person.

I have noted a few from the fifteenth century onwards :—Marg. Paston,
commaund, i. 246 ; Lord Berners, *methynke*, i. 250 ; Latimer, *methynke*,
Seven Sermons, 133 ; Ascham, *methincke*, Tox. 100 ; Q. Elizabeth, ' as
your secretarye *terme* it ', Lttrs. to J. VI, 30 ; Wentworth Pprs., ' my
cossen hear *take* great delight in fishing, and *ketch* many ', 47 ; ' the town
tell a world of stories of Lady Masham ', Peter W., 408.

The Endings of the Present Indicative Plural.

In M.E. the ending -*eþ*, -*iþ* in the Present Pl. is typical of the Southern
dialects, and -*en* of the Midland, especially of E. Midland. From the
middle of the thirteenth century onwards London texts, by the side of the
Southern -*eþ*, have a preponderance of the E. Midland -*en* type of Pres.
Pls. The weakened ending -*e*, with loss of final -*n*, was still further
weakened, sometimes, even in the fourteenth century, and from this type
our present-day form, without any suffix, is derived. Chaucer generally
writes -*en* in his prose, -*e* being rare. In his poetry both forms occur
very commonly, but in rhymes -*e* is almost universal.

The history of the Present Pl. during the Modern period is concerned
(1) with the gradual loss of the final -*n*, and the ultimate fixing of the
prevailing type as one with no ending at all ; (2) with the survival, for
a considerable period, alongside the -*en*, or the flexionless type, of the
ending ·*eth*, -*ith* ; (3) with the appearance of a Pl. ending in -*es*, -*ys*, -*s*.

Now this last is still, as it was in M.E., and even in O.E., a characteristic feature of the Northern dialects. Whether the use of this suffix,
sporadically, from about the middle of the sixteenth century in
Literary English, and in the colloquial speech of educated persons in the
South of England, is to be ascribed to Northern influence, is quite
another matter. We shall discuss this question later on.

The Present Indicative Plural in -en, -e.

We should expect, from what we know of M.E., to find that in the
fifteenth century -*en* or -*e* would be the sole, or at least the prevailing type of

ending in London English, and that -*eth*, -*ith*, &c., would occur only in texts written by Southerners. As a matter of fact, the latter suffix is by no means so rare in the fifteenth and sixteenth centuries as we might expect, even in the writings of those whom we have no reason to suspect of Regional tendencies. It would appear that the literary and official documents of the late fourteenth century do not give us an altogether true picture of actual speech habit in this respect, and that the -*iþ* Plurals must have survived in the colloquial speech of large sections of the population, over a considerable area, although expressed comparatively rarely in the written form of English. This type of ending survives long after the disappearance of -*n*. The appearance of the -*s* endings marks a further and later stage. These appear some time after the loss of -*n*. and at a period in which *ith*, &c., is a rarety.

It must be ascribed to the indirect influence of London speech, in its written form, that the -*en* type either very largely predominates, or is at least represented, from quite early in the fifteenth century, even in documents whose authors might be expected to stick to a pure Southern form.

Thus, Palladius (Essex) generally writes -*eth*, but has occasional -*en*; the Constable of Dynevor, by the side of *we fayleth*, 15, has also *they seyen* 'see', 16, and *hau* 'have', Ellis ii. 1 ; St. Editha has *slydith*, 8, but *dwelle*, 57 ; the Devonian Fortescue has only -*en*, -*yn*, or -*e* ; Shillingford has *semeth*, 12, *menyth*, 16, but more often -*en*, *requyren*, 30, *seyn* 'say', 40, 131, &c., *deserven*, 131, *touchyn*, 132 (-*en* occurs most commonly in the legal and official documents in the Shillingford Pprs., and in Shilling-ford's letter to the Chancellor ; this ending is commoner in the letter of the Bishop of Exeter than in S.'s own letters or those of his friends).

Turning to writers whom we might suspect of specific E. Midland tendencies:—Bokenam has -*e* or -*yn* ; William Paston, the judge, has -*en* or -*e* ; Marg. Paston has generally -*yn*—*ȝeowyn*, i. 168, or no ending—*ye thenk*, i. 224, but *makyth*, ii. 124 ; Gregory, the Cockney from Suffolk, -*yn*, -*e*, or no ending—*belevyn*, 75, *deputyn*, 124, *behote* 'promise', 125, *long*, 201, but also *longythe*, 134.

These writers, as we should expect, hardly differ from the London usage in this particular case.

We may now describe the characteristics of a certain number of typical Literary English texts. Hoccleve has only -*en* ; Rewle Sustr. Men. very commonly -*in*, *purchassin*, 81. 4, *longin*, 33. 2, &c., &c., but also *þey singiþ*, 110. 9, *þey etiþ*, 111. 17, *þey rediþ*, 116. 17 and 20 ; Bk. of Quint., -*en* with occasional -*iþ* ; State of Ireland, St. Pprs. of Hen. VIII, 1515, has frequent examples of -*yth*, but -*en* occasionally—*there bin more then 60 comties*, p. 1. Lord Surrey has *ben*, Aeneid, Bk. ii, 735. This is the latest -*en* form in prose in my collections until we get to Euphues, in which work I have noted *they loaden*, 144. This is a better example than that quoted by Bradley on p. 257 of his edition of Morris's Histori-cal Outlines, from Shakespeare—'and *waxen* in their mirth '—since the additional syllable is here added for the sake of the metre. The same applies to Wyatt's 'you that *blamen*', Tottel, 37. On the whole, Ben Jonson's remark in his English Grammar, that the ending -*en* was used ' till about the reign of Henry VIII ' is correct, but it should be qualified and limited to the beginning of the reign, for we must regard the examples just quoted from Surrey, Wyatt, and Euphues as literary archaisms, which do not represent the usage of the spoken language.   This applies also to Spenser's deliberate archaisms—*bene*, rhymes *tene, weene*, &c.   As late, however, as 1695 Congreve makes Ben Legend, a rough sailor, though a gentleman's son, say 'as we *sayn* at sea', Love for Love, Act III, Sc. vi.

Mention may be made of three fifteenth-century texts written in the South-West Midlands :—the English Register of Godstow Abbey (1450) has *-th* Pls., in *-ith* and *-eth*, very frequently, especially in the first, liturgical portions of the work, but also many in *-en*, and some in *-e* ; the English Register of Oseney Abbey, Oxfordshire, *c.* 1460, has *they hauen, þey holden*, 53, but *-n* is rather rare, *-e* being commoner, and *-þ* forms being apparently absent ; the Ordinances of Worcester have *-en* or *-e*.

The Central Midlands, as represented by the Coventry Leet Bk., have *-en, -yn.*

The Survival of Pres. Pls. in -eth, -ith.

We have seen that these are in use in documents over a very wide area, besides in the London and Literary English throughout the fifteenth century, we have now to trace them through the following century and beyond.   The chief examples I have noted are :—St. of Ireland, St. Pprs. Hen. VIII, iii, 1515, *-yth* is very common—e. g. *some callyth*, 1, *messengers comyth*, 14, *they payeth*, 5, &c., &c. ; Skelton, Magnyf., 'your clothes *smelleth* musty', 761, *Her eyen gray and stepe, Causeth* mine herte to lepe, Phyll. Sparowe, 1015 ; Sir Thos. Elyot, *besemeth*, 7, *harts lepeth*, 245, *people takethe comforte*, 45, *other foules and bestis which herdeth and flocketh*, 2. 210, *after exploitures hapneth occasions*, 2. 429 ; Lord Berners, Froissart, *other thynges lyeth at my hart*, 1. 194, *your Knightes abideth for you to wasshe*, 1. 195, *what weneth the Frenchmen*, 1. 328, *their husbandes payeth*, 1. 352 ; Archbp. Cranmer, *Your Lordships hath bene thorowly enformed*, Ellis i. 2. 172 ; Bp. Latimer, *the mountaines swelleth*, Seven Serm., 31, *goth*, 41, *kepeth*, 74 ; Cavendish, L. of Wolsey, *them that hath*, 245 ; Ascham occasionally uses *hath, doth* in Pl.—*as wild horses doth race*, Tox. 8 ; Q. Elizabeth, *the* ('they') *ar most deseeved that trusteth most in theirselves*, Ellis i. 2. 156, 1549 ; *who seekith . . . the may*, &c., Transl., *breakith*, Transl., 132 ; Sir Thos. Smith, *the father and mother sendeth them out in couples*, Rep. Angl. 24 ; Spenser, State of Ireland, *the upper garment which serving men weareth*, p. 623, col. 2 ; Euphues—*whose barkes seemeth*, 231, *pleasant sirroppes doth chiefliest infect a delicate taste*, 306.

In the seventeenth century the Verney Memoirs have a few examples:— *I believe others doth doe that*, Lady V., ii. 252, 1647, *Elders who . . . asketh them such questions*, Lady V., ii. 259, 1647.

It seems evident from these examples that the Southern *-th* Plurals survived longer in good usage than might be gathered from the late M.E. literary works.   This form is one of the Southern characteristics of the original London dialect which were gradually ousted by E. Midland encroachments, but it lingered long in the conservative usage of the upper classes of society.

Present Plurals in -s.

This form of the Pres. Indic. Pl., which survives to the present time as a vulgarism, is by no means very rare in the second half of the sixteenth century among writers of all classes, and was evidently in good colloquial usage well into the eighteenth century. I do not think that many students of English would be inclined to put down the present-day vulgarism to North country or Scotch influence, since it occurs very commonly among uneducated speakers in London and the South, whose speech, whatever may be its merits or defects, is at least untouched by Northern dialect. The explanation of this peculiarity is surely analogy with the Singular. The tendency is to reduce Sing. and Pl. to a common form, so that certain sections of the people inflect all Persons of both Sing. and Pl. with -s after the pattern of the 3rd Pers. Sing., while others drop the suffix even in the 3rd Sing., after the model of the uninflected 1st Pers. Sing. and the Pl. of all Persons.

But if this simple explanation of the present-day Pl. in -s be accepted, why should we reject it to explain the same form at an earlier date?

It would seem that the present-day vulgarism is the lineal traditional descendant of what was formerly an accepted form. The -s Plurals do not appear until the -s forms of the 3rd Sing. are already in use. They become more frequent in proportion as these become more and more firmly established in colloquial usage, though, in the written records which we possess they are never anything like so widespread as the Singular -s forms. Those who persist in regarding the sixteenth-century Plurals in -s as evidence of Northern influence on the English of the South must explain how and by what means that influence was exerted. The view would have had more to recommend it, had the forms first appeared after James VI of Scotland became King of England. In that case they might have been set down as a fashionable Court trick. But these Plurals are far older than the advent of James to the throne of this country.

The earliest example I have noted occurs, strangely enough, in the Report on the State of Ireland in St. Pprs. Hen. VIII, iii, 1515, p. 15, *the noble folk of the land shotes at hym.* This sentence is the more remarkable in that there are no 3rd Pers. Sing. in -s in this text, and that Pls. in -*ith* abound. It is just conceivable, though unlikely, that *folk* is here regarded as a Singular Collective Noun, and that the Verb is therefore also Singular. Sir Thomas Wyatt the Elder has *for swine so grones,* which rhymes *nones, bones,* Satire to Sir F. Bryan, 18, 1540. Bp. Latimer, in his Sermons, has a certain number of -s Plurals:—*standes,* 87, *some that liues,* 179, *there be some writers that saies,* 188, *some sayes,* 189. As we have seen above, the bishop often uses -s in the 3rd Sing. Machyn has *after them comys harolds,* 40. The only forms of the 3rd Sing. which I have found in this Diary end in -s (cf. p. 333), but they are so few that we cannot judge with certainty whether this was Machyn's usual form, nor how far the -s Plural may have been influenced by it. Lord Buckhurst, Induction, has 'And as the stone that drops of water *weares*', rhyming with *teares,* Noun, v. 12. Ascham has *the cordes haue nothyng to stop them, but whippes so far back,* &c.;

Queen Elizabeth has many examples, especially in her Translations, but some also in her later letters (to James VI).   A few examples :—*all our subjectes lokes after*, Lttrs. 31, *small flies stiks fast for wekenis*, L. 41, *your commissionars telz me*, ibid. 44, *sild recouers kings ther dominion*, ibid. 58 ; in the Translations we have :—*roring windz the seas perturbz*, 4, *all men hides them*, 132, *as the huntars rates ther houndz*, 134, *men that runs*, 135, &c., &c.   Thos. Wilson, Arte of Rhet., has *some speakes some spettes*, 220.   There are seventeen forms in -s after *some* on this one page.

The Verney Papers have *how things goes here*, Sir R. V., 1639 ; *couenantirs has forbidden any man to read it*, 240 ; Verney Memoirs—*My Lady and Sir tomos remembers their sarvices to you and Mrs. Gardiner*, Cary V., ii. 68, 1642, *both sides promisis*, &c., Lady Sussex, ii. 252, 1647, *the late noyses of riesings puts me in a fear*, &c., Cary Stewkley (Verney), iii. 439, 1659.

In the Wentworth Papers Lady W. and her son Peter both use these forms :—*which moste lauhgs at*, 52, 1706, *all people from the highist to the lowist stairs* (i. e. ' stares ') *after them*, 57 ; *several affirms*, 123 (Peter W.) ; *Lord Wentworth and Lady Hariot gives their duty to your Lordship*, Lady A. Wentworth, a child, 453, 1724 ;   *Lord Garsy and Mr. Varnum both coms in the somer thear*, 55 ; *all others sends fowls*, 59 ; *Peter and his wife comse tomorrow*, 127 ; *my letters that informs you*, 107 (Peter W.); *Two of the prettiest young peers in England . . . who, by the way, makes no pretty figure*, 395 (Peter W.) ; *Mrs. Lawson and Mrs. Oglethorpe gives their service to you*, 444 (Lord Bute).

Note.   The use of *is* and *was* with a Plural Subject will be dealt with under the Auxiliaries, p. 356.

The Infinitive.

The usual M.E. ending in the Midlands and South is -*en*, but forms without -*n* are found quite early.   A typical Southern ending of the Inf. is -*y*, -*ie*, &c., which represents the O.E. -*ian* suffix, and is generalized widely, especially in Verbs of French origin, in the dialects of the South-East and South-West.

The -*n* termination hardly survives in written documents beyond the third quarter of the fifteenth century, and by that time the examples are scarce.

All fifteenth-century writers use Infinitives in -*e*, even when they occasionally keep -*en* or -*yn*.   Hoccleve has *han, usen, synkyn, wedden* ; Const. of Dynevor, *to wetyn*, Ellis ii. 1. 14 ; Rewle Sustr. Men. is rather rich in -*n* forms—*to herin*, 90, &c., *þey schullen dwellin*, 94. 21, *we commaunde . . . senden, enioinen*, 95. 14, *bowen*, 113. 12, *knelyn*, 115. 38, &c. ; Fortescue generally has -*e* or no ending, e. g. *gyf*, but *helpen*, 152 ; Marg. Paston has numerous forms in -*n*—*ye vol askyn*, i. 49, *to heryn*, i. 67, *buyn* ' buy ', i. 68, *sellyn*, i. 69, &c., &c. ; Bokenam has *seen, delyvyrn, acceptyn, advertysyn, geuyn, lesyn*, &c.; Gregory has a fair number of -*n* forms—*usyn*, 82, *folowyn*, 91, *procedyn*, 99, *ken*, 99, *beryn*, 99, *doen*, 99, *setten, setlynne*, 117, and also rather strangely a few forms in -*y*—*delyvery*, 118, *answery*, 231 (twice), *ymageny*, 231 ; the Godstow Register usually has -*e* or no ending, but *fallyn*, 25 ; Caxton has very few examples of -*n*, but *ouertaken*, Jason 50. 5.   The -*y* type is found also in St. Editha—*to correcty*, 2383.

A late example in prose is *he and I wyll commen*, in a letter of Thos. Pery, 1539, Ellis ii. 2. 148.

A late survival, or rather revival, of *-en*, for metrical reasons, is seen in Lord Buckhurst's *I can accusen none*, Complaint of Duke of Buckingham, 147.

The Prefix y- in Past Participles.

This prefix, which is still much used by Chaucer, is comparatively rare in the poems of Hoccleve. In the Reg. of Pr. he writes *ypynchid*, *yput*, but generally omits the prefix in Strong Verbs. In the Minor Poems, however, we have *itake*, *ifalle*. On the whole during the fifteenth century the use of the prefix is chiefly confined to texts which show a more or less strongly marked Southern provincial influence, whether South-Eastern or South-Western. Thus it is frequent in the letter of the Constable of Dynevor Castle, in Shillingford, in the Register of Oseney, where it is almost universal in Strong and Weak Verbs, in the R. of Godstow, where, however, it is less frequent, especially in Strong Verbs. In St. Editha the prefix is often written and crossed out again in the MS., though it is also fairly often not erased, and often not written at all. In the South-East the prefix is very common in Palladius, but very rare in the much later Cely Papers ; the Suffolk dialect, as represented by Bokenam, shows no example of it, nor does Marg. Paston. Fortescue, from whom one might expect this Southernism, appears not to write *y-* at all in Strong Verbs and very rarely in Weak, though I have noted *i-blissed*, 155; Pecok seems to have no examples in vol. i of the Repressor, and there are none in the Ordinances of Worcester, nor those of Exeter.

Of texts written more specifically in the London dialect, the Suffolk man Gregory has a fair sprinkling of Past Participles, Strong and Weak, with *i-*, and Rewle of Sustr. Men. a few. Apparently Gregory's forms were not derived from his native dialect, so we must regard them as belonging to a rather archaic form of London speech. Caxton makes no use of the prefix, nor is it found in the later Cr. of Knt. of Bath, which is a better example on the whole of the higher type of London English. After this the prefix is only used by poets who are more or less deliberately archaic. An interesting form—*storm ybeten*—occurs in Skelton's Magnyfycence, a word which suggests the Spenserian period of Keats. Spenser's imitation of Chaucer is doubtless chiefly responsible for the occasional use of the *i*-forms by later poets.

VI

THE STRONG VERBS.

The following is but the slightest sketch of the development of these Verbs in the Modern period. The examples given of the forms of the members of each class are intended mainly to show on the one hand the survival of old forms, and on the other the adoption of those now in use. It is evident that a much larger collection of forms would be necessary to achieve, with anything like completeness, either of these objects. In fact a special monograph would be required, which I may possibly undertake when circumstances permit. The excellent monograph of Price on

Strong Verbs from Caxton to the End of the Elizabethan Period contains a great deal of material which I have not incorporated here, the following short account being based on part of my own collections. We want an account dealing with these Verbs from 1400 or so until the end of the eighteenth century. Caxton is not a good starting-point, nor is the end of the Elizabethan period the end of the story. I now regret that I did not make much larger collections from the Verney Memoirs and the Wentworth Papers, as well as from later eighteenth-century sources.

The apparent irregularities in the Strong Verbs during the Middle and Modern periods, compared with the conditions in O.E., are due to the working of analogy in various directions.

The fact that originally there were two, three, and in some cases four types in a single class of Verbs, and that there was a certain variety of treatment of each type according to Regional dialect, has given a very considerable number of possible types for the Preterite and Past Participle of some classes. Added to this there is the transference of Verbs from one class to another which while closely resembling it, yet differed from it in certain respects. Thus *speak* has been transferred to the class to which *break* belongs. The result of this was first to produce a new P. P. *spōken*, on the analogy of *broken*, and then to call into existence a new Preterite *broke* on the pattern of the new P. P.

During the M.E. period the tendency was to get rid of the distinction between the Singular and Plural in the Preterite in those classes where this originally existed. In the North and East Midland it was usually the old Singular Preterite which survived as the sole type for that tense. In the South-West, on the other hand, the type of the P. P. generally dominated the Preterite also.

It will be noticed that many Verbs have forms with both a long and a short vowel in the Pret. in the Early Modern period, a condition which is inherited from M.E. Thus we have both *spack* and *spāke*, *băd* and *bāde*, *săt* and *sāte*, &c. The explanation of this is simple. The short forms are in all these cases the normal developments of the O.E. forms—*sp(r)æc*, *bæd*, *sæt*, &c. In M.E. these forms were the only ones with a short vowel in the whole conjugation of each of these Verbs. It is perfectly natural, therefore, that some speakers should have extended the quantity of the Inf. and Pres. *spēken*, the Pret. Pl. *spēken*, and the P. P. *spēken*—*spōken* to the Pret. Sing., the solitary form which had a short vowel, pronouncing *spāk(e)* instead of *spăk*. Later, this new type *spāk(e)* was in its turn extended also to the Pret. Pl., so that *spēken* was eliminated and the distinction disappeared.

We see two distinct tendencies conflicting during the Modern period, namely, one to establish the type of the P. P. for the Pret. as well, and the other to eliminate the old P. P. type in favour of that of the Pret.

Those speakers who said *writ* in the Pret. exhibited the former tendency, while those who said *I have wrote* displayed the latter.

It has been pointed out that the old Pret. Pl. type rarely supersedes that of the Sing., unless the former be also that of the P. P., in which case it is assumed that it is the P. P. which is the basis of analogy, as the form more frequently used.

Thus the history of the Strong Verbs after the O.E. period is chiefly concerned with transference of Verbs from one class to another, with the elimination of this or that type, and with the ultimate distribution in a given dialect of the various types between the Pret. and P. P.

Many old Strong Verbs have passed into the Weak conjugation, e. g. *bake, sew,* &c. We notice a tendency to transfer others, e. g. *take, come, stand,* which did not, however, become established in the Standard Spoken or in the Literary form of English.

The converse process of a Weak Verb becoming Strong is rarer, but we note *strive—strove—striven* on the analogy of *thrive—throve—thriven,* &c. *Hide—hid—hidden* instead of O.E. *hȳdd,* M.E. *hĭdde,* is due to the influence of *ride—rid—ridden.* Here we note that *hid* was a perfectly normal Weak Pret. from *hide,* the vowel being shortened in M.E. before. the double consonant. *Rid,* a common Preterite, instead of *rode,* is due to the influence of the P. P. Having got *hide—hid,* it was inevitable that the agreement with *ride* should be completed by the formation of *hidden* as a P. P.

We see, even from the comparatively few examples given below, that the usage of the best writers in the sixteenth and even in the seventeenth and eighteenth centuries, in regard to the Strong Verbs, does not by any means coincide exactly with our own. Even at the present time there is a certain fluctuation. Thus, while we have eliminated *flang* as the Pret. of *fling,* and prefer the P. P. type, *sang, rang* are still in very wide use, although many speakers say *sung, rung,* allowing the P. P. type to carry the day as in the case of *flung.* Great hesitation exists in the conjugation of *wake.* What is the current form of the P. P. *?* Some speakers habitually use *waked,* others *woke,* others *woken.*

Such forms as *wrāte, drāve, strāke,* which occur sometimes in Cl. 1 in the sixteenth century are certainly not of Northern origin as is supposed by some. Apart from the very common occurrence of forms with *ā* in other classes—e. g. *sāte, bāre, spāke,* &c., side by side with *sat,* &c., which probably encouraged the use of *ā* as a vowel associated with the Pret., *wrāte,* &c., would arise naturally by the side of *wrăt* (with O.E. shortening) just as *sāte* and *spāke* arose by the side of *sat, spak,* and *gāve* by the side of *gaf.*

The analogy of *bāde* Pret. with a P. P. *bidden* may also have helped to form a Pret. *wrāte, strāke,* &c., in association with *written, stricken,* as also *sate* with a P. P. *sitten.*

It should be noted that the preservation or loss of *-en* in the P. P. is a matter of dialect originally. In M.E. the Southern dialects generally drop the *-n,* and Midland dialects retain it. Thus the variations between Verbs in this respect are the result of different competing Regional tendencies.

CLASS I. O.E. *ĭ—ā—ĭ—ĭ.* M.E. *ĭ—ō²—ĭ—ĭ.*

The Inf. and Pres. type of this Class shows no variation from the normal development of M.E. *ĭ,* and is invariably [*ai*]. It is therefore unnecessary to include examples.

Write.

Preterite. **wrōte,** &c. :—Pecok, *wroten* (Pl.); Shillingford, *wrote,* 8, *wrotte*, 61 ; Marg. Paston, *wrot*, i. 178, &c.; Latimer, *wrote*, 175, *wrot*, 175.

writ, &c. :—Euphues, *writ*, 304 ; Mrs. Eure, Verney Mem. ii. 87, *rit* (1642).

wrate :—Elyot, i. 131, 156, ii. 100.

Past Participle. **writt(en)**, &c. :—Hoccleve, *wryten* ; St. Editha, *wryten*, 33, *y-wryton*, 9 ; Bokenam, *wrytyn*, Pr. Marg. 4 ; Gregory, *wrytynne*, 61 ; Shillingford, *writyn*, 15 ; Gabr. Harvey, *writ*, Lttrs. 265 ; Euphues, *written*, 169 ; Mrs. Pulteney, V. Pprs. 222, *rit* (1639).

wrote, &c. :—Sir Edw. Howard, Ellis ii. 1. 216 (1513) ; Lady Mary M. Wortley, ' all the verses were *wrote* by me '.

Write. Lady Sussex uses *right* as a Pret., V. Mem. iv. 88, 1642.

Smite.

Preterite. **smote, smot** :—Gregory, *smote*, 76 ; Cr. of Dk. of York Knt. of Bath, *smot*, 399.

Past Part. **smyttyn**, Machyn, 14.

smete, Gregory, 77 ; **smetyn**, Gregory, 106 ; **smet**, Bokenam, Kath. 898.

smot, Shakespeare, L. L. L., rhymes with *not*.

Drive. St. Editha has Pret. Sing. *drof*, 36, Pret. Pl. *drovyn*, 3263, and *drevyn*, 54. The latter form occurs also in Shillingford, 97, and Short Engl. Chronicle, 71.

Abide. The normal Pret. Sing. *abode* occurs, St. Editha, 276, and. the Pl. *abydyn*, Bokenam, Crist. 673 ; Pecok has Sing. *abode*, and Pl. *abiden*, i. 20, *aboden*, i. 206 ; Marg. Paston, *abedyn* Pl., i. 111 ; Shillingford, *abode* Sing., 5 ; Latimer, *abode*, 188.

Past Participle. Marg. Paston, *abiden*, 41 ; also Fortescue, 135, and Shillingford, 41, and Skelton, Magnyfycence, 576 ; Marg. Paston has also *abedyn*, i. 81, also Short Engl. Chron. 130 ; Elyot has *aboden*, ii. 184.

Bite. The old Pret. *bôte* survives in the fifteenth century, Gregory, 202 ; Caxton, Jason, 69. 14.

Ride. Pret. *rod*, Marg. Paston, i. 77 ; Shillingford, *rode*, 5 ; Gregory, *roode*, 89 ; *rodde*, Lord Berners, i. 114 ; Machyn, *rod, rode*, 4.

rid, &c. :—Cranmer, Ellis i. 2. 37 ; Thos. Wilson, 140 ; Machyn also has *red*, 167.

Strike.

Inf., &c. By the side of *strike*, *strick* is also found :—Euphues, *to strick*, 239.

Preterite. **strōke** :—Cr. of Knt. of Bath, *stroke*, 400 ; Latimer, 94 ; Euphues, 251.

strake : strack :—Cr. of Knt. of Bath, *strakke*, 399, 400 (twice) ; Lord Berners, *strake*, i. 114, 140 ; J. Mason, *strake*, Ellis ii. 2. 59 ; Cavendish, L. of Wolsey, *strak*, 83.

streke :—St. Editha, 3739.

struck :—Machyn, 85.

Past Participle. **stricken**, &c. :—Machyn, *stryken*, 63 ; Euphues, *stricken*, 152, *striken*, 299.

strooken, &c. :—Thos. Wilson, *stroken*, 132 ; Sir T. Smith, *stroken*, Republ. 36 ; Euphues, *strooke*, 57, *stroken*, 162, 230.

strucken :—Honourable J. Dillon (of a ship), ' She had her bottome *strucken* out', Verney Pprs. 149.

CLASS II.   O.E. ēo, ēa, u, o ; M.E. ẹ̄, u (= [ȳ]), ō¹, u, o.

Choose. The Present and Inf. forms appear in three types—(1) *chēse* (with M.E. *ẹ̄¹*), which is characteristic of South-East and E. Midland ; (2) *ō* (M.E. *ō¹*) from a form with shifting of stress from the first to the second element of the diphthong, and the loss of the former :—*ẹ́o—ẹ́o—ō* ; (3) *ú* = [ȳ], which is a characteristic W. Midland and South-West treatment of *ēo* in M.E. Types (2) and (3) have no difference in pronunciation from the moment that [ȳ] has become [ū] (cf. p. 246), but the spelling with *u* probably indicates a late survival of (3). On the other hand, *u* may be written occasionally for type (2), according to the habit of writing *u* for O.E. *ō¹*. See pp. 234, &c. This is probably the explanation of the *chuse* spelling in writers who would hardly make use of type (3).

(1) Inf. and Pres., *to chees, chese*, &c., occur in Pallad. 4. 84, 99. 1059, &c. ; M. Paston, ii. 292, *I ches* ; Pecok, *chese* Subj., i. 112 ; Gregory, 230, Inf. ; Caxton, Jason, *for to chese*, 57. 32 ; Elyot, 51, *chesing* ; Lord Berners, i. 53.

(2) *chose, choose*, Lord Berners, i. 58 ; Latimer, Sev. Serm. 25 ; Ascham, Toxoph. 39 ; Euphues, *choose*, 139.

(3) *chuse*, &c., Pallad. 5. 123, Imperat. ; Lord Berners, i. 389 ; Machyn, *chuysse*, 17, *chusse*, 141 ; Thos. Wilson, A. of Rhet. 56 ; Euph. *chuse* Imperat., 229 ; Lady Rochester, Verney Mem. iii. 467 (1660).

The Preterite. The M.E. *chees, ches*, &c., with *ẹ̄²* [ē] from O.E. *ēa*, is gradually replaced by a form with *ō²*, formed on the analogy of the P. P. *chōsen*. This is the ancestor of the present form. The older form survives far into the fifteenth century, after which the *ō* form is most common. The occasional *chāse* must be explained by association with Vbs. of the *bear* class—Pret. *bāre*, P. P. *bōren*.

chees, &c., Hoccleve ; St. Editha, *chesen* (Pl.), 274 ; Gregory, *chesse* Pl., 190 ; Fortescue, *chese*, 112, 113.

chōse, &c., Pecok, i. 183 ; Gregory, *chosse*, 95, *they chosynne*, 96 ; Caxton, Jason, 94. 32 ; Lever, Serm. 35.

chāse, Pecok, *chas*, ii. 349, *chaas*, ii. ibid. ; Elyot, i. 214.

Past Participle. St. Editha still retains the old form *y-core*, 789, by the side of *y-chose*, 2207. There is no variety as regards the vowel, except that it occasionally appears to be short, as the following consonant is doubled, e. g. *chosse*, Gregory, 95 ; *chossen*, Machyn, 22 ; otherwise the only point of note is that, as in other Strong Vbs., the forms in *-e* alternate with those in *-en* :— *-e* occurs, Pecok, i. 111 ; Gregory, 71, 95 ; Lady Rochester, *choose*, V. Mem. iii. 467, 1660. Most writers, so far as my material goes, use the *-en* (*-yn*) type.

O.E. *gēotan—gēat—guton—goten* ' pour '.

This obsolete Vb. is still traceable in the word *ingot*, where *got* is derived from the P. P. Elyot preserves the fuller form of the P. P. in *yoten*, i. 48.

Lose. This Vb. had, originally, exactly the same vowel sequence as *choose*. It is conjugated as a Weak Vb. from early in the Modern period, the survivals of the old Strong Pret. and P. P. being rare. The latter survives as an Adjective in the compound *forlorn*.

Inf. and Pres. lese, &c., Pallad. 35. 248 ; Marg. Paston, i. 109, ii. 309, &c.; Fortescue, 118, *lesynge* Pres. Part., 138 ; Elyot, 34, *lese*; Lord Berners, *leese*, i. 28 ; Ascham, *lease*, Tox. 117, *leese*, ibid. 128, 158 (Subj.), *leeseth*, Tox. 158 ; Euphues, 193.
The other type appears as *loose*, 305.

Shoot. O.E. *scēōtan—scēāt—scuton—scoten* still retains the form with *ē*, comparable to *chēse, lēse*, in the fifteenth century, and is found in Marg. Paston—*schete*, i. 83, *shet*, i. 82. This lady also writes *schote*, i. 83. Gregory has *schute*, which may be a phonetic spelling for the *ō¹* type, as is most probable.
Gregory has a Weak Pret. *schot*, 204, and a P. P. *schottyn*, 58.

Float. O.E. *flēōtan*, &c.; Bk. of Quint. has *fletiþ* 3rd Pres. Sing.

Freeze. Milton in Trin. Coll. MS. writes *wherewith she freez'd her foes to congeal'd stone*. Comus 449. This, with the strange Weak Pret., is corrected from the original, which ran : *freezind wherewith*, &c., a very archaic form of Pres. Part. The old P.P. *frore* is used, P. L. ii, 595.

CLASS III.

O.E. *singan—sang—sungon—sungen*. Verbs of this Class have, on the whole, preserved three original types, though no longer distinguishing between Sing. and Pl. in the Pret. *Begin, spin, spring, swim, drink*, &c.
It is possible that *begin*, &c., besides *began*, in Pret. had also forms with a long vowel, on the analogy of Class IV—cf. *begane*, Pecok, Machyn, &c., *swame*, Lord Berners, by the side of *swamme*, Elyot, ii. 169.
In some Verbs of this Class the P. P. type penetrates to the Pret., and just as we now often have *rung, swum*, &c. in the Pret., we find *wonne*, Euphues, ' won ', 273, by the side of the then usual *wan* or *wanne*, which occurs very generally not only in Euphues itself, but also before, in Short Engl. Chron., *wanne*, 61, Gregory, 58, 71, Caxton, Jason, 11. 3, Lord Berners, Machyn, &c.
Lord Berners, i. 371, and Euphues, 88, both have *flang* where we now have *flung*, but Euphues already has *stung*, 68.
In the Vb. *find* the old distinction between Sing. and Pl. Pret.—O.E. *fånd*, M.E. *fond*; O.E. *fundon*, M.E. *founden*—is preserved far into the fifteenth century. Pecok has Sing. *fonde*, i. 101, Pl. *founden*, by the side of *fonden*, i. 242 ; Shillingford has *fonde*, 61, *founde*, 65. In the P. P., forms with or without *-n* occur throughout the fifteenth century—e. g. Gregory, *founde, foundyn*; Caxton, *founden*; Fortescue, *ffounde*; M. Paston, *fownd, fond*; Pecok and Ord. of Worcester, *founde*. Elyot has *founde*, i. 215, *founden*, 26, &c., &c. *Run*, in Inf., is a new formation; the ordinary M.E. type in Inf. and Pres. is *renne*, which is perhaps of Scand. origin. This persists as the more usual form throughout the fifteenth century and into the next century, and is found in Pallad., St. Editha, Bokenam, Pecok, Bk. of Quint., Fortescue, Cr. Knt. of Bath, and Cath. of Ar., the last but one having also *rynnyng* in Pres. Part. Lord Berners has *rynne* and *ryn*, and further, *ronne* (= *runne*), i. 163 and 358,

and *ronnyng*, i. 163. *Roon* is found in a letter of Sir Edw. Howard, Ellis ii. 1. 217, *to runne*, Ascham, Tox. 46, *ronne*, ibid. 103, but *rin* still occurs, Scholem. 54. Euphues has, apparently, only the *runne* type.

Come. O.E. *cuman—cōm—cam—cōmon—cāmon—cumen*.

Various types spring from the above. ᚱ

Pret. St. Editha has *cŏme* and *becŏme*, 25, Sing. 65, Pl. *cŏmen*, 58 ; Pecok, *cāmen*, *cāme*; Gregory has Pret. Pl. *cum*, 91, and a Pret. Sing. *come*, apparently = [kūm] from the *cŏmen* type; also *cam*, 91, a survival of old *cam* ; Caxton has *becăm*, 4. 24 Sing., and *cam*, 94. 32. Dr. Knight has *cam*, 196, and so has Sir T. Smith, Ellis ii. 3. 16. The P. P. is generally written *come*, which may represent either [kŭm] or [kūm].

That the O. and M.E. P. P. *cumen* survives is shown by the occasional spelling *comme*, &c. Gabriel Harvey had a new formation, *overcomd*, p. 3, as a P. P., and *ouercomed* occurs in the Te Deum in Edward VI's First and Second Prayer Books, and Shakespeare has *misbecom'd*, L. L. L. Pecok has *come*, Gregory, *ovyrcome*, 125, Machyn, *over-cum*, 70. Caxton has *comen* (Jason), and so has Elyot, ii. 144. Laneham's Lttr. (1575), *cummen* 33.

Climb. O.E. *clīmban—clămb—clŭmbon—clumben* ; M.E. *clīmb—clōmb—clŭmb*.

The Pret. :—*clāme* survives in Ascham, Tox. 76. The vowel is from an O.E. and M.E. unlengthened form *clămb*, with later lengthening on the analogy of the other tenses.

Hoccleve has the P. P. *clumben*, and Bokenam, *clomben*, Ann. 646.

Yield has a Pret. Pl. *yelde* in Gregory, 83, which apparently comes from the Late O.E. (Sthn.) *g̃æld*, M.E. *yēld*, type of the Singular, extended to Pl. also.

The P. P. *yolden* often occurs in Short Engl. Chron., and is found in Gregory as *i-yolde*, 79, *yolde*, 115, *yoldyn*, 115, and Elyot, ii. 220. Short Engl. Chron. has also *ylden*, 56, and Gregory has a Wk. P. P. *yoldyd*, 115. Spenser has P. P. *yold*, F. Q. vii. 7. 30.

Help. Caxton, Jason 102. 26, still has the old Pret. *halp*, also *helpe*, 76. 1, perhaps from O.E. South and South-East *healp*, M.E. *help*. A Pret. *holpe* is found in Robt. the Devil, 960, and in Shakespeare's Hen. IV, Pt. 1, 1. ii ; and *hop* Verney Mem. iii. 274 (1656). This is derived from the P.P. type.

The P. P. *holpe*(*n*) in M.E. is found without -*n* in Pecok, i. 284, with -*en*, &c., in Pallad., Gregory (*holpyn*), 207, Cr. Knt. of Bath, 400, Elyot, 117, Ascham, Tox. 43, &c., &c.

Fight. O.E. *feohtan* (*feht-*, *fiht-*)—*feaht—fuhton—fohten* ; M.E. *fihten—faht—fauht*; *fuhten* and *foughten*; *foughten*.

The Pret. *faught*(*e*) (M.E. Singular type) survives, Gregory, 82, &c. ; Caxton, Jason 66. 33 ; Short Engl. Chron. 68 ; Elyot, 179 ; the other type, *fought*, from the P. P., also occurs in Gregory and afterwards.

The P. P. retains the -*en* suffix in Ascham's *foughten*, Tox. 64.

CLASS IV.

Knead. The Strong P. P. *knōden* is preserved, Lever's Sermons, 46—*knoden into dough.*

Break. O.E. *brecan—bræc—bræcon—brocen*; M.E. *brēken, brak,*
and *brăk(e)—brēke* and *brōke—brōken.*

Preterite. During the whole of the fifteenth, sixteenth, and seventeenth
centuries *brāke* is the most frequent type, and, occasionally, *brăk.*
St. Editha, Pecok, Gregory, Cr. Knt. of Bath, Lord Berners, Latimer,
Euphues, &c., all have *brāke.* St. Editha still distinguishes the Pl. *brēkon,*
4410, from the Sing. type, and Gregory uses this type in the Sing., 202.

broke comes from the P. P. type. It is found already in Cr. Knt. of
Bath, 395.

Past Participle. The vowel is practically invariable from the M.E.
period onwards, being always the lengthened *ō.* There is, however,
a form *brake*, on the analogy of the Pret., found in Verney Mem. iv, used
both by Sir R. Verney, p. 134 (1665), and Dr. Denton, p. 223 (1676).
There is the usual fluctuation during the M.E. and Modern periods
between the forms *broke—broken.*

Speak, which originally belonged to Class V (O.E. *sprecan—spræc—
spræcon—sprecen*), has passed completely into that of *break*, and is best
considered under this Class. Its forms are identical with those of *break.*

The Pret. has both long and short forms as in M.E. St. Editha has
Sing. *spāke* and a Pl. *spēke,* 287, which doubtless preserves the original
Pl. type. The latter is rare, however, after the M.E. period. *Spāke* is
the usual type well into the seventeenth century. The type with a
short vowel, however, is also used by Pecok, *spak*, Caxton, *spack*, Jason
64. 30, Latimer, 115, and many others. The Rev. Mr. Aris uses *speake*
as a Pret., Verney Mem. iii. 136, 1655.

Past Participle. Spoke, spoken seem to be equally common down to and
during the eighteenth century. Sir J. Burgoyne has *spok,* V. Mem. ii.
217, 1642. Lord Chesterfield, writing in No. 100 of the *World,* 1754 (on
Johnson's Dictionary before it appeared), speaks of English as being
'studied as a learned language, though as yet but little *spoke*' in France
and Italy.

Marg. Paston still uses the archaic *spēke,* i. 77 (1449).

Bear and *steal* have pretty much the same history as the other Vbs. of
this Class, *bāre* and *stāle* long being the common form of the Pret.
Cr. of Knt. of Bath has *bēre* (Pret. Sing. and Pl., 391, 389), which may
be a phonetic spelling for *bāre*, or correspond to the old Pl. type.
Bokenam has Pret. Pl. *bēre. Stale* occurs throughout the fifteenth century
and in Cavendish, L. of Wolsey, 92.

CLASS V.

Give. O.E. *ġiefan, ġeaf, ġēafon—ġiefen* (W. Sax.); Non-W. Sax.:—
ġefan, ġeofan ; *ġæf, ġef; ġēfon* ; *ġefen, ġeofen.*

These forms give rise to correspondingly various types in M.E. and
Modern English.

The initial sound was an open consonant in O.E., and in M.E. is expressed by *ʒ*- or *y*-. By the side of these, forms with *g*-, expressing
a stop consonant, are common in M.E., which are probably due to Scandinavian influence. There is also an alternation between *i* and *ē* in the
vowel of the Inf. and Pres. Indic. The former may be of Scandinavian

origin, when the initial consonant is *g*, otherwise it must be derived from the Saxon type, or formed by analogy from the 2nd and 3rd Pers. Pres. The *gēve* forms are to be explained according to the statement on pp. 207-8.

Inf. and Pres. type. (1) yēve, ȝeue, &c. :—St. Editha 958, 1409, &c.; Pallad. (Imperat.) 19. 508; Bokenam, Marg. 1053, Eliz. 930 (*yeuyth*); Pecok, ȝeueth, 11, ȝeuen (Pl.), passim; Godstow Reg., *w. forȝeue*, 6; Marg. Paston, *yeve*, i. 268, *to ȝef*, i. 109, ȝeue, i. 67, ȝeuyn, i, 69; Shillingford, *yeve*, 27, *yeveth*, 29, &c.; Fortescue, 153, &c.

(2) gēve, &c. :—Pallad. Pr. 24. 656; Bokenam, Pr. Marg. 232 and 411; Pecok, passim; Marg. Paston, *geve*, ii. 218; Gregory, to *forgevyn*, 99; Shillingford, *geve* Inf., 20; Sir Thos. More, Ellis i. 1. 213, Inf., and *geveth*, i. 1. 200; Latimer, *to geue*, Ploughers 35, and Seven Serm. 22, *geuynge*, Ploughers 24; Edw. VI's First and Second Prayer Bks., *geue*, passim; Ascham, *geue*, Scholem. 115, 134, *geueth*, Tox. 39, 145; Cavendish, L. of Wolsey, 96, &c.; Gabriel Harvey, *gef* (= gēv?), 48; Q. Elizabeth, Lttrs. to J. VI, 2; Mrs. Basire, *geuing*, Corresp. 140 (1655).

(3) ȝive, yive :—Pecok; Bokenam, Imperat. *yiue*, Marg. 1123.

(4) ȝive, gyve, &c. :—Caxton, Jason 13. 2; Fortescue, *gyf* Inf., 129, *givith*, 139, *give* Pl., ibid.; Lord Berners, i. 22; Latimer, *gyue*, Ploughers 25, Ascham, *gyueth*, Tox. 28; Machyn, *gyfe*, *gyf* Subj.; Euphues, *giue*, 163, *giues*, 88, *to forgiue*, 90; Thos. Wilson (always); Q. Elizabeth, *gyve*, *give* (usual type).

Preterite.
Type (1). yaf, &c. :—St. Editha, ȝaffe, 81; Bokenam, *yaf*, Pr. Marg. 156, *þou youe*, Marg. 507, Pl. *youe(n)*, Agn. 441, Ann. 254; Shillingford, *yeaf*, 14; Marg. Paston, *yaffe*, ii. 215.

(2) gaf, &c. :—Wm. Paston, *gef*, i. 25 (= gaf with *e* written for [æ]?); Gregory, *gaffe*, 174; Caxton, Jason 12. 23, *gaf*.

(3) ȝāve :—Short Engl. Chron. 62; Marg. Paston, ȝave Pl., i. 109.

Sir Thos. Smith refers to both *yaf* and *yave* as antiquated.

(4) gave :—Gregory, 58; Caxton, Jason 3. 5; Bp. Knight, 204 (1512); Lord Berners; Ascham, Tox. 31; Latimer, *gaue*, Seven Serm., 36, *forgaue*, ibid. 57; Machyn, *gayf*, 3 (*ay* = ā, i. e. [ē or ē]?); Euphues, *gaue*, passim, *forgaue*, 175.

Past Participle.
(1) yēve(n) :—Hen. V, Letter in Lttrs. of Marg. of Anjou (1421); St. Editha, ȝeue, 499, *y-yeue*, 759; Pecok, ȝeue; Shillingford, 131; Lord Lovel's Will, *yeven*, L. D. D. 75. 27; Fortescue, *yeuen*, 152; Barlings Abbey Agreement, L. D. D. 135. 5; *y yeven*, Cely Pprs. 4; Oseney Reg., *iȝefe*, 6; Bury Wills, *yeuen* (1480).

(2) yōve(n) :—Bokenam, *youe*, Ann. 329; Pecok; Marg. Paston, ȝovyn, i. 112; Godstow Reg., *yoven*; Gregory, *yovyn*, 126; Sustr. Men., ȝouin, 96. 32; Irish Docs., Lttrs. and Pprs. i. 379, *youen*; also Bury Wills 77 (1492); *youe*, ibid. 77; Q. Elizabeth, *yeouen*, Argyle Lttrs. 32 (1595).

(3) gēve(n) :—M. Paston, i. 112; Gregory, *i-geve*, 64, *geve*, 96, *gevyn*,

96, 118; Fortescue, *geuen*, 136, 150, *geve*, 155; Bury Wills, *gevyn*, 82 (1595); Cr. Knt. of Bath, *geven*, 393, 398; Sir R. Wingfield, Ellis ii. 1. 212, *gevyn*; Edw. VI's First and Second Prayer Bks.; Latimer, *geuen*, Ploughers 20; Ascham, Tox. 13, 18, Scholem. 59, 134; Q. Elizabeth, Lttrs. 2; Mall Verney, V. Mem. ii. 214, *forgeven* (1655); Lady Went-worth, *geven*, W. Pprs. 40 (1705), 56 (1706), 64 (1708).

(4) **give(n)**, &c.:—*giffen*, Will of Lord Lovel, L. D. D. 86. 6 (1455); Caxton, Jason, *giue*, 70. 9, *gyuen*, 68. 18; Elyot, *giuen*, i. 215; Lord Berners, *gyven*, i. 171, &c., *forgyven*, i. 66; Cranmer, Ellis i. 2. 40; Ascham, *gyuen*, Tox. 19 (twice), 27; also *giuen*, which greatly prepon-derates over *geuen*; Machyn, *gyffyn*, 17; Euphues, *giuen*; Q. Elizabeth, Lttrs. to J. VI, 13; after the end of the sixteenth century, while *geuen*, &c., occurs, *given* is the predominant type.

(5) A type **gōvyn** is found occasionally, but I have only noted one example—from Gregory, 200. Bury Wills, 80, have a variant of this—*gwovyn* (1501). (6) *Geen*, Laneham's Lttr. 41.

In quite recent times the type *gave* was used as a P. P., though proba-bly never by the best speakers. Thus, Miss Austen, in Sense and Sensibility, chap. 24, makes Miss Lucy Steele write 'he has never *gave* me a moment's alarm', and 'it would have *gave* me such pleasure to meet you there'.

Bid and **forbid.** This Verb is derived from a blending of two O.E. Verbs, *biddan—bæd, bǣdon, beden* 'pray', and *bēodan—bēad—budon—boden* 'order', 'command', &c. The Pret. *bade*, pronounced both as [bæd], from the M.E. Singular type *bad*, and [beid] from a M.E. *bād*, with lengthen-ing on the analogy of the Pl. *bēden*, and the P. P. *bēden*, are easy to explain. The present-day P. P. found already in Late M.E. and becom-ing more frequent in the fifteenth and sixteenth centuries is more difficult. The only P. P.'s which agree with *bidden* are *written, ridden*, &c., of Class I. But it is not easy to see a point of association which can have led to the borrowing of a P. P. from this class by *bid*, unless it be the rarish *wrate*, &c.

Pres. and Inf. type. (1) *bidde, biddeth*, Pecok; Euphues, *forbiddeth*.
(2) *bēde, forbēdeth*, Pres. Subj., *forbede*, Pecok; Elyot, *God forbede*, ii. 141; Euphues, *bed* Inf. (variant of *bid*).
The *ē* forms are from O.E. *bēodan*. From this Verb also comes St. Editha's *bude*, 1520.

Preterite. (1) **bāde**:—Pecok, *forbāde*, i. 279; Marg. Paston, *ʒe bādeyn*, i. 69; Shillingford, *bāde* (Sing.), 7.
(2) **băd**:—M. Paston, *ʒe bad*, i. 77; Euphues; the last-mentioned source has also a Pret. *bidde*, 105.

Past Participle. (1) *bĕde*, Pecok, i. 7; Shillingford, *ybede*, 7.
(2) *bŏden*:—Pecok, *forbode*, i. 144, 145, *forboden*, i. 207; Shilling-ford, *forbode*, 44; Elyot, *forboden*, ii. 334. (3) Euphues has *forbidden*, 61.

Get. O.E. *ģietan* (non-W.Sax. *ģetan*) is only used compounded—*for-, be-, on-, ģietan.*
The parts are Pret. Sing. *-ģeat* (non-W. Sax. *-ģæt* and *-ģet*); Pret. Pl. *-ģēaton* (non-W. Sax. *-ģēton*); P. P. *-ģieten* (non-W. Sax. *-ģeten, -ģeoten*).

The use of this Verb uncompounded, and the stop *g*- instead of *y*- in the initial, are both the result of Scandinavian influence.   The *got*-forms are the result of confusion with Verbs of the *break* class, which always had -*o*- in the P. P.   The *got*-forms began in the P. P. and passed by the so-called 'Western' system of analogy into the Pret.

Infinitive Present.
(1) **yĕte**, &c.   This type appears to be rare in the Modern period in the uncompounded forms, but St. Editha has *for-ʒetone*, 2167, Pres. Pl.; Pecok, *forʒete*, Shillingford, *foryete* Imperat., 59.
(2) **gēte**:—Pallad., *gēte* (rhymes *sweete*), 14. 371 ; Bokenam, *forgete*, Marg. 464 ; Shillingford, *gete* Inf., 46 ; Marg. Paston, *gett*, ii. 239, *gete*, i. 48, *gettyn*, ii. 132, *to gyte*, ii. 179 (all Inf.) ; Lord Berners, *gette,* i. 29.

Preterite.
(1) **yat** :—St. Editha, *for-ʒat*, 453.

(2) **gat** :—St. Editha, *gatte*, 856 ; Gregory, *gatte* ; Lord Berners, *gatte*, i. 32 ; Latimer, *gat*, 179 ; Thos. Wilson, *forgat*, 49 ; Ascham, *gatte*, Scholem. 31.

(3) **gāte** :—Pecok, Fortescue, *gate*, 149 ;   Caxton, Jason 7. 21 ; Elyot, 180, *forgate*, ii. 139 ; Sir Thos. More, *forgate*, Ellis i. 1. 213 ; Latimer, *gate*, 57 ; Laneham's Lttr. (1575), 42.

(4) **got** :—Thos. Wilson, *begot*, 81.

(5) **gōte** :—Bokenam, *begotyn*, Crist. 676 ; Latimer, Seven Serm. 28. A Pret. Pl. *gēton* is found in Pecok, which is probably the lineal descendant of O.E. (non-W. Sax.) *gēton*.

Past Participle.
(1) **yĕte(n)** :—St. Editha, *yʒete*, 2744.
(2) **gēte(n)** :—Pecok, *geten* ; Fortescue, *getun*, 143.
(3) **gōten** :—It is not quite certain whether forms spelt with one *t* are in all cases long, but since it is said to be established by rhymes that the long type existed, and since this is the normal development of the vowel in an open syllable, I assume length unless the following consonant is doubled.   Caxton, Jason, *goten*, 8. 26 ; Fortescue, *gote*, 143, *goton*, 136, *gotyn*, 154 ; Gregory, *gotyn*, 134, *begotyn*, 70 ; Bp. Knight, *forgotyn*, 201.
(4) **gŏtte(n)** :—Elyot, *gotten*, 27 ; Lord Berners, i. 285, *gotte* ; Machyn, *gotten*, 52, *be-gotten*, 23 ; Ascham, *gotten*, Tox. 32 ; Latimer, 50, 78, &c. ; Lever, Sermons, 32 ; Gabriel Harvey, *gottin*, Lttrs. 17 ; Thos. Wilson, *gotten*, 202.

gotten is used by Lady Arabella in Vanbrugh's Journey to London, II. i, p. 345.
The American use of the suffix -*en* in the uncompounded form goes back to the current English of the sixteenth and seventeenth centuries.

Lie ' cumbo '.   O.E. *liċgean—læġ—lǣgon* (and *lāgon*) —*leġen* ; M.E. *liggen—lai—lain*.
The M.E. Pres. and Inf. type with *ġġ* (= [dž]) survives in Pecok, who has *leggith*, i. 29, *liggen* Pres. Pl., Pres. Part. *ligging*.
The P. P. *lyen*, &c., is used during the fifteenth and sixteenth centuries,

and occasionally in the seventeenth century :—Bokenam, *lyne*, Christ. 685; Cely Papers, *lyne*, 47; *lyen*, Elyot, i. 150; Cavendish, L. of Wolsey, 123; Creighton, Bp. of Bath and Wells, Verney Mem. iii. 92, 1670.

(M.E.) *Mēte* 'measure'. O.E. *metan—mæt—mǣton—meten.* The P. P. of this old Verb, *meaten*, occurs in Euphues, 92.

Sit. O.E. *sittan—sæt—sǣton—seten.*

Preterite. During the fifteenth and sixteenth centuries both *sate* and *sät* are in frequent use.

sate occurs in Gregory, 112, Short Engl. Chron. 53 (three times), Elyot ii. 157, Euphues, 52.

satte, &c., Gregory, 112, Cr. Knt. of Bath, 389, *satt*; Latimer, *satte*, 174, Machyn, *satt*, 43.

Euphues has also *set*, which is capable of more than one explanation. Lady Verney uses *sate*, V. Mem. ii. 306 (1647).

A P. P. *sitten* occurs in Hume's History of England, vol. vii, p. 353.

See. O.E. *sēon—seah* (and *sæh*)—*sāwon—sewen.* The M.E. Pret. forms are—Angl. *saugh*, and its variant, *saw*, from the *sæh* type, *seih* from a Southern *seh* type. There is also a form *sī* and *sih*, from the Pl. type *sēh*, *sǣh*, formed on the analogy of Angl. Pl. *sǣgon.* The old P. P. is generally abandoned in favour of a new form *sēne* from the O.E. Adj. *ġesēne*, non-W. Sax. *ġesēne* 'visible'.

The early Modern reflects the variety of forms found in M.E.

Preterite. St. Editha has, in Sing.:—*seyʒe*, 1016, *saye*, 823, *seye*, 907, *sey*, 2521, *sye*, 3153, *sawe*, 220, *saw*, 2112; in Pl.—*seyʒe*, 460, *seyen*, 2573. Bokenam has, in Sing.—*sey*, Marg. 1130, *sawe*, Magd. 1010, *saw*, Christ. 240; in Pl.—*seyn*, Pr. Marg. 345, *seyin*, Agn. 81. Marg. Paston has *sey* (Pl.), i. 113; Pecok, *thei sien*, i. 187, *sawen*, i. 246; Shillingford, *sigh*, 10, *sawe*, 67 (both Sing.); Cely Papers sometimes has *se*; Gregory, *sawe*, 110 (Sing.), *say*, 222 (Pl.); Cr. Knt. of Bath, *saytw*, 394 (Sing.); Bp. Fox of Winchester writes *see*, Ellis ii. 2. 5, *c.* 1520; Machyn, *say*, and often *see* Sing., *saw* Pl.; Aubrey has *I see*, i. 115. Lady Wentworth often writes *see*, especially in the phrase *as ever I see*, p. 57, &c.

Past Participle. St. Editha, *sene*, 473, *seyʒe*, 1502, *sey*, 2436, *y-sey*, 2440; Bokenam, *seyn*, Magd. 1058; Pecok, *seen*; Shillingford, *seyn*, 4, *sey*, 13; Marg. Paston, *sene*, ii. 82; Cr. Knt. of Bath, *sien*, 390, *seen*, 394.

CLASS VI.

Bake. O.E. *bacan—bōc—bōcon—bacen*; M.E. *bāken—bōke—bāken.* The old P. P. *bake* survives in Pecok, i. 67, Gregory, 141, and in Bp. Knight, 202. The latter writer has 'the bisket is almost *bake*' = the matter is nearly ripe.

Stand. O.E. *standan—stōd—stōdon—standen.* The old P. P. *stande*, &c., is used throughout the fifteenth century. A Weak form, especially in the compound *understanded*, is much in vogue in the sixteenth century, e. g. in the First Prayer Book, Preface. The Second Prayer Book has *understanden.*

Take. By the side of the universally used forms *take, taken, -yn*, in the P. P., Palladius has *taked*, used as a passive with an Auxiliary, 83. 630.

Lade. The P. P. *lade* occurs in Gregory, 175; *ouerloaden*, Wilson, 66, and *loaden* in Verney Mem. ii. 224, 1645, in a letter from Sir H. P. Newton.

Forsake. Sir T. Smith has Pret. *forsakid* in a letter, Ellis ii. 3. 10.

Laugh. O.E. *hlæhhan—hlōg—hlōgon.*
The old Strong Pret. *loughe* from *hlōh* survives in the fifteenth-century poem Robert the Devil, 872, and in Bokenam, *low*, Eliz. 737.

Gnaw, draw, slay have Prets. *gnōg—gnōgon, slōg—slōgon.* The forms *slew, drew*, which we now use exclusively, and the rather remarkable *gnew*, Robert the Devil, 200, are due to the influence of the reduplicating Verbs of the *blow, grow* class. *Slew* appears, Robert the Devil, 922 (coupled with *hue* 'hewed'), *slewe*, Caxton, Jason 11. 2, Gregory, 75, Machyn, *slew*, 102. On the other hand, *slow* from the *slōg* type occurs, Gregory, 79, and Fortescue, 117. *Drewe* occurs, Gregory, 58, *drue*, Lord Berners, i. 135, 136, *withdrue*, i. 153, *druw*, Machyn, 64. But Shillingford has *drowe*, 6, and Gregory, *withdrowe*, 84, from *drōg* type.
The P. P. of *draw* is *drane*, Machyn 4 (cf. p. 142); the normal is *drawen*, &c., cf. Gregory, *drave*, 58, *drawyn*, 186. Gregory has also a Weak form *drawyd*, 172.

CLASS VII.

THE So-CALLED REDUPLICATING VERBS.

Beat. O.E. *bēatan—bēot—bēoton—beaten.*
The Early Modern forms of Pres. and Pret. must have been [bet—bēt; bĭt] respectively.
The difference does not appear to be indicated by the spelling. Latimer has a Pret. *bet*, which may represent an early shortening from M.E. *bēt.* This would correspond to the present-day popular and dialectal *bet.* The latter could also be explained on the analogy of *meet—met*, &c.

Fall. O.E. *feallan—feoll—feollon—fallen.*
The very common M.E. *fill*, &c., which has not been satisfactorily explained, persists at least as late as the sixteenth century:—Hoccleve has *fille*; Shillingford, *fyll*, 19; Pecok, *fill, fillen, befill*; Caxton, *fylle*, Jason, 11. 8, *fill*, 99. 24; also Lord Berners, *fill*, i. 336, 398; and Cavendish, 6.
On the other hand, Bokenam has *fel, befel*, St. Editha, *felle*, 239, *fel*, 258. Lord Berners's usual form is *feel*, the normal development of O.E. *feoll*, of which *fell* is the shortened form. Lady Brill. Harley also has *feel* (1641), p. 119.

Hold. Comparable to *fill* from *feoll*, we find *hild* or *hyld* from *hēold*, Shillingford, 20; Gregory, 69, 179, *hylde*; Cr. Knt. of Bath, 389; Cavendish, 89. Lady Brill. Harley writes *heeld* (1638), p. 12. Cf. Milton's rhyme *shield-withheld*, and Spenser's *beheld* with *seeld* 'seldom'. This and *feel* above are survivals of M.E. *fēl, hēld.*

Shillingford has also *held*, 5, and Gregory, *helde*, 78, Lord Berners, *held*, i. 366, &c.; Marg. Paston has *huld*, ii. 191, a remarkable form to find in an Eastern dialect.

It is not surprising to find *hulte* in St. Editha, 852, &c., by the side of *helt*, 3206.

The P. P. is *iholde*, Godstow Reg.; *hald*, Marg. Paston; *holde*, 77, *hold*, 99, *holden*, 120, Shillingford; Euphues has *helde*, 304.

Hew. Robert the Devil has *hue* (and *slew*), 922, the descendant of M.E. *hēu* (cf. p. 242, on the spelling).

The P. P. in *-en* is normal in Early Modern *hewen*, Marg. Paston, ii. 251; Euphues, 111, &c., &c.

Know, blow, grow have quite regularly *knew, grew, blew*, &c., with variants *knyw, blue*, &c. Shillingford has a Weak Pret. *knawed*, 10 and 27.

The Pret. *shewe* from *show*, an old Weak Verb, occurs, Cavendish, L. of Wolsey, 185, doubtless on the analogy of this group. Euphues has the Strong P. P. *showen*, 202, 280, also *shewn*, 280.

CLASS VIII.

AUXILIARIES.

Be. The main points to be considered are the forms of the 3rd Pers. Pres. Indic. and of the Pl. Pres.

As regards the former, the old Southern form *bith*, &c., occurs here and there in the fifteenth century.

Shillingford has *bith*, Marg. Paston, *beth* (and *is*), but Pecok and Fortescue, *is*. This, indeed, is the usual form. The Pl. shows more variety, and the present-day *are*, derived from the E. Midlands, and ultimately from the North, comes only gradually into general use in London and the South.

The Southern Pl. *bith*, &c., was widely used in the fifteenth century, by the side of the Midland *bin, been*, or *be*.

The E. Midland texts of M.E. generally have *arn*, sometimes by the side of *ben*—thus, Genesis and Exodus (*arn* and *ben*), R. of Brunne (*are, ben*, and even *beþ*), Norf. Guilds (*arn*); in the fifteenth century Bokenam has *arn, ern*. William Paston, *arn*, Marg. Paston, *arn, ar, ben*, Lydgate, *arn*, Gregory, *ar* and *bene*. These writers are all from the E. Midlands, Bokenam definitely claiming to write the Suffolk speech, the others showing in many ways traces of their native dialect. In the letters of Q. Marg. of Anjou there is one from the Treasurer of Calais, who writes *er*, 16, other officers write *we aren*, by the side of *beeth*, and Henry V, in a letter of 1421, writes *ar*, p. 18. Other texts, with no very pronounced dialectal character, vary more or less. Short Engl. Chron. has *bethe*, Rewle Sustr. Men., *been*, Caxton, *ben*, but also *ye ar* (Jason), Cr. Dk. of York, *be, been*, Bk. of Quint., *ben*, Irish Documents in Letters and Papers, vol. i, *ben*. Shillingford has, by the side of occasional *ben*, the archaic *buth*, and also *beth*, Ord. of Worcester, *ben*, Godstow Register, *byn, ben*, Oseney Reg., *been*.

Early in the following century, a letter from Sir J. Wingfield, Ellis ii.
1 (1513) has *be*, while Bp. Knight (afterwards of Bath and Wells) (1512)
has *beth*(*e*) and *be*.   Lord Berners has *ben* and *are, arre, ar*.   The Will
of R. Bradley (Leics., 1533) still has *ben*, L. D. D. 162. 1.   Bp. Latimer,
be, bee commonly, rarely *are*, Machyn, *ar*, Ascham, *be*, often in Tox.,
while *are* occurs somewhat infrequently in Scholem. ; Wilson, Arte of
Rhet., has both *are* and *ben* frequently, Euphues, *are* and *be*, Q. Elizabeth,
ar and *be*.

With the negative, *be* was used late into the seventeenth century by
good speakers ; thus Col. Courtly, in Vanbrugh's Journey to London, says
if it ben't too long.   Otherwise, *are* seems the universal form of the Pl. in
the seventeenth century in good colloquial English.   I have noted no *be*
forms in the Verney Letters.

Confusion in use of is—are; was—were.

A tendency to extend the use of *is* to sentences in which there was a
Pl. subject is traceable in the sixteenth century and continues among
educated people well into the eighteenth century.   The -*s*- Plurals of
other verbs, referred to p. 340, may have been fostered partly by this
habit.   At the present time *is* with a Pl. subject is heard only among the
uneducated.

Sir Thomas Elyot writes *both body and soul is deformed*, Gouern. ii.
340; Sir Thos. Smith—*there is three wayes*, Rep. Angl. 64; Mrs. Isham,
Verney Mem. iii—*moste of our gentre is secured and took to Oxford*, 233,
1655; Sir Ed. Sydenham, ibid. ii—*all hopes of peace is now taken away*;
Edm. V.—*your delayes is out of your goodness*, V. Mem. ii. 132, 143;
Sir R. Verney—*my Cough and Cold is badd enough God helpe me*, iv. 326,
1685; Lady Strafford, Wentworth Pprs. 262—*Lord Marsam and Lord
Bathurst is named*; Lord Bute, Wentw. Pprs.—*when there is great folks,
fine words*, &c.

The construction *you was* was apparently much more common, and
there are indications of a more general tendency to extend the use of *was*
to the 3rd Pers. Pl. also.

Pope, in a letter to Lady Mary Montagu Wortley, dated Sept. 1,
1718, writes *I shall look upon you as so many years younger than you was :*
Lady Wentworth has *you was*, pp. 94, 118 ; Vermilla, in Fielding's Love
in several Masques, says—*pray, Sir, how was you cured of your love*,
Act iv, Sc. ii.   The habit was apparently passing into disrepute at the
beginning of the nineteenth century.   Miss Austen puts the construction
several times into the mouth of the rather vulgar Miss Lucy Steele in
Sense and Sensibility—*I felt almost as if you was an old acquaintance*,
vol. i, chap. 22 ; *I felt sure you was angry with me*, chap. 24 ; *if you was to
say to me*, &c., chap. 24.   The better-bred personages in this and others
of Miss Austen's books do not use this phrase.

I have noted a few examples of *was* with the 3rd Pers. Pls.   Sir
Thos. Seymour, 1544, *such sowders and maryners as was shept at
Harwyche*, St. Pprs. Hen. VIII, i, p. 781 ; Cavendish, L. of Wolsey, *the
wells whiche was*, 80 ; Nancy Nicholas, in Verney Mem., has *ye seconds*
(in a duel) *was*, iv. 230, 1683 ; Lady Sussex, *we was glade* ; in Wentw.

Pprs.—*they was*, 124, 1642; *The Duke of Kent and Lord Longville was,* 300 (Peter W.).

In Euphues appears the strange but quite explicable construction *art not you*, p. 180, where *you*, being used to a single person, takes the Singular form of the Verb. This is also the explanation of *you was*, though, as *they was* shows, there was a tendency to generalize this form of the Verb for both numbers.

The Vowel of Present-day *are*.

The M.E. *āre(n)* had undoubtedly originally a long vowel in stressed positions, as can be shown by rhymes. M.E. *āre* would result in present-day [eə], cf. M.E. *bāre*, which has become [beə], and *hāre*, which has become [heə]. This form was still in vulgar use down to the first half of the nineteenth century, as is seen from the spelling *air* in Dickens and other writers of his period. The ancestral form of this, from M.E. *āre* can also be proved by rhymes and spellings to have been in use at a much earlier date. Rede me, &c., rhymes *are—care*, Donne rhymes *are—faire*, Heroical Epistle, 21–2, with *aire*, ibid. 41–2, pp. 124–5; Mrs. Isham, in Verney Mem. iii, writes, *you air tow discrate*, p. 235, 1655, and Mrs. Sherrard writes *aier*, V. Mem. iii. 256, 1655; Cooper mentions *are, air, heir, ere* as all having the same sound.

This form is the basis of the negative *ain't* [eint], formerly written *an't*

The present-day pronunciation of *are* [ă] when stressed, [ə] in unstressed positions, is derived from the M.E. unstressed form *ăr(e)*. This became [ær] when M.E. *ă* was fronted (p. 196, &c., above) and was used both in Strong and Weak positions. In the former position the vowel underwent lengthening before -*r*, and the Early Modern combination [ǣr] was retracted subsequently to [ā(r)], cf. pp. 203–5, above.

This old Weak form, used in a stressed position, is seen in various rhymes in the sixteenth century and later, e. g. *are—warre*, Habington's Castara, 49; *farre—are*, Donne's Progr. of the Soul, First Aniv. 7–8.

Thus, it is evident that for a long time both types were in use, until one was finally eliminated in good usage.

Shall. The original difference in the vowels of the Sing. and Pl. of the Pres., which is found in Old and Middle English (*schal—schullen*) is preserved in texts from all sources down to the third quarter of the fifteenth century. During the greater part of this period *schall*, &c., occurs also in the Pl., and gradually the *schulle(n)* forms are altogether superseded by the Singular type.

The following Pl. forms may be noted:—Hoccleve, *schul, schol,* Pecok, *schulen* and *schal*, Shillingford, *shall*, Marg. Paston, *we sholle,* Rewle Sustr. Men., *schullin, schullen,* Bk. of Quint., *schulen* and *schal,* Gregory, *shulle* and *shalle*, Ord. of Worcester, *shullen,* Fortescue, *shul* and *shall*, Caxton, *shal, shull, shulle,* Jul. Berners, *shall.* Henceforward the Pl. seems to be everywhere levelled under the type of the Sing.

The 2nd Pers. Sing. is usually *shalt*, the traditional form, but Caxton has the analogical form *shalst*, Jason, 5. 20. Marg. Paston's *scholl* (Sing.) and *sholl* (Pl.) may have been formed on the analogy of the old form of the Pret.—*schōlde*, cf. *wol* from *wōlde*, though she does not usually write the Pret. in this way, or the *o* may be written for *u*, in which case the vowel has been introduced from the old Pl. type.   Finally, it is just possible that *o* represents the rounded vowel resulting from earlier *shaul*, for the explanation of which see p. 201, above.

The commonest spelling of the Pret. in the fifteenth century seems to be *schulde*, and this is used by nearly all the writers above cited. Shillingford, however, writes *sholde*, and Marg. Paston, *shoulde*.   It seems probable that this last, and the *ou* spellings, express [ū], which is that natural development of the vowel in M.E. *schŏlde* in stressed positions. The *l* was probably lost early, in unstressed positions at any rate, though the traditional spelling is rarely departed from in this word.   I have, however, noted *shud*, Elyot's Gouernour, 70, *shudd*, Gabr. Harvey's Lttrs. 3, and *shud*, in a letter of Cary Verney, V. Mem. ii. 67.   The vowel in the present-day Weak form of *should* shows that this is a new formation, in the Early Modern period, from the stressed form [ʃū(l)d].   The old spelling of the Pret. *shold* lasts far into the sixteenth century ; Latimer writes both *shold* and *should* ; Euphues also has both spellings.

Will.   The forms *wille*, *wile*, *wil*, &c., occur commonly in M.E., alongside *wule*, the vowel of which seems to be a rounding of *i* after *w*.   Chaucer has *wil*, but more commonly *wol*, which is very common in the fourteenth century.   It may be explained sometimes as a mere orthographical variant of *wule*, &c., but it is also often a distinct new form made on the analogy of the Pret. *wŏl-de*.   It is this that gives rise to the negative *won't* (for *wol not*).   Both *will* and *wol* occur throughout the fifteenth and sixteenth centuries, some writers using both forms, others chiefly *wol*, others only *will*, &c.   Pallad. has both, Bokenam, *wyl*, Marg. Paston, *wul* and *wol* ; St. Editha, *ychulle* (I will), *he wole* ; Sustr. Men., Fortescue, and Caxton, *wol*, *wole*.   Bp. Knight (1513) has *wil* in Pl. and *wol* in Sing., but the distinction is probably accidental.   Lord Berners has *wol*, Latimer, *wyl*, Cavendish, *wyll* and *wol*, Euphues, *wil*.

Can.   The O. and M.E. distinction between Sing. and Pl. survives in the fifteenth century to some extent ; Pecok has *cunnen* for the latter. Bokenam has *kun* for both Sing. and Pl., but also *kan* for the former.

The past tense is still *couthen* (Pl.) in Pecok, *couȝthe* in St. Editha, *cowde* in Bokenam, Marg. Paston, and Lord Berners.   The latter also writes *coulde*, and this remains the usual form, with occasional *colde*, for the sixteenth century and later.   The *l* has no historical justification, and is due to the analogy of *wolde*.

Elyot has a strange P. P. *kanned*, with the sense of *known*.

The Inf. is used after another Auxiliary throughout the fifteenth century, the old form, *kunne*, being used by Pecok, *kon* by Marg. Paston, *conne* by Caxton—as in *hit shall not conne kepe it secrete*, Jason, 13. 6.

May.   The old Pl. *mōwen*, as used in Chaucer's time, from O.E. *māgon*, survives throughout the first three quarters of the fifteenth century, and is found in Hoccleve, Shillingford, Pecok, Fortescue, and Caxton.   An Inf. *mōwen* 'to be able', is used after other Auxiliaries by Marg. Paston, Sustr. Men., Fortescue, and Caxton.

The past tense *mought* is found in Sir Thos. More (Ellis ii. 1. 289), Elyot, i. 164, passim, and Queen Elizabeth's early letters (*mougth*), Ellis i. 2. 157, 1549.

have.   See note on *have*, Appendix VI.

CHAPTER X

COLLOQUIAL IDIOM

THE uttered speech of private life is fluctuating and variable. In every period it varies according to the age, class, education, and habits of the speaker. His social experience, traditions and general background, his ordinary tastes and pursuits, his intellectual and moral cultivation are all reflected in each man's conversation. These factors determine and modify a man's mode of speech in innumerable ways. They may affect his pronunciation, the speed of his utterance, his choice of vocabulary, the shade of meaning he attaches to particular words, or turns of phrase, the character of such similes and metaphors as occur in his speech, his word order and the structure of his sentences.

But the individual speaker is also affected by the character of those to whom he speaks. He adjusts himself in a hundred subtle ways to the age, status, and mental attitude of the company in which he finds himself. His own state of mind, and the mode of its expression are unconsciously modified by and attuned to the varying degree of intimacy, agreement, and community of experience in which he may stand with his companions of the moment.

Thus an accomplished man of the world, in reality, speaks not one but many slightly different idioms, and passes easily and instinctively, often perhaps unknown to himself, from one to another, according to the exigence of circumstances. The man who does not possess, to some extent at least, this power of adjustment, is of necessity a stranger in every company but that of one particular type. No man who is not a fool will consider it proper to address a bevy of Bishops in precisely the same way as would be perfectly natural and suitable among a party of fox-hunting country gentlemen.

A learned man, accustomed to choose his own topics of conversation and dilate upon them at leisure in his College common room where he can count upon the civil forbearance of other people like himself, would be thought a tedious bore, and a dull one at that, if he carried his pompous verbiage into the Officers' Mess of a smart regiment. 'A meere scholler is but a woefull creature', says Sir Edmund Verney, in a letter in which he discusses a proposal that his son should be sent to Leyden, and observes concerning this—''tis too private for a youth of his yeares that must see company at convenient times, and studdy men as well as bookes, or else his bearing may make him rather ridiculous then esteemed'.

There is naturally a large body of colloquial expression which is common to all classes, scholars, sportsmen, officers, clerics, and the rest, but each class and interest has its own special way of expressing itself, which is more or less foreign to those outside it. The average colloquial speech of any age is at best a compromise between a variety of different jargons, each evolved in and current among the members of a particular section of the community, and each, within certain social limits, affects and is affected by the others.   Most men belong by their circumstances or inclinations to several speech-communities, and have little difficulty in maintaining themselves creditably in all of these.   The wider the social opportunities and experience of the individual, and the keener his lin-guistic instinct, the more readily does he adapt himself to the company in which he finds himself, and the more easily does he fall into line with its accepted traditions of speech and bearing.

But if so much variety in the details of colloquial usage exists in a single age, with such well-marked differences between the conventions of each, how much greater will be the gulf which separates the types of familiar conversation in different ages.   Do we realize that if we could, by the workings of some Time Machine, be suddenly transported back into the seventeenth century, most of us would find it extremely difficult to carry on, even among the kind of people most nearly corresponding with those with whom we are habitually associated in our present age, the simplest kind of decent social intercourse?   Even if the pronunciation of the sixteenth century offered no difficulty, almost every other element which goes to make up the medium of communication with our fellows would do so.

We should not know how to greet or take leave of those we met, how to express our thanks in an acceptable manner, how to ask a favour, pay a compliment, or send a polite message to a gentleman's wife.   We should be at a loss how to begin and end the simplest note, whether to an intimate friend, a near relative, or to a stranger.   We could not scold a footman, commend a child, express in appropriate terms admiration for a woman's beauty, or aversion to the opposite quality.   We should hesitate every moment how to address the person we were talking to, and should be embarassed for the equivalent of such instinctive phrases as—look here, old man; my dear chap; my dear Sir; excuse me; I beg your pardon; I'm awfully sorry; Oh, not at all; that's too bad; that's most amusing; you see; don't you know; and a hundred other trivial and meaningless expressions with which most men fill out their sentences.   Our innocent impulses of pleasure, approval, dislike, anger, disgust, and so on, would be nipped in the bud for want of words to express them.   How should we say, on the spur of the moment—what a pretty girl!; what an amusing play!; how clever and witty Mr. Jones is!; poor woman; that's a perfectly rotten book; I hate the way she dresses; look here, Sir, you had better take care what you say; Oh, shut up; I'm hanged if I'll do that; I'm very much obliged to you, I'm sure?

It is very probable that we perfectly grasp the equivalents of all these and a thousand others when we read them in the pages of Congreve and his contemporaries, but it is equally certain that the right expressions would not rise naturally to our lips as we required them, were we suddenly called upon to speak with My Lady Froth, or Mr. Brisk.

The fact is that we should feel thoroughly at sea in such company, and should soon discover that we had to learn a new language of polite society.

If we did not realize this, but insisted on speaking in our own way, we should be made to feel before long that we were outraging every convention and sense of decorum which that not very decorous age possessed. We should appear at once too familiar and too stiff and stilted; too prim and too outspoken; too pompous and too much lacking in ceremonious observance.

In any case we should cut a very sorry figure.

Now to exhibit, in a single chapter, even in the merest outline, the genius of the English colloquial idiom of several centuries, is an impossible task. Each century would need to be the subject of a thorough investigation, and all possible sources of information would require to be exploited to the full. Again, the various aspects of colloquial speech life must be examined, and the different elements arranged and grouped according to some principle of classification. Such a work, for a single age, would profitably occupy the time of a band of inquirers for many years, and even then it would be necessarily incomplete. As Mr. Henry Bradley has well remarked in his chapter on Shakespeare's Language :—
' At no period—not even in our own time, which has an unexampled abundance of prose fiction dealing with all aspects of contemporary life—has the colloquial vocabulary and idiom of the English Language been completely preserved in the literature. The homely expressions of everyday intercourse, the phrases of contemporary currency alluding to recent events, the slang words and uses of words characteristic of particular classes of society—all these have been but very imperfectly recorded in the writings of any age.'

A very perfunctory treatment of a vast subject is all that can be attempted here. If it suffices to interest a certain number of readers in the general question, and in some of the details here touched upon, so that they pursue the subject for themselves; if a few of these readers should be stimulated to devote some of their time to a systematic investigation of such parts of the matter here dealt with, or of others which are here omitted, then this short study will not have failed altogether of its object.

It is proposed to deal here with the subject in the following manner.

In the first place characteristic specimens will be given, of dialogue when this is available, otherwise of passages from letters of a colloquial character, to illustrate the general features and tone of familiar English from the fifteenth to the eighteenth centuries inclusive.

Following these specimens of whole passages, we shall attempt to illustrate certain special and particular elements in the conversation of everyday life. Those selected come principally under the following heads :—

Modes of greeting; farewells; compliments and complimentary banter; endearments; angry and abusive speeches among equals, or addressed to inferiors; expressions of approval and disapproval.

Oaths, imprecations, expletives, exclamatory and interjectional expressions; emphatics.

Preciosities, affectations, and euphemisms.

The term *Colloquial* is so far extended as to include formulas used in beginning and ending letters, nor are the examples of these confined entirely to purely familiar epistles written to intimates, but include also the beginnings and endings of letters of a more formal character.

In illustrating the colloquial style of the fifteenth century we have to be content, either with the account of conversations given in letters, or with such other passages from letters of the period as appear to be nearest to the speech of everyday life.

The following passages are from the Shillingford Letters, to which reference is repeatedly made in this book (see p. 65, &c.), and are extracted from the accounts given by the stout and genial Mayor of Exeter, in letters to his friends, of his conversations with the Chancellor during his visit to London.

Shillingford begins by referring to himself as 'the Mayer', but suddenly changes to the first person—*y*—in describing the actual meeting, again returning for a moment to the impersonal phrase.

John Shillingford.

'The Saterdey next (28 Oct. 1447) therafter the mayer came to Westminster sone apon ix. atte belle, and ther mette w^t my lorde Chanceller atte brode dore a litell fro the steire fote comyng fro the Sterrechamber, y yn the courte and by the dore knellyng and salutyng hym yn the moste godely wyse that y cowde and recommended yn to his gode and gracious lordship my feloship and all the comminalte, his awne peeple and bedmen of the Cite of Exceter. He seyde to the mayer ij tymes " Well come " and the iij^{de} tyme "Right well come Mayer" and helde the Mayer a grete while faste by the honde, and so went forth to his barge and w^t hym grete presse, lordis and other, &c. and yn especiall the tresorer of the kynges housholde, w^t wham he was at right grete pryvy communication. And therfor y, mayer, drowe me apart, and mette w^t hym at his goyng yn to his barge, and ther toke my leve of hym, seyyng these wordis, " My lord, y wolle awayte apon youre gode lordship and youre better leyser at another tyme". He seyde to me ayen, " Mayer, y pray yow hertely that ye do so, and that ye speke w^t the Chief Justyse and what that ever he will y woll be all redy". And thus departed.'—pp. 5, 6.

A little later:—

' Nerthelez y awayted my tyme and put me yn presse and went right to my lorde Chaunceller and seide, " My lorde y am come at your commaundement, but y se youre grete bysynesse is suche that ye may not attende". He seide " Noo, by his trauthe and that y myght right well se". Y seide " Yee, and that y was sory and hadde pyty of his grete vexacion". He seide " Mayer, y moste to morun ride by tyme to the Kyng, and come ayen this wyke: ye most awayte apon my comyng, and then y wol speke w^t the justise and attende for yow "', &c.—p. 7.

' He seyde " Come the morun Monedey" (the Chancellor was speaking on Sunday) . . . " the love of God " Y seyde the tyme was to shorte, and prayed hym of Wendysdey ; y enfourmed hym (of t)he grete malice and venym that they have spatte to me yn theire answeris as hit appereth yn a copy that y sende to yow of. My lorde seide, " Alagge alagge, why wolde they do so ? y woll sey right sharpely to ham therfor and y nogh ".'

Margery Brews.

The following brief extracts from the letters of Margery Brews, the affianced wife of John Paston (junior) are like a ray of sunlight in the dreary wilderness of business and litigation, which are the chief subjects of correspondence between the Pastons. Even this love-letter is not wholly free from the taint, but the girl's gentle affection for her lover is the prevailing note.

'Yf that ye cowde be content with that good and my por persone I wold be the meryest mayden on grounde, and yf ye thynke not your selffe soe satysfyed or that ye myght hafe much mor good, as I hafe undyrstonde be youe afor ; good trewe and lovyng volentyne, that ye take no such labur uppon yowe, as to come more for that matter, but let it passe, and never more to be spokyn of, as I may be your trewe lover and bedewoman during my lyfe.'—*Paston Letters*, iii, p. 172 (1477).

A few years later Mrs. Paston writes to her 'trewe and lovyng volentyne' :—

'My mother in lawe thynketh longe she here no word from you. She is in goode heale, blissed be God, and al yowr babees also. I marvel I here no word from you, weche greveth me ful evele. I sent you a letter be Basiour sone of Norwiche, wher of I have no word.' To this the young wife adds the touching postscript :—'Sir I pray yow if ye tary longe at London that it wil plese to sende for me, for I thynke longe sen I lay in your armes.'— *Paston Letters*, iii, p. 293 (1482).

Sir Thomas More.

No figure in the early part of Henry VIII's reign is more distinguished and at the same time more engaging than that of Sir Thomas More. A few typical records of his conversation, as preserved by his devoted biographer and son-in-law Roper, are chosen to illustrate the English of this time. The context is given so that the extracts may appear in Roper's own setting.

'Not long after this the Watter baylife of London (sometyme his servaunte) hereing, where he had beene at dinner, certayne Marchauntes liberally to rayle against his ould Master, waxed so discontented therwith, that he hastily came to him, and tould him what he had hard : "and were I Sir" (quoth he) "in such favour and authoritie with my Prince as you are, such men surely should not be suffered so villanously and falsly to misreport and slander me. Wherefore I would wish you to call them before you, and to there shame, for there lewde malice to punnish them." Who smilinge upon him sayde, "Mr Watter Baylie, would you have me punnish them by whome I receave more benefitt then by you all that be my frendes? Let them a Gods name speake as lewdly as they list of me, and shoote never soe many arrowes at me, so long as they do not hitt me, what am I the worse? But if the should once hitt me, then would it a little trouble me : howbeit, I trust, by Gods helpe, there shall none of them all be able to touch me. I have more cause, Mr Water Bayly (I assure thee) to pittie·them, then to be angrie with them." Such frutfull communication had he often tymes with his familier frendes. Soe on a tyme walking a long the Thames syde with me at Chelsey, in talkinge of other thinges he sayd to me, "Now, would to God, Sonne Roger, upon condition three things are well established in Christendome, I were put in a sacke, and here presently cast into the Thames." "What great thinges be these, Sir" quoth I, "that should move you so to wish?" "Wouldest thou know, sonne Roper, what they be" quoth he? "Yea marry, Sir, with a good will if it please you", quoth I. "I faith, they be these Sonne", quoth he. The first is, that where as the most part of Christian princes be at mortall warrs, they weare at universal peace. The second, that wheare the Church of Christ is at this present soare afflicted with many heresies and errors, it were well settled in an uniformity. The third, that where the Kinges matter of his marriage is now come into question, it were to the glory of God and quietnesse of all parties brought to a good conclusion : " where by, as I could gather, he judged, that otherwise it would be a disturbance to a great part of Christendome.'

' When Sir Thomas Moore had continued a good while in the Tower, my Ladye his wife obtayned license to see him, who at her first comminge like a simple woman, and somewhat worldlie too, with this manner of salutations bluntly saluted him, " What the good yeare, Mr Moore" quoth shee, " I marvell that you, that have beene allwayes hitherunto taken for soe wise a man, will now soe playe the foole to lye here in this close filthie prison, and be content to be shutt upp amonge myse and rattes, when you might be abroad at your libertie, and with the favour and good will both of the King and his Councell, if you would but doe as all the Bushopps and best learned of this Realme have done. And seeing you have at Chelsey a right fayre house, your librarie, your books, your gallerie, your garden, your orchards, and all other necessaries soe handsomely about you, where you might, in the companie of me your wife, your children, and houshould be merrie, I muse what a Gods name you meane here still thus fondlye to tarry." After he had a while quietly hard her, " I pray thee good Mrs Alice, tell me, tell me one thinge." " What is that ? " (quoth shee). " Is not this house as nighe heaven as myne owne ? " To whome shee, after her accustomed fashion, not likeinge such talke, answeared, " *Tille valle, Tille valle* " " How say you, Mrs Alice, is it not soe ? " quoth he. " *Bone deus, bone Deus*, man, will this geare never be left ? " quoth shee. " Well then Mrs Alice, if it be soe, it is verie well. For I see noe great cause whie I should soe much joye of my gaie house, or of any thinge belonginge thereunto, when, if I should but seaven yeares lye buried under ground, and then arise, and come thither againe, I should not fayle to finde some therin that would bidd me gett out of the doores, and tell me that weare none of myne. What cause have I then to like such an house as would soe soone forgett his master ? " Soe her perswasions moved him but a little.'

The last days of this good man on earth, and some of his sayings just before his death, are told with great simplicity by Roper. We cannot forbear to quote the affecting passage which tells of Sir Thomas More's last parting from his daughter, the writer's wife.

' When Sir Tho. Moore came from Westminster to the Towreward againe, his daughter my wife, desireous to see her father, whome shee thought shee should never see in this world after, and alsoe to have his finall blessinge, gave attendaunce aboutes the Towre wharfe, where shee knewe he should passe by, e're he could enter into the Towre. There tarriinge for his cominge home, as soone as shee sawe him, after his blessinges on her knees reverentlie receaved, shee hastinge towards, without consideration and care of her selfe, pressinge in amongest the midst of the thronge and the Companie of the Guard, that with Hollbards and Billes weare round about him, hastily ranne to him, and then openlye in the sight of all them embraced and tooke him about the necke, and kissed him, whoe well likeing her most daughterlye love and affection towards him, gave her his fatherlie blessinge, and manye goodlie words of comfort besides, from whome after shee was departed, shee not satisfied with the former sight of her deare father, havinge respecte neither to her self, nor to the presse of the people and multitude that were about him, suddenlye turned backe againe, and rann to him as before, tooke him about the necke, and divers tymes togeather most lovingley kissed him, and at last with a full heavie harte was fayne to departe from him ; the behouldinge whereof was to manye of them that were present thereat soe lamentable, that it made them for very sorrow to mourne and weepe.'

In his last letter to his ' dearely beloved daughter, written with a Cole ', Sir Thomas More refers to this incident :—' And I never liked your manners better, then when you kissed me last. For I like when daughterlie Love, and deare Charitie hath noe leasure to looke to worldlie Cui tesie '.

Next morning ' Sir Thomas even, and the Utas of St. Peeter in the yeare of our Lord God 1537 . . . earlie in the morninge, came to him Sir Thomas Pope, his singular frend, on messedge from the Kinge and his Councell, that hee should before nyne of the clocke in the same morninge suffer death, and that therefore fourthwith he should prepare himselfe thereto. " Mr Pope " sayth he, " for your good tydinges I most hartily thank you. I have beene allwayes bounden much to the Kinges Highnes for the benefitts and honors which he hath still from tyme to tyme most bounti- fully heaped upon mee, and yete more bounden I ame to his Grace for putting me into this place, where I have had convenient tyme and space to have remembraunce of my end, and soe helpe me God most of all Mr Pope, am I bound to his Highnes, that it pleased him so shortlie to ridd me of the miseries of this wretched world. And therefore will I not fayle most earnestlye to pray for his Grace both here, and alsoe in another world. . . . And I beseech you, good Mr Pope, to be a meane unto his Highnes, that my daughter Margarette may be present at my buriall." " The King is well contented allreadie " (quoth Mr Pope) " that your Wife, Children and other frendes shall have free libertie to be present thereat ". " O how much be- houlden " then said Sir Thomas Moore " am I to his Grace, that unto my poore buriall vouchsafeth to have so gratious Consideration." Wherewithall Mr Pope takeinge his leave of him could not refrayne from weepinge, which Sir Tho. Moore perceavinge, comforted him in this wise, " Quiete yourselfe good Mr Pope, and be not discomforted. For I trust that we shall once in heaven see each other full merily, where we shall bee sure to live and love togeather in joyfull blisse eternally."

Wolsey.

The *Life of Wolsey* (1557), by George Cavendish, a faithful and devoted servant of the Cardinal, who was with him on his death-bed, gives a wonderfully interesting picture of this remarkable man, in affluence and in adversity, and records a number of conversations which have a convincing air of verisimilitude. The following specimens are taken from the Kelmscott Press edition of 1893, which follows the spelling of the author's MS. in the British Museum.

' After ther departyng, my lord came to the sayd howsse of Eston to his lodgyng, where he had to supper with hyme dyvers of his frends of the court. And syttyng at supper, in came to hyme Doctor Stephyns, the secretary, late ambassitor unto Rome ; but to what entent he came I know not ; howbeit my lord toke it that he came bothe to dissembell a certeyn obedyence and love towards hyme, or ells to espie hys behaviour, and to here his commynycacion at supper. Not withstandyng my lord bade hyme well come, and commaundyd hyme to sytt down at the table to supper ; with whome my lord had thys commynycacion with hyme under thys maner. Mayster Secretary, quod my lord, ye be-welcome home owt of Itally ; whan came ye frome Rome ? Forsothe, quod he, I came home allmost a monethe agoo; and where quod my lord have you byn ever sence? Forsothe, quod he, folowyng the court this progresse. Than have ye hunted and had good game and pastyme. Forsothe, Syr, quod he, and so I have, I thanke the kyngs Majestie. What good greynounds have ye? quod my lord. I have some syr quod he. And thus in huntyng, and in lyke disports, passed they all ther commynycacion at supper. And after supper my lord and he talked secretly together until it was mydnyght or they departed.'—p. 143.

'Than all thyng beyng ordered as it is before reherced, my lord prepared hyme to depart by water. And before his departyng he commaundyd Syr William Gascoyne, his treasorer, to se these thyngs byfore remembred, delyverd safely to the kyng at his repayer. That don, the seyd Syr William seyd unto my lord. Syr I ame sorry for your grace, for I understand ye shall goo strayt way to the tower. Ys this the good comfort and councell, quod my lord, that ye can geve your mayster in adversitie? Yt hathe byn allwayes your naturall inclynacion to be very light of credytt, and mych more lighter in reporting of false newes, I wold ye shold knowe, Syr William, and all other suche blasphemers, that it is nothyng more false than that, for I never, thanks be to god, deserved by no wayes to come there under any arrest, allthoughe it hathe pleased the kyng to take my howse redy furnysshed for his pleasyr at this tyme. I wold all the world knewe, and so I confesse to have no thyng, other riches, honour, or dignyty, that hathe not growen of hyme and by hyme; therefore it is my verie dewtie to surrender the same to hyme agayn as his very owen, with al my hart, or ells I ware and onkynd servaunt. Therefore goo your wayes, and geve good attendaunce unto your charge, that no thyng be embeselled.'—p. 149.

'And the next day we removed to Sheffeld Parke, where therle of Shrewsbury lay within the loge, and all the way thetherward the people cried and lamented, as they dyd in all places as we rode byfore. And whan we came in to the parke of Sheffeld, nyghe to the logge, my lord of Shrewesbury, with my lady his wyfe, a trayn of gentillwomen, and all my lords gentilmen and yomen, standyng without the gatts of the logge to attend my lords commyng, to receyve hyme with myche honor; whome therle embraced, sayeng these words. My lord quod he, your grace is most hartely welcome unto me, and glade to se you in my poore loge; the whiche I have often desired; and myche more gladder if you had come after another sort. Ah, my gentill lord of Shrewesbury quod my lord, I hartely thanke you; and allthoughe I have no cause to rejoyce, yet as a sorowe full hart may joye, I rejoyce my chaunce, which is so good to come into the hands and custody of so noble a persone, whose approved honor and wysdome hathe byn allwayes right well knowen to all nobell estats. And Sir, howe soever my ongentill accusers hathe used ther accusations agenst me, yet I assure you, and so byfore your lordshipe and all the world do I protest, that my demeanor and procedyngs hathe byn just and loyall towards my soverayn and liege lord; of whose behaviour and doyngs your lordshipe hathe had good experyence; and evyn accordyng to my trowthe and faythfulnes, so I beseche god helpe me in this my calamytie. I dought nothyng of your trouthe, quod therle, therfore my lorde I beseche you be of good chere and feare not, for I have receyved letters from the kyng of his owen hand in your favour and entertaynyng the whiche you shall se. Sir, I ame nothyng sory but that I have not wherwith worthely to receyve you, and to entertayn you accordyng to your honour and my good wyll; but suche as I have ye are most hartely welcome therto, desiryng you to accept my good wyll accordyngly, for I wol not receyve you as a prisoner, but as my good lord, and the kyngs trewe faythfull subjecte; and here is my wyfe come to salute you. Whome my lord kyst barehedyd, and all hir gentilwomen; and toke my lords servaunts by the hands, as well gentilmen and yomen as other. Then these two lords went arme in arme into the logge, conductyng my lord into a fayer chamber at thend of a goodly gallery within a newe tower, and here my lord was lodged.'—p. 246.

Here are some short portions of dialogue between Wolsey and his friends, just before his death:

'Uppon Monday in the mornyng, as I stode by his bedds side, abought viii of the clocke, the wyndowes beyng cloose shett, havyng wake lights burnyng uppon the cupbord, I behyld hyme, as me seemed, drawyng fast to his end. He perceyved my shadowe uppon the wall by his bedds side, asked who was there. Sir I ame here, quod I. Howe do you? quod he to me. Very well Sir, if I myght se your grace well. What is it of the clocke? quod he to me. Forsothe Sir, quod I, it is past viii. of the clocke in the mornyng. Eight of the clocke, quod he, that cannot be, rehersing dyvers times eight of the clocke, eight of the clocke. Nay, nay, quod he at the last, it cannot be viii of the clocke, for by viii of the clocke ye shal loose your mayster; for my tyme drawyth nere that I must depart out of this world.' . . .—p. 265.

'Mayster Kyngston farewell. I can no moore, but whyshe all thyngs to have good successe. My tyme drawyth on fast. I may not tary with you. And forget not I pray you, what I have seyd and charged you with all: for whan I ame deade, ye shall peradventure remember my words myche better. And even with these words he began to drawe his speche at lengthe and his tong to fayle, his eyes beyng set in his hed, whos sight faylled hyme; than we began to put hyme in rembraunce of Christs passion, and sent for the Abbott of the place to annele hyme; who came with all spede and mynestred unto hyme all the servyce to the same belongyng; and caused also the gard to stand by, bothe to here hyme talk byfore his deathe, and also to bere wytnes of the same; and incontinent the clocke strake viii, at whiche tyme he gave uppe the gost, and thus departed he this present lyfe.'—p. 276.

Latimer.

The Sermons of Bp. Latimer present good examples of colloquial oratory, and the style is but little removed from the colloquial style of the period. The following are from the Sermon of the Ploughers, preached in 1548:

'For they that be lordes vyll yll go to plough. It is no mete office for them. It is not semyng for their state. Thus came up lordyng loiterers. Thus crept in vnprechinge prelates, and so haue they longe continued.

'For how many vnlearned prelates haue we now at this day? And no maruel. For if ye plough men yat now be, were made lordes they woulde cleane gyue ouer ploughinge, they woulde leaue of theyr labour and fall to lordyng outright, and let the plough stand. And then bothe ploughes nor walkyng nothyng shoulde be in the common weale but honger. For euer sence the Prelates were made Loordes and nobles, the ploughe standeth, there is no worke done, the people starue.

'Thei hauke, thei hunt, thei card, they dyce, they pastyme in theyr pre-lacies with galaunte gentlemen, with theyr daunsinge minyons, and with theyr freshe companions, so that ploughinge is set a syde. And by the lordinge and loytryng, preachynge and ploughinge is cleane gone . . .— pp. 24, 25.

'But nowe for the defaulte of vnpreaching prelates me thinke I coulde gesse what myghte be sayed for excusynge of them: They are so troubeled wyth Lordelye lyuynge, they be so placed in palacies, couched in courtes, ruffelynge in theyr rentes, daunceyng in theyr dominions, burdened with ambassages, pamperynge of theyr paunches lyke a monke that maketh his jubilie, mounchynge in their maungers, and moylynge in their gaye manoures and mansions, and so troubeled wyth loyterynge in theyr Lordeshyppes : that they canne not attende it. They are other wyse occupyed, some in the kynges matters, some are ambassadoures, some of the pryuie counsell, some to furnyshe the courte, some are Lordes of the Parliamente, some are presidentes, and some comptroleres of myntes. Well, well. Is thys theyr duetye? Is thys theyr offyce? Is thys theyr callyng? Should we haue ministers of the church to be comptrollers of the myntes? Is thys a meete office for a prieste that hath cure of soules? Is this hys charge? I woulde here aske one question : I would fayne knowe who comptrolleth the deuyll at home at his parishe, whyle he comptrolleth the mynte? If the Apostles mighte not leaue the office of preaching to be deacons, shall one leaue it for myntyng?'

Wilson's *Arte of Rhetorique* (1560) has a section 'Of deliting the hearers, and stirring them to laughter' in which are enumerated 'What are the kindes of sporting, or mouing to laughter'. The subject is illustrated by various 'pleasant' stories, which if few of them would now make us laugh, are at least couched in a very easy and colloquial style and enlivened by scraps of actual conversation. The most amusing element in the whole chapter is the attitude of the writer to the subject, and the combination of seriousness and scurrility with which it is handled.

'The occasion of laughter' says Wilson, 'and the meane that maketh us mery . . . is the fondnes, the filthines, the deformitie, and all such euill be-hauiour as we see to be in other? . . . Now when we would abashe a man for some words that he hath spoken, and can take none aduauntage of his person, or making of his bodie, we either doubt him at the first, and make him beleeue that he is no wiser then a Goose : or els we confute wholy his sayings with some pleasaunt iest, or els we extenuate and diminish his doings by some pretie meanes, or els we cast the like in his dish, and with some other devise, dash hym out of countenance : or last of all, we laugh him to scorne out right, and sometimes speake almost neuer a word, but only in continuaunce, shewe our selues pleasaunt'.—p. 136.

'A frend of mine, and a good fellowe, more honest then wealthie, yea and more pleasant then thriftie, hauing need of a nagge for his iourney that he had in hande, and being in the countrey, minded to go to Partnaie faire in Lincolnshire, not farre from the place where he then laie, and meeting by the way one of his acquaintaunce, told him his arrande, and asked him how horses went at the Faire. The other aunswered merely and saide, some trot sir, and some amble, as farre as I can see. If their paces be altered, I praye you tell me at our next meeting. And so rid away as fast as his horse could cary him, without saying any word more, whereat he then being alone, fel a laughing hartely to him self, and looked after a good while, vntil the other was out of sight.'—p. 140.

'A Gentleman hauing heard a Sermon at Paules, and being come home, was asked what the preacher said. The Gentleman answered he would first heare what his man could saie, who then waited vpon him, with his hatte and cloake, and calling his man to him, sayd, nowe sir, whate haue you brought from the Sermon. Forsothe good Maister, sayd the seruaunt your cloake and your hatte. A honest true dealing seruaunt out of doubt, plaine as a packsaddle, hauing a better soule to God, though his witte was simple, then those haue, that vnder the colour of hearing, giue them selues to priuie picking, and so bring other mens purses home in their bosomes, in the steade of other mens Sermons.'—pp. 141-2.

These two stories are intended to illustrate the point that ' We shall delite the hearers, when they looke for one answere, and we make them a cleane contrary, as though we would not seeme to vnderstand what they would haue '.

'Churlish aunsweres like the hearers sometimes very well. When the father was cast in judgement, the Sonne seeing him weepe: why weepe you Father? (quoth he) To whom his Father aunswered. What? Shall I sing I pray thee seeing by Lawe I am condemned to dye. Socrates likewise bieing mooued of his wife, because he should dye an innocent and guiltlesse in the Law: Why for shame woman (quoth he) wilt thou haue me to dye giltie and deseruing. When one had falne into a ditch, an other pitying his fall, asked him and saied: Alas how got you into that pit? Why Gods mother, quoth the other, doest thou aske me how I got in, nay tell me rather in the mischiefe, how I shall get out.'

The nearest approach to the colloquial style in **Bacon** is to be found in the *Apophthegms*, in which are scraps of conversation. A few may be quoted, if only on account of the author.

'Master Mason of Trinity College, sent his pupil to an other of the fellows, to borrow a book of him, who told him, "I am loth to lend my books out of my chamber, but if it please thy tutor to come and read upon it in my chamber, he shall as long as he will." It was winter, and some days after the same fellow sent to Mr Mason to borrow his bellows ; but Mr Mason said to his pupil, "I am loth to lend my bellows out of my chamber, but if thy tutor would come and blow the fire in my chamber, he shall as long as he will." —*Apophth.* 47, p. 113.

'There were fishermen drawing the river at Chelsea: Mr Bacon came thither by chance in the afternoon, and offered to buy their draught: they were willing. He asked them what they would take? They asked thirty shillings. Mr Bacon offered them ten. They refused it. Why then said Mr Bacon, I will be only a looker on. They drew and catched nothing. Saith Mr Bacon, Are not you mad fellows now, that might have had an angel in your purse, to have made merry withal, and to have warmed you thoroughly, and now you must go home with nothing. Ay but, saith the fishermen, we had hope then to make a better gain of it. Saith Mr Bacon, "Well my master, then I will tell you, hope is a good breakfast, but it is a bad supper."—p. 136.

Otway's Comedies have all the coarseness and raciness of dialogue of the latter half of the seventeenth century, and a pretty vein of genuine comicality. They are packed with the familiar slang and colloquialisms of the period. A few passages from *Friendship in Fashion* illustrate at once the speech and the manners of the day.

Enter LADY SQUEAMISH *at the Door.*

Sir Noble Clumsey. Hah, my Lady Cousin!—Faith Madam you see I am at it.

Malagene. The Devil's wit, I think; we could no sooner talk of wh— but she must come in, with a pox to her. Madam, your Ladyship's most humble Servant.

Lady Squ. Oh, odious! insufferable! who would have thought Cousin, you would have serv'd me so—fough, how he stinks of wine, I can smell him hither.—How have you the Patience to hear the Noise of Fiddles, and spend your time in nasty drinking?

Sir Noble. Hum! 'tis a good Creature: Lovely Lady, thou shalt take thy Glass.

Lady Squ. Uh gud ; murder! I had rather you had offered me a toad.

Sir N. Then Malagene, here's a Health to my Lady Cousin's Pelion upon Ossa. [*Drinks and breaks the Glass.*]

Ldy Squ. Lord, dear Mr Malagene what's that?

Mal. A certain Place Madam, in Greece, much talk't of by the Ancients; the noble Gentleman is well read.

Ldy Squ. Nay he's an ingenious Person I'll assure you.

Sir N. Now Lady bright, I am wholly thy Slave: Give me thy Hand, I'll go straight and begin my Grandmother's Kissing Dance; but first deign me the private Honour of thy Lip.

Ldy Squ. Nay, fie Sir Noble! how I hate you now! for shame be not so rude: I swear you are quite spoiled. Get you gone you good-natur'd Toad you. [*Exeunt.*]

. . . .

Malegene. . . . I'm a very good Mimick; I can act Punchinello, Scaramouchir, Harlequin, Prince Prettyman or anything. I can act the rumbling of a Wheel-barrow.

Valentine. The rumbling of a Wheel-barrow!

Mal. Ay, the rumbling of a Wheel-barrow, so I say—Nay more than that, I can act a Sow and Pigs, Saussages a broiling, a Shoulder of Mutton a roasting: I can act a fly in a Honey-pot.

Truman. That indeed must be the Effect of very curious Observation.

Mal. No, hang it, I never make it my business to observe anything, that is Mechanicke. But all this I do, you shall see me if you will: But here comes her Ladyship and Sir Noble.

Ldy Squ. Oh, dear Mr Truman, rescue me. Nay Sir Noble for Heav'n's sake.

Sir N. I tell thee Lady, I must embrace thee: Sir, do you know me! I am Sir Noble Clumsey: I am a Rogue of an Estate, and I live—Do you want any money? I have fifty pounds.

Val. Nay good Sir Noble, none of your Generosity we beseech you. The Lady, the Lady, Sir Noble.

Sir N. Nay, 'tis all one to me if you won't take it, there it is.—Hang Money, my Father was an Alderman.

Mal. 'Tis pity good Guineas should be spoil'd, Sir Noble, by your leave.
[*Picks up the Guineas.*]

Sir N. But, Sir, you will not keep my Money?

Mal. Oh, hang Money, Sir, your Father was an Alderman.

Sir N. Well, get thee gone for an Arch-Wag—I do but sham all this while:—but by Dad he's pure Company. . . .
. . . Lady, once more I say be civil, and come kiss me.

Val. Well done Sir Noble, to her, never spare.

Ldy Squ. I may be even with you tho for all this, Mr Valentine: Nay dear Sir Noble: Mr Truman, I'll swear he'll put me into Fits.

Sir N. No, but let me salute the Hem of thy Garmènt. Wilt thou marry me? [*Kneels.*]

Mal. Faith Madam do. let me make the Match.

Ldy Squ. Let me die Mr Malegene, you are. a strange Man, and I'll swear have a great deal of Wit. Lord, why don't you write?

Mal. Write? I thank your Ladyship for that with all my Heart. No I have a Finger in a Lampoon or so sometimes, that's all.

Truman. But he can act.

Ldy Squ. I'll swear, and so he does better than any one upon our Theatres; I have seen him. Oh the English Comedians are nothing, not comparable to the French or Italian: Besides we want Poets.

Sir N. Poets! Why I am a Poet; I have written three Acts of a Play, and have nam'd it already. 'Tis to be a Tragedy.

Ldy Squ. Oh Cousin, if you undertake to write a Tragedy, take my

Counsel: Be sure to say soft melting tender things in it that may be moving, and make your Lady's Characters virtuous whate'er you do.

Sir N. Moving! Why, I can never read it myself but it makes me laugh: well, 'tis the pretty'st Plot, and so full of Waggery.

Ldy Squ. Oh ridiculous!

Mal. But Knight, the Title; Knight, the Title.

Sir N. Why let me see; 'tis to be called The Merry Conceits of Love; or the Life and Death of the Emperor Charles the Fifth, with the Humours of his Dog Boabdillo.

Mal. Ha, ha, ha. . . .

Ldy Squ. But dear Mr Malagene, won't you let us see you act a little something of Harlequin? I'll swear you do it so naturally, it makes me think I'm at the Louvre or Whitehall all the time. [*Mal. acts.*] O Lord, don't, don't neither; I'll swear you'll make me burst. Was there ever anything so pleasant?

Trum. Was ever anything so affected and ridiculous? Her whole Life sure is a continued Scene of Impertinence. What a damn'd Creature is a decay'd Woman, with all the exquisite Silliness and Vanity of her Sex, yet none of the Charms! [*Mal. speaks in Punchinello's voice.*]

Ldy Squ. O Lord, that, that; that is a Pleasure intolerable. Well, let me die if I can hold out any longer.

A Comparison between the Stages, *with an Examen of the Generous Conqueror*, printed in 1702, is a dialogue between 'Two Gentlemen', Sullen and Ramble (see below), and 'a Critick', upon the plays of the day and others of an earlier date. The style is that of easy and natural familiar conversation, with little or no artificiality, and incidentally, the tract throws light upon contemporary manners and social habits. The following examples are designed to illustrate the colloquial handling of indifferent topics, and the small-talk of the early eighteenth century, as well as the treatment of the immediate subject of the essay.

Sullen. They may talk of the Country and what they will, but the Park for my money.

Ramble. In its proper Season I grant you, when the Mall is pav'd with lac'd shoes; when the Air is perfum'd with the rosie Breath of so many fine Ladies; when from one end to the other the Sight is entertain'd with nothing but Beauty, and the whole Prospect looks like an Opera.

Sull. And when is it out of Season Ramble?

Ram. When the Beauties desert it; when the absence of this charming Company makes it a Solitude: Then Sullen, the Park is to me no more than a Wilderness, a very Common; and a Grove in a country Garden with a pretty Lady is by much the pleasanter Landscape.

Sull. To a Man of your Quicksilver Constitution it may be so, and the Cuckoo in May may be Music t'ee a hundred Miles off, when all the Masters in Town can't divert you.

Ram. I love everything as Nature and the Nature of Pleasure has contriv'd it; I love the Town in Winter, because then the Country looks aged and deform'd; and I hate the Town in Summer, because then the Country is in its Glory, and looks like a Mistress just drest out for enjoyment.

Sull. Very well distinguish'd: Not like a Bride, but like a Mistress.

Ram. I distinguish 'em by that comparison because I love nothing well enough to be wedded to 't: I'm a Proteus in my Appetite, and love to change my Abode with my Inclination.

Sull. I differ from you for the very Reason you give for your change; the Town is evermore the same to me; and tho' the Season makes it look after another manner, yet still it has a Face to please me one way or other, and both Winter and Summer make it agreeable. —pp. 1-3.

COLLOQUIAL IDIOM

Here is a conversation during dinner at the 'Blew Posts'.

Critik. What have you order'd?

Ramb. A Brace of Carp stew'd, a piece of Lamb, and a Sallet; d'ee like it?

Crit. I like anything in the World that will indure Cutting: Prithee Mr Cook make haste or expect I shall Storm thy Kitchin.

Sull. Why thou'rt as hungry as if thou hadst been keeping Garrison in Mantua: I don't know whether Flesh and Blood is safe in thy Company.

Crit. I wish with all my Heart thou wert there, that thou mightst understand what it is to fast as I have done: Come, to our Places ... the blessed hour is come. ... Sit, sit ... fall to, Graces are out of Fashion.

Ramb. I wish the Charming Madam Subligny were here.

Crit. Gad so don't I: I had rather her Feet were pegg'd down to the Stage; at present my Appetite stands another way: Waiter, some Wine ... or I shall choak. ...

Sull. This Fellow eats like an Ostrich, the Bones of these great Fish are no more to him than the Bones of an Anchovy; they melt upon his Tongue like marrow Puddings.

Crit. Ay, you may talk, but I'm sure I find 'em not so gentle; here's one yet in my Throat will be my death; the Flask ... the Flask ...,

Ramb. But Critick, how did you like the Play last Night?

Crit. I'll tell you by and by, Lord Sir, you won't give a Man time to break his Fast: This Fish is such washy Meat ... a Man can't fix his knife in 't, it runs away from him as if it were still alive, and was afraid of the Hook: Put the Lamb this way.

Sull. The Rogue quarrels with the Fish, and yet you cou'd eat up the whole Pond; the late Whale at Cuckold's point, with all its oderiferous Garbadge, wou'd ha' been but a Meal to him: Well, how do you like the Lamb? does that feel your knife?

Crit. A little more substantial, and not much: Well, I shou'd certainly be starv'd if I were to feed with the French, I hate their thin slops, their Pottages, Frigaces, and Ragous, where a Man may bury his Hand in the Sauce, and dine upon Steam: No, no, commend me to King Jemmy's English Surloin, in whose gentle Flesh a Man may plunge a Case-knife to the tip of the Handle, and then draw out a Slice that will surfeit half a Score Yeoman of the Guard. Some Wine ye Dog ... there ... now I have slain the Giant; and now to your Question ... what was it you askt me?

Ramb. Won't you stay the Desert? Some Tarts and Cheese?

Crit. I abominate Tarts and Cheese, they're like a faint After-kiss, when a Man is sated with better Sport; there's no more Nourishment in 'em, than in the paring of an Apple. Here Waiter take away. ...

Ramb. Then remove every Thing but the Table-cloth.' ...

Ramb. Here Waiter—send to the Booksellers in Pell mell for the *Generous Conqueror* and make haste ... you say you know the Author Critick.

Crit. By sight I do, but no further; he's a Gentleman of good Extraction, and for ought I know, of good Sense.

Ramb. Surely that's not to be questioned; I take it for granted that a Man that can write a Play, must be a Man of good Sense.

Crit. That is not always a consequence. I have known many a singing Master have a worse voice than a Parish Clerk, and I know two dancing Masters at this time, that are directly Cripples: ... A Ship-builder may fit up a Man of War for the West Indies, and perhaps not know his Compas: Or a great Traveller, with Heylin, that writ the Geography of the whole World, may, like him, not know the way from the next Village to his own House.

Ramb. Your Comparisons are remote Mr Critick.

Crit. Not so remote as some successful Authors are from good sense:

Wit and Sense are no more the same than Wit and Humour; nay there is
even in Wit an uncertain Mode, a variable Fashion, that is as unstable as
the Fashion of our Cloaths : This may be prov'd by their Works who writ
a hundred Years ago, compar'd with some of the modern; Sir Philip Sidney,
Don, Overbury, nay Ben himself took singular delight in playing with their
Words : Sir Philip is everywhere in his Arcadia jugling, which certainly by
the example of so great a Man, proves that sort of Wit then in Fashion ; now
that kind of Wit is call'd Punning and Quibbling, and is become too low for
the Stage, nay even for ordinary Converse ; so that when we find a Man who
still loves that old fashion'd Custom, we make him remarkable, as who is
more remarkable than Capt. Swan.

Ramb. Nay, your Quibble does well now a Days, your best Comedies
tast of 'em ; the *Old Batchelor* is rank.

Crit. But 'tis every Day decreasing, and Queen Betty's Ruff and Fardin-
gale are not more exploded ; But Sense Gentlemen, is and will be the same
to the World's end.

Sull. And Nonsense is infinite, for England never had such a Stock and
such Variety.

Ramb. Yet I have heard the Poets that flourish'd in the last Reign but
two, complain of the same Calamity, and before that Reign the thing was the
same : All Ages have produced Murmurers ; and in the best of times you shall
hear the Trades-man cry—Alas Neighbour ! sad Times, very hard Times ...
not a Penny of Money stirring ... Trade is quite dead, and nothing but War
... War and Taxes ... when to my knowledge the gluttonous Rogue shall
drink his two Bottles at Dinner, and his Wife have half a Score of rich Suits,
a purse of Gold for the Gallant, and fifty Pounds worth of Gold and Silver
Lace on her under Petticoats.

Sull. Nay certainly, this that Ramble now speaks of is a great Truth;
those hypocritical Rogues are always grumbling ; and tho' our Nation never
had such a Trade, or so much Money, yet 'tis all too little for their voracious
Appetites : As I live—says he, I can't afford this Silk one Penny cheaper—
d'ee mind the Rogues Equivocation? as I live—that is, he lives like a Gentleman—but let him live like a Tradesman and be hang'd ; let him wear
a Frock, and his Wife a blew Apron.

Ramb. See, the Book's here : go Waiter and shut the Door.—pp. 76–9.

The dialogue of **Richardson**, 'sounynge in moral vertu', devoid of all
the lighter touches, is typical of the age that was beginning, the age of
reaction against the levities and negligences in speech and conduct
of the seventeenth and early eighteenth centuries.

The following conversation of rather an agitated character, between
a mother and daughter, is from Letter XVI, in *Clarissa Harlowe* (1748):

'. . . My mother came up to me. I love, she was pleased to say, to come
into *this* appartment.—No emotions child ! No flutters !—Am I not your
mother ?—Am I not your fond, your indulgent mother ?—Do not discompose
me by discomposing *yourself* ! Do not occasion *me* uneasiness, when I would
give *you* nothing but pleasure. Come my dear, we will go into your closet. . . .
Hear me out and then speak ; for I was going to expostulate. You are no
stranger to the end of Mr Solmes's visits—O Madam !—Hear me out ;
and then speak.—He is not indeed everything I wish him to be : but he is
a man of probity and has no vices—No vices Madam !—Hear me out child.—
You have not behaved much amiss to him : we have seen with pleasure that
you have not—O Madam, must I not now speak ! I shall have done presently.
—A young creature of your virtuous and *pious* turn, she was pleased to say,
cannot surely love a proflicate ; you love your brother too well, to wish to see
any one who had like to have killed him, and who threatened your uncles
and defies us all. You have had your own way six or seven times : we want

to secure you against a man so vile. Tell me (I have a *right* to know) whether you prefer this man to all others?—Yet God forbid that I should know you do; for such a declaration would make us all miserable. Yet tell me, are your affections engaged to this man?

I know what the inference would be if I had said they were not. You hesitate—You answer me not—You cannot answer me—*Rising*—Nevermore will I look upon you with an eye of favour—O Madam, Madam! Kill me not with your displeasure—I would not, I *need* not, hesitate one moment, did I not dread the inference, if I answer you as you wish.—Yet be that inference what it will, your threatened displeasure will make me speak. And I declare to you, that I know not my own heart if it be not absolutely free. And pray, let me ask my dearest Mamma, in what has my conduct been faulty, that like a giddy creature, I must be forced to marry, to save me from—from what? Let me beseech you Madam to be the Guardian of my reputation! Let not your Clarissa be precipitated into a state she wishes not to enter into with any man! And this upon a supposition that otherwise she shall marry herself, and disgrace her whole family.

When then, Clary [passing over the force of my plea] if your heart be free—O my beloved Mamma, let the usual generosity of your dear heart operate in my favour. Urge not upon me the inference that made me hesitate.

I won't be interrupted, Clary—You have seen in my behaviour to you, on this occasion, a truly maternal tenderness; you have observed that I have undertaken the task with some reluctance, because the man is not everything; and because I know you carry your notions of perfection in a man too high.—Dearest Madam, this one time excuse me! Is there then any danger that I should be guilty of an imprudent thing for the man's sake you hint at? Again interrupted! Am I to be questioned, and argued with? You know this won't do somewhere else. You *know* it won't. What reason then, ungenerous girl, can you have for arguing with me thus, but because you think from my indulgence to you you may?

What *can* I say? What *can* I do? What must that cause be that will not bear being argued upon?

Again! Clary Harlowe—

Dearest Madam forgive me: it was always my pride and my pleasure to obey you. But look upon that man—see but the disagreeableness of his person—Now, Clary, do I see whose person you have in your eye!—Now is Mᵣ Solmes, I see, but *comparatively* disagreeable; disagreeable only as another man has a much more specious person.

But, Madam, are not his manners equally so?—Is not his person the true representation of his mind?—That other man is not, shall not be, anything to me, release me from this one man, whom my heart, unbidden, resists.

Condition thus with your father. Will he bear, do you think, to be thus dialogued with? Have I not conjured you, as you value my peace—What is it that *I* do not give up?—This very task, because I apprehended you would not be *easily* persuaded, is a task *indeed* upon me. And will *you* give up nothing? Have you not refused as many as have been offered to you? If you would not have us guess for whom, comply; for comply you must, or be looked upon as in a state of defiance with your whole family. And saying thus she arose, and went from me.'

Miss Austen.

The following examples of Miss Austen's dialogue are not selected because they are the most sparkling conversations in her works, but rather because they appear to be typical of the way of speech of the period, and further they illustrate Miss Austen's incomparable art. The first passage is from *Emma*, which was written between 1811 and

1816. Mr. Woodhouse and his daughter have just received an invitation to dine with the Coles, enriched tradespeople who had settled in the neighbourhood. Emma's view of them was that they were 'very respectable in their way, but they ought to be taught that it was not for them to arrange the times on which the superior families would visit them'. On the present occasion, however, 'she was not absolutely without inclination for the party. The Coles expressed themselves so properly—there was so much real attention in the manner of it—so much consideration for her father.' Emma having decided in her own mind to accept the invitation—some of her intimate friends were going—it remained to explain to her father, the ailing and fussy Mr. Woodhouse, that he would be left alone without his daughter's company for the evening, as it was out of the question that he should accompany her. 'He was soon pretty well resigned.'

'" I am not fond of dinner-visiting" said he; "I never was. No more is Emma. Late hours do not agree with us. I am sorry M^r and Mrs Cole should have done it. I think it would be much better if they would come in one afternoon next summer and take their tea with us; take us in their afternoon walk, which they might do, as our hours are so reasonable, and yet get home without being out in the damp of the evening. The dews of a summer evening are what I would not expose anybody to. However as they are so very desirous to have dear Emma dine with them, and as you will both be there [this refers to his friend Mr Weston and his wife], and Mr Knightley too, to take care of her I cannot wish to prevent it, provided the weather be what it ought, neither damp, nor cold, nor windy." Then turning to Mrs Weston with a look of gentle reproach—"Ah, Miss Taylor, if you had not married, you would have staied at home with me."

"Well, Sir ", cried Mr Weston, "as I took Miss Taylor away, it is incumbent upon me to supply her place, if I can; and I will step to Mrs Goddard in a moment if you wish it." . . . With this treatment Mr Woodhouse was soon composed enough for talking as usual. "He should be happy to see Mrs Goddard. He had a great regard for Mrs Goddard; and Emma should write a line and invite her. James could take the note. But first there must be an answer written to Mrs Cole."

"You will make my excuses, my dear, as civilly as possible. You will say that I am quite an invalid, and go nowhere, and therefore must decline their obliging invitation; beginning with my *compliments*, of course. But you will do everything right. I need not tell you what is to be done. We must remember to let James know that the carriage will be wanted on Tuesday. I shall have no fears for you with him. We have never been there above once since the new approach was made; but still I have no doubt that James will take you very safely; and when you get there you must tell him at what time you would have him come for you again; and you had better name an early hour. You will not like staying late. You will get tired when tea is over."

"But you would not wish me to come away before I am tired, papa?"

"Oh no my love; but you will soon be tired. There will be a great many people talking at once. You will not like the noise."

"But my dear Sir," cried Mr Weston, "if Emma comes away early, it will be breaking up the party."

"And no great harm if it does" said Mr Woodhouse. "The sooner every party breaks up the better."

"But you do not consider how it may appear to the Coles. Emma's going away directly after tea might be giving offense. They are good-natured people, and think little of their own claims; but still they must feel that anybody's hurrying away is no great compliment; and Miss Woodhouse's

doing it would be more thought of than any other person's in the room.
You would not wish to disappoint and mortify the Coles, I am sure, sir;
friendly, good sort of people as ever lived, and who have been your neighbours
these *ten* years."

"No, upon no account in the world, Mr Weston, I am much obliged to
you for reminding me. I should be extremely sorry to be giving them any
pain. I know what worthy people they are. Perry tells me that Mr Cole
never touches malt liquor. You would not think it to look at him, but he is
bilious—Mr Cole is very bilious. No, I would not be the means of giving
them any pain. My dear Emma we must consider this. I am sure rather
than run any risk of hurting M^r and Mrs Cole you would stay a little longer
than you might wish. You will not regard being tired. You will be perfectly
safe, you know, among your friends.'

"Oh yes, papa. I have no fears at all for myself; and I should have no
scruples of staying as late as Mrs Weston, but on your account. I am only
afraid of your sitting up for me. I am not afraid of your not being exceedingly comfortable with Mrs Goddard. She loves piquet, you know; but
when she is gone home I am afraid you will be sitting up by yourself, instead
of going to bed at your usual time ; and the idea of that would entirely
destroy my comfort. You must promise me not to sit up." '

The next example is in a very different vein. It is from *Sense and
Sensibility* (chap. xxi) and records the mode of conversation of the
Miss Steeles. These two ladies are among Miss Austen's vulgar
characters, and their speech lacks the restraint and decorum which he
better-bred personages invariably exhibit. While the Miss Steeles' conversation is in sharp contrast with that of the Miss Dashwoods, with
whom they are here engaged, both in substance and manner, it evidently
passed muster among many of the associates of the latter, especially with
their cousin Sir John Middleton, in whose house, as relations of his
wife's, the Miss Steeles are staying. Apart from the vulgarity of thought,
the diction appears low when compared with that of most of Miss Austen's
characters. As a matter of fact it is largely the way of speech of the
better society of an earlier age, which has come down in the world, and
survives among a pretentious provincial bourgeoisie.

'"What a sweet woman Lady Middleton is " said Lucy Steele . . . "And
Sir John too" cried the elder sister, "what a charming man he is!" . . .
"And what a charming little family they have ! I never saw such fine children
in my life. I declare I quite doat upon them already, and indeed I am
always destractedly fond of children." "I should guess so" said Elinor
with a smile "from what I witnessed this morning."

"I have a notion" said Lucy, "you think the little Middletons rather too
much indulged ; perhaps they may be the outside of enough ; but it is natural
in Lady Middleton ; and for my part I love to see children full of life and
spirits ; I cannot bear them if they are tame and quiet."

"I confess" replied Elinor, "that while I am at Barton Park, I never
think of tame and quiet children with any abhorrence." '

.   .   .   .

"And how do you like Devonshire, Miss Dashwood? (said Miss Steele)
I suppose you were very sorry to leave Sussex."

In some surprise at the familiarity of this question, or at least in the
manner in which it was spoken, Elinor replied that she was.

"Norland is a prodigious beautiful place, is not it?" added Miss Steele.

"We have heard Sir John admire it excessively," said Lucy, who seemed
to think some apology necessary for the freedom of her sister. "I think

every one *must* admire it" replied Elinor, "who ever saw the place; though it is not to be supposed that any one can estimate its beauties as we do."

"And had you many smart beaux there? I suppose you have not so many in this part of the world; for my part I think they are a vast addition always."

"But why should you think" said Lucy, looking ashamed of her sister, "that there are not as many genteel young men in Devonshire as Sussex."

"Nay, my dear, I'm sure I don't pretend to say that there an't. I'm sure there's a vast many smart beaux in Exeter; but you know, how could I tell what smart beaux there might be about Norland? and I was only afraid the Miss Dashwoods might find it dull at Barton; if they had not so many as they used to have. But perhaps you young ladies may not care about beaux, and had as lief be without them as with them. For my part, I think they are vastly agreeable, provided they dress smart and behave civil. But I can't bear to see them dirty and nasty. Now, there's Mr Rose at Exeter, a prodigious smart young man, quite a beau, clerk to Mr Simpson, you know, and yet if you do but meet him of a morning, he is not fit to be seen. I suppose your brother was quite a beau, Miss Dashwood, before he married, as he was so rich?"

"Upon my word," replied Elinor, "I cannot tell you, for I do not perfectly comprehend the meaning of the word. But this I can say, that if he ever was a beau before he married, he is one still, for there is not the smallest alteration in him."

"Oh! dear! one never thinks of married men's being beaux—they have something else to do."

"Lord! Anne", cried her sister, "you can talk of nothing but beaux;—you will make Miss Dashwood believe you think of nothing else."'

It is not surprising that '"this specimen of the Miss Steeles" was enough. The vulgar freedom and folly of the eldest left her no recommendation and as Elinor was not blinded by the beauty, or the shrewd look of the youngest, to her want of real elegance and artlessness, she left the house without any wish of knowing them better'.

Greetings and Farewells.

Only the slightest indication can be given of the various modes of greeting and bidding farewell. These seem to have been very numerous, and less stereotyped in the fifteenth and sixteenth centuries than at present. It is not easy to be sure how soon the formulas which we now employ, or their ancestral forms, came into current use. The same form often serves both at meeting and parting.

In 1451, Agnes Paston records, in a letter, that 'after evynsonge, Angnes Ball com to me to my closett and *bad me good evyn*'. In the account, quoted above, p. 362, given by Shillingford of his meetings with the Chancellor, about 1447, he speaks of 'saluting hym yn the moste godely wyse that y coude' but does not tell us the form he used. The Chancellor, however, replies '*Welcome*, ij times, and the iij^de tyme "*Right wel come Mayer*", and helde the Mayer a grete while faste by the honde'.

In the sixteenth century a great deal of ceremonial embracing and kissing was in vogue. Wolsey and the King of France, according to Cavendish, rode forward to meet each other, and they embraced each other on horseback. Cavendish himself when he visits the castle of the Lord of Crépin, a great nobleman, in order to prepare a lodging for the Cardinal, is met by this great personage, who 'at his first coming embraced me, saying I was right heartily welcome'. Henry VIII was wont to walk with Sir Thomas More, 'with his arm about his neck'. The actual formula used in greeting and leave-taking is too often unrecorded. When the French Embassy departs from England, whom Wolsey has so splendidly entertained, Cavendish says—'My lord, after humble commendations had to the French King bade them adieu'. The Earl of Shrewsbury greets the Cardinal thus—'My Lord, your Grace is most heartily welcome unto me', and Wolsey replies 'Ah my gentle Lord of Shrewsbury, I heartily thank you'.

It is not until the appearance of plays that we find the actual forms of greeting recorded with frequency. In Roister Doister, there are a fair number :—*God keepe thee* worshipful Master Roister Doister ; Welcome my good wenche ; *God you saue and see* Nourse ; and the reply to this— Welcome friend Merrygreeke ; *Good night* Roger old knaue, *farewell* Roger old knaue ; *well met, I bid you right welcome.* A very favourite greeting is *God be with you.*

God continue your Lordship is a form of farewell in Chapman's Monsieur D'Olive, and *God-den* 'good evening', occurs in Middleton's Chaste Maid in Cheapside. Sir Walter Whorehound in the same play makes use of the formula '*I embrace your acquaintance Sir*', to which the reply is '*It vows your service Sir*'. Massinger's New Way to pay old Debts contains various formulas of greeting. *I am still your creature,* says Allworth to his step-mother Lady A. on taking leave ; of two old domestics he takes leave with '*my service to both*', and they reply '*ours waits on you*'. In reply to the simple *Farewell Tom,* of a friend, Allworth answers '*All joy stay with you*'. Sir Giles Overreach greets Lord Lovel with '*Good day to My Lord*' ; and the prototype of the modern *how are you* is seen in Lady Allworth's '*How dost thou Marrall?*' A graceful greeting in this play is '*You are happily encountered*'.

The later seventeenth-century comedies exhibit the characteristic urbanity of the age in their formulas of greeting and leave-taking.

'*A happy day to you Madam*', is Victoria's morning compliment to Mrs. Goodvile in Otway's Friendship in Fashion, and that lady replies— '*Dear Cousin, your humble servant*'. Sir Wilfull Witwoud in Congreve's Way of the World, says '*Save you Gentleman and Lady*' on entering a room. His younger brother, on meeting him, greets him with '*Your servant Brother*', and the knight replies '*Your servant! Why yours Sir, Your servant again ; 's heart, and your Friend and Servant to that*'. *I'm everlastingly your humble servant, deuce take me Madam,* says Mr. Brisk to Lady Froth, in the Double Dealer.

Your servant is a very usual formula at this period, on joining or leaving company. In Vanbrugh's Journey to London, Colonel Courtly on entering is greeted by Lady Headpiece—*Colonel your servant*; her daughter Miss Betty varies it with—*Your servant Colonel,* and the visitor replies to both—*Ladies, your most obedient.*

Mr. Trim, the formal coxcomb in Shadwell's Bury Fair, parts thus from his friends—*Sir, I kiss your hands* ; Mr. Wildish—*Sir your most humble servant*; Trim—*Mr Oldwit I am your most faithful servant*; Mr. Oldwit—*Your servant sweet Mr Trim.*

Your servant, madam good morrow to you, is Lady Arabella's greeting to Lady Headpiece, who replies—*And to you Madam* (Vanbrugh's Journey to London). The early eighteenth century appears not to differ materially from the preceding in its usage. Lord Formal in Fielding's Love in Several Masques, says *Ladies your most humble servant,* and Sir Apish in the same play—*Your Ladyship's everlasting creature.*

Epistolary Formulas.

The writing of letters, both familiar and formal, is such an inevitable part of everyday life, that it seems legitimate to include here some examples of the various methods of beginning and ending private letters from the early fifteenth century onwards. A proper and exhaustive treatment of the subject would demand a rather elaborate classification, according to the rank and status of both the writer and the recipient, and the relation in which they stood to each other—whether master and servant, or dependant, friend, subject, child, spouse, and so on. In the comparatively few examples here given, out of many thousands, nothing is attempted beyond a chronological arrangement. The status and relationship of the parties is, however, given as far as possible. We note that the formula employed is frequently a conventional and more or less fixed phrase which recurs, with slight variants, again and again. At other times the opening and closing phrases are of a more personal and individual character.

1418. *Archbp. Chichele to Hen. V.* Signs simply: your preest and bedeman.—Ellis, i. I. 5.

1425. *Will. Paston to* ——. Right worthy and worshepfull Sir. I recommaunde me to you, &c. Ends: Almyghty God have you in his governaunce. Your frend unknowen.—Past. Letters, i. 19-20.

1440. *Agnes to Will. Paston.* Inscribed: To my worshepful housbond W. Paston be this letter takyn. Dere housbond I reccommaunde me to yow. Ends: The Holy Trinite have you in governaunce.—P. L. i. 38-9.

1442-5. *Duke of Buckingham to Lord Beaumont.* Ryght worshipful and with all my herte right enterly beloved brother, I recomaunde me to you, thenking right hastili your good brotherhode for your gode and gentill letters. I beseche the blissid Trinite preserve you in honor and prosperite. Your trewe and feithfull broder H. Bukingham.—P. L. i. 61-2.

1443. *Margaret to John Paston.* Ryth worchipful husbon, I reccomande me to yow desyryng hertely to her of your wilfar. Almyth God have you in his kepyn and sende yow helth, Yorys M. Paston.—P. L. i. 48-9.

1444. *James Gresham to Will. Paston.* Please it your good Lordship to wete, &c. Ends: Wretyn right simply the Wednesday next to fore the Fest. By your most symple servaunt.—P. L. i. 50.

1444. *Duchess of Norfolk to J. Paston.* Ryght trusty and entirely welbeloved we grete you wel hertily as we kan . . . and siche agrement as, &c. . . . we shall duely performe yt with the myght of Jesu who haff you in his blissed keping.—P. L. i. 57.

1444. *Sir R. Chamberlayn to Agn. Paston.* Ryght worchepful cosyn, I comand me to you. And I beseche almyty God kepe you. Your Cosyn Sir Roger Chamberlain.

1445. *Agnes to Edm. Paston.* To myn welbelovid sone. I grete you wel. Be your Modre Angnes Paston.—i. 58, 59.

1449. *Marg. to John Paston.* Wretyn at Norwych in hast, Be your gronyng Wyff.—i. 76-7.

1449. *Same to same.* No mor I wryte to ʒow atte this tyme. Your Markaryte Paston.—i. 42-3.

1449. *Will. to John Paston.* Ends: Be ʒowre pore Broder.

1449. *Eliz. Clare to J. Paston.* No more I wrighte to ʒow at this tyme, but Holy Gost have ʒow in kepyng. Wretyn in haste on Seynt Peterys day be candel lyght, Be your Cosyn E. C.—P. L. i. 89-90.

1450. *Duke of Suffolk to his son.* My dear and only welbeloved sone. Your trewe and lovynge fader Suffolk.—P. L. i. 121-2.

1450. *Will. Lomme to J. Paston.* I prey you this bille may recomaunde me to mastrases your moder and wyfe. Wretyn yn gret hast at London.— P. L. i. 126.

1450. *J. Gresham to 'my Maister Whyte Esquyer'.* After due recomendacion I recomaund me to yow.

1450. *J. Paston to above.* James Gresham, I pray you labour for the, &c. —i. 145.

1450. *Justice Yelverton to Sir J. Fastolf.* By your old Servaunt William Yelverton Justice.—P. L. i. 166.

1453. *Agnes to J. Paston.* Sone I grete you well and send you Godys blessyng and myn. Wretyn at Norwych . . . in gret hast, Be your moder A. Paston.—P. L. i. 259.

1454. *J. Paston to Earl of Oxford.* Youre servaunte to his powr John Paston.—P. L. i. 276.

1454. *Lord Scales to J. Paston.* Our Lord have you in governaunce. Your frend The Lord Scales.—P. L. i. 289.

1454. *Thomas Howes to J. Paston.* I pray God kepe yow. Wryt at Castr hastly ij day of September, Your owne T. Howes.—P. L. i. 301.

1454. *The same.* Your chapleyn and bedeman Thomas Howes.—i. 318.

1455. *Sir J. Fastolf to Duke of Norfolk.* Writen at my pore place of Castre, Your humble man and servaunt.—P. L. i. 324.

1455. *J. Cudworth, Bp. of Lincoln, to J. Paston.* And Jesu preserve you, J. Bysshopp of Lincoln.—P. L. i. 350.

1456. *Archbp. Bourchier to Sir J. Fastolf.* The blissid Trinitee have you everlastingly in His keping, Written in my manoir of Lamehith, Your feithfull and trew Th. Cant.—P. L. i. 382.

1456 (Nephew to uncle). *H. Fylinglay to Sir J. Fastolf.* Ryght worshipful unkell and my ryght good master, I recommaund me to yow wyth all my servys. And Sir, my brother Paston and I have, &c. . . . Your nevew and servaunt.—P. L. i. 397.

1458. *John Jerningham to Marg. Paston.* Nomor I wryte unto you at this tyme. . . . Your owne umble servant and cosyn J. J.—P. L. i. 429.

1458 (Daughter to her mother). *Eliz. Poynings to Agn. Paston.* Right worshipful and my most entierly belovde moder, in the most lowly maner I recomaund me unto your gode moderhode. . . . And Jesu for his grete mercy save yow. By your humble daughter.—P. L. i. 434-5.

1469. *Chancellor and University of Oxford to Sir John Say.* Ryght worshipful our trusty and entierly welbeloued, after harty commendacyon. . . . Ends: yoͬ trew and harty louers The Chancellr and Thuniversite of Oxonford.—Ellis.

1477. *John Paston to his mother.* Your sone and humbyll servaunt P.— P. L. iii. 176.

1481-4. *Edm. Paston to his mother.* ʒour umble son and servant.— P. L. iii. 280.

1482. *J. Paston to his mother.* Your sone and trwest servaunt.—P. L. iii. 290.

1482. *Margery Paston to her husband.* No more to you at this tyme, Be your servaunt and bedewoman.— iii. 293.

1485. *Duke of Norfolk to J. Paston.* Welbelovyd frend I cummaund me to yow. . . . I shall content you at your metyng with me, Yower lover J. Norfolk.—iii. 320.

1485. *Eliz. Browne to J. Paston.* Your loving awnte E. B.

1485. *Duke of Suffolk to J. Paston.* Ryght welbeloved we grete you well. . . . Suffolk, yor frende.—iii. 324-5.

1490. *Bp. of Durham to Sir John Paston.* IHΣ. Xρς. Ryght wortchipful sire, and myne especial and of long tyme apprevyd, trusty and feythful frende, I in myne hertyeste wyse recommaunde me un to you. . . . Scribyllyd in the moste haste, at my castel or manoir of Aucland the xxvij of Januay. Your own trewe luffer and frende John Duresme.—iii. 363.

1490. *Lumen Haryson to Sir J. Paston.* Onerabyll and well be lovyd Knythe, I commend me on to ȝour masterchepe and to my lady ȝowyr wyffe. . . . No mor than God be wyth ȝow, L. H. at ȝouyr comawndment.

1503. *Q. Margaret of Scotland to her father Hen. VII.* My moste dere lorde and fader in the most humble wyse that I can thynke I recommaunde me unto your Grace besechyng you off your dayly blessyngys. . . . Wrytyn wyt the hand of your humble douter Margaret.—Ellis i. 1. 43.

Hen. VII to his Mother, the Countess of Richmond. Madam, my most enterely wilbeloved Lady and moder . . . with the hande of youre most humble and lovynge sone.—Ellis, i. 1. 43-5.

Margaret to Hen. VII. My oune suet and most deare kynge and all my worldly joy, yn as humble manner as y can thynke I recommand me to your Grace . . . by your feythful and trewe bedewoman, and humble modyr Margaret R.—Ellis, i. 1. 46.

1513. *Q. Margaret of Scotland to Hen. VIII.* Richt excellent, richt hie and mithy Prince, our derrist and best belovit Brothir. . . . Your louyn systar Margaret.—Ellis, i. 1. 65. (The Queen evidently employed a Scottish Secretary.)

1515. *Margaret to Wolsey.* Yours Margaret R.—Ellis, i. 1. 131.

1515. *Thos. Lord Howard, Lord Admiral, to Wolsey.* My owne gode Master Awlmosner. . . . Scrybeled in gret hast in the Mary Rose at Plymouth half o^r after xj at night . . . y^r own Thomas Howard.

c. **1515.** *West Bp. of Ely to Wolsey.* Myne especiall good Lorde in my most humble wise I recommaund me to your Grace besechyng you to contynue my gode Lorde, and I schall euer be as I am bounden your dayly bedeman. . . . Y^r chapelayn and bedman N I. Elien.

c. **1520.** *Archbp. Warham to Wolsey.* Please it yor moost honorable Grace to understand. . . . At your Graces commaundement, Willm. Cantuar.— Ellis, iii. 1. 230. Also : Euer, your own Willm. Cantuar.

Langland Bp. of Lincoln to Wolsey. My bownden duety mooste lowly remembrede unto Your good Grace. . . . Yo^r moste humble bedisman John Lincoln.—Ellis, iii. 1. 248.

Cath. of Aragon to Princess Mary. Doughter, I pray you thinke not, &c. —Ellis, i. 2. 19. . . . Your lovyng mother Katherine the Quene.

Archibald, E. of Angus. Addresses letter to Wolsey : To my lord Cardinallis grace of Ingland.—Ellis, iii. 1. 291.

1521. *Bp. Tunstal to Wolsey.* Addresses letter :—to the most reverend fader in God and his most singler good Lorde Cardinal.—Ellis, iii. 1. 273. Ends a letter : By your Gracys most humble bedeman Cuthbert Tunstall. —Ellis, iii. 1. 332.

1515 or 1521. *Duke of Buckingham to Wolsey.* Yorys to my power E. Bukynghain.

Gavin Douglas, Bp. of Dunkeld, to Wolsey. Zo^r chaplan wy^t his lawfull seruyse Gavin bischop of Dunkeld.—Ellis, iii. 1. 294. Zo^r humble servytor and Chaplein of Dunkeld.—Ellis, iii. 1. 296. Zo^r humble seruytor and dolorous Chaplan of Dunkeld.—Ellis, iii. 1. 303.

Wolsey to Gardiner (afterwards Bp. of Winchester). Ends : Your assurjd lover and bedysman T. Car^lis Ebor.—Ellis, i. 2. 6. Again: Wryttyn hastely at Asher with the rude and shackyng hand of your dayly bedysman and assuryd frende T. Car^lis Ebor.

1532. *Thos. Audley (Lord Keeper) to Cromwell.* Yo^r assured to his litell po^r Thomas Audeley Custos Sigilli.

Edw. E. of Hertford (afterwards Lord Protector). Thus I comit you to God hoo send yor lordshep as well to far as I would mi selfe . . . w^t the hand of yor lordshepis assured E. Hertford.

Hen. VIII to Catherine Parr. No more to you at thys tyme swethart both for lacke off tyme and gret occupation off bysynes, savyng we pray you in our name our harte blessyngs to all our chyldren, and recommendations to our cousin Marget and the rest off the laddis and gentyll women and to our Consell alsoo. Wryttyn with the hand off your lovyng howsbande Henry R. —Ellis, i. 2. 130.

Princess Mary to Cromwell. Marye Princesse. Maister Cromwell I commende me to you.—Ellis, i. 2. 24.

Prince Edward to Catherine Parr. Most honorable and entirely beloued mother. . . . Your Grace, whom God have ever in his most blessed keping. Your louing sonne, E. Prince.—Ellis, i. 2. 131.

1547. *Henry Radclyf, E. of Sussex, to his wife.* Madame with most lovyng and hertie commendations.—Ellis, i. 2. 137.

Princess Elizabeth to Edw. VI. Your Maiesties humble sistar to com- maundement Elizabeth.—Ellis, i. 2. 146; Your Maiesties most humble sistar Elizabeth.—Ellis, i. 1. 148.

Princess Elizabeth to Lord Protector. Your assured frende to my litel power Elizabeth.—Ellis, i. 2. 158.

Edward VI to Lord Protector Somerset. Derest Uncle. . . . Your good neuew Edward.—Ellis, ii. 1. 148.

Q. Mary to Lord Admiral Seymour. Your assured frende to my power Marye.—Ellis, i. 2. 153.

Princess Elizabeth to Q. Mary (on being ordered to the Tower). Your Highnes most faithful subjec that hath bine from the begining and wyl be to my ende, Elizabeth. (Transcr. of 1732).—Ellis, ii. 2. 257.

1553. *Princess Elizabeth to the Lords of the Council.* Your verye lovinge frende, Elizabeth.—Ellis, ii. 2. 213.

1554. *Henry Darnley to Q. Mary of England.* Your Maiesties moste bounden and obedient subjecte and servant Henry Darnley.

Queen Dowager to Lord Admiral Seymour. By her y^t ys and schalbe your humble true and lovyng wyffe duryng her lyf Kateryn the Quene.—Ellis, i. 2. 152.

Q. Mary to Marquis of Winchester. Your Mystresse assured Marye the Quene.—Ellis, ii. 2. 252.

Sir John Grey of Pyrgo to Sir William Cecil. It is a great while me thinkethe, Cowsine Cecill, since I sent unto you. . . . By your lovyng cousin and assured frynd John Grey.—Ellis, ii. 2. 73–4; Good cowsyne Cecill. . . . By yor lovyng Cousine and assured pouer frynd dowring lyfe John Grey.— Ellis, ii. 2. 276.

Lady Catherine Grey, Countess of Hertford, to Sir W. Cecil. Good cosyne Cecill. . . . Your assured frend and cosyne to my small power Katheryne Hartford.—Ellis, ii. 2. 278; Your poore cousyne and assured frend to my small power Katheryne Hartford.—Ellis, ii. 2. 287.

1564. *Sir W. Cecil to Sir Thos. Smith.* Your assured for ever W. Cecill. —Ellis, ii. 2. 295; Yours assured W. Cecill.—Ellis, ii. 2. 297; Your assured to command W. Cecill.—Ellis, ii. 2. 300.

1566. *Duchess of Somerset to Sir W. Cecil.* Good Mr Secretary, yf I have let you alone all thys whyle I pray you to thynke yt was to tary for my L. of Leycesters assistans. . . . I can nomore . . . and so do leave you to God Yo^r assured lovyng frynd Anne Somerset.—Ellis, ii. 2. 288.

Christopher Jonson, Master of Winchester, to Sir W. Cecil. Right honourable my duetie with all humblenesse consydered. . . . Your honoures most due to commande, Christopher Jonson.—Ellis, ii. 2. 313.

1569. *Lady Stanhope to Sir W. Cecil.* Right honorable, my humble dewtie premised. . . . Your honors most humblie bound Anne Stanhope.—Ellis, ii. 2. 324.

1574. *Sir Philip Sidney to the E. of Leicester.* Righte Honorable and my singular good Lorde and Uncle. . . . Your L. most obedi. . . . Philip Sidney.—Works, p. 345.

1576. *Sir Philip Sidney to Sir Francis Walsingham.* Righte Honorable . . . I most humbly recommende my selfe unto yow, and leaue yow to the Eternals most happy protection. . . . Yours humbly at commawndement Philipp Sidney.

1578. *Sir Philip Sidney to Edward Molineux, Esq.* (Secretary to Sir H. Sidney). Mr Molineux, Few words are best. My letters to my father have come to the eyes of some. Neither can I condemn any but you. . . . (The writer assures M. that if he reads any letter of his to his father 'without his commandment or my consent, I will thrust my dagger into you. And trust to it, for I speak it in earnest'. . . .) In the meantime farewell. From court this last of May 1578, By me Philip Sidney.—p. 328.

1580. *Sir Philip Sidney to his brother Robert.* My dear Brother . . . God bless you sweet boy and accomplish the joyful hope I conceive of you. . . . Lord! how I have babbled: once again farewell dearest brother. Your most loving and careful brother Philip Sidney.

1582. *Thomas Watson ' To the frendly Reader'* (in Passionate Centurie 'To Love). Courteous Reader . . . and so, for breuitie sake (I) aprubtlie make and end ; committing the to God, and my worke to thy fauour. Thine as thou art his, Thomas Watson.

Anne of Denmark to James I. Sir . . . So kissing your handes I remain she that will ever love Yow best, Anna R.—Ellis, i. 3. 97.

c. 1585. *Sir Philip to Walsingham.* Sir . . . your louing cosin and frend. In several letters to Walsingham Sidney signs 'your humble Son'.

1586. *Wm. Webbe to Ma.* (= 'Master') *Edward Sulyard Esquire* (Dedicatory Epistle to the Discourse of English Poetrie). May it please you Syr, thys once more to beare with my rudenes, &c. . . . I rest, Your worshippes faithfull Seruant W. W.

1593. *Edward Alleyn to his wife.* My good sweete mouse . . . and so swett mouse farwell.—Mem. of Edw. Alleyn, i. 36 ; my good sweetharte and loving mouse . . . thyn ever and no bodies else by god of heaven.—ibid.

1596. *Thos., Lord Buckhurst, afterwards Earl of Dorset, to Sir Robert Cecil.* Sir . . . Your very lo: frend T. Buckhurst.

1597. *Sir W. Raleigh to Cecil.* Sr I humblie thanke yow for your letter . . . Sr I pray love vs in your element and wee will love and honor yow in ours and every wher. And remayne to be comanded by yow for evermore W Ralegh.

1602. *Same to same.* Good Mr Secretary. . . . Thus. I rest, your very loving and assured frend T. Buckhurst.—Works, xxxiv-xi.

1603. *Same to same.* My very good Lord. . . . So I rest as you know, Ever yours T. Buckurst.

1605. *Same to same.* . . . I pray God for your health and for mine own and so rest Ever yours . . .

1607. *Same to the University of Oxford.* Your very loving friend and Chancellor T. Dorset.—xlvi.

c. 1608. *Sir Henry Wotton to Henry Prince of Wales.* Youre zealous poore servant H. W.—Ellis, i. 3. 100.

Q. Anne of Denmark to Sir George Villiers (afterwards Duke of Buckingham). My kind Dog. . . . So wishing you all happiness Anna R.—Ellis, i. 3. 100.

1611. *Charles Duke of York to Prince Henry.* Most loving Brother I long to see you. . . . Your H. most loving brother and obedient servant, Charles.—Ellis, i. 3. 96.

1612. *Prince Charles to James I.* Your M^{ties} most humble and most obedient sone and servant Charles.—Ellis, i. 3. 102.

Same to Villiers. Steenie, There is none that knowes me so well as yourself. . . . Your treu and constant loving frend Charles P.—Ellis, i. 3. 104.

King James to Buckingham or to Prince Charles. My onlie sweete and deare chylde I pray thee haiste thee home to thy deare dade by sunne setting at the furthest.—Ellis, i. 3. 120.

Same to Buckingham. My Steenie. . . . Your dear dade, gosseppe and stewarde.—Ellis, i. 3. 159.

Same to both. Sweet Boyes. . . . God blesse you both my sweete babes, and sende you a safe and happie returne, James R.—Ellis, i. 3. 121.

Prince Charles and Buckingham to James. Your Majesties most humble and obedient sone and servant Charles, and your humble slave and doge Steenie.—Ellis, i. 3. 122.

1623. *Buckingham to James.* Dere Dad, Gossope and Steward. . . . Your Majestyes most humble slave and doge Steenie.—Ellis, i. 3. 146-7.

1623. *Lord Herbert to James.* Your Sacred Majesties most obedient, most loyal, and most affectionate subjecte and servant, E. Herbert.

The letters of Sir John Suckling (Works, ii, Reeves & Turner) are mostly undated, but one to Davenant has the date 1629, and another to Sir Henry Vane that of 1632.

The general style is more modern in tone than those of any of the letters so far referred to. (See on Suckling's style, pp. 152-3.) The beginnings and endings, too, closely resemble and are sometimes identical with those of our own time.

To Davenant, Vane, and several other persons of both sexes, Suckling signs simply—'Your humble servant J. S.', or 'J. Suckling'. At least two, to a lady, end 'Your humblest servant'. The letter to Davenant begins 'Will'; that to Vane—'Right Honorable'. Several letters begin 'Madam', 'My Lord', one begins 'My noble friend', another 'My Noble Lord', several simply 'Sir'. The more fanciful letters, to Aglaura, begin 'Dear Princess', 'Fair Princess', 'My dear Dear', 'When I consider, my dear Princess', &c. One to a cousin begins 'Honest Charles'.

The habit of rounding off the concluding sentence of a letter so that the valedictory formula and the writer's name form an organic part of it, a habit very common in the eighteenth century—in Miss Burney, for instance—is found in Suckling's letters. For example : 'I am still the humble servant of my Lord —— that I was, and when I cease to be so, I must cease to be John Suckling'; 'yet could never think myself unfortunate, while I can write myself Aglaura her humble servant'; 'and should you leave that lodging, more wretched than Montferrat needs must be your humble servant J. S.', and so on.

The longwindedness and prolixity which generally distinguish the openings and closings of letters of the fifteenth and the greater part of the sixteenth century, begin to disappear before the end of the latter period. Suckling is as neat and concise as the letter-writers of the eighteenth century. 'Madam, your most humble and faithful servant' might serve for Dr. Johnson.

Most of our modern formulas were in use before the end of the first half of the seventeenth century, though some of the older phrases still survive. But we no longer find 'I commend me unto your good mastership, beseeching the Blessed Trinity to have you in his governance', and such-like lengthy introductions. The Correspondence of Dr. Basire (see pp. 163-4) is very instructive, as it covers the period from 1634 to 1675, by which latter date letters have practically reached their modern form. Dr. Basire writes in 1635-6 to Miss Frances Corbet, his fiancée, 'Deare Fanny', 'Deare Love ', ' Love', and ends ' Your most faithfull frend J. B.', ' Thy faithful frend and loving servaunt J. B.', 'Your assured frend and loving well-wisher J. B.', 'Your ever louing frend J. B.' When Miss Corbet has become his wife, he constantly writes to her in his exile which lasted from 1640 to 1661, letters which apart from our present purpose possess great human and historical interest. These letters generally begin 'My Dearest', and ' My deare Heart ', and he signs himself ' Your very louing husband', 'Yours, more than ever', ' Your faithful husband', ' My dearest, Your faithful friend ', ' Yours till death ', 'Meanewhile assure your selfe of the constant love of—My dearest—Your loyall husband '.

The lady to whom these affectionate letters were addressed, bore with wonderful patience and cheerfulness the anxieties and sufferings incident upon a state bordering on absolute want caused by her husband's deprivation of his living under the Commonwealth, his prolonged absence, together with the cares of a family of young children, and very indifferent health. She was a woman of great piety, and in her letters 'many a holy text around she strews ' in reply to the religious soliloquies of her husband. Her letters all begin ' My dearest ', and they often begin and close with pious exclamations and phrases—' Yours as much as euer in the Lord, No, more thene euer '; ' My dearest, I shall not faile to looke thos plases in the criptur, and pray for you as becometh your obedient wife and serunt in the Lord F. B.'; another letter is headed ' Jesu!', and ends—' I pray God send vs all a happy meting, I ham your faithful in the Lord, F. B.' Many of the letters are headed with the Sacred Name. Others of Mrs. Basire's letters end—' Farwall my dearest, I ham yours faithful for euer'; 'I euer remine Yours faithfull in the Lord'; ' So with my dayly prayers to God for you, I desire to remene your faithfull loveing and obedient wif'.

It may be worth while to give a few examples of beginnings and ends of letters from other persons in the Basire Correspondence, to illustrate the usage of the latter part of the seventeenth century.

These letters mostly bear, in the nature of an address, long superscriptions such as ' To the Reverend and ever Honoured Doctour Basire, Prebendary of the Cathedral Church in Durham. To be recommended to the Postmaster of Darneton' (p. 213, dated 1662).

This letter, from Prebendary Wrench of Durham, begins ' Sir', and ends—' Sir, Your faithfull and unfeigned humble Servant R. W.'

In the same year the Bishop of St. David's begins a letter to Dr. Basire —' Sir ', and ends—' Sir, youre uerie sincere friend and seruant, Wil. St. David's ', p. 219.

The Doctor's son begins—' Reverend Sir, and most loving Father ' and ends with the same formula, adding—' Your very obedient Son, P. B '.

p. **221**. To his Bishop (of Durham) Dr. Basire begins 'Right Rev. Father in God, and my very good Lord', ending 'I am still, My L^d, Your L^{ps}. faithfull Servant Isaac Basire'. In 1666 the Bishop of Carlisle, Dr. Rainbow, evidently an old friend of Dr. B.'s, begins 'Good Mr. Archdeacon', and ends 'I commend you and yours to God's grace and remaine, Your very faithfull frend Edw. Carliol', p. 254.

In 1668 the Bishop of Durham begins 'Mr Archdeacon' and ends 'In the interim I shall not be wanting at this distance to doe all I can, who am, Sir, Your very loving ffriend and servant Jo. Duresme', p. 273. Dr. Barlow, Provost of Queen's, begins 'My Reverend Friend', and ends 'Your prayers are desired for, Sir, Your affectionate friend and Seruant, Tho. Barlow', p. 302 (1673). Dr. Basire begins a letter to this gentleman—'Rev. Sir and my Dear Friend'... ending 'I remain, Reverend Sir, Your affectionate frend, and faithful servant'. To his son Isaac, he writes in 1664—'Beloved Son', ending—'So prays your very lovinge and painfull Father, Isaac Basire'.

Having now brought our examples of the various types of epistolary formulas down to within measurable distance of our own practice, we must leave this branch of our subject. Space forbids us to examine and illustrate here the letters of the eighteenth century, but this is the less necessary as these are very generally accessible. The letters of that age, formal or intimate, but always so courteous in their formulas, are known to most readers. Some allusion has already been made (pp. 20-1) to the tinge of ceremoniousness in address, even among friends, which survives far into the eighteenth century, and may be seen in the letters of Lady Mary Montagu, of Gray, and Horace Walpole, while as late as the end of the century we find in the letters of Cowper, unsurpassed perhaps among this kind of literature for grace and charm, that combination of stateliness with intimacy which has now long passed away.

Exclamations, Expletives, Oaths, &c.

Under these heads comes a wide range of expressions, from such as are mere exclamations with little or no meaning for him who utters or for him who hears them, or words and phrases added, by way of emphasis, to an assertion, to others of a more formidable character which are deliberately uttered as an expression of spleen, disappointment, or rage, with a definitely blasphemous or injurious intention. In an age like ours, where good breeding, as a rule, permits only exclamations of the mildest and most meaningless kind, to express temporary annoyance, disgust, surprise, or pleasure, the more full-blooded utterances of a former age are apt to strike us as excessive. Exclamations which to those who used them meant no more than 'By Jove' or 'my word' do to us, would now, if they were revived appear almost like rather blasphemous irreverence. It must be recognized, however, that swearing, from its mildest to its most outrageous forms, has its own fashions. These vary from age to age and from class to class. In every age there are expressions which are permissible among well-bred people, and others which are not. In certain circles an expression may be regarded with dislike, not so much because of any intrinsic wickedness attributed to it, as merely because it is vulgar. Thus there are many sections of society at the present time where such an expression as ' *O Crikey* ' is not in use. No one would now pretend that in its present form, whatever may underlie it, this exclamation is peculiarly blasphemous, but many persons would regard it with disfavour as being merely rather silly and distinctly vulgar. It is not a gentleman's expression. On the other hand, ' *Good Heavens* ', or ' *Good Gracious* ', while equally innocuous in meaning and intention, would pass muster perhaps, except among those who object, as many do, to anything more forcible than ' *dear me* '.

Human nature, even when most restrained, seems occasionally to require some meaningless phrase to relieve its sudden emotions, and the more devoid of all association with the cause of the emotion the better will the exclamation serve its purpose. Thus some find solace in such a formula as ' *O my little hat!* ' which has the advantage of being neither particularly funny nor of overstepping the limits of the nicest decorum, unless indeed these be passed by the mere act of expressing any emotion at all. It is really quite beside the mark to point out that utterances of this kind are senseless. It is of the very essence of such outbursts—the mere bubbles on the fountain of feeling—that they are quite unrelated to any definite situation. There is a certain adjective, most offensive to polite ears, which plays apparently the chief rôle in the vocabulary of large sections of the community. It seems to argue a certain poverty of linguistic resource when we find that this word is used by the same speakers both to mean absolutely nothing—being placed before every noun, and often adverbially before all adjectives—and also to mean a great deal—everything indeed that is unpleasant in the highest degree. It is rather a curious fact that the word in question while always impossible, except perhaps when used as it were in inverted commas, in such a way that the speaker dissociates himself from all responsibility for, or proprietorship in it, would be felt to be rather more than ordinarily intolerable, if it were used by an otherwise polite speaker as an absolutely meaningless adjective prefixed at random to most of the nouns in a sentence, and worse than if it were used deliberately, with a settled and full intent. There is something very terrible in an oath torn from its proper home and suddenly implanted in the wrong social atmosphere. In these circumstances the alien form is endowed by the hearers with mysterious and uncanny meanings; it chills the blood and raises gooseflesh.

We do not propose here to penetrate into the sombre history of blasphemy proper, nor to exhibit the development through the last few centuries of the ever-changing fashions of profanity. At every period there has been, as Chaucer knew—

> a companye
> Of yonge folk, that haunteden folye,
> As ryot, hasard, stewes and tavernes,
> Wher-as with harpes, lutes and giternes,
> They daunce and pleye at dees both day and night,
> And ete also and drinken over hir might,
> Thurgh which they doon the devel sacrifyse
> Within the develes tempel in cursed wyse,
> By superfluitee abhominable;

Hir othes been so grete and so dampnable,
That it is grisly for to here hem swere;
Our blissed lordes body they to-tere;
Hem thoughte Jewes rent him noght y-nough.

We are concerned, for the most part, with the milder sort of expressions which serve to decorate discourse, without symbolizing any strong
feeling on the part of those who utter them. Some of the expletives
which in former ages were used upon the slightest occasion, would
certainly appear unnecessarily forcible for mere exclamations at the
present day, and the fact that such expressions were formerly used so
lightly, and with no blasphemous intention, shows how frequent must
have been their employment for familiarity to have robbed them of all
meaning.

So saintly a person as Sir Thomas More was accustomed, according
to the reports given of his conversation by his son-in-law, to make use
of such formulas as *a Gods name*, p. xvi; *would to God*, ibid.; *in good
faith*, xxviii, but compared with some of the other personages mentioned
in his *Life*, he is very sparing of such phrases. The Duke of Norfolk,
'his singular deare friend', coming to dine with Sir Thomas on one
occasion, 'fortuned to find him at Church singinge in the quiere with
a surplas on his backe; to whome after service, as the(y) went home
togither arme in arme, the duke said, "*God body, God body*, My lord
Chauncellor, a parish Clark, a parish Clarke!"'

On another occasion the same Duke said to him '*By the Masse*,
Mr Moore, it is perillous strivinge with Princes ... for *by Gode's body*,
Mr Moore, Indignatio principis mors est', p. xxxix. In the conversation
in prison, with his wife, quoted above, p. 364, we find that the good
gentlewoman 'after her accustomed fashion' gives vent to such exclamations as '*What the good yeare* Mr Moore': '*Tille valle, tille valle*'; '*Bone
deus, bone Deus man*', 'I muse *what a God's name* you meane here thus
fondly to tarry'. At the trial of Sir Thomas More, the Lord Chief
Justice swears *by St. Julian*—'that was ever his oath', p. li.

'*Tilly-fally*, Sir John, ne'er tell me', and 'What the good year!' are
both also said by Mrs. Quickly in Henry IV, Pt. II, ii. 4. *Marry*, which
means no more than 'indeed', was a universally used expletive in the
sixteenth century. Roper uses it in speaking to More, Wolsey uses it,
according to Cavendish; it is frequent in Roister Doister, and is constantly in the mouths of Sir John Falstaff and his merry companions.
*By sweete Sanct Anne, by cocke, by gog, by cocks precious potstick, kocks
nownes, by the armes of Caleys*, and the more formidable *by the passion of
God Sir do not so*, all occur in Roister Doister, and further such exclamations as *O Lorde, hoigh dagh!, I dare sweare, I shall so God me saue,
I make God a vow* (also written *avow*), *would Christ I had*, &c. Meaningless imprecations like *the Devil take me, a mischiefe take his token and him
and thee too* are sprinkled about the dialogue of this play. The later plays
of the great period offer a mine of material of this kind, but only a few
can be mentioned here. *What a Devil* (instead of *the Devil*), *what a pox,
by'r lady, z'ounds, s'blood, God's body, by the mass, a plague on thee*, are
among the expressions in the First Part of Henry IV. In the Second

Part Mr. Justice Shallow swears by *cock and pie*. By the side of these
are mild formulas such as *I'm a Jew else, I'm a rogue if I drink today*.

In Chapman's comedies there is a rich sprinkling both of the slighter
forms of exclamatory phrases, as well as of the more serious kind. Of
the former we may note *y faith, bir lord, bir lady, by the Lord, How the
divell* (instead of how *a* devil), all in A Humorous Day's Mirth; *ile be
sworne*, All Fooles; of the latter kind of expression *Gods precious soles*,
H. D. M.; *s'foot, s'bodie, God's my life*, Mons. D'Olive; *Gods my passion*,
H. D. M.; *swounds, zwoundes*, Gentleman Usher. '

Massinger's New Way to pay old Debts has *'slight, 'sdeath*, and a fore-
shadowing of the form of asseveration so common in the later seventeenth
century in the phrase—' If I know the mystery . . . may I perish ', ii. 2.

It is to the dramatists of the later seventeenth and early eighteenth
century that the curious inquirer will go for expletives and exclamatory
expressions of the greatest variety.   Otway, Congreve, and Vanbrugh
appear to excel all their predecessors and contemporaries in the fertility
of their invention in this respect.   It is indeed probable that while some
of the sayings of Mr. Caper, my Lady Squeamish, my Lady Plyant,
my Lord Foppington, and others of their kidney, are the creations of the
writers who call these ' strange pleasant creatures' into existence, many
others were actually current coin among the fops and fine ladies of the
period.   Even if many phrases used by these characters are artificial concoctions of the dramatists they nevertheless are in keeping with, and
express the spirit and manners of the age.   If Mr. Galsworthy or
Mr. Bernard Shaw were to invent corresponding slang at the present
day, it would be very different from that of the so-called Restoration
Dramatists.   The bulk of the following selection of expletives and oaths is
taken from the plays of Otway, Congreve, Wycherley, Mrs. Aphra Behn,
Vanbrugh, and Farquhar.   A few occur in Shadwell, and many more
are common to all writers of comedies.   These are undoubtedly genuine
current expressions some of which survive.

Among the more racy and amusing are :—

Let me die : ' Let me die your Ladyship obliges me beyond expression '
(Mr. Saunter in Otway's Friendship in Fashion) ; ' Let me die, you have
a great deal of wit' (Lady Froth, Congreve's Double Dealer); also
much used by Melantha, an affected lady in Dryden's Marriage à la
Mode.

Let me perish—' I'm your humble servant let me perish ' (Brisk, Double
Dealer); also used by Wycherley, Love in a Wood.

Strike me speechless⎱
Strike me dumb   ⎰—Lord Foppington (Vanbrugh's Relapse).

Death and eternal tartures Sir, I vow the packet's (= pocket) too high
(Lord Foppington).

Burn me if I do (Farquhar, Way to win him).

Rat me, ' rat my packet handkerchief (Lord Foppington).

Never stir—' Never stir if it did not' (Caper, Otway, Friendship in
Love) ; ' Thou shalt enjoy me always, dear, dear friend, never stir '.

I'll take my death you're handsomer ' (Mrs. Millamont, Congreve, Way
of the World).

As I'm a Person (Lady Wishfort, Way of the World).

Stap my vitals (Lord Foppington; very frequent).

Split my windpipe—Lord Foppington gives his brother his blessing, on finding that the latter has married by a trick the lady he had designed for himself—'You have married a woman beautiful in her person, charming in her airs, prudent in her conduct, canstant in her inclinations, and of a nice marality split my windpipe '.

As I hope to breathe (Lady Lurewell, Farquhar, Sir Harry Wildair).

I'm a Dog if do (Wittmore in Mrs. Behn's Sir Patient Fancy).

By the Universe (Wycherley, Country Wife).

I swear and declare (Lady Plyant); *I swear and vow* (Sir Paul Plyant, Double Dealer); *I do protest and vow* (Sir Credulous Easy, Aphra Behn's Sir Patient Fancy); *I protest I swoon at ceremony* (Lady Fancyfull, Vanbrugh, Provok'd Wife); *I profess ingenuously* a very discreet young man (Mrs. Aphra Behn, Sir Patient Fancy).

Gads my life (Lady Plyant).

O Crimine (Lady Plyant).

O Jeminy (Wycherley, Mrs. Pinchwife, Country Wife).

Gad take me, between you and I, I was deaf on both ears for three weeks after (Sir Humphrey, Shadwell, Bury Fair).

I'll lay my Life he deserves your assistance (Mrs. Sullen, Farquhar, Beaux' Strategem).

By the Lord Harry (Sir Jos. Wittol, Congreve, Old Bachelor).

By the universe (Wycherley, Mrs. Pinchwife, Country Wife).

Gadzooks (Heartfree, Vanbrugh, Provok'd Wife); *Gad's Bud* (Sir Paul Plyant, Double Dealer); *Gud soons* (Lady Arabella, Vanbrugh, Journey to London); *Marry-gep* (Widow Blackacre, Wycherley, Plain Dealer); *'sheart* (Sir Wilful, Congreve, Way of the World); *Eh Gud, eh Gud* (Mrs. Fantast, Shadwell, Bury Fair); *Zoz* I was a modest fool; *adszoz* (Sir Credulous Easy, Devonshire Knight, Aphra Behn, Sir Petulant Fancy); *'D's diggers Sir* (a groom in Sir Petulant Fancy); *'sheart* (Sir Wilf. Witwoud, Congreve, Way of the World); *od'sheart* (Sir Noble Clumsey, Otway, Friendship in Fashion); *Adsheart* (Sir Jos. Wittol, Congreve, Old Bachelor); *Gadswouns* (Oldfox, Plain Dealer). By the side of *marry*, frequent in the sixteenth and seventeenth centuries, the curious expression *Marry come up my dirty cousin* occurs in Swift's Polite Conversations (said by the young lady), and again in Fielding's Tom Jones—said by the lady's maid Mrs. Honor. With this compare *marry gep* above, which probably stands for 'go up '.

Such expressions as *Lard* are frequent in the seventeenth-century comedies, and the very modern-sounding *as sure as a gun* is said by Sir Paul Plyant in the Double Dealer.

The comedies of Dryden contain but few of the more or less mild, and fashionable, semi-bantering exclamatory expressions which enliven the pages of many of his contemporaries; he sticks on the whole to the more permanent oaths—*'sdeath, 'sblood*, &c. It must be allowed that the dialogue of Dryden's comedies is inferior to that of Otway or Congreve in brilliancy and natural ease, and that it probably does not reflect the familiar colloquial English of the period so faithfully as the conversation in the works of these writers. Dryden himself says, in the Defense of the Essay of Dramatic Poesy, 'I know I am not so fitted by Nature to write Comedy: I want that Gaiety of Humour which is required to it. My Conversation is slow and dull, my Humour Saturnine and reserv'd: In short, I am none of those who endeavour to break all Jests in Company, or make Repartees'.

It may be noted that the frequent use—almost in every sentence—of such phrases as *let me perish, burn me,* and other meaningless interjections of this order, is attributed by the dramatists only to the most frivolous fops and the most affected women of fashion. The more serious characters, so far as such exist in the later seventeenth-century comedies, are addicted rather to the weightier and more sober sort of swearing. It is perhaps unnecessary to pursue this subject beyond the first third of the eighteenth century. Farquhar has many of the mannerisms of his slightly older contemporaries, and some stronger expressions, e. g. 'There was a neighbour's daughter I had a *woundy* kindness for', Truman, in Twin Rivals; but Fielding in his numerous comedies has but few of the objurgatory catchwords of the earlier generation. Swearing, both of the lighter kind as well as of the deliberately profane variety, appears to have diminished in intensity, apart from the stage country squire, such as Squire Badger in Don Quixote, who says *'Sbodlikins* and *ecod,* and Squire Western, whose artless profanity is notorious. Ladies in these plays, and in Swift's Polite Conversations, still say *lard, O Lud,* and *la,* and *mercy, 'sbubs, God bless my eyesight,* but the rich variety of expression which we find in Lady Squeamish and her friends has vanished. Some few of the old mouth-filling oaths, such as *zounds, 'sdeath,* and so on, still linger in Goldsmith and Sheridan, but the number of these available for a gentleman was very limited by the end of the century. From the beginning of the nineteenth century it would seem that nearly all the old oaths died out in good society, as having come to be considered, from unfamiliarity, either too profane or else too devoid of content to serve any purpose. It seems to be the case that the serious oaths survive longest, or at any rate die hardest, while each age produces its own ephemeral formulas of mere light expletive and asseveration.

Hyperbole; Compliments; Approval; Disapproval; Abuse, &c.

Very characteristic of a particular age is the language of hyperbole and exaggeration as found in phrases expressive on the one hand of compliments, pleasure, approval, amusement, and so on, and of disgust, dislike, anger, and kindred emotions, on the other. Incidentally, the study of the different modes of expressing such feelings as these leads us also to observe the varying fashion in intensives, corresponding to the present-day *awfully, frightfully,* and the rest, and in exaggeration generally, especially in paying compliments.

The following illustrations are chiefly drawn from the seventeenth century, which offers a considerable wealth of material.

It is wonderful what a variety of expressions have been in use, more or less transitorily, at different periods, as intensives, meaning no more than *very, very much,* &c. *Rarely* in Chapman's Gentleman Usher— '*How did you like me aunt? O rarely, rarely*', 'Oh lord, that, that is

a pleasure *intolerable*', Lady Squeamish in Otway's Friendship in Love ;
'Let me die if that was not *extravagantly pleasant* (= very amusing),
ibid. ; 'I vow he himself sings a tune *extreme prettily*', ibid.: 'I love
dancing *immoderately*', ibid. ; 'O dear 'tis *violent hot*', ibid. ; 'Deuce take
me if your Ladyship has not the art of surprising the most naturally in
the world—I hope you'll *make me happy* in communicating the Poem',
Brisk in Congreve's Double Dealer ; 'With the reserve of my Honour,
I assure you Mr Careless, I *don't know anything in the World* I would
refuse to a Person *so meritorious*—You'll pardon my want of expression',
Lady Plyant in Double Dealer; to which Careless replies—'O your
Ladyship is *abounding in all Excellence*, particularly that of Phrase ; My
Lady Froth is very well in her Accomplishments—But it is *when my
Lady Plyant is not thought of—if that can ever be*' ; Lady Plyant :—
'O you overcome me—*That is so excessive*' ; Brisk, asked to write notes
to Lady Froth's Poems, cries 'With all my Heart and Soul, and *proud of
the vast Honour* let me perish'. 'I swear Mr Careless you are *very
alluring*, and say so many fine Things, and nothing is *so moving* as a fine
Thing. . . . Well, sure if I escape your Importunities, I *shall value myself*
as long as I live, I swear ; Lady Plyant. The following bit of dialogue
between Lady Froth and Mr. Brisk illustrates the fashionable mode of
bandying exaggerated, but rather hollow compliments.

'*Ldy F.* Ah *Gallantry to the last degree*—Mr Brisk was ever anything so
well bred as My Lord ? *Brisk*—Never anything but your Ladyship let me
perish. *Ldy F.* O prettily turned again ; let me die but you have a great
deal of Wit. Mr Mellefont don't you think Mr Brisk has a World of Wit ?
Mellefont—O yes Madam. *Brisk*—O dear Madam—*Ldy F.* An *infinite
deal!* *Brisk*. O Heaven Madam. *Ldy F.* More Wit — than Body.
Brisk—I'm *everlastingly your humble Servant*, deuce take me Madam."

Lady Fancyful in Vanbrugh's Provok'd Wife contrives to pay herself
a pretty compliment in lamenting the ravages of her beauty and the consequent pretended annoyance to herself—'To confess the truth to you,
I'm so *everlastingly fatigued* with the addresses of unfortunate gentlemen
that were it not for the *extravagancy* of the example, I should e'en tear
out these wicked eyes with my own fingers, to make both myself and
mankind easy'.

Swift's Polite Conversations consist of a wonderful string of slang
words, phrases, and *clichés*, all of which we may suppose to have been
current in the conversation of the more frivolous part of Society in the
early eighteenth century. The word *pure* is used for *very*—'this almond
pudden is *pure good*' ; also as an Adj., in the sense of *excellent*, as in 'by
Dad he's *pure Company*', Sir Noble Clumsey's summing-up of the 'Arch-
Wag' Malagene. *To divert* in the characteristic sense of 'amuse',
and instead of this—'Well ladies and gentlemen, you are pleased *to divert*
yourselves'. Lady Wentworth in 1706 speaks of her 'munckey' as
'full of *devertin* tricks', and twenty years earlier Cary Stewkley (Verney),
taxed by her brother with a propensity for gambling, writes 'whot dus
becom a gentilwoman as plays only for *divartion* I hope I know'.

The idiomatic use of *obliging* is shown in the Polite Conversations, by
Lady Smart, who remarks, in answer to rather excessive praise of her
house—'My lord, your lordship is always *very obliging*' ; in the same

sense Lady Squeamish says 'I sweare Mr. Malagene you are a *very obliging person*'.

Extreme amusement, and approval of the persons who provoke it, are frequently expressed with considerable exaggeration of phrase. Some instances are quoted above, but a few more may be added. '*A you mad slave you, you are a tickling Actor*', says Vincentio to Pogio in Chapman's Gentleman Usher.

Mr. Oldwit, in Shadwell's Bury Fair, professes great delight at the buffoonery of Sir Humphrey :—' Forbear, pray forbear; *you'll be the death of me; I shall break a vein* if I keep you company, *you arch Wag you*. . . . Well Sir Humphrey Noddy, go thy ways, thou art the archest Wit and Wag. I must forswear thy Company, *thou'lt kill me else*.' The arch wag asks ' What is the World worth without Wit and Waggery and Mirth ?', and describing some prank he had played before an admiring friend, remarks—' If you'd seen his Lordship laugh! I thought my Lord *would have killed himself*. He desired me at last to forbear; he *was not able to endure it*.' ' Why what a *notable Wag's* this ' is said sarcastically in Mrs. Aphra Behn's Sir Patient Fancy.

The passages quoted above, pp. 369–71, from Otway's Friendship in Love illustrate the modes of expressing an appreciation of ' Waggery '.

In the tract Reasons of Mr. Bays for changing his religion (1688), Mr. Bays (Dryden) remarks *à propos* of something he intends to write—'*you'll half kill yourselves with laughing* at the conceit ', and again ' I protest Mr Crites you are enough to make anybody *split with laughing*'. Similarly ' Miss ' in Polite Conversation declares—' Well, I swear *you'll make one die with laughing*'.

The language of abuse, disparagement, contempt, and disapproval, whether real or in the nature of banter, is equally characteristic.

The following is uttered with genuine anger, by Malagene Goodvile in Otway's Friendship in Love, to the musicians who are entertaining the company—' Hold, hold, what insufferable rascals are these ? Why you scurvy thrashing scraping mongrels, ye make a worse noise than crampt hedgehogs. 'Sdeath ye dogs, can't you play more as a gentleman sings ? '

The seventeenth-century beaux and fine ladies were adepts in the art of backbiting, and of conveying in a few words a most unpleasant picture of an absent friend—' O my Lady Toothless' cries Mr. Brisk in the Double Dealer, ' O she 's a *mortifying spectacle*, she 's always chewing the cud like an old Ewe '; ' Fie Mr Brisk, Eringos for her cough ' protests Cynthia; *Lady Froth* :—' Then that t'other great strapping Lady— I can't hit of her name; the old fat fool that paints so *exorbitantly* '; *Brisk* :—' I know whom you mean—But deuce take me I can't hit of her Name neither—Paints d'ye say ? Why she lays it on with a trowel.'

Mr. Brisk knows well how to ' just hint a fault '—' Don't you apprehend me My Lord ? Careless is a very honest fellow, but harkee—you understand me—somewhat heavy, a little shallow or so '.

Lady Froth has a picturesque vocabulary to express disapproval— ' O Filthy Mr Sneer? he 's a nauseous figure, a most fulsamic Fop '. *Nauseous* and *filthy* are favourite words in this period, but are often used so as to convey little or no specific meaning, or in a tone of rather affectionate

banter. ' He 's one of those nauseous offerers at wit ', Wycherley's Country
Wife ; 'A man must endeavour to look wholesome' says Lord Foppington
in Vanbrugh's Relapse, 'lest he make so nauseous a figure in the side
box, the ladies should be compelled to turn their eyes upon the Play ';
again the same nobleman remarks 'While I was but a Knight I was
a very nauseous fellow ' ; and, speaking to his tailor—' I shall never be
reconciled to this nauseous packet '. A remarkable use of the verb, to
express a simple aversion, is found in Mrs. Millamont's *I nauseate* walking ;
'tis a country divertion ' (Congreve, Way of the World).

In the Old Bachelor, Belinda, speaking of Belmour with whom she is
in love, cries out, at the suggestion of such a possibility—' Filthy Fellow !
. . . Oh I love your hideous fancy ! Ha, ha, ha, love a Man !' In the
same play Lucy the maid calls her lover, Setter, ' Beast, filthy toad'
during an exchange of civilities. ' Foh, you filthy toad ! nay, now I've
done jesting ' says Mrs. Squeamish in the Country Wife, when Horner
kisses her. ' Out upon you for a filthy creature ' cries ' Miss ' in the
Polite Conversations, in reply to the graceful banter of Neverout.

Toad is a term of endearment among these ladies : ' I love to torment
the confounded toad' says Lady Fidget, speaking of Mr. Horner for
whom she has a very pronounced weakness. ' Get you gone you good-
natur'd toad you' is Lady Squeamish's reply to the rather *outré* compliments of Sir Noble.

Plague (Vb.), *plaguy*, *plaguily* are favourite expressions in Polite Conversations. Lord Sparkish complains to his host—' My Lord, this venison
is plaguily peppered'; ' 'Sbubs, Madam, I have burnt my hand with your
plaguy kettle ' says Neverout, and the Colonel observes, with satisfaction,
that ' her Ladyship was plaguily bamb'd '. ' Don't be so teizing ; you
plague a body so ! can't you keep your filthy hands to yourself?' is
a playful rap administered by ' Miss ' to Neverout.

Strange is another word used very indefinitely but suggesting mild
disapproval—' I vow you'll make me hate you if you talk so strangely, but
let me die, I can't last longer ' says Lady Squeamish, implying a certain
degree of impropriety, which nevertheless makes her laugh ; again, she
says, 'I'll vow and swear my cousin Sir Noble is a strange pleasant
creature '.

We have an example above of *exorbitantly* in the sense of 'out-
rageously', and the adjective is also used in the same sense—' Most
exorbitant and amazing' is Lady Fantast's comment, in Bury Fair, upon
her husband's outburst against her airs and graces. We may close this
series of illustrations, which might be extended almost indefinitely, with
two from the Verney Memoirs, which contain idiomatic uses that have
long since disappeared. Susan Verney, wishing to say that her sister's
husband is a bad-tempered disagreeble fellow, writes 'poore peg has
married a very humersome cros boy as ever I see ' (Mem. ii. 361; 1647).
Edmund Verney, Sir Ralph's heir, having had a quarrel with a neighbouring squire concerning boundaries and rights of way, describes him
as ' very malicious and stomachfull ' (Mem. iv. 177, 1682). The phrase
'as ever I see' is common in the Verney letters, and also in the Wentworth Papers.

Preciosity, &c.

We close this chapter with some examples of seventeenth-century preciosity and euphemism. The most characteristic specimens of this kind of affected speech are put by the writers into the mouths of female characters, and of these we select Shadwell's Lady Fantast and her daughter (Bury Fair), Otway's Lady Squeamish, Congreve's Lady Wishfort, and Vanbrugh's Lady Fancyful in the Provok'd Wife. Some of the sayings of a few minor characters may be added; the waiting-maids of these characters are nearly as elegant, and only less absurd than their mistresses.

Luce, Lady Fantast's woman, summons the latter's stepdaughter as follows :—' Madam, my Lady Madam Fantast, having attir'd herself in her morning habiliments, is ambitious of the honour of your Ladyship's Company to survey the Fair'; and she thus announces to her mistress the coming of Mrs. Gertrude the stepdaughter:—' Madame, Mrs Gatty will kiss your Ladyship's hands here incontinently'. The ladies Fantast, highly respectable as they are in conduct, are as arrant, pretentious, and affected minxes as can be found, in manner and speech, given to interlarding their conversation with sham French, and still more dubious Latin. Says the daughter—' To all that which the World calls Wit and Breeding, I have always had a natural Tendency, a *penchen*, derived, as the learned say, *ex traduce*, from your Ladyship : besides the great Prevalence of your Ladyship's most shining Example has perpetually stimulated me, to the sacrificing all my Endeavours towards the attaining of those inestimable Jewels ; than which, nothing in the Universe can be so much *a mon gre*, as the French say. And for Beauty, Madam, the stock I am enrich'd with, comes by Emanation from your Ladyship, who has been long held a Paragon of Perfection : most *Charmant*, most *Tuant.*' ' Ah my dear Child' replies the old lady, ' I! alas, alas ! Time has been, and yet I am not quite gone'. . . . When Gertrude her stepsister, an attractive and sensible girl, comes in Mrs. Fantast greets her with ' Sweet Madam Gatty, I have some minutes impatiently expected your Arrival, that I might do myself the Great Honour to kiss your hands and enjoy the Favour of your Company into the Fair ; which I see out of my Window, begins to fill apace.'

To this piece of affectation Gatty replies very sensibly, ' I got ready as soon as e'er I could, and am now come to wait on you', but old Lady Fantast takes her to task, with ' Oh, fie, Daughter! will you never attain to mine, and my dear Daughter's Examples, to a more polite way of Expression, and a nicer form of Breeding? Fie, fie; I come to wait on you! You should have said; I assure you Madam the Honour is all on my side; and I cannot be ambitious of a greater, than the sweet Society of so excellent a Person. This is Breeding.' ' Breeding!' exclaims Gatty, ' Why this had been a Flam, a meer Flam'. And with this judgement, we may leave My Lady Fantast.

We pass next to Lady Squeamish, who is rather ironically described by Goodvile as ' the most exact Observer of Decorums and Decency alive '. Her manner of greeting the ladies on entering, along with her cousin Sir Noble Clumsey, if it has the polish, has also the insincerity of her age—'Dear Madam Goodvile, ten thousand Happinesses wait on you! Fair Madam Victoria, sweet charming Camilla, which way shall I express my Service to you?—Cousin your honour, your honour to the Ladies.— *Sir Noble*:—Ladies as low as Knee can bend, or Head can bow, I salute you all: And Gallants, I am your most humble, most obliged, and most devoted Servant.'

The character of this charming lady, as well as her taste in language, is well exhibited in the following dialogue between her and Victoria.

'Oh my dear Victoria! the most unlook'd for Happiness! the pleasant'st Accident! the strangest Discovery! the very thought of it were enough to cure Melancholy. Valentine and Camilla, Camilla and Valentine, ha, ha, ha,

Vict. Dear Madam, what is't so transports you?

Ldy Squ. Nay 'tis too precious to be communicated: Hold me, hold me, or I shall die with laughter—ha, ha, ha, Camilla and Valentine, Valentine and Camilla, ha, ha, ha—O dear, my Heart's broke.

Vict. Good Madam refrain your Mirth a little, and let me know the Story, that I may have a share in it.

Ldy Squ. An Assignation, an Assignation tonight in the lower Garden;—by strong good Fortune I overheard it all just now—but to think of the pleasant Consequences that will happen, drives me into an Excess of Joy beyond all sufferance.

Vict. Madame in all probability the pleasant'st Consequence is like to be theirs, if any body's; and I cannot guess how it should touch your Ladyship in the least.

Ldy Squ. O Lord, how can you be so dull? Why, at the very Hour and Place appointed will I greet Valentine in Camilla's stead, before she can be there herself; then when she comes, expose her Infamy to the World, till I have thorowly revenged my self for all the base Injuries her Lover has done me.

Vict. But Madam, can you endure to be so malicious?

Ldy Squ. That, that's the dear Pleasure of the thing; for I vow I'd sooner die ten thousand Deaths, if I thought I should hazard the least Temptation to the prejudice of my Honour.

Vict. But why should your Ladyship run into the mouth of Danger? Who knows what scurvy lurking Devil may stand in readiness, and seize your Virtue before you are aware of him?

Ldy Squ. Temptation? No, I'd have you know I scorn Temptation: I durst trust myself in a Convent amongst a Kennel of cramm'd Friers: Besides, that ungrateful ill-bred fellow Valentine is my mortal Aversion, more odious to me than foul weather on a May-day, or ill smell in a Morning. . . . No, were I inclined to entertain Addresses, I assure you I need not want for Servants; for I swear I am so perplexed with Billet-Doux every day, I know not which way to turn myself: Besides there's no Fidelity, no Honour in Mankind. O dear Victoria! whatever you do, never let Love come near your Heart: Tho really I think true Love is the greatest Pleasure in the World.'

And so we let Lady Squeamish go her ways for a brazen jilt, and an affected, humoursome baggage. If any one wishes to know whither her ways led her, let him read the play.

Only one more example of foppish refinement of speech from this play—the remarks of the whimsical Mr. Caper to Sir Noble Clumsey, who coming in drunk, takes him for a dancing-master —'I thought you had known me' says he, rather ruefully, but adds, brightening —'I doubt you may be a little overtaken. Faith, dear Heart, I'm glad to see you so merry!'

The character of Lady Wishfort in the Way of the World is perhaps one of the best that Congreve has drawn; her conversation in spite of the deliberate affectation in phrase is vivid and racy, and for all its preciosity has a naturalness which puts it among the triumphs of Congreve's art. He contrives to bring out to the full the absurdity of the lady's mannerisms, in feeling and expression, to combine these with vigour and ease of diction, and to give to the whole that polish of which he is the unquestioned master in his own age and for long after.

The position of Lady Wishfort is that of an elderly lady of great outward propriety of conduct, and a steadfast observer of decorum, in speech no less than in manners. Her equanimity is considerably upset by the news that an elderly knight has fallen in love with her portrait, and wishes to press his suit with the original. The pretended knight is really a valet in disguise, and the whole intrigue has been planned, for reasons into which we need not enter here, by a rascally nephew of Lady Wishfort's. This, however, is not discovered until the lover has had an interview with the sighing fair. The first extract reveals the lady discussing the coming visit with Foible her maid (who is in the plot).

'I shall never recompose my Features to receive Sir Rowland with any Oeconomy of Face. . . . I'm absolutely decayed. Look, Foible.

Foible. Your Ladyship has frown'd a little too rashly, indeed Madam. There are some Cracks discernible in the white Varnish.

Lady W. Let me see the Glass—Cracks say'st thou? Why I am arrantly flead (e. g. flayed)—I look like an old peel'd Wall. Thou must repair me Foible before Sir Rowland comes, or I shall never keep up to my picture.

F. I warrant you, Madam; a little Art once made your picture like you; and now a little of the same Art must make you like your Picture. Your Picture must sit for you, Madam.

Lady W. But art thou sure Sir Rowland will not fail to come? Or will he not fail when he does come? Will he be importunate, Foible, and push? For if he should not be importunate . . . I shall never break Decorums—I shall die with Confusion; if I am forc'd to advance—O no, I can never advance. . . . I shall swoon if he should expect Advances. No, I hope Sir Rowland is better bred than to put a Lady to the Necessity of breaking her Forms. I won't be too coy neither.—I won't give him Despair—But a little Disdain is not amiss; a little Scorn is alluring.—*Foible.*—A little Scorn becomes your Ladyship.—*Lady W.* Yes, but Tenderness becomes me best.—A Sort of a Dyingness—You see that Picture has a Sort of a — Ha Foible!—A Swimmingness in the Eyes—Yes, I'll look so—My Neice affects it but she wants Features. Is Sir Rowland handsom? Let my Toilet be remov'd—I'll dress above. I'll receive Sir Rowland here. Is he handsom? Don't answer me. I won't know: I'll be surpris'd; He'll be taken by Surprise.—*Foible*—By Storm Madam. Sir Rowland's a brisk Man.—*Lady W.* —Is he! O then he'll importune, if he's a brisk Man. I shall save Decorums if Sir Rowland importunes. I have a mortal Terror at the Apprehension of offending against Decorums. O I'm glad he's a brisk Man. Let my things be remov'd good Foible.'

The next passage reveals the lady ready dressed, and expectant of Sir Rowland's arrival.

— 'Well, and how do I look Foible!—*F.* Most killing well, Madam. *Lady W.* Well, and how shall I receive him? In what Figure shall I give

his Heart the first Impression? There is a great deal in the first Impression.
Shall I sit?—No, I won't sit—I'll walk—ay I'll walk from the door upon his
Entrance; and then turn full upon him—No, that will be too sudden. I'll
lie, ay I'll lie down—I'll receive him in my little Dressing-Room. There's
a Couch—Yes, yes, I'll give the first Impression on a Couch—I won't lie
neither, but loll, and lean upon one Elbow; with one Foot a little dangling
off, jogging in a thoughtful Way—Yes—Yes—and then as soon as he appears,
start, ay, start and be surpris'd, and rise to meet him in a pretty Disorder—
Yes—O, nothing is more alluring than a Levee from a Couch in some Confusion—It shews the Foot to Advantage, and furnishes with Blushes and
recomposing Airs beyond Comparison. Hark! there's a Coach.'

But it is when *l'heure du Berger* draws near, as she supposes, that
Lady Wishfort rises to the sublimest heights of expression :—

'Well, Sir Rowland, you have the Way,—you are no Novice in the Labyrinth
of Love—You have the Clue—But as I'm a Person, Sir Rowland, you must
not attribute my yielding to any sinister Appetite, or Indigestion of Widow-
hood; nor impute my Complacency to any Lethargy of Continence—I hope
you don't think me prone to any iteration of Nuptials—If you do, I protest
I must recede—or think that I have made a Prostitution of Decorums, but
in the Vehemence of Compassion, or to save the Life of a Person of so much
Importance—Or else you wrong my Condescension—If you think the least
Scruple of Carnality was an Ingredient, or that—'.

Here Foible enters and announces that the Dancers are ready, and thus
puts an end to the scene at its supreme moment of beauty — and
absurdity. Even Congreve could not remain at that level any longer.

It is worth while to record that in this play, a maid, well called *Mincing*,
announces—'Mem, I am come to acquaint your Laship that Dinner is
impatient'. The hostess invites her guests to go into dinner with the
phrase—'Gentlemen, will you walk?'

This chapter and book cannot better conclude than with a typical piece
of seventeenth-century formality. May it symbolize at once the author's
leave-taking of the reader and the eagerness of the latter to pursue the
subject for himself.

The passage is from the Provok'd Wife :—

'*Lady Fancyful.* Madam, your humble servant, I must take my leave.
Lady Brute. What, going already madam?
Ldy F. I must beg you'll excuse me this once; for really I have eighteen
visits this afternoon. . . . (*Going*) Nay, you shan't go one step out of
the room.
Ldy B. Indeed I'll wait upon you down.
Ldy F. No, sweet Lady Brute, you know I swoon at ceremony.
Ldy B. Pray give me leave—*Ldy F.* You know I won't—*Ldy B.*—You
know I must.—*Ldy F.*—Indeed you shan't—Indeed I will—Indeed you shan't
—*Ldy B.*—Indeed I will.
Ldy F. Indeed you shan't. Indeed, indeed, indeed, you shan't.'
                    [*Exit running. They follow.*]

APPENDIX I

P. 168.

Gill's Account of English ' Long a '.

Middle English *ā*, in *name, take, bacon, capon,* &c., is regularly transcribed by Gill with the symbol *ä*, the dots indicating length. "This sound ", says Gill, " the Germans express by *aa*, as in *maal* ' feast ', *haar* ' hair '. On the face of it one might suppose that Gill intended to assert that the English sound of this vowel in his day, or at any rate in his own pronunciation, was still the same as in M.E. Against this we have evidence which goes to show that one hundred and fifty years before Gill's time, at a modest estimate, M.E. ā was fronted, and levelled under the sound of M.E. [ē̯]. See pp 194-196 above. If this be so, then Gill's statement is very misleading. His speech may, indeed, have been old-fashioned, after all, he was born in 1565, but it is going rather far to suppose that he himself still spoke M.E.! Again, we know that Gill was in very many respects an accurate and candid observer, and it is incredible that he should have described as a back what was actually a front vowel. He certainly does not use these terms, nor even ' guttural and palatal ', but he must have recognized the difference perfectly well. Let it be remembered that Gill distinguishes consistently between M.E. [ē̯] and [ê], writing ë for the former, and ï for the latter ; that long and short vowels are throughout his book accurately distinguished ; that he recognizes the existence of syllabic *-l, -n, -r* ; that he records the difference between stressed and unstressed forms of auxiliaries and personal pronouns ; that in his examples of the pronunciation of the Mopsae he records what we know to have really existed, though we may think that Gill is pedantic in condemning as foppish and affected, what was actually pretty universally established in his time.

It appears to me far more probable that Gill was mistaken in regard to the quality of the German vowel in ' *maal* ', &c., than that he should have been so totally deaf to the sound of the English vowel in *name,* &c., as his identification of the two vowels seems to suggest. Why, he actually makes his Mopsae pronounce M.E. *ā* as ë in *Këpn* and *Këmbrik.* He himself prefers *ä* in these words. I suggest that Gill had the archaic pronunciation [ǣ] for old *ā,* that to him, as to all Englishmen of his day, [ā] was an unknown sound, difficult to hear accurately, and to reproduce, and that he heard this unfamiliar vowel as [ǣ] his own sound, expressed by the same letter. Many Englishmen at the present time regularly substitute the short vowel [æ] for [a] when pronouncing French, German, Welsh, and so on. If Gill misheard, and mispronounced, German [ā] as suggested, his identification of it with the English ' long *a* ' was perfectly natural.

It is surprising enough that Gill should himself still have pronounced his *ä* as [ǣ], and this may have been due to some dialect influence, whether social or regional. We may perhaps conclude, if we accept the above interpretation of his symbol *ä,* that his short *a* expressed [æ]. He distinguishes the strong and weak forms of *have* as ' häv ' and ' hav ' respectively, and there is nothing to show that the vowels differed otherwise than in quantity. It was impossible for one who was not a phonetician to describe [æ] whether long or short. Thirty years or so after Gill, Wallis put *ă* among the ' palatal ' vowels, and it was not till thirty years later still that Cooper unequivocally describes this sound as a low front.

APPENDIX II

Various notes on Vowels of Stressed Syllables.

P. 194, line 13 from bottom.

Some regard the spelling *credyll* as suspect, and suggest that the *e* here is not for M.E. *ā* at all, but that it represents a M.E. *ē̆.* The ground for this is *crĕdel* which occurs in Promptorium (Norf. 1440), *credil* appears in Seven

Sages (c. 1425). The origin of *ē* here, from O.E. *ă*, is not very clear, if it be other than M.E. *ā* fronted.

P. 202.

Rounded Vowel in **wrath**.

Milton evidently used the same vowel as Cooper. In his autograph MS. (Ode on Circumcision 23), he first wrote *wrauth*, though he altered this to *wrath*, but in Morgan MS. in lines 54, 110, 220, where the scribe first wrote *wrath*, a subsequent corrector has inserted *u*. Miss Darbishire says the spelling *wrauth* has been preserved by the printer in nearly every other place in P. L.

P. 223.

Variant Pronunciations of **high** and **height**.

The present form *high* [*hai*] goes back to M.E. *high*; the spelling *height* to a M.E. type with *ei*. The pronunciation of the latter has been influenced by that of *high*. Milton's spelling *highth* (P. L. i. 92, 2, 82, &c.), shows the same influence, and no doubt expresses [haiþ] But a ME. *heigh* also existed, and would give Modern *hey* = [hei], cp. *Heywood*, &c. Price (1668) says that *high* and *hay* are pronounced alike ; Mrs. Adams, Later Verney Letters, i. 3, writes—*my rent I own is too hey for me* (1697). Habington, Castara, 96 (1634), rhymes *height—state* ; Cooper (1685) puts *height* and *weight* together ; Dryden *height—fate*, also Dyer, Grongar Hill, 33–34 (1726) ; Baker (1725) says *height* is pronounced both ' *hite* ', and ' *hait* '. Thus both types of both words survived.

Note that the pronunciation of *eye* goes back to M.E. *īye*, whereas the spelling is from M.E. *ēye* which would normally give Mod. [*ei*].

P. 230, line 19.

Diphthonging of M.E. **ū** in Northern English.

It is not quite accurate to say that no diphthonging has taken place in the Mod. Dialects of the North. H. Orton, *Sth. Durh. Dialect*, § 133, gives the regular isolative development of *ū* in Byers Green as [*öu*], as in [bröun, döük, köu, (h)öus], &c., &c., for O.E. *brūn, dūce* ' duck ', *cū, hūs*, &c. He regards this, however, as ' only a very recent ' modification. One might indeed be inclined to regard the diphthonging in these words as an imitation of Standard English, were it not for [döuk], which shows the survival and development of long *ū* where Southern English has the shortened form. In § 387 Orton adduces forms to show at least the beginning of diphthonging in the dialects of Lorton, Kendal, and Stokesley. Thus Northern diphthonging of *ū*, such as it is, appears to be late, only incipient, and confined to a restricted area.

P. 239.

Pronunciation of Rome.

Swift rhymes this word with *gloom*, and Pope writes:—
> *From the same foes at last both felt their doom,*
> *And the same Age saw Learning fall and Rome.*
>   Ess. on Crit., 685.

Lady Gardiner has the inverted spelling *in the rome of*—Later V. Letters i, p. 110 (1702). Walker, Dictionary (4th Ed., 1806) says ' the *o* of this word seems irrevocably fixed in the English sound of the letter in *move* and *prove*'.

Pp. 243, 244.

The Survival of the Sound [**ȳ**] in English.

While many of the spellings quoted—*youes*, &c.—undoubtedly point to [jū] in such words as early as the sixteenth century, the statement of Voltaire should be noted. He says that, in spite of the corruption of English vowels, *u* retains the sound which it has in French, and that *true* is pronounced *tru* [ȳ] not *trou* [ū]. (See the article, *Langage*, in the *Dictionnaire Philosophique*.) Voltaire was in England from 1725 to 1728, and was perfectly conversant with English usage. If we believe him, we must conclude that the old, front pronunciation of this vowel still survived among some speakers, right into the eighteenth century, although others, and perhaps a larger number, pronounced [ū, jū]. Pope's rhyme *blooms—perfumes*, Eloisa, 217–18, and Lady Winchilsea's *comes* (= [kūmz] and *perfumes* To Ldy Worsley at Longleat, are both in favour of [pəfjūmz].

Pp. 248–9.

M.E. **ai** and **ā**, and see also M.E. ē̆, pp. 209, &c., above.

Later spellings showing levelling of M.E. ē̆, ā, ai. From Later Verney Letters, vol. i :—*ea* for *ā*, *St. Jeamsis Park* (1697), p. 37 ; *to have her bed mead* (1700), p. 75. *ea* for *ai*, *my two meads*, 48 (twice) (1699), and 69 (twice) (1700) ; *a* for *ai*, *well ared*, 36 (1699) ; *a* for ē̆, *for my own ware*, 37 (1699) ; *ay* for ē̆, *beyon say*, ' sea ', 107 (1702).

P. 253.

Vowels Un-shortened or Lengthened.

The Letters of Lady Brill. Harley have a number of interesting spellings indicating long vowels.

I.
Spellings and Rhymes Showing Retention of Old Long Vowels as such.

(The following spellings are all from Lady Brill. Harley, except where otherwise stated:—
neeuer, forgoot, P.P., p. 3 (1627) ; *to geet* ' get ', p. 20 (1638 ; cp. Shakespeare's rhyme *get—heat* ; *heeld* ' held ', p. 13 (1638) ; *fooute* ' foot ', p. 56 (1639) ; *sheeding blood*, p. 43 (1639) ; *I toucke*, p. 86 (1639) ; *so weet a day*, p. 89 (1640), (cp. Milton's rhyme *wet—great*, Pens. 8, and *eat—wet*, Pens. 80); *feel* ' fell ', 119 (1641) ; *hoot* ' hot ', p. 121 (1641); *freend*, Letter from Sir Harry Vane in Lady Brill. Harley's Letters, p. 236 (1650).

2.
Spellings and Rhymes Implying Later Lengthening.

reest (n.), Ldy. B. H. p. 2 (1625); Milton rhymed *rest* with *feast*, Cowley with *least ; beest* ' best ', p. 5 (1629), cp. *beast* ' best ', Mrs. Basire, p. 137 (1654) ; Cowley rhymed *best—least—east* ; Ldy. B. H. *loos* ' loss ', p. 31 (1638), also p. 71 (1639) ; *loost*, P.P. (ibid.); Spenser rhymed *lost—boast*, Drayton with *coast*, Dryden with *boast*, and *coast ; the hors coost me £8*, p. 199 (1643) ; Hodges, 1643, says *coast—cost* are pronounced alike.

APPENDIX III

Reduction or Loss of Vowels in Unstressed Positions. Especially in Seventeenth and Early Eighteenth Centuries.

The Endings -en, -on.

These endings are differently treated in ordinary speech, and in poetry, according to the consonant which precedes.

I (a) When the word ends in a stop, whether voiceless or voiced, the ending may become a mere syllabic *-n* : thus *ridden, written, golden, open, beckon*, &c., may become [ridn, ritn, gouldn, oupn, bekn], all consisting of two syllables, but with no vowel in the second syllable.

(b) The same is true when -*en* follows a voiceless open consonant—*listen,
orphan, often,* &c., may become [l*i*sn, ɔfn], &c.

The reason why -*n* in these positions constitutes a fresh syllable is
that it is a very sonorous sound, more so than a stop, or a voiceless open
consonant, whereas a stop following a vowel—as in *bid*—involves a
reduction of sonority, then, if -*n* be uttered immediately after this, a fresh
increase of sonority, and therefore a new syllable, results, as in [b*i*dn].
For these reasons final -*n* in all the above words, and others in which
similar conditions exist, is always syllabic, and cannot be otherwise.

2   *Combination   Stop* + -**en** + *Vowel.*

If -*n*, otherwise syllabic, be followed by another suffix beginning with
a vowel such as -*ing*, -*er*, or -*est*, the -*n* tends to lose its syllabic quality,
by virtue of the greater sonority of the following vowel, and to become
purely consonantal. Thus *opening* [óupn*i*ŋ], *reckoning* [rɛkn*i*ŋ],
listener [l*i*snə] are all in ordinary speech pronounced with two, not
three syllables.

A similar loss of the syllabic quality of -*n* may also occur in a breath-
group in which the following word begins with a vowel. Thus *hidden
in a tree* may become [h*i*d n*i*n ə trī] (four syllables) instead of [h*i*dn *i*n
ə trī] (five).

3   -**en** -**on** *Preceded by a Voiced Open Consonant.*

(a) In such words as *even, heaven, driven, chosen, prison, risen, reason,* the
final -*n* is often uttered so as not to form a syllable. This is made
possible by the fact that the difference in sonority between a voiced
open consonant and -*n* is so slight that no increase in sonority is perceived
in passing from one to the other. This monophthongic pronunciation of
risen, heaven, &c., is perhaps less usual to-day than formerly, and in
every-day speech, now, we probably utter a slightly syllabic -*n* in spite
of the preceding voiced open consonant. The poets, however, often
find it convenient to pronounce *heaven, heavens,* &c. as a single syllable
in their lines.

(b) When a suffix beginning with a consonant follows, the single syllable
in the first part of the word may remain as such, and *heavenly,* &c.,
may function in verse as two syllables, and not as three.

4   *The Series Voiced Open Consonant* + -**en** + *Vowel.*

If -*n*, as we saw above (2) following a stop, or voiceless open consonant,
often loses its syllabic quality when a vowel follows, still more certainly
does this happen with the class of words just considered. Thus if *even,*
prison, &c., are often single syllables in verse, this character is generally
secured to them beyond doubt in the compounds, *evening   prisoner*
[ívn*i*ŋ pr*i*znə]. When the same series occurs in a breath-group, the
syllabic quality of -*n* readily disappears. Thus, *Even in our ashes* consists of five syllables, and not of six in Gray's line, and the series *prison
ordained* in *to these rebellious here thir pris'on ordain'd* P. L. 71, the
metre requires [pr*i*z nɔdeind] exactly as in [pr*i*znə].

5   **Fallen, swolen, stolen.**

These words are now usually pronounced as two syllables [fɔ́lən,
swoulən, stoulən], at any rate, at the end of a sentence, and before
consonants—*fallen through,* &c. But when they occur before vowels
they are often monosyllables—*fallen in, stolen away, swolen up.* On the
other hand, Milton and his contemporaries seem to have pronounced
them as monosyllables in all positions. Thus:—

> *Fall'n cherube to be weak is miserable.*
> 　　　　　　　　　　　　　—P. L. i, 167, also in 92.

But swolne with wind and the rank mist they draw.
                                                    —Lyc. 126.
Stolne on his wing my three and twentith year.
                                          —Sonnet on 23rd Birthday.

In the last line the following vowel would in any case tend to ensure the purely consonantal character of -*n*.

The reason why these three words can easily become monophthongs is that there is no increase of sonority in -*n* as compared with -*l*-. If two syllables are required by the metre in a line of verse, a mere syllabic -*n* hardly constitutes a satisfactory syllable coming after -*l*-, and we should probably prefer to pronounce [fɔ͞lən], &c., as in Dryden's :—

Fallen, fallen, fallen, fallen,
Fallen from his high estate.
                                          Alexander's Feast. 77–8.

These principles are applied in their verse, and often recognized in the spelling, by many poets, and with remarkable, though not complete, consistency by Milton. For a discussion of Milton's spellings of the -*en* and -*on* words, reference should be made to the remarks of Miss Helen Darbishire in the Introduction to her edition of the Morgan MS. of Bk. I of P. L., pp. xxviii, and xxxiii and xxxiv, and further to H. C. Wyld, *The Significance of* 'n *and* -en *in Milton's Spelling*, Englische Studien, 1935, pp. 138–48.

It is pointed out by Miss Darbishire that Alexander Gill, Milton's headmaster at St. Paul's, recognizes in *Logonomia* (1621), pp. 134–5 of Reprint, that -*n*, -*l*, -*r* could each constitute a syllable, without any vowel in front of them. What Gill does not appear to notice is that these sounds when final are not always syllabic. (See remarks under 3, 4, and 5 above).

Gill in his phonetic transcriptions writes simply -*n* in words of all our classes—*brökn, göldn, lesn, oxn* ; *chösn, prizn, sëzn, hevn* ; *stöln*, &c., &c., and does not call attention to the fact that -*n* is not necessarily a syllable in words of classes 3 and 5. Yet he makes no difference in the spelling of *hevn* between —*And thundring dʒöv that hyh in hevn duth dwel*, where the word is a single syllable, and—*Thinking tu skäl the hëvn of hir hart*, where it is two. The mark of length on *hëvn* in the last line may possibly represent an actual pronunciation, from M.E. *hëven*.

Milton's Spellings.

We may take it that the spellings in Trin. Coll. MS. represent what Milton intended, since these are in his own handwriting, though, indeed, he is not perfectly consistent.

The spellings in the Morgan MS., and in the early editions, are on the whole what Milton wanted, and they show evidence of careful revision.

Milton might have used the symbol '*n* to represent a genuine syllabic -*n* (in *trod'n*, &c.), and have distinguished from this the -*n* which did not form a syllable (in *heavn*, &c.) by writing the latter always with plain -*n*. Unfortunately, he does not make this distinction, but writes '*n* or *n* indifferently for syllabic and non-syllabic -*n*. '*n*, however, is much more frequent for both. Milton further occasionally, though rarely, writes -*ŏn*, -*ĕn*, or -'*on*, -'*en*, to indicate the loss of the syllable. Lastly, he sometimes, both in Trin. MS., and in Morgan, writes -*en* when no syllable is required by the verse. In some cases the early editions are more in accordance with Milton's principles than the MS.

A few examples of the various classes of words from the poetry:—
Class 1 (*a*). *Stop* + -*en* (syllabic -*n*).
Of that forbidd'n tree whose mortal taste
                                          Morgan MS., 2.

(The original scribe wrote *forbidden*. An apostrophe in a darker ink has been added above the line, between -*d*- and -*n*. Miss Darbishire sees a stroke deleting the *e*, but this is practically invisible in the facsimile.)
Op'n'd into the hill a spacious wound.
                                          —Morgan MS., 689.

Like night, and dark'n'd all the Land of Nile.
                                        —Morgan MS., 343.
          Thy firm unshak'n virtue ever brings.
                                        —Sonnet to Fairfax, Trin. MS.

Sudden.

We may note that Gill writes *sudaine*, and Milton *suddaine*, Com., 552, 954, and elsewhere, and also *sudden*, Lyc., 74. Gill never writes *sudn* for this word, nor Milton *sudd'n*. Both prefer the Spenserian and M.E. spelling with *-ain(e)*. This form may go back to an earlier type with the older system of stressing upon the second syllable. This type, when the accent was subsequently shifted to the first syllable, at any rate among some speakers, might retain the ' clear ' vowel in the second syllable longer than words in which this had always been unstressed. Gill and Milton then, appear not to have reduced this syllable to a syllabic *-n*. That other, more colloquial speakers did so, however, is shown by Mrs. Isham's spelling *suddnly* (1644), cit. p. 272 above.

Class 2. *Series stop + -en-, -on- + vowel (loss of syllabic quality).*
     From Trin. Coll. MS. (no apostrophe) :—
          Of calling shapes and beckning shadows dire.
                                                  Com., 207.

          Of other care they little reckning make.
                                                  Lyc., 116.

          batning our flocks with the fresh dews of night.
                                                  Lyc., 29.

     From Morgan MS. (with or without apostrophe) :—
          Likning his Maker to the grazed ox.
                                        —586 (1st Ed., *Lik'ning*).
          Distends with pride and hardning in his strength.
                                                  —572.

(Note that in line 662 the scribe first wrote :—*open or understood, must be resolv'd*, but corrected to *op'n*, which Miss Darbishire in her note on this line thinks was what Milton intended. I must venture to differ, because *op'n* suggests a syllabic *-n*. But this, before the following vowel, would tend to become [ōpnər ándəstúd], that is, a syllable too few. Milton must have desired, as the metre requires, [ōpen ɔr] .)

Class 3 (*a*). *Series Voiced Open Consonant + -n (non-syllabic -n).*
     From Morgan MS. :—
          Eternal spirits : or have ye chos'n this place
                                                  —318.
          Of glory obscur'd : as when the sun new ris'n
                                                  —594.
          Swarm'd and were strait'nd till the signal giv'n.
                                                  —776.
          Driv'n backward slope thir poynting spires and rowld
                                                  —223.

(1st Ed. *drivn*; this spelling occurs also in the prose notes in Trin. MS.)
          Cornice or frieze with bossy sculptures grav'n
                                                  —716.

          In the beginning how the Heav'ns and Earth.
                                                  —9.

(I have counted twenty-nine examples of *Heav'n* so spelt, and one of *Heav'nly*, in Morgan M.S.)
     From Trin. Coll. MS. :—
          now the top of heav'n doth hold.
                                                  Com., 94.

(Without apostrophe)
          and give resounding grace to all heavns harmonies
                                                  Com., 243.

          till oft converse with heavnly habitants.
                                                  Com., 459.

Class 4. *Series as in 3 Followed by a Vowel.*

In line 71, cited above under No. 4, in preliminary statement of the various classes of words, the metre shows that the phrase *prison ordain'd* is to be uttered as three syllables. (*Note.*—There are other instances of this type of spelling in Milton, where a vowel, though written, has an apostrophe placed before or over it, to indicate that the syllable is elided : thus— *That he, the supream Good, tŏ whome all things ill,* Com., 217 ; *to' inveigle and invite th' unwary sense,* (Com., 538 ; *th' all giver would be' unthankt, would be unprais'd,* Com., 723.

It will be noted later that such spellings are frequent in Cowley.

In Morgan MS., 211, *risen* is left uncorrected, but has been amended to *ris'n* in the 1st and 2nd Editions. The following vowel ensures a monosyllable, as the metre demands—*Had risen or heav'd his head, but that the will.* A similar mis-writing occurs in a similar series in Morgan MS., 680. *From Heav'n for even in Heav'n.* Here the 1st Ed. has *ev'n.* In Trin MS., Com. 786, the necessarily monophthongic *heav'n* is so written— *ne'ere looks to heav'n amidst his gorgeous feast,* Com., 786, and also in Lyc., 84 . . . *in heav'n expect thy meed.*

In Lyc., 34, *cloven* is written *clov'n* by Milton himself, although the metre requires two syllables. Possibly the apostrophe is not intended as a cancelling mark. Even so, *cloven* would seem to be a better spelling.

In Morgan MS., 248, it is written:—

> *Whom reason hath equald, force hath made supream.*

The word *reason* is a monosyllable here as the metre requires, and the phonetic surroundings demand. *Hath* in an unstressed position would normally lose its *h-*, and the series, in Milton's pronunciation, was [rēznə ρ ĭkwəld]. The scribe should have written *reas'n, reasn,* or *reas'on.* Trin. Coll. MS. has *Evning,* Lyc., 30.

Class 5. *The fallen, stolen Group.*

This group as monophthongs has already been illustrated above. It may be noted that Morgan MS. has *fal'n* at least three times, 84, 282, 330, and in Milton's own hand *faln,* in the prose notes of Trin. Coll. MS. (poems on Scriptural subjects).

Milton's Pronunciation of - en + -on when Not Syllabic -n.

The details just discussed are important because, while of interest from a purely textual point of view, they have also a far wider significance. They have a bearing on Milton's actual pronunciation, and as similar spellings before, and after, and during his time show, this pronunciation was not confined to the poet, and to his schoolmaster Gill, but were normal in colloquial sixteenth- and seventeenth-century English.

But if it is desirable to learn that Milton generally pronounced *heaven,* and *prison,* &c., as monosyllables, and *trodden, open* with a mere syllabic -n, it will seem no less desirable to attempt at least to form some idea of how Milton pronounced the second syllable of *heaven* etc. when dissyllabic, and so written:—

> *And Powers that earst in Heaven sat on thrones.*
> —Morgan MS., 360.

Or

> *Thir glory witherd. As when Heavens fire*
> —ibid., 612.

Or

> *Pour'd never from her frozen loynes, to passe*
> —352.

Again, when his scribe writes, without correction:—

> *And broken chariot wheeles, so thick bestrown*

and

> —311,

> *Darkens the streets then wander forth the sonnes*
> —501,

it may be asked, why not *brok'n* and *dark'ns*, since these spellings would suggest perfectly adequate dissyllables ? It is at least arguable that Milton intended something more here, and in many other lines where *-en* is written after stop consonants, than merely a syllabic *-n*. The effect is finer, and more weighty in these lines if the suffix be pronounced as either [ən] or [ɛn]. But even if this be thought a mere refinement, there is still *heaven* and other words of this group to be reckoned with.

A glance at pp. 271-2 above shows that the ending *-en*, both in *heaven*, &c. (after voiced open consonants) and also in such words as *open, written*, &c. (after stops) is often written *-in*, or *-yn*, in the fifteenth and sixteenth centuries. The examples collected from seventeenth-century sources are, unfortunately, less numerous. Some additional examples may now be given from sources of fifteenth to seventeenth century. In the Paston Letters *-yn* seems to be the usual form in all writers. A few may be quoted. Marg. Paston has, amongst many others, *gotyn*, P. P. iii. 295 (1482) ; *tokyn* (n) twice, iii. 95 (1483) ; the Duke of Suffolk has *hevyn* ' heaven ', i. 122 (1450) ; and the Prior of Bromholm has *writtin*, P. P. i. 79 (1449). From the sixteenth century we may add *tokyns* in a letter of John Herrick, the poet's father ; from the seventeenth—*aspin*, Gill (1621), p. 111. 13; *oftin*, Lady Brill. Harley, 321 (1639) ; *-men* appears as *-min* in Gill (in the pronunciation of the ' Mopsae ', in *gintlmin* p. 38. 8, and in *townsmin*, Lady Brill. Harley, 98 (1640).

Turning to spellings for *-on* (see pp. 275-6 above) we may add to the examples there given ; from Paston Letters, *rekyn* (vb.), Sir J. Paston, ii. 321 (1468) ; *poysened*, ii. 93 (Mem. on French Prisoners). From sixteenth century: comes *prysin*, several times, Lady Hungerford, 265-6 (1569).

From the available evidence we are probably safe in supposing that many speakers, at least, from the fifteenth century onwards, pronounced *heaven*, *prison*, &c., as [hɛvin, prizin] when they did not pronounce the words as monosyllables, and *often, open, reckon*, &c., as [ɔftin, ōpin, rɛkin] when the unstressed syllables here were not reduced to mere syllabic *-n*.

Spellings Resembling, or Identical with those of Gill and Milton.

(1) **-en** *in P. P.*

(*a*) Monosyllabic *swolne*, and *faln(e)* are so printed in the early editions of Spenser ; *faln* is actually written by Mrs. Isham, Verney Mem. i. (1639), and by Mrs. Basire, 135 (1654).

(*b*) *Givn*, Mrs. Isham, Verney Mem. i (1639); *thouzn* '1000', Cooper (1685).

(2) **-on, -en** + *Vowel in Suffix : Loss of Syllabic Quality* (see examples from Milton above).

Gill spells *rekning* ; Lady Brill. Harley *reckning*, 18 (1638) ; Dryden spells *reck'ning*. A very early example of this type occurs in the Paston Letters, *rekning*, Sir J. Paston, ii. 348 (1469).

Gill has *oftner*, so also Lady Brill. Harley, 84 (1640).

(3) *Voiced Open Consonant* + **-on, -en,** *followed by a Vowel.*

The word *prisoner* is spelt *prizner* by Gill ; *prisner*, according to Miss Darbishire, is Milton's spelling. With these we may compare *prisner*, Lady Brill. Harley, 11 (1638), and *prisnors, -ners*, 205 (1643) ; *prisners* (twice), Mrs. Isham, Verney Mem. ii. 203 (1644) ; *presnor*, Mrs. Basire, 108 (1651).

A similar loss of a syllable under the same conditions is seen in *reasnabell*, Lady Brill. Harley, 12 (1638), 55 (1639), and 97 (1640).

The same lady also writes *seasning*, and *seasned*, 53 (1639).

Syllabic **-l**.

Gill recognized the existence of this sound as of syllabic *-n*. He habitually spells—*trubl, fibl, girdl, litl, intangl, tikl, humblness*, &c., &c. Milton expresses this sound by '*l*, and *l*', in his autograph MS. and in the Morgan MS. Thus:—*myrt'ls*,

Lyc. 2 ;   strangl'd, Com. 729 ; humbl'd (prose Notes, 'Adam unparadised' in Trin. Coll. MS. ; wrincl'd, corrected by Milton from wrinkled, in cancelled line in Comus ; stabl'd, Com. 534. The spelling haze'l, Lyc. 42, no doubt represents [hēzl], the e being merely an indication that the vowel in preceding syllable is long. In the Morgan MS. I have noted doubl'd, 485 ; manacl'd, 426 ; troubl'd, 557 and 616 ; rifl'd, 687 ; fabl'd, 741.

Spenser, or his printers, usually prefer the other type—trembled [tremblid], sprinkled, handled, &c. I have noted a fair number of -l'd spellings in Chapman's plays—e.g., speckl'd, baffl'd, mangl'd, stifl'd, &c., &c. And further, what must be intended for syllabic -l in the Paston Letters, peepll, i. 166–7, Justice Yelverton (1450). As a matter of fact, the ordinary spelling -le, people, &c., can hardly have ever expressed anything else but syllabic -l. Side by side with the above spelling, however, the writers of the Paston Letters constantly write peepil, and peeple.

It should be noted that Gill does not write batl for battle, but batails, 113, 12, &c., and that Milton writes the word battaile, Com. 654, and also battel, and cp. imbatteld, Morgan MS., 130. He does, however, write battlements, Morgan MS., 742. Here we must assume syllabic -l-. In the other spellings, the M.E. type battáile is perpetuated, and the forms suggest that the shifting of stress to the first syllable took place, among some speakers, too late for a complete reduction of the second syllable to mere syllabic -l.

Milton writes in his own hand, navill 'navel', Com., 550, and in all places evil(l).

Syllabic -r.

From the fifteenth-century spellings cited on pp. 270–1 above it appears that the ending -er after a consonant is variously written -yr, -ur, of which the former seems to predominate. In addition, there are a few spellings without a vowel—fadr, massangr, remembr, undr, watre, murdre, from Marg. Paston, Sir J. Fortescue and Caxton. To these may now be added (all from Paston Letters) :—Arblastr, i. 128, J. Denyes (1450) ; remembr, ii. 93, J. Paston the Elder (1462) ; 'my nonne propr goodes', i. 133, J. Payne (1465) ; her aftr, iii. 14, Sir J. Paston (1471). It seems probable that such spellings express a syllabic -r.

The variant spellings may all have been intended to express more or less this same sound—either syllabic -r, or an indeterminate vowel followed by a weak consonantal -r. Our present pronunciation [ə(r)] is, in fact, very old. It may have arisen direct from the weakening of syllabic -r.

Gill writes the ending -er as such—biter, beter, fader, &c., and Milton, I think, does not use such spellings as bettr, bittr. I have noted the isolated spelling betr in the Verney Mem. ii. 319, in a letter of Mrs. Sherrard (1657). This lady's pronunciation, as well as that of Gill and of Milton, and their later contemporaries, was most likely [bɛtə].

Loss of Vowel Before -r- in Unstressed Syllables when a Vowel Follows.

I have noted robrys, robbryys in Paston Letters, ii. 32, Marg. Paston (1469). Spenser's flowring (F. Q., 2, 7, 16) may be a case in point, cp. Milton's flowrets, Lyc., 133 (Trin. Coll. MS.) ; and watrie, Lyc., 12, and watry, Morgan MS., 397, certainly are. Other examples of vowel loss before r + vowel in Milton are imbroidrie, Lyc., 148, and emrald, Com., 894.

Milton often omits the vowel before -r- when -in follows, sometimes putting an apostrophe, sometimes not:—Trin. Coll. MS., hov'ring; Com., 214, wondring in Notes for Poems on O.T. subjects. On the other hand, slandering occurs in the same Notes, and suffering in Morgan MS., 158, and hovering, ibid., 345, where the metre requires only two syllables in each instance.

Morgan MS. has also adventrous, 13 ; weltring, 78 ; thundring, 233 ; bord'ring 219, &c.

In Com., 79, Milton first wrote adventurous, but on consideration, struck out u before -r- and put an apostrophe ; in Com., 609, he writes ventrous. Note that Milton writes venter (vb.), Com., 228.

Similar spellings seem not to be used by Gill.

The loss of a syllable before -*r*- is common in poetry in the seventeenth century and later.

Cowley sometimes omits the vowel letter, putting an apostrophe to mark the omission of it and of the syllable—*vict'ry, gen'rous, conqu'rours* ; sometimes writes the letter but puts an apostrophe before it, to show that the syllable is lost for which it stands—*iv'ory* (one syllable), *rig'orus* (two syllables), *Mem'ory* (two syllables), *Lux'ury* (two syllables), *discov'ering* (three syllables), *quiv'ering* (two syllables), &c. With this practice, cp. Milton's spellings *prisòn or-* &c., cited above, p. 405.

Dryden cuts out the letter and puts an apostrophe when a syllable is lost— *ign'rant, rev'rence, fev'rish,* &c. Swift has many similar spellings—*shiv'ring, vent'ring, iv'ry, nat'ral.*

-er, -our + -ed.

Spenser's printers usually prefer the types *nombred, slumbred, offred. suffred,* &c., or, without elision of the vowel before the -*r, slombered, scattered. the type answerd, deliver'd,* &c., being rarer. Milton, however, prefers the latter type. The Trin. Coll. MS. has *enter'd,* Circumcis., ii ; altered from *entered* ; *enterd,* in Plan for P. L., *murder'd, martyr'd,* Notes, O.E. History, *discover'd, cover'd,* Poems on Scriptural subjects ; *hinderd, honourd,* ' Lttr. to a Freind '.

The scribe of Morgan MS. has written *endanger'd,* 131, *shatter'd,* 202, *answer'd,* 272, *scatter'd,* 326, *scepter'd,* 734, *cover'd,* 763 ; further, without an apostrophe, *scatterd,* 304, *witherd,* 612, *enterd,* 731. This is the less archaic, more colloquial type. Such forms as *scatter'd, labour'd, conquer'd, endanger'd, honorde, severd,* and so on, are found in Donne, Herrick, Chapman, Cowley, and Dryden.

I have noted *sufferde,* P. P. Verney Mem. ii. 81, Lady Sussex (1642), and the same lady writes *a retierde life,* ii. 153 (1643).

Loss of Unstressed Syllable in Other Words.

Business. Gill spells *biznes,* 88. 29, 89. 2 (Reprint). Milton's usual spelling is *buisness,* in Trin. Coll. MS. Com., 109, in Notes for Poems on Scriptural subjects, in a cancelled passage, Com., 18, and in Morgan MS., 150 (*buis'nesse*), and elsewhere. Miss Darbishire suggests that Milton got this spelling (as regards the dropping of -*i*- in the middle of the word) from Gill. But this was in Milton's day, as now, the ordinary pronunciation (to judge by the spellings). I have collected the following examples :— *bisnis,* Mrs. Pulteney (later Mrs. Eure), Verney Papers, 222 (1638) ; also *bisnes,* Verney Mem. i. 157 (1643) ; *buisnes,* Lady Brill. Harley, 3, 5, 10 (1627 and 1638) ; also *biusnes,* 75 (1639) ; both spellings, the only ones, occur constantly in this lady's letters. She often transposes the order of letters, but in this case, she may merely have put the dot in the wrong place ; *busnis,* Lady Vere, Lady Brill.'s Letters, 213 (1641) ; *bisnes,* and *besness,* Mrs. Basire, 109 (1651) ; *busnes,* Holmes, the Verneys' Steward, Verney Mem. ii, 411 (1659). Dryden and Swift constantly print *bus'ness.*

Cov'nant(*s*), Milton's own MS., Circumcis., 21, and Comus, 682.

Tapstrie hall, Com., 224 ; Cowley, *tap'estry,* Dav. iii.

Venson, Lady Brill. Harley, 62 (1639) ; Chapman, Emp. of Germany ; Jones (1701) says *i* not pronounced in this word.

Exemnation, Lady Brill. Harley, 69.

Med'cinall, Milton, Com. 636.

Abslate, ' absolute ', Lady Sydenham, Verney Mem. ii. 102 (1641).

Compny, Lady Hobart, Verney Mem. iii. 407 (1657).

Inno'cent, unusu'al, annu'al, om'nous, all in Cowley ; *cab'net, filth'ness,* Dryden.

APPENDIX IV

Points Connected with the Consonants.

Loss of -1 in **should** and **would**. (See Ch. viii., p. 297.)

I am now convinced that the loss of *-l-* in these words occurred primarily in unstressed positions, and that these weak types without *-l-* were later generalized in all positions. On the other hand, it is established both by rhymes and by the statements of grammarians that pronunciations with *-l-* were still current among some speakers, at any rate in stressed forms, after the evidence of occasional spellings proves that the *-l-* had ceased to be pronounced in weak positions. I may note here a very early example of the loss of *-l-* in *should*, which is spelt *schyd* three times in a letter from Robert, Prior of Bromholm, written in 1449, Paston Letters, i. 78. This is nearly one hundred years earlier than the form from Elyot's *Gouernour* quoted on p. 297 above, but there is no reason to doubt its genuineness, especially as the vowel is also evidently reduced in the weak position. Our present-day unstressed [ʃəd] is a normal development of earlier [ʃud, ʃad]. The present-day stressed form [ʃud] may well be from an earlier [ʃud] with the later vowel shortening as in [stud] from earlier [stūd]. See p. 238 above. Our [wud] may be explained in the same way from earlier [wūd], which indeed is vouched for by Hodges (1643), who says that the word is pronounced like *wood*, and *wooed*. The *u* in this word would, in any case, be preserved from the un-rounding discussed on p. 232 above by the initial *w-*. Milton in the *Letter to a freind* writes *woud* in his autograph MS. (= [wūd] ?).

Waller, *Summer Island*, 49–50, rhymes *would—mud*, which seems to imply for the former a short vowel and no *-l-*. Possibly *m-* here preserved a rounded vowel in *mud* as *w-* has done in *would*.

l retained.

By the side of the *-l*-less type of pronunciation, there is, I think, evidence equally unequivocal for the existence in the sixteenth and seventeenth centuries, of another pronunciation, with *-l-*, not only in *should* and *would*, but also in *could*. It may perhaps have been assumed by some that in the last word, the *-l-* was purely graphic, and due to the *written forms* of the other two. But the analogy went deeper than that, and influenced the pronunciation also; indeed it may have begun in the spoken language during the sixteenth century. Let us consider first the evidence of the rhymes for each word.

Could is rhymed by Spenser with *behold, mould, behold, gould* ' gold ', *hould*, also with *should* and *would* ; by Drayton with *behold*. Dryden rhymed *could* with *good*.

Would is rhymed with *hold, behold* by Wyatt ; with *mould, tould* ' told ', *gold, hold*, by Spenser ; with *hold, behold* by Drayton.

Should is rhymed by Wyatt with *behold, hold, gold* ; by Shakespeare with *cool'd* (V. and A., 385, &c.) ; by Spenser with *mould, hold, behold*.

Several of the seventeenth-century grammarians testify to pronunciations with *-l-*. Gill (1621) transcribes *wūld, shūld, kūld* (*ū*=[*ǖ*]). Price (1662) puts *could, cold*, and *cool'd* together ; Wharton (1653) writes *woold, coold, shoold* as expressing this pronunciation, and Cooper (1685) says that *could* is pronounced like *cool'd*.

On the other hand, Milton in the Sonnet To my freind Mr. Hen. Laws, dated February 9, 1645 (second draft) writes *coudest*, crosses this out, and writes *cou'dst*, which seems to suggest that he did not pronounce *-l-* in this word, though it is true it is not very strongly stressed in the line. P. 301.

Metathesis of -r- (hunderd, apurn, &c.)

Hundred is not infrequently written *hundurd, hunderd*, &c., in the seventeenth century, and the pronunciation which this suggests is attested by grammarians' statements, and by such rhymes as Tennyson's in the Charge of the Light

Brigade—*thunder'd, wonder'd* with *hundred*. Among many old people of good breeding this pronunciation survived into the present century. *Hundird* occurs Stonor Papers i, 71 (1465). Milton may well have said [handə(r)d], though the evidence for this is rather weak. Miss Darbyshire believes he intended to write *hunderd*, or to have it written and printed. The fact is that although this spelling never occurs in Milton's own handwriting (cp. *hundred* in Arcades 22), this is printed *hunderd* in the Ed. of 1645, in the *Errata* of 1668 Ed. of P.L. i. 760, and in the 2nd Ed. in the text. In the Morgan MS. of Bk. I of P.L. 709 *hundred* is altered to *hunderd*. This, however, is cancelled in favour of *row of*. (See Miss D.'s note on this line in her Ed. of the MS.) There is good ground for believing that this MS. was written and corrected under Milton's own direction. Miss Darbyshire has also found various examples of *hunderd* in Milton's prose works. I have noted the following spellings of the word :—1635, *hundered*, Hon. James Dillon (twice), Verney Papers 165 ; 1639, *hunderd*, Sir Edm. Verney, Verney Papers 246, and Lady Brill. Harley Letters, p. 40 ; this lady also writes *hundered* ;. 1642 *hondard*, Cary Gardiner, Verney Mem.. ii. 63 ; 1685, Cooper transcribes *hundurd* ; 1701, Jones says that the sound *-erd* is written *-red* in *hundred*. Walker, Pronouncing Dictionary (4th Ed.), 1806, gives *hundred* as the ' solemn ', *hundurd* as the colloquial pronunciation also *aprurn, saffurn*. *In addition to Saffurn* cit. above p. 301, the spelling *safern* occurs in Gill's Logonomia, p. 112. 5, in a transcription of F.Q. 1. ii. 7, where Spenser's text has *saffron*.

Gill also writes *breðern,* 129, 5 and 6 ; Mrs. Basire, 135 (1654) writes *brethern*.

APPENDIX V

P. 329.

Weak Forms of **their (thir, thyr, ther).**

Miss Darbishire has traced the history of Milton's spellings, *thire*, and *thir*, in an elaborate Appendix (pp. 71–4) to her edition of Morgan MS. Speaking generally, the former spelling is used in the earlier portion of Trin. Coll. MS., and the second in that part written in and after 1642, and in subsequent editions of Milton's works supervised by the poet. The strong form *their* is used but sparingly, thus, for instance, in Morgan MS. it occurs only five times, while *thir* is written sixty-four times. The early printed editions of all the Books of P.L. show a similar disparity in the use of *thir* and *their*. It must be said at once that the difference between *thire* and *thir* has no significance for the pronunciation, however interesting it may be to the textual critic. We are concerned here with Milton's preference for the weak form, probably pronounced [ðə(r)]. An interesting point noted by Miss Darbishire (p. 70) is that when Milton dictated *thir*, his scribe heard it as *the*, and thus wrote it, e.g. *With singed top thir stately growth though bare* (Morgan MS. 614) where *thir* has been corrected from *the*. This makes it highly probable that *-r* was not pronounced here by the poet. Both of Milton's favourite spellings are found among others of his contemporaries. Thus, in the Letters of Mrs. Basire :—*thire* (1651), 109, and 112 (1653) ; *thyr* (1655), 142, and (1656), 147. Elsewhere the same lady writes *ther* (1654), 138.

The most frequent weak form which I have noted is *ther* :—Lady Brill. Harley, 1638 ; Lady Sussex, Verney Mem. ii. 82, &c. (1642) ; Mrs. Adams (1697) in V. Letters of eighteenth century, i. See other early examples of weak forms of *they, their*, p. 329 above.

Milton's Use of Spelling **their.**

The weak form *thir* is generally used, ' correctly ' enough, that is in unstressed positions. It is, however, at least once written where contrasting stress seems to require the strong form, e.g.,

And with thir darknesse durst affront his light.
—P.L. i. 391 (Morgan MS.).

On the other hand, *their* is by no means written with perfect consistency only in stressed position. In fact it appears in, at most, two passages in this position in Morgan MS. :—

> *Who from the pit of Hell*
> *Roaming to seek their prey on earth durst fix*
> *Their seats long after next the seat of God.*
>
> P.L. i. 381–4.

In the last line *their seats* is certainly contrasted with *the seat of God*. In the second line *their* is probably unstressed. In the following line it may be questioned whether *their* is really stressed :—*Osiris, Isis, Orus, and their train.*—P. L. i. 478. Miss Darbishire does not recognize this as one of the passages in which *their* is justified. She regards lines 391, and 384, as the only places where the strong form is *certainly* required. (See her *Introduction* to Morgan MS. p. xvii.)

APPENDIX VI

P. 358.

Strong and Weak Forms of **Have**.

The normal stressed form from M.E. *hāve* was [hēv] in E.Mod. Gill usually spells *hāv* in his transcriptions, but also recognized the weak form, with short vowel—transcribed *hav*, e.g., *I hav born, drunk, fled*, but also in *what hŏp hav J ?*

The later poets rhyme the strong form with *grave, save, gave*, &c., just as Chaucer rhymes *have—grave*, &c. These rhymes occur in Spenser, Shakespeare, Drayton, Donne, Milton, Waller, Cowley, Dryden, to mention no more. This form has now been lost, except in the compound *behave*, in Sthn. and Standard English. Its equivalent survives, however, in Scots. *hae* [hē].

The present-day stressed *have* [hæv] is from a generalisation of the old weak type, and from this new weak forms [həv, əv] and, after vowels, [v] have been developed.

In the seventeenth and early eighteenth century a weak form *a* = [ə] was current. Thus—*then I thought she would a done*, Mrs. Isham, Verney Papers, 262 (1639) ; *I shud a bin silent*, Cary Verney (Gardiner), Verney Mem. ii. 67 (1642) ; *anoufe to a broke a mans hart*, Mrs. Isham, Verney Mem. ii. 200 (1644) ; *I mit a come to a seean you*, Mrs. Basire, Letters, 139 (1653).

Swift ridicules *I thot to ha come*, as a fashionable absurdity, *Tatler*, 1710. The same type is also objected to by Swift in the negative construction *I han't don't*, ' have not done it ' (1710, *Tatler*, No. 230). Peter Wentworth not infrequently uses this negative, e.g., Wentworth Papers, 86 (1709), and ibid. (1711), 231.

The form *a* for unstressed *have* is far older than the seventeenth century, however, and the following examples from the fifteenth-century Paston Letters may be noted :—*I wold full fayn a ben*, Earl of Oxford, i. 143 (1450); (they) *wold a slayne hym*, W. Wayte, i. 151 (1450) ; *if he wold a named it.* J. Osbern, i. 215 (1451) ; *he myght a ben holpyn*, Marg. Paston, iii. 24 (1471).

INDEX

SUBJECT INDEX

ă (M.E.) in Mod. English, 196, &c. ; becomes *au* before -*l*, 201 ; rounded after *w-*, *wh-*, 201, &c. ; rounding not shown in rhymes of 16th and 17th c., 203 ; lengthened before -*s*, -*f*, -*þ*, and -*r* and cons., 203.

ā (M.E.), Fronting of, 194, &c.

Accidence, M.E., East Midlands, 31 ; Southern, 36 ; Kentish and S.E., 40 ; from 15th c., ch. ix. See also under various parts of speech.

Addition of Consonants, finally after -*r*, -*n*, -*m*, -*l*, -*s*, -*f*, 309 ; medially before consonant groups, ib.

Adjectives, Plurals in -*s*, 324 ; Comparative and Superlative, 325 ; mutated Comp. and Superl., 325-6 ; irregular forms of, 326.

ai (M.E.) in Mod. period, 247 ; Mulcaster on different pronunciation of, by men and women, 249 ; treatment of in unstressed syllables, 260, 266, 279, 280.

Ascham, Roger, his account of learning and talents of Edward VI, Elizabeth, and Lady Jane Grey, 104 ; exhorts Cecil to cultivate English, 110 ; language of *Toxophilus* and *Scholemaster*, 127-31.

Aspirate, loss of, 294-6 ; addition of, 310.

au (M.E.) in Mod. period, 251 ; in unstressed sylls., 260, 278.

Aubrey describes appearance, voice, and accent of Sir Walter Raleigh, 109.

Austen, Jane, idiom and spirit of her age faithfully reflected in her dialogue, 185 ; her characters probably spoke according to Walker's principles, 186 ; examples of her dialogue, 374-7.

Auxiliary Verbs, 355.

b, loss of between cons., and between cons. and vowel, 302, 303 ; loss of when final, 304.

Bacon, *Essay on Friendship* quoted, 149 ; recommends slow, drawling speech, 156 ; his more colloquial style illustrated, 369.

Baker, William (*Rules for True Spelling*, 1724), gives valuable information on unstressed syllables, 175 ; on consonant combinations, 176.

Basire, Dr., Correspondence of, invaluable for study of 17th c. English, 164 ; letters from Dr. and Mrs. B. quoted, 385, 386.

Batchelor (*Orthoepical Analysis*, 1809), first notes diphthong in *make*, &c., 196 ; warns against 'refinement' of pronouncing *lad* as *led*, &c., 199.

Behn, Mrs. Aphra, cit. passim, 389-93, &c.

Berners, Lord, account of language of his transl. of Froissart, 117-19.

Bertram (Royal English-Danish Gr., 1753) on vowel in *book*, *look*, *hood*, *foot*, and in *blood*, *flood*, *soot*, 237 ; on vowel in *burn*, 299.

Bokenam's *Lives of Saints* (Suffolk, 1443), 77.

Boleyn, Queen Anne, shares with her daughter Queen Elizabeth the habit of writing *desiar*, 137.

Bradley, Dr. Henry, on colloquial idiom in literature, 361.

Brews (Paston), Margery, examples of her epistolary style, 362.

Browne, Sir Thomas, examples of his style, 151 ; his mannerisms less marked in some of his Prefaces, 152.

Burney, Miss Fanny, her opinion of Walker, 181.

Butler, Rev. Charles (*English Grammar*, 1634), account of his teaching, 170-1.

Catherine of Aragon, Reception of, 90.

Cavendish, George, Language of his *Life of Wolsey*, 121-3 ; records Wolsey's conversation, 365-7.

Caxton, William, wrote in London English but did not create literary English, 62 ; a Kentishman, 86 ; adopts conventional scribal spelling, and does not innovate, 87 ; commanded to amend his English, 88 ; stilted style of his translations, 88-9 ; features of his dialect, 87.

Cely Papers, language of, 79.

Chapman's *Mons. D'Olive*, 378 ; *Humorous Day's Mirth*, 389 ; *Gentleman Usher*, 389.

Chaucer, uses London Court dialect of his day, 52 ; character of this, 53, &c. ;

WORD INDEX

SUPPLEMENTARY INDEX
TO NEW MATERIAL

Words, &c., marked N *will be found in the footnotes; those marked* App. *in the Appendices.*

SUBJECT INDEX

WORD INDEX

Words, &c., marked N *will be found in the footnotes; those marked* App. *in the Appendices.*